THE COLLECTED WORKS OF
Grey Owl

*Three Complete and
Unabridged
Canadian Classics*

GREY OWL

 PROSPERO
B·O·O·K·S
A DIVISION OF CHAPTERS INC.

Men of the Last Frontier first published in 1931 in Canada by Macmillan of Canada.

Sajo and the Beaver People first published in 1935 in Canada by Macmillan of Canada.

Pilgrims of the Wild first published in 1935 in Canada by Macmillan of Canada.

Canadian Cataloguing in Publication Data

Grey Owl, 1888-1938
    The collected works of Grey Owl

Contents: The men of the last frontier – Pilgrims of the wild – Sajo and the beaver people.

ISBN 1-55267-006-6

1. Canada, Northern – Description and travel. 2. Canada, Western – Description and travel. 3. Natural history – Canada. 4. Beavers. 5. Indians of North America – Canada. 6. Grey Owl, 1888-1938. I. Title.

FC3205.3.G735 2000   917.1   C99-932790-9   F1060.9.G74 2000

THE CANADA COUNCIL | LE CONSEIL DES ARTS
FOR THE ARTS | DU CANADA
SINCE 1957 | DEPUIS 1957

The publisher gratefully acknowledges the support of the Canada Council for the Arts and the Ontario Arts Council for its publishing program.

Canada

We acknowledge the financial support of the Government of Canada through the Book Publishing Industry Development Program (BPIDP) for our publishing activities.

This collection produced for Prospero Books, a division of Chapters Inc., 90 Ronson Drive, Etobicoke, Ontario M9W 1C1.

Key Porter Books Limited
70 The Esplanade
Toronto, Ontario
Canada M5E 1R2

www.keyporter.com

Design: Peter Maher
Electronic formatting: Jean Peters

Printed and bound in Canada

00 01 02 03 6 5 4 3 2

Contents

The Men of the Last Frontier / 1

Pilgrims of the Wild / 225

Sajo and the Beaver People / 421

By Grey Owl

The Men of the Last Frontier (1931)
Pilgrims of the Wild (1934)
Sajo and the Beaver People (1935)
Tales from an Empty Cabin (1936)

The Men of the
Last Frontier

Contents

Prologue / 3

I. The Vanguard / 5
II. The Land of Shadows / 25
III. The Trail / 41
IV. The Still-Hunt / 69
V. On Being Lost / 91
VI. The Fall of the Leaf / 109
VII. The Tale of the Beaver People / 119
VIII. The Altar of Mammon / I39
IX. The House of McGinnis / 159
X. The Trail of Two Sunsets / 173
Epilogue / 213

Prologue

A DEEP SLOW-FLOWING RIVER; SILENT, SMOOTH AS MOLTEN glass; on either bank a forest, dark, shadowy and mysterious.

The face of Nature as it was since the Beginning; all creation down the eons of unmeasured time, brooding in ineffable calm, infinite majesty, and a breathless and unutterable silence.

So it has lain for countless ages, dreaming, dwelling on the memories of untold tales no longer remembered, wise with the wisdom of uncounted years of waiting.

Overhead an eagle manoeuvres in the eye of the sun, and in the shadows on the shore an otter lies asleep.

Far-off in midstream appears a tiny dot, growing larger and larger as it approaches, and presently a bark canoe, yellow as an autumn leaf, and floating as lightly, speeds by. The sun glints sharply at regular intervals on paddles swung with swift and tireless strokes, by six brown, high-featured savages. Eagle feathers bob in unison, copper-hued backs bend and sway, driving forward the fragile craft, high of prow and stern, with a leaping undulation that is the poetry of motion.

In the centre stands a white man, bedizened with the remnants of the lace and ruffles of the courts of Europe. His cheeks are hollow and his frame gaunt. His skin is streaked with blood from the bites of myriad flies, but he recks not of it; his burning gaze is fixed ahead: Westward, Westward, from whence the river flows.

A few minutes and the bump and swish of paddles become inaudible.

3

The canoe diminishes again to a speck and disappears into the unknown. And the tiny waves of its passing find their way to shore, and so die. The two wild creatures stare in idle curiosity, and return each to his occupation: the eagle to his undisturbed soaring, the otter to his interrupted sleeping: and little know that, for a moment, they have gazed on History.

And so, unostentatiously, without pomp or ceremony, all unknown to the teeming millions of the Eastern Hemisphere, the long closed portals of the Western World swing open.

I
The Vanguard

"I live not in myself, but I become
Portion of that around me; and to me
High mountains are a feeling, but the hum
Of human cities torture; I can see
Nothing to loathe in Nature, save to be
A link reluctant in a fleshly chain,
Class'd among creatures, when the soul can flee,
And with the sky, the peak, the heaving plain
Of ocean, or the stars, mingle, and not in vain."
LORD BYRON

CHAPTER ONE

The Vanguard

DURING THE LAST TWENTY YEARS OR SO, WITH EMIGRATION pouring its thousands of newcomers into Canada to seek fresh homes, the world has been wont to consider the Dominion as a settled country, largely shorn of its forests, and given over almost entirely to farming, mining, manufacturing, and like industries.

Certainly the Canada of to-day can boast of unlimited opportunities for those who are willing to work, and there can be found in her cities and small towns a civilization as prosaic and matter-of-fact as exists in many older and longer-settled countries. There is big business; there are mining developments and engineering projects second to none in the world. Several finely equipped railroads span her from coast to coast. The mountains have been conquered, mighty rivers dammed, and vast reaches of prairie and woodland denuded of their game and brought under the plough. There are few improvements or inventions of modern times that are not in common use, even in sparsely settled districts.

All this is known to the world at large, and the word "Canada" is synonymous with "Prosperity" and "Advancement." These things coupled with the almost unequalled natural resources yet remaining at her command, have placed Canada in the forefront of the colonies that help to make the British Empire.

Those of us who enjoy the high privilege of participation in the benefits accruing from the development of a land of such riches, and unequalled opportunity, are apt to think but little, or fail, perhaps, even to be cognizant of the ceaseless warfare that for three centuries has been carried on in the van of the Great Advance. Without it the triumphant march of to-day might have been long deferred, or at least limited to a far smaller area. This bitter contest is still being waged without intermission, by a thin handful of devoted souls, on the far-flung borderland beyond the fringe of Civilization, where they are still adding additional, and alas, final, verses to the soul-inspiring saga of the Great North-West.

The mechanical mind of the efficient engineer who designs marvellous bridges, constructs huge dams, lays out our railroads, or makes extensive surveys—however well suited to his particular calling—very seldom possesses that sixth sense which seems to be the peculiar attribute of the pathfinder. Many of the mountain passes, and skilfully selected routes bearing the names of prominent men supposed to have discovered them, were the century-old trails of trappers and other frontiersmen whose names we never hear.

Not for the borderman are the rich rewards of honour, material profit and national prominence, which fall rather to those who follow with the more conspicuous achievements of construction, and, too often, destruction. Not for gain does he pursue his thankless task, for he is satisfied if he makes the wherewithal to live; neither for renown, for he lives obscurely, and often dies a strange death, alone. And no press notices sing his praises, and no monument is raised over his often unburied body.

He who leads the precarious life of skirmisher or scout on the No-Man's-Land beyond the Frontier, becomes so imbued with the spirit of his environment, that when the advance guard of the new era sweeps down on him with its flow of humanity and modern contrivance, he finds he cannot adapt himself to the new conditions. Accustomed to loneliness and seclusion, when his wanderings are curtailed, he forthwith gathers his few belongings and, like the Arab, folds his tent and steals silently away. Thus he moves on, stage by stage, with his furred and feathered associates, to fresh untrammelled horizons; where he explores, lays his trails, and unearths secret places to his heart's content, blazing the way for civilization, and again retiring before it when it comes.

This is the spirit of the true Pioneer. This is the urge that drove Champlain, Raleigh, Livingstone, and Cook into the four corners of the earth; the unquenchable ambition to conquer new territory, to pass where never yet trod foot of man.

Of all the various kinds of bordermen that pass their days Back of Beyond, undoubtedly the most accomplished and useful as a pathfinder is the trapper. He antedates all others. Men of the type of Boone, Crockett, Bridger, and Cody still exist to-day, undergoing the same hardships, eating the same foods, travelling by the same means, as did their forerunners, and talking languages and using methods handed down from the dim obscurity of the past, by the past-masters in the first and most romantic trade that North America ever knew, that of the hunter. The trapper of to-day has no longer the menace of the hostile savage to contend with, but he is in many ways under infinitely greater difficulties than was the woodsman of an earlier day.

From the time of the conquest of Canada until about fifty years ago, the land now under cultivation was covered with hardwood and pine forests with little or no undergrowth or other obstructions to retard progress. The woods-runner of that period had the best of timber for manufacturing his equipment. As a contrast, I once saw in the far North a party of Indians equipped with tamarac axe-handles and poplar toboggans; a condition of affairs about on a par with using wooden wheels on a locomotive, or cardboard soles on boots. The woods in those days were full of deer, a more prolific animal than the moose, far more easy to handle when killed, and with a much more useful hide. The old-time trapper had not far to go for his hunt, once settled in his district, and he had no competition whatsoever.

The modern hunter has to cover more ground, largely by means of trails laboriously cut through tangled undergrowth, sometimes not setting over three or four effective traps in a ten-mile line. The country so far North is more broken, the rivers rougher, the climate more severe; the forest, amounting in some places to little more than a ragged jungle, offers resistances unknown to the traveller of earlier days. Steel traps have supplanted to a large extent the wooden deadfall, and the snare, and better firearms have simplified still-hunting;* but game is scarcer, and harder to approach, except in very remote sections.

Conditions have changed, and the terrain has shifted, but the kind

* Stalking.

of a man who follows the chase for a living remains the same; the desire to penetrate far-away hidden spots, the urge to wander, is there as it was in his prototype of two hundred years ago. The real trapper (by which I mean the man who spends his days up beyond the Strong Woods, not the part-time hunter, or "railroad" trapper out for a quick fortune) is as much an integral part of the woods as are the animals themselves. In tune with his surroundings, wise in the lore of the Indian, he reads and correctly interprets the cryptograms in the book that lies open before him, scanning the face of Nature and forestalling her moods to his advantage. Dependent entirely on himself, he must be resourceful, ready to change plan at a moment's notice, turning adverse circumstances and reverses to what slight advantage he may. The hardships and privations of the trapper's life have developed in him a determination, a dogged perseverance, and a bulldog tenacity of purpose not often necessary in other walks of life. At the outset, before the commencement of the hunt, the trapper may have to spend one or two months in getting supplies to his ground, after spending most of the summer searching for a likely spot. His exploration work is of great value to those who follow him, but it is all lost time to him. He expects, and receives, nothing for his labours, but counts it all in the day's work, and hopes his ground will produce the goods. On such trips these men are sometimes called on to perform seemingly impossible feats, and probably no trip coming inside my recollection would illustrate this better than the journey undertaken by a white man and an Indian, three winters ago in Northern Quebec.

These men came from further south and, having made no allowance for the difference in climate, on their arrival found the freeze-up already in progress. Travelling during this period is considered by even the most enduring as being almost, if not quite, impossible.

Nothing daunted, these two hardy souls commenced their pilgrimage, for it was nothing less. Each had a canoe-load of about 600 lbs. On the first lake they found ice, which, whilst not capable of bearing a man, effectually prevented the passage of a canoe. This had to be broken, the two men armed with poles first breaking a channel in an empty canoe, from one expanse of open water to another. This entailed the unloading of 600 lbs.

of baggage on any kind of shore, into the snow, and the reloading of it on the return of the empty canoe; work enough, if frequently performed. They proceeded thus at the rate of about three miles a day, carrying the loads and canoes over seven portages. It snowed steadily day and night, increasing the difficulties on portages, making camping out a misery, and preventing at the same time the ice from becoming thick enough to walk on.

For five days they continued this struggle, making camp every night after dark, soaking wet and exhausted. It now turned colder, and this did not improve the ice under its clogging mass of snow water, while in the channel so laboriously broken, the cakes of ice and slush often cemented together, during the return trip, into a stronger barrier than the original ice had been. Held up at length on the shores of an eight-mile lake by these conditions, they passed around the entire shoreline of one side of the lake on snow-shoes, the ice being too weak to carry them otherwise, and even then, within a few feet of the shore, driving their axes through the ice at one blow every few feet. A full day was consumed on the outward journey, and they returned by the light of a clouded moon, splashed to the head, their garments freezing as they walked. But they were well repaid, as the water flooded the ice around the holes they had cut, and slushed up the snow on it. The whole mass froze through, forming a kind of bridge, over which they passed in safety, drawing the canoes and loads in relays on improvised sleighs.

This style of progress, alternating with the usual portages, continued for several more days, one man going through the ice in deep water, and being with difficulty rescued. The men were in no danger from starvation, but wrestling with hundred-pound bags of provisions under such trying conditions, and carrying ice-laden canoes over portages on snowshoes, was too severe a labour to be long continued. Worn-out and discouraged by their seemingly hopeless task, too far in to turn back, not far enough advanced to remain, faced by the prospect of passing the best part of the winter on a main route denuded of game, these companions in tribulation plodded with bitter determination, slowly, painfully, but persistently ahead.

Mile by mile, yard by yard, foot by foot, it seemed, those mountainous loads proceeded on their way, as two steely-eyed, grimfaced men opposed their puny efforts to the vindictive Power that vainly inhibited their further progress.

Their objective was a fast-running river, some forty miles in from the steel*, knowledge of which had caused them to retain their canoes, in the hopes of finding it unfrozen. This proved to be the case, and on its current they travelled in ease and comfort, as far, in two days, as they had previously done in the two weeks that they had been on the trail. When the water no longer suited their direction, they camped several days to rest up; and winter coming on in real earnest, they cached their now useless canoes, and making sleighs moved on into their ground by easy stages.

My own first introduction to a district celebrated for its topographical irregularities was a muskeg two miles long, of the same width and of indeterminate depth. These muskegs are frequently little more than moss-covered bogs that offer not one solid piece of footing in miles. Between two of us we juggled close on nine hundred pounds of equipment and provisions across this morass, besides a large freighting canoe, taking three days to complete the task. It rained the whole time, so we were wet on both sides, at both ends, and in the middle. Two nights camp had to be made on a quaking bog, where a small cluster of stunted spruce offered shelter and a little dry wood, whilst mosquitoes in countless myriads swarmed on us from the pools of slime on every side.

At no place in this swamp could we carry over a hundred pounds, owing to the treacherous nature of the footing, this increasing the number of trips.

On one occasion, bogged to the knees, I was unable to extricate myself, and, unwilling to drop my load in the mud, had to wait in this position till my partner passed on his return trip. The whole thing was a hideous nightmare. Four trips apiece we made by quarter-mile stretches, and the labour involved was nothing short of terrific. Yet the, feat, if so it could be called, excited no comment; such things are commonly done.

☙☙☙

MEN FOLLOWING THE TRAP LINE BECOME SO INURED TO THE severe conditions prevailing, and the unremitting exertion connected

*Railroads

with the continuous travelling, that they can undergo, without serious inconvenience, discomforts and hardships that would kill an ordinary man. The exigencies of a life devoted to wrestling a living from an unyielding and ungenerous wilderness, make frequent feats of endurance a matter of course; yet the severity of the life itself, unartificial, healthy, aboriginal almost, engenders the nervous force necessary to the performance of them. Laziness under these conditions is an impossibility, as even to exist requires, at times, a daily expenditure of energy not always given by the wage-earner to a day's work.

In the summer long trips have to be made by canoe and portage into the interior in search of hunting-grounds, whilst swarms of mosquitoes and black flies make life almost unendurable. In late summer, or early Fall, canoes are loaded down with little less than half a ton of supplies, and have to be run down rapids, or poled up them according to direction, and paddled over big lakes in all kinds of weather, into the selected territory. At every portage the whole outfit must be unloaded, packed across the carry by means of a leather headpiece attached to two ten-foot thongs and known as a "tump line," in loads of from one to three hundred pounds each trip, according to the kind of trail. The canoe is then reloaded and the paddling renewed. No rests are taken on these portages; recuperation is supposed, on the sound theory that a change is as good as a rest, to take place on the return trip for another load.

In these late days game is far to seek, and it is sometimes necessary to go in two or three hundred miles over thirty, forty, or fifty portages, only perhaps to find, with the coming of snow, that what had appeared to be a rich territory when visited on an exploration trip, is now barren, the game having migrated in the interim. The hunter who finds himself caught in such a predicament may be hard put to it to make his expenses, and his whole year is a loss.

The hunting ground reached, a log cabin is built, trails laid out, caches of provisions distributed to outlying points, where tents or other shelters for one-night stands are to be located. Traps are set, meat killed and brought in. Once the snow commences to fall, trails have to be kept open, and traps examined and broken out after every storm, to the number of perhaps two hundred or so, extending over an aggregate of thirty or forty miles of lines. And this is over and above the constant cutting of wood, cooking, tanning of hides, and other routine work.

Expeditions have to be made into far districts with a toboggan loaded with a tent, stove, blankets, and a few provisions, drawn by dogs. This outfit will be set up every night on top of the snow, the only preparation being to tramp the surface solid with snowshoes, and to lay on it a thick layer of balsam brush. Every morning this will be all pulled down again, and loaded, and trail broken ahead of the dogs for another day; and so on for a week at a time.

A man if alone, and going far, needs all the available space in his canoe for provisions, and must often do without dogs, having no room for them. On these side trips he must therefore draw his own toboggan. As he has also to break his own trail, he travels light, taking only a sheet of canvas for a windbreak, and one blanket, sleeping out all night in temperatures often as low as 60 degrees below zero.

Making camp thus is a matter of two or three hours' hard work, and this after a day's hard travelling. The snow has to be dug out over an area of about ten feet each way, as the fire would speedily sink below the level of the camp to the ground otherwise; and not the least labour is the cutting of the large quantity of wood required. Nor dare the trapper lose time to cook, eat, or rest until the last job is done, lest he be caught in the dark with insufficient wood, or otherwise unprepared for the blistering deadly cold.

For there is One who is watching him, has watched him since he entered the woods, waiting for just some such contingency: the grim Spirit of the Silent North, who stalks each lonely traveller's footsteps relentless and implacable, whose will is law in the White Silence. They who enter his Kingdom do well to tread with circumspection.

Once fixed for the night, his hunger satisfied and his pipe going, the refreshed man takes his ease. He is no longer alone, for his dancing fire serves as both friend and comforter; and as he sits and watches the billowing smoke clouds make pictures in the air, he thinks not of the labours of the day just done, but plans the morrow's trip with enthusiasm. Thus he is content, and his scheme of existence, shorn of all the multitudinous complexities of modern life, suffices him; he retains his peace of mind and thinks the cost in hardship well repaid.

During the dead days of mid-winter, when game does not run, the time hangs heavy, and loneliness is often such that only high-pressure activity keeps the mind from wandering into the black abyss of introspection. So that, as a man is more alone with himself in the confinement of the camp, he stays out during all the hours of daylight, and often many of those of darkness, in all weathers, traversing the empty streets of the forest, where the tracks of beasts are as messages from friends, and the very trees seem living entities.

A man so much alone looks kindly on the numerous small birds and animals that congregate around his cabins and camping places. Squirrels that eye him knowingly from the eaves of his roof, chattering and quivering with some violent emotion the while, are tolerated until they become a pest. Ermine are suffered to enter the camp at will through some hidden crack, to flicker noiselessly around in flashes of white, bobbing up almost simultaneously in widely separated spots, thus giving the impression that there are two of them, where there is only one, or that they are able to appear in two places at the one time. Chickadees in little flocks chirrup their "Don't-give-a-darn—Don't-give-a-darn" at him at every stop, and— trail companion that sticketh closer than a brother—the whiskey-jack commits, unpunished, his numerous depredations. This whiskey-jack is a small bird, about the size of a blackbird, but he has more mischief in his small body than there is in a whole bag of cats. He is a scamp, but a likeable rascal, at that. He mocks the calls of other birds and steals bait, or any small articles left around the camp. He loves human company, and, at the first smoke of a camp-fire, he appears mysteriously from nowhere, like a small grey shadow, and perches on a limb, generally right over the trapper's lunch place, knocking snow down his neck or into the cooking as he lights. He has a foolish little song he whistles which is supposed, no doubt, to charm the hunter into giving him a part of his meal. This he generally gets, but does not eat, carrying it away and cacheing it; so he is never full, and stays until the last morsel has disappeared.

A lonely man cannot resist the little bird's begging, and he, as he gets fed, becomes bolder and, should the man move away to fix the fire, will even steal out of the lunch bag. If shoo'ed away, Mr. Whiskey Jack will fly up squawking into a branch and maybe knock some more snow down the trapper's neck, or on to his mitts which he is carefully drying.

A pleasant hour having been spent in this way, the trapper moves on, thinking himself well rid of this impish familiar, and continues baiting his sets. Friend whiskey-jack follows silently and invisibly behind, flying from tree to tree. When the trapper stops and baits his trap, the nuisance watches until he is gone, and just as carefully unbaits it, removing the meat piece by piece, and cacheing it—and so all along the line for miles. And when the trapper returns to his fire place, there is his chum, sitting innocently up on a limb, singing his crazy song, waiting for some more to eat. At one camp I had, there were five or six of these birds, and they used to follow me out on the trail in this way; and in selecting their portion from any moose-meat there was, believe me, they knew the steak from the neck. A man alone for months is glad of their company, in spite of the trouble they make; and for me their friendliness and cheerful whistling have brightened many a lonesome camp fire.

By some dispensation of Providence the unpleasant happenings, the freezings, the burnings, the starvation trips, and the terrific labour are soon forgotten, only the successes and triumphs are remembered. Were it otherwise, not one man in ten would return to the bush after the first trip. A man may be soaking wet, half-frozen, hungry and tired, landed on some inhospitable neck of the woods, vowing that a man is a fool to so abuse himself. Yet, let him but make a fire, get a sheet of canvas between himself and the elements, and a dish of hot tea under his belt, and his previous state of misery will fade from his mind; and he will remark to his partner, his dogs, or his tea-pail, that "Home was never like this," or that "This is the life."

He overcomes his difficulties by skill and cunning, rather than by force, taking a leaf from the Indian's book, thus husbanding his energies against the time when he is tried by the supreme tests of endurance, which occur frequently enough. A saving sense of humour eradicates all feeling of self-pity in times of stress, the only feeling being that elation which one lone man may experience at prevailing against overwhelming odds, and the only comments passed are a few quaint remarks on the queer tricks of Fate. The more lurid flows of profanity are reserved for trivial occurrences, where the energy thus expended will not be missed.

This optimistic state of mind must be carried to the point where—if he lose a canoe-load of goods through miscalculation, or incorrect handling

in a rapids, or should a toboggan piled with necessaries, and what few luxuries he permits himself, go through the ice after being hauled eighty miles
or so—he must be glad it was not worse, see only the silver lining, and
remember he did not drown. Also that he is lucky to, perhaps, have saved a
few matches in a waterproof case, or that he kept his hat dry maybe.

He who lives by the hunt must be patient, and of a monumental calm.
The constant petty annoyances incident to everyday travel, trivial in themselves, become by constant repetition exasperating to a degree, and would
soon drive an irritable man to the verge of insanity. Being much alone, this
modern Spartan subjects himself to a discipline as severe as that demanded
of any soldier, for he cannot allow his emotions ever to gain the upper hand,
lest they get complete control, and that way madness lies. His unceasing vigilance and watchfulness, by constant practice, become almost automatic.
Even in sleep this awareness of what is transpiring around him is subconsciously continued, so that a slight noise, as of the passage of some animal,
or the abrupt cessation of a familiar sound, bring instant wakefulness.

They who would catch a woodsman of the old school asleep do well
to come carelessly and with much noise. A stealthy approach seems to
establish some telepathic communication with the subconscious mind of
one who lives with Nature. This faculty is borrowed from the animals,
and is common amongst Indians. To creep up on a sleeping animal,
except in a canoe, is an impossibility. Domesticated wild animals, lying
asleep, perhaps in the midst of all kinds of noise, will, if gazed at intently,
become uneasy and awaken.

A man's progress through the woods is heralded before him as the
advance of a plague would be down a crowded thoroughfare, and he who
would cope with senses so much more delicately balanced than his own
must needs develop, to some extent, the alertness of the beasts he chases.

Also, he must develop to a remarkable degree the tenacity of life that
they possess. Deer shot through the heart have been known to rush
blindly on for a hundred yards, dead to all intents and purposes. I have
followed moose, shot through the lungs and otherwise wounded, that
travelled doggedly on for miles before falling. So with man, it has sometimes occurred that, having lost everything by some accident, frequent
enough in the unwritten history of the woods, lone bushmen have been

known to stagger out of the wilderness in a dying condition, having striven painfully for days to get to some human habitation, the will to live alone having sustained them until they might safely collapse.

The case is well known of the Scotch half-breed, who was caught by the leg in a bear trap weighing perhaps twenty-five pounds, and fastened to a large tally-pole. He cut through the heavy birch clog with his hunting-knife, no mean feat even for a well man; he then made a sling to hold the leg and trap clear of the ground, and, with the teeth lacerating him at every move, made his way to civilization on improvised crutches—only to die during the night within reach of help, just outside the town limits.

∾∾∾

IN A TERRITORY BEYOND THE JURISDICTION OF THE POLICE, life is simplified down to a few basic principles. Laws become more or less unnecessary, except the few unwritten ones which are tacitly observed; and ostracism, or worse, is the penalty for infringement. In such an elementary state of society complete strangers, meeting, have no means of judging one another save by a few simple direct actions, and it is well to avoid even the appearance of wrongdoing. Witness the case in earlier days of the prospector, who, on meeting a party on the trail, reached quickly towards his hip, and was immediately shot. It transpired that he had merely been in the act of drawing his flask to offer a round of drinks, but the suspicious action, as related by the witness, entirely exonerated his assailant.

Generally speaking your woodsman does not steal.

In the first place, a man usually has all the necessaries or he could not be in the woods at all, also, he has faith in his fellow man, and in the unwritten law that he himself obeys. To take a certain amount of food, to carry a man on to the nearest base of supplies, is not considered other than excusable. In fact, deserted shacks are often found to contain a small supply of essentials, left there by the departing owners with that very end in view. Caches containing goods worth hundreds of dollars are often exposed to view, although sheltered from the weather; and passersby will make repairs to the keep-over if necessary, in the same spirit in which they expect to get it done for them by others.

Once stealing is commenced by a few amateurs and thoughtless or ignorant vandals, the tradition of centuries crumbles, the barriers are down, and stealing becomes the king of outdoor sports. A rifled cache in the woods calls for reprisals of a severe nature and, unless justice can weed out the offenders, sometimes leads to grim tragedy enacted beneath the larch and spruce trees, who keep their secret well; mute witnesses, condoning by their silence a justice as certain and inexorable as the retributions of Nature itself.

Two years ago a white trapper, situated two hundred and forty miles north of the railroad in the Abitibi district, returned one night to his camp to find it destroyed in such a way as to be no longer habitable. Worse, every last ounce of his provision was gone, together with a spare canoe, a tent, and small stove, with which he could have made out to live, on a strictly meat diet, all winter. His remaining stove was smashed beyond possibility of repair.

The man was in a serious position. He had with him a little food left from his trip, enough only for a couple of days at the most. It was the time of year when, owing to ice conditions, travel by canoe was almost impossible. Soon the intense cold of winter, in that parallel, would be upon him and without shelter he must succumb, starvation or no. The time of the raid had obviously been selected with regard to this. Somehow he got out to the "Front," how is not known, except that he arrived in rags, and in a starving condition. I have talked with the man in question, but beyond stating that it "was no picnic" he will not speak of the trip.

The *casus belli* was known to be the disputed ownership of a rich hunting-ground, and the intention of the raiders evidently was that he should never leave the spot alive. The following winter, in the same district, the two parties met, six men all told; threats were exchanged over the muzzles of loaded rifles, and a pitched battle seemed imminent. But the affair had attracted the attention of the Mounted Police and itching trigger-fingers had to be controlled in this instance. Arrests were made and a trial staged. Justice, unable to differentiate between the claims of either side, dropped the case; but such things are never forgotten nor forgiven.

This affair was a modification of the old "Longue Traverse," a scheme adopted by the despotic representatives of a big fur company in earlier days, whereby undesirables, such as freetraders, encroaching trappers and others, were captured, their outfit confiscated, and themselves turned loose with a rifle and a few rounds of ammunition, to find their way on foot, hundreds of miles, to the nearest town. And often enough a pair of Indian killers, earning thereby, perhaps, a rebate on their debt, followed stealthily behind to watch the dying struggles of a starving man with callous apathy, or grimly stalk him day by day, and later shoot him.

A man who has successfully overcome the difficulties, and endured the privations of the trap-line for a few years, can no more quit it than the confirmed gambler can leave his gaming. Trapping is, after all, a gamble on a large scale, the trapper's life and outfit against the strength of the wilderness and its presiding genii, to win a living; and in the hazard he experiences a rare pleasure.

Nor is his life without its compensations. He may climb a mountain, and look as far as the eye can reach, out over illimitable leagues of forested hill and valley stretching into the dim distance, with a feeling of ownership, and there is none to say him nay. And to all intents and purposes it is his, therein to work his will; surely a vast enough estate to satisfy the most land-hungry, and with no taxes or upkeep attached to it. His sole title to possession is the hard-won supremacy he has attained to by unremitting toil, as potent for him as any letters patent could be. The sense of untrammelled freedom and a wild independence, inculcated by wanderings over an unlimited area, enter his soul, unfitting him for any other walk of life. His is the sport of kings, and he is free as no king ever was.

He scans the face of the wilderness, and there gets his inspiration. The pale disc of the moon shining through the interlaced limbs of a leafless tree; the silhouette of tall distant pines against the frosty sky; the long shadows cast by a winter sunset across the white expanse of a snowbound lake, all strike a chord which finds a ready response in his breast. He may not be able, or willing, to express his feelings to the world, but they indubitably impress his unspoken thoughts. The sublimity, the immensity, and the silent majesty of his surroundings influence his character, and the trapper is often a quiet thoughtful man, set in his ways, and not overly given to conversation.

Many are the tales told of his taciturnity; exaggerated accounts, no doubt, many of them, but typical. There is the story of the old-timer, who, in years of solitary wandering, had happened on a particularly pleasant camping ground and was preparing to pass the night there. Presently he saw coming a canoe, and soon a stranger, attracted no doubt by his smoke and the knowledge of the presence of another of his kind in the interminable waste, edged his canoe ashore and landed.

"Fine evening," said the stranger, probably his first speech for months.

"Yeah," replied the old-timer.

"Gosh darned fine camping ground you got here," added the new arrival.

"Uh huh." The habit of a lifetime was not to be so easily broken.

The other man commenced to unload his canoe, and whilst he so busied himself, endeavoured to warm the chill atmosphere by cheerful conversation.

"They's a war in China; d'jy'a hear about it?" he queried.

Receiving no answer he looked up to see his newly-found companion, deliberately folding his blankets, and pulling down his tent, evidently so lately erected.

"What in hell's wrong," he demanded in pained surprise. "Not goin' away, a'ir you?"

"Yes, I' m going away," was the answer. "They's too darn much discussion around here to suit my fancy."

It is related of a man of my acquaintance that on an occasion being informed politely that it was "a great day" he gave no answer; and on the remark being repeated, replied—"I'm not denying it, am I? I don't aim to have no argyment with you!"

Men who follow this life will follow no other, and the interests of the outside world, current events, the doings of the great and the near-great, affect them not at all. I remember being of a party where one of the guides was asked how he could go such long periods without news from the "front," as the railroad is called, the death of a noted film star being cited as an example of such news.

"I don't give a continental hoot," said he, "if Douglas Fairbanks eats his beans with a knife or a shovel. As for that fillum guy you say died, too much of a good thing killed him I guess. Me I'm O.K. here, and I won't die till I'm dam good and ready."

Those used to the polite evasions and diplomatic social intrigue of a higher state of society find the average frontiersman disconcertingly direct in speech on occasion, yet his tact and acumen have been such that in days gone by he was able to deal successfully with savage leaders, past-masters in all the arts of subtlety, where the trained diplomats of Europe failed.

Proud generals have sought his advice on the eve of decisive battles, and without his leadership the successful crossing of the western plains by the great wagon trains of fifty years ago would have been well-nigh impossible. There are no longer any savages or generals contesting for the possession of this country but he still, to-day, shoulders responsibilities as great and as important. He is entrusted with the care of brigades of canoes loaded with valuable cargoes destined for the scene of important development work, and highly trained engineers turn to him for advice when map and compass fail.

Even at this late day, the arts of woodcraft are practised as originally acquired from the Indian, whose highly specialized faculties his white contemporary has more or less successfully emulated. Having for neighbours a people who carry drums to celebrate the Wabeno and wear charms to ward off evil spirits, the white trapper has naturally imbibed some of their lesser superstitions. If he has bad luck he is none too sure that he is not conjured by some enemy. He feels that there is no actual harm done by cutting out the knee-caps from the hind legs of his beaver carcases and burning them, or by placing a small portion of tobacco in the brain-box of a bear he kills and hanging the skull on a tree.

Sometimes old hands, soured by the disappointments of several bad seasons in succession, will proclaim that they have quit the game, are off the trail for life. But come Fall, the smell of a smoky wood-fire, or the sight of some portion of well-used equipment, companion of many a long and arduous journey, brings up a chain of recollection, and the hunt is on again.

One of the most successful trappers I ever knew was visited with about all the bad luck that could be crowded into one season. The beaver in his district developed a degree of sagacity unusual even in those animals. They evaded his sets persistently, springing traps, and stealing bait with monotonous regularity. A swarm of rabbits descended on the land, and on nearly every occasion on which a valuable animal entered a trap house, the rabbits were there first, getting themselves caught, and providing an excellent chain of free lunches to the fur bearers, who disdainfully refused his other lures. Omitting to remove a greased plug from the muzzle one day, he blew the end off the best rifle in the world, as he was wont to call it. Early in the Fall a cloudburst had transformed a dry creek into a raging torrent, carrying away a tent and complete outfit erected as a branch camp in an outlying district. A man of Indian training, he was superstitiously inclined, as is common; so, when, after slicing one of his feet with an axe, he found one of his dogs eating the bones of one of the few beaver he had caught*, he commenced to figure that there was a nigger in the woodpile somewhere, and left the woods, selling most of his gear.

The next year, resolving to try his luck once more, he reassembled an outfit, and hit the trail for over the hills and far away; only to find one morning, his canoe, left overnight at the far end of a portage, completely stripped of its canvas by a bear. Apprehensive of what further disaster might lie in store, he patched up the canoe, returned to town, and sold out completely. He had been a saving man, so he built him a nifty bakeshop, and did well selling bread to the people of the village.

Coming on Fall, 1 tried to persuade him to come in with me, saying 1 would lend him the equipment, but he stood firm to his decision. As I was leaving town for the last time I paused at his little shop in passing. It was a cool day in Indian Summer, the tang of Autumn was in the air, and a bluish haze softened the outlines of the wooded hills across the lake, which, calm as a sheet of glass, reflected the forest that crowded down to its very edge in reds, yellows, and russet browns. The sun was shining brightly, but without heat, through the smoke of woodfires from the houses of our little town, as it hung in wisps and whorls in the still air.

The old fellow was standing outside his door, looking beyond the smoke, into the distant hills, gay in their autumn colouring. I held out my hand to bid him farewell, and just then came a chill puff of wind, from nowhere at all, blowing some yellow leaves from a bush to our feet where they eddied momentarily and went fluttering and rustling down the empty street. He followed them with his eyes. Turning suddenly, he

*Among the more primitive Indians and trappers it is considered derogatory to the beaver, on account of his high intelligence, that a dog should eat any part of the carcase, especially the bones. The carcases must all be returned to the water, or, if eaten by man, the bones restored to their element.

struck my hand aside. "Hell," said he. "Good-bye nothin'! gimme some traps an' a gun, I'm comin' with you!"

There are exceptions, but the professional hunter and woods-runner seen at the trading posts is rarely the shaggy, bearded, roaring individual depicted in the movies and some books; but a quiet, purposeful-eyed man, out in town, after the hunt, to have a good time in his own way.

Rarely does he leave the bush in the winter months, unless perhaps at New Year, and I have seen some lively times at trappers' conventions at that season. Habits of silence and watchfulness make him a somewhat taciturn person, but when in congenial company, and his tongue perhaps loosened by a few applications of the New Year's spirit, the effect of the gloom of shadowy forests fades temporarily away, and the repression of word and action gives way to a boisterous hilarity.

Some save their gains, others engage in a well-earned spree, as has been customary with frontiersmen from time immemorial. On these occasions they spend money like water, and indulge in generosities that would stagger a city worker, seeming to place little value on the money so hardly earned.

His short holiday over, some morning at daybreak the trapper loads his toboggan and harnesses up his team, amidst the barking and howling of huskies, near huskies, and just plain dogs, and is gone. He has no thought of the money he spent, the good times he had, or didn't have; true to type his mind is on the trail ahead. And as he passes the first fringe of the forest, which is never any great distance from these outposts of civilization, he enters the enchanted world of which he is as much a part as the ancient trees, the eternal snows, and the dancing Northern Lights. The magic of the winter wilderness descends on him like a cloak, and the waiting hush that covers the face of Nature, reaches out and engulfs him.

An anachronism, belonging to a day long past, he marches back down the avenues of time, a hundred years in as many steps. With a glance at the sun for direction, and eye to the lie of the land easiest for his dogs, feeling for signs of an unseen and drifted trail with his feet, he swings along on his big snow-shoes, out across the Frontier, beyond the ken of mortal man, to be no more seen in the meagre civilization he has left behind, till the suns of springtime shall have melted the snowdrifts from the hillsides, and cleared the lakes of ice.

Whether treading bitter trails, or resting securely in warm log cabins; faltering over empty barrens with, staring eyes; hollow-cheeked with hunger or with hands dyed to the wrist with the rich blood of newly killed meat; fighting for life with desperate strokes in the hungry white water, or floating peacefully along some slow, winding river; these men of the Last Frontier are toilsomely, patiently, but indubitably laying the stepping-stones by which will pass the multitudes of future ages.

On the outskirts of the Empire this gallant little band of men still carries on the game that is almost played. The personnel changes as the years roll on, but the spirit remains the same. Each succeeding generation takes up the work that is laid down by those who pass along, leaving behind them traditions and a standard of achievement that must be lived up to by those who would claim a membership in the brotherhood of the Keepers of the Trails; bequeathing something of their courage, self-sacrifice, and devotion to a cause, to those who follow.

These are the soldiers of the Border Lands. Whether recruited from pioneer stock, and to the manner born, or from the ranks of the wage earners; whether scion of a noble house, or the scapegrace who, on account of some thoughtless act has left the haunts of men, or, perchance, a rolling-stone to whom adventure is as the breath of life; each and every one is playing his allotted part in that heroic struggle which is making possible the fulfilment of the greater and more lasting purpose of the future.

We, to-day, of this generation, are seeing the last of the free trappers; a race of men, who, in passing, will turn the last page in the story of true adventure on this continent, closing forever the book of romance in Canadian History. The forest cannot much longer stand before the conquering march of modernity, and soon we shall witness the vanishing of a mighty wilderness.

And the fast Frontiersman, its offspring, driven back further and further towards the North into the far-flung reaches where are only desolation and barrenness, must, like the forest that evolved him, bow his head to the inevitable and perish with it. And he will leave behind him only his deserted, empty trails, and the ashes of his dead camp fires, as landmarks for the oncoming millions. And with him will go his friend the Indian to be a memory of days and a life that are past beyond recall.

The Land of Shadows

"Full in the passage of the vale above
A sable silent solemn forest stood
Where nought but shadowy forms were seen to move."

CHAPTER TWO

The Land of Shadows

SIDE BY SIDE WITH THE MODERN CANADA THERE LIES THE last battle-ground in the long-drawn-out, bitter struggle between the primeval and civilization. I speak not of those picturesque territories, within easy reach of transport facilities, where a sportsman may penetrate with a moccasined taciturn Indian, or a weather-beaten and equally reticent white man, and get his deer, or his fishing; places where, in inaccessible spots, lone white pines, one-time kings of all the forest, gaze in brooding melancholy out over the land that once was theirs. In such districts, traversed by accurately mapped water routes and well-cut portages, all the necessities and most of the luxuries of civilization may be transported with little difficulty.

But to those on whom the magic lure of far horizons has cast its spell, such places lack the thrill of the uncharted regions. Far beyond the fringe of burnt and lumbered wastes adjacent to the railroads, there lies another Canada little known, unvisited except by the few who are willing to submit to the hardships, loneliness, and toil of long journeys in a land where civilization has left no mark and opened no trails, and where there are no means of subsistence other than those provided by Nature.

Large areas of this section are barren of game, no small consideration to the adventurer caught by the exigencies of travel, for an extended period, in such a district. The greater part, however, is a veritable sportsman's paradise, untouched except by the passing hunter, or explorer; those hardy spirits for whom no privation is too severe, and no labour so arduous as to prevent them from assuaging the wanderlust that grips them and drives them out into the remaining waste places, where the devastating axe has not yet commenced its deadly work, out beyond the Height of Land, over the Great Divide.

This "Backbone of Canada" so called, sometimes known as the Haute Terre, stretches across the full breadth of the continent, East and West, dividing the waters that run south from those that run north to the Arctic Sea. In like manner it forms a line of demarcation between the prosaic realities of a land of everyday affairs, and the enchantment of a realm of high adventure, unconquered, almost unknown, and unpeopled except by a few scattered bands of Indians and wandering trappers.

This hinterland yet remains a virgin wilderness lying spread out over half a continent; a dark, forbidding panorama of continuous forest, with here and there a glistening lake set like a splash of quicksilver amongst the tumbled hills. A harsher, sterner land, this, than the smiling Southland; where manhood and experience are put to the supreme test, where the age-old law of the survival of the fittest holds sway, and where strength without cunning is of no avail. A region of illimitable distance, unknown lakes, hidden rivers, and unrecorded happenings; and changed in no marked way since the white man discovered America.

Here, even in these modern days, lies a land of Romance, gripping the imagination with its immensity, its boundless possibilities and its magic of untried adventure. Thus it has lain since the world was young, enveloped in a mystery beyond understanding, and immersed in silence, absolute, unbroken, and all-embracing; a silence intensified rather than relieved by the muted whisperings of occasional light forest airs in the tree-tops far overhead.

Should the traveller in these solitudes happen to arrive at the edge of one of those high granite cliffs common to the country and look around him, he will see, not the familiar deciduous trees of the south, but will find that he is surrounded, hemmed in on all sides, by apparently endless black forests of spruce, stately trees, cathedral-like with their tall spires above, and their gloomy aisles below. He will see them as far as the eye can reach, covering hill, valley, and ridge, spreading in a green carpet over the face of the earth. Paraded in mass formation, standing stiffly, yet gracefully, to attention, and opposing a wellnigh impenetrable barrier to the further encroachments of civilization, until they too shall fall before the axe, a burnt offering on the altar of the God of Mammon.

In places this mighty close-packed host divides to sweep in huge undulating waves along the borders of vast inland seas, the far shores of which show only as a thin, dark line shimmering and dancing in the summer heat. These large lakes on the Northern watershed are shallow for the most part, and on that account dangerous to navigate. But in spots are deep holes, places where cliffs hundreds of feet high run sheer down to the water's edge, and on to unfathomed depths below. Risen from the lofty crags by the frosts of centuries, fallen rocks, some of them of stupendous size, lie on some submerged ledge like piles of broken masonry, faintly visible in the clear water, far below. And from out the dark fissures and shadowy caverns among them, slide long, grey, monstrous forms; for here is the home of the great lake trout of the region, taken sometimes as high as forty pounds in weight.

In places long low stretches of flat rock reach up out of the water, entering the wall of forest at a gentle incline. Their smooth surface is studded with a scattered growth of jackpines, fashioned into weird shapes by the wind, and, because standing apart, wide and spreading of limb, affording a grateful shade after long heats at the paddle on the glaring expanse of lake. These are the summer camping grounds of the floating caravans, and off these points a man may catch enough fish for a meal in the time it takes another to make the preparations to cook them.

In the spring time, in sheltered bays, lean and sinuous pike of inordinate size, hungry-looking and rapacious, lie like submarines awash, basking in the sunlight. Shooting them at this season is exciting sport, as only the large ones have this habit, and fish up to fifty inches in length are common.

Here and there, too, the sable carpet of evergreen treetops is gashed by long shining ribbons of white, as mighty rivers tumble and roar their way to Hudson's Bay, walled in on either side by their palisades of spruce trees, whose lofty arches give back the clatter of rapids or echo to the thunder of the falls.

Far beneath the steeple tops, below the fanlike layers of interlaced limbs that form a vaulted roof through which the sunlight never penetrates, lies a land of shadows. Darkened aisles and corridors lead on to nowhere. A gloomy labyrinth of smooth, grey columns stretches in every direction into the dimness until the view is shut off by the wall of trees that seems to forbid the further progress of the intruder. This barrier opens up before him, as he goes forward, but closes down behind him as though, having committed himself to advance he may not now retire; it hems him in on either side at a given distance as he proceeds, a mute, but ever-present escort. Here, in the endless mazes of these halls of silence, is neither time nor distance, nor direction.

Here exists a phantom world of unreality, where obstacles crumble beneath the touch and formless undefinable objects loom up vaguely in the middle distance, fading to nothingness on near approach. Elusive creatures whose every movement is furtive, light of foot, springy, effortless of gait, go their soundless ways; grey ghosts that materialize and vanish on the instant, melting into the shadows at the sight of man, to stand observing him from skilfully selected cover.

Above, below, and on all sides is moss; moss in a carpet, deadening the footfall of the traveller, giving beneath his step, and baffling by its very lack of opposition his efforts to progress. Moss stands in waist-high hummocks, around which detours must be made. Moss in festoons hangs from the dead lower limbs of the trees, like the hangings in some ancient and deserted temple. And a temple it is, raised to the god of silence, of a stillness that so dominates the consciousness that the wanderer who threads its deserted naves treads warily, lest he break unnecessarily a hush that has held sway since time began.

In places the dense growth of spruce gives way to sandy plains, where, more open but still a heavy enough forest, are stretches of jackpine. Here the gnarled and uncouth limbs, and the ragged grotesquely twisted tops of these deformed hybrids, throw fantastic shadows at the full of the moon on the floor of this devil's dance-hall,—shadows in and out of which flit the Puck-wah-jeesh in their goblin dances, as they hold high revel to the tune of their soundless drums, and plot fresh mischief against the Indian.

∾ ∾ ∾

NOT ALL THE WILD LANDS GLOOM IN SULLEN SHADOW. THERE are vistas, unbelievably beautiful, to be seen beyond the boles of giant trees edging some declivity, of sun-drenched valleys, or wide expanse of plain, blue with its luscious carpet of berries. Occasional grassy glades, oases in the sameness of the sunless grottos surrounding them, refresh the mind and eye, seeming intimate and friendly after the aloofness of the stately forest.

Huge burns, of ancient time and unknown origin, lie like scars, across the landscape. Here all the foundation and structure of the earth's surface, hitherto jealously hidden, lies naked and exposed. Smooth round mountains bare of vegetation, upthrust of Keewaydin*, the oldest known rock, rear themselves above the arid waste, monuments to the mighty upheaval that belched them forth from the bowels of the earth. High broken cliffs and precipitous crags of red granite flank the boulder-strewn gulleys, and dried-out stream beds. Immense masses of rock, cracked open by the intense heat of forgotten fires, lie fallen apart, choking the valleys. No movement of a living beast, no sound of a bird, relieves the staring desolation. This is the world as it was after the age of ice, the scratches and gouges of its slow passage still visible on the now solid rocks. Here, a prospector, skilled in the science of metals, may find his Eldorado.

The culminating reward of the fruitless labour of a lifetime may stand out freely for all to see in one of those white bands of quartz that shine so glassily on the mountain side, and indication of untold riches may lie beneath the surface of a handful of gravel, to be exposed by some careless movement of a foot, or perhaps by the lighting of a fire.

There are ridges, becoming rarer as one journeys towards the Arctic Circle, of birch and poplar, cheerful with their bright trunks, and sun-spotted leafy floor, so familiar below the Height of Land. Here are singing birds and partridges, and also the main routes of moose and bears in summer; their trail, as well beaten as any portage, affording a never-failing guide to a lake or river. These are the Hills of the Whispering Leaves of the Indians, so called because of the continuous rustling flutter of the poplar

*An Indian word meaning land of the N.W. Wind, or the wind itself. The name is applied generally to the North Country beyond the Height of Land, and is also the name of this rock (Keewatin) in mineralogy.

leaves, shivering and trembling in the lightest current of air, in contrast to the motionless foliage of the conifers which so monopolise the landscape.

It is in such places, near a pleasant, sunny lake, or by a cheerful, shouting brook, that the red men spend the lazy days of the short north-country summer, resting from the arduous toil of the long winter. Nor are they idle, for now they are already preparing equipment for next winter's hunt; tanning hides for clothing and making their cunningly devised snowshoes and toboggans, against the time when the Hunting Winds hold sway. And during the long afterglow which precedes the coming of darkness in these high latitudes, they sit by smoky fires and listen to some white-haired teller of the tales of ancient days, when in one lift of traps a man might half-fill a canoe with beaver, or spear sufficient sturgeon for his winter needs in a single night.

In places the forest dwindles down to small trees which, giving way to moss and sage brush, thin out and eventually disappear altogether, and the country opens out into one of those immense muskegs or swamps which make overland travel in whole sections of this territory impossible in the summer time. These consist mostly of stretches composed of deep, thin mud, covered with slushy moss, and perhaps sparsely dotted with stunted, twisted trees. Bright green, inviting-looking fields show up in places, luring the inexperienced into their maw with their deceptive promise of good footing. These last are seemingly bottomless, and constitute a real danger to man or beast, excepting the lordly moose, who, by some unknown means is able to walk over, or swim through, such places unscathed. There are holes between hummocks that are filled with noisome stagnant water, which would engulf a man. The whole thing is practically a floating bog, yet the only good water to be found, perhaps for miles around, is in just such places, to be obtained in the small pitcher plants which grow thickly, with about as much as an eggcup will hold in each.

But the main part of the country is clothed in its dark-green robe of spruce trees. They stand in serried rows around every lake, and wall in every river to the banks, darkening them with their shadows, still sentinels on guard from everlasting.

∾∾∾

IN THE FASTNESSES OF THIS RAPIDLY FADING FRONTIER, THE last on this continent, reigns the Spirit of the North Land. Enthroned behind the distant mountains with the cohorts and legions of his last grand army massed about him, he sallies forth, brooding over the length and breadth of the land, seeking whom he may destroy, ever devising new means for the elimination of the invaders of his chosen realm. His is not the spectacular kill by the shedding of blood, not the shock of honest battle in the open, but by devious ways and subtle methods he obtains his ends. Securely entrenched behind the bristling ramparts of the forest, with all the unleashed forces of the primeval at his command, he primes his deadly weapons, and spreads his entanglements, his obstacles, and his snares; nor are they always vainly set.

Through them the invader must pick his way with the delicacy and assurance of one who walks barefoot amongst naked knives. Some of his weapons are merely annoyances, irritating but bearable; others are harassing to the point of obsession, wearing out the body and mind, and lessening the resisting power of a man; others, yet, bring swift death, or the long slow agonies of those who would die but cannot.

A stiff, wiry growth of sage brush, knee-deep and tangled, cumbers the ground over large areas. Mosquitoes, black flies, moose flies, and sand flies in relentless swarms make the forest almost uninhabitable for three months of the four of which the summer consists. The immense inland seas, shallow and exposed, are frequently whipped to fury on short notice, or none at all, by terrific storms, which, gathering force over the Height of Land, lash these northern latitudes with unbelievable fury. Forest fires, irresistible, all-devouring, sweep at times through the close-set resinous timber at railroad speed, leaving in their wake a devastation of bare hills and smoking stumps; desperate indeed is the plight of the voyageur so trapped far from water. Frequently miles of rapids have to be negotiated, where only the greatest skill and courage, coupled with days at a time of heart-breaking and exhausting labour, can gain the objective. In winter snow often lies six feet deep in the woods and at the railroad, a hundred or so miles to the south, sixty-five degrees below zero (Fahr.) is no uncommon temperature. A rise in temperature often precipitates a blizzard, and these winter storms are so violent as to destroy whole areas of timber by sheer weight alone; the solitary trapper caught on the trail by one of these tempests, with little or no warning, especially if crossing any large lake, is in grave danger. His dogs, blinded and half-choked by the wind-driven masses of snow, cannot face the storm. Himself unable to break trail through the mounting drifts, or to keep his direction through the whirling white wall that surrounds him at the distance of a few feet, he may, if far from land, perish miserably.

Perhaps, wisely relying on his dogs to lead him ashore, he may, if lucky, find wood and shelter enough for his protection. A broken axe handle under these conditions would be not only an inconvenience, but a disaster with probably fatal results. Here, with his toboggan sheet for a windbreak, a bed of hastily laid brush, and a pile of wood sufficient to do all night, gathered with infinite labour, he can make some kind of a stand to live out the storm.

The howling wind fills his shelter with blinding smoke, and the fire only serves to melt the snow as it accumulates on blankets, food and clothing, wetting everything; cooking is impossible, and content with a pail of tea and perhaps some thawed-out fish intended for dog feed, he and his shivering huskies crouch by the fire all the long night. And often enough the cold light of morning breaks on a shelter half-filled with drifting snow, a fire long since extinguished, and a pack of whining wolf-dogs waiting in vain to be harnessed up, later to run wild with the wolves.

The waterways that form a network over large sections are the lines of travel of not only man, but of mink, otter, and other animals, who go their rounds as regularly as any man. Further back in the hills range fisher, marten and wolves, in their never-ceasing hunt for meat to abate their continuous hunger. In sheltered spots among heavy timber, the giant moose yards up in small herds. Although they are six feet high at the shoulder the snow lies at times so deep in the forest that they are unable to navigate, moving only a few yards daily, eating and sleeping alternately. As they move they plough a trench through the snow about three feet wide, and maybe five feet deep, a pitfall for those who travel at night. Here they stay until spring thaws leave them free to wander back to their favourite haunts of lily ponds and marshes.

These animals grow, in the season between June and September, sets of horns of from thirty to sixty or seventy inches' spread, losing them again in January. They put up terrific battles among themselves in the fall, and dead moose are a common sight in the woods at that season, with at least one bear in attendance on the feast so provided, fattening up for the long winter sleep.

Back off main routes in lonely ponds, or on dammed-up streams in hidden gullies, communities of beaver work all summer against the coming of winter, passing the cold dead months of the year, as a reward for their prodigious labour, well fed and in comfort and warmth. The shores of lakes, swamps and the edges of the frozen fen lands, are the hunting grounds of lynxes and foxes, for in such places abound the snowshoe rabbits, their prey.

In a wilderness apparently without life there is a teeming population continuously on the move, yet a man may travel for days at a time and see nothing but the trees around him, and hear nothing save the sounds he himself makes. For here man is the only alien, the arch-enemy from whom all the dwellers in this sanctuary flee, as from pollution. Apprised of his approach by senses trained to register the least discordant note in the symmetry of their surroundings, they disappear long before he arrives in the vicinity. All along his line of travel this is going on and hardly ever is he permitted to see or hear the living creatures that surround him on every side.

Animals seem to be able to distinguish instantly the slightest noise made by man, from that of any other forest dweller. The laughing owls may hoot in uncouth cackling whoops; a beaver may waken the echoes with a resounding smack of his tail on the water; a tree may fall with a crash, or a moose walk carelessly along rattling the underbrush, or smashing dry sticks underfoot, and cause no more commotion than the shake of an ear or the flick of a tail. But let a man so much as break a twig or rustle the dry grass of a beaver meadow, and all living creatures within earshot will, each according to his kind, sink beneath the surface of the water without a ripple, fade soundlessly into the shadows, leap with astonishing bounds to cover, or freeze into immobility, if their colour scheme harmonizes sufficiently well with the immediate background.

There are two notable exceptions to this, however; the skunk and the porcupine. The latter beast is dumb cousin to the beaver, whom he resembles very closely except for the tail, the webbed hind feet, and his bristles. But it seems that when the brains were handed out between the two of them, the porcupine was absent and the beaver got them all. With no regard for personal safety, to him strange noises or the smell of cooking, are as music and ambrosia; and a camp will not be very long pitched, in a country where they abound, before a "porky " will be over to make his inspection. Save for an insatiable appetite for canoe gunwales, paddles, leather goods, provisions of all kinds, anything made of wood, canvas, paper,—or perhaps it were easier to say everything not made of iron or steel,—and for a bad habit he has of leaving barbed quills lying around carelessly, he is a harmless enough beast. Skunks are also friendly, and if undisturbed are as goodnatured as a cat. They also have the community spirit, but this can be carried too far, as in the instance when I awoke one morning to find a number one extra large specimen curled up on my blankets. I made several attempts to rise and on each occasion he became very agitated, so 1 had to lie in bed until he was pleased to go.

To the majority of the dwellers in the centres of civilization the animals inhabiting the waste places are nothing more than savage creatures, wandering aimlessly about, with no thought beyond the satisfaction of one or two animal appetites. But closer observation reveals the fact that nearly all of them have more native intelligence than those animals that have spent many generations dependent on man, and amongst the higher orders among them their "personal" relations are such that the word "brute" as term of contempt is somewhat of a misnomer. Ferocious as many of them undoubtedly are when in pursuit of their prey, they all have their lighter moments, and their lives are almost as well regulated as those of human beings living under the same conditions.

They form strong attachments amongst themselves. Beaver work in shifts, keep a clean house, and hold rapid fire conversations together; coons wash their food before eating it. Most of them keep trails, especially beaver, deer, and bears, and in the case of the latter animal they blaze the boundaries of their territories in places by biting and tearing bark off trees, and it is known that they do not encroach on each other. They will climb a tree for the express purpose of sliding down again, doing this repeatedly for no other reason than the kick they get out of it. Otter also play together, and will climb a steep bank and slide down into the water uttering sharp barks of enjoyment, climb up, and slide again, much after the fashion of human beings on a toboggan slide; they, too, travel in well-defined territories, passing certain spots every eight or nine days with the regularity of clockwork. Crows, gulls and eagles will fly into the wind during a gale, and then turning, allow themselves to be blown down wind at dizzy speed, flying back upwind and repeating the performance until satisfied. Wolves when hunting exhibit team work similar to that employed by football players, send out scouts, obey the orders of a leader, and will gambol and play on the ice precisely as do pedigreed collies on a lawn.

Man is not the only trapper in the wilderness. There are insects that dig holes into which their prey falls and is captured before he can get out. Water spiders set nets shaped like saxophones, the large end facing upstream, to catch anything floating down, and round the curve, in the small end, waits the spider. Wolves divide their forces to capture deer, and I saw one of them drive a deer across a stream, whilst another waited in the brush on the other side for him to land. I know of another occasion on which three wolves cornered a caribou on a fair-sized lake. In the timber the snow was too soft for either wolves or caribou to make much headway. It was April and the ice was clear of snow and slippery as glass. A caribou's hoof is hollowed out in such a way that it grips the ice, but the wolves had difficulty in making any speed. The caribou ran round and round the lake, a distance of several miles each trip, thinking, no doubt, to tire the wolves; but two would rest whilst one chased the caribou, taking each his turn until the deer dropped from exhaustion.

Of the creatures that inhabit the woods, by far the lesser number are of a predatory nature. The majority consists of the varieties of deer, the rodents, and the smaller birds. Nature is cruel, and the flesh-eating animals and birds kill their prey in the most bloodthirsty manner, tearing off and eating portions of meat before the unfortunate animal is dead. The thought of this considerably lessens the compunction one might feel in trapping carnivorous animals, as they are only getting a dose of their own medicine and do not undergo a tithe of the sufferings they inflict on their victims, often hastening their own end by paroxysms of fury.

ɔ ɔ ɔ

ALTHOUGH THIS COUNTRY OFFERS SUCH RESISTANCES TO overland travel during the short summer of the region, with the coming of winter, with its ice and snow, which are apt to cause stagnation in settled areas, all these difficulties cease. Once the freeze-up comes, and the woods are in the grip of winter, and snowshoes can be used, usually early in November, a man may go where he will without let or hindrance. Moss, sage-brush and muskeg no longer retard progress.

The one-time gloomy forest becomes cheerful in its bright mantle of snow, the weight of which bears down the fanlike foliage of the evergreens, letting in the sunlight, and what once were shadowed crypts become avenues of light. Swift dog-teams race down the snowy highways between the trees, where in summer men plodded wearily over the insecure footing at the rate of perhaps a mile an hour. Once snow commences to fall no creature may move without leaving the signs of his passage. All the goings, the comings, the joys, and the tragedies of the forest folk are printed there for the experienced eye to read. Nothing intrigues the imagination of a hunter so much as the sight of fresh tracks. There in the snow is a story; but, although the characters are so plainly written, he must needs be an expert who would interpret them.

Easily distinguishable to the initiated are the tracks of each variety of beast, say, the peculiar trail of an otter; three or four hops and a slide, more short hops and another slide, sometimes yards in length. The lynx leaves tracks which in point of size might well pass for those of a small lion; the leaping progression of Wapoose the white rabbit, whose exaggerated hind feet have gained for him the title of "snowshoe" rabbit, shows everywhere. These feet are partially webbed, and have a large spread, enabling him to pass without sinking over the softest snow, and where a single track shows plainly, it much resembles that of some gigantic bird of prey.

Very common are the delicate, paired footprints of the ermine; and similar, but larger, and not so numerous, are those of the fisher, and marten; common too are the neat, mincing footmarks of the fox, spaced, like those of the lynx, exactly in line, and as regularly as the "tuck" of a drum. Often can be seen where an owl has swooped down on a skurrying rabbit, his imprint plainly showing where he missed his stroke and landed in the snow, the rabbit doubling, twisting, racing, screeching with mortal fear, and the owl, in muffled deadly silence, following every twist and turn, but unable to strike. Here and there the drag of a wing, the scrape of wicked claws, show plainly the progress of the struggle. For fifty yards or so this may go on, and at the end, a torn skin, the heavier bones, and the entrails. For your owl is fastidious and skins his victims, alive, taking only the best of the meat.

From now on the trapper, with the tell-tale tracks to guide him, can place his snares to greater advantage at the various crossings and routes, now easily discovered, which animals as well as human beings devise to facilitate their ceaseless travels.

Soon comes the time of the Dead Days. The wind no longer whispers and sighs through the tree-tops, deadened by their load of snow, and the silence, intense enough before the coming of winter, now becomes the dominating feature of the landscape. In these padded corridors sound has no penetration and the stillness becomes almost opaque. It is as though one walked through an endless vaulted chamber, walled, roofed and paved with silence. Unconsciously one listens, waiting, straining to hear some sound which seems imminent, but never actually occurs, and all Nature seems to stand with bated breath, waiting momentarily for the occurrence of some long-threatened incident. The swish of the snow-shoes, and the light rustle of garments are thrown back thinly to the ear, and the crack of a rifle is chopped off short in a dull thud.

Storm after storm piles the snow higher and higher on the stratified limbs of the spruce, until the mounting roll of snow meets the burdened limb next above it. Other storms smooth off the irregularities with a finishing blanket of snow, and the trees become transformed into immense pointed columns of white. Those of smaller growth, completely covered, show only as squat pillars and mounds fantastically sculptured by the keen-edged winds into the semblance of weird statuary.

Beautiful as this Arctic forest appears in the daytime, it is only by moonlight, when much travelling is done to avoid the cutting winds of the daylight hours, that the true witchery of the winter wilderness grips the imagination. Seen by the eerie light of the moon, the motionless, snow-shrouded trees that line the trail, loom on either hand like grim spectres, gruesomely arrayed, each in his winding-sheet, staring sardonically down on the hurrying wayfarer. In the diffused uncertain light the freakish artistry of the wind appears like the work of some demented sculptor, and the trail becomes a gallery of grinning masks and uncouth featureless forms, as of dwellers in a world of goblins turned suddenly to stone.

Athwart the shafts of moonlight, from out the shadows, move sound-less forms with baleful gleaming eyes, wraiths that flicker before the vision for a moment and are gone. The Canada lynx, great grey ghost of the Northland; the huge white Labrador wolf; white rabbits, white weasels, the silvery ptarmigan: pale phantoms of the white silence. A phantasy in white in a world that is dead.

And in the moonlight, too, is death. The full of the moon is the period of most intense cold, and there have been men who, already exhausted by a day's travel, and carrying on by night, half-asleep as they walked, their senses lulled by the treacherous glow, decided to sleep for just a little while on a warm-looking snow bank, and so slept on forever. So Muji-Manito, the Evil Genius of the North, cold and pitiless, malignantly tri-umphant, adds another victim to his gruesome tally.

Then later, when the moon has set, in that stark still hour between the darkness and the dawn, the snow gives back the pale sepulchral glare of the Northern Lights; and by their unearthly illumination, those who dance the Dance of the Deadmen* perform their ghostly evolutions, before the vast and solumn audience of spruce.

And then the stillness is broken by the music of the wolves, whose unerring instinct senses tragedy. It comes, a low moaning, stealing through the thin and brittle air, swelling in crescendo to a volume of sound, then dying away in a sobbing wail across the empty solitudes; echoing from hill to hill in fading repetition, until the reiteration of sound is lost in the immensity of immeasurable distance.

*Indian name for the Northern Lights.

And as the last dying echo fades to nothing, the silence settles down layer by layer, pouring across the vast deserted auditorium in billow after billow, until all sound is completely choked beyond apparent possibility of repetition. And the wolves move on to their ghastly feast, and the frozen wastes resume their endless waiting; the Deadmen dance their grisly dance on high, and the glittering spruce stand silently and watch.

This then is the Canada that lies back of your civilization, the wild, fierce land of desperate struggle and untold hardship, where Romance holds sway as it did when Canada was one vast hunting ground. This is the last stronghold of the Red Gods, the heritage of the born adventurer. In this austere and savage region men are sometimes broken, or aged beyond their years; yet to those who are able to tune in on their surroundings, and care to learn the lessons that it teaches, it can become a land of wild, romantic beauty and adventure.

Up beyond the wavering line of the Last Frontier lies not merely a region of trees, rocks and water, but a rich treasure-house, open to all who dare the ordeal of entry, and transformed by the cosmic sorcery of the infinite into a land of magic glades and spirit-haunted lakes, of undiscovered fortunes, and sunset dreams come true.

This is the face of Nature, unchanged since it left the hands of its Maker, a soundless, endless river, flowing forever onward in the perpetual cycle which is the immutable law of the universe.

Not much longer can the forest hope to stem the tide of progress; change is on every hand. Every year those who follow the receding Border further and further back, see one by one the links with the old days being severed, as the demands of a teeming civilization reach tentacles into the very heart of the Wild Lands. And we who stand regretfully and watch, must either adapt ourselves to the new conditions, or, preferably, follow the ever-thinning line of last defence into the shadows, where soon will vanish every last one of the Dwellers amongst the Leaves.

The Trail

"Send not your foolish and feeble; send me your strong and your sane,
Strong for the red rage of battle; sane, for I harry them sore."
SERVICE

CHAPTER THREE

The Trail

THE TRAIL! YOU VISUALIZE A SMOOTH, NARROW PATH meandering in and out between stately trees; lightfooted Indians slipping noiselessly by; a highway between two points unknown; a winding road to dreams, romance, and mystery.

It can be that. It can also be the faintly discernible, at times invisible, crushing of dry moss on sun-scorched rocks, with little or no other indication of the passage there of generations of wandering tribesmen. It may be but a few broken twigs, turned leaves, or bent grasses, displaced by the single passage of some adventurer, which, slowly twisting back to their former position, are no more disturbed by the foot of man; or a well-defined, beaten main route, hard-packed by the traffic of centuries; the smooth and easy road to disaster, or the rough and arduous road to fortune.

On it may pass the wealth of a nation, from some fabulously rich Eldorado, or the staggering wreck of a beaten man, broken on the wheel of incompetence or misfortune. The Trail is the stage on which all the drama, the burlesque, the tragedy, and the comedy of the wilderness is played. On these narrow paths that thread their secret ways through hidden places, are performed epic deeds of courage and self-sacrifice and incredible acts of treachery and cowardice.

On the Trail the soul of a man is stripped bare and naked, exposed for all to see, and here his true nature will come out, let him dissemble never so wisely. The pleasant and versatile companion of a social entertainment

may exhibit unsuspected traits of pusillanimity, and weakness of character, when put to the test; and the unassuming, self-effacing "wallflower"
may show an unexpected fund of resourcefulness, and by sheer strength of
ill perform prodigies of valour which his sturdier brethren shrink from.

Night and day the Trail makes its insistent demands on the ingenuity,
the resourcefulness, and the endurance of a man. Work on the Trail is
synonymous with the contact between an irresistible force and an
immovable object. The issue is entirely in the air until the last incident of
that particular trip is closed. The whole course of a journey may be
changed, or increased hardship caused, by such apparent trivialities as a
change of wind, or the passing away of clouds from the face of the sun.
An hour lost may mean a day or more beyond schedule at the other end,
with attendant shortage of supplies. Careless travelling is too dearly paid
for to be indulged in. No rests are taken; the easier sections of the route
providing sufficient respite from toil and permitting recuperation of
energy to expend on the difficulties ahead. Abandoned loads, non-
completion of self-appointed tasks, mistakes in direction or in selection
of routes, involving delay, are all blots on the record of efficiency, for
which payment is extorted to the last pound of flesh. Although the
rewards of the game are rich to those who conform to the rules, the
penalties of disobedience are often swift, sure and terrible. And let not the
heedless be unduly optimistic that at times the discipline appears to
slacken, that the barriers seem to be down, and all is going well. This is
but subterfuge, an attempt to catch him off guard, to deal a lightning
bodyblow, or a foul. For the Trail is like unto a fickle officer, who to-day
apparently condones breaches of discipline, to visit sudden and dispro-
portionate penalties for the least infringement on the morrow.

Every year takes its toll of life by bad ice, intense cold, or misadventure. Quarrels over hunting grounds terminating fatally are not
unknown, the Spirit of the Northland meanwhile sitting by and grinning
ghoulishly to see his enemies destroy one another.

Often a rifle or other imperishable article of equipment, exposed by
the low water of a hot summer, or the remains of a canoe hung high and
dry by spring floods, points to some error in judgement that explains an
almost forgotten disappearance. Some bones and a few mildewed rags at

a long-dead camp fire, discovered by a wandering Indian, will account for one canoe that failed to show up after the spring hunt.

Even the very silence, most negative of all the passively resistant qualities of the country, claims its victims. The unearthly lack of sound is such a strain on the nerves of those unaccustomed to it that men have been known to go insane under its influence, and have had to be brought out to the railroad.

The Trail is the one and only means of entry to the land of promise of the North, and on it all must pass a critical inspection. Newcomers must undergo the severe scrutiny of the presiding powers, and all who enter are subjected to trial by ordeal, from which only the chosen few emerge unscathed. And to those who by their own unaided efforts do so prevail the jealously guarded portals of the treasure-house are thrown open without reserve; and there is a twice-fold value on the recompense so hardly won, and, once attained to, so lavishly bestowed.

Nor are the rewards thus gained always material. Let it not be imagined that riches dog the footsteps of the successful frontiersman. His ambition to become supreme, get quickly rich and retire early, if he had any such idea, is soon lost sight of in the lively and unceasing contest he must enter into, if he would qualify for admission to the fraternity of the forest.

Up beyond the Height of Land, no man may expect any exemption or immunity on account of his superiority, as such; he has to prove his case. Often he exhibits less common sense than the animals, and of them all he is the most helpless in the face of the vigorous conditions that obtain. When he has conquered these he has accomplished something worth while.

The spiritual satisfaction, the intellectual pleasure, and the knowledge of power that comes with victory over a valiant but ruthless adversary, which accrue after years of submission to the acid test of wilderness life, give the veteran woodsman a capacity for a clean, wholesome enjoyment of living that riches sometimes fail to bring. And looking back on his past struggles, through which he has risen successfully to a position of equality with the dwellers of the waste lands, he would not trade his experience for wealth. He enters into his inheritance with a mind tempered to the fullest appreciation of it, and says to himself that it was worth his while.

On the Trail life is stripped of the non-essentials; existence is in the raw, where in aye is an aye, and a no, no; and no trick of speech, or mannerism or cherished self-deception, can gain one jot or tittle of preferment. Under these conditions a man subordinates that part of him that feels and suffers, to the will to conquer, retaining only that part which takes cognizance of the exigencies of travel, and the means adopted to overcome them. There is none to tell him what he shall or shall not do, yet he has the hardest master a man can well work for—himself.

Long periods of intense concentration of will on one line of endeavour, together with the entire subjection of all that is physical to the fulfillment of the big idea, produce, in time, a type of mind that can be subdued by death alone, and cases have been known of stricken men who, dead to all intents and purposes, staggered on an appreciable distance before finally collapsing.

ᘍᘍᘍ

OUT FROM TOWN; THE WARMTH, THE LAUGHTER, THE comfort left behind. Past half-finished barns, and snowy deserts of burnt stumps; past the squalid habitations of the alien, while the inmates stare out with animal curiosity; and so beyond, the works of man, to where the woods become thicker and thicker, and all is clean, and silent, and shining white—the winter Trail.

Trees filing by in endless, orderly review, opening up before, passing on either hand, and closing in irrevocably behind. That night a camp under the stars. Then, the hasty breakfast in the dark, breaking of camp in the knife-edged cold of dawn; shivering, whining huskies squirming impatiently whilst numb fingers fumble with toboggan strings, and the leather thongs of dog harness. Then away!

Strings of dogs swinging into line; a couple of swift, slashing dog fights, the shouts of the drivers, cracking of whips, and an eventual settling down to business. The swing and soft sough of snowshoes in the loose snow, the rattle of frame on frame. Then the sun rises. Glittering jewels of frost shivering on the pointed spruce-tops, like the gay ornaments on Christmas trees. The breath jets into the crackling air like little clouds of smoke, and rises off the dogs. Onward, onward, speed, speed, for the hands are still numb, and the cold strikes the face like volleys of broken glass; and we have far to go to-day.

So, for an hour; we begin to warm up. Suddenly ahead, the thud of a rifle, the answering crack leaping with appalling reverberations amongst the surrounding hills. Shouts up front; someone has shot a caribou. Good! fresh meat for supper.

Two of the more lightly laden teams drop out, and their owners commence expertly to skin and dress the kill; as their hands become numb they will plunge them to the elbows in the warm blood for a minute, and resume their work.

More hours; steep hills where men take poles and push on the load ahead of them, to help the dogs; on the down grades, tail ropes are loosed, and men bear back with all their weight, some falling, others dragged on their snowshoes as on a surf-board, amidst the shouts and yells of the brigade and the excited yapping of the dogs as they race madly to keep ahead of the flying toboggan. Meanwhile the Trail unwinds from some inexhaustible reel up front, passes swiftly underfoot and on behind, while the trees whirl swiftly by.

Then another stop; what is this? "Dinner," say the trail breakers; well, they ought to know, they are bearing the brunt of the work. Quick, crackling fires, tea made from melted snow, whilst the dogs take the opportunity to bite the ice balls off their feet; most of them are wearing moccasins, evidence of thoughtful owners; for men, red or white, have always a heart for a dog. Pipes are lighted, and all hands relax utterly and smoke contentedly—for a few minutes.

Meanwhile, a word for the husky. Lean, rangy, slant-eyed and tough as whalebone, hitched in teams of four; over muskegs and across frozen lakes; tails up, tongues hanging, straining against the harness, bracing themselves at the curves, trailwise and always hungry, these faithful animals haul their loads all day for incredible distances. Not overly ornamental in appearance, inclined to savagery and deadly fighting, and thieves of no mean ability, these half-bred wolves are as necessary to transport in the North as horses were in the West in the early days. On more than a few occasions, they have been the means of saving life by their uncanny knowledge of ice, and unerring sense of direction.

And now the short rest is over, and we swing into position as the teams go by, and are away. Hours, miles, white monotony, and a keen, steady wind; lake and portage, gully and riverbank; sometimes the crest of a bare hill from which a fleeting glimpse of the surrounding country is obtained. Limitless, endless, empty distance before, behind, and on either hand.

Later a trail turns in from the left, a thin winding ribbon, dwindling to a thread, to nothingness, across a lake, the far shores of which show but faintly, coming from out of the Keewaydin, the storied, mystic North. The trail is well packed by snowshoes of all sizes, men, women and children; Indians.

Good going now; the trail breakers, glad of the respite, drop behind. On the hard trail the snowshoes commence to sing.

Smoke ahead; teepees, windbreaks; the Indian camp. Sharp vicious barking, howling, and then an unspeakable uproar as a herd of wolf-dogs swoops down on the caravan. Shrill scolding of squaws, who belabour lustily with burning sticks, restoring comparative quiet. Black-eyed, round-faced children stand aloof, whispering in soft voices. Maidens with head shawls peep from canvas doorways; buxom old ladies declaim loudly, as they cook at open fires. A tall spare man with Egyptian features, and long black hair, intones gravely in an ancient language, and we understand that we are invited to share the camp ground; the place is well sheltered, and we are told, there is much wood, moose-meat. But we cannot stay; the mail is with us, and travels on schedule; to-night we camp at Kettle Rapids, to-morrow at Thieving Bear.

"Will we take tea"? We surely will, for who can refuse tea on the Trail? Large steaming bowls, and strong.

Away again; more hours, more miles. The teams with the meat have caught up, and the party redoubles its speed; it is getting colder and the men commence to trot. The snowshoes sing shriller now as the *babiche** tightens in the frost, and speed, and more speed is the slogan. Another lake; long, narrow, and bordered by glittering spruce-trees garbed in white; the great sun, hanging low above them, dyeing their tops blood red.

And as the sun goes down, the shadows creep softly out of the woods to the feet of the runners, and beyond. The wind drops and the cold quickens.

*The rawhide thongs that compose the knitted filling or web of the snowshoe.

One man drops out; there is blood on his moccasins. Incorrectly dressed, his feet have chafed with the rub of the bridles and have been bleeding for an hour. Another man steps aside and joins the first; as no one of the brotherhood of trail runners can be left alone in distress; an unbreakable law. But the mail man is satisfied, so all hands stop for the night.

Out axes and after the drywood, boys! A mighty clamour of steel biting into wood. Large piles of spruce boughs make their appearance. Semicircular windbreaks of canvas stretched over poles cluster before a central fire, eight feet long. Smoke billows up to a certain height, to open out in a spreading, rolling canopy over the camp.

Dogs are fed with frozen fish or moose meat, this their only meal in twenty-four hours.

It has now been dark a long time, but wood is still being cut; eventually quiet settles down and the men sleep; but not the dogs. It seems they never sleep. One of them finds a morsel of something eatable; a swift rush and he is fighting at least six others. Howls, snarls, sharp, shrill yapping as of wolves; then curses, shouts, thuds, and silent scurrying retreats; for your husky does not yelp when beaten, but is a skilful dodger.

Once more, quiet. And then the moon rises, pale, and very large, and seemingly no further away than the back of the next ridge, the ragged outline of the shrouded trees standing sharply out across its face.

From around the fire, where each takes his turn at replenishing, come sounds of sleep. The bizarre shadows cast by the shifting flames dance in and out the tree-trunks, and white snowshoe rabbits appear and disappear silently within the circle of light, unseen by the dogs who have crept up near the fire, dozing with the eye nearest it.

The moon rises high and resumes its normal size. The cold grips the land with the bite of chilled steel; trees crack in the frost like scattering rifle-fire. Then, later, as the moon sets, a thin wailing comes stealing across the empty wastes, wavering in strophe and anti-strophe, increasing in volume as voice after voice takes up the burden; the song of the wolves. And simultaneously, as at a given signal, in the wide dance hall of the sky above, the Dead commence to tread their stately measures. Flickeringly and hesitantly at first; but, as the moonlight disappears, the unearthly nebulous host stretches in the files of a ghostly array, which has the whole

horizon for its manoeuvring, swiftly undulating, spreading and con-
tracting, advancing and retreating in formless evolution, marching in
column of route across the face of the Northern sky, swaying in a lambent, flickering horde to the tune of the unheard rhythm that rocks the
universe. At times they seem to hover in the tree tops, almost, it would
seem, within reach, and the ear seems to get the illusion of sound; so that
the listener strains to hear the ghostly music, almost, but not quite audible, to which the spectral company is performing.

A little later the mail man gets up, scans the stars, and pronounces it
time to rise. An hour and a half, or less, and all is ready. As the day breaks,
the last team disappears around a bend in the trail. And nothing remains
but a few bare poles, flattened piles of brush, and a dead fire, and, stretching either way into the chill, white silence, the Trail.

Such, in normal circumstances, is the Trail in winter. A few days soft
weather, however, or a rainstorm, may bring conditions which make travelling virtually impossible. Yet a man caught out in such shape must do
the impossible; he must go on. Goaded on by the knowledge of a rapidly
diminishing food supply, or the certainty of more bad weather, he must
keep moving; for this is the Trail, and will be served.

One season, having located a pocket of marten and lynx, which, being
within a short distance of the railroad, had been overlooked, another
man and myself hunted there all winter. We made frequent trips to town,
a distance of twelve miles, often covering the route in four hours or less.

Hearing from a passing Indian that there was talk of a close season
being suddenly declared, we decided to take out our fur, and dispose of it
while it was still legal, and so avoid a heavy loss. This was late in April, and
the ice was on the point of going out, but there were yet four feet of snow
in the bush.

We started before daylight one morning, so as to cross most of the lakes
before the sun took the stiffening out of the night's frost. There was open
water of varying widths and depths around the shores of every lake, and we
crawled out over this on poles, drawing the poles with us for use in making our landing. A light blow easily punctured the ice in any place, excepting on our winter trail, which, padded down solid by the numerous trips
back and forth to town, formed a bridge over which we passed, most of the

time erect, and with little danger. An hour after sunrise, a south wind sprang up, the sky clouded over, and it commenced to rain. The bottom went out of the ice bridges, necessitating walking the shores of each remaining lake, and on land the trail would no longer support our weight.

Where we had so blithely passed at a three-miles-an-hour gait in winter, we now crawled painfully along by inches, going through to the knee at each step, the snowshoes often having to be extricated by hand. The surface held until we put just so much weight on it, when it let us through at every step with a shock that was like to jar every rib loose from our backbones. Off the trail the snow was of the consistency of thick porridge, and progress there impossible.

We heartily cursed the originator of an untimely close season, who, no doubt, sat at home in warmth and comfort, whilst we, his victims, wet to the skin, our snowshoes heavy with slush, our feet and legs numb with ice-water, crept slowly on. The water slushed in and out of our porous moccasins; but there was little we could do beyond wringing them and our socks out, and so occasionally getting relief for a few minutes, and also keeping moving. At that, we were no worse off than the man who walked all day in ice-water with holes in his boots, claiming that he preferred them that way, as he did not have to take them off to empty them.

Every so often we made a lunch, and drank tea, and our progress was so slow that on one occasion, on making a halt, we could look back, and still see the smoke of our last fire, made two hours before. And this is to say nothing of the load. We took turns to draw the toboggan, which could not stay on the trail, since the sides having given out it was peaked in the centre. Thus the toboggan ran on its side most of the time, upsetting frequently, and the friction producing contrary to common supposition, cold instead of heat, it became coated with ice, and drew with all the spring and buoyancy of a watersoaked log. Frequent adjustments had to be made to snowshoe-bridles with numb hands, the increased weight of the snowshoes breaking the tough leather repeatedly.

Resting was not desirable, except at a fire, as we became chilled to the bone in a few minutes; and, dark coming on with several miles yet to go, we pressed on as best we might. The jar of constantly going through the trail was nauseating us, and we had almost decided to camp for the night in the rain, when there loomed up in the gloom a large grey animal, standing fair in the centre of the trail ahead. We reached simultaneously for the rifle, but the animal came towards us with every appearance of confidence, and turned out to be a big Indian dog, out on a night prowl for rabbits.

Had this occurred in days gone by, no doubt we should have subscribed for a shrine at the place, in honour of some saint or other; as it was we said nothing, but seized the unfortunate beast, and quickly stripping the tump line off the toboggan, with multiple knots fashioned a dog harness, and hitched up our new-found friend. Showing no regret for his interrupted hunt, he hauled along right manfully, whilst we, unable to do enough for our deliverer, kept the toboggan on the trail, as far as was humanly possible, with poles. About that time, the wind changed to the North, the sky cleared, and it commenced to freeze, and with all these things in our favour, we made the remainder of the trip with ease, having spent seventeen and a half hours of misery to cover about ten miles up to that point.

In the woods nothing can be obtained except by effort, often very severe and prolonged, at times almost beyond human endurance. Nothing will occur of its own volition to assist, no kindly passer-by will give you a lift, no timely occurrence will obviate the necessity of forging ahead, no lucky accident will remove an obstruction. Of course, a man can always give up, make fire, eat his provision, rest, and then slink back to camp, beaten and dishonoured; but that is unthinkable.

As you sit on your load to rest, searching the skyline for some encouraging indication of progress, it is borne home to you most irrefutably that all the money in the world cannot hire a single hand to help you, and that no power on earth, save your own aching feet, will cause the scenery to go sailing by, or take one solitary inch off the weary miles ahead. And as you sit in chill discomfort, your body bowed down from the weight of your load, your mind depressed by the incubus of the slavish labour yet to do, you realize that the longer the rest, so much longer you remain on the Trail. The thought goads you on to further efforts. Those packs will never move themselves, and the fact that they may contain skins worth a small fortune obtains for you no respite.

In civilization, if you showed your peltries, attention would be showered on you; willing hands would lift you to your feet. Deep in the forest your valuable pack becomes a useless burden, except for the pinch or two of tea and the few bites of greased bannock it may contain, which are worth, to you, more than all the gold in Araby.

At times you are fain to give up, and abandon your hardly-won treasure, of which you would give the half for one mile of good footing or the privilege of going to sleep for an hour. But you must struggle on; exhaustion may be such that further movement seems impossible, or you may have injuries that cause exquisite torture with every movement; but that trip must be finished, or in the latter event, fire must be lighted and camp of some kind made.

The beautiful marten stole gracing the shoulders of the elegantly dressed woman in Bond Street or on Broadway might, if it were able, tell a tale its owner little guesses.

∾∾∾

AT TIMES THE SPIRIT OF THE NORTHLAND, TIRING OF HIS heavy role, turns mountebank, and with sardonic humour he fashions mirages, travesties of the landscape they belie, and very baffling to one not acquainted with the topography of the district. Whole ridges of trees disappear from view, and across empty fields of ice a solid wall of forest presents itself, to melt into nothing, and be replaced perhaps by an expanse of open water which apparently bars further advance. It takes considerable steadiness of mind to march on into a section of landscape which you know not to be there, and so discredit the evidence of your senses.

Meanwhile this devil-turned-wizard conjures forests out of the ether, blots out mountains, and balances islands precariously one on another. A puerile occupation for an evil genius bent on destruction, yet men have been cajoled to death on bad ice by these tactics.

In a strange country, during the more vivid of these performances, it is as well to make camp, and leave the mummer to his clowning, until he allows the landscape to resume its normal contours.

After a more or less eventful visit to the "front," a companion and myself decided to desist from our efforts to relieve the stagnation of currency in the district, to return to the bush, and have a square meal.

My associate, not content with a few days' hilarity, had been looking too earnestly and too long on the wine when it was sixty-five over proof, and had tried to promote the health of the community by depriving it of its whiskey supply. The morning of the first day of the trip in was an epic of heroism on his part; and a good deal of the time he was not at all sure if his surroundings were real or the offspring of a slightly warped vision. I was not in a position to be of much assistance, having troubles of my own. But he kept on doggedly placing his feet one ahead of the other, until we arrived at the shores of a fair-sized lake.

Here a mirage was in progress. An island we well knew to be there was nowhere to be seen, and a dignified and solemn row of ancient trees, old enough probably to know better, were poised above the level of the surrounding scenery, head down.

My companion took a look at the manifestation, his eyes distended and his jaw dropped.

"Cripes," said he. "Do you see what I see?"

I replied that I thought I did. He shook his head.

"You don't see the half of it," he said. "This is the limit; I'm goin' back!"

Sometimes in winter a trail hidden by successive storms, or invisible in the darkness, has to be felt out step by step for miles at a time; and that at a speed little, if any less, than that attained to on good footing and during the daylight hours. The trail itself, if once passed over previously, is harder than the surrounding snow and a slight give of the shoe, slightly off on one side, is sensed, and the error rectified without pause, at the next step. Thus a man and his outfit are enabled to pass dryshod over lakes that are often otherwise a sea of slush beneath the field of snow. A few steps into this and showshoes and toboggan become a mass of slush which immediately freezes, making progress impossible and involving the loss of an hour or more. This feat of feeling the way is common enough, but calls for intense concentration, and much resembles walking swiftly on a hidden tightrope; so much so, that a trapper will say with regard to a trip, that he went so many miles, of which he walked so much "on the tightrope." The strain attached to this form of exercise is such that on making a halt, one's frame is distinctly felt to relax. I have walked miles in this way, and then suddenly realized that my hands had been gripped tight all during the stretch in an effort, apparently, to hold the body free of the legs, as one who sits on eggs, dressed in his best, would do.

Under these conditions, the trail being most of the time invisible, a man travels to as much advantage in the night as in the daytime; more, in fact, as he is not constantly deceiving himself with fancied indications of the trail which land him into trouble.

As much travelling is done at night, almost, as in day; in summer to avoid the heavy winds of the daylight hours on large bodies of water, and in winter, because, owing to the length of the nights, much less wood is required for those who sleep out in daytime; also, the searing winds that generally go down with the sun, are avoided.

There is a peculiar, indescribable charm attached to night journeying that is handed down to some of us from the dawn of time; few can realize, without the experience, the feeling of wildness and barbaric freedom that possesses the soul of one who travels alone in the dark, out on the edge of the world; when anything may happen, beasts of all kinds are abroad, and flitting shapes appear and disappear, dimly seen by the light of the stars.

In a country where so little happens to break the monotony of wilderness travel, small occurrences, trivialities almost, become momentous occasions. The passage of a band of wolves at an unusual place, the distant sighting of an otter, a change of wind even. This is borne out in the nomenclature of sections of trail, and prominent features of the scenery. Such names as Hell's Gate, Steel River, Devil's Eddy, Smoky Falls, Lazy Beaver, Place-where-the-Devil-laughed, Dancing Portage, Hungry Hall, Lost Indian, are all apt reminders of the perhaps one outstanding incident that made history in that particular spot or region.

But the greatest thrill of all is that of suddenly finding strange footprints in a section where no signs of man, other than your own, have been seen for half a year. Fresh snowshoe tracks turning in, and going your way, perhaps. This opens up a wide field of speculation. You undergo all the sensations experienced by Robinson Crusoe on his discovery of the well-known footprint. A man, one of your kind, and not long gone by; he slushed up the trail in one place, and it is not yet frozen!

A man, yes; but who? Frenchman? Indian? assuredly not the latter, his tracks would be unmistakable. A wandering fur-buyer? The Mounted Police? Surely they are not going to be narrow-minded about that little affair last spring at Bisco. The Prince of Wales? Maybe; they say he is in Canada just now.

Anyhow this has got to be investigated. You quicken your steps, and two hours later you smell smoke, and suddenly come on a blazing fire, with a tea pail suspended over it. It is only Old Bill from the Wild Cat Hills; but anyway, Bill is a good old plug, and is just back up from "Canada," and he may have some news, or a letter.

Bill has no letters and less news, but he has a few chocolate bars, priceless treasures, which he shares, and a new brand of tobacco that would asphyxiate a horse, which he also endeavours to share. We eat and talk awhile, then Bill, who draws his own toboggan, gathers up his belongings, ducks into his tump line, and slipping with deft ankle movements into the bridles of an immense pair of trail breakers*, shoes of an Indian rig, waves his hand, and is away. For Bill turns off here; he is leaving the Wild Cat Hills, and is going, foot-loose and free, to some far range as yet unexplored.

And as I stand and watch him go, I am lonesome a little, for the thought strikes me that Bill is old and may not come back. And so, bending forward against the creaking leather, snow flying in little puffs from his big snowshoes, he goes. Leaving behind him as he proceeds that winding, ever-lengthening, narrow ribbon, the Trail, his one obsession for days to come, the only thing that connects him with his fellow-man, and one that the first storm will obliterate.

Down the hollow tunnels between snow-laden trees, over unmarked wastes, he picks his way by instinct; cynosure of all the hostile eyes that stare coldly out from shadowy recesses. Pushing doggedly on, across windlashed lakes, with their scurrying drift, and whirling, breath-taking snow-devils, past bald glistening mountains that stand guard at the portals of some mighty river. A moving speck, creeping across the face of the earth, he goes on to unknown destinations.

Day by day he penetrates deeper and deeper into the Kingdom of the Spirit of the North, where, jealous of such encroachment on his domain, with a thousand imps of mischief to do his bidding, master of all the

*Large snowshoes.

powers of evil, the brooding Killer grimly bides his time; nor does he always wait in vain.

∾∾∾

A SMALL, RED BUILDING OVERSHADOWED BY A LARGE canoe-shed, on the flat top of a rocky point; at the water's edge a dock at which float a number of canoes in various stages of loading. Men pass from the shed to the dock with bags of flour, sacks of beans, tents, blankets, boxes and bundles.

In the shade of the wide-topped jackpines, a knot of townspeople watch the busy scene, their eyes turned often to the door of the little red building. The laden men, too, often glance that way; all present wear an air of expectancy.

Presently the canoes are all loaded, the shed closed, and the men dispose themselves to wait. Some of these are attired in new mackinaw or khaki, and knee-boots; others, to whom, it is obvious, the proccedings are no novelty, wear the faded canvas clothing and the moccasins, or other heelless footwear, of the professional canoeman.

Soon the door of the diminutive office opens, and there steps out from it a man, weather-beaten, lean and wiry as a greyhound, dynamic energy apparent in every movement, indomitable will stamped on every feature. He closes the building as though for a long time; for not once again during five months will any of these men return to this spot, unless dismissed the Service, for this is the official Head Quarters of the Government Forest Rangers, the wiry man their Chief.

Seventy-five miles in is their distributing point, and from it these thirty men will successfully police from fire an area of ten thousand square miles. The Chief shoulders a heavy packsack, and steps quickly down to the dock with the lithe swing of an Indian. He glances appraisingly over his little band.

"Are we ready?" he asks.

It seems we are. He embarks in the rear canoe, for the trip ahead is long and arduous, and he must shepherd his men, unknown quantities many of them. Paddles are dipped, the veterans leading, and the flotilla is in motion. The bunched canoes string out, gain speed; the sun flashes on wet paddles, kneeling men sway to the stroke, and the canoes leap ahead in low undulations. The brigade is on its way, off on the Summer Trail.

The first objective is a long black point ahead, apparently the end of the lake. The point is reached, rounded, and another stretch of lake appears, with a similar point beyond. Hours of paddling, and no noticeable change in the scenery. A treadmill—but no stops.

Paddles, by pairs, click in unison with the regularity of clockwork; never a stroke is missed. Hours pass. The seasoned canoemen in front are setting a pace that never changes, never will change. They seem to have solved the problem of perpetual motion. The sun, a copper ball, burns its way across the sky, beating down on unshaded faces and bare forearms, and its reflected image on the glassy water stares into eyes puckered to mere slits against the scorching glare. The Chief, with his sternsman, a supple, slant-eyed Cree, brings up the rear, watching his men estimating their efficiency. Some parts of his patrol are difficult, and he must place his rangers judiciously.

Between two broken hills the lake narrows to a deep bay and finally comes to an end. Here a well-beaten, but not wide, path winds up a gully by carefully selected grades. Canoes are unloaded, and mountainous piles of baggage start up the ravine, as men assume their burdens and move off. This is the portage so long looked for as a change from the interminable paddling. And a change it certainly is. Everything, canoes and all, must be carried by man-power to the other side. Let us hope it is a short one. With our two hundred odd pounds apiece, by general consent conceded to be a "man's load," we commence the carry. An easy grade at first, but becoming rapidly more arduous as the two hundred and some pounds take their toll of nerve and muscle, with each successive upward step. Here the curse of Adam is fulfilled to the letter; sweat commences to pour into the eyes, down the body, dripping off the forearms. Vicious insects light and bite on contact. One hand is engaged in pulling forward and down on the top load to support the head, the other contains an axe or a pail of lard; so the flies stay until surfeited, and blood runs freely with the sweat. Up, and up, and then some. Surely this cannot go on much longer! But it does. Up on the crest, finally, where is a cool breeze; thank God for that; tear open the shirt and let it in.

Then down a declivity where the energy expended to keep from being rushed into uncontrollable speed, is apparently greater than the effort of climbing; the thought of a slip with that load is intolerable. Then a level spot, badly cluttered with boulders, and stones that move underfoot, where one walks with the precise steps of a cat, as a false step may mean a broken leg.

Men returning empty, carrying coiled tump lines, stand aside and give the trail to the burdened ones. No words are spoken on meeting; talking has become an effort, and the toilsome paddling of the forenoon now appears, by contrast, to have been little more than a light and healthful pastime.

At last, piles of bags and boxes lying in scattered heaps, but without confusion; the end, no doubt. You unload, and look around, and see no lake; only a continuation of that never-to-be-sufficiently-damned trail. This, then, is not the end, only a stage.* How many more? True to the code you will not ask, but take what comes and like it; you coil your line and return. After all it was worth carrying that jag† if only to experience the feeling of comfort walking back without it. You step aside at intervals for heavily laden men; some of them have four hundred pounds and over. Incredible, but there are the bags—count them; a hundred of flour in each. These men trot, with short, choppy steps, but smoothly, evenly, without jar, whilst breath whistles through distended nostrils, and eyes devoid of expression stare glassily at the footing.

Several trips like this, then the canoes are taken. These, carried one to a man, do not stop at the stage, but, an easier load, seventy pounds perhaps, go on to the next stop, so that precious privilege, rest walking back, will not be forfeited. Otherwise a stoppage would be necessary at the dump before again picking up a load, and delays are neither tolerated, nor expected; the sooner it is over the better; resting merely prolongs the agony. Stage after stage; stifling heat in a breathless scorching tunnel. Our hopes of a short portage have long ago faded entirely. Where is the end of this thing? Maybe there is no end.

And eventually every last piece and pound is dumped on the shores of

*Portages are divided into convenient sections, and the dump at the end of each section is called a stage.
†Load.

a lake. Weary men make fire, cook, and wash the brassy film from their throats with hot tea. Hot tea on a broiling day!—yet the system calls for it. The lake is very small; not much respite here; load up, unload, and pack across again.

A new hand asks how many portages there are, and we hear it said that on this first leg of the journey there are fifteen more, and that the next one is called "Brandy" and admitted to be a bad one. We subsequently find this admission to be correct, but at the time, in view of our experiences on the last portage, we are all agog with interest as to what special features this alcoholic jaunt has in store.

We are not long in finding out. Almost a mile in length with five sharp grades arranged without regard for staging or symmetry, it has also a steep slope at the far end, which, being equal in sum to the aggregate of the hills so painfully climbed, at one fell swoop kicks your gains from beneath your feet, and lands you panting and half-dead back at the same level from which you started. So this is Brandy. She is, as we heard, a man-killer; and well named, for it is quite conceivable that more than one stricken man has found himself compelled to reach for his flask, before finally vanquishing this monster.

On the way back, after the first trip, we see the new man. He sits on a log with his head in his hands, exhausted, dejected. He can go no further. The Trail, ever on the watch, has weighed him in the balance, and he is found wanting. He will be sent back; for this is the Trail, where none may falter or linger, or evade the issue. For the time being he must do what he can, as to leave him is out of the question, but the weeding-out process has commenced.

On the third day we enter the pineries. Hills black with pine to the water's edge. Rock walls hundreds of feet in height and crowned with pine, falling sheer down into deep water. Pine, in mass formation, standing solemn, dignified, kings of all the forest; a sea of black sweeping tops swinging to the North; myriads of dark arms pointing one way, Northward, to journey's end; as though in prophetic spirit they see their doom approaching, and would flee before it to the last stronghold of the Red Gods. We are now entering the area for which this corps will be held responsible till late Fall, and two canoe crews receive their instructions, and leave the brigade, taking each their separate way to a designated patrol district.

Indian signs now become frequent; teepee poles amongst the pine trees, in the glades, and on the beaches; caches raised high on scaffolds in sheltered spots; trail signs, marking a route; shoulder bones of moose hanging in pairs at camp grounds; bear skulls grinning out over the lake from prominent points. If you are stuck for tobacco you will find some in the empty brain box; but no bushman will take it; reprisals for vandalism of that kind may entail endless trouble. I once heard a white guide severely reprove a half-breed belonging to his party, who, wishing to show contempt for such customs, and considering himself above them, took one of these skulls down and commenced to fill his pipe from it. The guide gave in no uncertain terms his opinion of the unsportsmanlike proceeding.

This is an Indian country; and at evening the double staccato beat of a drum swells and ebbs through the still air, faint but very clear, yet unaccountably indeterminate as to direction. A strangely stirring sound, giving an eerie quality to the surroundings. Those pines heard that sound three hundred years ago, when they were saplings; beneath these very trees the Iroquois war parties planned their devilish work, to a similar rhythm. We had thought these things were no longer done. The Cree is questioned, but he blinks owlishly, and has suddenly forgotten his English. The following day shows no sign of living Indians, but here and there is a grave with its birch-bark covering, and personal effects; always in a grove of red pines, and facing towards the sunset. Moose are seen every day now, and two men told off to fish when the evening halt is made, generally return in half an hour, or less, with enough fish for the entire party's meal.

Immense bodies of water many miles in length alternate with carries of from a hundred yards to three miles, so that there are stretches where we pray for a portage, and portages where we pray for a stretch. The pine-clad mountains begin to close in on the route, the water deepens, narrows, and commences to flow steadily.

We are now on the head of a mighty river, which drains all this region, and soon the portages become shorter, but more precipitous, and are flanked on one side or the other by a wicked rapids. Some of these can be run; but not all are experts, and the Chief will not allow valuable cargoes and, perhaps, useful lives to be sacrificed in order that some man of uncertain ability may try to qualify as a canoeman. Rocks that would rip the bottom from a canoe at a touch, lie in wait, invisible, just below the surface, but indications of their position are apparent only to the practised eye. Eddies, that would engulf a pine tree, tug at the frail canoe essaying to drag it into the vortex. Treacherous cross-currents snatch viciously at the paddles; deceptive, smooth-looking, oily stretches break suddenly into six-foot pitches.

But there are amongst us some who have earned the right to follow their own judgment in such matters; these now take control of the situation. They are the "white water men," to whom the thunderous roar of a rapids, and the smell of spray flying in the face, are as the intoxication of strong drink. To such as these considerations of life and limb loom small compared with the maddening thrill of eluding and conquering the frenzied clawing and grasping of tons of hungry, rushing waters; yet coupled with this stern joy of battle is a skill and a professional pride that counts the wetting of a load, or the taking of too much water, an ineradicable disgrace.

None but those who have experienced it can guess the joyous daredeviltry of picking a precarious channel at racing speed between serried rows of jagged rocks, spiteful as shark's teeth. Few may know the feeling of savage exultation which possesses a man when the accumulated experience of years, with a split-second decision formed after a momentary glimpse through driven, blinding spume into some seething turmoil, and a perfect coordination between hand and eye, result in, perhaps, the one quick but effective thrust of the paddle or pole, that spells the difference between a successful run, and disaster. And as the canoe careens, and sidles, and plunges its way to safety, the pent-up emotions of its crew find expression in the whoops and shouts of the white canoemen, and the short, sharp yelps of the Indians, their answer to the challenge of the rapids. And the thundering waters drop back with a sullen growl, and a man may lean on his paddle, and look back and say, "Well, that was not too bad."

I know men who would camp a night at a bad rapids in order to have the sun in the right place for running, not able to resist picking up the gauntlet so arrogantly flung at their feet by some stretch of water that had already taken its toll of human life. But this hazardous pastime is not one to be entered upon lightly by those not knowing their danger, or who knowing it, overrate their own prowess. For a man well skilled in the game, with many years of hard apprenticeship to his credit, is sometimes called on to pay the extreme penalty; and a broken paddle, an unexpected obstruction, or sheer hard luck, may accomplish what the might of the river never could contrive.

Swept clear of his canoe, still living yet a dead man, he is whirled swiftly down; then comes the quick terrible realization of his awful extremity, that he is beyond aid, that this is the end. And the arches of the forest that have echoed to the shouts of triumph of those who run successfully, mockingly give back the cry of agony of the latest of that which knows no pity or remorse. A few swift seconds, and the black waters have thrown aside their plaything, limp and lifeless in the pool below, whilst the ring of trees round it stand all unheeding, or watch in silent apathy. And as if the act had been ordained from ages past, the silence of a thousand years resumes its sway; the pendulum of unmeasured time continues its sweep of the universe, and the soundless symphony of the infinite plays on.

ຄຄຄ

MEN REACT DIFFERENTLY TO THE NEAR APPROACH OF certain death. One, an Indian, laughed inordinately all during the last half-minute of his time on earth, and the ghastly bubbling gurgle as his mouth reached the level of the water, before it closed over his head for ever, will stay in my memory for many a day, as it doubtless will in the minds of all of us who had to stand helplessly by, and see him swept over a sixty-foot fall.

Another, also unable to swim, strangely, but undeniably, the usual thing with men who spend their lives in a canoe, after swamping in heavy water came to the surface with his hat on. Upon this hat he immediately clapped his hand, holding it in position and fighting for his life with one hand only, until he sank.

In another instance two men attempted to negotiate a dangerous place with a full load, in high water. The canoe filled, and, loaded down with traps, guns, flour, a stove and other heavy articles, it immediately sank. One of the partners seized a bundle, which held him up for a few seconds only, when he disappeared, to remain under the ice all winter. The other as a powerful swimmer, and after losing much time and vitality in an effort to rescue his companion, he commenced to fail in the icy water and made for land. Exhaustion was such, that, a short distance from shore, he gave up, allowing himself to sink. Not far below the surface his feet struck a rock, and he was able to retain his footing there, partly submerged, until sufficiently rested to make the remaining distance to safety.

Yet not always does the grim reaper stalk in the wake of misadventure which, if he be absent, is often in the nature of an entertainment for the lookers-on. A timely sense of humour has taken the sting from many a bitter misfortune, for out on the endless Trail, the line between tragedy and comedy is very finely drawn. A look, a word, anything that will crack a laugh in faces drawn with anxiety, no matter at whose expense, will often make a burlesque out of what would otherwise be an intolerable situation.

For instance, no one could ask for a more humorous and elevating exhibition than I myself once gave, before an interested audience of sixteen Fire Rangers. Upset by an unfortunate move, for which my partner and I were equally to blame, 1 swung out of the canoe as it capsized, keeping hold of the stern, and going down the rest of the swift water like the tail of a comet, amidst the sarcastic comment of the assembled Rangers. My bowsman was wearing heavy boots instead of moccasins, and in a kneeling position, the usual one in a canoe, his stiff footwear had become wedged beneath the thwart. He must have been almost a minute under the overturned canoe, unable to extricate himself, and in grave danger of drowning, when, with what little assistance I could give, he somehow got loose. Bewildered, he climbed onto the canoe, which being old and heavy, immediately sank, and me with it.

I am an indifferent swimmer, if any, and this was a dangerous eddy, and deep; there were no hand holds to speak of. So, although it rolled and twisted considerably in the cross current, I stayed with the canoe, on the chance that it would float up, as without it I would be a dead loss anyhow; and soon my head broke water again. The attentive concourse on the river bank, who were in nowise disturbed, evidently thinking we were giving an aquatic performance for their benefit to lighten the cares of a heavy day, were highly diverted, until my companion, on my return to the surface, swam ashore, where his condition apprised them of the true state of affairs. In a matter of seconds a canoe was racing towards me, whilst its occupants shouted encouragement. About this time I was in pretty bad shape, having taken much water, and my hold on the canoe was weakening; so I commenced to shout lustily, suggesting speed. To my horror, one of the men suddenly ceased paddling and commenced to laugh.

"Say," said he. "Why don't you stand up?"

And amidst the cheers and shouts of the appreciative assemblage, I stood up in about three feet of water. I had been floating with my legs out ahead of me, and had drifted backwards within a few yards of the shore.

Then there is the official whom I saw sitting in a canoe which had run aground and filled. Wet to the waist, he sat in the water with both feet elevated above the gunwales.

"What in hell you doin' there?" angrily demanded his assistant, who stood on the rock, submerged to the knees.

"Keeping my feet dry," replied the official with chattering teeth.

Many of the prospectors are old "desert rats" and plainsmen, used to horses and knowing but little about canoes. One such, not realizing the chances he was taking, attempted the negotiation of a difficult piece of fast water with the loaded canoe, whilst his companion crossed the portage. Unable to distinguish the channel, the prospector ran foul of a swift shallows; and, on getting out to lighten the load, he was swept off his feet and nearly carried away. The canoe swung sideways and filled, to the gunwales, and, with part of its contents, was salvaged only after an hour's hard work. An inventory was taken of the remaining goods, which were found to be thoroughly soaked. The man who had walked did not berate his crestfallen companion, who was responsible for the mishap, merely remarking disgustedly:

"We needn't have gone to all that trouble, we could have got that stuff just as wet letting it down on a rope."

The Height of Land is, for some reason, the breeding place of storms of a severity and suddenness that makes a familiarity with the signs preceding them imperative to those whose itineraries include lakes of any size. As one of the members of a heavily freighted brigade, caught in the centre of a lake forty-nine miles in length by one of these unexpected tempests, I once had this forcibly illustrated for me.

We were crossing at the narrowest stretch, a distance of fifteen miles, and were at about the centre, when, with very little warning, a gale sprang up which steadily increased until we were unable to ride it any longer. The waves had a twenty-four-mile sweep at us, yet we could have juggled our way to some bay that offered shelter, only for the fact that the lake being shallow, there was little buoyancy in the water, and the waves struck in rapid succession, with no sea-room between them. The canoes began to take water in quantities, and the danger of swamping was imminent, so we jettisoned the half of our valuable cargoes, and ran down wind to a small, bare rock island. Erecting tents was impossible without poles, so we bunched the canoes together and spread the tents over them. Here, with no wood, no brush, exposed to a continuous hurricane, we spent two days and a night. As the remains of our loads were the heavier packages that had been in the bottom of the canoes, and consisted in each case of flour, beans, and salt pork, all of which require cooking to be palatable, we came near to starving in the midst of plenty, and were mighty glad on the following night to make the mainland, and cook a few meals.

I have seen masses of water the height of a pine tree and ten yards across, spiraling and spinning across the centre of lakes at terrific speed in the spring of the year. With them a canoe has little chance. I once saw a point of heavy timber, perhaps thirty acres in extent, whipped, and lashed, and torn into nothing but a pile of roots and broken tree-stumps, in the space of fifteen seconds.

I saw a gap the width of a street, tearing itself at the speed of an express train through a hardwood forest, birch and maple trees, three feet through, being twisted around until they fell. Strange to say the few white pine escaped unscathed, standing around mournfully afterwards as though appraising the damage. In this instance there was a settlement near, in which a farmer claimed to have seen his pig-pen, pigs and all, go sailing away into the unknown. On being asked how far the building was carried, he replied that he didn't know, but that it must have been quite far, because the pigs did not return for a week.

In a country of this description it is well to pitch camp, even if only for a night, with due regard for possible falling timber or cloud-bursts; in dealing with the unsleeping, subtle Enemy, ready to take advantage of the least error, it is well to overlook nothing.

A storm of this kind, at night, with nothing but a flimsy canvas tent between men and the elements, is a matter for some anxiety. The fierce rattle of the rain on the feeble shelter, the howling of the wind, the splintering crash of falling trees, which, should one fall on the tent, would crush every soul within it, make speech impossible. The blackness is intensified by each successive flash of lightning which sears its way between the rolling mass of thunder-heads, the air driven by the appalling impact between the heavenly artillery and the legions of silence. It is an orgy of sound; as though in very truth the wild women* on their winged steeds were racing madly through the upper air, screeching their warcries, and scattering wreck and desolation in their wake.

With the passing of the storm comes the low menacing murmur of some swollen stream, growing to a sullen roar as a yellow torrent of water overflows its bed, forcing its way through a ravine, sweeping all before it. That insistent muttering must not go unheeded, for there lies danger. Trees will be sucked into the flood; banks will be undermined, and tons of earth and boulders, and forest litter, will slide into the river channel, on occasion taking with them tents, canoes, complete outfits, and the human souls who deemed their feeble arrangements sufficient to cope with the elements.

Thus, with little preliminary, the Master of Destruction† ruthlessly eliminates those who so place themselves at his disposal; for at such times he scours the wilderness for victims, that he may gather in a rare harvest while the time is ripe.

To those who dwell in the region that lies north of the Haut Terre, which heaves and surges, and plunges its way two thousand miles westward across the across the face of the continent, the settled portions of the Dominion are situated in another sphere. This is not surprising, when it is considered that a traveller may leave London and be in Montreal in less time than it takes many trappers to reach civilization from their hunting-grounds. Most frontiersmen refer to all and any part of this vast Hinterland as the Keewaydin; a fitting name, of Indian origin, meaning the North-West Wind, also the place from which it comes. Only the populated areas are referred to as "Canada."

Canada, to many of them, is a remote place from whence come bags

*Valkyries.
†The brooding, relentless evil Spirit of the Northland, which every Indian believes haunts the northern vastnesses with a view to the destruction of all travellers.

of flour and barrels of salt pork, men with pale skins, real money, and new khaki clothing; a land of yawning sawmills, and hustling crowds, where none may eat or sleep without price; and where, does a man but pause to gaze on the wonders all about him, he is requested to "move on," and so perforce must join the hurrying throng which seems so busy going nowhere, coming from nowhere.

A surge of loneliness sweeps over him as he gazes at the unfriendly faces that surround him, and he furtively assures himself that his return ticket is inside his hat-band, and wonders when is the next North-bound train. Supercilious bell-boys accept his lavish gratuities, and openly deride him; fawning waiters place him at obscure and indifferently tended tables, marvel at the size of his tips, and smirk behind his back. For he is a marked man. His clothes are often old-fashioned and he lacks the assurance of the town-bred man. He has not the pre-occupied stare of the city dweller; his gaze is beyond you, as at some distant prospect, his eyes have seen far into things that few men dream of. Some know him for what he is, but by far the greater part merely find him different, and immediately ostracise him.

He on whom the Trail has left its mark is not as the common run of men. Eyes wrinkled at the corners prove him one who habitually faces sun and wind. Fingers curved with the pressure of pole, paddle and tump line; a restless glance that never stays for long on one object, the gaze of a bird or a wild thing, searching, searching; legs bowed a little from packing, and the lift and swing of wide snowshoes; an indescribable freedom of gait. These are the hallmarks by which you may know him.

There is another type; unwashed, unshaven, ragged individuals appear at the "steel" at intervals, generally men who being in for only a short time are able to stand that kind of thing for a limited period. They are a libel on the men they seek to emulate, wishing to give the impression that they are seasoned veterans, which they succeed in doing about as well as a soldier would if he appeared in public covered with blood and gaping wounds, or an actor if he walked the streets in motley.

Many, young on the trail, do some very remarkable feats, and impose on themselves undue hardship, refusing to make the best of things, and indulging in spectacular and altogether unnecessary heroisms. They go to the woods in the same spirit as some men go to war, as to a circus. But the carnival spirit soon wears off as they learn that sleeping on hard rocks when plenty of brush is handy, or walking in ice-water without due cause, however brave a tale it makes in the telling, will never take a mile off the day's journey, nor add a single ounce to their efficiency.

The Trail, then, is not merely a connecting link between widely distant points, it becomes an idea, a symbol of self-sacrifice and deathless determination, an ideal to be lived up to, a creed from which none may falter. It obsesses a man to the utmost fibre of his being, the impelling force that drives him on to unrecorded feats, the uncompromising taskmaster whom none may gainsay; who quickens men's brains to shift, device, and stratagem, purging their bodies of sloth, and their minds of weak desires.

Stars paling in the East, breath that whistles through the nostrils like steam. Tug of the tump line, swing of the snowshoes; tracks in the snow, every one a story; hissing, slanting sheets of snow; swift rattle of snowshoes over an unseen rail in the dark. A strip of canvas, a long fire, and a roof of smoke. Silence.

Canoes gliding between palisades of rock. Teepees, smoke-dyed, on a smooth point amongst the red pines; inscrutable faces peering out. Two wooden crosses at a rapids. Dim trails. Tug of the tump line again: always.

Old tea pails, worn snowshoes, hanging on limbs, their work is well done; throw them not down on the ground. Little fires by darkling streams. Slow wind of evening hovering in the tree tops, passing on to nowhere. Gay, caparisoned clouds moving in review, under the setting sun. Fading day. Pictures forming and fading in glowing embers. Voices in the running waters, calling, calling. The lone cry of a loon from an unseen lake. Peace, contentment. This is the Trail.

Tear down the tent and the shelter,
Stars pale for the breaking of day,
Far over the hills lies Canada,
Let us be on our way.
TRAIL SONG

The Still-Hunt

"Deep in the jungle vast and dim,
That knew not a white man's feet,
I smelt the odour of sun-warmed fur,
Musky, savage and sweet."

CHAPTER FOUR

The Still-Hunt

NAPOLEON, SO HISTORY INFORMS US, SAID THAT AN ARMY travels on its stomach. He was right; Napoleon knew his stuff. More than that, this statement goes for Empires too, and the building of them, or any other line of human endeavour requiring a large expenditure of physical energy. The Bible itself is full of references as to how, when and where its people ate.

On the Frontier eating a meal is not the ceremonial affair of politely restrained appetite and dainty selection seen in the best hotels and restaurants, but an honest-to-God shovelling in of fuel at a stopping-place, to enable the machinery to complete its journey, or its task. There the food supply is the most important consideration, and starvation is not merely going hungry for a few days, but becomes a fatal proposition. Civilization will not let you starve; the wilderness will, and glad of the opportunity.

Flour beans, lard, tea, and a certain amounts of sugar, with salt pork, may be transported in sufficient quantities to suffice for all winter, in a single canoe, for a single man.

But meat seems to be the only food, modern opinion to the contrary notwithstanding, which will supply the amount of energy needed to meet the climatic conditions, and successfully to withstand the constant hardship, which are two of the main features of existence in some parts of Northern Canada, and as much so to-day as ever they were in the early days. Without it the whole line of the offensive against the powers of the great white silence

70

would perceptibly weaken; and meat boiled, fried, dried, smoked, or just plain frozen, is what this thin line of attack is moving up on.

This does not condone the indiscriminate slaughter of moose, deer and other meat animals. Game protection is very strictly enforced in this country, and to-day the sportsman who comes out of the woods with his quota of trophies, while he leaves several hundred pounds of the best of meat to spoil in the woods, is counted guilty of a crime. The practice of supplying the crews of railroad construction and lumber camps with wild meat, fortunately not universal, is also to be much condemned. The companies, or contractors operating, are bearing the expense of boarding their crews, and the saving effected by the use of free meat is simply so much profit for the company, whose legitimate gains should not be so increased at the expense of the country, besides it does some honest tradesman out of his dues; and transportation facilities are no problem to this kind of pioneering.

It is no longer, as it was thirty years ago, a matter of seeing how much game one can kill to ascertain the number of different ways in which a stricken animal may hit the ground. Parts of this North country are swarming with game, but also, large areas of it are not. I have traversed regions a hundred miles in width where no track or other sign of animal life was to be seen save that of rabbits. The population of game animals, if evenly distributed, would not be as dense as it now appears to be, but there is enough meat in the North, in most places, to enable the pathfinders and the first fringe of scattering settlers, to live, and, if taken with discretion, not diminish the supply.

One sizeable moose will provide a man with meat for well over half the winter, and each settler family, with one moose per member, may, with due care, have the best of meat during all the cold months. With the coming of civilization and increased transportation facilities, hunting would no longer be necessary, and animals of all kinds could be preserved in perpetuity.

Pot-hunter is a term of reproach through all the length and breadth of the sporting world, as differentiating between the man who hunts for meat and the man who hunts for sport. But hunting to fill the pots of those families, who, as representatives of an entire people, are bravely struggling against adverse conditions and leading a life of deprivation and heavy labour, in their endeavour to bring some semblance of prosperity to a bleak and savage wilderness, is nothing to be held up to public scorn. These settlers and the trail-makers further afield are the people who are actually laying the foundation of an Empire overseas, subsisting for the most part on few enough of the necessaries of life; people to whom a large quantity of lard is as riches, and dried apples a luxury. Salt pork, which goes under the various euphonious titles of "Chicago Chicken," "Rattlesnake Pork" (on the supposition, based on the flavour, that the pigs it came from were fed on rattlesnakes), or just plain "sow-belly," whilst eatable to a hungry man, is no relish.

For these settlers to kill, subject to the liberal game laws of the different Provinces, an occasional moose to alleviate somewhat the monotony of beans and bannock to enable them to carry on cheerfully, is just as praiseworthy in principle as are the stupendous slaughters made by persons of high degree in Europe, where we may see recorded single bags of deer, bears and wild boars, large enough to keep an able-bodied pioneer family in meat for five years. It is understood that these huge piles of meat are given to the poor, to hospitals and other deserving institutions, which undoubtedly exonerates the men involved; so here, again, the much maligned pot gets in its nefarious work, without which such taking of animal life would be a shameful waste.

In the North, the failure of the fall moose hunt is as much of a catastrophe as the blighting of a wheat crop would be in more organised areas. Pot-hunting it is truly; but sport? Yes; the greatest sport in the world; the meat hunt of the Makers of a Nation.

Not so spectacular, this still-hunt, as were the great buffalo hunts of the emigrant trains crossing the plains, half a century ago, but every bit as much a part of the history of the development of the continent. As on to-day's frontier, the settler then was not as expert as his neighbour, the Indian, but by hook or by crook, he got his meat, and so does his successor to-day. An old-time buffalo hunt was an inspiring sight. The strings of light-riding savages on their painted ponies, probably the best irregular light mounted infantry the world has ever seen, naked to the waist, vieing with each other in spectacular and hazardous stunts, exhibiting a skill in horsemanship never attained to by trained cavalry; the black sea of rolling humps, and bobbing heads, the billowing clouds of dust through which the fringe of wild, yelling horsemen were intermittently visible; the rumbling of innumerable hoofs, and, in the case of white men, the thudding of the heavy buffalo guns, combined to produce a volume of barbaric uproar, and a spectacle of wild confusion and savagery that had its duplicate in no part of the world.

The Indian and the settler killed, generally speaking, only enough for their needs. Then buffalo hides became of value, a dollar a piece or less. Immediately every man with the price of a camp outfit, a couple of wagons, a few horses and a gun, took to the buffalo country and, under pretence of clearing the plains for agricultural purposes, these animals were slaughtered without mercy. Right-minded people arose and condemned the perpetration of such a heinous crime as the destruction of an entire species to satisfy the greed of a few men. The United States Government, however, took no steps to prevent it, one official even suggesting placing a bounty on the buffalo, as it was understood that their destruction would settle once and for all the vexing and ever-present Indian problem.

It is worthy of note that at this time, Canada, with a large Indian population, had no such problem. The Blackfeet domiciled on both sides of the international boundary, whilst raiding trapper camps and committing depredations on the American side, respected the peace treaty they had made with Canada. This proves conclusively that a little tact and consideration could have accomplished with the Indians what bodies of armed troops could not.

Although no bounties were actually offered, the policy of destruction was carried out to the letter. The Indians, friendly or otherwise, took the war-path in defence of their ancient birthright; retaliatory tactics of the utmost cruelty were carried out against them, and some tribes were wiped almost out of existence. For several years, not many, the prairie became a shambles. The buffalo were eventually corralled in the state of Texas on one of their annual migrations, and one spring they failed to appear on the Canadian plains. The Indian problem was settled for all time.

A whole species of a useful and noble animal had been destroyed, and an entire race of intelligent and courageous people decimated and brought into subjection, in the space of a number of years that could be counted on the fingers of a man's two hands.

Allowing at a conservative estimate two hundred pounds of meat to each beast, and considering the semi-official computation of their number, which was around ten million head, it can easily be computed that two hundred million pounds of first-class meat, excepting the little that could have been eaten by the hunters themselves, was allowed to rot on the prairie. Add to this the greed and cruelty of the act, and the pitiable spectacle of the thousands of calves dying of neglect, or becoming a prey to wolves. This, however, is not the kind of empire-building of which I like to speak, and serves as a very poor example of my subject. This hetacomb, too, was hardly a still-hunt.

It is not given to all to acquire skill in this most thrilling of sports. He who would become proficient at it must learn to move as a shadow, his actions smooth as oil, and his senses set to a hair-trigger touch; for the forest is argus-eyed, and of an unsleeping vigilance, and must always see him first.

Still-hunting is an art learned from the Indian, an accomplishment in which few white men excel, save only those who have spent many days in the lodges of those silent, thoughtful people, or consorted much with those who have. I can almost hear the howl of protest going up from a host of pseudo-bushmen, whose experience is confined to running moose down in deep snow, blundering on them in sections where they are numerous, or shooting them at the water's edge, which anybody can do. I repeat that the average white man is not a good still-hunter.

There are exceptions; famous guides, celebrated for their skill in "calling,"* crafty as the savage whose tricks they have acquired, men who have earned a reputation of never coming out without their moose are to be met in bush communities in all parts of Canada; but they are as outstanding there as is a genius in a colony of artists. But all must take off their hats to the Indian. His own evasive, subtle mind fits him admirably to cope with the cunning and elusive nature of such animals as moose and deer. Indeed, it is probable that his type of mentality has been evolved by just such exercises during many generations, for the red man is primarily

*Moose can be called to a firing position by experts, in the right season.

a hunter. Few but he are able, without snow, and in most cases, even with it, to track and locate a moose without scaring the animal (in which case he is gone, and as impossible to overtake as a train would be), for no moose, unless bogged to the shoulders in snow, has ever been taken by tracking him down from behind. Not all are mentally fitted to enter into the intricacies of move and countermove, advance, circle, and retreat which must be studied in each case, or to guess the necessary allowance for the changing of a scarcely perceptible breath of wind.

Busy workers have not the time to acquire the knowledge that warns of too close an approach to a disadvantageous firing position, nor have they, unless they live as close to Nature as their swarthy brethren, the instinct that evinces itself in the culminating achievement of knowing the exact position of the moose in relation to himself, before the last two or three steps are to be made that will expose the hunter, and give him his shot at a quarry that he has stalked for an hour. And all this without sight, sound, or indication of the presence of moose, excepting perhaps some week-old tracks and nibbled branches, and in a section, such as moose commonly resort to, where a man is lucky to be able to see ten feet ahead of him.

It takes no little skill also to enter a "yard" of moose, padded down with tracks as numerous as those of cows in a pasture, and make a specific set at one particular beast. Yet this is necessary; hit or miss, rambling tactics meeting with no more success than firing into the centre of a flock of ducks ever does. The least carelessness of approach, the rattle of cartridges in the pocket, the slapping of a twig on the clothing, or even too much mental concentration on the animal itself, causing uneasiness, will alike result in a sudden flurry and crackling of twigs and brush, the measured, rapidly diminishing thump of hoofs driven by legs working like piston-rods, the distant crash as some rotten tree gives way before the driving weight of flesh, bone, and muscle, and then utter silence. And like as not without a hair of the quarry having been seen.

The actual shooting is child's play. More moose are killed at fifty feet by good hunters, than at a hundred yards by good shots. A moose is not a hard target, and once seen, looms up amongst the undergrowth like the side of a barn. The difficult part is to get to see him. On the still-hunt the sum and substance of the hunter's efforts are to see the animal before it sees him; to closely approach a moose without his being aware of your presence is an impossible feat, as indeed it is with any other of these dwellers amongst the leaves. But like all the other types of deer, unless rendered frantic by the scent of man, his curiosity gets the better of him; he will stay until he gets a fleeting glimpse of what he is running away from. That is the hunter's only chance of success.

All animals that live in the wilderness are provided with a set of protective habits which the skilled hunter, having knowledge of them, turns to his advantage. Beaver, when ashore, post a guard; not much advantage there, you think. But standing upright as he does in some prominent position, he draws attention, where the working party in the woods would have escaped notice. Both beaver and otter plunge into the water if alarmed or caught in a trap (in this case a stone is provided which keeps them there, to drown). Foxes rely on their great speed and run in full view, offering excellent rifle practice. Deer contrive to keep a tree or some brush between their line of flight and their enemy, and the experienced hunter will immediately run to the clump of foliage and shoot unseen from behind it.

Moose feed downwind, watch closely behind them but neglect to a certain extent the ground ahead. When about to rest they form a loop in their trail, and lie hidden beside it, where they can keep an eye on it, manoeuvring to get the wind from their late feeding ground. These things we know, and act accordingly. We decide on the animal we want, and make a series of fifty-yard loops, knowing better than to follow directly in the tracks, the end of each arc striking his trail, which is a most tortuous affair winding in and out as he selects his feed. We do this with due regard for the wind, all along his line of travel, touching it every so often, until we overshoot where we suppose the trail ought to be. This shows—provided our calculations are correct, our direction good, and if we are lucky—that our moose is somewhere within that curve. It has now become a ticklish proposition.

We must not strike his tracks near where he is lying down (he cannot be said to sleep), for this is the very trap he has laid for us. If we go too far on our loop we may get on the windward side (I think that is the term; I am no sailor). Pie for the moose again. Probably he is even now watching us. To know when we are approaching that position between our game and the tell-tale current of air is where that hazard comes in which makes moose-hunting one of the most fascinating sports.

All around you the forest is grey, brown and motionless. For hours past there has been visible no sign of life, nor apparently will there ever be. A dead, empty, silent world of wiry underbrush, dry leaves, and endless rows of trees. You stumble and on the instant the dun-coloured woods spring suddenly to life with a crash, as the slightly darker shadow you had mistaken for an upturned root takes on volition; and a monstrous black shape, with palmated horns stretched a man's length apart, hurtles through tangled thickets and over or through waist-high fallen timber, according to its resisting power. Almost pre-historic in appearance, weighing perhaps half a ton, with hanging black bell, massive forequarters, bristling mane, and flashing white flanks, this high-stepping pacer ascends the steep side of a knoll, and on the summit he stops, slowly swings the ponderous head, and deliberately, arrogantly looks you over. Swiftly he turns and is away, this time for good, stepping, not fast but with tireless regularity, unchanging speed, and disregard for obstacles, that will carry him miles in the two hours that he will run.

And you suddenly realize that you have an undischarged rifle in your hands, and that your moose is now well on his way to Abitibi. And mixed with your disappointment, if you are a sportsman, is the alleviating thought that the noble creature still has his life and freedom, and that there are other days and other moose.

I know of no greater thrill than that, after two or three hours of careful stalking with all the chances against me, of sighting my game, alert, poised for that one move that means disappearance; and with this comes the sudden realization that in an infinitesimal period of time will come success or failure. The distance, and the probable position of a vital spot in relation to the parts that are visible, must be judged instantly, and simultaneously. The heavy breathing incidental to the exertion of moving noiselessly through a jungle of tangled undergrowth and among fallen timber must be controlled. And regardless of poor footing, whether balanced precariously on a tottering log, or with bent back and twisted neck peering between up-turned roots, that rifle must come swiftly forward and up. I pull—no, squeeze—the trigger, as certain earnest, uniformed souls informed me in the past, all in one sweeping motion; the wilderness awakes to the crash of the rifle, and the moose disappears. The report comes as a cataclysmic uproar after the abysmal silence, and aghast at the sacrilege, the startled blue-jays and whiskey-jacks screech, and chatter, and whistle. I go forward with leaps and bounds, pumping in another cartridge, as moose rarely succumb to the first shot. But I find I do not need the extra bullet. There is nothing there to shoot. An animal larger than a horse has disappeared without a trace, save some twisted leaves and a few tracks which look damnably healthy. There is no blood, but I follow for a mile, maybe, in the hopes of a paunch wound, until the trail becomes too involved to follow.

I have failed. Disaster, no less. And I feel pretty flat, and inefficient, and empty-bellied.

Worst of all, I must go back to camp, and explain the miss to a critical and unsympathetic listener, who is just as hungry as I am, and in no shape to listen to reason. Experiences of that kind exercise a very chastening effect on the self-esteem; also it takes very few of them to satisfy any man's gambling instinct.

∿∿∿

A BIG BULL RACING THROUGH CLOSE TIMBER WITH A SET OF antlers fifty or sixty inches across is a sight worth travelling far to see. He will swing his head from side to side in avoidance of limbs, duck and sway as gracefully as a trained charger with a master-hand at the bridle, seeming to know by instinct spaces between trees where he may pass with his armament.

It is by observing a series of spots of this description that a man may estimate the size of the bull he is after.

The tracks of bull and cow are distinguishable by the difference in shape of the hoofs; the bull being stub-toed forward, and the cow being narrow-footed fore and aft. Also the bull swings his front feet out and back into line when running; this is plain to be seen with snow on the ground of any depth; furthermore the cow feeds on small trees by passing around them, the bull by straddling them and breaking them down.

Tracking on bare ground is the acme of the finesse of the still-hunt, especially in a dry country; and tracking in winter is not always as simple as would appear. More than a little skill is sometimes required to determine whether the animal that made the tracks was going or coming. This is carried to the point, where, with two feet of snow over month-old tracks, visible in the first place only as dimples, an expert may, by digging out the snow with his hands, ascertain which way the moose was going; yet to the uninitiated tracks an hour old present an unsolvable problem as to direction, as, if the snow be deep, the tracks fill in immediately and show only as a series of long narrow slots having each two ends identical in appearance. The secret is this, that the rear edge of the hind leg leaves a sharper, narrower impression in the back end of the slot than does the more rounded forward side. This can be felt out only with the bare hands; a ten-minute occupation of heroic achievement, on a windy day on a bleak hillside, in a temperature of twenty-five below zero. Nevertheless a very useful accomplishment, as in the months of deep snow a herd may be yarded up a mile from tracks made earlier in the season.

But should the herd have travelled back and forth in the same tracks, as they invariably do, we have confusion again. In that case they must be followed either way to a considerable hill; here, if going downhill they separate, taking generous strides, or if uphill, short ones. Loose snow is thrown forward and out from the slots, and is an unfailing guide if visible, but an hour's sharp wind will eradicate that indication save to the trained eye.

Assuredly the hunt is no occupation for a pessimist, as he would most undoubtedly find a cloud to every silver lining.

There are many ways of killing moose, but most of them can be effected only at times of the year when it would be impossible to keep the meat, unless the party was large enough to use up the meat in a couple of days, or, as in the case of Indians, it could be properly smoked.

In the summer when they come down to water in the early morning and late evening, moose are easily approached with due care. They stand submerged to the belly, and dig up with the long protruding upper lip, the roots of waterlilies, which much resemble elongated pineapples. Whilst eyes and ears are thus out of commission the canoeman will paddle swiftly in against the wind, until with a mighty splurge the huge head is raised, the water spraying from the wide antlers, running off the "pans" in miniature cataracts, when all movement in the canoes ceases, and they drift noiselessly like idle leaves, controlled by the paddles operated under water. The moose lowers his head again, and the canoes creep up closer now, more cautiously, care being taken not to allow the animal a broadside view. On one of the occasions when he raises his head the moose is bound to become aware of the danger, but by then the hunters have arrived within rifle shot of the shore; so, allowed to provide his own transportation to dry land, he is killed before he enters the bush.

In the mating season moose may be called down from the hills by one skilled in the art, and threshing in the underbush with an old discarded moose-horn will sometimes arouse the pugnacity of a reluctant bull; but when he comes it is as well to be prepared to shoot fast and straight.

Many sportsmen become afflicted with a peculiar malady known as buck-fever when confronted suddenly by the game they have sought so assiduously. The mental strain of senses keyed to the highest pitch, coupled with the quivering expectation of a show-down at any moment, is such that this "fever" induces them either to pump the magazine empty without firing a shot or forget to use the sights, or become totally incapable of pressing the trigger. Gentlemen of that temperament had better by far let fallen moose-horns lie when in the woods during the early part of October. They certainly are lacking, in the *sang froid* of a prominent business man I once guided on a hunt.

He was a man who liked a drink, and liked it at pretty regular intervals, when on his vacation. Included in the commissariat was a case of the best whiskey. Every morning when we started out a bottle was placed in the bow of the canoe and from it he gathered inspiration from time to time, becoming at moments completely intoxicated, as he averred, with the scenery. The agreement was that when the Scotch was gone the hunt was over, and, head or no, we were to return to town. It was not a good moose country. I had hunted all I knew how, and had raised nothing, and my professional reputation was at stake. The day of the last bottle arrived, and our game was still at large. As we started for the railroad I was in anything but a jubilant mood, when, on rounding a point, a large bull of fair spread stood facing us on the foreshore: at a distance of not over a hundred feet. I jammed my paddle into the sand-bar, effectually stopping the canoe, and almost whooped with joy; but my companion, who was pretty well lit by this time, gazed fixedly at the creature, now evidently making preparations to move off.

I urged an immediate shot. In response to my entreaties this human distillery seized his rifle and tried to line his sights. Failing, he tried again, and fumbled at the trigger, but the "scenery" was too strong for him. The animal, apparently fascinated by the performance, had paused, and was looking on. The man was about to make another attempt when he put the gun down, and raising his hand he addressed the moose.

"Wait a minute," said he.

Reaching down into the canoe he handed me over his shoulder not the rifle but the bottle, saying as he did so, "Let's have another drink first!"

After the first frosts bull moose are pugnaciously inclined towards all the world, and more than one man has been known to spend a night up a tree, whilst a moose ramped and raved at the foot of it till daylight. Whether these men were in any actual danger, or were scared stiff and afraid to take any chances, it is impossible to say, but I have always found that a hostile moose, if approached boldly down wind, so that he gets the man-scent, will move off, threateningly, but none the less finally. Although the person of a man may cause them to doubt their prowess, they will cheerfully attack horses and waggons, domestic bulls, and even railroad locomotives.

Bull moose are quite frequently found killed by trains at that time of the year, and they have been known to contest the right of way with an automobile, which had at last to be driven around them. A laden man seems to arouse their ire, as a government ranger, carrying a canoe across a portage once discovered.

It was his first trip over, and, no doubt attracted by the scratching sound caused by the canoe rubbing on brush as it was carried, this lord of the forest planted himself square in the middle of the portage, and refused to give the ranger the trail. The bush was too ragged to permit of a detour, so the harassed man, none too sure of what might occur, put down his canoe. The moose presently turned and walked up the trail slowly, and the man then picked up his canoe again, and followed. Gaining confidence, he touched his lordship on the rump with the prow of the canoe, to hasten progress; and then the fun commenced. The infuriated animal turned on him, this time with intent. He threw his canoe to the side, and ran at top speed down the portage, with the moose close behind. (It could be mentioned here, that those animals are at a distinct disadvantage on level going; had the ranger entered the bush, he would have been overtaken in twenty steps.)

At a steep cut-off he clutched a small tree, swung himself off the trail, and rolled down the declivity; the moose luckily, kept on going. After a while the ranger went back, inspected his canoe, which was intact, and put it out of sight, and it was as well that he did. He then returned to his belongings to find his friend standing guard over a torn and trampled pile of dunnage which he could in no way approach. He commenced to throw rocks at this white elephant, who, entering into the spirit of the game rushed him up the trail again, he swinging off in the same place as before. This time he stayed there. The moose patrolled the portage all the hours of darkness, and the ranger spent the night without food or shelter.

A moose, should he definitely make up his mind to attack, could make short work of a man. They often kill one another, using their antlers for the purpose, but on lesser adversaries they use their front feet, rearing up and striking terrific blows. I once saw an old bull, supposedly feeble and an easy prey, driven out into shallow water by two wolves, where they attempted to hamstring him. He enticed them out into deeper water, and turning, literally tore one of them to pieces. Fear of wounding the moose prevented me from shooting the other, which escaped.

When enraged a bull moose is an awe-inspiring sight, with his flaring superstructure, rolling eyes, ears laid back, and top lip lifted in a kind of a snarl. Every hair on his back bristles up like a mane, and at such times he emits his challenging call—O-waugh! O-waugh!; a deep cavernous sound, with a wild, blood-stirring hint of savagery and power. This sound, like the howling of wolves, or the celebrated war-whoop when heard at a safe distance, or from a position of security, or perhaps in the latter case, at an exhibition, is not so very alarming. But, if alone and far from human habitation in some trackless waste, perhaps in the dark, with the certainty that you yourself are the object of the hue and cry, the effect on the nervous system is quite different, and is apt to cause a sudden rush of blood to the head, leaving the feet cold. The sounds, invested with that indescribable atavistic quality that only wild things can produce, under these conditions, are, to say the least, a little weakening.

Once, and once only, was I ever in any serious danger from the attack of a moose. On this occasion, needing meat, I was looking for moose-tracks. Finding some indications, I had, after only a short still-hunt, come on to two of them, a cow and a well-grown calf, at the edge of a beaver pond. I shot the calf, which suited my requirements, it being yet warm weather, and the cow made two or three runs at me, but was easily scared away by a few shots fired in the air; I felt safe enough as I had in my pocket some spare cartridges, tied in a little buckskin bag to keep them from rattling.

Whilst skinning the kill I noticed a beaver swimming towards me, his curiosity aroused by the shooting probably, as I suppose that the crack of a rifle had never been heard before in all that region. The beaver was unprime and the hide valueless, but, becoming interested in his movements, I sat down on the bank and watched him. Quite absorbed in my pastime I was suddenly startled by a slight crackling behind me, followed immediately by the hollow, coughing grunt of an angry bull moose. The sound was no novelty to me, but never before had it carried, to my ear, the note of menace that it now did. No thunderous bellowing roar of a lion could convey half the murderous intent expressed in the cold malevolence of that sound behind my back. It chilled me to the marrow, and the hair crept on my scalp. I jumped to my feet and whirled with a yell calculated to jar the horns off the creature's head, but which produced not the slightest effect. He stood facing me, every hair on his body erect, his eyes red with hate. He commenced rubbing his hocks together, sure signal of a charge, and I smelt distinctly the sickening, musky odour these animals emit when about to fight.

Afraid to make a sudden movement, for fear of precipitating an attack, I reached stealthily for my rifle, jerked it to my hip, pumping as

I did so, and fired; that is, I pulled the trigger, and almost before the answering click told me the gun was empty it flashed into my brain like an arrow from hell that I had emptied the magazine in driving away the cow.

But the spell was broken. The moose moved; so did I.

He had me between himself and the pond, with a margin of about ten feet in my favour. Once in the water, my chances I knew, would be poor; so I made pretty good time down the edge of it, and the moose ran parallel to me; we seemed to be pretty evenly matched for speed. At the end of the pond I turned, quickly jumped the creek, and made for a stretch of flat, steeply sloping rock, where I could not be cornered up; this was covered with a scattered growth of small jackpines, which, whilst not large enough to climb, offered dodging facilities. This move brought the moose directly behind me.

Still running, I got out my bag of cartridges, and pulled the string with my mouth: the knot jammed; I slackened my speed and tore at the bag with my teeth, ripping it, and spilling most of the cartridges. Ramming a shell into the breech I spun quickly round to find that the moose had stopped also, startled at my sudden move, and at about the same distance as before. I took quick aim, ready to shoot, but his rage was spent, and his former pugnacity gave way to uneasiness. I knew now that the danger was over, although I was obliged to sting him in the flank before I could get rid of him.

∾ ∾ ∾

IN THE COURSE OF A HUNT EVERY DETAIL LIABLE TO HAVE A bearing on the situation must be noted; such as the roll of the land forming pockets where the wind may eddy; the direction of the different vagrant air currents, or a shift in the wind itself, must be tested for, generally by means of wetting a finger and holding it up, the side which the wind is coming from becoming immediately cool; or if there be snow, by throwing up handfuls and watching its drift.

Care must be taken that an approach is not made up a steep hill where your quarry will sight you before you can see enough of him to cover with your foresight; also that you do not stand out in prominent relief, in the full glare of the sun, or find yourself obliged to shoot into it.

I remember seeing a much-needed buck saunter off into the bush in plain sight, owing to the fact that I faced the setting sun on a lake shore, and every time I raised my rifle the deer completely disappeared, swallowed up in the glare.

Trivial occurrences, that would appear to have no connection with the hunt whatever, may be of the utmost importance. The cawing of a few crows once led to a kill which was the realization of the dream of years to the sportsman I accompanied on the trip. It was in a burnt country, and my companion was unsuitably clad as to his feet in a pair of heavy, hard-soled boots, and in the dry, brittle ruck of the fire was making a terrific noise. We had heard that exciting terrible sound, the clashing of huge antlers as two bulls fought to the death, about half a mile back; and we were now closely approaching our estimation of the position of this battle, which had ceased. I asked my companion to stand still for a moment so that we could listen a while, and he unfortunately chose a brittle log to stand on, which gave way with a crash. Remarking meekly that he "made more noise standing still than some people did running," the unfortunate man urged me to try my luck alone.

Just at that moment we heard faintly a continuous, low sound, about two hundred yards to the south of us. This, after listening attentively, we made out to be the sound of crows, flocking together at some spot. This probably meant that some animal lay dead there, in all likelihood a moose, killed in a fight. My friend took courage on hearing the good news, and decided to see the thing through. As we listened, getting our bearings and testing the wind repeatedly, the sound changed to a scolding, and the birds seemed to scatter and take the air, as though disturbed. Better all the time; this argued a living moose, no doubt inspecting his victim, as they do periodically when victorious.

We laid our plan of approach and started away, and when we were within about twenty-five yards of the disturbance, the crows took flight, and we came suddenly out in plain view of a pool of water, in which lay a moose, very dead, and for a long time since, which it took no skill to determine. Seated in the water, feeding on the ill-smelling carcass, was about the biggest black bear I had seen for a long time, he being the cause of all the uproar. Although it was not my hunt, the other man being for a moment spellbound, and with good reason, for it was a remarkable sight, I immediately shot the bear. On receiving the second bullet, he raced into an unburned patch of larches, where we eventually found him dead. This clump we circled, to find his point of egress, if any, as a wounded bear is apt to be dangerous, and we were as yet uncertain of his demise.

We had no more than half completed our detour when we heard that deep-throated gurgling cough that so thrills the hunter to the core of his being, and, it seemed, almost at our elbows. Turning we saw two big bulls looking down on us from the top of a knoll not fifteen yards away. Here this sportsman redeemed himself. The biggest bull did not offer him a very good target, but sensibly taking the smaller one that did, he dropped his moose neatly and cleanly with a well-placed bullet.

Some men are stricken with buck fever after the shooting is all over. One man, when I knocked down a badly wounded bull that would otherwise have suffered for hours and given us a long and useless chase, his gun empty, and thinking his game was escaping him, had been in despair. He became so excited on seeing the moose fall, and his trophy assured, that he started searching in all his pockets with fluttering hands, ejaculating disjointedly:

"You saved the day; you sure did, I appreciate that; believe me I do. I-I-yes sir, I must do something for you; something worth while, that you'll remember me by." Having at last located what he was searching for, he finally pulled out a gold cigarette-case, and opening it, he held it towards me. "Here," he said, "have a cigarette, you deserve it!"

I had no intention of accepting a gift offered in such circumstances, but his concluding words caused me to show some astonishment, and, noticing it, he suddenly became aware of the situation his excitement had tricked him into, and we both enjoyed a hearty laugh over the incident and I kept the cigarette to remember him by.

Being accustomed to hunting on the plains, where the game is in pockets, in gulleys, river bottoms, or in bluffs of poplar or willows, and thus standing partly located at the outset, and where it is more a matter of good shooting than good hunting, I found the still-hunt, as practised by the Northern Indians, an entirely different proposition. I know of no set of conditions to which the ancient simile of the needle in the haystack could be better applied.

My first experience was a good many years ago, with a young Ojibway, yet in his teens. He had all the quiet and confident bearing that goes with conscious ability, moved like a shadow, and addressed me not at all. From the outset he was in no hurry, spending much time listening to the wind above, and inspecting the ground below, both apparently inconsequent proceedings as there seemed to be no wind and the only visible tracks, to the reading of which I was no stranger, were old ones and plain to be seen. However, his tardiness suited me as, coming from a territory where walking is not popular, and with the slippery, stiff-soled moccasins of the plains Indian on my feet, I was quite well occupied keeping him in sight as it was, and sincerely hoped nothing would occur to increase his speed.

We proceeded in a fairly direct line of travel for maybe an hour, when on a sudden he stopped and, motioning me to come, showed me the fresh tracks of a cow moose. Our progress now became more circuitous and rambling, and he wandered apparently quite aimlessly around, listening meanwhile for a non-existent wind.

It-was during the Fall of the year, and I found the wonderfully coloured woods a fairyland after the bare, brown prairie, and the dry harsh mountains protruding from blistering belts of sand. I was having a good time and, moose or no moose, the gyrations of my gnome-like and elusive companion intrigued me to the limit. Presently he stopped in a glade, and looked around, smiling with the air of one exhibiting a long-sought treasure. I also looked around, but did not smile, as I recognized the spot as the one at which he had discovered the moose track. I had been twisted often enough in my calculations in the wild lands to guess what that meant.

"Ki-onitchi-kataig, we are lost," I said.

He shook his head, and pointing to the moose track held up two fingers.

So that was it, he had in the circling discovered another moose. I had not seen him go through any motions indicative of a person discovering anything, moose or man, but supposed he must know what he was about. Maybe, I reflected, if we went around again, we could add another moose to the tally, and then surround them and make a general slaughter. The stripling now made some preparations. He took off his outside shirt and his hat, tying a folded handkerchief of indefinite colour around his bobbed hair. He hung his discarded clothing, with his blanket-cloth gun case on a limb, and this mark of confidence in his ability to find the place again induced me also to remove and hang up my coat and hat; it seemed we must be about to hurry.

But my elfin guide stood motionless, apparently lost in thought, formulating his plans; and as he stood, a study in black and tan, and faded buckskin, under the bronze dome of a giant birch tree, I thought that if only some great artist were there with skilful brush to commit to canvas the wondrous colour scheme, the shades, the shadows, the slanting streams of subdued light, the attitude of my primitive companion, wild, negligent, yet alert, furtive almost, like the creatures he was hunting, the masterpiece would result that could well be representative of a race, and of an epoch that will soon be with the things which are no longer, lost forever.

The moment passed and he moved on.

Our progress was now very slow. Twice I ascertained that we were covering short sections of our previous itinerary, back-tracking in spots, making endless half-circles on a base line itself anything but straight.

On our left came a breath of sound, a slight rustle, and on the instant the boy sank into the woods like a hot knife through butter. Presently he returned, smiled his thin smile, and made the sign of a fox's tail. More half-circles. He commenced testing for the wind with a wet finger, and crumbling leaves in his hands allowed the dust to drift. The result was almost imperceptible. He seemed to gather some satisfactory information from the manoeuvre, however, as he nodded his head and went on.

Bars of sunlight hovered here and there as the trellised roof of leaves wavered and swayed, and in the more open it filtered through, to lie in golden pools upon the forest floor. These he skirted stealthily, keeping in the gloom on their borders with that instinct of self-effacement which alike to the predatory or the furtive, spells success or safety.

He tested for wind more frequently now, on one occasion stopping and creeping backwards on his tracks, as though backing out of some sacred precinct that he had inadvertently entered. He circled out, and back into the same spot by another direction, a matter of yards only, and, selecting a spot in a wall of small evergreens, suddenly raised his rifle and fired.

At the same instant I saw a patch of coarse hair resolve itself into a huge brown body, as a cow moose surged through the balsams, blood streaming from nose and mouth, to sink down within twenty feet.

The Ojibway blew the smoke out of his rifle.

"Meheu," he said, speaking for the first time. "It is done."

On Being Lost

"Vainly walked he through the forest...
In the snow beheld no footprints,
In the ghastly gleaming forest
Fell, and could not rise from weakness,
Perished there from cold and hunger."
LONGFELLOW

CHAPTER FIVE

On Being Lost

THREE YEARS AGO, ON A NIGHT IN SPRING, A MAN WENT down from his camp fifty yards to the river to get a pail of water and has never been seen since.

A year before the time of writing, in this district, a deer-hunter took an afternoon stroll and was discovered eleven days later, by one of a gang of twenty-five men who scoured the woods for him for twenty miles around.

In the first case the man strayed off the water-trail in the dark, and not arriving at the shack he attempted to correct his mistake and took a short-cut, only to arrive back to the river at another point. He again endeavoured to strike the camp but, angling too much to his right, missed it. So much was learned by the finding of the pail at the river bank, and by his tracks. After that he entered a country of burnt, bare rocks, and small patches of green swamp, and he is there yet.

The second man, having killed a deer, remained where he was, erected a shelter and kept a fire. Beyond the mental strain incident to his adventure he was in good condition when found. Wherein lies the secret of the difference between being correctly and incorrectly lost.

The safest course, with night coming on, and being still astray, is for one to stop, make a fire, and as comfortable a camp as maybe, and wait for daylight, with the feeling of security that it brings after the uncertainties and exaggerated forebodings of a long night. Then, perhaps, bearings can be taken to better advantage, and the sun may be shining, although it may now, after half a day of extended and aimless ramblings, be impossible for the wanderer to determine in which direction a start should be made.

Even so, he may strike for low land, and if his camp is not situated on it he will have at least an idea where it should lie. The inability of the average man to retain a record of his itinerary to the rear, whilst he selects his route ahead, is responsible for more loss of life in the woods than any other factor, excepting perhaps fire. This is so well recognized that one of the Provinces has passed a law prohibiting the killing of porcupines except in cases of emergency, they being the only animal that can be killed by a starving man without weapons.

A man may start on a bright, sunshiny day, with all confidence, to make his way to some as yet undiscovered lake or river, or to look over a section of country, and find his trip going very satisfactorily. Inviting glades, offering good travelling, open up in every direction: gulleys lead on miraculously from one to another in just the right directions; and an occasional glance at the sun, or the lie of the land, affords all the indication of route necessary. The course is smooth, the wheels are greased, and he slides merrily on his way.

Having lured him in so far with fair promise, the fickle landscape now decides to play one from the bottom of the deck. The going becomes thicker during the next half-hour, and the ground inclined to be swampy, with quite a few mosquitoes present. The interest aroused by these features induces a slight relaxing of concentration, and during such period of pre-occupation the sun guilefully seizes on this as the psychological moment at which to disappear. The travelling becomes worse, much worse. Dwarf tamarac,* spruce and cedar have now superseded the more generous and tractable hardwoods, and standing close-packed, with interlaced limbs, they form an entanglement from the feet up, through which a man is hard put to it to force a passage. Overhead is an impenetrable mass of twisted branches, through which the perspiring man vainly endeavours to get a glimpse of the sun, only to discover that it is gone. From the high ground further back he has seen a ridge of hardwood across the swamp, perhaps a mile away or more, where the footing will be good; so he presses on for this.

*American larch.

He fights his way through the tangled growth for hours, it seems, and appears to be no nearer the slope of deciduous timber than he ever was. He now, wisely, decides to eat and think it over; so making a fire, and infusing his tea with swamp water, he builds himself a meal.

After this, and a smoke, being now refreshed, he goes forward with renewed energy and zeal. This, in time, wears off; there is no improvement in the going, he seems to arrive nowhere, and would be much cheered by the sight of a familiar landmark. This, however, is not forthcoming; but presently he smells smoke. Wondering who but one in his own predicament would make a fire in such a jungle, he trails up the smoke, finding an odd footprint to encourage him; he will at least see a man, who may know the district. He arrives at the fire, and no one is there, but there are tracks leading away which he commences to follow, on the run. All at once he notices something oddly familiar in the shape of a spruce top he is climbing over, and with sudden misgiving he sets his moccasined foot into one of the stranger's footprints, to find that they fit perfectly; the tracks are his own. He has been tracking himself down to his own fire-place!

Mixed with the feeling of affront at the scurvy trick that is making a laughingstock of him for all the forest, is more than a hint of uneasiness, and, taking careful observations, he starts out anew, this time more slowly and coolly. An hour finds him back at the long-dead fire. With a sudden burst of speed in what he hopes is the right direction, he puts this now thoroughly distasteful piece of scenery behind him, tearing and ripping his way through this endless maze, that seems somehow to cover all Northern Canada. He frequently maps out his line of march with a stick in the mud, and spends much time in abstruse calculations; but it is only a matter of time till he returns, torn, exasperated, scarcely believing his eyes, to this hub of the wheel on which he is being spun so helplessly.

And on him dawns, with sickening certainty, the indisputable fact that he is lost. He becomes a little panicky, for this begins to be serious.

He appears to be unable to get away from this spot, as though held by a powerful magnet which allows him to wander at will just so far out, drawing him inexorably back at intervals. He is caught in the grip of the endless circle, which from being a mere geometrical figure has now become an engine which may well encompass his destruction. As these thoughts pass swiftly, fear enters his heart. If wise, he will now get him a quantity of boughs, and construct a lean-to, gather a pile of wood, and pass the night in comfort, hoping for the re-appearance of the sun in the morning. Or he may blindly obey the almost uncontrollable impulse of the lost, to run madly, tearing through underbrush regardless of clothing and skin, so as to get as far from the hateful spot as possible, and go on, and on, and on—to nowhere. He will almost inevitably take the wrong direction, at last breaking away from that deadly circle, in which case his speed only serves to plunge him deeper and deeper into a wilderness that stretches to the Arctic Sea. Darkness finds him exhausted, and almost incapable of making camp, and when the sun rises the next morning, his calculations, if he has any, are so involved, that he knows not whether to travel facing the sun, with his back to it, or across it.

He may be later stumbled upon, by the merest accident, by some member of a search party, or by his partner, if the latter is a skilful tracker; or again, he may find his way to a large body of water and wait to be picked up by some Indian or other passer-by. This within a reasonable distance of civilization. If far in the woods he will wander hopelessly on, sometimes in circles, at times within measurable distance of his camp, past spots with which he is familiar, but is no longer in a condition to recognize. The singing of the birds becomes a mockery in his ears; they, and everything around him, are carrying on as usual, each in its own accustomed manner of living, and yet he, the lord of creation, is the only creature present who is utterly and completely subjugated by his surroundings. Hunger gnaws his vitals, and hot waves of blood surge through his brain, leaving him weak and dizzy. Still he must keep on, always; he may yet strike some trapper's cabin or Indian encampment; even his deserted fireplace, once so odious, now appears in the light of a haven of refuge.

As the hours pass swiftly on, and the setting of another sun finds him no nearer safety, his mind becomes obsessed by strange fancies; the grey whiskey-jacks, trail companions on more fortunate trips, flickering across his line of vision like disembodied spirits, whispering together as they watch him, become birds of evil omen, sent to mock him with their whistling. Luminous rotting stumps, glowing in the darkness with ghostly phosphorescence, seem like the figments of a disordered dream; and a grey owl, floating soundlessly on muffled wings, has all the semblance of an apparition with yellow, gleaming eyes. The little distant red spots, like fire, that every tired man sees at night, are to him real enough to cause him to chase them for long distances in the falling dusk, spending his waning strength, and undergoing the added mental torture of disappointment. The whole world of trees, and shadows, and dark labyrinth becomes a place of phantasma and fevered imaginings, and his soul becomes possessed by a shuddering dread that no known danger of ordinary woods travel could account for. The sepulchral glow of the moon transforms the midnight forest into an inferno of ghostly light, pregnant with unnamable supernatural possibilities.

As he grows weaker he becomes the victim of hallucinations, and is beset by a form of insanity, the "madness of the woods," in which the dim arches become peopled with flitting shapes and formless apparitions. Gargoyle faces leer and grimace at him from out the shadows; Indians appear, stare momentarily beyond him as though he were invisible, to disappear again, eluding his frantic efforts to attract their attention. Acquaintances stand beckoning in the distance who, when he approaches, retreat yet further, and beckon again, finally fading to nothingness, or walking callously out of sight. And he shouts frenziedly that they may stop and wait for him, at which the woods become suddenly deserted, and his voice echoes hollowly through the endless, empty ramifications, which have now assumed the appearance of a tomb.

And there hangs over him as he blindly staggers onward, a Presence, an evil loathsome thing, which, as though to mark him as its own, envelops him with its shadow; following him like a hideous vampire, or some foul, carrion bird, waiting but for the moment when he will drop, watching with a terrible smile. For the ghoul that sits enthroned behind the ramparts of the North, holds always in his hand the strands of his entanglements, sleeping not at all, lest, of those who stumble unawares within them, there should one escape.

For another day, perhaps two, or even three, he stumbles on; muttering, at times raving; falling, getting up, only to fall again; crawling at last in that resistless urge of the lost to keep on while there is yet life; and always just ahead dangles the will-o'-the-wisp of hope, never fulfilled.

And if ever found, his bones will indicate his dying posture as that of a creeping man.

༄ ༄ ༄

IN NORTHERN QUEBEC, DURING ONE OF THE MINING RUSHES
which are yet in progress, a prospector came out to the railroad to report
his partner lost. This had happened six weeks before his arrival at the
"front." He had spared no effort, and had used every means that mortal
man could devise to recover his companion, but without avail. As this
had happened in a territory that could only be reached by something
over two hundred and fifty miles of a rough and difficult route, which it
would take at least two weeks to cover, it was considered useless to make
any further attempt, as the man had no doubt been long dead.

The prospector, however, had his doubts. Both men were experienced
bushmen, although perhaps not gifted with that sense of direction which
not even all Indians possess. Being no tenderfoot, the missing man would
not be likely to make any further false moves after the initial one of getting lost, and this thought had kept alive a spark of hope.

For two weeks the bereft man could not get his friend out of his mind;
often he dreamed of him. After one of these dreams, more vivid than the
rest, in which he saw his partner crawling, in the last extremity, along the
sandy beach on the shores of a shallow lake, he decided to revisit the
ground, having been lucky in his prospecting, by means of an airplane. In
a few hours he was hovering over the scene of the mishap.

Nearly every lake in the district was visited for signs of life, but none
of them answered the description of the dream lake. Eventually the pilot,
fearing to run out of gasoline, advised a return. Influenced by his vision,
as indeed he had been in deciding to make the trip, the miner asked the
aviator to fly low over a cluster of lakes about twenty miles from the original camp site, one of them being plainly shallow, and having sand
beaches down one side.

And, as they passed over the sheet of water, they saw a creeping thing,
moving slowly along on the beach, stopping, and moving on. At that distance it could have been a bear, or a wolf hunting for food, and they were
about to swing off to the south and civilization when they decided to
make one last attempt and investigate.

Three minutes later the two men were confronted by an evidence of human endurance almost past belief. Practically naked, his body and face bloated with the bites of mosquitoes he no longer had the strength to fight, his two month's beard clotted with blood and filled with a writhing mass of black flies, emaciated to the last degree, the missing man, for it was he, was even yet far from dead.

But, after sixty-two days of suffering such as few men are called on to endure, this man who would not die could no longer reason. He stared dully at his rescuers, and would have passed on, creeping on hands and knees. And he was headed North, going further and further away from the possibility of rescue with every painful step.

Very gently he was carried, still feebly resisting, to the waiting plane, and in two hours was in safety.

Later the rescued man told how, confused by the non-appearance of the sun for several days, he had wandered in circles from which he could not break away, until he commenced to follow lake shores, and the banks of rivers, expecting them to lead him to some body of water that he knew.

On the re-appearance of the sun, after about a week, he was so far gone as to become possessed by the idea that it was rising and setting in the wrong places, and travelled, accordingly, north instead of south, continuing in that direction long after he had ceased consciously to influence his wanderings. For food he had dammed small streams and set a weir of sticks in a pool below, easily catching the fish left in the drained creek bed. During the weeks of the sucker run, he fared not too badly, as suckers are a sizeable fish of two or three pounds weight, and fish, even if raw, will support life. Later this run ceased, and the suckers returned to deep water. He was then obliged to subsist on roots and an occasional partridge killed with a stone, until he became too weak to throw at them.

He next set rabbit snares of spruce root, most of which the rabbits ate; so he rubbed balsam gum on them, which rabbits do not like, and occasionally was lucky. Soon, however, he lacked the strength to accomplish these things, and from that on lived almost entirely on the inside bark of birch trees. So far north there are miles of country where birch trees will not grow, so he was often without even that inadequate diet. At last he was crawling not over a couple of hundred yards a day, if his last day's tracks were any indication. To travel six or eight days without food is an ordeal few survive, and only those who have undergone starvation, coupled with the labour of travelling when in a weakened condition, can have any idea of what this man went through.

His mind a blank, at times losing sight of the object of his progress, daily he crept further and further away from safety. And there is no doubt that insanity would eventually have accomplished what starvation apparently could not.

This "madness of the woods" that drives men to destruction, when a little calm thinking and observation would have saved the day, attacks alike the weak-willed and the strong, the city man and the bush-whacker, when, after a certain length of time, they find themselves unable to break away from the invisible power that seems to hold them within a definite restricted area from which they cannot get away, or else lures them deeper and deeper into the wilderness. Men old on the trail recognize the symptoms and combat them before their reasoning powers become so warped that they are no longer to be relied on.

This peripatetic obsession causes men to have strange thoughts. Under its influence they will doubt the efficiency of a compass, will argue against the known facts, fail to recognize places with which they are perfectly familiar.

One lumber-jack foreman who became twisted in his calculations, struck a strange road, followed it, and arrived at a camp, and not till he entered it and recognized some of the men, did he realize that the camp was his own. Some men lost for long periods, and having been lucky enough to kill sufficient game to live on, although alive and well seem to lose their reasoning powers entirely. At the sight of men they will run, and are with difficulty caught, and with staring eyes and wild struggles try to free themselves and escape.

Only those who, relying on no compass, spend long years of wandering in the unmarked wastes of a wild country, acquire the knack, or rather the science, of travelling by the blind signs of the wilderness. Ordinary woodsmen of the lumber-jack type, whose work seldom calls them off a logging road, are as easily lost as a townsman. Timber cruisers, engineers and surveyors are all compass men. Their type of work

makes necessary the continuous use of this instrument, and they do little travelling without it.

It is only amongst men of the trapper or prospector type that we find
developed that instinctive sense of direction, which is a priceless gift to
those who possess it.

Travelling in an unpeopled wilderness calls for an intense concentration on the trail behind, a due regard for the country ahead and a memory that recalls every turn made, and that can recognize a ridge, gulley, or
stream crossed previously and at another place. Swinging off the route to
avoid swamps, and other deviations must be accomplished without losing
sight of the one general direction, meanwhile the trail unrolls behind like
a ball of yarn, one end of which is at the camp and the other in your hand.

If the sun is out it is an infallible guide, provided proper allowance is
made for its movement. In returning by the same route no attempt is made
to cover the same ground, unless convenient, so long as creeks, ridges, flats
and other features are recognized as they occur, and provided you remember
at about what angle you traversed them. Every man has a tendency to work
too much to either left or right, and knowing that, he must work against it.

The tops of the pine trees on the crest of ridges point uniformly
north-east; in level bush, if open to the wind, the undergrowth has a "set"
to it which can sometimes be detected. The bark is thicker and the rings
in the timber closer together on the north side of trees in exposed places.
Do not forget that water always runs downhill; moose and deer tracks in
March are mostly found on a southern exposure; the snow of the last
storm is generally banked on the side of the trees opposite from the direction of the wind it came with, which you will, of course, have noted; and
the general trend, or "lie" of the country in all Northern Canada is north-
east and south-west. Taking an average on all this data, some pretty accurate travelling can be done.

These are some of the indications by which Indians travel, nor have
they any God-given superiority over other men in this respect. Only
intensive training and habits of acute observation bring them to the pitch
of excellence to which they often attain. One generation out of their environment and the faculty is as dead as it is in most white men. There is as
much difference between travelling by compass and picking a trail by a

study of details such as were just mentioned, as there is between a problem in mathematics and a work of art.

A compass calls for progression in straight lines, over all obstacles, or if around them by offsetting so many paces and recovering that distance, the obstruction once passed; a purely mechanical process. Little advantage can be taken of the lie of the land, and a man is more or less fettered in his movements.

There are highly important operations and improvements taking place all along the frontier which would be almost impossible without this device and very accurate results are obtained by its use in mapping out the country; but for ordinary travelling purposes he is freer who uses the sun, the wind, the roll of mountains and the sweep of the earth's surface as his guides, and from them he imbibes a moiety of that sixth sense which warns of danger and miscalculation, so that a species of instinct is evolved—whereby a man may be said to feel that he is wrong—almost as infallible, and more flexible of application than any instrument can be, and to it a man may turn when all else fails. This is developed to a remarkable degree in some individuals.

Of all the snares which Nature has set to entangle the footsteps of the unwary the most effective is the perfidious short-cut. Men well tried in woodcraft succumb to its specious beguilements in the endeavour to save a few hours and corresponding miles. I firmly believe there never yet was a short-cut that did not have an impassable swamp, an unscalable mountain or an impenetrable jungle situated somewhere about its middle, causing detours, the sum of which amount to more than the length of the original trail. This is so well recognized that the mere mention of the word "short-cut" will raise a smile in any camp. Often an old trail that seems to have been well used long ago, after leading you on for miles in the hopes of arriving somewhere eventually, will degenerate into a deer path, then to a rabbit runway, and finally disappear down a hole, under a root.

∾ ∾ ∾

AFTER MANY YEARS IN THE WOODS WITH THE MOST efficient instructors at the work that a man could well have, I find that I cannot yet relax my vigilance, either of thought or eye, for very many minutes before I become involved in a series of errors that would speedily land me into the orbit of the endless circle. I find it impossible to hold any kind of connected conversation and travel to advantage. In the dark especially, if the mind slips a cog and loses one or more of the filaments of the invisible thread, it is impossible to recover them, and nothing then remains but to stop, make fire, and wait for daylight.

My first experience in this line was far from heroic. I remember well my initial trial trip with an Indian friend who had volunteered for the difficult task of transforming an indifferent plainsman into some kind of a woodsman. We sat on a high rocky knoll on which were a few burnt pines, on one of which we had hung up the packsack. All around us were other knolls with burnt stubs scattered over them. The lower ground between them was covered with a heavy second growth of small birch and poplars, willows and alders. My task was to leave the hill on which we were seated, cross a flat, and climb another, identical in appearance, even to its dead trees, distant about three hundred yards. Nothing, I considered, could well be easier, even without the sun which I had to help me.

I descended the slope and struck through the small growth at its foot, and soon found that I was entangled above, below and on all sides by a clawing, clutching mass of twisted and wiry undergrowth through which I threshed with mighty struggles. After about twenty minutes I saw the welcome shine of bare rock, and was glad enough to get into the open again. I climbed the knoll, and there, to my astonishment, sat my friend and mentor at the foot of one of the chicos*, calmly smoking, and apparently not having turned a hair in his swift trip through the jungle.

I owned myself beaten, remarking that he must have made pretty good time to have arrived at the spot ahead of me. He looked mildly surprised, and replied that he had not arrived at any place, not having as yet moved. I hardly believed him until I saw the packsack where I myself had hung it, and my humiliation was complete when I realized that I had walked right down into that flat and turned round and walked right out again.

This was my first acquaintance with the charming endless circle. It was not my last, and even to-day it sneaks alongside of me through the

*A dry standing tree of good size. "Chico" is of French origin, and is now a recognized word in bush phraseology.

forest like a spinning lariat, hopefully waiting for the day when I shall place my foot within. And these days I hold that imaginary ball of twine very tightly in one hand, whilst scrutinizing the landscape ahead with a view to my proposed route, and I fight flies with the other.

My tutors have turned me out, so they consider, a finished product, and in certain circumstances I am able to contrive, devise and stand from under with the best of them; yet even to-day there are times when my failure to apply the lessons so painstakingly taught me, if known, would be the cause of much disappointment and terse but apt comment spoken through the blue smoke-haze in certain shadowy lodges, beneath the sombre spruces.

As late as four years ago I was guilty of a piece of bad judgment, or several of them, that left a considerable blot on my record, already none too spotless, and came near to settling for all time my earthly problems. The occasion was one on which it became necessary, owing to the destruction of a hunting ground by fire, to move several hundred miles to the north, and, in so doing, I failed to make the necessary allowance for changed climatic conditions. This resulted in my arriving behind the season, and finding the trading post out of many things, and its stock, much depleted, consisting mainly of culled or damaged goods remaining after the Indians, now long departed for their hunting grounds, had taken their pick. Amongst these left-overs was a one and only pair of moose-hide mitts, too small to be of much use. Having at that time no hides of my own, these I was obliged to take; the initial mistake and one for which, later, I dearly paid.

I was able to locate a ground with the assistance of the post manager and a very inaccurate map, and had a bad two weeks getting in with my stuff, fighting ice and snow-storms all the way, a matter of seventy miles or more. The trapping was fair, but the ground, being small, was soon hunted out, necessitating long trips into the interior in search of fur.

There had been much soft weather after the preliminary cold snap, and I started out on an exploration trip on a wet, soggy day, on which dragging and lifting the slushed snowshoes was a heavy enough labour. I perspired profusely, and on leaving the chain of lakes on which my cabin was situated for the overland trip to other waters, I hung up my outside shirt and leggings and proceeded without them, a piece of foolishness bordering on the criminal.

It soon commenced to snow heavily, and so continued for the rest of the day; a wet, heavy snowfall which in my half-clothed condition, quickly wetted me to the skin. With that lack of commonsense for which some people are remarkable, I carried on obstinately. Late that afternoon I found beaver. Not waiting to set any traps, as a cessation of movement, and dabbling elbow deep in ice-water meant a clammy chill which I was in no mood to endure, I made fire and drank tea, and thus fortified, commenced the return trip.

All went well for the first few miles. The sky cleared, and it turned colder, which, whilst it froze my outer clothing, made it windproof, and lightened the heavy going considerably, the snow no longer clogging my snowshoes. The moon would rise shortly and everything was coming my way. I anticipated an easy journey home; I had found beaver of a potential value amounting to some hundreds of dollars, and a little wetting damped my spirits not at all.

The fact that I was probably two hundred miles directly north of my accustomed range, and in a country of severe and sudden storms and erratic changes in temperature, did not enter into my calculations.

My outbound route had been very circuitous, and at a point where I thought it would be to my advantage I attempted the old, oft-tried, and justly notorious expedient of a short-cut in the dark. On such a night, calm, clear and frosty, nothing could possibly go wrong, and I expected to strike my own tracks in a patch of timber near the lake where my clothing was, and so on home. Half an hour from that time, in my wet condition, I became chilled with the now rapidly increasing cold, and was again obliged to make fire in a small gulley, where I waited the coming of the moon.

A chill wind arose, whistling bleakly over the deserted solitude, and I shivered over my fire, seemingly unable to get warm. The eastern sky lightened, and soon the ragged outline of the pointed spruce stood darkly silhouetted against the great moon, now creeping up over the ridge, and commencing to flood the little valley with a lambent glow. The uncertain illumination lent an appearance of illusive unreality to the surroundings which affected me strangely, and I began to have some misgivings as to the advisability of going further that night.

As the pale disc cleared the hills the shadows shortened and I made out to see a small sluggish stream, picking its somnolent way amongst snow-covered hummocks of moss and scattered clumps of larches. The prospect was not inviting, so not waiting to dry my mitts and moccasins, I prepared myself for a fast trip to my clothes, and abandoned my fire;

two more mistakes either one of which, under the circumstances, was sufficient for my undoing.

I examined the creek and having ascertained the direction of its flow, decided to go downstream, as long as its direction suited me; and turning my back on my sheltered nook, with its abundance of dry wood and friendly twinkling fire, I started on a very memorable journey. And at my elbow, as I walked, there sounded a still, small voice which said plainly and insistently, "Do not go; stay by the fire; there you are safe; do not go"; the voice, so often disregarded, of discretion, making a last bid to stay the tragedy of errors now about to be consummated.

The going was bad. There was not enough snow to level the inequalities of the ground, and the floor of the gulley was plentifully bestrewn with broken rock piles, studded with large hummocks, and pitted with holes; and, the moon only serving in this instance to increase the shadow cast by these obstacles, I stumbled and fell repeatedly, arising from each fall chilled to the bone.

Presently the stream meandered off to the right, out of my projected line of travel, and the sides of the ravine fell away into low undulations, which flattened out and eventually disappeared altogether. I realized that I was on the borders of one of those immense muskegs with which this North Country abounds. I proceed on my way, hoping that I would soon emerge into a belt of timber, which in that region would indicate the proximity of a lake, but none was to be seen save a small clump of spruce to my right and far ahead; and on all sides the white, endless fields of snow lay stretched in dreary monotony.

The moon, having become hazy whilst I was yet at the fire, was now circled by a band of rainbow hue, and before long became completely obscured; a storm threatened and soon became imminent. A low moaning sound could be heard to the north, increasing every minute, and I bitterly regretted leaving my late camp ground; but, as there was yet enough light to distinguish the details of the scenery, such as they were, with that fatuous optimism that has driven many a man out over the edge of the Great Beyond, I cast behind me the last atom of discretion and pushed forward with all possible speed.

Suddenly, with the whistling and screaming of a myriad hell-bound demons, the blizzard struck, sweeping down from the north in a choking, blinding wall of snow and zero hurricane, lashing the surface of the muskeg into a whirling frenzied mass of hissing snow-devils, sticking to my frozen and inadequate clothing in a coat of white, and effectually blotting out every vestige of the landscape.

Staggered by the first onslaught, I quickly recovered and, realizing the seriousness of the situation, I took a firm grip on my reasoning powers, whilst my mind subconsciously searched the screeching ether for some indication of direction.

In the open the wind eddied and rushed in from every side, and no bearings could be taken from it, but I thought I could detect above the other sounds of the tempest, the deeper roar of wind in the block of timber, now distant about half a mile. With this as a guide I continued on my journey, my objective now the shelter of the grove in question.

Bent almost double, gasping for breath, my clothing caked with frozen snow, becoming rapidly exhausted, I knew that, dressed as I was, I could not long survive in such a storm.

The insistent barrier of the wind became a menace, a tangible, vindictive influence bent on my destruction. All the power and spite of the hurricane seemed centred on my person with the intention of holding me back, delaying me until my numbed limbs refused further duty, driving me down, down in between the snow mounds, where, shrieking with triumph, it would overwhelm me with a whirling mass of white, and soon nothing would remain save the roar of the wind, the scurrying drift, and the endless, empty waste of snow.

Coupled with this cheerful reflection was the thought that perhaps, after all, my senses were deceived concerning the supposed position of that bluff of timber, and this spurred me on to renewed speed, if such a word could be applied to my groping progress. My arms became numb to the elbow, and my legs to the knee. My eyelids repeatedly stuck together with rime which I rubbed off with frozen mitts; and I stumbled on, knowing I must never fall.

The wind seemed to redouble its fury, and the wall of resistance that it opposed to my efforts seemed more and more a malicious attempt to detain me until I no longer had the strength to fight it. So that it became a personal issue between the tempest and myself; it with all the howling fury of unleashed omnipotent power, and I with all the hate, and bitterness and determination its buffeting had aroused in me.

How long this continued I do not know, but suffice it that in time I heard with certainty the roar of wind-tossed tree tops, and soon a black wall of forest rose up before me, and I knew that I now had a fighting chance. I quickly skirted a section of the belt of evergreens, looking up in an endeavour to find a bare pole protruding through the black tops, indicating a dry tree, but could distinguish nothing. Entering the grove I quickly chipped various trees, tasting the chips for dry wood; every one stuck to my lips, showing them to be green and impossible to start a fire with. A deadly fear entered my heart; supposing there was no dry wood, what then?

I commenced a frantic but methodical search, tapping boles with my axe for the ring of dry timber, but without avail.

Meanwhile the cold was biting deeper and deeper, and I was well aware that any wood found after the lapse of another twenty minutes would be useless, as I should by that time be unable to light a fire.

In a kind of a panic I ran out into the open, and, the storm having abated somewhat, I saw, to my unspeakable relief, a tall dry tamarac standing no great distance away, and hidden from me till then.

I attacked it furiously with my axe and now found that my wet mitts had frozen into such a shape that it was almost impossible to chop. I made several strokes, and the axe twisted in my grip and no more than dinged the tamarac, hardest of dry woods.

Once a glancing blow struck my foot, shearing through moccasin and blanket sock, drawing blood. Eventually the axe flew out of my numbed hands entirely and I lost precious seconds recovering it. There was only one alternative; I must chop barehanded. This I did, felling the tree, and continuing cutting it up until my fingers began to freeze. And then I found that my mitts, already too small, had so shrunken with the frost that now, hard as iron, *I could not put them on again.*

I stood for a moment, as the deadly import of this entered my brain with damning finality. I was confronted with the stark staring fact that I could no longer use my hands; and around my feet the snow was stained with an ever-widening patch of blood. I was as near to death as mortal man may be and yet live.

The storm had passed. The Northern Lights commenced their flickering dance. The landscape had now assumed an appearance of hypocritical solemnity; the moon also appeared, to lend the proper air of sanctimonious propriety fitting to the occasion, and the capering corpses* in the northern hemisphere mocked with their grotesque gyrations my abortive movements.

I marvelled somewhat that in this present day and age of achievement, with civilization at its peak, I should be beyond its help, dying in a way, and owing to conditions long supposed to be out of date. I got a slight "kick" out the notion, and thus exhilarated suddenly decided that this was no time and no place to die. I intended to be no spectacle for a gallery of ghouls, nor did I propose to submit dumbly to the decrees of one whom I had yet to meet— The Devil of the North forsooth, with all his power and his might!

I laughed aloud, for I had a trump card; two of them, in fact, one up each sleeve; he should not freeze my hands, and so destroy me. I decided that I would freeze my hands myself. And so I did, cutting up and splitting, until my hands became bereft of power and feeling, fully believing that I had lost my fingers to save my life.

I made a fire. The agony of it as the circulation made its way through the seared flesh; and the fear of a horrible death by blood-poisoning, or a useless existence without hands! For a man finds these things hard to accept with the calmness expected of him, and I am perhaps of softer mould than some.

Gibbering madmen have before now dragged their hideous deformities out to the haunts of man to exhibit them as payment exacted for lesser follies than I had committed that night. My fingers were frozen and my foot cut to the bone, but not badly enough to cause permanent injury, although I could hunt no more that winter.

I later found that the muskeg skirted the lake, and the next morning as I moved out I discovered that the clump of spruce that I had originally intended to pass by was an offshoot of the forest that I was looking for, and that I had spent the night, half-frozen, within a rifle-shot of my discarded clothes.

So I am still in doubt as to whether that blizzard was intended to destroy me, or if it was not merely one of those rough, but friendly attempts to set us on the right road, that we sometimes suffer at the hands of our friends.

*Indian name of the Northern Lights, "Dance of the Dead Men."

VI

The Fall of the Leaf

" Now the Four-Way Lodge is open,
Now the Hunting Winds are loosed."

CHAPTER SIX

The Fall of the Leaf

MUCH HAS BEEN WRITTEN CONCERNING THE BEAUTIES AND the joys of spring. Poets have glorified that time of flowers, and budding leaves, and frisking lambs in every language. I have, however, formed the opinion, after observing a good many of them, that spring is a time of the year to be regarded as something to look back on, or forward to, but not to enjoy. In the snow countries it is a season of floods, wet feet, bad trails, transportation difficulties, and shortage of supplies.

Easter is a favourite season for breaking ice, and carrying canoes on snowshoes over portages flooded with slush; whilst the weather is a nightmare of wet snowstorms and chill rains, or, if warm and clear the resultant thaw produces torrents of melted snow water and shaky ice. By the time these conditions mend equipment has been damaged far more than by the wear and tear of a whole year of honest travel. Men's patience is worn to a frazzle, and the seeds of a wasting sickness are often laid in the system of those who perforce must sleep out in the rain or not sleep at all.

Here, spring is a time of the year when the marriage market is weak, bootleggers' receipts are high, and those of the Church very low. I think the habitants* have a saint whose speciality it is to care for travellers at this season. I should much like to meet him, and discuss the matter quietly as between gentlemen, without witnesses.

Rarely do we hear favourably, in poetry or in prose, of that season

*French-Canadian settlers.

called by some the "death of the year," and too often looked forward to with misgiving as the precursor of dread Winter, the Fall. To those who may view its splendours in a forest untouched by the hand of man, autumn means much more than just the transition between the closing of summer and the coming of winter. In a country composed, as Canada is, largely of wild lands it means above all the opening of the hunting season, with the breaking of the monotony of civilized life, and all the freedom for the indulging of primitive instincts that goes with it.

It is a time of painted forests decked out in all the gay panoply of Indian Summer, of blue haze which lends enchantment to distant prospects, and of hills robed in flaring tints, which, in spite of their brilliance, merge and blend to form the inimitable colour scheme which, once every year, heralds the sad but wondrous spectacle of the falling of the leaves. Motionless days of landscapes bathed in waiting silence; the composed and breathing calm of an immense congregation attending the passing of a beloved one, waiting reverently until the last rites have been completed; for this is the farewell of the leaves to the forest which they have for a time adorned. Their task performed, with brave colours flying they go down in obedience to the immutable law of forest life, later to nourish the parent stem that gave them birth. And in the settled hush that precedes their passing, even the march of time itself seems halted, that there may be no unseemly haste in their disposal, whose life has been so short.

In the endless spruce forests of the High North, much of the beauty of Fall is lost, and passing suddenly out of the gloomy evergreens onto a rare ridge of birch and poplar, with their copper and bronze effects, is like stepping out of a cave into a capacious, many-pillared antechamber draped in cloth of gold. It is only in the hardwood forests of beech, maple and giant black birch yet remaining in certain areas, that the full beauty of the Fall of the Leaf can be appreciated. It was once my fortune to make a trip at this season, in a reserved area of some three thousand square miles in extent, in the heart of the strong woods country, below the Ottawa River. A lovely region it was, and is, of peaceful, rock-girdled lakes, deep, clear, and teeming with trout; and of rich forests of immense trees reaching in a smooth billowing tide in every direction. Here was not the horrific sepulchral gloom of the goblin-haunted spruce country, nor the crowded formation of hostile array. The trees, huge of trunk and massive of high-flung limb, stood decorously apart, affording passage for several men abreast; and the dimness was rather that of some enchanted palace seen only in a dream, and in which chords of stately music could be expected to resound at any moment.

The wide and spreading tops met overhead to form a leafy canopy that was a blaze of prismatic colour, as though the lofty pillars supported a roof of stained glass, through which the sunlight filtered here and there, shedding a dim but mellow glow upon the forest floor.

Between the well-ordered files one walked without obstruction, and in momentary expectation of a fleeting view of some living creature, of the many who dwelt herein. Every step opened up new vistas through the open woodland, the level bottom of which was relieved by terraces edged with small firs that loomed up blackly in the riot of colour, and occasional smooth white boulders which stood crowned by grey and hoary beeches with gnarled limbs, and serpentine, protruding roots, standing like effigies or statues carved from blocks of marble in some old castle garden. There the figure of a man was belittled, dwarfed to insignificant proportions, by the grandeur, and the vast and looming bulk of the objects by which he was surrounded.

At intervals the dimness was brightened, at about twice the height of a man, by the bright tinted foliage of dogwood, and moose-maple saplings. The gloom made the stems invisible at a little distance, and where the shafts of sunlight struck them, these gay clusters appeared like Japanese lanterns of every imaginable shape and hue, suspended in mid-air to light the ancient halls for some carnival or revel. In the wider spaces between the smooth grey hardwoods, stood the bodies of huge white pine, fluted red-brown columns upwards of six feet across, rearing their bulk up through the roof of leaves, to be shut off completely from further view; yet raising their gigantic proportions another half a hundred feet above the sea of forest, to the great plumed heads that bowed to the eastward each and every one, as though each morning they would salute the rising sun.

Although in the dimness of the ancient forest no breeze stirred the leaves of the young maples, far above, the air was never still. And through the dark masses of the noble sweeping tops of the pine trees, a steady wind played in a deep, prolonged and wavering note, as of the plucked strings of an unseen distant harp; gently humming like the low notes of an organ played softly, dying away to a whisper; swelling again in diapason through the vast transept of the temple of silence, the unceasing waves of sound echoing and resounding across the immeasurable sweep of the universe.

No moose were to be seen in this region, but every once in so often, a group of deer leaped out of sight, with sharp whistles, and spectacular display of white tails.

The air was filled with the low sound of falling leaves, as they made their hesitant way to earth, adding little by little to a variegated carpet already ankle deep. And as they came spinning, floating, and spiralling down like golden snowflakes, the sound of their continuous, subdued, rustling transformed the stately forest into a shadowed, whispering gallery, in which it seemed as though the ancient trees would tell in muted accents the age-old secrets of days gone by, did one but have the ears to understand.

∾∾∾

TO THE FOREST DWELLERS, AUTUMN, WITH ITS SIGHTS, ITS sounds, its smells, its tang, which like good wine, sends the blood coursing and tingling through the veins, with its urge to be up and doing, and the zest and savour of its brittle air, is more than a season; it has become a national institution.

The signs of its coming are eagerly noted by all in whom one drop yet remains of the blood of long gone savage ancestors. Over the whole of North America the first frosts, where they occur, are a signal for the overhauling of weapons of all kinds, and the assembling of implements of the chase. Men step lighter, as with kindling eye they seem to emulate the hustle, the bustle, and the preparation of all living creatures in response to the stirring call of this magic season. For now the Hunting Winds are loosed to course at will along the highways of the forest, stirring the indolent to action, and quickening the impulses with their heady bouquet.

Now the Four-Way Lodge is open, and out from its portals pour the spirits of all the mighty hunters of the Long Forgotten Days, to range again the ancient hunting-grounds. And when a chill wisp of a breeze sweeps down into the forest, and scooping up a handful of leaves, spins them around for a moment in a madly whirling eddy, and of a sudden lets them drop, many will say that it is the shade of some departed hunter who dances a ghostly measure to the tune of the hunting winds.

The woods are full of crisp rustlings, as small beasts scamper over frosted, crackling leaves, intent on the completion of self-appointed tasks. The surface of the waters is broken by clusters of ducks and water-fowl of all kinds, noisily congregated for the fall migration. Along the shorelines, ever-widening V's forge silently ahead, as beaver and muskrats, alert, ready to sink soundlessly out of sight on the least alarm, conduct their various operations. Porcupines amble along trustfully in the open, regardless of danger; and, partly owing to their bristling armour and greatly owing to the luck of fools, generally escape unscathed. Back in the hills any number of bears are breaking off boughs and shredding birch-bark, to line dens that a man could be well satisfied to sleep in.

In the blaze of the declining sun the hills seem crested with fire, as the level rays strike the scarlet of the maples on the ridges. The russet of the whispering sedge-grasses on the river-flats and marshlands and the yellow of the wild hay in the beaver meadows, take on a metallic sheen, like bur-nished golden filigree, in which is set some placid sheet of water, reflecting on its glassy surface an inverted, flaming forest, and the hue of the evening sky, pink with its promise of frost, as the short day draws to its close.

The light mists of evening that begin to rise in the fen-lands are per-meated with the aromatic scent of dried cherry leaves, and the spicy odour of the sage. With the near approach of darkness everything that had life is in movement, preparing for the great change soon to come, and the air is full or subdued sound, barely audible but insistent, as a myriad creatures of every size and species comb the face of the earth for the wherewithal to pass the winter, now so close upon them.

Slight noises in the distance have a startling penetration in the thin and buoyant air, and the passage of a squirrel over the dry leaves creates a disturbance out of all proportion to his size. Swift creatures, no longer silent-footed, rattle noisily across the brittle carpet on important errands. The crackle of brush, the sharp, alarmed whistle of a deer, and the whirring flight of a family of partridges, herald the approach of some creature larger than common, and a bull moose, in all the savage splendour of bristling mane and wide-spread antlers, stalks out beyond the tree-line onto the strip of grasses that border the lake, and calls his challenge, bidding defiance to all the world. His summons unanswered, he threshes mightily in the tall reeds, twisting and tearing saplings with deep grunts and hollow rattling of horns, in the futile rage of his unfulfilled desire for combat. Shortly he stops to listen, and, seeming to detect some dissonance in the scheme of his surroundings, he becomes uneasy, and retires, though with hesitation. And then, reason enough for the moose's trepidation, there comes stealing in from the south a low-set, slim canoe, loaded to the gunwales, slipping silently along, propelled by the deft, light strokes of the practised canoeman.

And on the instant all sound ceases, and silence falls, abruptly as the sudden quenching of a light.

The light craft skirts the shore amidst the idly floating leaves, and its progress is as soundless as theirs, yet no movement rewards the vigilance of the man kneeling in its stern; the policy of proscription declared against this arch-enemy of all living creatures, this pariah of the society of the woods, could not be more completely carried out were he some noisome pestilence stalking through the kingdom of the wild.

The canoe lands at an open point of jack-pines and the man unloads, erects his tent with a few swift movements, and soon the glimmer of his camp fire lights the now rapidly falling dusk, and its smoke hangs in banks and wisps over the water, edging the wreaths of mist with blue.

Darkness settles and the fire dies. The stars, large and far apart, seem almost within reach, and the blade of the low-hung moon lies on its back just clear of the needle-pointed spruce that crown an eminence. And overhead the long wavering lines of wild geese pass at frequent intervals from the north with discordant clamour, as they retreat before an enemy with whom they have already been in action, and whose further advance is now imminent.

And as the night wears on and the moon sinks behind the hill, the population of the woods recommences its interrupted labours.

Small, earnest forest people in unnumbered multitudes race back and forth from cache to cache. The faintly discernible sounds of the daylight hours increase in volume during the stillness of the night, and are punctuated by distinguishable noises that much intrigue the curiosity of the listener; the distant screaming of a rabbit being prepared for cold storage by some successful butcher; the "plop," and rustle, and scratch, as muskrats, like little gnomes, with short swift runs and hops work feverishly at their harvesting; the thumps and thuds, draggings and scrapings, and the low murmur of voices, as the gangs in the beaver-works labour prodigiously to complete their preparations....

But as daylight commenced to show in the east, these noises gradually ceased and day broke over an empty forest devoid of life or sound, save for a small flock of black ducks at their morning toilet and a porcupine, who had been appeasing his insatiable appetite for leather with a tump line, forgotten outside the tent on the point.

There was some slight commotion within the tent and a stream of smoke issued from the long, narrow stove pipe projecting from it. The porcupine, interested in this new development, stared stupidly at the smoke for a while, then, taking a few last bites out of the canoe gunwale in passing, lumbered off with the consciousness of a good night's work well done.

At this juncture the man emerged from the tent, and the sight of the ruined tump line evoked a string of caustic remarks, arranged with the alliterative proficiency of one well versed in the art. The porcupine listened in pained surprise for a moment, and withdrew tactfully further into the timber; and, with a preliminary four-foot jump, the black ducks took the air and, circling the shoreline once, hit for the south.

The man viewed the angry-looking sunrise with misgiving. Wasting but little time on his hasty breakfast, he soon loaded up and headed for the north. The ice rimming the shores of his landing place had had to be broken with a pole to get the canoe into the water, and the rime that had settled on the beaver hay was heavy enough to show the passage, during the night, of a fox. These signs increased his apprehension, for he had also heard the all-night passage of the wild geese. Well he knew the penalty he might pay for having, in his ambition, penetrated so far before settling for the winter. He was caught in a network of small waters soon to be frozen, and tie him up for the Fall hunt. The special devil to whom is allotted the control of the legions of Winter, might wantonly loose them on a waiting world at any moment that his whim suggested. Soon he would throw up his ramparts and entanglements, effectually blocking all attempts at progress, sealing all hands into whatever neck-of-the-woods they were caught in, until winter was sufficiently advanced to release them. For this particular devil is well skilled at his game. Not his, as yet, a barrage of heavy storms, deep snow and zero wind. Coarse work, that, so early in the bout; anyhow, these men seemed to weather well on such stuff. Better, at first, a little display of skill, the deft touch of the artist; snow enough to cause a burdened man to slip on a sidehill, ice enough to cajole him out onto the water to try conclusions, and then to fail with a canoe badly scratched, and cut; cold enough to freeze the one bag of much treasured potatoes, but not sufficient to make good ice.

Thus Ka-peboan-ka, keeper of Keewayedin, the North-West Wind, rewards the effrontery of those who deem their small goings and comings should enter into the calculations of the Red Gods.

The man's prognostications seemed about to prove only too true. Before noon of that day, ragged strips of grey clouds tore across a leaden sky, to the accompaniment of a shrill whining storm-wind that ripped the last leaves from the hardwoods, where they had hung but tenuously for days, ready to drop at the first volley of the advancing hosts of winter. And all Nature stood by in hole, and den, and matted evergreen covert, or builded house, waiting for that moment against which all had prepared for forty days or more: excepting man. He, the most intelligent and gifted of living creatures, alone was not ready. Abroad with a heavy outfit and unprepared, of all things having life he was to be the sole victim of the cataclysm now about to occur.

In two days a devastating change had come over the landscape. Gone from the uplands was the wonderfully blended colour scheme. There only remained a few garish patches of red splotched here and there, like dabs of paint scattered at random on a grey canvas, and only serving to accentuate the stark nakedness of the bare limbs through which the wind whistled and thrummed. Gone was the carnival note of the gay hanging lanterns of the dogwoods, as they stood now extinguished, in the empty halls of their revel. Before the chilling blast clouds of dead leaves eddied and volleyed down the roofless naves, flying at times in whirling masses high above the crest of the forest. And slanting, hissing down from the North, sifting through the naked limbs of the hardwoods, there rattled onto the fallen leaves a few hard flakes of the first snow. And Ka-peboan-ka, the old, the mischievous, the boisterous, having gloated long enough over his all-too-effective work, rubbed his hands gleefully, and entered the lists for the final bout with the crimson and brown youth,* whose warm smile was fast fading as he weakened, this time to fall and rise no more.

And Ka-peboan-ka threw over the body his white mantle, and danced a whirlwind dance of triumph, till the air about him became filled with flying snowflakes. And countless leagues of grey and purple landscape petrified and turned slowly white, as he blew his whistling blasts of icy breath into the four corners of the earth. In the morning the sun rose glittering but without warmth on a world blanketed beneath a heavy pall of snow.

Winter was on.

*Indian personification of Indian Summer.

The Tale of the Beaver People

"Of all beasts he learned the language
Learned their names and all their secrets
How the beavers built their lodges."
LONGFELLOW

CHAPTER SEVEN

The Tale of the Beaver People

ON THE SHORES OF A NAMELESS LAKE I CROUCHED AND shivered in the wet sagebrush. It was breaking day; the smell of the dawn was in the air, and a clammy mist enveloped the land, through which, in spots, individual trees showed as shadows, faintly, if near at hand. Further than that nothing was visible.

Low, mysterious noises came to my ear, and as the light waxed stronger these became louder, so as to be distinguishable; the leap of a fish; the quacking of a couple of ducks in a reed-bed; the staccato, nervous tapping of a woodpecker; a distant hollow crash in the depth of the forest; a slight rustle in the bushes behind me as a weasel peered out with extended neck, to vanish suddenly, appearing instantaneously ten feet away almost before his disappearance had been registered by the eye.

The mist commenced to rise, and a current of air stirred the poplar leaves to a light fluttering. The ducks became partly visible, and seen through the vapour they seemed to float on air, and to be of inordinate size.

I shivered some more.

Under the influence of the slight breeze the fog billowed slowly back exposing the little sheet of water; the wavering line of the hills on the far shore appeared and disappeared within its folds, and the crest of the ridges seemed to float on its surface like long, low islands. To the East was clear of fog and the streaks of clouds that hung there, as I watched, turned slowly pink. Not ten feet away, on a log, a muskrat rubbed himself dry with vigorous strokes, and as he scrubbed mightily I could hear his little gusts of breath in the thin air. A flock of whistlers volleyed overhead with bullet velocity, circled the pond and lit on the water with a slithering splash; a kingfisher dived like an emerald streak at the rise of a speckled trout, and, missing his stroke, flew with a chattering laugh to a dry limb. And at the discordant sound came the first notes of the plaintive song of the Canada bird, a haunting melody that ceases in full flight, the remainder of the song tantalisingly left unsung as though the singer had become suddenly weary: a prelude in minor cadence. And from all around, and across the pond, these broken melodies burst out in answering lament, while the burden of song was taken up by one after another trilling voice. There poured out the rippling lilt of the American robin, suggestive of the clear purling of running water; the three deep golden notes of some unknown songster, the first three chords of an obbligato plucked from the strings of a bass viol. Others, now indistinguishable for very volume, joined in as the slowly rising sun rolled up the curtain of the mist on the grand overture conducted by the Master Musician, that is the coming of day, in the unspoiled reaches of the northern wilds.

I drew the blanket-case off my rifle and pumped a shell into the breech. I was there with a purpose: for the time was that of the spring hunt, and this was a beaver-pond. Two deer appeared in the reeds in a little bay, necks craned, nostrils working as they essayed with delicate senses to detect the flaw in the perfectly balanced structure of the surroundings which I constituted. I did not need them; and moreover, did they take flight with hoarse whistles and noisy leapings all living creatures within earshot would be immediately absorbed by the landscape, and my hunt ended. But I am an old hand at the game, and, having chosen a position with that end in view, was not to be seen, heard, or smelled.

Yet the scene around me had its influence, and a guilty feeling possessed me as I realized that of all present in that place of peace and clean content, I was the only profane thing, an ogre lurking to destroy. The half-grown ferns and evergreen sedge grasses through which the early breeze whispered, would, if I had my way, soon be smeared with the blood of some animal, who was viewing, perhaps with feelings akin to my own, the dawning of another day; to be his last. Strange thoughts, maybe, coming from a trapper, one whose trade it is to kill; but be it known to you that he who lives much alone within the portals of the temple of Nature learns to think, and deeply, of things which seldom come within the scope of ordinary life. Much killing brings in time, no longer triumph, but a revulsion of feeling.

I have seen old hunters, with their hair silvered by the passage of many winters, who, on killing a deer would stroke the dead muzzle with every appearance of regret. Indians frequently address an animal they are about to kill in terms of apology for the act.

However, be that as it may, with the passing of the mist from the face of the mountains, I saw a large beaver swimming a short distance away. This was my game; gone were my scruples, and my humane ideas fled like leaves before the wind. Giving the searching call of these animals, I cocked my rifle and waited.

At the call he stopped, raising himself in the water to sniff; and on the summons being repeated he swam directly towards me into the very jaws of destruction. At about fifteen feet I had a good view of him as he slowed down, trying to catch some indication of a possible companion, and the beautiful dark fur apprised me of a hide that would well repay my early morning sortie. The beaver regarded me steadily, again raising himself to catch an expected scent, and not getting it he turned lazily to swim away. He was at my mercy, and I had his head snugly set between the forks of my rear sight, when my heart contracted at the thought of taking life on such a morning. The creature was happy, glad to be in God's good sunlight, free after a winter of darkness to breathe the pure air of the dawn. He had the right to live here, even as I had, yea, even a greater claim, for he was there before me.

I conquered my momentary weakness; for, after all, a light pressure on the trigger, a crashing impact, would save him many days of useless labour. Yet hesitated, and as I finally laid my rifle down, he sank without a ripple, out of sight. And I became suddenly conscious of the paeans of praise and triumph of the feathered choir about me, temporarily unheard in my lust to kill; and it seemed as though all Nature sang in benediction of an act which had kept inviolate a sanctuary, and saved a perfect hour from desecration.

I went home to my cabin and ate my breakfast with greater satisfaction than the most expertly accomplished kill had ever given me; and, call it what you will, weakness, vacillation, or the first glimmerings of conscience in a life hitherto devoted to the shedding of blood, since the later experiences I have had with these animals I look back on the incident with no regret.

ᖰᖰᖰ

AT ONE TIME BEAVER WERE TO THE NORTH WHAT GOLD WAS to the west. In the early mining camps gold was the only medium of exchange; and from time immemorial at the northern trading posts a beaver hide was the only currency which remained always at par, and by its unchanging value, all other furs were judged. It took so many other hides to equal a beaver skin; and its value was one dollar. Counters were threaded on a string, each worth a dollar, and called "beaver," and as the hunter sold his fur its equivalent in "beaver" counters was pushed along the string. No money changed hands. So many discs were replaced in settlement of the hunting-debt, and as the trapper bought his provisions the remaining "beaver" were run back down again, one by one, a dollar at a time, until they were all back where they belonged, and the trade completed.

They usually went back down the string a good deal faster than they came up, and the story is told of the hunter with two bales of fur who thus paid his debt, spoke twice, and owed a hundred dollars. Although pelts were cheap provisions were not. I have spoken with men, not such very old men either, who traded marten, now selling as high as forty dollars, at the rate of four to a beaver, or twenty-five cents each.

A hunter must have had to bring in a stupendous amount of fur to buy even the barest necessities, when we consider the prices that even today obtain at many of the distant posts; a twenty-five pound bag of flour, $5.00; salt pork, $1.00 a pound; tea, $3.00 a pound; candles, 25¢ each; sugar, 50¢ a pound; 5 lb. pail of lard, $4.50; a pair of trousers, $25.00; and so on. The oft-told tale of piling beaver hides to the height of the muzzle of a gun in order to purchase the weapon, although frequently denied, is perfectly true. Many old Indians living to-day possess guns they bought that way. It is not so generally known that some unscrupulous traders increased the price by lengthening the barrels, necessitating the cutting off of a length with a file before the weapon could be used.

Although beaver do not exist to-day in sufficient quantities to constitute a hunt, up till ten years ago they were the chief means of subsistence of an army of white hunters, and thousands of Indians. Since their practical extermination the Northern Ojibways are in want, and many of the bands have had to be rationed by the Government to prevent their actual starvation.

The first, and for over a hundred years, the only business in which Canada was engaged was the fur trade, of which the beaver was the mainstay; and its history affords one of the most romantic phases in the development of the North American Continent.

The specimens of beaver pelts exhibited to Charles of England influenced him to grant the famous Hudson Bay Company's Charter, apportioning to them probably the largest land grant ever awarded any one concern. Attracted by the rich spoils of the trade, other companies sprang up. Jealousies ensued, and pitched battles between the trappers of rival factions were a common occurrence. Men fought, murdered, starved and froze to death, took perilous trips into unknown wildernesses, and braved the horrors of Indian warfare, lured on by the rich returns of the beaver trade. Men foreswore one another, cheated, murdered, robbed, and lied to gain possession of bales of these pelts, which could not have been more ardently fought for had each hair on them been composed of gold.

The Indians, meanwhile, incensed at the wholesale slaughter of their sacred animal, inflamed by the sight of large bands of men fighting for something that belonged to none of them, took pay from either side, and swooped down on outgoing caravans, annihilating them utterly, and burning peltries valued at hundreds of thousands of dollars. Often, glad of a chance to strike a blow at the beaver man, the common enemy, they showed a proper regard for symmetry by also destroying the other party that had hired them, thus restoring the balance of Nature. Ghastly torturing and other diabolical atrocities, incident to the massacre of trappers in their winter camps, discouraged hunting, and crippled the trade for a period; but with the entire extinction of the buffalo the Indian him-self was obliged to turn and help destroy his ancient friends in order to live. Betrayed by their protectors the beaver did not long survive, and soon they were no more seen in the land wherein they had dwelt so long.

Profiting by this lesson, forty years later, most of the Provinces on the Canadian side of the line declared a closed season on beaver, of indefinite duration. Thus protected they gradually increased until at the outbreak of the World War they were as numerous in the Eastern Provinces as they ever had been in the West. I am not an old man, but I have seen the day when the forest streams and lakes of Northern Ontario and Quebec were peopled by millions of these animals. Every creek and pond had its colony of the Beaver People. And then once again, and for the last time, this harassed and devoted animal was subjected to a persecution that it is hard to credit could be possible in these enlightened days of preservation and conservation. The beaver season was thrown open and the hunt was on.

Men, who could well have made their living in other ways, quit their regular occupations and took the trail. It was the story of the buffalo over again. In this case instead of an expensive outfit of horses and wag-ons, only a cheap licence, a few traps, some provisions and a canoe were needed, opening up widely the field to all and sundry.

The woods were full of trappers. Their snowshoe trails formed a net-work of destruction over all the face of the wilderness, into the farthest recesses of the north. Trails were broken out to civilization, packed hard as a rock by long strings of toboggans and sleighs drawn by wolf-dogs, and loaded with skins; trails over which passed thousands and thousands of beaver hides on their way to the market. Beaver houses were dyna-mited by those whose intelligence could not grasp the niceties of beaver trapping, or who had not the hardihood to stand the immersion of bare arms in ice-water during zero weather; for the setting of beaver traps in mid-winter is no occupation for one with tender hands or a taste for tea-fights. Dams were broken after the freeze-up, and sometimes the entire defences, feed house, and dam were destroyed, and those beaver not cap-tured froze to death or starved in their ruined works, whilst all around was death, and ruin, and destruction.

Relentless spring hunters killed the mother beavers, allowing the little ones to starve, which, apart from the brutality of the act, destroyed all chances of replenishment. Unskilful methods allowed undrowned beaver to twist out of traps, leaving in the jaws some shattered bone and a length of sinew, condemning the maimed creatures to do all their work with one or both front feet cut off; equivalent in its effect to cutting off the hands of a man.

I once saw a beaver with both front feet and one hind foot cut off in this way. He had been doing his pitiful best to collect materials for his building. He was quite far from the water and unable to escape me, and although it was late summer and the hide of no value, I put him out of misery with a well-placed bullet.

Clean trapping became a thing of the past and unsportsmanlike methods were used such as removing the raft of feed so that the beaver must take bait or starve; and the spring pole, a contrivance which jerks the unfortunate animal into the air, to hang for hours by one foot just clear of the water, to die in prolonged agony from thirst. To inflict such torture on this almost human animal is a revolting crime which few regular white hunters and no Indian will stoop to.

I remember once, on stopping to make camp, hearing a sound like the moaning of a child a few yards away, and I rushed to the spot with all possible speed, knowing bear traps to be out in the district. I found a beaver suspended in this manner, jammed into the crotch of a limb, held there by the spring pole, and moaning feebly. I took it down, and found it to be a female heavy with young, and in a dying condition; my attempts at resuscitation were without avail, and shortly after three lives passed into the discard.

The Government of Ontario imposed a limit on the number to be killed, and attempted, futilely, to enforce it; but means were found to evade this ruling, and men whose allowance called for ten hides came out with a hundred. There is some sorcery in a beaver hide akin to that which a nugget of gold is credited with possessing, and the atmosphere of the trade in these skins is permeated with all the romance and the evil, the rapacity and adventurous glamour, attendant on a gold-rush. Other fur, more easily caught, more valuable perhaps, may increase beyond all bounds, and attract no attention save that of the professional trapper, but at the word "beaver," every man on the frontier springs to attention, every ear is cocked. The lifting of the embargo in Ontario precipitated a rush, which whilst not so concentrated, was very little, if any, less than that of '98 to the Yukon. Fleets, flotillas, and brigades of canoes were strung out over the surface of the lakes in a region of many thousand square miles, dropping off individually here and there into chosen territories, and emerging with spectacular hunts unknown in earlier days. The plots and counter-plots, the intrigues and evasions connected with the tricks of the trade, resembled the diplomatic ramifications of a nation at war.

History repeated itself. Fatal quarrels over hunting grounds were not unknown, and men otherwise honest, bitten by the bug of greed and the prospect of easy money, stooped to unheard-of acts of depravity for the sake of a few hides.

Meanwhile the trappers reaped a harvest, but not for long. Beaver in whole sections disappeared and eyes were turned on the Indian countries. The red men, as before, looked on, but this time with alarm. Unable any longer to fight for this animal, which, whilst no longer sacred was their very means of existence, they were compelled to join in the destruction, and ruin their own hunting grounds before others got ahead of them and took everything. For ten years the slaughter went on, and then beaver became scarce.

The part-time hunter, out for a quick fortune, left the woods full of poison baits, and polluted with piles of carcasses, and returned to his regular occupation. The Indian hunting grounds and those of the regular white trappers had been invaded and depleted of game. The immense number of dog-teams in use necessitated the killing of large numbers of moose for feed, and they also began to be scarce. Professional hunters, both red and white, even if only to protect their own interests, take only a certain proportion of the fur, and trapping grounds are maintained in perpetuity. The invaders had taken everything.

To-day, in the greater part of the vast wilderness of Northern Canada, beaver are almost extinct; they are fast going the way of the buffalo. But their houses, their dams, and all their works, will long remain as a reproach and a heavy indictment against the shameful waste perpetrated by man, in his exploitation of the wild lands and the dwellers therein. Few people know, or perhaps care, how close we are to losing most of the links with the pioneer days of old; the beaver is one of the few remaining reminders of that past Canadian history of which we are justly proud, and he is entitled to some small niche in the hall of fame. He has earned the right to our protection whilst we yet have the power to exercise it, and if we fail him it will not be long before he is beyond our jurisdiction for all time.

The system that has depleted the fur resources of Canada to a point almost of annihilation, is uncontrolled competitive hunting and trapping by transient white trappers.

The carefully-farmed hunting territories of the Indians and the resident white trappers (the latter being greatly in the minority, and having in most cases a proprietary interest in the preservation of fur and game, playing the game much as the Indian played it) were, from 1915 on, invaded by hordes of get-rich-quick vandals who, caring for nothing much but the immediate profits, swept like the scourge they were across the face of northern Canada.

These men were in no way professional hunters; their places were in the ranks of other industries, where they should have stayed. The Indian and the dyed-in-the-wool genuine woodsmen, unsuited by a long life under wilderness conditions to another occupation, and unable to make such a revolutionary change in their manner of living, now find themselves without the means of subsistence.

Misinformed and apparently not greatly interested provincial governments aided and abetted this destructive and unwarranted encroachment on the rights of their native populations who were dependent entirely on the proceeds of the chase, by gathering a rich if temporary harvest in licences, royalties, etc. A few futile laws were passed, of which the main incentive of enforcement often seemed to be the collection of fines rather than prevention. Money alone can never adequately pay the people of Canada for the loss of their wild life, from either the commercial, or recreational, or the sentimental point of view.

We read of the man who opened up the goose to get all the golden eggs at once, and the resultant depression in the golden-egg market that followed. The two cases are similar.

We blame the United States for their short-sighted policy in permitting the slaughter of the buffalo as a means of solving the Indian problem of that time, yet we have allowed, for a paltry consideration in dollars and cents, and greatly owing to our criminal negligence in acquainting ourselves with the self-evident facts of the case, the almost entire destruction of our once numerous fur-bearing and game animals. Nor did this policy settle any Indian problem, there being none at the time, but it created one that is daily becoming more serious. The white man's burden will soon be no idle dream, and will have to be assumed with what cheerful resignation you can muster.

We must not fail to remember that we are still our brother's keeper, and having carelessly allowed this same brother to be robbed of his rights and very means of existence (solemnly agreed by treaty to be inalienable and perpetual, whereby he was a self-supporting producer, a contributor to the wealth of the country and an unofficial game warden and conservationist whose knowledge of wild life would have been invaluable) we must now support him. And this will complete his downfall by the degrading "dole" system.

At a meeting I attended lately, it was stated by a competent authority that there were more trappers in the woods during this last two years than ever before. The fact that they paid for their licences does not in any way compensate either the natives or the country at large for the loss in wild life consequent on this wholesale slaughter.

The only remedy would seem to be the removal from the woods of all white trappers except those who could prove that they had no alternative occupation, had followed trapping for a livelihood previous to 1914 (thus eliminating the draft evaders and others who hid in the woods during the war) and returned men of the voluntary enlistment class. It is not perhaps generally known that the draft evaders in some sections constitute the majority of the more destructive element in the woods to-day. Forced to earn a livelihood by some means in their seclusion, and fur being high at the time, they learned to trap in a kind of way. They constitute a grave menace to our fur and game resources, as their unskilful methods make necessary wholesale destruction on all sides in order to obtain a percentage of the fur, leaving in their path a shambles of unfound bodies, many of them poisoned, or crippled animals, which, unable to cope with the severe conditions thus imposed on them, eventually die in misery and starvation.

Regulations should be drawn up with due regard for conditions governing the various districts, these to be ascertained from genuine woodsmen and the more prominent and responsible men of native communities. Suggestions from such sources would have obviated a good deal of faulty legislation. Those entrusted with the making of our game laws seem never to become acquainted with the true facts until it is almost too late, following the progress of affairs about a lap behind.

Regulations, once made, should be rigorously enforced, and penalties should include fines and imprisonment, as many illegal trappers put by the amount of a possible fine as a part of their ordinary expenses.

There is another point of view to be considered. If the depletion of our game animals goes on much longer at the present rate, specimens of wild life will soon be seen only in zoos and menageries.

How much more elevating and instructive is it to get a glimpse— however fleeting—of an animal in its native haunts than the lengthy contemplation of poor melancholy captives eking out a thwarted existence under unnatural conditions? Fur farms may perpetuate the fur industry eventually unless the ruinous policy of selling, for large and immediate profits, breeding animals to foreign markets is continued. But these semi-domesticated de-natured specimens will never represent to the true lover of Nature the wild beauty and freedom of the dwellers in the Silent Places, nor will they ever repopulate the dreary empty wastes that will be all that are left to us when the remaining Little Brethren have been immolated on the altars of Greed and Ignorance, and the priceless heritage of both the Indian and the white man destroyed for all time.

In wanderings during the last five years, extending between, and including, the Districts of Algoma in the Province of Ontario and Misstassini in the Province of Quebec, and covering an itinerary of perhaps two thousand miles, I have seen not over a dozen signs of beaver. I was so struck by this evidence of the practical extinction of our national animal, that my journey, originally undertaken with the intention of finding a hunting ground, became more of a crusade, conducted with the object of discovering a small colony of beaver not claimed by some other hunter, the motive being no longer to trap, but to preserve them.

I have been fortunate enough to discover two small families. With them, and a few hand-raised specimens in my possession, I am attempting the somewhat hopeless task of repopulating a district otherwise denuded of game. It is a little saddening to see on every hand the deserted works, the broken dams, and the empty houses, monuments to the thwarted industry of an animal which played such an important part in the history of the Dominion.

Did the public have by any chance the opportunity of studying this little beast who seems almost able to think, possesses a power of speech in which little but the articulation of words is lacking, and a capacity for suffering possible only to a high grade of intelligence, popular opinion would demand the declaration of a close season of indefinite duration over the whole Dominion.

Did the Provinces collaborate on any such scheme, there would be no sale for beaver skins, and the only source of supply being thus closed, poaching would be profitless. Even from a materialistic point of view this would be of great benefit, as after a long, it is to be feared a very long, period a carefully regulated beaver hunt could be arranged that would be a source of revenue of some account.

$$\infty\infty\infty$$

IT IS GENERALLY CONCEDED THAT THE BEAVER WAS BY FAR the most interesting and intelligent of all the creatures that at one time abounded in the vast wilderness of forest, plain and mountain that was Canada before the coming of the white man.

Although in the north they are now reduced to a few individuals and small families scattered thinly in certain inaccessible districts, there has been established for many years, a game reserve of about three thousand square miles, where these and all other animals indigenous to the region are as numerous as they were fifty years ago. I refer to the Algonquin Provincial Park in Ontario. This game sanctuary is guarded in the strictest manner by a very competent staff of Rangers, and it is a saying in the region that it would be easier to get away with murder than to escape the consequences of killing a beaver in their patrol area.

This little worker of the wild has been much honoured. He ranks with the maple leaf as representative of the Dominion, and has won a place as one of Canada's national emblems, by the example he gives of industry, adaptability, and dogged perseverance; attributes well worthy of emulation by those who undertake to wrest a living from the untamed soil of a new country. He is the Imperialist of the animal world. He maintains a home and hearth, and from it he sends out every year a pair of emigrants who search far and wide for new fields to conquer; who explore, discover, occupy, and improve, to the benefit of all concerned.

The Indian, who lived by the killing of animals, held his hand when it came to the beaver. Bloody wars were waged on his behalf by his redskinned protectors, until the improvements of civilization raised economic difficulties only to be met by the sale of beaver skins, with starvation as the alternative.

The red men considered them as themselves and dignified their Little Talking Brothers with the name of The Beaver People, and even in these degenerate days of traders, whiskey, and lost tradition, there are yet old men amongst the nations who will not sit to a table where beaver meat is served, while those who now eat him and sell his hide will allow no dog to eat his bones, and the remains, feet, tail, bones and entrails, are carefully committed to the element from which they came, the water.

It would seem that by evolution or some other process, these creatures have developed a degree of mental ability superior to that of any other living animal, with the possible exception of the elephant.

Most animals blindly follow an instinct and a set of habits, and react without mental effort to certain inhibitions and desires. In the case of the beaver, these purely animal attributes are supplemented by a sagacity which so resembles the workings of the human mind that it is quite generally believed, by those who know most about them, that they are endowed to a certain extent with reasoning powers. The fact that they build dams and houses, and collect feed is sometimes quoted as evidence of this; but muskrats also erect cabins and store food in much the same manner. Yet where do you find any other creature but man who can fall a tree in a desired direction, selecting only those which can conveniently be brought to the ground? For rarely do we find trees lodged or hung up by full-grown beaver; the smaller ones are responsible for most of the lodged trees. Instinct causes them to build their dams in the form of an arc, but by what means do they gain the knowledge that causes them to arrange that curve in a concave or a convex formation, according to the water-pressure?

Some tame beaver objected strongly to the window in my winter camp, and were everlastingly endeavouring to push up to it articles of all kinds, evidently thinking it was an opening, which it is their nature to close up. That was to be expected. But they overstepped the bounds of natural impulse, and entered the realm of calculation, when they dragged firewood over, and piled it under the window until they had reached its level, and on this improvised scaffold they eventually accomplished their purpose, completely covering the window with piled-up bedding. Whenever the door was open they tried every means of barricading the opening, but found they could never get the aperture filled. One day I returned with a pail of water in each hand to find the door closed, having to set down my pails to open it. I went in, and my curiosity aroused, watched the performance. As soon as I was clear, one of the beaver started to push on some sacking he had collected at the foot of the door, and slowly but surely closed it. And this he often did from then on. Instinct? Maybe.

Their general system of working is similar in most cases, and the methods used are the same. However, in the bush no two places are alike, and it requires no little ingenuity on the part of a man to adapt himself to the varying circumstances, yet the beaver can adjust himself to a multiplicity of different conditions, and is able to overcome all the difficulties arising, meeting his problems much in the way a man would.

Their strength is phenomenal and they can draw a stick which, in proportion, a man could not shift with his hands; and to move it sideways they will go to each extremity alternately, poise the end over their head and throw it an appreciable distance. I have seen two small beaver struggling down a runway with a poplar log, heaviest of soft woods, of such a size that only the top of their backs and heads were visible above it.

Shooting them when they are so engaged, a common practice, somehow seems to me in these latter days, like firing from ambush on children at play, or shooting poor harmless labourers at work in the fields.

The beaver is a home-loving beast and will travel far overland, around the shores of lakes and up streams, searching for a suitable place to build. Once settled where there is enough feed, and good opportunities to construct a dam, a family is liable to stay in that immediate district for many years. The young, at the age of two years, leave home, and separating, pick each a mate from another family, build themselves a house and dam, and settle down to housekeeping; staying together for life, a period of perhaps fifteen years. At the end of the third year they attain full growth, being then three feet and a half long with the tail, and weighing about thirty-five pounds. In the spring the mother has her young, the male making a separate house for them and keeping the dam in repair. The last year's kittens leave the pond, going always downstream, and wander around all summer, returning about August to assist in the work of getting ready for the winter. The first part of these preparations is to build a dam, low to begin with, and being made higher as needed. The main object of this structure is to give a good depth of water, in which feed may be kept all winter without freezing, and heavy green sticks are often piled on top of the raft of supplies, which is generally attached to the house, in order to sink it as much as possible. Also by this means the water is flooded back into the timber they intend to fall, enabling them to work close to the water and facilitating escape from danger.

Much has been said concerning the timber they are supposed to spoil in this way, but the shores of a lake are hardly ever low enough to allow any more than the first narrow fringe of trees close to the water to be drowned, and that is generally of little value commercially.

The immense amount of work that is put into a dam must be seen to be realized. Some of these are eight feet high, a hundred yards long, and six feet through at the base, tapering up to a scant foot at the water level. Pits are dug near the ends from which are carried the materials to prevent seepage, and a judicious admixture of large stones adds the necessary stiffening at the water-lines. Canals are channelled out, trees felled near them, neatly limbed, cut up, and all but the heavier portions drawn to the water and floated away. The heightened water facilitates this operation, and besides thus fulfilling his own purpose, the beaver is performing a service for man that, too late, is now being recognized.

Many a useful short-cut on a circuitous canoe route, effecting a saving of hours, and even days, a matter of the greatest importance in the proper policing of the valuable forests against fire, has become impracticable since the beaver were removed, as the dams fell out of repair, and streams became too shallow for navigation by canoes.

The house alone is a monument of concentrated effort. The entrance is under water, and on a foundation raised to the water level, and heightened as the water rises, sticks of every kind are stacked criss-cross in a dome-shaped pile some eight feet high and from ten to twenty-five feet in width at the base. These materials are placed without regard to interior accommodation, the interstices filled with soil, and the centre is cut out from the inside, all hands chewing away at the interlaced sticks until there is room enough in the interior for a space around the waterhole for a feeding place, and for a platform near the walls for sleeping quarters. The beds are made of long shavings, thin as paper, which they tear off sticks; each beaver has his bed and keeps his place.

Pieces of feed are cut off the raft outside under the ice, and peeled in the house, the discarded sticks being carried out through a branch in the main entrance, as are the beds on becoming too soggy. Should the water sink below the level of the feeding place the loss is at once detected, and the dam inspected and repaired. Thus they are easy to catch by making a small break in the dam and setting a trap in the aperture. On discovering the break they will immediately set to work to repair it without loss of time, and get into the trap. When it closes on them they jump at once into deep water and, a large stone having been attached to the trap, they stay there and drown, taking about twenty minutes to die; a poor reward for a lifetime of useful industry.

Late in the Fall the house is well plastered with mud, and it is by observing the time of this operation that it is possible to forecast the near approach of the freeze-up.

And it is the contemplation of this diligence and perseverance, this courageous surmounting of all difficulties at no matter what cost in labour, that has, with other considerations, earned the beaver, as far as I am concerned, immunity for all time. I cannot see that my vaunted superiority as a man entitles me to disregard the lesson that he teaches, and profiting thereby, I do not feel that I have any longer the right to destroy the worker or his works performed with such devotion.

Many years have I builded, and hewed, and banked, and laboriously carried in my supplies in readiness for the winter, and all around me the Beaver People were doing the same thing by much the same methods, little knowing that their work was all for nought, and that they were doomed beforehand never to enjoy the comfort they well earned with such slavish labour.

I recollect how once I sat eating a lunch at an open fire on the shores of a beautiful little mountain lake, and beside me, in the sunlight, lay the body of a fine big beaver I had just caught. I well remember, too, the feeling of regret that possessed me for the first time, as I watched the wind playing in the dead beaver's hair, as it had done when he had been happy, sunning himself on the shores of his pond, so soon to become a dirty swamp, now that he was taken.

In spite of his clever devices for protection, the beaver, by the very nature of his work signs his own death warrant. The evidences of his wisdom and industry, for which he is so lauded, have been after all, only sign-posts on the road to extinction. Everywhere his bright new stumps show up. His graded trails, where they enter the water, form ideal sets for traps and he can be laid in wait for and shot in his canals. Even with six feet of snow blanketing the winter forest, it can be easily discovered whether a beaver-house is occupied or not, by digging some snow off the top of the house and exposing the large hollow space melted by the exhalations from within. The store of feed so carefully put by, may prove his undoing, and he be caught near it by a skilfully placed trap. Surely he merits a better fate than this, that he should drown miserably three feet from his companions and his empty bed, whilst his body lies there until claimed by the hunter, later to pass, on the toboggan on its way to the hungry maw of the city, the home he worked so hard to build, the quiet and peace of the little pond that knew him and that he loved so well.

This then is the tale of the Beaver People, a tale that is almost told. Soon all that will remain of this once numerous clan of little brethren of the waste places will be their representative in his place of honour on the flag of Canada. After all an empty mockery, for, although held up to symbolize the Spirit of Industry of a people, that same people has allowed him to be done to death on every hand, and by every means. Once a priceless exhibit displayed for a king's approval, the object of the devotion of an entire race, and wielding the balance of power over a large continent, he is now a fugitive. Unable to follow his wonted occupation, lest his work show his presence, scarcely he dares to eat except in secrecy, lest he bring retribution swift and terrible for a careless move. Lurking in holes and corners, in muddy ponds and deep unpenetrable swamps, he dodges the traps, snares, spring poles, nets, and every imaginable device set to encompass his destruction, to wipe him off the face of the earth.

Playful and good-natured, persevering and patient, the scattered remnants of the beaver colonies carry on, futilely working out their destiny until such time as they too will fall a victim to the greed of man. And so they will pass from sight as if they had never been, leaving a gap in the cycle of wilderness life that cannot be filled. They will vanish into the past out of which they came, beyond the long-forgotten days, from whence, if we let them go, they can never be recalled.

The Altar of Mammon

And the smoke rose slowly, slowly
Through the tranquil air of morning

Ever rising, rising, rising
Till it broke against the heaven
And rolled outward all around it.
LONGFELLOW

CHAPTER EIGHT
The Altar of Mammon

AWAY BACK AROUND 1870 OR MAYBE 1880, FOR INDIANS PAY little attention to dates, a large war-party of Sioux and Blackfeet Indians from the Western plains penetrated as far east as North-Western Ontario. Some of the more vivid incidents connected with their arrival so impressed the Crees of that district that, from then on, they kept a permanent guard on an eminence, in order that, in the event of a return visit, they might be prepared to welcome their guests in a suitable manner.

The mountain became known as Sioux Lookout, a name it, together with the town at its foot, retains to this day, and the lookout is still a lookout, not for hostiles, but for that far more deadly enemy, fire.

When the marauders returned home from their barbering expedition, they referred to Canada, with Indian aptitude, as the Land of the Red Sunset; and the suitability of the name is as apparent now at the setting of the sun on nearly every summer day as it was then. In the summer months the sun goes down daily a blood-red ball, seen through a pall of smoke at varying distances, painted in garish hue by the vapour emanating from the destruction of one of Canada's most valuable assets, her timberlands.

As a woman's hair is—or was—her chief adornment, so Canada's crowning glory is her forests, or what remains of them. With her timber gone, the potential wealth of the Dominion would be halved, and her industries cut down by one-third; yet the forest is being daily offered up for a burnt sacrifice to the false gods of greed and waste, and the birthright of future generations is being squandered by its trustees. Not only is the interest, the merchantable timber arriving at maturity, being used up faster than it accumulates, but the capital, the main body of the forest, is fast disappearing. Year by year for three-quarters of a century, this useless and costly destruction has been going on for five months out of every year; sometimes in widely separated districts, at others in a seething wall of flame that stretches clear across the greater part of Canada.

This is no exaggeration; in large cities such as Montreal, Toronto and Ottawa the sun has been noticeably darkened on more than one occasion by the smoke of fires two hundred miles away. Whole towns such as Haileybury, Liskeard, Cochrane, and many others, have been swept off the face of the earth. Mining camps such as Porcupine and Golden City have been burnt with loss of life running into three figures. In the latter case, I happened to be in the district, and at a distance of twenty miles I distinctly heard the roar of the flames, little knowing the holocaust that was taking place. The smoke was such that it was impossible to see a quarter of a mile on the lakes, and all travelling had to be suspended except by those familiar with the country. A shortage of canoes compelled hundreds of people to enter the lake by which the town was situated, where they extended in a living chain, holding hands to support each other, dipping their bodies from time to time under the surface to wet their clothes. Many of these were suffocated by smoke, those near the shore were badly scorched, and some were drowned. Relief trains sent up to the end of the steel were got through with difficulty, being on occasion derailed by the twisted metals, and in the tank of one locomotive that could be driven no further on account of the heat, a man was later found scalded to death.

I assisted in the work of recovering some of the bodies scattered through the charred forest, prospectors caught far from water by the sudden rush of fire; they were mostly in crouching positions, with the hands held over the face, sights terrible to see. This particular fire travelled, in spots, at an estimated speed of forty miles an hour, creating a hurricane of its own, and during the short time of its duration, laid waste an area as large as the South of England.

When it is considered that catastrophes such as these can be, and mostly are, caused by a carelessly discarded cigarette or match, unextinguished camp fires, or some other simple and preventable cause, and that useful lives and valuable timber, running into untold sums, can be destroyed by the criminal neglect of one individual, it is not very hard to see that fire protection in Canada has become a matter of the gravest importance.

No longer is the settler in danger of massacre, although in some districts wolves menace his stock, but in what is known as the "backwoods," which includes all that region of half-cleared farms on the fringe of the forest proper, his life and property are in danger from forest fires as never before.

The Governments of the various provinces keep in the woods, during the danger period, forces of men equipped with every contrivance that could possibly be brought to bear on fires at such distances from vehicular transportation. In days now happily gone by, Fire Ranging was more or less of a farce. By the patronage system, then in vogue, men were often appointed to the staff of the Service who by trade were entirely unsuited to the position. In those days the way a man cast his vote was considered of more importance than the service he could give in the field, and those who had the responsibility of seeing the work done, or were genuinely interested, were hampered by the vote-peddlers. The rank and file consisted mostly of college students out to make enough money to see them through their winter courses; estimable fellows, all of them, but just as much out of place in their new environment as an Indian or a trapper would have been had he gone to their colleges and tried to assume the *rôle* of professor. Most of them were unused to a canoe, the only means of transportation, excepting for the little knowledge they might have picked up at summer resorts or at a boating club. The time that should have been spent patrolling the beat was expended in futile endeavours to do their own cooking, keep from getting lost, and generally take care of themselves; and many of them unfortunately looked on the expedition as a frolic, or else a chance to get a few lessons in woodcraft, and be paid for it.

Meanwhile Canada was burning up.

Some of the chiefs and their assistants were highly efficient men, who took their responsibilities very much to heart; and there were a few men of undoubted ability salted through the heterogeneous mass of inefficiency, but they were not common; and alone these men could do little. So, every spring, there was the elevating exhibition of ten or a dozen canoes starting out on an expedition intended to protect the most valuable, and at the same time the most perishable asset that particular Province owned, with a good two-thirds of its personnel now dipping a paddle in the water for the first time in their lives. And so the procession wobbled and weaved along the route, herded on its unwilling way by a harassed, discouraged, and vitriolic Chief, who tore his hair, and raved and pleaded at every portage. He was held answerable for the proper distribution of his men by a certain date, and in the case I have in mind he got them there, God knows how.

In one instance a young man who had passed, on an Ontario Reserve, what must have been a most uncomfortable summer between the flies, the loneliness, and a very exaggerated fear of wild beasts, on his return home caused to be published in a Toronto newspaper an account of his experiences. Among other things he related how an inhuman and relentless Chief had banished him and his partner to a remote and "very undeveloped" district, where they were frequently lost, and at one time were obliged to lock themselves in, while a ferocious lynx of large size laid siege to their camp for an entire day. As further evidence of the Chief's brutality he stated that some rangers who had been discharged had been obliged to find their way out without a guide! It is to be supposed that they found the lack of a footman also very distressing at times. This was about eighteen years ago, and although, apparently, taken seriously at the time the story would not be published in these days, except as a joke, as it is well known that there are no authentic accounts of lynx, unless in a trap, ever attacking a man, and the Forest Ranger of to-day is certainly in no need of a guide. But this gives an idea of the protection that one of Canada's most heavily forested regions was getting up to a not so very distant date.

This has all been changed. The fire-fighting machinery is now one of the most efficient and highly organized branches of the government service. Only men of known ability are employed. Districts where much travelling is done are patrolled by airplanes, which are also used for transporting fire-fighting apparatus to places to which it would be otherwise impossible to move it. Steel towers, hauled in sections by dog-teams during the winter, are erected on commanding situations and connected by telephone, and in them sentinels are posted every day of summer.

Portages are kept in first-class condition, and short-cuts established, so that gangs of men and equipment may be rushed to the scene of a fire in the shortest possible time. Professional woodsmen and Indians are kept on the pay-roll for the express purpose of discovering blocks of valuable timber, and opening up routes to them.

A hundred miles each side of the railroad, in wild districts, is protected in the most intensive manner; beyond that the type of man who is responsible for most of the fires is rarely found. Those who have sufficient experience to enable them to penetrate farther than the Rangers go, will neither intentionally nor carelessly set a fire.

In case of fire a government ranger of the lowest rank has power, in emergency, to call to his aid all the able-bodied men he needs, employed or otherwise, and he takes charge of the situation, although paradoxically they receive more wages for the duration of the fire than he does. All this comes a little late, but something may be saved.

The numerous lumber camps situated on the fringe between civilization and the true wilderness have long been known for their hospitality, their generosity to Indians, and the readiness of their crews to assist in cases of distressed travellers, and in the event of fire. No man need go hungry or want for a bed when passing through the lumbering districts, and weary trappers have rested in them for days, regaling themselves with cooking such as only the old-time camp cooks know how to put up, free of any charge.

Most of the companies are honest in their dealings with timber on Crown lands, but unfortunately some of these concerns have passed out of the hands of the big-hearted lumber kings, and under a new regime fail to keep up the traditions. There are a number of them now being operated by foreign amalgamations with huge sums of money behind them, and having no special interest in the country, their only concern being to get what can be got whilst the getting is good. They employ labour certainly, as long as it lasts, even as the beaver supported a large population for a time and are gone now. The two cases are parallel.

The white pine, king of all the Forest, at one time the mainstay of the lumber industry, is now only existent in a few remote districts, or in reserves set aside by a wise government. But the pine is hard to save.

Politics have still a little to say, for it is a profitable tree, and many are the hungry eyes turned on the rolling dark green forest of the reserved lands. Certain unscrupulous lumber companies, of foreign origin, have been the cause of fires designed to scorch large areas of timber on Crown lands. Burnt timber must be immediately sold or it will become a total loss. The burning of an old lumber camp, and the sacrifice of some logging gear in the fire establishes innocence on the part of the company, and they come into possession of a nice, juicy cut of timber which rightly belongs to the public. The money is paid over but the pine is none the less gone.

I remember once visiting a lumber camp belonging to a foreign company, to obtain details of a fire that had taken place on their cuttings. Somehow or another it did not transpire what my business at the camp was, but we, the camp bosses and myself, fell into an argument as to whether the timber on a certain lake in the Forest Reserve would ever be cut. They declared that it surely would, and I stoutly maintained that it would not.

"The Government won't sell," I finished triumphantly.

"They'll sell if it burns, won't they," said one of the bosses with a knowing wink, not knowing what I represented. Two summers later a large block of timber adjacent to the lake was burnt and the district for miles around has passed into the hands of its enemies.

A letter appeared not long ago in a prominent newspaper in a Canadian City, in which it was pointed out that the reports being circulated concerning the alleged shortage of pine were hurting the lumber industry. It will be far worse hurt when the pine are gone, which will be before very long, and most of the old white pine companies are even now turning their attention to pulp, which, whilst not quite so profitable, employs as much labour, the main issue. It were better so than that the people of Canada should be robbed of the pleasure of having at least one or two National Parks in a state of Nature, if they serve only the purpose of a monument to the forest that is gone, a memento of the Canada that was in the days of the Last Frontier. Let us, before it is too late, learn a lesson from the tale of the beaver and the buffalo. The forest is a beaten enemy to whom we can well afford to be generous.

Too many regard the wilderness as only a place of wild animals and wilder men, and cluttered with a growth that must somehow be got rid of. Yet it is, to those who know its ways, a living, breathing reality, and has a soul that may be understood, and it may yet occur to some, that part of the duty of those who destroy it for the general good is to preserve at least a memory of it and its inhabitants, and what they stood for.

The question of re-forestation immediately crops up.

I feel that the planting of a few acres of seedlings to compensate for the destruction of thousands of square miles of virgin timber, whilst a worthy thought, and one that should be extensively carried out, seems much like placing two cents in the bank after having squandered a million. Let us keep on with the good work by all means, but why not at the same time devise means to save a little of what we have?

This re-forestation may salve the consciences of those who would ruthlessly sell or cut the last pine tree, but by the time the seedlings arrive at maturity, a matter of a hundred and fifty years or more, the rabble of all nations will occupy so much territory that the trees will have no room to grow.

No one seems to have thought of ascertaining just how long a soil impoverished by being systematically denuded of its natural fertilizer, by the removal of all mature timber, will reproduce a forest worthy of the name. In these domestic woodlands there will fall no logs to rot and nourish the trees growing to take their places, especially in the unproductive barrens to which the interests of practical forestry have been relegated by the somewhat over-zealous land-hunters.

We have already to-day examples of this depreciation in "land-power" in some of the great wheat-growing areas of the West. The ruinous "scratch-the-land-and-reap-a-fortune" policy of the propagandists of settlement schemes in the past has been followed only too closely; and, insufficiently fertilized, the soil, having given all it had, is beginning to run out.

There are to-day in Canada large concerns that in the guise of a benevolent interest in Wild Life, and under cover of a wordy forest preservation campaign (of which re-forestation, *not* conservation, is the keynote), are amalgamating in order to gain possession of practically all of Canada's remaining forests.

And, let us be warned, they are succeeding handsomely.

Enormous areas are already beyond the jurisdiction of the people. As a sop to public opinion the benefits of re-forestation are dwelt on, not as a contributing factor in silviculture (and a very necessary one it is), but as a substitute for the timber they wish to remove. According to those interested the forests will burn, fall down, decay, or rot on the stump if they are not cut immediately, and in return they will plant comparatively infinitesimal areas with tiny trees, to replace the fast disappearing forests on which they are fattening.

So we have the highly-diverting spectacle of one man, standing in the midst of ten million acres of stumps and arid desolation, planting with a shovel a little tree ten inches high, to be the cornerstone of a new and synthetic forest, urged on to the deed by a deputation of smug and smiling profiteers, who do not really care if the tree matures or not—unless their descendants are to be engaged in the lumbering business.

How have the mighty fallen, and will continue to fall!

Even the policy of girdling* the hardwood species where they are not useful as firebreaks, woods whose beautiful fall colouring and grateful shade are a tradition in Canada, has been advocated to allow the growth of more easily merchantable species in their place at some future date. The virtual drying-up of springs, lakes, creeks and even fair-sized rivers consequent on this wholesale removal of forest growth, we hear nothing about.

Even an Act of Parliament to preserve a few hundred square miles of Canada's natural scenery intact for the benefit of the people, has to be fought through a number of sessions before it can wrest from destruction beauty spots of inestimable value to the nation, the benefits of which will accrue to the greater number and for all time, not only temporarily to an individual or a company.

And until the politics in which the issue is obscured are kept out of the matter and replaced by public-spirited altruism and a genuine forest conservation policy, the will of the people will be over-ridden, and the forest will continue to fall before the hosts of the God of Mammon, until the last tree is laid in the dust.

No punishment can be severe enough to atone for the deliberate or

*Removing a ring of bark entirely around a tree, on which it dies.

careless setting of fire, and how little this is realized even to-day is illustrated by the decision, handed down, of a magistrate in a middle-sized town, when a man charged with having a bottle of whiskey in his possession during a prohibition wave was fined two hundred dollars, and another guilty of setting fire, and destroying several thousand dollars' worth of timber, paid only ten dollars and costs.

I may seem to overemphasize this point, and perhaps could be accused of speaking too strongly, but if you had seen, as I have, noble forests reduced in a few hours to arid desert sparsely dotted with the twisted, tortured skeletons of once were trees, things of living beauty, (or if you are very practically minded, things of high value), excuse could no doubt be found for my zeal.

I know a little lake, called by the Indians the Place of Calling Waters, a blue gem, circled, as I once saw it, by a yellow beach of sand and set in a valley of ancient spruce and birches. In the middle distance a dark pine stood out in silhouette, with its twisted arms thrown out against the Western sky, and the haze of evening dimmed the bristling outline of the wooded mountains.

It is different now. The glade is cut and the lake polluted. The giant pine no longer flaunts his banner-like limbs in the face of the burning sun, and the mountain has become a pile of sterile rocks, covered with a skeleton forest of burnt rampikes, whose harsh outlines no haze can ever soften. And the cause? A "Hunky"* colony.

Beauty spots such as this little Lake of Calling Waters, groves redolent with the clean smell of the leaves, carpeted in Spring with a myriad flowers, must soon be laid waste and trampled underfoot by the unsavoury hordes of Southern Europe, and their silence broken by a babel of uncouth tongues.

A frenzied and misdirected immigration policy, *encouraged by the demands of a wage-cutting type of employer by no means rare, and promoted by shipping and transportation companies whose only interest is to collect fares,* is fast filling up Canada with a polyglot jamboree of lan-

*Bohunk, a term applied to S. E. Europeans. They are rated as of the lowest grade of intelligence by U. S. Government standards. It is known that they frequently cause fires deliberately, in order to obtain employment fighting them.

guages, among which English is by no means the predominate feature. The unskilled labour market in Canada is glutted. Every city has its unemployment problem. Prosperity there is, but not enough to provide a livelihood for the adult male population of all Europe.

If the United States found it hard to absorb the immense quantities of immigrants landing on her shores, and was obliged to institute the quota, a wise act. There is room in Canada for some of the surplus population of the British Isles, and employment for them, but, at the present rate of increase from other sources, the population will soon, if it does not already, exceed the supply of labour that the country has to offer. Later, when the harm has been done, measures similar to those now in use on the other side of the line may have to be adopted, and the Briton, arriving here and finding the country overstocked, will naturally ask "Where do we go from here?"

The South-eastern European will work for less than the "white" races, and has therefore to a very extent supplanted the old-time, happy-go-lucky lumber-jack of song and story. This is to say nothing of other occupations he has seized on and monopolized, for no one will work with him.

He lowers the standard of living by existing under conditions that the English-speaking and French-Canadian nationalities would not tolerate, and in order to live the cheaper, in places where he boards himself, will kill every living creature from a whiskey-jack up, to eke out his niggardly diet.

The "Bohunk" or "Bolshie" is seldom seen without a home-made cigarette, hanging from his lower lip, which he will carelessly spit out into the inflammable forest litter. For days perhaps the dry muck will smoulder along, until a breeze springs up and fans the "smudge" into a blaze which leaps quickly from one resinous tree to another, till the whole forest is in flames.

This type herds together in communities where the whole output of his labour is just sufficient to support life, and generally in sections where the timber he cuts and destroys is worth infinitely more than his contribution to the wealth of the country.

At the present time, in some sections, timber as a national asset is worthy of far more consideration than the attempts at agriculture carried on in the same area. Forest regions of the backwoods, of the semi-cultivated type, abound with deserted farms, which, having run out owing to poor soil, serve no purpose save that of creating a fire hazard when overgrown with wild hay.

I venture to say, and I am upheld in this by recent findings of expert silviculturists, that a large percentage of the land now under so-called cultivation in forest regions, would be of far greater value under timber, and should never have been opened for settlement in the first place.

Agricultural over-production has, in some parts of the country, reached such a pitch that many farmers are feeding the best of grain to their cattle and pigs as being a more profitable method of disposal than selling it, whilst as an example of market prices, they must sell eggs at 5 and 10 cents a dozen and butter at 15 cents a pound, as against 40 cents and 35 cents in former times. Many farmers with large holdings are mortgaged to the hilt. These are cold facts and will bear investigation; and although those who are engaged in the emigrant trade (for so it can well be called) may not agree with these statements, bankers and others doing business in these areas will.

And yet with a world-wide business depression in full swing, and an unemployment tally of many thousands to account for, we allow transportation concerns to issue flamboyant literature far and wide with a view to attracting to these shores boatloads of unwanted foreign-born "settlers." A period of readjustment and retrenchment, followed up by properly balanced and strictly enforced immigration legislation, will be necessary before any influx of unskilled, ignorant peasantry can be looked on with equanimity by the citizens of this Dominion.

The forest-fire menace in Canada is very real, yet the continued carelessness of unintelligent vandals, who get into the country simply because they have so much money, can't speak English, and do not happen to have consumption or a wooden leg, is destroying as much, if not more, valuable timber than is cut for useful purposes. Hundreds of square miles of the finest forests now remaining on the American Continent, trees that were old when Wolfe stormed the citadel at Quebec, will be carelessly burnt every summer to provide a Roman holiday for an alien race. It would not be fair to blame the "Hunky" for all the fires, but with less of him the fire risk would be much reduced.

As an example of the spirit of some of these foreigners who, in certain districts, infest our forest countries, I will give an experience of my own. It fell to my lot to be passing a lumber crew just as a fire, of which they themselves were the originators, entered the green bush adjacent to their cuttings and was fast eating its way into the Government Reserve. As a Ranger it became my duty to take charge of the situation and I was obliged to call on the entire crew of two camps, some eighty or ninety men all told. When they assembled I saw at a glance that every man-jack was a Bohunk.

My troops were useless from the start. They shambled along with hands in pockets, or unwillingly holding shovels or axes, babbling and cackling in their own language. I caught more than one covert glance and sneering inflection cast my way and looked for trouble. I distributed them as best I could, an operation which much resembled that of lining up a herd of pigs on a skating-rink, and turned them loose on the fire.

While passing along the edge of the burn, noting the wind, direction the fire was taking, locating water and such things, I noticed the two fore-men, Germans, (good solid citizens they were too), two French cooks and some choreboys working like demons at a spot otherwise deserted. The foremen should have been foreing, the cooks cooking and the chore-boys choring, but it transpired that the Bolsheviek had deserted in a body and had taken the bush, hiding out from the distasteful job, and these men had turned out to fight the fire alone.

"The Soviet sons-of-dogs," swore one German. "Wait till I get them birds into the big timber!"

I routed out all the slackers I could find, and passed up and down the entire fighting-line, wheedling, threatening and cursing, until at last I became so exasperated that I threw the light axe I carried at one of the most impudent of them, close enough to startle him, where it stuck into a cedar with a good solid "chuck," an Indian trick, and hitherto used only as a pastime. This created some impression, and by brandishing the axe, and a fluent use of all the profanity I could invent, better results were obtained.

And this was the spirit with which these men, aspiring to become cit-izens of a new and progressive country, met an emergency that was destroying their very means of livelihood, and for which they themselves were responsible.

I fail to see what right men such as these have to a share in the unearned increment of Canada, whilst the English-speaking and French-Canadian workers are shouldered aside to make room for them. It will keep Canada busy absorbing the British population she is getting, a people who would have the interests of the country at heart, without having to divide up their birthright among a clamouring multitude of undesirables, who should never have gotten past the immigration barriers.

❧ ❧ ❧

FOR A WOODSMAN TO REVISIT A COUNTRY THAT HE ONCE knew as virgin and find it has been destroyed by fire is like coming home and finding the house burnt. Trappers and Indians rarely set fire; if they did their occupation would be soon gone. No man will burn his own property, and the proprietary feeling of these people towards their stamping grounds is very real. Most of them are the best unofficial Fire Rangers we have.

It is a serious misfortune, nay, a catastrophe of sweeping proportions, for a trapper to be burnt out, or see his territory going up in smoke. I know whereof I speak, having had the distress of seeing the greater portion of a well-loved and familiar landscape destroyed by a fire in the space of forty-eight hours, I myself and several others barely escaping with our lives, and this necessitated my moving out of the district entirely. I was in the Fire Service at the time, and on going out to the village for provisions was detained by the Chief as smoke had been observed in a district with which he knew me to be familiar. That same evening an Indian, having paddled fifty miles without stopping, save for portages, came in and reported the exact location of the fire, which had come from somewhere south and west, and was fast eating its way into my hunting ground.

The next day a gang of hastily hired rangers and Indians started for the scene of the trouble. The main route was very circuitous, and more than once my fortunate knowledge of the presence of beaver enabled us to make use of several short-cuts, the dams being in good condition, and the shallow creeks, otherwise unnavigable, being well flooded. With these things in our favour we arrived within ten miles of our objective late on the first day and we began to hear the roar of the fire. That night, as we camped, sparks and large flakes of dead ashes fell into the tenting ground, and the sky was lit up by the terrible, but beautiful and vivid glare of a sea of flames. Much delayed by numerous portages, it was not until noon the next day that we were within measurable distance of the conflagration, which was a "hum-dinger." There was a considerable mountain between us and the fire, and along the foot of this we tugged and hauled heavily loaded canoes up a shallow river, plugged with old fallen timber. Sparks, brands and burning birch bark fell about us unheeded. Sweating white men cursed and heaved, and passed scathing remarks on the owner of the country who did not keep his rivers in shape—myself. Patient, silent Indians juggled canoes and their loads with marvellous dexterity from one point of least resistance to another. Men of four nations waded in mud to the knees, broke paddles and ripped canvas from canoe-bottoms, unreprimanded by an eloquent and forceful Chief.

At his desire I described a short route to the fire area, and he swiftly made his plans and disposed his forces. My allotted sector, with two Crees, was the mountain, at the foot of which a couple of men made camp. Once up the mountain, from which we had a plain view of the camp, we separated, each taking a different direction, in order to get three observation angles on the fire from the eminence. Once alone, and in a fever of anxiety concerning my possible losses, I plunged ahead at full speed, angling towards the greatest volume of sound. I must mention here, that being used to moccasins, I was much hampered by a pair of stiff hard-soled larrigans which I had donned for fire-fighting purposes, and in which at times I was at some pains to keep on my feet.

I was suddenly startled by the sight of a bear which lumbered by me, bound for the river. A rabbit raced almost between my legs, then another and another. The roar had become deafening, and the heat almost unbearable, and I strained every muscle to attain the western, or far, crest of the mountain, before it became untenable for my purpose. I saw another galloping rabbit, and noticed curiously that it was passing from the left, when it should have been coming head on. A partridge flew, again from my left, struck a tree, and fell to the ground, scorched, blinded, and gasping. It I killed in mercy.

Just then I detected a sharper undertone of sound underlying the deeper heavy roar ahead of me, and on looking to the left and behind me, towards the line of flight of the bird, from whence it seemed to come, I saw the thin crackling line of a ground-fire creeping swiftly towards me like a molten carpet, now within a hundred yards of me, and backed at no great distance by a seething wall of flames. The fire had met me more than halfway, and had thrown out a flanking party. I was neatly trapped.

I turned and incontinently fled, making for the widest part of the V of flames, as the main conflagration had now caught up. And here is where my hard-soled 'packs* came in. Unused to boots, I found I could not run on the slippery jack-pine needles without losing time, and it took all of whatever will-power I may possess to tone my movements down to a swift walk, and curb my desire to race, and scramble, and tear my way regardless of boots, direction or anything else, just run—run. The flames were now on three sides of me, and my clothes were becoming brittle. Fortunately the intense heat kept the smoke up so that if I could keep my distance I was in no danger of suffocation; the danger lay in a very probable enveloping movement by the enemy.

I saw some harrowing sights. Dumb creatures endeavouring to save their lives from the one element against which all are helpless, some succeeding, others not. I saw tiny partridges in huddled groups, some lying on their backs with leaves in their claws, beneath which they deemed themselves invisible, realizing that there was danger somewhere, and using the only protection that they knew. And—I know of no greater love that a mother can have than this—I saw the hen bird sitting dumbly by, unable to herd the little creatures to safety, waiting to burn with them.

The smoke darkened the brightness of noonday, but the cavern of flames lit up the immediate surroundings with a dull red glow. I was keeping ahead of the fire but my direction began to be a matter of doubt. "Follow the animals," I kept thinking; but all that could had gone by, and now there were no more. I forced back my terrible fear. I caught myself saying, "You can't make me run, you—you can't make me run," and there

*Shoepacks, also larrigans; an oil-tanned moccasin of heavy leather, sometimes having a boot-like sole.

I was running and slipping and stumbling in my deadly footwear; and with a jerk I slowed, or rather accelerated to my swiftest walk.

More partridges, eyeing me dumbly from low limbs, and the chicks huddled beneath: oh the pity of it! Two more rabbits: follow them, follow them, fast! A small muskeg showed up; I raced for it expecting a pond: there was none. Past the muskeg and on. The growth of small cypress that cluttered the forest here became very thick. Surrounded by smoke, now commencing to billow down with the back-draught of the fire, my brain reeling with the heat, with the horror of what was too probably to be my funeral pyre driving me on, I scrambled desperately ahead, with no thought but to keep the advancing flanks of the destroyer behind me.

My feet seemed leaden, and my head a shell, light and empty, as I squirmed with desperate contortions to force a way through the continuous barrier, like a cane-brake, of small trees. I could no longer keep any specific direction, but knew I must now be far past the camp. I thought momentarily of my two companions; I had long since passed the area they had been assigned to. And then, breaking at length through the last of the barrier of saplings, I burst out on to the eastern brow of the mountain. Fire goes but slowly down a hill, so I took time to breathe, and looking down could see the camp; and from its proximity I knew that my ordeal by fire had not lasted over twenty minutes, if that, though I would have sworn that it had occupied an hour.

The camp ground itself was a scene of the utmost confusion. Tents were being pulled down by main force and jammed into canoes, sometimes poles and all; pots, blankets, baggage and equipment of all kinds, seemed, at that distance, to be picked up in quantities and dumped onto the nearest craft.

I descended the mountain, the fire commencing to creep over its edge, and found waiting for me with a canoe one of the Crees who had gone up with me. He had seen me coming out on the summit, expecting me there as he watched the course of the fire. He grinned and spoke in English:

"Hot like hell, eh?"

"Some," I replied soberly, as I felt the split and scorched back of my canvas shirt.

On the river just above the camp was a live beaver-dam, and it came as a timely assistance in aiding us to make our getaway, deepening the river so that we reached without loss of time a mile and a half portage leading inland to a large lake. This, one of my main trails, was in good shape, and we moved over it at nothing less than a trot. To check the fire was impossible without a change of wind, and in any case reinforcements were necessary.

The Chief and one man commenced the return trip to get help, and from what I saw of the river afterwards, and judging by the two men's description, the first part of the journey must have been something in the nature of running the gauntlet. The fire had crossed the river for most of its length in the interim, and was yet burning on both sides in many places. The aftermath of a fire is often as dangerous as the element itself, as trees, tottering on burnt-out stumps or severed roots, fall without warning. On the section of the stream where the log-jams were, necessitating delays, these men were in danger of being killed or injured at any minute, as trees fell without warning across the river, and into it. On the lower reaches the fire was still burning, but here the water was fortunately deeper, and when some blaze hotter than common was encountered, the men crouched, half-submerged under the overturned canoe, which lying with its gunwales completely under water, afforded an airtight shelter as long as the canvas should last, or until the blaze died down. They told of a big bull moose with scorched hair and staring eyes, that fell exhausted into the water, and lay there sucking air into the tortured lungs in great gasps, paying no more attention to the canoe than had it been a floating chip. I saw on those waters dozens, no less, of small birds of all kinds floating dead along the river banks and young things such as half-fledged waterfowl, tiny squirrels, and odd humming-birds, that had made the water only to drown or die of suffocation; a pitiful sight.

Moose we found dead—by the smell, a week later—that for some unexplainable reason had died within reach of water, but no bears, although these latter were making full use of the banquet all ready cooked and served for their convenience.

My camp and complete outfit were saved, but my heart was saddened by the thought of the terrible loss of life amongst my poor beasts, and the destruction of the noble jack-pine forest in which I had roamed so long.

Amongst the Indians on this expedition there was an old man, a conjurer, whose name means "The Little Child." He was the oldest man in the party, and the leadership of this "little child" in matters of bush technique was tacitly accepted by all. This ancient carried a drum. He took charge of the Indians in a very effective manner, but did no work. The Chief had noticed this, and had asked me to speak for him concerning the matter, and the following conversation ensued:

"Little Child, why do you not work, as the others are doing."

"Because," replied Little Child, "I am here for another purpose."

"But," said the Chief, "I thought you were here to fight fire."

Little Child shook his head, and speaking gently, as to one who is mentally deficient, said:

"You do not understand. I am not here to fight that fire; I am here to put it out!"

The two ideas being synonymous in the executive's long experience, he found this a little puzzling.

"What do you mean by that?" he asked.

"Wait and see," replied the Indian.

Knowing better than to give direct orders to one of his race the Chief went on his way; but I waited, and I saw. What actually happened was remarkable enough. The weather had been hot, the sun shining without intermission for many days, and there was every sign of these conditions lasting indefinitely. This made our work the harder. Nevertheless, the next day Little Child deserted the party, taking his drum. As he left he said to me:

"I am now going to put out the fire. Two days, maybe three; wait and see!"

He secreted himself a mile away on a hill, and during two evenings and the whole of two nights we heard that drum, with never a break in its rhythm; tum-tum, tum-tum, tum-tum, tum-tum; the double staccato beat of the conjuror. The nights were very calm, and we heard, thinly, the high-pitched undulations of a three or four-note chant continuously repeated. Incessantly, without change it came and went, swelled and flattened to a prolonged minor note, and commenced again; until some of the white men, who were not used to that kind of thing, began to feel uneasy as to what it could mean. The Crees and Ojibways lapsed into a listless apathy, but none the less, each one of them could have posed for a statue intended to portray intense attention. At noon of the third day Little Child came down, put his drum into a gaily decorated case, and demanded something to eat. He had not broken his fast during three days. After he had eaten he said:

"I will now sleep. Tonight it will rain; tomorrow there will be no fire. Meheu! it is finished."

Some time after midnight all hands awoke to a torrential downpour that streamed over the dried earth and under tents, to soak up through groundsheets and blankets; but we cared not, our work was done; the fire was out.

And Little Child had made a reputation as being either a magician of satanic abilities, or the best weather-prophet in Eastern North America.

The House of McGinnis

"On the sunny banks of it,
Thoughtful little creatures sit."
STEVENSON

CHAPTER NINE

The House of McGinnis

A LOUD THUD, A CRASH, THE TINKLE OF BROKEN GLASS, THEN silence. A sound as of a hand-saw being run at great speed by an expert, a bumping, dragging noise and a vicious rattling; then another crash; more silence.

"And what," asked my guest as we neared the camp, "is that; an earthquake?"

"That," I answered, with some misgiving, "is the beaver, the ones you are coming to see!"

We entered the cabin, and the scene within was something to be remembered, the devastation resembling that left in the wake of a young whirlwind. The table was down, and the utensils it had held had disappeared; a four-foot stick of wood protruded through a shattered window, and below the one that remained a quantity of wood had been piled, affording facilities for the effective use of a battering ram. The washstand had been dissected and neatly piled in the bunk from which the blankets had been removed, these being included in a miscellany of articles such as dishes, moccasins, and so forth, with which the stove was barricaded. With hurried apologies to my visitor I assessed the damage, but beyond the disarrangements just mentioned, there was no serious harm done; that is, so far, no lives had been lost. I had been away two days, being delayed by soft weather, which, with its exhilarating effect on these animals, accounted for the delirious attack on my humble fixtures.

There was no sign of the raiders, they having retreated to their house at the presence of a stranger; but later they appeared and were introduced, and again retired, hopping and capering like little round gnomes, taking with them the peace offerings of chocolate and apples which they accepted, after considerable diplomatic manoeuvering, from my companion.

McGinty and McGinnis, having put their house in order, were receiving from five to half past, the guest providing the luncheon.

After open water on until early in June, the spring hunt is in full swing on the frontier, and towards the end of that period the young beaver are born. The mother, who lives at this time in a separate lodge built and tended by the male or buck beaver, being generally larger than the rest of the family is much sought after. She is easily caught close to the house, and drowns at the entrance, whilst the kittens within listen in terror to her frantic struggles to escape. Crying continuously in child-like wails, they wait in vain for the big kindly brown body that is supporting their feeble existence, till the thin little voices are stilled, and two pitifully small bundles of fur cease to move, and lie in the house to rot.

A neighbouring hunter once came to me and asked if I would come and remove a live beaver from a trap from which the drowning-stone had come loose. After several hours' travelling we arrived at the spot, when my companion refused to go to the trap, saying he could not bring himself to inflict any further torture on the suffering creature.

"Wait till you see," he told me.

I went to the place he described, and this is what I saw.

The beaver, a large female, moaning with pain, was shaking the trap that was firmly clamped on one front foot, and with the other she held close to her breast, nursing it, a small kitten beaver, who, poor little fellow, little knew how close he was to having his last meal.

I liberated her as gently as possible, and she made no effort to bite me.

With a sharp blow of my axe I severed the crushed and useless paw, when, parched with thirst, she immediately commenced to drink the blood which flowed from the wound as though it had been water. She then made slowly and painfully for the lake, only to return for the young one, who had become intensely interested in my footwear and was with difficulty prevailed on to enter the water. My companion approved of my action, although he had lost a valuable hide; he had seen the young one there, he said, and his heart had turned to water. This experience gave me some food for thought, and had its effect in hastening a decision I later arrived at, to quit the beaver hunt altogether.

Since that occurrence I have been the means of saving several pairs of small lives by following the carcase-strewn trails of the spring hunters, keeping the period they get further entertained little fellows for about a year, after which too reckless with the furniture to be any as guests.

Only those who have had the opportunity of studying living specimens over an extended period can obtain any idea of the almost human mentality of these likeable little creatures. Destructive they are, and their activities have much the same effect on the camp that two small animated sawmills running loose would have. They resemble somewhat an army tank, being built on much the same lines, and progressing in a similar manner, over or through anything that is in the way. After the first six months they can sink themselves through a six inch log at a remarkable speed, biting lengthways with the grain of the wood for three or four inches, cutting the cross section at each end and pulling out the chip.

They roam around the camp, and, with no evil intent but apparently from just sheer joy of living, take large slices out of table-legs, and chairs, and nice long splinters out of the walls, and their progress is marked by little piles and strings of chips. This in the fore part of the evening. After "lights out" the more serious work commences, such as the removal of deerskin rugs, the transferring of firewood from behind the stove into the middle of the floor, or the improvement of some waterproof footwear by the addition of a little openwork on the soles. They will gnaw a hole in a box of groceries to investigate, and are very fond of toilet soap, one brand in particular preferred, owing, no doubt, to the flavour incident to its school-girl complexion-giving qualities.

In winter they will not leave the camp and I sink a small bath tub in the floor for them, as they need water constantly. They make a practice of lying in the tub eating their sticks and birch tops, later climbing into the bunk to dry themselves. To accomplish this they sit upright and squeeze and scrub the entire body. The water never penetrates beyond the guard hairs into the fur, but I suppose half a pint is no exaggeration of the amount of water one of them will squeeze out of his coat.

Tiring of this performance, I once removed the bench by which they climbed into the bunk and prepared for a good night's rest at last. I had got so used to the continuous racket they created all night, between the drying off periods, that, like the sailor who hired a man to throw pails of water against the walls of his house all night while on shore, I could not sleep so well without the familiar sounds, and during the night I awoke to an ominous silence. With a premonition of evil I lit the lamp and on taking stock saw one of my much-prized Hudson Bay blankets hanging over the edge of the bunk, and cut into an assortment of fantastic patterns, the result of their efforts to climb into the bed. The regularity of the designs startled me, and I began to wonder if I had gone suddenly insane, as nothing short of human agency, it seemed, could have cut those loops and triangles so symmetrically. Closer examination showed that the effect had been produced by their gathering the blanket in bunches with their forepaws, and cutting out a few pieces from the pucker, with more or less pleasing results.

Apparently realizing, by the tone of certain carelessly worded remarks which I allowed to escape me, that they had gone a little too far this time, the guilty parties had tactfully retired to their trench under the wall, awaiting developments. This excavation they had made themselves. In building the camp I had made an aperture in the bottom log, and constructed outside it, at great trouble, what was, I considered, a pretty good imitation of a beaver house. The first night in they had inspected my work, found it unsuitable, and proceeded to block up the entrance with sacking. They then commenced operations under the bunk, cutting a hole in the floor for the purpose, and digging out the soil. This dirt they trundled up from the depths, pushing it ahead of them, walking with the hind feet only, the fore-paws and chin being used to hold the mass together. Whilst thus engaged they rather resembled automatic wheelbarrows. They brought up, on each journey, perhaps the full of a two-quart measure apiece of earth, which was painstakingly spread on the floor as it accumulated; as the tunnel was dug out for about six feet beyond the wall, there was quite an amount of dirt brought into the shack, and there were times when I, also, was quite busy with a shovel.

They took my interference in good part, hopping and capering about my feet in their clumsy way, much as I imagine elephants would gambol. They eventually got pretty well organized, one sleeping and the other working in shifts of two or three hours each.

After about a week of this a large mound of earth was eventually patted down smooth and solid near the water supply, and operations apparently brought to a satisfactory conclusion; so I considered that we should all now take a good rest. But the beaver is not a restful animal. Doubtless they had been warned by those advertisements that remind us that "those soft foods are ruining our teeth," for anything that offered resistance enough was bitten, the harder the better. Anything that gave good toothholds was hauled, and everything that could be pushed was pushed high, west, and sideways. Quantities of birch-bark were carried into the bunk and shredded, this contribution to the sleeping accommodation supposedly entitling them to a share of the blankets. They apparently took notice that I put wood into the stove at intervals, and in a spirit, no doubt, of co-operation, at times they piled various articles against the stove. Once when I had been out for a short time, I returned to find the camp full of smoke, and a pillow, a deerskin rug, and a map of some value to me, piled around the stove, and all badly scorched. Eventually I was obliged to erect a wire screen for safety.

It is remarkable that in spite of the orgy of destruction that went on for the first two weeks in camp, the door, an easy target, was not molested, and nothing was cut that would occasion an air leak into the camp. It is their nature to bank up against the intrusion of cold, and any loose materials that they could gather would be piled along the foot of the door, where there was a certain amount of draught. They barred the door so effectually on one occasion that I had to remove a window to enter the cabin.

Some morning, at daylight. I would awaken to find one on each side of me sleeping, lying on their backs snoring like any human. At intervals during sleep they sharpen their teeth in readiness for the next onslaught. When working, if the teeth do not seem to be in good shape, they pause for half a minute or so and sharpen them, repeating this until they are suited. The skull is fitted with longitudinal slot which allows for the necessary motion of the jaws, and the resultant grinding is much like the whetting of an axe.

The sound of an axe or knife being filed struck them with terror, and they would drop everything and run to me for protection, evidently thinking the noise came from some large animal whetting its teeth.

Beaver are the most persevering creatures I know of, man not excepted, and any job which they undertake is never abandoned until completed or proved impossible. They conduct their operations with all the serious intentness and economy of movement of trained artisans, and at the conclusion of each stage, small adjustments are made, and little pats and pushes given, either expressing satisfaction with the work or testing its solidity, I know not which.

These queer little people are also good housekeepers. Branches brought in for their feed are immediately seized on and piled to one side of the entrance to their abode. After feeding on pancakes or bread pudding, which they dearly love, the dish is pushed away into some far corner, alone with the peeled sticks and other used portions of feed. Their beds, consisting of sacks, which they tear to shreds, mixed with shredded birch-bark and long, very fine shavings cut from the floor, after being used for a period, are brought out and scattered on the floor, apparently to dry, and taken in again after a couple of days. They spend long periods on their toilet. One of the toes of the webbed hind feet is jointed so as to bend in any direction, and is fitted with a kind of double claw; with this they comb their entire coat.

They seem capable of great affection, which they show by grasping my clothing with their strong forepaws, very hands in function, pushing their heads into some corner of my somewhat angular personality, bleating and whimpering. At times they clamour for attention, and if taken notice of they shake their heads from side to side, rolling on their backs with squeals of joy. If left alone for as long as twenty-four hours, on my return they are very subdued until I talk to them, when they at once commence their uncouth gambols and their queer wrestling.

They conduct these wrestling matches—for they can be called nothing else—by rising on their hind feet, supported by the tail, while the forepaws are locked in neck and under-arm holds, looking like dancers. In this position they strain and push, each striving to overcome the other, until one begins to give way, walking backwards, still erect, pushed by his adversary. Then, perhaps by the judicious use of his tail, he recovers, prevails, and the walk commences in the opposite direction. They go at this for all they are worth, and the changes in the expression of their voices, according to the luck they are having, are remarkably plain. This performance resembles a violently aggressive fox-trot about as closely as it does anything else, and is continued until one or the other allows his tail to double under him and is bowled over, protesting loudly.

One peculiarity they have is that, when hungry, they do not fawn as most domestic animals do, but complain loudly, standing on their hind legs and grasping at the dish. If the food is withheld they scold shrilly, beating the air with their forepaws. Also, if in their work they fail in some object such as the placing of a stick, they jerk the limbs and head violently and show every sign of irritation, resuming the attempt with an impetuous violence that either makes or breaks. But as a rule they are very tractable, and after feeding will follow one all over the camp, and at times are rather a nuisance in their desire to be taken up and petted.

The male beaver has, to a certain extent, the protective instinct that dogs possess, but not of course so highly developed. I had no knowledge of this until one day I happened to be resting on my blankets on the floor after a trip—a common custom in the woods—and lying with his head on my shoulder was a six months old buck beaver. An Indian friend came in, and busied himself in some way that brought him close to my head, on the opposite side from my furry chum. Immediately the latter crossed over and stationed himself between the man's feet and my person. My friend found it necessary to pass around me, and the beaver made a quick short-cut across my face, and again took post between us. Noticing this, and thinking it might be coincidence, my companion returned to his former position, and the beaver returned also, again using my face for a runway, blowing and hissing his disapproval. It is the more remarkable in that the man was a frequent visitor, and on the best of terms with both animals, playing with them by the hour during my absence.

Another time I received a visit from a passing hunter, and on his entrance, the female beaver, always more docile than her mate, must needs go over and make an inspection of the newcomer. The male also went towards him, with every sign of disapproval, and on the stranger stooping to pat the other, reached out with his hand-like forepaw, and endeavoured to pluck her away.

Beaver are far from being the dumb creatures that most animals are. While working they are continually murmuring and muttering, even if alone, and if some distance apart occasionally signal their position by short, sharp cries. It is very rarely that speaking to them does not elicit some kind of answer.

They have a large range of distinctly different sounds. The emotions of rage, sorrow, fear, joy, and contentment are expressed quite differently, and are easily recognized after a short period of observation. Often when a conversation is being carried on they will join in with their vocal gymnastics, and the resemblance to the human voice is almost uncanny to those not accustomed to hearing it, and has been partly the cause of their undoing, as they are a very easy animal to imitate. When in trouble they whimper in the most dolorous fashion, and become altogether disconsolate. They have an imitative faculty of a sort, as any kind of bustle or quick moving around results in a like activity on their part, entailing a good deal of unnecessary gathering and pushing and dragging.

In common with most animals when tamed, beaver will answer to a name. In Canada an Irishman is known as "a Mick," and the Indian word for beaver, Ahmik, is identical in pronunciation. So I gave them Irish names, of which the two most notable were McGinty and McGinnis, names they got to know very well, and they were suitable in more ways than one, as they both had peppery tempers, and would fight at the drop of the hat anything or anybody, regardless of size, always excepting each other or myself.

My camp became known as "The House of McGinnis," although McGinty, whimsical, mischevious as a flock of monkeys, being the female was really the boss of the place; and although I am deficient in the art of making the best mouse-traps, all the world hereabouts has made a beaten path to my door on their account.

In the spring they become very restless, and nothing short of confinement in a wire pen will hold them. If allowed to go they will travel far and wide; they do not forget their old home, but will return after three or four weeks, and feed all around the camp, using it as a head-quarters and eventually settling in the vicinity.

I turned the two Mc's loose last spring and they made themselves a small house and a dam on a pond in a little valley back of a mountain called the Elephant, and would come when called and enter the cabin, which practice they have continued till the present time. They would always answer at intervals all the way down the lake, a not loud but very clear and penetrating sound, much like two notes of a violin sounded together, which changed to the "hoo! hoo!" of welcome as they landed. They have ventriloquial powers, as have some other creatures in the forest country, and at times it was impossible to tell the direction from which they were coming. This no doubt is a protection against the prying ears of certain beasts with a taste for beaver meat.

Domesticated beaver will under no circumstances bite a human being, and if annoyed they will hold a finger between their dangerous teeth, exerting only just so much pressure, screeching with rage meanwhile. At a sharp exclamation they will release their hold. They are no mean adversaries in a fight, striking a series of quick raking blows with the heavy pointed claws of the front feet, and they have been known to kill dogs with one slashing bite of their razor-edged teeth, aimed always at the throat.

In the wild state they mate for life, and in captivity they show the same fidelity to the hand that reared them. They are a "one-man dog," accepting neither food nor favour from strangers, puffing and blowing their dissatisfaction at the near approach of one they do not know; yet this little beast, with the mind of a man and the ways of a child, can work his way very deeply into the affections of those who get to know him, and I have been offered sums of money out of all proportion to their actual value, but cannot bring myself to sell them into captivity.

It is a remarkable fact that the hand-raised beaver do not, to my knowledge, associate with their own kind, building for themselves within a short distance of others, but never on the same pond.

It is indeed difficult to guess what mental processes take place back of the bright beady eyes in those thick skulls. It is hard to doubt that they are governed by something more than instinct, as they sit and ponder, seeming to deliberate before making some move. But undoubtedly this same instinct is very strong, as, turned loose at the age of a year, and with no experience, they conduct their affairs with the efficiency, though lacking for a time the ingenuity, of their wild brethren; but it leaves much to be accounted for.

Indians become much attached to them as pets, and refer to them as "Little Indians." I know of a young girl who had a much-loved pair of young beaver, that once in their daily swim were swept away on the spring flood; and were unable to return, as their habit generally was. It was at a time of year when the deep snow lining the creek beds was underlaid by a foot or so of icy water, and snowshoes would not bear up. Yet this child negotiated several miles of streamland under these conditions, through the tangled growth of willows and alders, crawling on her hands and knees for long distances over the hollow snowbanks. In spite of this device to distribute her weight, she broke through repeatedly and waded in the icy slush, only, on overtaking them, to find her little friends unable to make shore. She was overtaken by her people, who found it no easy task to dissuade her from further useless exposure, and she was obliged to return to the camp without her pets, whom she mourned as for lost friends.

It speaks well for the race that, within a reasonable area around the village, no traps were set that spring by the hunters, and the following fall the two beaver were located. By common consent of white hunter and Indian alike, they were spared until a half-breed heard the story. He agreed with the rest not to molest them, but, with the lack of sportsmanship which, unfortunately, characterizes so many of his type, at the first opportunity killed them both.

Up the lake half a mile from my camp there lives a little beaver, the remaining one of a pair one of which died last summer. He spends his nights with me, sharing my bed and board. He seems to miss his small companion that is gone, and has none of the lighthearted devilry of his forerunners. I fixed up an old beaver house, placed a large quantity of feed for him, and turned him loose. But he will not stay loose. Every night until the ice came he was at the camp door at dark.

He is a sad little creature as he sits forlornly on the floor. He has none of the non-subcutaneous beauty that so undermines the talent of certain screen idols, yet who knows but that in the wee old-fashioned brain there is not some dim recollection of happy days of romping and tumbling with just such another clumsy ball of fur in the deep, cool grass on the river bank. And as he regards me gravely, sitting on my feet the while, my heart goes out to the little waif who does not want to be free, and I pick him up and pass my hand over the rich, dark fur, and he sighs contentedly and immediately falls asleep to dream of cool waters, and mud, of poplar leaves and pancakes.

He is small, weighing perhaps ten pounds, but of the two of us he is the better bushman, mainly on account of a few simple things that he can do and I cannot—for instance break ice with my head, cut wood with my teeth, or find my way under half a mile of ice to an unmarked hole in the dark; all very useful accomplishments in this walk of life.

His visits are more irregular now as no doubt it is a ticklish job negotiating that lengthy swim without coming up for air. I was anxious to observe how he was able to do this, so watched him for several hours with a flashlight. His method was to create a considerable disturbance at the waterhole until a bubble of air had formed at its edge under the ice. To this, when large enough he attached himself, and swam away with it. The bladder of air enveloped his head and most of his back; at intervals he would make holes in the ice, probably to renew the air supply. This occurred three times in the fifteen or so minutes it took him to cover the distance.

When the ice gets thicker this performance will become impossible, and he will pass the winter in the house of McGinnis, who, with McGinty the sly, the capricious and the inquisitive, has now a lodge of his own designing, on a lake not a mile from this camp. I often wonder if my oldtimers remember their trips in a box over many portages, the six hundred mile train ride, the journey which they made inside a stove when the canoe swamped and they nearly drowned. Or if they have a passing thought for the torn deerskin rugs, and the cut table legs, and the chewed blankets; the wrestling matches, and the long sleeps on a warm soft bed;

or if they will ever know of the big empty space they left when they went away, as they lie in their small mud hut on the little round pond where the Elephant Mountain stands guard.*

To-day I kill no more beaver, but am bent on repairing in some small measure the damage done in younger and more thoughtless days; replacing at least a part of what I have destroyed, restoring dried-out lakes to their fullness of contented families, bringing life where is nought but desolation. That I may hear in the long evenings, as in the old days, the splash of huge flat tails on the water as the working parties change shift; the queer childlike cries as they wrestle on the leaves beneath the silvery poplars that are their life, the crooning of the mothers within the lodges tending their young. That I may see the dark and gloomy forest shores shining again with Wasacsena,† the brightness of newly peeled sticks, and visit and marvel over the carefully dug-canals and the sand pits. And perhaps at times I may glimpse a wise old head, the head of Mishomis, the Old Man, as a pair of bright black eyes, not unfriendly, but always cautious, watch covertly my every move from out the shadows near the shore. And I shall know that I am not, after all, alone in this mighty wilderness, whilst I have for neighbours the happy colonies of Ahmik, The Beaver People.

*These beaver are still with the writer, visiting camp regularly several times day and night, and are so domesticated that, even after six months at a time of isolation in their winter lodge, they emerge in spring perfectly tame.
†Indian word for shining appearance of timber, denuded of bark, lying along the shoreline; caused by beaver, ice scraping or natural driftwood.

The Trail of Two Sunsets

"I beheld our nations scattered,

Saw the remnants of our people
weeping westward wild and woeful,
Like the cloud-rack of a tempest,
Like the withered leaves of Autumn."
LONGFELLOW

Longfellow surely grasped the true spirit of the wilderness when he wrote Hiawatha, *and shows a knowledge of Indian life and customs that is uncommon. So much is this recognized among Indians that, at this late day, and since many years, the poem has been perpetuated by them in the form of a yearly play, held in its natural setting of woods and waters at a place called Derbarato on Lake Huron, where, these people claim, Longfellow spent a long time gathering his material, living amongst them meanwhile. There are some hundred performers, amongst whom no article of white man's clothing, and no word of English is permitted during the week of the celebration. Their rendering of the Indian Songs is worth going far to hear. These are the Garden River Ojibways and Algonquins; I have hunted a good deal with these people in the Mississauga River country, and once on an occasion when I assisted in promoting a tribal celebration at Biscotasing, Ontario, a number of them travelled nearly two hundred miles by canoe to take part in it.*

CHAPTER TEN

The Trail of Two Sunsets

BACK IN 1876 WHEN THE COMBINED FORCES OF THE SIOUX, the Cheyennes, and the Pawnees defeated General Custer in the ill-advised fiasco which resulted in the demolition of his entire command, the wiser chiefs, having formed by that time a pretty fair idea of the methods of reprisal likely to be handed out, advised the departure from that place of the warriors involved.

Their scheme of holding Custer as a hostage against retaliation by the whites had been thwarted by that General blowing out his brains on the field of battle: a historical fact, long known only to the Indians themselves. And so, like guilty children who have only too successfully opposed the authority of their elders, they fled before the expected retribution, to Canada.

They had learned the bitter lesson that although a battle won by the white man's soldiers was considered a victory, a combat in which the Indians prevailed was termed a massacre. Their chiefs were hanged for anticipation in honest battle, whilst atrocities committed by the troops, such as took place at Klamath Lake and Wounded knee, went unpunished. It speaks well for the policy of the Canadian government towards Indians that these people saw Canada in the light of a sanctuary. As a result of the just and considerate treatment of the tribes coming under British control the Canadian frontier was, with the exception of the abortive Riel Rebellion, singularly free from the brutalities, the injustice, the massacres, and the prolonged wars that so characterized the settling of the Western United States. But all that is over now. The Indian is an outcast in his native land, and the Indian population on both sides of the line is at peace for always, if a condition of gradual wasting away and dis-integration can be so called.

A moiety have adopted the white man's ways, not always with success, and mostly with attendant degeneracy and lowering of national integrity; although individuals, even so, have risen to remarkable heights.

No longer do they produce great war chiefs, such as Tecumseh, Crowfoot, Dull Knife, and a hundred others, the necessity for them hav-ing long passed, but of the large number in the Canadian Expeditionary Force, more than one received a commission, were N.C.O.'s, and as snipers many distinguished themselves, one, to my personal knowledge, winning the V.C. Lately in the United States a man of Indian blood, Curtis by name, came close to the Presidential chair, and Pauline Johnstone, or Tekahionwake to give her her tribal name, is Canada's fore-most poetess. Dr. Orokonateka became head of the Foresters, next to the Masons the most powerful organized society in Canada; there is an Indian artist of note, and Buffalo-Child Long-Lance is by no means the only Indian author. These are of course outstanding examples and, con-sidering the small number of the race yet remaining, compare well numerically with the white man's achievements; for these people, and some others not mentioned, must be taken seriously, and not at all in the spirit of the old gentleman who once visited a college maintained for the education of Indians. On his tour of inspection he came across a young tribesman who was working away at a carpenter's bench. Astonished at the sight of an Indian engaged in such an occupation, he stared for a time and at length exclaimed:

"This is extraordinary; are you an Indian?"

The young man admitted he was.

"And are you civilized?" continued the old gentleman.

"No," replied the Indian, "are you?"

Another incident of the kind occurred at an exhibition where a Sioux chieftain, attired in the regalia to which his rank entitled him, was dis-playing some handiwork of his tribe. He had much impressed those visitors who had come in contact with him by his quiet and gentlemanly bearing, and one of these, a lady of authentic Puritan ancestry, remarked patronizingly:

"An Indian warrior; how antique."

And the Indian looked at her and replied: "Yes, madam, 'antique' is correct. As residents of this country our people have at least the merit of antiquity."

Indian Chiefs, however able, have not, and never did have, absolute authority over their bands; they acted in an advisory capacity, and, their ideas being once accepted, the people placed themselves under their direction for that particular battle or journey; but the opinion of a whole tribe might run counter to the chief's policy, in which case the matter was decided by vote. This has given rise to the general impression that Indians are not amenable to discipline, but their records in the late war disproves this, and there is no doubt that had they been able to forget their tribal differences and jealousies and become properly organized, they could have put up a resistance that would have gained them better terms than they received, at the hands of their conquerors.

At the outbreak of war, a number of young men of the band with which I hunted, offered their services. Most of them could speak no English, and few had ever made a journey of any kind, save a canoe. One patriotic soul, Pot-Mouth by name, offered to provide his own rifle, tent and blankets. After several weeks in a training camp, where, owing to the retiring disposition of the forest-bred, he fared badly, this doughty warrior showed up one day at the trading post, in full uniform, purchased a quantity of supplies, and hit for his hunting ground. On his return for a second load he found an escort awaiting him and he was brought to trial as a deserter.

Through an interpreter, he stated, in his defence, that the board was poor, and that the officers had too much to say; so, there being as yet no sign of hostilities, he had decided to quit the job until the fighting started. He was leniently dealt with, and served as a sniper until "the job" was finished, having acquired in the meantime a good record, and a flow of profanity that could wither a cactus.

This independence of spirit has prevented the Indians as a race from entering the field of unskilled labour, but the members of some tribes have shown an aptitude for certain occupations requiring skill and activities.

The Iroquois of Caughnawauga are amongst the best bridge-builders in Canada; as canoemen the Crees, Ojibways and Algonquins can be approached by no white man save, with few exceptions, those they themselves have trained; and although not companionable as guides they command a high wage where serious trips into difficult territories are contemplated.

There exists with a certain type of woodsman, not however in the majority, a distinct hostility towards the Indian, often the result of jealousy of the latter's undoubted superiority in woodcraft. They evince a good-natured contempt for the Indian's abilities in the woods, mainly because, not having travelled with him, they have not the faintest idea of the extent of his powers nor of the deep insight into the ways of the wilderness that he possesses, entailing knowledge of things of which they themselves have never even heard. For the red man does not parade his accumulated knowledge of two thousand years. He is by nature cautious, and an opportunist, seizing on every available means to attain his ends, working unobtrusively by the line of least resistance; and his methods of progress are such that a large band may pass through a whole district without being seen.

He is accused of pusillanimity because he follows the shore line of a lake when beating into a tempest, his purpose being to take advantage of the eddies and back currents of wind which exist there; whilst the tyro plunges boldly and obstinately down the centre of the lake, bucking the full force of the elements, shipping water and wetting his outfit, and often becoming wind-bound, or at least arriving at his destination some hours late.

This people, who knew the fine art of canoeing when in England bold knights fought for the favour of fair ladies, do not need to run rapids to gain experience, and will not do so, thereby risking water-soaked provisions, unless they may gain time by so doing. But, on the necessity arising, they face, without hesitation, white water and storms that their detractors would not for a moment consider. For this is their daily life; the novelty of the game was worn off somewhere around 1066, and they no more pass their time doing unnecessary stunts, than an expert runner would sprint to his daily work in a series of hundred yard dashes.

The genuine woodsman knows these things, and does not disdain to learn from his swarthy brother, attaining often a degree of excellence that causes even his teachers to look to their laurels. The Indian is not to be judged by the standards of civilization, and those who cast aspersion on his skill or manhood, from the fund of their slight experience, know not whereof they speak. In his own line he is supreme, and few know his worth who have not travelled with him. The Indian is rarely seen in lumber camps, for he was never an axeman to compare with the French-Canadian; but in river-driving, the operation of herding a half-million or so of logs down a river swollen with melted snows, and generously strewn with rapids, an occupation requiring a degree of quick-footed daring and swift judgment, he excels.

His knowledge of the idiosyncrasies of swift water is unsurpassed, and although less spectacular than his Gallic contemporary, awakened from his lethargy by the lively competition with his vivacious co-worker, he enters into the spirit of the game with zest. The famous Mohawk drivers are much in demand by companies whose holdings necessitate long drives of timber down rough and dangerous rivers such as the Ottawa, the Gatineau, the Madawaska and other famous streams.

Civilization has had a certain influence on the more primitive Indians of the north in some districts, but rarely for good, as witness the shiftless, vagabond families living in squalid misery on some of the small reserves, where they are neither flesh, fish, nor fowl, nor yet good red Indian.

The Indian, and I refer now only to him whose life is spent in the Land of Shadows, although a dreamer and a visionary in his idle moments, is a being who lives by constant struggle against the elements, and some very signal virtues are called forth by the demands of his life. As many a business man, on quitting his chosen sphere of activity, becomes more or less atrophied, so the Indian, removed from his familiar occupations, and having no occasion for the exercise of his highly specialized faculties and ideas, loses out entirely.

Those Indians before mentioned who have attained national prominence belong to tribes whose geographical position was in their favour; civilization has made them fairly prosperous, and, excepting Long Lance who is, though educated, a splendid savage, they have two or three generations of civilization already behind them. Some are so fortunately situated as to have oil found on their reserves with the result that they are actually wealthy. But the Indians of the far north live much as their grandfathers did; they are too far behind to catch up in this generation and at the present rate of decrease they will not long outlive the frontier that is so rapidly disappearing.

To effect in a few years an advancement in them that it has taken the white man two thousand years to accomplish would entail their removal; and to wrench them loose from their surroundings and suddenly project them into the pitiless, competitive maelstrom of modern life would be equivalent to curing a sick man by hanging him, or loading a sinner into a sixteen-inch gun and shooting him up into heaven. Or, to come back to earth, requesting the Indian to exchange the skilful manipulation of pole, paddle, and snowshoe, in which his soul rejoices, for the drudgery of a shovel on a small backwoods farm, the first step in the reclaiming of which requires him to destroy the forest on which he looks as a home, is to ask an artist to dig graves, for an artist he surely is in his line, and the grave would be his own.

The coming of civilization does not surround the northern tribes with prosperous farmers or the multifarious chances of employment as it did in more favoured districts; it merely destroys their means of livelihood, without offering the compensations of the more productive areas.

Left to his own devices in civilization the Indian is a child let loose in a house of terrors. As a solace he indulges in the doubtful amusements of those only too ready to instruct him, and lacking their judgment, untrained in the technique of vice, he becomes a victim of depravity. Unable to discern the fine line between the evasions and misrepresentations with which civilized man disguises his thoughts, and downright dishonesty, he becomes shiftless and unreliable. The few words of English he learns consist mainly of profanity, so we have the illuminating object-lesson of a race just emerging from a state of savagery turning to the languages of the white man for oaths that their own does not contain. Some few have been brought out to the front and partially educated, but almost invariably they return to the tent or the teepee, and the crackling wood fires, to the land of endless trails, tumbling water, and crimson sunsets.

The Indian readily falls a victim to consumption when he substitutes a poor imitation of the white man's way of living for his own; as he gropes blindly around in the maze of complications that surround him, he selects badly; and undernourished and inadequately clothed, his impoverished system absorbs the first disease that comes along.

Submission to the unalterable facts of a hard life have given the Indian a subdued mien, which his bold and vigorous features belie, quite out of keeping with his fierce and tireless energy when roused. He is the freeman of a vast continent, the First American. Innovation intrudes itself all about him, but he changes not. To those who undertake his regeneration he listens gravely and attentively, whilst retaining his own opinion; inflexible as the changeless courses of Nature which flow around him. If the Indian accepts one or another of the white man's various religions, he does so with reservations. He fails to see what lasting benefit can be derived from a gospel of love and peace, the adherents to the many sects of which are ready to fly at one another's throats over a discussion as to which is the shortest road to hell. An Algonquin once innocently asked me what did I suppose the white man had done in the past that he was unable to approach his God save through an interpreter?

He is Catholic or Protestant with cheerful impartiality, according to whichever minister gets to him first, practising the required rites at intervals, in public, and is easily persuaded to give sums of money for the building of churches. For he is a simple man, he thinks there may be something in this hell business after all, and he, with his bush experience, takes nothing for granted and likes to play safe. Yet he retains his own views, and secretly communes with his omnipresent deity, and propitiates his evil spirit, whilst the white man, too, often works for his own particular devil quite cheerfully, and at times with enthusiasm. I once lived in a small town where the Indians hunting to the north of the railroad track were Protestants and those to the south of it were Catholics; a matter of geography. I remember, too, a Cree Indian, well advanced and able to speak good English, although unable to write, who dictated to me a letter addressed to a Protestant minister in which he reminded the churchman of a promise to help in case of need. The need had now arisen, and the Cree asked for the loan of a hundred dollars, or some such trifling sum, I forget exactly, and to intimidate the good parson into granting his request, he threatened, in the event of a refusal, to turn Catholic.

Under the white man's scheme of existence the Indian is asked to forget his language, his simple conception of the Great Spirit, and his few remaining customs, which if it were demanded of the Hindus, the Boers, the Irish or the French-Canadians, would without doubt cause a rebellion.

And as he sits and glooms beneath the arches of the forest before his little smoky fires, he coughs his hacking cough and stares dumbly out into the dancing shadows, wondering, now that his spirits are forbidden him, why the white man's God that dispossessed them does not fulfil the oft-repeated promise of the missions. Yet their loyalty is such that they recognize no Provincial authority, but look to Ottawa, the seat of Dominion Government, as directly representing the King, who to them is no Royal personage, but Gitche Okima, literally the Great Chief, a father who cannot fail them.

Since the war I have attended councils where no white men were present, the opening ceremony of which was to place on floor the Union Jack, the assembly seating themselves in a circle around it, and each speaker advanced to the edge of the flag and there had his say.

Very recently I listened to an altercation between a band of Indians and an ecclesiastic who had lowered the dignity of his Church, and entirely lost the confidence of his flock by his extortionate methods of retailing high-priced salvation. During the discussion the "Black Robe" stated that the British Government had nothing to do with the Indians, and that they were directly responsible to the Church for any benefits they had received, including the introduction of moose and beaver into the country. And an old chief arose, and speaking for his assembled people, said with grave emphasis:

"When King George tells us that, we will believe it!"

And no matter how pious, earnest and sincere a man of God may undertake the task, it will take years of patient labour and devotion to eradicate the effect of this untimely speech on a people to whose minds a statement once made can in no wise be withdrawn.

☙ ☙ ☙

THE OJIBWAYS ARE PROBABLY THE MOST NUMEROUS OF THE tribes that roam the vast Hinterland north of the fifty-first parallel; and regardless of wars, rumours of wars, and the rise and fall of nations, oblivious of the price of eggs, champagne, and razor blades, they wander the length and breadth of the land, which, with the one proviso of game being in plenty, is at once to them a kingdom and a paradise. They overcome with apparent ease the almost insuperable difficulties incidental to a life in this land of violent struggle for existence. By a process of elimination, the result of many generations of experience, they have arrived at a system of economy of effort, a reserving of power for emergencies, and an almost infallible skill in the detection of the weak points in Nature's armour, that makes for the highest degree of efficiency.

Gaunt Crees, in lesser numbers, hollow-cheeked, high-shouldered fellows, skilled in the art of speed, ranged this region with burning ambition and distance-devouring stride. The light wiry Ojibway, with his crew of good and evil spirits, his omens, and his portents continually dogging his footsteps, packed unbelievable loads over unthinkable trails or no trails at all, and insinuated himself by devious ways into the most inaccessible fastnesses. Then came the white man, cheerful, humorous, undismayed by gods, devils or distance; working mightily, hacking his way through by main force where the Indian sidled past with scarcely a trace, pushing onward by sheer grit and bulldog courage.

Subdued by no consideration of the passage here before him of the wise and mighty men of former generations, there being in his case none, he forged ahead and lugged the outfit along. And if his lack of skill in the discovery of game left the larder kind of low at times, he starved like the gentleman he was, and dared the wilderness to beat him. And always he left behind permanent works; laboriously hewn trails, log cabins, small clearances and often large burns, while his russet-skinned, sloe-eyed contemporaries with their easy swing and resilient methods, looked askance at his ruinous progress, and wished him evil. And they retired unobtrusively before him to where as yet, for a little time, the enchanted glades were not disfigured by unsightly stumps, nor the whispering echoes rudely awakened by the crash of falling timber, and other unseemly uproar. The passage of the paleface through his ancestral territories is, to the Indian, in effect, what the arrival of the German Army would have been to a conquered England. To them his progress is marked by a devastation comparable only with that left in the wake of a plague in a crowded metropolis.

His coming changed the short springy carpet of buffalo-grass that covered the prairie into a tangle of coarse wild hay, shoulder high. The groves of the forest became dismal clearances of burnt and blackened skeleton trees, and the jewelled lakes were dammed and transformed into bodies of unclean water, bordered by partly submerged rampikes, and unsightly heaps of dead trees, where, in the event of a sudden storm, landing was dangerous if not impossible. Fish died in the pollution, and game of all kinds migrated to other regions.

For the Indian the woods are peopled with spirits, voices, and mysterious influences. To him the Spirit of the North, a brooding, sullen destroyer who glooms over the land like a shadow of death, is very real. How this destructive demon retains his supremacy over the forces of nature in face of the Indian's ever-present God, to whom he can apply at a moment's notice, is as easily explained as is the uninterrupted prosperity enjoyed by the Satan of the white man. Certain dark ravines are mausoleums in which dwell the shades of savage ancestors. Individual trees and rocks assume a personality, and a quiet glade is the abode of some departed friend, human or animal. The ghostly flickering of the Northern Lights he calls the Dance of the Dead Men, and in the Talking Waters of a rapids he hears the voices of the Old Men of bygone days. The thunder is a bird, and the May-may-gwense, mischievous bush fairies, tangle the traveller's footsteps, spring his traps and put out his fires. Headless skeletons run shouting through the woods at night, and in some dark and swirling eddy dead men swim, at the full of the moon. The Windigo, a half-human, flesh-eating creature, scours the lake shores looking for those who sleep carelessly without a fire, and makes sleeping out in some sections a thing of horror.

Thunder Cape rears its thirteen hundred feet of impossible grandeur up out of Lake Superior, fitting bastion to the wall of seismic masonry that swells and plunges its tortuous way across the lone land to add its mass to the Great Divide, which, swinging eastward for a thousand miles and westward for a thousand more, was erected by the Red Gods to be an impregnable rampart to the jealously guarded treasure house of the north. And here beneath this solid mass of the oldest known rock sleeps Hayowentha, or as sometimes called, Hiawatha. He was the great and wise prophet of the Indians, a gentle soul who called the animals Little Brothers, worked for the betterment of mankind, and went around doing good.*

When the first white-winged vessel landed on these shores, he left his people in sorrow at their approaching doom, which they would not take means to avert, with his dogs, his beaver, and his birds, and his canoe, and entered the mighty rock, there to sleep, waking but once a year, until finally he comes forth to effect the emancipation of his people.

Every Fall he releases the Hunting Winds, and opens the Four Way Lodge, coursing for a night through the forest he tried to save, with his furred and feathered familiars, and guarded by a host of wolves. And at such times the Indians can detect in the antiphony of the song of the wolf-pack, the deeper baying of Hiawatha's hell-dogs; they can hear the muted swish of wings of ghost-birds, and across the hills echoes the clear flute-like call of phantom beaver, from wastes where never beaver was before.

And so we see the Indian cluttered up and retarded by a host of inhibitions, as he was formerly by ceremonial, so that he will put off an important trip on account of a dream, as in former days he delayed a battle to recover a few venerated bones and trinkets, or lost sight of a cause in the fulfilment of some useless vow. The Indian's God does not reside in the inaccessible heights of majestic indifference of most deities. The Indian feels his presence all his waking hours, not precisely as a god, but as an all powerful, benevolent Spirit, whose outward manifestation is the face of nature. An intimate kind of a Spirit who sends a message in the sighing of the North-west Wind, may plant a hidden motive in the action of a beast for man to profit by, or disturb the course of nature to save a life. They do not fear him, for this God jogs at their elbow, and is a friend, nor do they worship him, save through the sun, a tree, a rock, or a range of hills, which to them are the outward and visible signs of the Power that lives and breathes in all creation.

The Indian believes that his dead are not gone from him, that they live invisible, but ever-present, in selected spots, to which, in trouble, he will

*See note on p. 174.

repair and spend hours in meditation. The little girl who lost her pet beaver, as related a few pages back, begged the hunter who had killed them to show her where the bodies lay. She preserved the skulls and all the bones, hanging them, in a birch-bark box decorated with porcupine quills, in some secret resort, where she spent hours at a time, and where none were permitted to disturb her.

Great fighting chiefs of former days carried medicine pouches containing a few bits of feathers and small bones, and other apparently useless remnants, as sacred, however, in their eyes, as some religious relics are to a devout congregation.

The band of white thrown across a lake at night by the moonbeams, is, to the red man, the path that little children and small animals take when they die; the Silver Trail to the Land of Spirits. All others take the Sunset Trail.

The conception of the Indian's heaven generally held is erroneous. The Happy Hunting Ground, so called, is not a place of care-free slaughter, but a, let us hope not too mythical, region where hunting is no longer necessary, and where men and the animals live together in amity, as was supposed to be in the beginning. For the Indians were always conservationists, the first there ever were in this country. They are blamed for the existing shortage of wild life, yet when these people were the most numerous, on the arrival here of the white man, the forests and plains swarmed with game. Few Indians are left to-day, yet every period of a few years sees some interesting or valuable animal practically wiped off the map.

The Provinces of Canada have at last decided, now that some varieties of animals and timber are on the point of disappearance, to get together and try to evolve some means of preserving Canada's rapidly dwindling natural forest resources. The stable door is about to be closed, the horse having long gone. How slowly we move!

Let us hope that in this judicious and altogether praiseworthy attempt to save something from the wreckage, money will not talk as loud as it generally does when the public welfare and the interests of some branches of big business come into conflict.

There is a kindred feeling between the Indians and the animals which is hard to understand in the face of their former cruel and relentless methods of warfare; but these wars were almost always waged in the defence of those things they held most dear; their freedom, their game, and their sacred spots. Behind a masklike visage the Indian hides a disposition as emotional as that of a Latin. Men who carried dripping scalps at their belts, their bodies streaked with the blood of dead enemies, fought for the preservation of individual trees, and wept at the grave of a friend. When the real bush Indians kill they often address the body before cutting it up, and perform some little service, such as placing the head in a comfortable position or brushing snow from the dead face, whenever they pass that way. They hang up the skull of a bear and place tobacco in it, in propitiation, and if they catch any of the meat they hang the shoulder blades on a tree, first painting two black stripes on them, running parallel to show that their thoughts were not against the bear's, but with them. There is a little bird that stays around campfires, in the trees' hopping from the stem of one leaf to another, as if inspecting them; he is called the Counter of the Leaves, and must on no account be killed. All savagery, no doubt, but not more savage than a civilization that permits the continuance of bull fighting, where worn-out working horses, as a reward for their long service, are, when wounded in the unequal contest, patched up until killed by the bull—blindfolded, that they may not evade the thrust that disembowels them, their vocal chords destroyed so as not to upset by their screaming the delicate nerves of a cowardly and degenerate audience, who, elated by the knowledge that helpless dumb creatures are being tortured for their amusement, shout their brutal satisfaction. And this on the very day they set apart to worship the white man's God of mercy and love! Indians never did these things. Frightful torments they inflicted, or submitted to, according to the luck of war, but to inflict such brutalities on an animal as a pastime seemingly never occurred to them.

Indians are in tune with their surroundings, and that accounts to a large extent for their ability in the old days to detect the foreign element in the atmosphere of the woods and plains. A movement where all should be still; a disturbance of the colour scheme; a disarrangement in the set of the leaves; the frayed edge of a newly-broken stick, speak loud to the Indian's eye. They have catalogued and docketed every possible combination of shape, sound, and colour possible in their surroundings, and any deviation from these, however slight, at once strikes a dissonance, as a false note in an orchestra of many instruments is plain to the ear of a musician. An approaching change of weather affects them as it does the animals, and they readily take on the moods of Nature, rain and dull weather seeming to cast a gloom over a whole community. A change of wind they forecast quite accurately and even if sleeping the changed atmospheric conditions brought about by its turning from the South to the North awaken the older people, and they will say, "It is Keewaydin; the North Wind is blowing."

To them the North-west wind is paramount; it is the Wind of Winds; it stands for good trails and clear skies, and puts a bracing quality into the atmosphere that makes any extreme of temperature endurable. They sniff it with distended nostrils as one quaffs a refreshing drink, and inhale deeply of it, as though it were some elixir that cured all bodily ills. From it they seem to gather some sort of inspiration, for it speaks to them of that vast, lone land, down from which it sweeps, which, no matter what advances civilization may make, no one will ever know quite all about.

The red man's whole attitude towards Nature can be summed up in the words of an old man, my companion during many years of travel:

"When the wind speaks to the leaves, the Indian hears—and understands."

The singing of the wolves is not to him the dreadful sound that it is to some. The wolf and his song are as much a part of the great wilderness as the Indian himself, for they are hunters too, and suffer from cold and hunger, and travel long hard trails, as he does.

The wild frenzy of a hurrying rapids, the buffeting, whistling masses of snow whirling across the winter lakes, are to him a spectacle in which he is taking an active part, a rough but friendly contest amid surroundings with which he is familiar, and which he feels will not betray him, does he but obey the rules of the game.

With the heroic atmosphere of war removed and the Cooperesque halo of nobility dissipated by continuous propinquity, the red man loses much of his romantic appeal. But as one gets to know this strange people, with their simplicity, their silence, and their almost Oriental mysticism, other and unsuspected qualities become apparent, which compel the

admiration of even those who make much of their faults. Doggedly persevering, of an uncomplaining endurance and an infinite patience,
scrupulously honest for the most part, and possessed by a singleness of
purpose that permits no deviation from a course of action once decided
on, they are as changeless as the face of the wilderness, and as silent
almost, and much given to deep thinking, not of the future, but—fatal to
the existence of the individual or of a nation—of the past. The future
holds nothing for them, and they live in the days gone by. The Indian
stands adamant as the very hills, while the tide of progress swells around
him, and unable to melt and flow with it, he, like the beaver and the buffalo with whose history his own destiny has been so identified, will be
engulfed and swept away. And then all the heart-burnings and endless
complaints of the land-hungry over the few acres of soil that are given him
in return for the freedom of a continent, will be at an end for all time.

And it almost were better that he so should go, whilst he yet holds his
proud position of supremacy in the arts of forest lore, and retains his wild
independence and his freedom in the environment for which he is so
eminently fitted. It is better that he should follow where the adventurer
and the free trapper already point the way, to where the receding, ever
shrinking line of the Last Frontier is fading into the dimness of the past.
Better thus, than that he should be thrown into the grinding wheels of
the mill of modernity, to be spewed out a nondescript, undistinguishable
from the mediocrity that surrounds him, a reproach to the memory of a
noble race. Better to leave him, for the short time that remains to him, to
his recollections, his animals, and his elfin-haunted groves, and when the
end comes, his race will meet it as a people, with the same stoic calm with
which they met it individually when defeated in war in former times.

∾ ∾ ∾

THE OLD DAYS ARE NOT SO FAR BEHIND. THE MOST STIRRING
period in the history of the old frontier is removed from the present only
by a period frequently covered by the span of one human life. I have
talked with an old woman who remembered, for she has long joined the
great majority, the first matches introduced to her people. They were the

kind, still in use in the woods, known as eight-day matches, as on being struck they simmered along for an interminable period before finally bursting into flames. After the interesting entertainment of seeing them lit she retrieved the sticks and took them home to demonstrate the new marvel, but much to her disappointment she could not make them work.

She told me much of the ancient history of the Iroquois and remembered the war parties going out, and as a child, during a battle she hid with the rest of the children and the women in the fields of squashes and corn which the Indians maintained around their villages.

One old man of the Ojibway with the prolonged name of Neejinnekai-apeechi-geejiguk, or to make a long story short, "Both-ends-of-the-day," witnessed the Iroquois raids of 1835 or thereabouts in the Temagami region. He was a man to whom none could listen without attention, and was a living link with a past of which only too little is known. Although he died in distressing circumstances a good many years ago, I remember him well, as I last saw him; straight as an arrow and active as a young man in spite of his years, he had an unusually developed faculty for seeing in the dark, which accounts for his name, which inferred that day and night were all one to him. I recollect that he carried an alarm clock inside his shirt for a watch, and when once, at a dance, he fell asleep, some mischievous youngster set the alarm, and he created the diversion of the evening when the sudden racket within his shirt woke him up. In reality the first touch of the little urchin had awakened him, but he purposely feigned continued sleep till the alarm should go off, for he had a keen sense of humour, which Indians possess more often than they get credit for. He was also fond of the society of young children, but he once showed me some grisly relics that invested his character with quite a different aspect; and from then on there seemed to lurk behind his cheery smile at times a savage grin.

He would sit for hours outside his camp, tapping a small drum, singing ancient songs in a language no one understood; and sometimes he would lay the drum aside, and to those who had assembled to hear his songs, he would tell of things that students of Canadian history would have given much to hear; of ways and means now long forgotten; tales of the wild Nottaways in bark canoes that held a dozen men; of shaven-headed Iroquois who crept at dawn into a sleeping village and slew all within it before they could awaken. He told of a woman who having crossed a portage some distance from camp, was fishing, and whilst so engaged, saw land at the portage, canoe-load after canoe-load of Mohawk warriors, who secreted their canoes, and effacing the signs of their passage, lay hidden in deadly silence, awaiting the proper hour to strike. That she had been observed she took for granted; but she reasoned, and rightly, that the enemy would not risk killing her, as, if missing, a search for her might reveal the war-party. She decided to return to camp by way of the portage, her passport to safety being her pretended ignorance there of enemies. So this courageous and sagacious woman landed, picked up her own canoe, and walked the full length of the trail, knowing that in the dark forest on either hand, lay a hundred warriors thirsting for her blood, and that the least faltering or sign of fear would cause her instant death, and precipitate an attack on the village. Her steadiness of mien led the invaders to imagine themselves undiscovered, and she made the trip unmolested. Thus she was able to warn her people who made such good use of the hours of darkness that when at dawn the Iroquois made their attack they found only an empty village.

Judging by some of the old man's narratives, apparently these far-famed warriors were not as uniformly successful as we have been led to believe. It appears that they made a practice of taking along a captive as a guide in his own territory, knocking him on the head when his sphere of usefulness was ended, and taking another in the new district. These conscripted guides sometimes put their knowledge of the country to a good account, as on the occasion when a large canoe, loaded with warriors, arrived near the head of a falls, which was hidden from sight by a curve. The guides, there were two of them in this case, informed their captors that this was a rapids that could be run by those who were acquainted with the channel, and they took the steering positions, formulating, as they did so, a plan, with swift mutterings in their own language, unheard in the roar of the falls. The water ran dark and swift between high rock walls, except at one spot where there was a line of boulders reaching from the shore out into the channel. Increasing the speed of the canoes as much as possible, the Ojibways jumped off the now racing craft as it passed the stepping stones, and the remainder of the crew, struggling desperately to stem the current, were swept over the falls. Those that did not drown were killed with stones by their erstwhile guides, who had raced over the portage with that end in view. And great was the glory thereof. The incident obtained for that place the name of Iroquois Falls, which it retains to this day.

During the winter a band of them, arriving back in camp after an arduous and fruitless man-hunt, fatigued by the use of snowshoes unsuited to conditions so far North, asked their guide, a woman, what steps her people took to relieve the cramps that afflicted their legs after such heavy snowshoeing. She informed them that the method generally adopted was to lie with their legs elevated, with the ankles on cross-bars, feet towards the fire. This they did. Exhausted, they fell asleep. The woman wetted and stretched some rawhide thongs, lightly bound their ankles to the bars, and put on a good fire. Soon the thongs dried and shrunk; holding them with a grip like iron, and she killed them all before they could extricate themselves. Taking all the provision she needed, this very able woman proceeded to another war party she knew to be in the vicinity, as vicinities go in that country, a matter of fifty miles or so, and gave herself up as a prisoner. She soon gained the confidence of her captors, and once, coming home tired, they committed the indiscretion of falling asleep in her presence. She thereupon burnt all the snowshoes except one pair, on which she escaped, leaving them as much marooned in six feet of snow as any crew of shipwrecked sailors on a desert island could be, and they were later found and killed by a jubilant band of Algonquins.

The descendants of these same Iroquois today are living near Montreal, and are staging a comeback, reviving their ancient customs, dress and dances, and this movement is becoming widespread. In the West, blanketted, bonnetted warriors are no longer an uncommon sight, college graduates though some of them may be; and big Indian conventions are being held, to which all the tribes send delegates, where the English language is not permitted, none but tribal dress is worn, and at which the long forbidden Sun Dance is now permitted, minus the self-torturing feature. Always the most interesting thing to me at these revivals is the sight of the old men with their long braided hair, in some cases white with the passage of three-quarters of a century, dressed in the regalia that was at one time the only garb they knew, and wearing war-bonnets that they earned, when each feather represented the accomplishment of some deed of courage, or of skill. They may not be able to compete with the younger men in their supple posturings, but they are living for a while once more the old life that has so long been taken away from them. And I often wonder what stirring memories, and perchance what melancholy recollections of the past, are awakened behind those inscrutable old eyes and wrinkled faces, as they raise their quavering voices in the "Buffalo Song" in a land of cattle, or tread, in mimic wardance, measures to which they stepped in deadly earnest half a century ago.

℘℘℘

MANY YEARS AGO I CAST IN MY LOT WITH THAT NATION known under the various appellations of Chippeways, Algonquins, Londucks, and Ojibways. A blood-brother proved and sworn, by moose-head feast, wordless chant, and ancient ritual was I named before a gaily decorated and attentive concourse, when Ne-ganik-abo, "Man-that-stands-ahead," whom none living remember as a young man, danced the conjurors' dance beneath the spruce trees, before an open fire, danced the ancient steps to the throb of drums, the wailing of reed pipes, and the rhymmical skirring of turtle shell rattles; danced alone before a sacred bear-skull set beneath a painted rawhide shield, whose bizarre device might have graced the tomb of some long-dead Pharaoh. And as the chanting rose and fell in endless reiteration, the flitting shadows of his weird contortions danced a witches' dance between the serried tree-trunks. The smoke hung in a white pall short of the spreading limbs of the towering trees, and with a hundred pairs of beady eyes upon me, I stepped out beneath it when called on. And not one feral visage relaxed in recognition, as, absorbed in the mystery of their ritual they intoned the almost forgotten cadences.

"Hi-Heeh, Hi-Heh, Ho! Hi-Heh, Hi-Heh, Ha! Hi-Hey, Hi-Hey, Ho! Hi-Ho, Hi-Ho, Ha!" and on and on in endless repetition, until the monotony of the sounds had the same effect on the mind that the unvarying and measured markings of a snake have on the eye. The sensation of stepping into the motionless ring was that of suddenly entering a temple devoted to the worship of some pagan deity, where the walls were lined with images cast in bronze; and there I proudly received the name they had devised, which the old man now bestowed upon me.

At that the drums changed their rhythm and the whole assemblage, hitherto so still, commenced to move with a concerted swaying, rocking motion, in time to the thunder of the drums, and the circle commenced to revolve about me. The chant broke into a series of rapidly ascending minor notes, which dropped from the climax to the hollow, prolonged hoot of the owl whose name I now bore.

"Hoh-hoh, hoh-hooooooo! Hoh-hoh, hoh-hoooooo!" The weird cries trailed off into the empty halls of the forest, while faster and faster grew the dance before the bear skull; and the drummers, and those who played the rattles, and the circle round about, moved in unison to the constantly accelerating tempo that the old man gave them, till the swift thudding of many feet made a thunder of its own, and the glade became a whirling mass of colour; and ever the chant grew louder, until with a long-drawn out quavering yell, "Ahi, yah-ah-ah-ah-ah," all movement ceased, and like the dropping of a curtain, silence fell.

This band is sadly reduced. The lonely graves beneath the giant red pines are more numerous to-day; they are a fading people. Not long from now will come one sunset, their last; far from the graves of their fathers they are awaiting with stolid calm what, to them, is the inevitable. To leave them, to stand from under, to desert the sinking ship, were a craven act, unthinkable. All of whatsoever I may know of the way of the wild they have taught me.

Neganikabo, my mentor, my kindly instructor, my companion in untold hardship and nameless tribulation, has the magic invisible veil of mystery from across the face of the forest, that I might learn its uttermost secrets, and has laid open before me the book of Nature for me to read; and in my bungling way I have profited by his lessons, but the half is not yet done. I have followed him when snowshoes sank into the soft snow halfway to the knee, mile after weary mile, to sleep at night behind a square of canvas; this for five days and nights, it snowing steadily most of the time, and with nothing to eat but strips of dried moose-meat, and teas made from boiled leaves of the Labrador sage. I have negotiated dangerous rapids under his tuition, when at each run, after the irrevocable step of entering, I doubted much that I would make the foot alive. He has led me many hours of travel with birch bark flares at night, and more than once entire nights in an unknown country without them. Once, soon after the freeze-up, and with the ice in bad condition, we returned late in the evening to our sahaagan,* to be greeted by a heap of charred fragments, and bare poles on which small portions of canvas were still smouldering.

Our fire, which we supposed we had extinguished, had worked under the peaty forest soil, and sprung up in the centre of the camp, destroying every last ounce of provisions, the blankets, and the shelter itself. Greatest of our losses was that of several mink and a red fox, the latter not entirely destroyed, but now scorched black; my first black fox, and, I might add, my last. As a storm threatened the old man started on the day and a half's journey to the village in the darkness, over ice that few would have attempted by daylight, judging it by the sound only, singing in bad spots in an undertone, a song suitable to the conditions; such as "I see the trail like a thread, I see it, I see it," or "I feel water close, I feel water." Meanwhile all I could see was the surrounding blackness, and the only thing I felt was a sinking sensation in the pit of my stomach when the tap of his pole indicated bad ice.

I have seen him, in the spring of the year, when all ice is treacherous, after half a day of juggling between canoe, sleigh, and snowshoes, walk out on to the next lake, that by all the law should have been as bad as the last one, and glancing casually across it say:

"This ice is good."

His faculties of observation, as with most Indians, were very keen; nothing seemed to escape him. He could detect game invisible to me, yet his gaze was not piercing, rather it was comprehensive, all-embracing, effortless as is the eye of a camera, registering every detail in a moment of time. He often made fire with bow and spindle, habitually carried flint and steel, and seemed to have knowledge of the speech of some animals, calling them almost at will in the right season. He carried a beaded pouch

*Semi-circular canvas shelter.

which contained, among other trinkets, some small beaver bones. In spite of the unprecedented advances in latter years of the price of beaver skins, on account of some belief he held he would not kill these animals, even when in want; and he would stand at times outside their lodges, seeming to converse with them. Not a good shot with firearms, yet he would get so close to his quarry without their knowledge, that an old muzzle-loading beaver-gun (so called from the method of purchase) fulfilled all his requirements for game of all sizes, partridges included. For your Indian, in common with the white hunter, shoots his birds sitting; but he uses a bullet, and the mark is its head, a sporting enough proposition for a man with an empty belly. He showed me, in the course of years, did I but have the head to hold it all, what a man may learn in a long life of observation and applied experience.

He had his humorous occasions too. With a party of moose-hunters we were standing on the abrupt edge of a hill, the face of which had fallen away and lay in a mass of broken fragments at the foot, crowned with a few small jackpines, shoulder high. Across the valley was a ridge crested with a row of immense white pines, seedlings, perhaps, in the days when the Plymouth Brethren dodged flights of arrows on their way to church. One of the tourists had shown great curiosity with regard to the venerable guide, and had pestered me with endless questions regarding him. The old man knew no English but I think he got the gist of the conversation, for at last, on being asked his age, he pointed across to the big pines.

"Tell that man," he said, "that when I was a boy those trees were so small that I could reach out and shake them—so!" and grasping one of the jackpine saplings he shook it violently back and forth.

ℭℭℭ

HE WHO LANDS HIS CANOE AT A SEMI-PERMANENT INDIAN village at any hour after daylight will find few, if any, of the men at home. At the first sign of dawn the hunters are away, for more game may be taken in the two hours after the break of day than in all the rest of the twenty-four together.

Returning at noon the visitor is very apt to find the inhabitants half-sleeping, and the camp basking silently in the sunlight without a sign of life; save perhaps some old woman who sits smoking and dreaming by the slowly smouldering fire; and he will hear no sound save the drowsy hum of insects and the metallic shrilling of the cicadas* in the tree-tops. For this is the hour of rest. Quite often these people have done half a day's work when the rest of the world was in bed, and when an Indian is not actually engaged in some branch of his strenuous occupation, he relaxes utterly and completely. The women do all the camp work, and this is what no doubt gives rise to the legend of Indian laziness. Did a man lay his hand to the maintenance of camp, once it is erected, he would be laughed out of countenance by his womenfolk and sent about his business.

These villages are all movable, for this is a nomadic people. Rarely do they build cabins save in the vicinity of a trading post. Tents, wind-breaks and birch-bark shelters are scattered amongst the growth of umbrella-toped jack-pines, on a low point midway of a lake set deep into an amphitheatre of emerald hills. Here and there a tall teepee, its upper half dyed a deep umber by the smoke of years, looms above its lesser brethren. On the foreshore a variety of canoes are drawn up, the canvas-covered type predominating, but some of them are of birch-bark, dyed red with alder sap, with black strips of gum at the seams. And in the background is the inevitable dark, towering wall of evergreen forest.

Hudson Bay blankets, half an inch thick, and green, blue, black, red or white, according to the owner's taste, hanging out on poles to air before each lodge, give a brilliant note of colour. Women in voluminous plaid dresses and multicoloured head shawls, move from tent to tent, sewing, baking endless bannocks, or working everlastingly at half-tanned hides. In an open space near the centre of the village is standing a rack of poles, ten feet long and six high, festooned with numerous strips of moose-meat, and on it, split open from the back, hangs a giant sturgeon the length of a man. Beneath this rack a long slow fire is burning, the cool smoke hovering in amongst the meat and fish, adding to it a savour and a zest that no bottled condiment can impart. Men, some with clipped heads, others bobbed, older men with long black braids, gather around this central

*This insect resembles an enormous house-fly about two inches long, with the wings obliquely down the body. It sucks the sap of trees.

place, whittling out muskrat stretchers* with crooked-knives, mending nets, sitting around and smoking, or just sitting around. Half-naked children play in the dust with half-tame huskies; a crow, tied by the leg with a length of thong to a cross pole, squaking discordantly at intervals.

Two tumbling bear cubs run loose; one, his face covered with flour, chased by an enraged woman with a cudgel; a month-old wolf, his nature already asserting itself, creeps up on a cat, twice his size, which lies sleeping, its head in the shade of a small square of birch-bark it has found; for so do even domestic animals adapt themselves to this manner of life and turn opportunist; next winter some of the dogs will feign a limp, or unaccountably fall sick, on being hitched up for the first trip.

As the sun climbs down towards the rim of hills the men bestir themselves, and at intervals, in parties of two, or singly, take their guns and light axes, slip down on noiseless moccasined feet to the shore, and paddle silently away, Some will be back at dark, others at midnight; a few have taken small neat packs and will be gone several days. No goodbyes have been said, no stir has taken place; they just steal away as the spirit moves them; when one turns to speak they are not there; that is all.

As the day falls, smudges are lit to the windward, a protection from the swarms of mosquitoes that now descend on the camp, and volumes of smoke envelope the point through which the tents are dimly visible. Tiny beavers are brought down to the lake for their daily swim, whilst young boys stand guard with clubs to keep the dogs away, or take canoes and herd the stragglers in, for there are voracious pike of immense size in these waters that would make short work of a month-old kit. Nets are set, everything eatable, and many things not considered to be so, are hung up out of reach of the dogs, and the business of the day is ended. Little, twinkling fires spring to life and the pale illumination of tallow dips within the lodges gives the village from the distance the appearance of a gathering of fireflies. And on the canvas wall the shadows of those within depict their every movement, and through them every sound escapes, so that one's neighbour's doings are so obvious, and his conversation so audible, as to be no longer intriguing. The same principle that is the doom of prudery and prohibition, in this case ensures a privacy that four stone walls do not always give.

*Frames for stretching hides.

Then some morning at daybreak the whole village is in motion. Blankets are folded and teepees pulled down, fires are extinguished with countless pails of water. Children, now fully dressed, commence carrying down the smaller bundles to the canoes. The tenting place has become monotonous; the fish have moved to deeper water, also a woman heard a squirrel chattering during the night; a bad omen. So the camp is to be moved.

The dogs, viewing the preparations with disfavour, howl dolorously, for to them this means a long and arduous journey around the edge of the lake to the next stop, whilst their masters sit at ease in the smooth-running canoes. For Indians, unless on a flying trip, travel within easy reach of the shore line, as offering better observation of the movements of game; and this is a country of sudden and violent tempests, a consideration of some account, with women and children aboard. Should the shore deviate too far from the line of travel, room will be made, temporarily, for the dogs.

There is no unseemly haste in this breaking of camp. Every individual has his or her allotted task; not a move is wasted. Quietly, smoothly, without bustle or confusion, the canoes are loaded, and in little more than an hour from the time of rising nothing remains of a village of perhaps ten or fifteen families, save the damp steam rising from deluged fires and the racks of bare poles, piled clear of the ground for future use.

The scene at a portage is a lively one. Colourful as a band of gypsies, men, women and children are strung out over the trail, decked with inordinate loads of every imaginable description. Men with a hundred pounds of flour and a tin stove take a canoe for a binder; others take from two hundred pounds up, of solid weight. Women carry tents and huge rolls of blankets with apparent ease, their hands filled with light but irksome utensils. The squaws take their share of the labour as a matter of course, and to suggest to them that packing is no job for a woman would be to meet with instant ridicule.

Children carry their own packs with miniature tump lines, taking their work as seriously as do their elders. Some women carry infants on their backs, laced on to flat padded boards fitted with an outring in such a manner that the child is protected in case of a fall, from which dangles a wooden home-made doll or other simple toy. These mothers carry no other load, but to them, having their hands free, is delegated the difficult and diplomatic task of herding, leading and hazing along the trail those of the multifarious pets that cannot be carried in bags or boxes, assisted by the children. I have seen cats perched contentedly on top of a roll of bedding, stealing a ride, crows carried on poles like banners, full-grown beaver led on a chain, tiny bears running loose, not daring to leave the outfit, and once a young girl with an owl laced tightly into a baby's cradle, the poor creature being supposedly highly honoured.

The younger men vie with one another in tests of speed and endurance, while the seasoned veterans move along with measured step and a smooth effortless progression that never falters or changes. These people are considered to be half-savage, which probably they are, yet contrast their expenditure of effort on behalf of the young of wild animals that fall into their hands, with the behaviour of a family of civilized Indians, who bought a bear cub from some of their more primitive brethren, expecting to sell it at a high figure to tourists. Failing in this, they had no more use for it, and unwilling to let it go, as it had cost them money, they neglected the poor little creature, and it died of thirst chained to a tree within a few feet of the lake shore.

A large percentage of the Indians of mixed blood who live near the railroad (this does not include those bush Indians who of necessity trade at railroad posts) are rascals; their native cunning in the chase is diverted into improper channels, and they become merely sly and lazy. They lack the dignity, the honesty, and the mental stability of the genuine forest dwellers, whose reputation as a race has suffered much at the hands of this type.

Indian winter camps in the Keewaydin district differ little from their summer villages. They erect their habitations in more sheltered places, but tents and wigwams are the only shelters, the former warmed by small tin stoves that give a surprising heat, and the latter by an open fire inside, with sometimes the stove as well. The lodges are banked high with snow and are a good deal warmer than would be supposed. But once the stove dies it is only a matter of a few minutes till the cold swoops down like a descending scimitar of chilled steel, down through the flimsy canvas, on into the ground beneath the sleepers, freezing it solid as a rock, searching out every nook and cranny in the weak defences, petrifying everything.

And over the camp hangs a mist of hoar frost, whilst the wolves beyond the ridges bay the moon, and the trees crack with reports like gunshots in the iron grip of ninety degrees of frost. Although permanent for the period of deep snow, the entire camp may be loaded on toboggans and moved at an hour's notice. Stretched out in file across the surface of frozen lakes, half hidden by drifting snow, these winter caravans travel sometimes hundreds of miles. They literally march, these people, and almost always in step, each stepping between the tracks of his predecessor, an action which in time becomes second nature, so that the trail, by the packing of many snowshoes, becomes a solid springy road, on which the dogs are able to put forth their best efforts. And in the van, leading a procession perhaps a quarter of a mile in length, are the trail breakers, often young girls and boys of from twelve years of age up. This seems like cruelty, but it is no colder at the head of the caravan than at the rear, and these children pass lightly over the snow without hardship to themselves, packing the trail; and the entire outfit travels easily behind them, where otherwise men would have to take turns to break a trail a foot in depth, at the rate of a mile an hour. These youngsters take a pride in their work and contest hotly for the leadership, a coveted honour.

Every night camp must be made in any weather. A heavy carpet of spruce or balsam boughs supports the tents and provides a floor on the surface of several feet of snow; stoves are quickly put up, wood cut and the cooking done, and the dogs, once fed, dig themselves in for the night. The various tasks are all performed with the speed and efficiency of long practice; and in a remarkably short space of time the camp assumes an appearance of permanence and comfort; only, in the morning, to be taken down and loaded up for the next leg of a journey that is never quite completed, summer or winter.

To follow these restless people in their ceaseless wanderings, is to spend long weeks of terrific labour, alternating with lazy days of basking in the sun, and games, and dancing. Periods of want are offset by days and nights of feasting. I have seen times when small birds and squirrels were snared for their meat, dogs were eaten as they died of hunger, and wailing children cried for the food their starving mothers could not give. And on a day a lucky hunter found a herd of moose, and pinched faces became broad with smiles, and people ate, and ate, till they could eat no more, a herd of brown youngsters with laughing shoe-button eyes, sat around a fire of their own, each with his broiled moose-rib, hands and faces well smeared with grease. Juicy steaks were impaled on sticks planted at an angle before the fires, and when they had sizzled awhile, one ate the meat with his fingers, and wiped his hands on the stick.

Generally the more primitive Indian camps are well regulated and the housekeeping, although often untidy, is clean, but in cases of this kind, aboriginal standards are the only ones followed for the time being, and everybody is happy—until the next time. In these communities, provision, on becoming short, becomes common property, as meat is at any time. No one claims a kill as his own exclusively, each family sending a representative to collect their share and those unable to leave have it brought to them. Each also takes his turn to supply, and on this account, another young fellow and myself, our turn arriving, undertook to do our bit.

It was the time of first ice, and the travelling was of the best, with less than six inches of snow. We took two days' provisions, intending to return by a short-cut the third day. And here is where the mice and men, so often mentioned, sustained their well-known reputation. We were poor prophets. The second night it turned soft, and there was an unprecedented snowfall of at least two feet. The lakes slushed up and the bush was clogged with wet snow. We had brought no snowshoes, we had not killed a moose, we had nothing to eat save the remains of our last meal, and were at least twenty miles from the village; an interesting problem any way you look at it. It took us four days and a half to get back, during which time we ate one partridge and two squirrels. These last we ate raw in order to get all there was in them. Once we found a thin strip of dried moose-meat hanging on a rack at an old camp ground; it was no bigger than your thumb, and must have been old enough to vote, being much like a stick of wood.

We commenced to become weak, taking long rests which ate into our time, and when it was necessary to cross over a log larger than common, we sat on it and looked at one another for long periods. I thought frequently of the squirrel skins which we had thrown away; apart from the hair there had been nothing wrong with them. We were much tempted to commit the indiscretion of eating snow, and sometimes chewed the scrapings off the inside bark of yellow birch. This, however, induced thirst, and drinking ice-water under these conditions is sometimes fatal. In the course of our wanderings we arrived at a spot where a moose had been killed that Fall, and we dug the bones out of the snow, scorched them for a while on a fire, broke them open, and devoured the rotten marrow with relish.

These exercises occupied four days. At noon on the next day we met a rescue party supplied with snowshoes, but we were unable to use them, as we were now deathly sick from our last meal, and had to ride the dog teams. But for an old woman who understood the use of herbal medicines we should probably have died. I can never be caught in precisely the same predicament again, as since that experience I keep my snowshoes within reach whilst there is ice on the lake.

But the pitfalls are many and various. Violent and unseasonable changes of weather may catch unprepared those who live precariously on the edge of things, and inflict severe hardship; and even Indians, who have made the weather a separate study, are not altogether immune.

Five canoes of us, all heavily laden, were caught on a river that was rapidly freezing up, and thinking to beat out the ice, we made no camp, but continued on our journey in the darkness, until, unable to break ice any further we were actually frozen in near the shore. We had to chop the canoes out by firelight, make a cache, and wait for daylight. This was only the middle of October, and one of the party froze the ends of all the fingers of one hand.

The next day, taking what we could carry, we started overland on a twenty-five mile journey to our destination, where we had camps already built, walking on good ice all of the last day. On our arrival we commenced setting traps, intending to return with toboggans, at the first snow, for our goods. We had worked only a couple of days, when the unnatural conditions changed, the ice went out with heavy rain, and we were well marooned on a large island, on which the camps were situated, with but little food and no canoes.

We stayed here for three weeks living mostly on fish, until the second and permanent freeze-up released us, when we drew in our huge loads by relays, losing the early Fall hunt in the process.

෮෮෮

AS IS COMMON WITH ALL SAVAGE PEOPLES, AND SOME NOT SO
savage, there was prevalent amongst the Indians, not so long ago, the
practice of the arts of the medicine-man, or conjuror, and even to-day
every Indian community has at least one exponent of the black arts.
Undoubtedly most of these wizards are nothing more than quacks and
charlatans who, working on the credulity of their less well-informed
tribesmen, have indulged a taste for the occult with attendant increase in
prestige. This exploitation of the ignorant is common enough in the
administration of most of the many religions with which man has seen fit
to cloud his clear perception of things infinite; but in the case of the
Indian these practices have no bearing on religion, and the medicine-
man is simply a magician. In most cases he is merely tolerated on the off-
chance that there may be something in it, since nobody wants to be
caught with his boots off, yet amongst the Indian mystics are men who
sincerely believe in their own powers; and powers some of them have
without a doubt over and above those of common men.

I have seen some startling performances, but believe that they all
come under the heading of either sleight-of-hand, or hypnotism, or perhaps in some instances, telepathy. In the first place the Indian is by the
nature of his environment psychic and imaginative to the last degree.
The ceaseless and monotonous beating of a drum for hours, which precedes nearly all these seances, exercises an influence on him which leaves
him in a very receptive condition for the hypnotic influence. I was present at a gathering where an old medicine-man caused a handkerchief to
be hidden, by a stranger, at a distance but in his presence. Taking from the
crowd a youth of his own race, he placed both hands on the lad's shoulders and gazed steadily into his eyes perhaps for a minute. At this point
the beating of a drum, which had continued without a break for at least
an hour, ceased. On being released the young Indian walked out of sight
as though dazed, but without hesitation, soon returning with the handkerchief. This was repeated with several different articles in various hiding places, with only one failure.

Collusion between the conjuror and the stranger was impossible, as the former could speak no English, and the latter was a tourist passing by on a trip. No word passed the old man's lips, but the boy seemed to fall very easily under his influence, and was no doubt a familiar subject.

On another occasion, before a small but sceptical assemblage, a noted conjuror sat facing a disc of stretched rawhide, distant from him about ten paces. I assisted in hanging immediately in front of the disc, about a foot apart, three tanned moose hides, which suspended loosely from a beam, formed a target that was almost bullet-proof. Yet before the eyes of all, this man took a shaftless bone arrowhead, and with a quick flirt of his hand drove it apparently through the hides. On pulling them aside the arrowhead was seen to be imbedded in the disc, and no hole or other mark could be discerned on the skins. None present were able to detect the trick, and it was suggested that the performance had been an example of group hypnotism, of which, in that case, I was one of the victims together with several highly mystified tourists.

There have been cases where a conjuror has put a curse on one who has offended him, such as bad luck in hunting, accidental maiming with an axe or knife, sickness, or even death. Fear of the supposed power, causing a lack of confidence in his ability to break the spell cast on him, has caused many a victim unconsciously to bring about his own undoing, and so fulfil the curse. The hypnotic power of a drum at a certain pitch of sound, beaten regularly and without intermission, is not generally known. Some of these magicians claim the uncanny ability of calling to them by this means those who are far out of earshot of the sound. It is not beyond the realms of possibility, perhaps, that reduction to a clairvoyant or psychic condition—if such a condition exists—by voluntary starvation, the monotonous beat of the drum, and continuous mental concentration on the one idea over a period of thirty hours or more, may enable a strong-willed man to project his thoughts through space, forcing his ego in waves across the ether, willing himself to be felt hour after hour, until the object of these intense mental efforts to be heard feels an influence, he knows not what, that inevitably draws him to a certain spot.

An experience, yet very fresh in my mind, befell me not long since, and, although not offered as a proof of these things, yet could be of interest to those who make a study of telepathy or thought transference, and might give food for thought to others. My opinion in the matter is of no value, and the occurrence could easily be accounted a coincidence, or the result of a reaction to nostalgia. It was in autumn, a season when everyone is more of less tempted to indulge in reflection and recollection, and I was taking a few days of relaxation between the finish of a strenuous summer's exploration in search of a hunting-ground, and the commencement of the Fall trip in with my supplies. I passed the peaceful lazy days of Indian Summer gathering up energy for the trials to come, mostly sitting before my tent, smoking and thinking, as our custom is when idle. Meanwhile I found my mind constantly dwelling on the scenes of my younger days, and particularly on a certain lake, now widely known for the picturesque beauty of its shores. More and more frequently my thoughts reverted to the well-remembered scene, until I thought of little else in my waking hours, and sleeping, dreamed of it. Recollections crowded down upon me, and there rose vividly and persistently before my mind the image of my wise and ancient companion of former days, whom I should never see again. It was on those waters that I had embarked on the restless wandering life of a trapper, and a feeling akin to homesickness, which I found myself unable to conquer, at last decided me to visit that place once more, although I knew the inhabitants had long ago departed. Little more than a day's travel by canoe brought me to the last portage, which comes out on to the lake I sought at the deserted camping-ground.

As I neared the end of the carry I became conscious of some peculiar quality in the silence, which I felt but could not define. Coming out onto the open lake shore and my hearing no longer impeded by the canoe, I knew this for the measured, persistent throbbing of an Indian drum, which, whilst distant, seemed to come from no particular direction. The sound brought back a flood of reminiscences of long-departed days amongst the simple, kindly people of my adoption, of whom no recent sign remained, though the graveyard showed a pitiful increase.

Here, under these very trees I had feasted, and gamed, and danced with those of whom many now rested in that silent grove, with its miniature birch-bark huts which had contained food, and its remnants of personal belongings, laid in bark receptacles by trusting friends, for use on the journey to the Other Side.

Only the teepee and tent poles, rotten and fallen long since, and the shallow moss-grown depressions left by the fires of many years, marked the site of what had once been a populous village of human souls. And as I gazed on the familiar scene, my feelings reflected the mood of the place, which seemed immersed in a brooding melancholy.

The leasing of the surrounding waters to a fishing concern, resulting in a shortage of the food supply of the Indian, and the proximity of a new railroad with its attendant horde of amateur trappers, leaving in their wake a ravished area of poison and broken beaver-dams, had driven the occupants of the glade from their ancestral home forever. I thought of my old associate, and what his feelings would be were he alive to see the ruin and decay that had encompassed his little band; he whose rigid adherence to the customs of his race had long kept his people from that contamination of the wilderness and its dwellers, which seems to be, only too often, inherent in the advance of civilization in its earlier stages. A feeling of sadness pervaded me, and I began to wish I had not come.

I had felt influenced in some unaccountable way to make this pilgrimage, and, now, having arrived, I decided to make the best of it, and proceeded to make fire and prepare my shelter for the night. And as I worked the monotonous beat of the drum, at first merging itself into the scheme of things, as does the ticking of a clock in a silent room, so as to be at times unnoticed, became insistent, obtruding itself on my senses, weaving a spell about me, until I found myself moving about my various tasks in time to it. During the still night the sound, now fainter, now louder, never ceasing with its changeless rhythm, dominated my consciousness, sleeping and waking, and the figments of my half-formed dreams danced in the darkness to its tune.

Unable to rest I went down and sat by the water's edge. The ceaseless hypnotic throbbing permeated the air with its magic of a bygone day, and in the amphitheatre of the dusky hills that rimmed the lake, seemed to sound a chord, to which the tympans of Nature vibrated, to strike a master note which, if prolonged enough, could rock the fabric of the wilderness to its foundations. I felt as one must who is becoming hypnotized. Education and the influences of civilization slipped from me like a discarded garment, as the atavistic syncopated pulsing thrilled me, arousing half-forgotten instincts, and stirring my blood to be dead. Back down the years the memories trooped upon me, effacing the veneer of semi-culture I had acquired; memories of barbarous nights when the lines of half-naked dancers postured and side-stepped through the figures of the Wabeno, between the long fires; bowed, and writhed, and stamped as they chanted a chorus that was old before the white man came, to the thudding of one-sided drums, the thin wailing of reed whistles, the piping of hollow wing-bones of eagles, and the clinking rattle of dried deer-hoofs. High-pitched yells and ululations rang sharply against the roof of the forest, and long quavering whoops trailed off into the recesses of the mountains, echoing back and forth across the empty hills in fading repetitions; dying away at times to the whisper of wind through the dry grasses of the fenlands, swelling again to a rhythmic uproar; continuing without intermission, until after two nights and a day the drums were stilled; and then the feasts of moose-meat—

Late the next day the sound abruptly ceased, and towards evening a bark canoe drifted gently ashore at the landing-place, and with a guttural exclamation of greeting there rose before me my friend of many days— Ne-ganik-abo, Stands First.

My emotions were not a little mixed, as I had thought of him as long ago gathered to his fathers. Many years had passed since we first had bent to the paddle and slept beneath the stars together. An aged man from my earliest recollection of him, he now seemed of another day and age, which indeed he was, and changed beyond belief. Dressed in old and faded overalls and shirt, he retained only the footwear of his people, a pair of beautifully beaded moccasins, and a medicine pouch decorated with porcupine quills. His hair, now white, framed a face the colour of old mahogany, patrician in cast, and almost fleshless; the eyes alone lent life to the mask-like visage, which was seamed with a thousand wrinkles. He sat at the fire and smoked awhile, seeming to rest, for he was very feeble.

He refused my offers of food, and, it not being customary for younger men to open a conversation, I waited until he first should speak; which, his smoke finished, he did, standing, and emphasizing his remarks with the restrained but expressive gestures of an Indian.

"Washaquonasin, Grey Owl, I see you do not forget. I called, and, of them all, you came."

Up to this moment I had thought of no such thing, but there now flashed through my mind the tales I had heard. Was this the explanation of my unaccountable urge to visit the lake? I remembered that this place had been accessible to me any day for years, yet I had chosen this particular time to come. Coincidence? I became conscious of a slight feeling of uneasiness. He continued:

"Three days have I called and none came; this is the last day, the day of Two Sunsets; to-night I go away from here; to-morrow you would not have found me. My son, I have seen many snows come and go; to me you are a young man, and most of what I say will pass by your ears like the piping of frogs, or the tapping of a woodpecker on a hollow tree; yet of all my people, you are the only one who remembers the way of our race. I was a warrior once, and fought the blue-coated soldiers on a day when a river ran red with blood, and none escaped. This is many years past. Three of us returned here; we formed ourselves a blood-brotherhood, that of the Beaver, called after our bravest warrior, killed in the battle. Of them, I alone remain. When you were named, I made you a blood-brother of the clan; remember that."

He looked searchingly at me for a moment. This, then, was the reason for his attitude towards these animals, and I knew that I might never set another beaver trap, did I choose to remain true to the creed of this society of the Dead. For the old man's weakness was such that it was evident that soon, not he, but I, would be the last of the clan of the Beaver.

He said a few words in a language unintelligible to me and resumed:

"Since then I have seen many changes; I have seen the skin teepees replaced by houses; the snowshoe trail by the railroad; and now the winged canoe of the white man flies with the wild geese amongst the clouds. I am now very old. Old age is a time of rest and meditation, yet I find myself surrounded by changes that keep me moving; at no place can I rest, and ponder peacefully on the past. Long ago my people left this lake where I was born. I played as a child on this very beach, and in these forests I learned the wisdom of the Old Men. Here I will leave my bones that the Medicine Spirits may see that there is one that has not forgotten that he is an Indian."

He paused and seemed to listen.

Came a sound, a murmuring from the distance, a wind that stirred the tree-tops overhead; the sleeping forest half-awakened, sighed, and as the sound passed onward, slept again. And all around the golden and red leaves of the birch and maples, the spots of sunlight on the forest floor; and the thin blue wisp of smoke trailing up and up from the dying fire, up through the leaves and on beyond them. And far overhead the Unseen Musician improvised a low rambling melody in the many-stringed lyre of the pine-tops, and its soft humming, and the quiet lap, lap of the wavelets on the sandy shore, mingled with the old man's voice as he intoned in soft gutturals, with all the imagery to which his language lends itself.

"I hear a sound: the wind speaks to the leaves. No! it is the spirit of an Indian, looking for a place to rest, and there is none! The sky is red at night with the fire of burning forests. The beaver are gone, and there are no more singing birds; they cannot sing in the dry limbs of dead trees, and the Indian cannot live in a land of rotting stumps. The setting sun throws a red path across the water; there lies the trail to the Land of Spirits; along it I soon must follow my people. When the deep snows come I will dance the Dance of the Dead Men in the northern sky."

The latter part of his speech seemed only indirectly intended for me; rather he thought aloud. He spoke of his past life, his old-time friends, and of days beyond the memory of living man. He dwelt on the time when his band could count half a hundred lodges, and told of his struggles to keep his people steadfast; and he seemed to wander a little, till I got the purport of his words: he was painting the picture of a vanishing race. He seemed no longer aware of his surroundings, and somehow gave the impression of talking to an invisible audience, of which I was not one. And his voice gathered some arresting quality from his theme, so that even the motionless trees about him seemed to stand and listen. And my previous intimacy faded into the background; and he seemed no longer a man, but a prophet, the patriarchal ruler of a vanished people, a reincarnation of the fabled Hiawatha.

And from his words there seemed to spring a pageant in the air behind him, of days gone by; of mighty men, long dead, whose deeds now lived again; of lines of naked braves filing by in the crouching hop and shuffle of the war-dance; of clouds of mounted warriors with waving ghostly bonnets, passing in review to strains of wild unearthly music. Of a buckskin-coated figure, with long yellow hair, surrounded by the bodies of dead men dressed in blue, standing alone in an inferno of screaming, racing savages, painted ponies, and whirling dust-clouds; in his ears the terrible shuddering chorus of the death-hulloo;* a pistol raised to his head for the last act.

His voice lost its martial note, and the fire died from the old eyes, momentarily aflame with the memory of the historic combat. And then the scene changed. Endless forests marching, marching, tops swaying to the tune of the Hunting Winds; brigades of yellow bark canoes loaded high with skins, floating down swift rivers walled with granite; four-footed creatures, now rare, trooping by in all their rich variety; the quiet lodges of a peaceful people, lodges before whose doors stood racks of sturgeon, moose and deer-meat. Then—the coming of the railroad; unnumbered leagues of noble forest falling before a sea of flames; scattered bands of a broken, bewildered people driven like leaves before the wind and then—to-day! And as he ceased the scenes faded, and the figures were gone; and he stood again alone; a forlorn, lonely old man.

I fumbled in my mind for words to express my thoughts, when turning, he walked the few steps beyond the edge of the forest to the sandy lake shore, and stood facing the glimmering ribbon of red cast on the still water by the now rapidly setting sun. In the crimson glow, the broken, patched canoe became a thing of beauty, and the withered, time-worn figure in its tattered clothing, silhouetted against the brilliance, seemed to take on again something of the wild freedom of his youth in its posture. With the simple dignity of a savage chieftain he raised his right hand, palm out, and bowed his head, as though in benediction of the scene before him, saluting the western sky with that greeting with which the Indian met the first white man, the ancient and almost forgotten Peace Sign. And as he so stood,

*So called by the whites. A rhythmic yelling, almost a chant, used by Indians to signalize victory and the taking of scalps.

embracing into his audience with a single gesture, the peaceful sleeping lake, the dark legions of the forest, and the brooding hills, he cried in a loud, clear voice, as to a vast and unseen assemblage:

"I stand on the Trail of Two Sunsets. To-night the sun sets for the White Man for a day. Soon another sun will set for the Indian; and it will be forever. There is a cloud across the face of the sky, and it shadows our trail to the end."

He dropped his head, and sitting down beside his canoe, seemed lost in reverie. And the rim of the burning sun sank behind the distant hill-tops, and the last vestige of the red beam disappeared from the surface of the water.

I waited respectfully till the aged chieftain should see fit to address me again, when another thought struck me, and with a chill not altogether accounted for by the cool of evening, I walked quickly over and laid my hand on his shoulder.

His arm slipped gently down from the gunwale to his side. He was dead.

I buried him the next day in his old canoe, with his muzzle-loading gun, his old-fashioned axe, and his beaded pouch of relics by his side, in the smooth ground beneath the birches near the lake-shore, where he may hear the singing birds trill in rippling melody their evensong, in the sad days of the Fall of the Leaf, and the North-West wind may bring a message from the Great Lone Land beyond.

And there he will always be, facing towards the West, so that the rays of the setting sun to which he turned so wistfully in his last moments, may, at the close of every summer day, bathe his resting-place, in the Glory of his Sunset Trail.

Epilogue

Epilogue

AT THE BROW OF A HIGH EMINENCE STOOD TWO MEN, THEIR figures etched sharply against the sky of a day now near its close. Beside them lay two bundles, rolled as though in readiness for a long and immediate journey.

To the south lay spread out a smiling valley of farmlands, dotted thickly with the habitations of man; and at the foot of the declivity far below, were half-cleared fields, in which lay piles of burning roots and prostrate tree-trunks. And there came up faintly to the ears of the men the ring of axes and the crash of falling timber, as an antlike swarm hewed at the face of the forest, eating into it, as a rising flood eats into a wall of sand.

Beyond the valley, in the distance, stood a mighty city, its tall buildings rising in huge piles of masonry heaped up against the skyline, whilst from its bowels rose the dull roar and whirr of massed machinery, and a confused hum as of a myriad bees within a gigantic hive. Towering smokestacks belched forth heavy clouds of rolling black smoke, which hung over the city like a dark canopy, and spreading out over the farm lands, shadowed them.

On the other side the mountain descended in a gradual slope to the level of the dark waves of an endless forest, the tree-covered hills rolling into the north, row on row, rank on rank, sweeping on in ever-lessening undulation until they merged into the dimness of the horizon. The ocean of evergreens opened out as it neared the foot of the descent, to flank a long open meadow of beaver hay, down the full length of which there wound a long ribbon of a trail, winding and twisting its way amongst the yellow grasses towards the north, until, visible only as a thread where it entered the woods, the trees crowded down upon it, engulfed it, and swallowed it up, so that it could be no more seen.

The man nearest the edge of the cliff stood leaning on his rifle, gazing out over the tilled fields, towards the city beyond. His grey eyes were narrow, and stamped at the corners with crowsfeet, hallmark of one who has peered into the glare of a thousand suns, and faced the blizzards of many winters. His face, tanned to the colour of leather, was hollow-checked, ascetic almost. Once his glance strayed involuntarily to the panorama of forest that lay spread out behind him, but his eyes again sought the distant city, as though drawn by some powerful attraction.

The other, a tall spare man, his long-black hair confined at the temples by a buckskin band, and with the vigorous features and calm bearing of an Indian, regarded not the city, but stood motionless, his gaze roaming over the sweep and swell of the wilderness; and at his feet were the charred sticks of a fire, now extinguished. He had the air of one who waits.

Presently he turned and touched the white man on the shoulder, and pointing to the west, spoke in his native language.

"The sun is setting, my ears are filled with the sound of falling trees; it is enough. See ! the shadows lengthen; let us go."

And as the slow wind of evening passed over the land, there seemed to come an answering murmur from the hosts of the forest, saying, "Let us go: let us go."

And the concerted waving movement of the myriad tree tops in the breeze likened them to an immense and restless concourse, gathered together for some great migration, awaiting but the signal for departure.

For a moment longer the frontiersman stood irresolute, and then with a gesture of finality, his face set in the stern lines of one who has made a sweeping and unalterable decision, he assumed his pack and turning his back forever on the haunts of man, followed the Indian, now already on his way.

And their moccasined feet left no track as they followed the winding trail, and as they marched steadily away, their figures grew smaller and smaller, diminished, dwindled, dwindled, until at last, no longer distinguishable in the gathering dusk, they vanished into the shadows amongst the trees.

And there nothing remained of their passing, save the empty trail, and the ashes of their long-dead fire.

In the darkness from over all the length and breadth of the wild lands there came a murmur, and the air was filled with the sound of a mighty rustling and a crepitation, as of an innumerable multitude in motion. And the dark masses of the forest seemed to roll up behind those who had already gone before, to recede like the outgoing waves of an ebbing tide, as though, defeated at last, they retired before the Juggernaut that was now upon them, fleeing in the face of the doom that had threatened them for now three hundred years.

And with them went all of the wild that had life, following the last fading line of the Vanishing Frontier, Northward, Northward, ever Northward, back into the days that are long forgotten, slipping away over the hills into the purple distance, beyond the Land of Shadows, into the sunset.

A young Archie Belaney in Hastings, England, at the turn of the century. Belaney would later emigrate to Canada and assume the name "Grey Owl." *Photographer Unknown (Glenbow Archives / NA-5502-1)*

Grey Owl would often use his canoes to traverse the lakes and rivers of Saskatchewan in his job as honorary ranger. *W.J. Oliver (Glenbow Archives / NA-4868-210)*

Grey Owl with one of his tamed orphaned beavers at Lake Ajawaan, Saskatchewan. *W.J. Oliver (Glenbow Archives / NA-4868-214)*

A canoe was considered a valuable resource to the guides, trappers and conservationists of the North. Grey Owl used his to traverse many of the lakes and rivers around Canada. *W.J. Oliver (Glenbow Archives / NA-3680-5)*

Anahareo, pictured here with Grey Owl *circa* 1933, was a Native Ojibway who lived with Grey Owl sporadically for many years. They had one daughter. *W.J. Oliver (Glenbow Archives / NA-4868-205)*

Grey Owl, seen here *circa* 1930, was often nervous that one of his beavers would jump from the canoe while he was paddling about the lakes and rivers of Saskatchewan. *Photographer Unknown (Glenbow Archives / NA-3680-8)*

From his cabin window, Grey Owl watches one of his tamed beavers work on its house, *circa* 1933–34. *W.J. Oliver (Glenbow Archives / NA-3680-7)*

The orphaned beavers that Grey Owl adopted were eventually welcomed into the family. This beaver joins in the meal with Grey Owl and his family, *circa* 1933–34. *W.J. Oliver (Glenbow Archives / NA-4868-203)*

Grey Owl, seen here *circa* 1933, first decided to adopt a baby beaver after saving one whose parents had been killed by trappers. Shortly afterwards, he decided to start a sanctuary for orphaned beavers. *W.J. Oliver (Glenbow Archives / NA-4868-212)*

Grey Owl shares a picnic with Anahareo and his friend, William J. Oliver. Ajawaan, Saskatchewan, circa 1933–34. *Photographer Unknown (Glenbow Archives / NA-4868-202)*

It was at this table that Grey Owl wrote his stories. Note the beaver house on the floor next to him. Beavers were an integral part of his life and often appeared in his writing. *Circa 1933–34. W.J. Oliver (Glenbow Archives / NA-3680-6)*

Grey Owl will be fondly remembered as both a mystery and a legend. His love of nature and the Canadian wilderness, and his stories of life as a guide, have become part of the canon of Canadian nature writing. *W.J. Oliver (Glenbow Archives / NA-3680-3)*

Pilgrims of the Wild

Contents

BOOK ONE • TOULADI
Preface / 228
Prologue /232
I. How Anahareo Had Her Way / 236
II. How We Undertook a New Responsibility / 251
III. How the Pilgrimage Commenced / 261
IV. How We Came to Touladi / 276
V. How We Crossed the Slough of Despond / 284
VI. How We Built the House of McGinnis / 298
VII. How McGinty and McGinnis Opened a New Door / 305
VIII. How We Made Christmas / 316
IX. How We Came to the Depths / 329

BOOK TWO • QUEEN OF THE BEAVER PEOPLE
I. How Anahareo Left Touladi / 342
II. How the Queen and I Spent the Winter / 352
III. The Coming of Rawhide / 368
IV. The Dark Hour and the Dawn / 384
V. How We Left Rawhide Lake / 395
VI. How the Pilgrimage was Ended / 410
Epilogue / 417

BOOK ONE

TOULADI

My road calls me, lures me
    West, east, south, and north;
Most roads lead me homewards,
    My road leads me forth
       To add more miles to the tally
          Of grey miles left behind,
      In quest of that one beauty
        God put me here to find.

—John Masefield

Preface

THIS IS PRIMARILY AN ANIMAL STORY; IT IS ALSO THE STORY OF two people, and their struggle to emerge from the chaos into which the failure of the fur trade, and the breaking down of the old proprietary system of hunting grounds, plunged the Indian people, and not a few whites, during the last two decades. Their means of livelihood destroyed by fire and the invasion of hordes of transient trappers and cheap fur buyers, these two, a man and a woman, newly married and with no prospects, broke loose from their surroundings taking with them all that was left to them of the once vast heritage of their people,—their equipment and two small animals as pets.

Outcasts in their own country, wandering in what amounted to a foreign land, they tried desperately to fit somewhere into this new picture. Their devotion to these creatures that represented to them the very soul of their lost environment, eventually proved to be their salvation.

All the places are actual, the story known to not a few; characters are real, and if named receive, save in one instance, their proper appellations.

In order to properly grasp the spirit in which this book is written, it is necessary to remember that though it is not altogether an Indian story, it has an Indian background. The considering attitude towards all nature which appears throughout the work, is best explained by a quotation from John G. Gifford's "Story of the Seminole War."

"The meaning of sovereignty is not very clear to primitive peoples, especially to the Indian. He rarely dominated the things around

228

him; he was a part of nature and not its boss." Hewitt says of the Indian:

"In his own country...he is a harmonious element in a landscape that is incomparable in its nobility of colour and mass and feeling of the Unchangeable. He never dominates it as does the European his environment, but belongs there as do the mesas, skies, sunshine, spaces and the other living creatures. He takes his part in it with the clouds, winds, rocks, plants, birds and beasts, with drum beat and chant and symbolic gesture, keeping time with the seasons, moving in orderly procession with nature, *holding to the unity of life in all things,* seeking no superior place for himself but merely a state of harmony with all created things...the most rhythmic life...that is lived among the races of men." This viewpoint is not peculiar to people of native blood but is often found in those of other races who have resided for many years in the wilderness.

The idea of domination and submission, though now passing out of date in nearly every walk of life, is hard to disassociate, in the minds of some, from the contact between civilized man and beings in a state of nature. This was forcibly illustrated in a late radio broadcast during which, in a play dealing with frontier conditions, an actor who portrayed the part of Indian guide was heard to address the head (not the leader, as is generally supposed, the guide being of necessity in that capacity) of the party, in an awed voice, as "Master." But the more tolerant and unaspiring, though perhaps less ambitious view-point of the Indian must be taken into consideration, if the reader is to fully appreciate the rather unusual tenor of the narrative.

Interpretations of the more obscure mental processes of the animal characters that run through the story, are of necessity comparative; such attempts at delineation are difficult, and often inadequate, without some parallel to draw them by ; but the great majority of the descriptions of animal psychology are very clear and positive. Those manifestations that were at the time inexplicable have been construed in the light of later investigation and experience, so as to preserve the unity of impression of the narrative.

In the rather ill-considered rush we have been in to exploit our natural resources, we have taken little trouble to examine into the capabilities and possibilities of the wild creatures involved in it, save in so far as the findings were of commercial value. Therefore much that is interesting has been overlooked. The kinship between the human race and the rest of our natural fauna becomes very apparent to those of us who sojourn among the latter for any length of time; alarmingly so to those whose attitude has hitherto been governed by the well-worn and much abused phrase that "Man shall have dominion over all." However I do not draw comparisons between man and beast, save in a few instances which are too remarkable to be overlooked. Nor do I ascribe human attributes to animals. If any of their qualities are found to closely approximate some of our own, it is because they have, unknown to us, always possessed them, and the fault lies in our not having discovered sooner that these characteristics were not after all exclusively human, any more than are a number of others to which we have by long usage become accustomed.

My fingers, well toasted at many an open fire, and stiffened a little by the paddle and the pull of a loaded toboggan, are ill suited for the task I set them to. In this writing game I find myself in the dangerous situation of a man who has played his first game of poker and won a small jackpot, and who is now sitting in on another round having rather disastrous possibilities. To each his craft and calling, nor should we grudge another his ability; none the less, did I have the power to expertly carry out what I have here attempted, or had another, more skilled in letters and who knew this story well, have undertaken it, it would have been better done.

To me the rifle has ever been mightier than the pen. The feel of a canoe gunnell at the thigh, the splash of flying spray in the face, the rhythm of the snowshoe trail, the beckoning of far-off hills and valleys, the majesty of the tempest, the calm and silent presence of the trees that seem to muse and ponder in their silence; the trust and confidene of small living creatures, the company of simple men; these have been my inspiration and my guide. Without them I am nothing. To these and to my teachers, men of a type that is rapidly passing from the face of the earth, belongs the credit for whatever there may be that is worthy in this work of mine.

And should any part of it provide an hour of pleasure to just a few of those who love the Great Outdoors, or who have a kindly thought for a simple people or for a lowly animal, or should I perchance touch somewhere a chord of sympathy, or make some slight appeal to the sense of fair play of any of those true Sportsmen to whom Wild Life owes so much to-day, I will count my work, with all its imperfections, as having been worth while.

WA-SHA-QUON-ASIN (GREY OWL)
Beaver Lodge
Prince Albert National Park
Saskatchewan
November 7th, 1933

Prologue

OUTSIDE A WINDOW FROM WHICH THE SASH HAS BEEN removed stands a man, alert, silent, watchful.

The cabin beside which he keeps post faces out onto a lake, its frontage at the water's edge. The slopes of the surrounding hills are covered with a heavy forest, the tall grey poplars and giant spruce standing close in a dark and serried palisade about the camp.

The water is calm and unruffled; the lake appears to sleep. There is no sound and no movement save the desultory journeyings of a squirrel, engaged in salvaging cones he has been dropping from the spruce tops.

In front of the man, and directed through the aperture into the building, is a motion picture camera, trained on the door which is closed. The interior of the building is equipped with the rude but comfortable furnishings, and the simple utensils of a woodsman's home, for the greater part of the dwelling is given over to human occupancy, and is a permanent abode, although it has one peculiarity. Across one end of it is a large erection having the appearance of a massive earthwork, shoulder high and occupying easily one-third of the floor space.

Outside, in strategic positions commanding the door and the approach from the lake, are other men, holding cameras. Inside the building a man sits in a chair, waiting. Suddenly:

"All right! here he comes," cries a watcher. The man at the window sights his machine afresh, makes small adjustments and stands poised, ready. There can now be heard, approaching the entrance, a heavy measured tread. The camera man's face becomes suddenly tense, the camera commences to whir and simultaneously with a resounding thump the door is thrown widely open and there steps over the threshold, not the leading lady of a cast of players, not the handsome hero of a screen romance, nor yet the villain, but a full-grown beaver, erect, and bearing in his arms a load of earth and sticks.

Walking upright like a man, steadily, purposefully, looking neither to the right nor to the left, past the stove, round the table, between the benches, he pursues his undeviating way towards the earthwork, advancing with the resolute step of an unfaltering and unchangeable purpose. The camera swings, follows him, grinding. But for that sound and the thudding of the beaver's heavy steps, there is silence. Straight up the side of the lodge, for such the earthwork is, the beaver marches, deposits his load, tamps it in with his hands; he pushes in a stick to bind it, cuts off the protruding end and potters at some small repairs. At this moment another and a larger beaver enters hauling a six foot stick which she skilfully manoeuvers through the opening, drawing it over to the house and up the side of it. The two animals work with the heavy pole, placing it; they are very particular and take some time at this. Meanwhile the man in the chair rises, shuts the door and resumes his seat.

The camera drones on.

Another beaver, small, brisk, business-like, emerges from a hole in the side of the lodge, places two sticks very carefully, looks around, becomes fidgety and scampers in again. The operator's face is a study; he is getting it all. Yesterday he got a moose passing through the door yard, the day before a group of muskrats.

The two big beaver at last finish their job to their complete satisfaction; and now their purposeful, sober mien deserts them. On all fours and at a little trot, they run over to the seated man and stand erect beside him, looking up at him. Their enquiring faces reach waist high on him as he sits. They must weigh one hundred pounds between the two of them. The larger one, the female, plucks at his sleeve trying to attract his attention. The camera grinds steadily and the beavers undoubtedly hear it. But they pay no heed; this is their fourth year at the business.

The man strokes the animals' heads.

"Well! how is it going today, old-timers?" he asks.

A series of short, sharp, ejaculations from the larger one as she pulls impatiently at his hand with her forepaws.

"All right, here's your apple," says the man, and seizing the offering, she runs, hops, and trots over to the door, opens it inwards, with a quick pull at a leather loop, and runs outside. The other, her consort, patient, more sedate, gently takes his apple, and slips quietly out.

The camera at the window stops. Outside other machines click and drone according to their kind, as the expert passes from one to another of his sentries for down at the so-lately deserted waterfront, a scant thirty feet away, are more beavers, swimming, playing, eating.

All at once one of them stands upright, sniffing the air, listening, a stiff brown pillar of attention; a foreign scent has drifted down from that dark unknown forest with its threat of a thousand dangers. Without warning the beaver leaps into the water with a terrific plunge, slaps his tail. Immediately there is a violent commotion, cries, splashes, heavy thudding of broad flat tails, and in a moment not a beaver is to be seen.

Silence falls, the water quickly subsides. There is nothing visible, though the machines are cocked and ready. But their work is finished. They will get nothing more today.

Far out on the lake, but out of range, black heads bob up; V's stream away from them as the workers, not seriously alarmed after all, proceed to the scene of their various occupations.

It has all been very casual, in a way. No rehearsing has been done, no commands given; the actors have done just about as they liked. The beaver are free and unrestrained and could be gone beyond all hope of recovery in an hour. But they prefer to stay here, and year by year have made this place their home, have even built their domicile within the human habitation, a subterranean passage leading from it to the bottom of the lake.

Extraordinary behaviour for an animal supposed to be wild and unapproachable! Perhaps it is. But the story that lies behind this little scene is even stranger.

Yet it is a very simple one, of happenings and small but queer events that did not much affect the history of the world, or of a whole town full of people, or even a room full, but which were so very important to those who played a part in them.

It is not a tale of heroism, or hazard, or very high accomplishment, but has more to tell of loyalty and tolerance, and gentle wistful beasts; and of the bond between a woman and a man. There is much joy in it, a little sorrow, some loneliness and struggle, and some rare good fun. It plumbed the depths of human souls and sometimes touched the heights, and much of everything that goes between.

I know that story very well, and how it all began, in the Unforgotten Days of Long Ago.

And because it is a tale of ways and means and a manner of living which you may be unfamiliar with, its strangeness may compensate in some degree for my lack of skill in the telling of it.

CHAPTER ONE

How Anahareo Had Her Way

THE TOWN OF BISCO WAS DROPPING FAST ASTERN AS I DIPPED and swung my paddle, driving my light, fast canoe steadily Northward to the Height of Land. It was not much of a town as towns go. It had no sidewalks, and no roads, and consisted mainly of a Hudson's Bay store, a saw mill, probably fifty houses scattered on a rocky hillside, and an Indian encampment in a sheltered bay of Biscotasing Lake, on the shores of which this village stood. But it was rather a noted little place, as, being situated within measureable distance of the headwaters of a number of turbulent rivers such as the Spanish, the White, the Mississauga, the Mattawgami, the Ground-hog and others, and being moreover the gate-way to a maze of water routes that stretch Southward to lakes Huron and Superior, and Northward to the Arctic ocean, the fame of its canoemen was widely known. That part of the District of Algoma, in the Province of Ontario, had until lately been one of the best fur-producing territories in Northern Canada, but an influx of get-rich-quick transient hunters had depleted the fur-bearing animals almost to the point of extinction, and times were not what they had been.

Reduced though it might be, none the less this isolated post had been my home town for the fifteen years since I had drifted down from the North, if coming out to sell fur and replenish supplies twice a year can be said to establish citizenship. I had seen my best years in the vast forests and on the intricate waterways that commenced at its back door and stretched many hundreds of miles into the interior, and was leaving behind me friendships with both red men and white, that had been cemented by year after year of trial by ordeal in the crucible of hardship; and I was feeling a little choked up and lonely.

The farewell celebrations had been a little lively, and I was not the only one leaving town that evening, but none of the others were coming my way; they were all headed in the opposite direction, to their stamping grounds on the distant Mississauga whose pine-crowned cliffs, maple crested ridges, and wild fierce rapids I might never see again. So I thought as I plugged along, the little swirling eddies that slid from my paddle singing a low whispering dirge in the silence of that Spring night.

Less than a dozen miles brought me to the first portage. Certain hints dropped by the Hudson's Bay Manager, who was also Chief of Police (he was, in fact, the whole force; he could serve a warrant so you'd never feel the jar, but was, in certain circumstances, a gentleman to be avoided), made it seem advisable to cross this immediately. It was four miles long and I had two loads, outfit and canoe. But the footing was good and there was a moon. In the ensuing labour a lot of my depression of spirits oozed through my pores in the form of perspiration. It was an arduous trip, eight miles loaded and four empty on the middle return journey; but it was completed soon after sunrise when I made camp, slept till noon, and then proceeded on my pilgrimage.

A disastrous bush fire had swept my hunting ground leaving it a barren area of cracked rock, burnt out stumps and tortured tree trunks, and I was bound North and East to the far off, supposedly fruitful ranges of the Abitibi district in Northern Quebec; a vast country which, so rumour had it, was little explored and was populated only by a few wandering bands of Ojibway[1] Indians. Much of my route lay through a country I had known. It was now almost unrecognizable. A railroad had been built through part of it. There were huge burns, areas of bare rocks and twisted rampikes, miles of staring desolation. Riff-raff bushmen, dirty, unkempt; stolid European peasantry tearing down the forest; settlers on stone farms (two crops a year—one snow and the other rocks) existing, no more. The change was nearly unbelievable. Immured in the fastness of

[1] Pronounced O-*jib*-way, accented on the second syllable.

the Mississauga I had not known what had been going on. I passed on uneasy, fearful, wondering what lay ahead. There was plenty!

Old Fort Mattawgami, the river dammed, was flooded out, all under water save the little Mission Church which stood awash on a knoll; I had a noon meal on its steps, sorrowfully. Another trading post, a startling new pale-looking affair, stood on the far shore on high land. I passed it by at half a mile; Old Man Miller wasn't there anyway, he was living in Gogama on a pension from the Company,[1] still worrying about his old Post.

I met some old-time faces, men who had made history in these parts; I got the news such as it was. It sounded to me more like a Book of Doom. Flying Post was on its last legs, its Indians dispersed. Alec. McLeod, factor at Elbow Lake, who so wore his thigh with the paddle that cancer had set in and the leg had to be amputated—cursing, roaring, mighty McLeod that no man could ever outface and few could follow—dead. Ancient John Buffalo on the Montreal River, a trapper of the old régime, almost a landmark in the country, dead these many years. Snape, who ran Moose Factory at a time when a round trip from the front took six weeks fast voyaging, now manager of a Company[1] store in a small town, his ankle broken and badly knit—off the trail for keeps. Andy Luke, who habitually carried 400 lbs. on a portage and who had made big hunts that were a byword in the land, *working on the railroad as a labourer,* his son Sam, lean, wiry Sam with the speed and endurance of a greyhound, a wizard in a canoe, doing odd jobs. Big Alec Langevin, six feet two in his summer moccasins to whom fifty miles on snowshoes was a small matter, gone away to Quebec for marten. I later met him there—on his way back.

Tommy Saville, the White Indian, adopted by the Ojibways when young and who had made and spent a fortune in a gold rush, living in a house in a town, eating his heart out for the trail, sneaking down cellar to boil a pail of tea over a little fire of shavings—to get the feel of it again: people thought him queer—

What did it all mean; was the whole Wilderness falling about our ears?

I kept going. Further on the tale improved but little. Shining tree and Gowganda, rich camps of earlier days, far from the railroad and

[1] Hudson's Bay Company.

undisturbed by the hodge-podge and the hurly-burly of the march of progress, were still kept alive by many of the old originals, waiting for a break, hoping with the perennial optimism of the dyed-in-the-wool prospector, for a new strike to keep the old camp going. The whole Gowganda lake area had been burnt to the bare rock. White Duck, who had carried the mail in the early days, had passed into a legend.

One reunion was notable and all too short, with Billy Guppy, that king of all woodsmen, respected by all men, red and white, and whom the Indians called Pijeense—The Little Lynx. Time had changed him in no discernible way; he alluded to the subject of our last conversation, held fifteen years before. He still clung to his traditions and always would.

I encountered Indians, white woodsmen, real prospectors, each meeting an experience. But when their conversation turned to future plans there were evidences of a vague foreboding in their speech. No man felt secure. Fire, railroads, power projects, the aeroplane, they were tearing the old life apart. The Frontier was rolling back like a receding tide. I must hurry.

Four hundred miles travel brought me to a town on the Temiskaming and Northern Ontario Railway which, when I first saw it, had been a frontier post. Before the coming of the steel, rare sportsmen and adventurers, seeking the freedom and spiritual satisfaction to be found in an untouched virgin territory, had come here at intervals. We guided them, a strange, new, interesting job; these men had been our comrades on the trail. We talked about such a trip all Winter, and showed each other the letters we got from our patrons. The place was now a populous tourist resort. An automobile highway was in the making. I took a job here; the party was a good one, people from New York, with all the genial good fellowship of the American on a vacation. But there was a false note. Guides were no longer companions, they were lackeys, footmen, toadies; a kind of below-stairs snobbery had sprung up among them,—kid-glove guiding; some of them actually wore white cotton gloves at their work. Old-timers talked about it, shook their heads—but they had to follow suit; fur was gone and this now emasculated occupation was their only means of subsistence.

My main outfit had been sent around to this place by freight; I shipped it ahead three hundred miles, replenished my supplies and left, in my heart rebellion and disillusionment. This place held memories I had hoped to renew. I pitied the pine trees standing there. They had to stay.

The Frontier was on its way. So was I.

I had billed my freight to a point on the Transcontinental where I arrived a month later, renewed my food supply and sent the outfit another stage ahead. In this manner, touching the railroad at strategic points, a journey was made that covered approximately two thousand miles. This occupied two years, during which time I wandered on in the summer time, and trapped with more or less success wherever Fall caught me.

The waters began to go crossways of my projected line of travel rather than with it, necessitating an inordinate amount of portaging; so that the last leg of the journey was made ignominiously on a train, with the outfit in the baggage car, out of which the canoe regarded me reproachfully at every stop. There was, however, another very compelling reason for this dereliction; my correspondence, usually nonexistent, now demanded constant attention. At a summer resort where I had guided for a short time the year before, there had been a girl, a cultured, talented and personable young woman of the Iroquois, a cut or two above me perhaps, but not, I hoped, on that account unattainable. The affair was quite wanting in the vicissitudes and the harrowing, but stirring episodes that are said to usually beset the path of high romance. The course of true love ran exasperatingly smooth; I sent the lady a railroad ticket, she came up on a pullman and we were married, precisely according to plan. The complications started afterwards.

In order that the blame will not attach in the wrong places, I must here give a brief outline of two very conflicting personalities. We were, in many ways, exact opposites. In my young days I had received some pretty intensive home tuition from an ever-blessed aunt, but had shown little aptitude save in geography, history and English. In the latter subject the ground work had been solid, and as I now see, very skilfully laid. But I had so far taken no trouble to build on it. Most of my time from middle youth on, had been spent in solitude or largely amongst a people whose language was not English, and confused by regional dialects. Only a retentive memory and a passion for reading had kept alive this early training, and my precise and somewhat stilted English was, like a stiff and ceremonious suit of Sunday best, something to be taken out of the closet and worn on occasion, and its use ended, returned to the limbo of unneeded things. I was careless in my speech and quickly resented any infringement on what I considered to be my personal freedom. This last trait had been intensified by the discipline endured in the army. I had been one of those unusual people, so seldom met with in stories, who was not an officer, did not attract the attention of the higher command, entered the army as a private and left it as one. I had come back to the woods with my efficiency much impaired, and my outlook on things generally had been in no way improved by the job of sniper that I had held, and the sole educational effect the war had been to convince me of the utter futility of civilization. Most of my views, whilst free and unconventional were correspondingly narrow.

My wife Gertrude, who will be referred to from now on by her tribal name of Anahareo, was not highly educated, save in that broader sense which is much to be desired, and is not always the result of schooling. She had a passion for advancement, uplift, and a proper use of words and took a lively interest in world events. She was a direct descendant of hereditary Iroquois chiefs, and her father was one of the original Mohawk rivermen who had helped to make history along the Ottawa in the days of the great square-timber rafts; she came of a proud race. She was strictly modern, as modern went at that time, a good dancer and conversationalist, and, a particular dresser herself, she naturally wanted me to always look my best. My idea of looking my best was to wear my hair long, have plenty of fringes on my buckskins, to allow one tassel of my Hudson Bay sash to hang behind like a tail, and to have the front of my shirt decorated with an oblique row of safety pins on each side, as a Cossack wears his ammunition, to be intriguingly glimpsed at times beneath a leather vest. These things were very dear to me, and as to the safety pins, why, they were real handy and served a useful as well as an ornamental purpose, being used to hang up my clothes to dry at night. Other peculiarities born of long habit, and hitherto unnoticed, now became very obvious. I could not, or would not, carry on any conversation at all whilst in a canoe, and preferred to walk in single file, trail fashion as, like most bush people, I continually bumped into anyone who walked beside me; as a concession the lady was, in this case, always allowed to walk in front. These features were brought to my attention one by one, and it is easily seen that our honeymoon, spent with a load of supplies on the way into a hunting ground, must have been unusual and interesting.

Out at the front[1] it had been found that I could never learn to dance ball-room style, but could in an emergency, with proper assistance, get through the figures of a quadrille without any serious results. I could also dance the Grass Dance[2] to a drum, and sing the Wabeno[3] very creditably. In the other matters I submitted, rather tamely as I now remember it, and as a reward was allowed to retain the fringes and the braided hair. I was being made over for my own good, and it was a bitter pill. But far, far more was yet to come; though even today I sometimes furtively wear the safety pins and the tail, and get great comfort from it.

I speedily discovered that I was married to no butterfly, in spite of her modernistic ideas, and found that my companion could swing an axe as well as she could a lip-stick, and was able to put up a tent in good shape, make quick fire, and could rig a tump-line and get a load across in good time, even if she did have to sit down and powder her nose at the other end of the portage. She habitually wore breeches, a custom not at that time so universal amongst women as it is now, and one that I did not in those days look on with any great approval. The apparel of our own women ran heavily to voluminous plaid skirts and gay tartan head shawls. This one wore top boots and a mackinaw shirt, and somehow achieved an appearance of rough and ready competence, borne out in her behaviour, that was quite without that odious suggestion of mannishness which only too often accompanies these departures from feminine tradition. As a wedding present I had bought her some yards of heavy serge or broadcloth, or something of the kind, but in view of her rig-out I began to feel that a rifle or an axe would have been more appropriate. But she pounced on the dress-goods at once, and with a pair of scissors in her mouth and a pencil in her hand, she suspended the cloth against her body, where it was held by a stiff breeze that was blowing, and marking the outline where the wind shaped the goods against her form, proceeded to cut them out. I stood by in rather

---

[1] The "front"; a term used by trappers and others to designate the railroad, jumping-off place, or other border of civilization; an abbreviation of "frontier."

[2] Grass Dance: Part of the War-Dance.

[3] Wabeno: Indian Ceremonial Dance accompanied by singing.

apprehensive silence and viewed the apparent slaughter of this very excellent material, for which I had payed a very excellent price, but out of which there was presently constructed (the word aptly describes the process) one of the best fitting and most elegant-looking pair of breeches anyone could wish for; and while she was not very much of an expert at out-door cooking, I soon found that I had procured me a really first-class needle-women.

She had brought up with her, as a dowry, a large packsack well stuffed with clothes, an ominous-looking volume entitled "The Power of Will," five small tattered booklets comprising "The Irving Writing System," under the mistaken impression that they were "Hints for Housewives," and an exceedingly good felt hat which I gained possession of and still wear on special occasions.

The literary booklets were an oversight and belonged to her sister, who had a husband with a flair for writing, and we had considered sending them back, though we never did; which, it afterwards turned out, was just as well.

This new wife of mine must have been very lonely at times, though she never said so. Once she suggested that we have a radio. This made me vaguely uncomfortable. We all had an idea in those days that radio caused electrical disturbances that had a bad effect on the weather, so that on account of some gigolo with corrugated hair singing "Ting-a-ling" or "You've got me crying again" in Montreal or Los Angeles, a bunch of good men had bad snowshoeing all winter. So I tactfully sidestepped the idea and we viewed the sunset through the one window of our cabin for relaxation; at that, these sunsets were often pretty good to look at. Eating was lots of fun too. We arose before daylight and often travelled all night. Snowshoes and toboggan, or canoe, were cared for almost like they had been horses, while the little woman waited patiently, wishing it was time to eat. She was, she said, becoming jealous of the bush. There was one particular ridge that I visited often and spoke highly of (value about two hundred dollars) as it was the abode of a number of marten, and my frequent visits there occupied whatever spare time I had. For this spot she had a special hatred and I, in my blind stupidity, could not see the reason.

We ate, slept, and dreamed lines of traps, and in the evenings laid out trails and pored over maps, or made preparations for the next day's excursion. I was engrossed by my work and talked of little else. The stern discipline of the trail ruled also in the cabin. The trail was my religion, and like any other fanatic I tried to force my views on even the one I loved. Altogether there were the makings of a first-class domestic tragedy.

But the exigencies of constant travel and the demands made by our manner of living, left little time for temperamental readjustments, and the hurry and drive of the Fall and early Winter trapping occupied the full of our days, until one evening just before Christmas, I returned from a short trip to find my proud and gallant Anahareo in a dishevelled and disconsolate heap upon the bunk, with a tear-stained face and her eyes swollen and red from weeping. And then the whole thing came out, everything, piece by piece. At first I could not understand; everything had seemed to be going first class. I had been a most appreciative husband, not at all indifferent or unattentive as the real Indians often were. This woman had won my lasting respect and admiration with her courage in the face of unaccustomed hardships, and I had let her know it. But that, it was now revealed, was not at all what she wanted. Respect! The dead got that. Admiration! What was that!—You admired scenery. We lived, it appeared, with all the sociability of sleigh dogs: we ate our meals with the same relish we enjoyed throwing wood through a stove-door.

And I listened amazedly to this strange contradictory creature that could sleep out in the rain with a smile, and cry over a lack of ceremony at meal times.

There was more, much more. Trap lines, plans! plans!—plans to inflict torture and death and then to go out and boast of it! I was startled at this latter accusation, and a little indignant. I was trying my best to earn us a living; a man had to kill whatever way he could, and all he could; fur was getting low. But the truth peered out in a most unwelcome fashion from between the lines of this recital, and when it was done I marched out of the house to visit my pet ridge, hurt, bewildered, and not a little angry. I made a fire up there and sat and smoked and thought the matter over while I skinned a marten, and fought my battle out alone as Anahareo had done this many days. And all at once I saw myself as I was, saw clearly the selfishness that had been bred in me during a life of solitary wandering, and realized how narrow was the rut that I had got into.

Even my niggardly attentions had been only the scraps, the leavings, the tag ends left over from the spent emotions of the day, that I was offering to this woman who had given her happiness into my hands. And I went down that mountain trail at a run, my dignity, my accursed self-assurance thrown to the winds, and arrived home with my snowshoes nearly smoking, hoping I was not too late. You guessed it; I was not. And from that day, on which I recognized to some extent my woeful shortcomings and what they might have led to, and made some effort to overcome them, could be counted the first steps in a regeneration that worked a revolution in our whole scheme of existence.

Don't imagine that there was any sudden and complete renunciation such as overcomes the luckless and often temporarily aberrated victim of a highly emotionalized revival meeting; this would have been, at best, but temporary. It was a slow, hard process fraught with many mental upheavals and self-examinations, and numerous back-slidings and reversals to type, and it involved a self-discipline as severe as any that the trail, with all its stern severities, had ever imposed upon me. But I emerged from each conflict, I hoped, the better for it, and was not without assistance.

And so the threatening clouds of disaster that were darker and more real than I at the time suspected, rolled clean away. We worked as hard as ever, but I left the job outside the home where it belonged and we took a pride in our little cabin and made ornaments for it, and talked of many things that we had never before had time to even mention. We found our necessary partings longer now, and in our travels, where our trails forked, the one who arrived at the crossing first, spelt out a foolish message for the other in the snow; and we were very happy, at last. And Anahareo became her old self once again. But I never did. And the lesson never was lost, and from it sprang results such as we had never dreamed of, and it had a bearing on all the strange events that followed after.

Anahareo from now on followed the trap trails regularly and we were boon companions. Although it was her first Winter at this rather strenuous occupation, she soon became so adept that she was able to take her turn at breaking trail, took care of side lines herself, and was altogether a good deal more of an assistance than some men partners I have had. She was strong and hardy, but this did not prevent her from realizing more and more keenly the cruelties of her new profession. The sight of frozen twisted forms contorted in shapes of agony, and the spectacle of submissive despairful beasts being knocked senseless with an axe handle, and hung up in a noose to choke out any remaining spark of life while the set was being made ready for a fresh victim, moved her to deep compassion. And worse, to her mind, were the great numbers of harmless birds and squirrels caught accidentally and to no good purpose, and often still alive, some screaming, others wailing feebly in their torment. And strangely, it was to be noticed that some of these animals seemed to sense her feeling, and on more than one occasion a doomed animal would look not towards me, to the death that was so near, but at her, staring as though in dumb hopeless appeal to her for the mercy it must have known that I would never give. I remember particularly a lynx that after the stroke screamed out like a woman, and not yet dead, tried to crawl to her in the anguish of its last extremity.

These things made her very unhappy, which was a mild surprise to me, as I had supposed that, being of full Indian blood, she would have at least as much apathy for the sufferings of these animals that were providing us with the means to live, as had I myself.

I had long ago invested the creatures of the forest with a personality. This was the inevitable result of a life spent wandering over the vast reaches of a still, silent land in which they were the only form of animate life, and sprang from early training and folklore. Yet this concession gained them no respite, and although I never killed needlessly and was as merciful as was possible under the circumstances, the urge of debts to be paid, money to spend, and prestige to be maintained, lent power to the axe handle and cunning to the hands that otherwise might have faltered on occasion. Always I had pitied, but had closed my mind to all thoughts of compassion save in retrospect.

But my point of view was slowly changing. Forced at last to stop and look around and take stock, obliged now to think of someone else besides myself, I stepped out of my case hardened shell and rubbed my eyes to get a clearer vision, and saw many things that had hitherto escaped me in my remorseless striving for achievement. My surroundings began to have a different aspect. Up till now the fate of those creatures amongst whom my life had been spent had mattered only in so far as they contributed to my prowess as a hunter. Now my newly awakened consideration for something else besides myself, was branching out most disastrously it seemed. I began to have a faint distaste for my bloody occupation. This was resolutely quenched, though the eventual outcome was inescapable.

Even in those less enlightened days, at a time when I actually believed that radio was spoiling the hunt by affecting the climate, I was perhaps not without a certain sense of justice which, though not recognized as such at the time, evinced itself in strange ways. A primitive and imaginative ancestry had not been without its influence. There were certain precepts, amounting to superstitions, that were strictly adhered to at no matter what cost in time and trouble. You may not take them very seriously, but to me they amounted to a good deal, and were often performed with quite a solemn ritual. No bear was killed without some portion of the carcass, generally the skull or shoulder bones, being hung up in a prominent place somewhere in his former range. The bodies of beaver were laid in supposedly comfortable positions and the hands, feet and tail, severed for convenience in skinning, were laid beside or on the body. Whenever possible the body, with these appendages securely tied to it, was committed to the water through a hole laboriously cut in the ice. Those eaten had the knee-caps, unusual adjuncts for an animal, removed and most religiously burnt. All these ceremonies are practised by semi-civilized, and even more advanced Indians over a wide area; and should anyone be tactless enough to enquire the reason why they do these things, the answer if any, will be:

"Ozaam tapskoche anicianabé, mahween—because they are so much like Indians."

I had however other customs of my own invention, and kept rigidly two self-imposed rules. I would allow no sportsman I guided to photograph a wounded animal until it was dead, and any animal that should chance to be brought to camp alive, must be resuscitated and let go. So when I one Spring captured a month old wolf cub I took him home to the cabin and kept him alive, intending to free him when he was old enough to fend for himself. He was a forlorn little creature, and although I was kind to him he was never happy. He had two sole amusements: one was chewing an old moccasin under the bed, the nearest approach to playing that he ever got; the other was staring by the hour at the cabin walls, staring with his slanting, inscrutable eyes unfocused as though gazing, not at the dark walls of his prison but on beyond them, on into the far distance, to some far distant prospect of his earlier memory. He paid me scant attention save to accept food, but kept on gazing with his veiled eyes until his view was shut off by the sides of the box in which he lay and died.

And so perhaps he came at last to his Promised Land, upon which he had looked so wistfully and so long.

At the termination of the Winter trapping season we went out to sell our fur. Prices had fallen, and were going down every week or so. Although we did not realize it, the day of the trapper was almost done. The handwriting was on the wall, but although it had been painstakingly inscribed there by ourselves, none of us were able to read it.

The hunting ground we were working had been previously trapped over by a noted hunter the Winter before, and between that and the low prices we only took fur to the value of about six hundred dollars; not a great sum in comparison to what I had been in the habit of making during these boom years. There would be little left over after the debt was settled and a summer's provisions purchased, not enough to start out in pursuit of that willow-the-wisp, the virgin, untapped hunting ground that every trapper sees visions of, gets reports about, sees on maps, but never quite catches up to. So I decided on a Spring hunt to replenish the exchequer, something that went a little against even my principles, as a hunt at that time of the year was looked on as both destructive and cruel by the better class of trapper. But there was a family of beaver remaining over from the organized slaughter of the year before, and like too many of my kind, I salved my conscience by saying that I may as well clean them out before someone else stepped in and took them.

Delayed over a week at the post by the late arrival of a buyer, and more time being consumed by the journey in, we did not arrive back at our ground until the last of May. The hunt should have been over by now, and I was a little disturbed over the hardship I could not now avoid inflicting, as the young beaver were most certainly born by now, and would perish after the old ones were removed. This proved to be the case.

Whilst making a set at an old, renovated beaver house where I knew the female to be, I heard faintly the thin piping voices of kitten beavers. In apparent clumsiness, I allowed my paddle to drop with a rattle on the canoe gunnell with the intention of hiding the sound, but Anahareo had heard it and begged me to lift the trap, and allow the baby beaver to have their mother and live. I felt a momentary pang myself, as I had never before killed a beaver at this time on that account, but continued with my work. We needed the money.

The next morning I lifted the bodies of three drowned beaver. The mother was missing however, one trap being unaccounted for. I found where the chain had been broken, and dragged for the body unsuccessfully, later breaking the dam and partly draining the pond, but without avail. She would be the largest and most valuable, so I bemoaned my loss and forgot the life that had been destroyed for nothing, and the helpless kittens left to starve. After a whole day spent in a fruitless search, I removed all traps and equipment and proceeded to camp, having no intention whatever of returning; but the next day, after skinning and stretching the catch, for no reason at all I changed my mind. So inauspiciously do important events intrude themselves into our lives. I portaged back to the ruined pond that would never again be good for anything, and we paddled over to the old beaver house in an effort to discover if the female had succeeded in getting back there, but could find no indication either by sight or sound of her presence.

So we turned to go, finally and for good. As we were leaving I heard behind me a light splash, and looking back saw what appeared to be a muskrat lying on top of the water alongside of the house. Determined to make this wasted day pay, I threw up my gun, and standing up in the canoe to get a better aim, prepared to shoot. At that distance a man could never miss and my finger was about to press the trigger when the creature gave a low cry, and at the same instant I saw, right in my line of fire another, who gave out the same peculiar call. They could both be gotten with the one charge of shot. They gave voice again, and this time the sound was unmistakeable—they were young beaver! I lowered my gun and said:

"There are your kittens."

The instinct of a woman spoke out at once.

"Let us save them," cried Anahareo excitedly, and then in a lower voice, "It is up to us, after what we've done."

And truly what had been done here looked now to be an act of brutal savagery. And with some confused thought of giving back what I had taken, some dim idea of atonement, I answered,

"Yes; we have to. Let's take them home." It seemed the only fitting thing to do.

This was not such an easy matter as the kittens were well able to take care of themselves in the water, being older than I had thought. By the exercise of considerable patience and ingenuity we eventually caught them, and dropped them aboard, two funny-looking furry creatures with little scaly tails and exaggerated hind feet, that weighed less than half a pound apiece, and that tramped sedately up and down the bottom of the canoe with that steady, persistent, purposeful walk that we were later to know so well. We looked at them in a kind of dumbfounded bewilderment, feeling much as if we had caught a pair of white elephants, hardly knowing what to do with them. And certainly we had not the faintest inkling of the far-reaching effects their unceremonious entry into our affairs was to have.

Had my finger pressed but lightly on the trigger that fateful morning, these two tiny creatures, whose coming saved from slaughter so many of their kin who followed them and materially changed the lives of several people, would have passed like two wisps from some wandering breeze, back into the Great Unknown from which they had so short a time before set out.

CHAPTER TWO

How We Understook a New Responsibility

IT IS ONLY FAIR TO SAY THAT AT THE TIME WE DID NOT KNOW what we were letting ourselves in for. From the very commencement it was plain that this experiment was to be no picnic. Any preconceived ideas either of us had on the raising and handling of pets had to be radically changed. These were no cringing terror stricken wild things with feral eyes that cowered fearfully in dark corners, but a pair of very wide awake, aggressive personalities, who fastened themselves on us as their protectors. They gave themselves completely into our hands, and proceeded to levy unceasing demands on our attention. They allowed us at no time to forget the responsibilities that we had incurred, and before long they had us trained to sleep with one eye open and one hand on the milk can. Feeding them was a problem. They would not drink the diluted milk out of a dish, and having no feeding bottle we conceived the idea of loading a slim twig with the sweet milk out of the can, closing the beaver's mouth over it with our fingers, and pulling out the stick. Masticating this sticky mass kept them interested for long periods at a time, and they did not need much of it, so this scheme simplified matters considerably. They were very gentle, and they had a kind of naive disarming friendliness of disposition that took it quite for granted that they belonged, and that we were well disposed towards them and would see them through.

After feeding times they desired to be picked up and fondled and it was not long before they made this a regular habit, falling asleep in odd places such as the inside of an open shirt, half way up a sleeve, or draped around a person's neck. Should they be removed from these places they would immediately awaken and return in the most determined manner, and if placed in their box they awoke at once, and with piercing outcries demanded to be again taken up, grasping our hands and lifting themselves up by means of them. If their cries were disregarded they would eventually lapse into unconsciousness, but the passage near the box of either one of us restored them to immediate and vociferous wakefulness. They soon got to know our voices, and would answer concertedly with loud exclamations when spoken to. We allowed them to roam around the tent at will, and occasionally on their rambles they would become lost and parted. Their bold self-confidence would then quickly desert them, and they became lonely and would call frantically for help, and on being placed together they would throw themselves on their backs with wiggles and squeals of joy, and lie down together holding tightly on to each other's fur. Often as they lay sleeping we would speak to them for the fun of having them awaken and answer us, which they invariably did, in their shrill childish treble. Should this, however, occur too often they would become very impatient and express their annoyance in no uncertain terms. Their voices were really the most remarkable thing about them, much resembling the cries of a human infant, without the volume but with a greater variety of expression, and at all hours of the day and night there was liable to be some kind of a new sound issuing from the interior of the box. The best known and easiest to recognize of these was the loud, long and very insistent call for lunch, which chorus broke out about every two hours.

These whimsical little creatures early showed evidence of qualities and capabilities that at once arrested our attention and it was not long before our diminutive charges became attached to us, and, I am free to confess, we to them. Each had a special liking for one of us, and continued faithful to his choice. They lavished this affection on us in a number of curious ways, such as upsetting the box, as soon as they were big enough to do so, and rushing out at us as we passed, or creeping into our blankets at night and cuddling up to us. They would generally lie on our bodies, one on each of us, the favoured position being a rather inconvenient one across the throat. If alarmed whilst out and around, they would come gliding along belly to the ground, each to his chosen friend, and sit quietly as two mice until the supposed danger had passed.

They were continually escaping, and the first few times this happened we hunted for them high and low, feeling ourselves pretty smart to ferret out two such small objects from the underbrush. But our anxiety and subsequent gratification were both quite unnecessary, as we discovered that on hearing us in the brush they would run towards us of their own accord. On this account we became over-confident, and one morning, having failed to close the box before retiring, we awoke to find their chamber empty, and no sign of a beaver any place in the tent. A prolonged and wide search failed to locate the wanderers. We hunted all that day both by canoe and on land, and remained out all night, going back to the tent every so often in the somewhat vain expectation that they might have returned in the meantime. It seemed hard to believe that they would desert us like that, attached to us as they seemed to be, but after all they were wild animals, they were well able to travel and feed themselves, and could now probably get along without us. We felt a little hurt about it. Maybe too, they could not return; there were plenty of hawks and owls, and an otter would make short work of them. Realizing at last that they had been gone over thirty hours, and that if living, they would now be far beyond our reach, we gave up the search and went home to get some sleep, not a little sad—and there in the tent, all unconscious of the excitement of which they were the cause, sat the two deserters on the bed, soaking wet, and squeezing the water out of their coats on to the blankets.

After this experience we simply pitched our camp near any old lake, and with due regard for predatory birds and beasts, we let them come and go as they pleased. They would walk down to the lake with that methodical step of theirs, bathe, swim, and play in the reeds awhile and return, plodding solemnly up and down the water trail together, like two little old men out for a constitutional. They were good housekeepers too. By this time they were beyond the milk stage, and to supplement their natural diet we fed them once a day on porridge and each had his dish, which when empty, was pushed over to the side of the tent, and the instinct for stacking used material as far out of the way as possible caused them to try and rear the plates against the wall. This was not easy to do, but they persisted at it and very often succeeded.

At three months of age they ceased to be of any further trouble to us save for the daily feed of porridge, an insatiable and very active curiosity regarding the contents of provision bags and boxes, the frequent desire for petting that seemed to fill some great want in their lives, and the habit they had of coming into our beds, soaking wet, at all hours of the night.

They were scrupulously clean, were gentle and good natured, they gave out no odour whatever, and were altogether the best conducted pair of little people one could wish to live with. They were very self-effacing, and a good deal of the time were neither to be seen nor heard; but always there came moments, generally about sun down, when they seemed to feel the need of some attention, and getting to know of this we made a point of giving it to them. And they would give little bleats and play with our hands, nibble our finger tips and climb on us, so far as climbing was possible to them, with many absurd but genuine evidences of real affection.

This desire to be made much of, the appeal in their voices, the habit they had of playing with a lock of hair, a button or a buckskin fringe, made them seem very childlike to us. These mushy spells did not as a rule last very long, and soon satisfied they would go about their business and perhaps not show up till daylight, weary, wet, and very sleepy.

That Anahareo should become devoted if not actually addicted to them, is not at all remarkable; but my own attitude towards them was something quite beyond my expectations, and was even likely to have a compromising effect on our chief means of livelihood—the beaver hunt. I wondered at times if it was quite manly to feel as I did towards these small beasts. But I was able to call to my rescue the recollection of an ugly pock-marked Indian, a huge, evil appearing man I had always disliked, but who spent a whole day in the rain searching for a young beaver he had lost; and when he recovered it, he came home in the pouring rain in his shirt sleeves carrying the shivering little creature wrapped up in his coat. Yet another had shot a good lead-dog for killing a beaver he had kept for two years as a pet. Evidently the little devils had a way of working on a person's sympathies, and at the commencement I was a little sly and furtive about them when Anahareo was around. Their utter dependence on our good will claimed all of any chivalry we had. Their little sneezes and childish coughs, their little whimpers and small appealing noises of affection, their instant and pathetically eager response to any kindness, their tiny clinging hand-like forepaws, their sometimes impatiently stamping feet, and their little bursts of independence, all seemed to touch a chord of tenderness for the small and helpless that lays dormant in every human heart. Riotously happy for the most part, they were at odd times subject to fits of peevishness and irritation, during which they quarrelled and slapped at one another and at us, but these moods were of short duration and were, we found, the result of improper feeding, which was later to have more serious results. Their hands—one can call them nothing else—were nearly as effective as our own more perfect members would be, in the uses they were put to. They could pick up very small objects with them, manipulate sticks and stones, strike, push, and heave with them and they had a very firm grasp which it was difficult to disengage. When peeling a stick they used them both to twist the stem with supple wrist movements, while the teeth rapidly whittled off the succulent bark as it went by, much after the fashion of a lathe.

They were greedy little fellows and were constantly trying to steal from one another. These attempts however were never very serious, and seldom were successful, as the owner of the stick was always well prepared, and on the approach of his companion, welcome enough at all other times, he would set up a vigorous vocal protest which continued long after the object of them had given up all thought of plunder. They would none the less allow us to approach and handle them freely whilst eating, without any complaint, but if we attempted to lay hold of their wooden sandwich they would let out a sharp ejaculation or two, and promptly turn their backs on us.

Should we be away up the lake for any length of time, we would, on our return, call them whilst yet some distance away, and they would come to meet the canoe, answering the call with long high-pitched cries, and on close approach would reach up to us with outstretched hands in eager expectancy, grasping our fingers and looking up at us and making the most uncommon sounds. For we always made it a practice to bring along little bits of sweet things we made for them, and they would lie in the water eating them with loud enjoyment and a very audible smacking of lips. This usage gave us nearly as much pleasure as it gave to them, the more especially when we found that whether satisfied or not they did not leave us, but would try to get aboard the canoe, and on being lifted in, the tail providing a very convenient handle for the purpose, they would clamber over our persons with every sign of pleasure. And if the treats in any way improved the welcome we received, show me the very good friend whose heart is not the warmer towards you when you set him at your table!

Yet, on reflection, it struck me as passing strange that we, representatives of two tribes who, above all others, had each in their day made the war-trail a thing of horror (an art, by the way, in which the whole world is at present busy in perfecting itself), should be wearing ourselves to a frazzle over the likes and dislikes of two miserable little creatures that were not, according to civilized standards, worth the powder to blow them to hell.

Towards the middle of Summer it became necessary to go out to the railroad to confer with others of my calling on the possibilities of the coming Winter. On this journey, whilst in the canoe, we let the beaver run loose as they were not able to climb out of it. On the portages they were dumped into a grain bag, and dangled from a thwart of the inverted canoe. One of these carries was two miles in length, and they cried the whole way while mosquitoes settled on the bag in swarms. Having no longer a box, at camping grounds we hung them up in the bag near a fire to keep the mosquitoes from them, so they were at times pretty well smoked. They slept nearly all the time and ate nothing, but arrived in fair shape except that they were a little groggy. An Indian who came to see them said they were dying, but an hour or two in the water restored them. It was now necessary to confine them both day and night, owing to the presence of a multitude of idle sleigh dogs that formed the larger part of the population of the village. They expressed their disapprobation of this treatment by promptly eating their way out of everything we tried to keep them in, so that they had me busy providing boxes which lasted, if they were good, one night.

Another trip had yet to be made to the trapping camp for some equipment that remained there, so we left the beaver in care of a friend who locked them carefully into an outhouse built of logs. We returned a few days later with our load, and as soon as we disembarked Anahareo went to visit the beaver, whilst I crossed immediately over to the store to obtain a good strong box, as we expected to board a train that evening. I was met on my way back by a pale and distraught Anahareo.... The beaver were gone! They had eaten through the timbers at the thin place where two logs rested one on the other, and gone on a tour. Our friend was greatly disturbed at their loss, knowing how we prized them. He muzzled a beaver dog, an animal especially trained to hunt them, and set out to trail them down. I commenced to comb the surrounding woods, covering the ground in the direction of the lake which was some considerable distance away. The beaver had not been gone long, and could, under ordinary circumstances, have been easily recovered; the danger was grave only on account of the huskies of which there were dozens, and cheap-skate hunters who would kill anything on sight.

We were not long away before one of the beaver, the female, showed up in the yard, and when seen was picking her way nonchalantly amongst several dogs, some of whom were commencing to circle warily behind her. With a shout and a wild leap Anahareo threw herself between them, and grabbing up the startled beaver ran for the nearest door, pursued by the enemy. This I learned on my return from an unsuccessful search. And when the hunting dog returned and was found to have also failed,[1] we, Anahareo and I, looked at one another silently and with one common thought—the little male whose curiosity and wandering habits had got him into hot water continually, had made just one trip too many. The big strong box looked pretty large and empty with one small lonely kitten beaver crouched unhappily in a corner of it. They had never been apart more than a few minutes all their short lives, and this one was wailing querulously in the way they had when lonesome, or in some trouble.

I hunted all evening without avail. The train we were to have taken passed on without us, and it would very soon be dark. The place was swarming with huskies, hunting dogs and —— dogs, most of them half starved, and the kitten would have made no more than a mouthful for any of them. The chances were poor. I had never realized until now how much the little fellows had gotten in under my skin. The lost waif was my own particular chum, and I was going to miss him. Yet I could not believe but what he had somehow made the grade and got to the lake, distant

---

[1] The very young of most animals, as a protection against predatory beasts, are odourless.

though it was. They had blundered complacently through a number of tough situations from the time of their birth on, and—there—sure enough, across a narrow bay I saw a dark brown object on the shore line, dimly seen in the rapidly falling dusk—just in time! I gave several loud calls and instantly, not from the direction of this brown object at all, but from a spot not a stone's throw ahead of me, came an answer, a most dolorous wailing. The willows were very thick and I could see nothing, but I advanced, calling every few steps and getting an answer each time, until with eyes bulging and hair erect, the wanderer burst through the leaves and threw himself at my feet. I picked up the little furry body and held him close to my shirt, while he uttered barely audible whimpering sounds and burrowed his nose into my neck. He was bone dry, so that although he must have been on the point of entering the water, he had allowed himself to be called away from it by the sound of a voice that he knew. Never before, and only once since, have I had the same feeling of relief at the recovery of anything lost.

Anahareo of course was overjoyed. And now the so-big box had its small quota of inhabitants, and from it there arose sounds of strife as the reunited couple quarrelled lustily over some sweet biscuits we had bought to celebrate the occasion. And as I watched them disporting themselves in happy unconsciousness of any danger past, present or future, I found it strange and a little disquieting that these animals, that had seemed heretofore to have only one use, and that I had destroyed by hundreds, should turn out to be so likeable, should so arouse the protective instinct of a man who was their natural enemy.

From a purely economic viewpoint, I had long been opposed to the wholesale slaughter now going forward, which was indeed almost at an end for want of victims. But this was different. These beasts had feelings and could express them very well; they could talk, they had affection, they knew what it was to be happy, to be lonely—why, they were little people! And they must be all like that. All this tallied with the incredible stories I had heard in younger days, and perhaps accounted for the veneration that our people, when savage, had held them in, calling them "Beaver People," "Little Indians" and "Talking Mothers." Indian mothers, bereaved of an infant, had suckled baby beavers at their breasts and thus gained some solace. I had seen them myself cared for tenderly by those whose hands they had fallen into. And I would have left them to die with never a thought, an intention that seemed now to have been something nearly barbarous. Well, we had to live, and anyway they were all right. To make sure I looked inside the box, and carefully securing the lid, went to bed.

That night they gnawed their way out of their new domicile and, weary with this, and that, and one thing and another, were found the next morning fast asleep along side of it.

Having again missed our train, with the freakish irresponsibility common to our kind when not seriously employed we decided to miss a few more and stay for the weekend. The news concerning our menagerie had spread, and we were approached by a fur dealer who wanted to see what we had. There were, he said, a pair of other young beaver that an Indian had turned into a store keeper in part payment of his debt, and he himself had intended to buy them. They were not, he said, in good shape and might die, and he would not touch them unless shipped to him at the present owner's risk. He was much taken with ours, as they were in first-class condition, and he made us a good offer. This of course we did not accept; although we were getting short of money we had no notion of parting with them.

But we did go to see the other kittens, first putting our own under a heavily weighted galvanized wash tub, and setting a guard over them with orders to show them to nobody. The place we were going to was a combined general store and hotel, but its principal source of revenue was the sale of contraband liquor. This bootlegger was not a bad fellow at heart, and he gave away as much whiskey as he ever sold. He was a very devout man too, and had in his private chamber a kind of altar with a candle burning continuously before it. Here he was in the habit of holding family worship, and it was no uncommon thing for him to rise from his knees and repair behind his grocery counter, sell a bottle of liquor to a customer, and return to his devotions, being careful to bless himself before entering the sacred chamber. These people, who had bought the new kittens, had no idea of how to look after them, and the little creatures were in utter misery. They were plainly in a dying condition, crying weakly without ceasing. When we reached inside the box they clutched our fingers in their tiny hands with pitiful cries of distress, as though begging the best they knew how for somebody, anybody, to take away this great trouble that had fallen upon them, to keep them from the black abyss into which they were sinking.

I could pity, but not condemn. I had not the right; at the old beaver house I had nearly done this very thing myself.

"If only they would let us have them," whispered Anahareo, "just to die in the box with ours beside them, so they wouldn't be lonely."

"We'll buy them." I turned to the store keeper, "How much do you want for them?"

"Plenty," he countered. "How much you got?"

I told him. "Not enough," he said. He had to live too.

Anahareo offered to care for them, suggesting shrewdly that they would be worth more if they recovered. This overture also was refused. The merchant had sent for a license to enable him to ship them to the dealer we had met, and would, he stated, be satisfied if the beavers lived until the deal was settled, and they safely on their way. If they then succumbed it would be, he considered, a good joke on the buyer. This, I might add, was a fair example of the ethics of more than a few of the bucket-shop fur buyers that the late boom in prices had produced.

But the kittens did not live, fortunately perhaps, and without water, proper food or care of any kind, one little prisoner was found on the Sunday morning lifeless in his cell, and the other lay dead beside a water pail that he had crawled to for the life-giving fluid that he could not reach.

And it seemed to me like very close to desecration, when the two little wasted forms that belonged in the clean sweet freedom of the Silent Places were thrown, dead and despised, into a dirty bucket of slops.

And later, as I looked in on the two small creatures that were so dependent on me, I knew that never would I sell them into bondage, and that living or dead they should be forever free. I thought too, of that other brown body lying squandered and lifeless on the bottom of their home-pond with its paw, so much like a hand, clamped in one of my traps. My gesture of atonement, made half in earnest at the time, now began to have a deeper meaning. And let times be never so hard in days to come, rather than be a party to such a scene as I had just witnessed in that sordid bootleg joint, I would myself go hungry.

I think it was at that moment that I finally decided to quit the beaver hunt for good.

CHAPTER THREE

How the Pilgrimage Commenced

THIS DECISION OF MINE TO GIVE UP BEAVER TRAPPING WAS not a hasty one. Beaver was an animal on which I had depended almost entirely for my living. They had been so identified with my own destiny as to be something in the light of a patron beast, far more so than an owl, a detestable bird whose name had been imposed on me only on account of my nocturnal habits. Although I had ably assisted at the destruction of this beast, now that he was in danger of extinction in the North, I had a sudden feeling of regret, something of that vacant feeling of bereavement that comes upon us on the disappearance of a familiar land mark, or on the decease of some spirited, well-respected enemy. Thus the hide hunters must have felt as the last buffalo dropped, so that some of them abjured forever the rifle and the knife, and strained every nerve to bring them back again. Even as veteran Indian fighters, better able to appreciate the qualities of their late foe now that he was down, reached out a helping hand to raise him up again.

One hundred thousand square miles of country in Ontario was dry of beaver, and save for their deserted works it was as if there never had been any. I had travelled nearly two thousand miles by canoe through a reputed beaver country to find only here and there a thinly populated colony, or odd survivors living alone. I had sat in council with the Simon Lake Ojibways and had talked with other bands from Grand Lake Victoria. Waswanipis from the Megiskan, Obijuwans from the head of the St. Maurice, wide-ranging half-breeds from far-off Peribonka, they all carried the same tale. The beaver were going fast; in large areas they were already gone. Was this then, to be the end? Beaver stood for something vital, something essential in this wilderness, were a component part of it; they *were* the wilderness. With them gone it would be empty; without them it would be not a wilderness but a waste. And I, to whom the railroad and the plough were anathema, had done all I could, along with the vandals, cheap fur traders, and low grade bushmen, to help put the country into shape for their reception.

The exuberant recklessness of my earlier days was past and gone, those lonely, wild and heedless days in the vast and empty silences, when I had been sufficient unto myself, leaving death behind me everywhere. I was beginning to ponder more and more deeply on the unfairness and injustice of trapping these animals. The influx of hordes of incompetent amateur trappers that high fur prices had inflicted on the country, I had looked on with uneasiness for some years past as a menace to the profession, and had constantly deplored the brutality of their methods. The regular trapper, if he knows his business at all, sets for beaver only under the ice, so the animal is invariably and cleanly drowned, or else escapes the trap uninjured. A dead animal, decently killed was no great matter, but a crippled beast was a crime and the woods were full of them.

A number of incidents had contributed to this line of thought. About the first of these was the sight of a mother beaver nursing one of her kittens whilst fast by one foot in a trap. She was moaning with pain, yet when I liberated her, minus a foot, she waited nearby for the tardy and inquisitive kitten, seeming by her actions to realize that she had nothing to fear from me. Suspended in the air by a spring-pole, I found another female—a beast that cried out in a voice strangely human when I took her down, and died with one of my fingers tightly grasped in her uninjured paw. She had been about to become a mother. This spring-pole is a particularly fiendish contrivance that jerks the unfortunate creature out of the water to hang there. The animal is uninjured and may remain there for days until it dies of thirst and exhaustion. Frequently birds will pick out the eyes before the animal is dead. These and other methods equally brutal are adopted by unskilled hunters who can get their beaver no other way, and these instances were only two out of dozens to be seen on every hand.

These inhumanities aroused in me a strange feeling; it was that these persecuted creatures no longer appeared to me as lawful prey, but as co-dwellers in this wilderness that was being so despoiled, the wilderness that was so relentless yet so noble an antagonist. They too fought against its hardships and made their home in it; we all, man and beast, were comrades-in-arms. To see them so abused awoke in me a kind of loyalty or *esprit-de-corps*, so that for me to continue my own operations against them along with these alien interlopers who had nothing in common with any of us, now seemed like some form of treason, almost as though I were a renegade who assisted an invader to despoil his unarmed fellow-country men. It would be more fitting that I should sue for a permanent peace with all the Dwellers Amongst the Leaves and throw in my lot with them against this unprincipled enemy that stooped to such dishonest meanness. There seemed to be something grossly unfair and unjust about the whole affair.

Besides the decimation of game, there were other deplorable features of this infestation. Stealing commenced, beginning with pilfering on trap-lines; soon caches were being robbed of equipment, and trappers came in to their grounds to find themselves without snowshoes, stoves, blankets or traps. Camps were cleaned out of supplies and were left in a filthy condition; even canoes were stolen. The old traditions began to crumble. Men began to be wary and mistrustful; some locked their cabins, a thing that bit very deeply into the old free spirit of hospitality of the real woodsmen. In those days we figured that a man who built his camp in a hidden spot or locked his door, was not only an outlander, but he was not to be trusted. Now, and shamefully, it seemed to have become necessary. To rob a cache was the unforgivable thing, and the odd man was shot. It was a sign of the times—the country was getting civilized.

The little beavers are born any time from the middle of May to the first week in June. Beaver hides are still prime at that season in Northern areas. So the Spring hunt is still on, and transients swept through the country like a relentless scourge, invading the territories of others, killing off the mother beaver who are easily caught at that time, and passed on to fresh fields leaving the baby beavers to starve by hundreds. Apart from the barbarity of this method, it had done more in a decade to annihilate the beaver, than the Winter trapping of centuries. Often the woebegone little creatures, already some time without food, would attempt to follow the hunter's canoe as he paddled away with the body of their mother, wailing despairfully but ineffectually. It is to be said in favour of natives that they nearly always adopted these orphans. But their story had always been pitiful, even to the apathetic Indians—a craving for attention, a clutching of little forepaws, confinement, neglect, and after a few weeks almost inevitable death, wailing to the last, with unforgettable voices that seemed somehow to yet be faintly audible long after they were still and the little thwarted lives had passed into the discard.

I had rescued a number myself. I remember one little fellow, who used to sleep rolled up in a furry ball on the side of my head, all night; and when I turned over he would awaken, and passing across my forehead as I rolled, would arrive at the other side all set, there to fall asleep again. He used to climb up on my shoulder, and as I worked around, cooking or whatnot, he would lie draped across the back of my neck and I often ate my meals with him there. But he was a sick little beaver, and became at last too weak to do these things and died one day in my hand, still trying feebly to climb up to his old familiar place.

Two others were with me for three weeks and were exceptionally playful and chummy, and could not bear to be three feet apart. They used to follow me around, tight to my heels, coaxing plaintively to be noticed, until they too, suddenly drooped and died. Right to the last they had their tiny paws clutched in each other's fur, as though to be sure they were not parted even on this the last of all their journeyings.

I had watched fat little beavers sitting up like queer diminutive Buddhas on a river bank, solemnly wagging their heads at the rising sun, while the mother lay by and crooned at them, plucking them towards her at intervals and rolling on her back from time to time, murmuring with contentment, happy with her young and the sheer joy of living.

The spectacle of a crippled beaver with only one hind leg and three stumps, doing his best to carry on, had moved me to put him out of his misery. Every year in March, when they sometimes came out on the surface, I had laid in wait for beaver and killed them with a club, and their resignation in the face of death was always disturbing; some of them had tried to shelter their heads from the blow with their hands. One, badly wounded with shot, had swam ashore within a few feet of me, and had lain there looking up at me so that I had boggled the execution most horribly. The incident had haunted me for days.

I was getting sick of the constant butchery, and the sight of the ruined works so toilsomely erected, the accusing loneliness of the empty beaver ghost-towns, and the utter desolation of the ravaged colonies was saddening to any thinking man. But this had not, however, prevented me from going on to the next lodge and setting my traps as carefully as ever; and like many another good business man I had justified myself, and had resolutely closed my mind to any thought of the hardships I might be inflicting in the course of my profitable undertakings. They had seemed to me to be just foolish dupes who took my proffered lures, beasts that were put on earth for my convenience, dumb brutes that didn't know the difference. And now had come these small and willing captives, with their almost child-like intimacies and murmurings of affection, their rollicking good fellowship with not only each other but ourselves, their keen awareness, their air of knowing what it was all about. They seemed to be almost like little folk from some other planet, whose language we could not yet quite understand. To kill such creatures seemed monstrous. I would do no more of it. Instead of persecuting them further I would study them, see just what there really was to them. I perhaps could start a colony of my own; these animals could not be permitted to pass completely from the face of this wilderness. I thought of Michael Pablo and the buffalo. His idea had borne fruit: why should not mine? But this matter took some figuring. There was nothing simple about it. I had first to discover a family of beaver not already claimed by some other hunter, and then hold them against comers, by no means an easy task. I would tame them; so far an unheard of proceeding, but I had faith in the crazy scheme, and was convinced by what I knew of our little fellows that this was possible. It was like to be a hungry, thankless job, unless I could locate in a good fur country that would provide us a livelihood, in which case it would swarm with trappers and I would have to be my own game warden, with consequent and highly unpleasant antagonisms. I would undoubtedly be looked on as a renegade; but my mind was made up, and I would attempt to go through with it.

Meanwhile my equipment consisted of two small beaver and a bill at the grocery store.

I broke the news to Anahareo with some misgivings.

"Well!" I informed her, with what assurance I could muster. "We got a new job. I'm off the beaver hunt for good."

"I wish you meant it," she replied skeptically.

"It's true enough though; I'm through," I insisted. "I am now the President, Treasurer, and sole member of the Society of the Beaver People. How about a donation?"

"Donations are going to be pretty thin," she laughed, "but I am glad. I never hoped you'd do that. What'll you do now?"

I told her my plans, adding,

"It may go hard with us—we might have to pull in the belt a few notches. Are you game?"

"Of course," she replied. "We'll both work at it."

Good old Anahareo! Not much on the skillet, but right there with bells on when work was required to be done.

Meanwhile other interests had arisen that might eventually have some bearing on this question of a livelihood. For some time there had been staying with us an old Algonquin Indian by the name of David White Stone, who came from Ontario as we ourselves did. Though we had never met before, we were acquainted with him and he with us, by means of that far reaching and mysterious, but highly efficient moccasin telegraph system, peculiar to primitive peoples, whereby a man's character and history are known with uncanny accuracy over whole territories where he has never even appeared. He was representative of that type of Indian that has assimilated much of the white man's knowledge, whilst retaining nearly all the characteristics of his race. He spoke English and French fluently, but with a marked accent. He was a tall, hard, wiry man, but had the moderate movements and retiring disposition of his kind. He was possessed of an unusual sense of humour, a pair of extremely penetrating eyes, and could howl more like a wolf than any man I ever heard. When in his cups he could sing the Mass very passably, and he had a shot gun which threw shot so close, that "You could pick a man out of a crowd with it." Whilst in these fortunately rare fits of religious fervour he became very desirous of demonstrating the powers of this unusual weapon. In his youth the famous Iroquois raids into Northern Ontario were still spoken of, and he was not at all sure that some bands of them did not lay hidden in some inaccessible fastnesses, planning further mischief. He had assisted in the laying out of the Canadian Pacific Railway, and had been present when Edward Prince of Wales with his picked canoemen, had started from Mattawa on his historic canoe trip along the old fur route down the Ottawa River to Montreal. He still believed that in some mysterious, far-off, undiscovered region, there was game without end—and gold. For Dave was a prospector, and the year before had found a mine, at present unstaked and unrecorded. Now mining leaves me cold as a rule and I know little of it; for though I had followed several mining rushes including the spectacular Cobalt stampede of 1906, it had been as a packer and canoeman only, and I had felt, at the time, slightly contemptuous of those misguided people who were grubbing in the rocks and dirt with such eagerness. But an essayer pronounced Dave's samples to be so rich that they interested even me. Evenings we talked over this mine, and squinted knowingly through a glass at the samples, and pored over maps. And the old man's enthusiasm so fired the imagination of Anaharco, who comes of a family of prospectors, that I think the only thing that stopped them from starting out on an expedition at eleven o'clock one night, was the impossibility of obtaining supplies at that hour. With some difficulty I persuaded them to at least consider waiting till Spring, when we might have a stake, and then we'd all go. That was his plan, share and share alike. Then we'd cash in, get us a good outfit, and head North to take our pick of the wild country beyond the reach of civilization; for we all still believed that there was game "in them thar' hills." We all soberly discussed the arrangements that would be necessary for the beaver, who would be big by then, quite as though they were two growing children whose welfare had to be considered in any plans we made. David used to play with them by the hour, teaching them their manners and officiating at their games. I had not divulged my ultimate scheme to him, as I was possessed of a

superstition that any plan which was broached to a party not directly connected with it would never be carried out.

It had been raining steadily in that part of Quebec for three straight
summers, and living in a tent we were always damp and none too comfortable. The Indians were dying like flies from tuberculosis and other ills
that this weather was greatly responsible for. Their hunting grounds had
been invaded and depleted by "railroad" trappers, and those that were
not starving were so undernourished that they had no longer any resistance against the diseases that civilization had brought to them. The
Indian doctor from Ottawa had his hands full, and he advised us to get
away from these conditions before we fell a victim to them.

A piece of luck in the shape of a hunting party, offered the wherewithal to make the move, so we hired out with them, beaver and all. The
beaver became at once the mascots of the party and had a whale of a
time, getting acquainted with the sportsmen, cutting holes in tents and
tarpaulins, stealing bread, getting into the butter and eggs, and being a
general nuisance. We let them go at nights, and they got lost pretty regularly, as we moved camp often and these constant changes in the surroundings confused them. But they always arrived home somehow,
entering the wrong tent at three o'clock one morning, one of them clambering over a sleeping man and trailing his wet body from nose to tail
over the man's face. This caused a passing sensation and some momentary but caustic comment. Towards the end of the trip the party ran low
in provisions, and the beaver were much envied, as, their kind of food
growing all around them, they were for several days the only members of
the expedition who had enough to eat.

About this time we met up with a Micmac Indian who hailed from
New Brunswick. His name was, we will say, Joe Isaac. He was actually
called by some other biblical appellation, but I refrain using it here out of
respect for his feelings, should he ever peruse this account. However, he
read, he said, nothing but the best of literature, so that leaves me fairly
safe. In my wanderings I have met numbers of pretty fair liars, artistic
and otherwise, and of these he was by far the most accomplished. He was
a natural and to the manner born; one of those men who holds you in a
kind of a trance, and whom you must believe as you hear him, even

though after you escaped the spell gradually worked off, and you began to see the light. He allowed it to leak out in conversation that he was a professional athlete, and admitted that he was pretty good, and "would go behind no man's back to say so." And he was good, there was no denying it; he was a very supple man. He had made his living at this profession, but he took first prizes so consistently that at last he had been barred all over the continent. He was at present merely passing the time till this ban should be lifted, as working, he said, took the spring out of his bones. No place could be mentioned but he had been there at some time or another; if you had been there yourself, and confounded his statements, he escaped confusion by the simple expedient of changing the name of the place. He had scars supposed to have been received in battle, but which turned out to be the result of a surgical operation. His experiences seemed a little crowded for his apparent years, but by careful calculation on that basis we were able to compute his age at about one hundred and eighteen. Altogether a man of parts.

This is a portrait of the gentleman who was to be responsible for our next adventure. Amongst other regions, he had been in a district known as Temiscouata, and as it happened he really had. Of this spot he talked long and lavishly. He had boats on the Touladi lakes there, owned a hunting lodge, his credit was good at all stores, and he had friends who would welcome with open arms any friends of his. I discounted his possessions, and discreetly divided the sum of his descriptions by about six, and found that even then this Temiscouata or Touladi or whatever the place was called, must be quite a spot. And it was at that.

Anyway it was a new location, we had never been there before, and it was far away, therefore as good a place as any. And of course there was bound to be a hunt there. I don't know where we got the idea that all of Canada was swarming with game; Lord knows we did enough moving around trying to follow it up. It appeared from what Joe told us at one of his seances, that the settlements there were in an impoverished condition owing to the encroachments of wild animals. The deer were so numerous that they destroyed much of the crops. The fishermen on the lakes were at their wits end owing to a plague of mink and otter that had lately descended on the country. Saw logs arrived at the mill, after passing through this beaver-infested territory, all gouged up by their teeth marks. There was also a species of man-eating cat for which the Government offered a rich bounty. After this enumeration he fell into one of his shorter, and more reflective silences, during which, no doubt, further material was being gathered. I took the opportunity to put a little cross-examination.

"Did you say there was beaver there, Joe?" I asked him casually. Joe settled himself in his seat so as to better take up the recoil, and cocked his lip for a broadside.

"Beaver!" said he, his eye kindling—and then he was away. He was most impressive; it was nice to hear him talk. He warmed to his subject. Yes, beaver were very numerous. So numerous in fact that they were over-crowded in some of the smaller streams. It was said that some of them, on this account had to live out, and grew as a protection short hair on their tails, like otters. These specimens, it appeared, were known as "grass beaver." On being further interrogated, he admitted that he could not vouch for this from personal observation. Why he should balk at so small a matter was mildly surprising, but we supposed that like any other master of his art, he knew his limits.[1]

This Temiscouata being near his native territory, he had not perhaps, for that reason, viewed it through quite the same golden haze that adorned the more distant areas, and some little part of his description was supported by fact. Otherwise this story could not have been written. But the discrepancies were many and varied, as will be seen. But his yarns were attractive, I'll say that for them, and well told too. With my conservation idea in mind, I was a little insistent in my cross-examining concerning beaver, and once he bared his arm and looked thoughtfully at a scar. I think he had a notion to tell me it was a beaver bite, received in some fight with a herd, or band, or covey, or whatever formation they went in, of the land or grass variety. I hastily changed the subject. He was always very hurt if you disbelieved him, and I didn't press the matter, as

[1] The writer has since read an account by V. B. Cawston in which he describes just such an animal, existing in the southern interior of British Columbia. He intimates that they need little water, and states that they cut grass and dry it for hay. They are, he says, the size of a ground-hog and have a short tufted tail. An opportunity is offered here for some interesting research.

there were sure to be a few of them anyway, and one family was all I needed for the nucleus of my project.

So maps were got out again, routes were drawn with sticks in the sand, and we talked and ate Temiscouata and Touladi for about a week.

Trappers' tales! How well we know them, how we love to hear them—and tell them! How, knowing better, do we delight to sail away on some wild goose chase that promises little profit and much adventure—because Peter Handspike says he knew a hunter who was in a country where beaver were so thick, mind you, and the cuttings so heavy and piled so high, that in getting over them a man fell and broke two of his legs—yes sir, broke his two legs and died there. And (here's the secret) no one had hunted there since! And now beaver was as thick as that—(the fingers of both hands held clustered before the face and peered through with difficulty, indicating the closely packed masses of beaver)—and the snowshoeing was the best you ever saw!

Dave used to stand by and listen to these monstrous falsehoods, chuckling quietly to himself, and although he was the wisest of us all he never contradicted them—afraid, he said, to spoil a good thing.

The fact that these yarns could at best be only partly true, and were only half-believed, made little difference. Always there was the lure of the Unknown, the appeal to the wandering spirit, amounting to a passion, that possessed every last one of our kind to the core of his being. The suggestion was about all that was needed, and a sketchy description or two, to start the ball rolling. A map was considered the choicest kind of literature, intriguing possibilities to be read in every outline. While men openly derided the tall tales they listened to with such avidity, they made, hasty and secret preparations to act on them, and took a chance.

Gamblers all—let's go!! And so to Temiscouata we went.

Poor old Dave nearly cried when we left. We felt like deserters leaving him, but we couldn't rake up the amount of his ticket. We had barely our own fares and other expenses, and must ourselves depend on getting a hunting debt in a strange place. The old fellow was negotiating the sale of his canoe and the famous "crowd-gun" to raise the price. I had myself just traded in an old canoe, companion of a good few years on the trail, for a new pair of snowshoes, and I knew about how he felt. So we said good-bye to our friend, promising to send for him as soon as we had made a couple of good lifts on our trap-line.

We took a complete outfit—canoe, snowshoes, guns, cookery, everything. The beaver went in a tin-lined box with a dish for water secured in one corner, and we had a large bundle of poplar for them in the baggage car. When it became necessary to change cars, I carried them in the box on my back, by means of a tump line. In Quebec city we fed them on the station platform, attracting thereby a large crowd, and there was talk of "wild animals insufficiently caged." We hustled them away from there, and took refuge in a kind of a one-man restaurant, where the waitress in charge kindly offered me sanctuary. A reporter gouged us for our life history, refused to believe us and gave us his opinion that we were cleverly masquerading, warning us that there was a law against it. The beaver, restive from long confinement and excited no doubt by the noise, commenced to gnaw at the lining of their box, and only ceased when it was in motion. Fearing they would damage their teeth, I rigged my tump line and walked up and down with them. We crossed the river on the ferry steamer, and while on board I had to stand with the box of beaver on the tump line, whilst they cried out in long continuous wails and scrambled around, and spilled water down my back. We drew a lot of attention, some of it unwelcome, but most of it friendly. We got a lot of fun out of watching the expression on the faces of those close to us as they tried, without seeming to do so, to locate the source of the crying. One gentleman, being at the time well lubricated, asked us why, in the name of God did we not let the child out of the box like Christian people.

Eventually we were all safely stowed away on a train again and this was very little the result of any skill or management on my part, although I belong to that class of traveller who is always very much on time, but was greatly owing to the kindness to strangers, and the desire to help out, that we were to find characterises the population of the Eastern part of the Province of Quebec.

The train pulled out, the beaver quit lamenting, and we began to look about us. To my uneasiness I saw that the train was headed more and more South and East, and through a well settled country; a dismal outlook. Here and there stood occasional lone trees, recognizable in their build as originals remaining from the vast forests that must have once possessed this region, and reflecting in their lonesome and forlorn appearance something, I thought, of our own case. Crossing the St. Lawrence, that great river that in its lower reaches so definitely divides highlands of the wild Laurentians from the tamer low country to the South, had seemed an irrevocable step, and I had felt as though we were cutting ourselves off forever from our country and friends. It had been like crossing a bridge into a forbidden country, or passing a milestone on a road leading to destruction past which it was impossible to return. The hypnotic effect of Joe Isaac's oracular utterances had pretty well worn off, and now, as the swiftly revolving wheels clicked off the hurrying miles with deadly finality, we were penetrating deeper and deeper into what was to all intents and purposes a foreign country. This, I reflected with bitter irony, was how a captured animal felt when he was torn from his native heath and shipped away in a crate.

A train ride was no new experience to me. Beneath the sheltering wing of irascible but benevolent old Bill Cody, or under the stern protective discipline of an army, I had seen plenty territory through the windows of a day coach, and in later days, on the occasional trips made to such small centres as Sudbury and Chapleau, I had considered myself a pretty seasoned traveller. The looks of the country through which the train had passed on these occasions had been of little interest, and had been surveyed with the feeling of rather detached complacency with which we had always viewed the somewhat abortive intrusions of the settlers. But this was a different matter; it was to be no joy ride. There was the serious consideration of a livelihood, and there was more than myself to think of. The difference was that between seeing a mock battle in the movies, and suddenly finding oneself under fire in a front line trench. My accustomed manner of living had in no way equipped me to earn a livelihood under the conditions that obtained here. We were going South-East and it would get worse. I looked towards the three living creatures for whose well-being I was responsible, and began to feel considerable doubt as to the wisdom of this venture. Anahareo looked up from an aperture in the beaver box in which her face was buried, and caught my anxious glance. Instantly she asked:

"What are you worrying about now? We are going to make out all right."

"But the country, look at it. Is that your idea of a hunting ground?" I asked, supplementing, "And the train swinging Souther all the time."

"It'll change," she said. "I bet Temiscouata is just all bush."

"Maybe, maybe," I said, adding cheerfully, that is, as cheerfully as possible, "Oh! but sure we'll make out, sure we will." I thought a while. "I'll go see the conductor."

We thought this might be a good idea, so setting out I trailed this official down to the news agent's stand, and there cornered him up. He turned out to be a genial person with very optimistic views, and I got some reassurance there, but not too much.

"Your ticket calls for Cabano," he stated, "and all your stuff is right with you on the baggage car, so you can't do much about it. I know that Temiscouata country, it's not bad at all. Not much to hunt mebbe, but easy to live in. Good folks down there." He then added considerately, and I hoped truthfully, "If it's bush you're looking for, you'll find plenty. That's the trouble with it, too much bush."

Too much bush!

I returned to Anahareo.

"Well, what does the conductor think of it?" she asked.

"Says there's too much bush down there," said I. "The man's dotin'; probably thinks a few miles of poplar scrub is a forest."

And the farms, and towns, and factories, and macadamized roads continued to go streaking by, and we sat mighty close together on our seat, Anahareo and I, looking pretty pale around the gills, and viewing with increasing disquietude this country that was so different from our own wild friendly Northland. And the two little creatures in the box at our feet, our sole living tie with the woods and waters that were now so far away, seemed very close to us in spirit. They were part and parcel of this adventure now, members of this expedition that was not just two humans and two small animals, but a little company of four, pilgrims together in an alien land.

We changed trains again at Rivière du Loup, and although we swung due South from there, we began to glimpse heartening, though as yet distant views of purple wooded hills and the glimmer of an occasional lake. We even saw an Indian, but had no chance to speak to him.

Our two small companions in tribulation now began to show the effects of the journey, and the sympathetic conductor permitted us to break some train rules on their behalf, allowing us to turn them loose in the nearly empty coach, where they paraded solemnly up and down the aisle. He suggested that we go into the baggage car with them, where the air was fresher. This change and some fresh water (the entire contents of the cooler) brightened them up considerably. Water and fresh air seemed to always have a more revivifying effect on them than food. They had not eaten for a long time, nor for that matter had we, in our anxiety. On learning of this the train crew shared their lunches with us and helped feed the beaver, and I think, between the beaver and us, they gave away most of their dinner. Thus the noblesse of Old Quebec.

This friendly treatment and the sight of big Temiscouata Lake, flanked on the opposite shore by a high green mountain that was shaped like an elephant's back and crowned with pine trees, had a very cheering effect on our spirits. And as we neared our destination we saw stretching from the East shore of the Lake, and as far away as the eye could reach, the rolling sweep of a sure-enough, honest-to-God forest.

I loaded the outfit on the wagon that was to take us to the lake, and we moved off. The town was small, obviously a bush town. There were farms on this side, but there across the water was our environment, and plenty of it apparently. Things were beginning to shape up a good deal better. But I had still a lot of contriving to do. We had only about a month's provisions with us, and we would have to eat this Winter until we brought out some kind of a hunt. Everything depended on my getting a hunter's debt.

After I had paid the teamster I put back into the pocket of my buckskin coat our entire fortune, consisting of exactly one dollar and forty-five cents.

CHAPTER FOUR

How We Came to Touladi

THE TOWN OF CABANO WAS A TYPICAL FRENCH CANADIAN village, rambling picturesquely along the lake shore in the lee of a high forested ridge.

It was a pleasant sunny place, and had none of that chilling aloofness about it that so daunts the newcomer in many towns of its size; nor did the people who walked its streets have that harried look so often seen on the face of the city dweller. The very appearance of its tree-shaded board sidewalks and unpretentious but neat wooden dwellings, somehow suggested a spirit of good will and hospitality, as houses and clothes not unusually reflect the personality of those who occupy them. The town's most prominent features were a saw-mill, without which it would have had no reason for being, and a tall stone church that stood high on a knoll above the rest of the village, which seemed to nestle in the shelter of it.

As we passed through the streets with all our worldly goods piled on the accompanying wagon, we encountered numbers of people, all of whom were speaking French. No English was to be heard, and it was apparent that what little of the language I had picked up in France, consisting of about forty words, would have to be brushed up and the forty words put through their paces before very long. We heard the word *sauvages*—Indians— repeated several different times as the speakers looked us over. Evidently we were objects of interest, but although they were frankly curious, there was nothing impolite or unmannerly in the demeanour towards us of even the

276

most inquisitive amongst them. On the contrary it was characteristic that once, when we tried to pass a group that had been conversing on the sidewalk with the wholehearted vivacity common to their nationality, they stepped down into the road to let us by, while the ladies bowed and murmured their excuses and the men tipped their hats to us.

The far or Eastern shore of the lake was solid bush without visible habitations. Across there somewhere was Touladi,[1] gateway to our hopes, the river we had come so far to see. We decided to go there immediately and make camp. A heavy sea was rolling, and a party of people who were boarding the ferry boat, expressed concern that we should attempt the crossing in our, to them, frail canoe. We figured to put our canoe wherever a boat could go, and a whole lot of places no boat could ever go, so taking half our load and the beaver, we paddled across and landed in a quiet bay just around a point from the ferry landing. This ferry, under the name of St. Jean Baptiste (nearly everything carried the name of some saint in this country), plied back and forth over the mile wide crossing, and was the connecting link between Cabano and a single road that wound for fifteen miles through the woods to another and far smaller town. This hamlet consisted of about a hundred families, and was the last outpost of civilization; situated on the Touladi river, it was also accessible by canoe. St. John the Baptist followed us across, making heavy weather of it, bringing the remainder of our outfit and a few passengers. Meanwhile we turned the beaver loose for the exercise they sorely needed. They at once scrambled down to the lake where, awed perhaps by the presence of so much water after the rather arid interlude of the past week, they contented themselves with running up and down along the edge of it, and making occasional dashes into the lake and out again.

Not long after, we heard voices approaching around the bend, and the same people who had advised us against attempting the lake, came over to us in a state of the greatest concern as to our welfare, they having lost sight of the canoe and supposing us wrecked. They were cultured French people, and one of them spoke English fluently. And their expressions of genuine relief and their friendly interest, coming after the forebodings and utter loneliness of the past few days, and the thought that these people

[1] Pronounced Toolady.

really cared what happened to us, gave me a queer unaccustomed feeling in my throat, and neither of us could find any words. But when they opened up a basket they had brought and spread out cookies, and sandwiches and candies, saying that we must be hungry after our long trip, and offered them to us so graciously that it was impossible to refuse them, I saw Anahareo's eyes glistening with tears that were very near the surface.

The beaver, who had so far remained unobserved, created a diversion at this point by coming up from the lake with a view to inspecting the gathering, and the ladies cried "Oh! oh! look at the pets. Oh! *voyez les babettes!*" and stooped to fondle them with swift little pats, and then became afraid of them and ran from them, and the kittens, of course, scampered after them. Then the beavers in turn became also a little alarmed, and took to the lake and splashed water over the people with their tails, which caused more excitement. So that it was quite a merry party that day on the shores of Old Temiscouata; but I fear that our visitors found us very dumb and boorish in our bewilderment. They had a journey to make and presently took their leave, first getting us to write down out names in Indian and in English, and persuaded us to draw each a picture of our patron beast or namesake. So that Anahareo, who is called Pony by those that know her, made the outline of a little horse, and I portrayed a solemn and rather cadaverous-looking owl. And as a parting gift they left with us a box full of cakes and a bottle of wine—"For *souper, pour* your sup-per—think of us—" and their exclamations to one another could be heard long after they had rounded the point.

And as we watched them go we did not feel so lonely any more, and these kind people perhaps never knew how much they had helped to cheer the hearts of the two exiles that were out on this pilgrimage—or was it a crusade?—of which the end was not yet in sight. We had not, so far, made even a beginning, and our stuff was scattered all over; so we busied ourselves making camp, and built a pen for the "babettes," as we had heard some shooting and feared to leave them loose too long at a time.

The lake calmed down and that evening we had another visitor, a man in a skiff who brought us some small trout. He spoke not at all, having apparently no English, but smiled and nodded and offered his fish as he stood in his boat. I endeavoured to thank him as best I could in what

I took to be pretty fair French, my proficiency in the language existing mostly in just such polite phrases as were suitable to this occasion. I knew the words conveyed my meaning correctly, but he evidently did not understand me. I repeated, slowly and distinctly, but he merely smiled and shook his head.

"That's queer," I said to Anahareo, perplexedly. "I'm saying it all right. He doesn't understand his own language."

"I guess maybe he does," she replied, "perhaps if you tried what you know of it he might."

"Well, what's wrong?" I asked, getting a little indignant. "I'm talking French ain't I, and correct too."

"Of course it was correct," she agreed, "but you were talking Indian." Well, I had known it wasn't English anyway; but our guest spoke up.

"That is quite all right," he said, in perfect English, "the mistake is mine. I thought you spoke only Indian."

During the time we camped there we had a number of visitors, people coming over in boats to see us, some of them, we subsequently discovered, important citizens of the place. Apart from a certain amount of natural curiosity, these people seemed to feel that here were strangers within their gate who must be made to feel at home, and they went out of their way to do it. Moreover some of them came bearing gifts. One brought us some potatoes, another a bottle of very creditable moonshine whiskey; yet another supplied us with the names of certain people he thought we should be aware of. A fur buyer from a neighbouring town came across with overtures to trade for the beaver, offering supplies sufficient to last till the New Year.

But whether impelled by curiosity, business, or pure friendliness, nearly all were courteous and considerate. There were a couple of unfortunate incidents, but that was to be expected, and without them it would all have been quite too good to be true. All this was a little unexpected, as my experiences with the few French Canadians I had met in the far North had not always been so fortunate. This may have been on account of the contact with a very unsavoury class of so-called trapper, greatly recruited from the draft-evading class of 1917–18, that had invaded the wilderness, and the Frenchman, with his mercurial temperament, was quick to take new and not always desirable impressions. But these people were different. This was Old Quebec of the seigneuries with three centuries of *noblesse oblige* behind it. They were in their own environment, and spent their lives in a little universe all their own, and as is common with any living creature under the sun in like circumstances, were at their best. We may philosophise and moralise concerning the short-comings of man when submitted to the acid test of adversity, and thereby perhaps we may get the measure of a man. Yet hardships make a dour people as a rule, and it is mighty pleasant to sometimes consort with those who, being in happier circumstances, are better able to present the world with a smiling face, and whose possible reactions to our own particular code are really none of our concern.

I had not as yet approached any store for a debt, and so far no merchants had contested for the honour of supplying me with a hundred dollars' worth of provisions on long term credit. This was apparently not that kind of a town, and I saw no sign of any regular fur buying establishment. The store keepers here probably did not realize that there was such a thing in business as a hunting debt, and I knew that this was going to be a hard one to raise. Time was moving along, and the leaves were already turning; I would soon have to get down to it. Meanwhile I had amassed a considerable amount of information regarding the country. This did not quite tally with the glowing accounts we had heard, but its sources were more reliable. We were told the forest that commenced at the crest of the elephant-like mountain, stretched from the mouth of the Touladi river clear into New Brunswick, and almost to the Atlantic Ocean. This was all to the good. But Mr.—ah—Jacob, or Solomon, or Beelzebub, had been a little too enthusiastic, and was astray in a few minor details. He had owned no hunting camp, let alone a lodge; his fleet of boats was non-existent, farmers were not complaining of any depredations by fur bearing animals, (though deer did actually steal a little hay) and as to man-eating cats,— come to think of it, there was a man who had a grandfather that—but why spoil a good story; he may want to tell it again.

An Irish timber cruiser who knew the surrounding country inside out, informed us that if we went in forty or fifty miles we *might* get a few mink and foxes, and the odd otter. There were, he stated, a few families of beaver at widely separated points; they were the only worth while hunt.

And I was not to hunt them, by self-imposed, unbreakable decree. It was plain that I was going to keep my pledge under no very easy terms. Anyhow I was now sure of my colony, and with the rest of the fur to work on we perhaps could live. That was about all a fellow did anyway in this happy-go-lucky existence,—live, and see lots of country, and work mighty hard at it, and enjoy it too. A big stake or a small one, the results were about the same. I have never yet in all my travels met a retired trapper living on his means.

And now a fresh trouble hove into the offing. The beaver went bald, and in a big way. For a long time they had been rubbing and scratching continuously, day and night, pulling out their fur by handfuls, and in a short time they were as innocent of hair as a pair of snakes, save for a narrow mane that extended out of reach down the centre of their backs. This gave them rather the appearance of the shaven-headed Indians we see depicted in the history books, Anahareo's own particular tribe being generally specified. So we gave them the first of all the many names they later had, and called them Little Iroquois. However, the matter was serious enough. They became listless, refused to eat, and began to fight shy of water, all bad signs with these animals. We sought the advice of a doctor. It was his opinion that we should feed them no more porridge as it was no doubt over-heating their blood, in their inactive state, and might eventually kill them. It was bad enough the way it was. Winter was not far off and they had no coats. The doctor gave us a box of salve, and recommended a well known baby's food that would relieve their condition. He charged nothing for either the advice or the ointment, saying, in his precise scholastic English,

"I am an old soldier; I never take money from any of the boys. If you are sick come and see me, it will cost you nothing. I am always your friend."

Which was lucky. I had just thirty cents, enough perhaps for the baby food. And to-day I would have to negotiate that debt. A neighbouring store had the kind of tonic food we needed for our invalids, and the merchant wrapped it up.

"*Soixante et quinze*," he said. Seventy five cents. I looked at it. It might have as well been seventy five dollars. And across the lake our two little buddies were waiting in their misery. We had to have it, and with a courage I had not known I possessed,

"Will you charge it?" I asked. I tried hard to radiate an air of confidence, but felt a good deal like a man waiting for the well-known sudden stop at the end of the fall.

"*Mais certainement Monsieur—en suite?*"

I turned to Anahareo who seemed to have the better ear for French.

"What's that he says?" I asked her. He answered the question himself.

"Is there anything else?"

I crossed my fingers, touched wood, changed feet, and could have used some prayers if I'd had any. He was asking for it, so I took the bull by the horns.

"I'm going in to hunt on the Touladi. I want a Winter's provisions." Well, there it was.

"What part?" he asked.

"The Horton branch," I answered, and that was all I knew about it.

"Oh! yes," said the merchant, "nice country," and reaching for his order book, stood with his pencil poised—ready. Just like that.

I went out of there owing a hundred and twenty odd dollars, fixed for the winter. When we got outside,

"Let's open up the champagne," said Anahareo.

ɷ ɷ ɷ

WHEN WE RETURNED TO CAMP WE FOUND THE LITTLE beavers as we had left them, sitting pitiful, silent and naked, drooping in their pen. There was none of the grotesque gambolling with which they had formerly welcomed our home comings, and when the pen was opened they showed no inclination to come out of it. Carefully we applied the salve, spreading it over their little scabby bodies. This treatment induced a fresh attack of irritation, and their rubbing and scratching at this served to massage the ointment well into the hide. We cooked up a decoction of the tonic. Beaver are an impossible animal to feed forcibly, and we were greatly relieved to find that after picking up a few tentative handfuls and smelling it, that they ate a quantity. Before that day was over they perked up considerably and took the medicated food with relish, and in a couple more days had regained much of their former good spirits. I have never known anything alive having the recuperative powers these two animals possessed. From my subsequent experience with kitten beavers, I now realize that with the heroic treatment that we, in our ignorance, meted out to them, they should have been dead long ago. Inside of a month they had their full complement of hair, and it was to be noticed from then on, that they were no longer subject to fits of peevishness. But this was later. Just now, two trips with a heavily loaded canoe would have to be made into the woods with our formidable commissariat, and as we did not yet know precisely where we were headed for, no further time was to be lost. After giving the convalescents three days to get on their feet, I drew the half of our supplies, and one clear Fall morning we broke camp.

And with a touch of frost in the air, a light mist on the water, and with the golden and crimson leaves falling all about us, we eased the nose of our canoe into the current of Touladi, and our gallant little company of four headed for Over the Hills and Far Away, bound for an unknown destination.

CHAPTER FIVE

How We Crossed the Slough of Despond

THE RIVER WAS NOT ONE OF DEEP WATER AND FREQUENT heavy rapids such as I had been accustomed to working on, but was shallow and very swift, and the poling, whilst neither difficult nor dangerous, was pretty steady. Standing for hours at a time in a canoe, the usual position in poling, can become very tiresome. We were a little overloaded, and it took us a full day bucking the current to make the reputed nine miles to a chain of waters known as the Touladi Lakes. This very welcome change provided an opportunity to kneel down and paddle a while. Another half day in slack water brought us to the hamlet where we were to get the precise information that would determine our further route.

Here again a church, seeming very large for so small a population, was the predominating feature of the landscape, affording by its omnipresence a standing promise of that benign moral support that the habitant finds so helpful in his toilsome existence.

On the outskirts we met the real habitant type, some of them with their knowledge of the world confined to the area of their tiny farms and the utterances of their spiritual advisers. Those that might be aptly termed the headmen of this community were kindly, hospitable and progressive; one of them, despite the handicap of having only one arm, was a nimble fellow who took automobiles apart and made them into motor sleighs, had erected a small electric light plant, and built and owned the ferry boat on Temiscouata. But there were not a few who looked askance at the passing Indians from behind half closed doors or windows, or else stood staring in utter and silent curiosity; some of them, if on the road, went so far as to check their horses to our pace, and drove slowly beside us as we walked, getting a good eyeful while they could.

On the river bank was a Company store belonging to the mill owners, and they allowed us to cache our stuff in their store-houses. Enquiries elicited the information that we would have to go in another thirty miles to the mouth of Stony Creek. At the head of this stream was a lake that was recommended as a good location, as the immediate district had not been lumbered over. There were said to be a few mink, otter, and foxes in the country and the lake was the abode of a family of beaver, reputed to be the only one in the entire region. It was noticeable that as we penetrated deeper into this country, so the game retreated before us, spread out, and grew less. We learned also that the river forked here, and the branch that we were to ascend was so swift and shallow that a heavily laden canoe was out of the question, and we must have the bulk of our outfit taken by team over a lumber road that followed the river. Coming from a country where roads and teams do not flourish, I rebelled inwardly at thus having to back down, but a look at the river convinced me that it was the only course. It was not a country where people travelled by the methods we were using, and the reasons for this were later to become very apparent. The team was to cost ten dollars, which we did not have. But optimism is contagious, especially if it be extremely cheerful, and this country seemed imbued with it; so we felt that we would raise it somehow, and we did. On the way back to collect the remainder of our outfit, we came on to a red fox swimming across the river. He had nearly gained the opposite shore when, our canoe suddenly appearing around the bend, he did what a wolf or a fox will nearly always do if alarmed whilst in the water, he turned and swam back as fast as he possibly could to his starting point. We captured him, put him in a bag, and later sold him alive for a ten dollar bill. It seemed somehow like a betrayal; he had been free, like us, and the money had no sooner changed hands than I wished I had killed the poor beast outright, and sold the hide instead. The dealer, who had made a special trip for the fox, was the same one who previously had wished to make a

trade for the beaver, and at this time, whilst he supposed us to be in selling humour he made a further offer, raising his bid to a hundred dollars,
cash. He was very insistent and not an easy man to refuse, but the beaver
were now five months old and had become so much a part of our lives,
that I think no sum of money however large would have tempted us. They
now weighed about eight pounds apiece but were not up to normal size,
being stunted by lack of exercise, swimming especially. But their teeth had
not suffered on this account, and having outgrown their tin-lined box,
they had become something of a problem while in transit. Once while we
were crossing a lake they opened up their receptacle, spilling out into the
lake, and we had to lose nearly half a day waiting until they were pleased
to give themselves up. As snow already lay on the ground, and ice was
beginning to form in sheltered spots we could not afford any loss of time;
so we hit on an entirely new idea. We put them in the tin stove we had, an
oblong box-like arrangement without an oven, lashing the lids on tightly
and securing the door. We fed them through the stove-pipe hole, out of
which the loud, long, and well-known lunch call would issue from time to
time. This expedient was the most convenient arrangement we had so far
devised, as they roamed the surrounding waters all night while the stove
was in use, and in the day time, when it came time to move, they disappeared into it and became simply a part of the regular load. They got to
look on this as their routine, going obediently into their tin house and settling down to sleep on their brush beds. And only for this device they
would most certainly have lost their lives.

Having made arrangements to have our load go round by sleigh to the
mouth of our home-stream-to-be, we proceeded up river in the canoe.
There had been several heavy snowfalls and Winter had arrived in good
earnest. The canoe became quickly coated with ice, and the accumulations
that formed on the steel shod pole thickened it into a club that splashed
water at every stroke, so that the gunnell was a solid mass of ice and the
bottom of the canoe was like a skating rink. Under these conditions, standing in the narrow slippery stern, the usual attitude for the sternsman in poling, was a ticklish business. We had aboard only a camping outfit and the
beaver in their tin prison. These few things, including the canoe, could
have gone on the load, but our dignity would not permit this, and I think

that nothing can be so humiliating to a good canoe as to be ignominiously hauled, upside down, alongside of a perfectly navigable body of water. But worse was to befall it, and not at all in accordance with the best traditions. Putting extra pressure on the pole in an especially stiff piece of fast water, my moccasins, frozen and slippery as glass, shot from under me on the icy canoe bottom and I fell flat on my face in the river. I managed to twist clear of the canoe to avoid upsetting it, but this availed little as the light craft, out of control, swung side on, filled, and was forced to the bottom by the pressure. Anahareo, who was kneeling rolled clear, head first. Instantly we both regained our feet—swift work to be done, a matter of seconds! Somewhere under that rushing icy flood, perhaps already gone, was the stove and in it the beaver were securely locked without a chance for their lives.

Packs, some air remaining in them momentarily, commenced to float up, and soon the canoe, becoming empty would shift and begin to buckle. We disregarded all this and groped desperately, shoulder deep. Anahareo was swept off her feet once, recovering by some miracle of agility. A beaver suddenly immersed drowns as quickly as any other beast, and we had searched for a full minute. And I think we lost our heads a little for a moment, for suddenly we were holding up the dripping stove between us, although we could never remember the act of finding it, and Anahareo was crying out

"They're alive! they're alive!" while I stood stupidly, clutching in my free hand, as though it were a talisman, the handle of our new tea pail, while the pail itself, with the lid on, was bobbing merrily off with our immediate supply of lard, on its way to New Brunswick. The temperature was far below freezing; the water was icy cold and tore at our legs, so that we were like to lose our foothold and be swept away.

The river bank was some five rods away but Anahareo, by the judicious use of her pole, arrived there safely with the stove and its now frantic occupants. Three times she ran the gauntlet of the frigid racing torrent, getting all our stuff ashore, while I, being of longer gear, did the salvaging and raised the canoe. Fortunately it was a staunch craft, and although some sheathing and several ribs were smashed, the canvas was whole and the canoe still serviceable.

But we had little time for congratulations. It was freezing hard, and ice was forming on everything including our clothes. We were both soaked to the hide and the beaver in their almost hairless condition were in danger of perishing. Some of the blankets were partly dry, having been in the centre of the bundle, so I wrapped up Anahareo and the beaver together in them, and left them lie there in the snow while I rustled some wood and got an immense fire going, working on the run while the clothes froze on my back. Once the outer clothing is frozen a certain measure of warmth is possible inside them, but I must have resembled a frenziedly active tin-man, and no doubt the whole business, if viewed from a warm safe spot would have been highly entertaining to an onlooker. It had been a narrow escape for our pets, for if they had been in a light wooden box they would have been swept away immediately and been battered to death before they could have gnawed their way out, or I have got the canoe ready and under way. Anyhow it was all over now, and such is life in the woods that what with the great warm fire, a cooking pot half full of tea and a pan full of deer meat, we were again happy and as well off as ever; while the two deep-sea divers sat warm and comfortable on new bedding in their tin hut, eating some candies that were reserved for special occasions, and making a great noise about it.

We had lost nothing save the tea pail and a small package of lard, and even two panes of glass tied on to a washboard were recovered intact some distance down stream. My self-esteem, however, had received a severe set-back, for I had committed what, to a canoeman, was in the light of a major crime, which I am here expiating by telling about it from the house-tops.

Inside of a couple of hours we were again on our way, partly dry and as confident as ever, and looked on our mishap as now amounting to a little more than a slightly longer dinner hour than we usually allowed ourselves. We spent most of that night drying our equipment, while our two furless companions showed no disposition to enter the water, having probably had enough of it for the time being; but seemingly hard put to find some other outlet for their abounding energies, they dug themselves a long tunnel in the side of the hill before they went to sleep.

Early the next day we arrived at our cache, left there by the team, which had gone back. Across the river from it was Stony Creek at the head of which was Birch Lake, our final stopping place. Here we received something in the nature of a surprise, and also an explanation of the reason why canoes were not as popular in this country as we thought they should be. Those who had recommended this stream as a means of reaching our hunting territory had told us that it was eight miles long, but had omitted to mention that it was three feet wide and possibly six inches deep.

We could no longer use the canoe.

This was, as the fella' said, not a situation but a predicament. It was six miles overland to the lake, there was half a foot of snow on the ground, we had at least eight hundred pounds of freight which would now have to be carried the entire distance piecemeal. The joke was on us.

The country in the immediate vicinity had been heavily lumbered, and the slash, we knew, extended to within a short distance of the lake in question. The green country commenced there and our hunt would lay from there on, so we had little choice but to keep going. Packing is one of my regular occupations, but the idea of taking this terrific carry all in one bite, especially in a cut-over country, was a little staggering. And there was more than myself to consider. I had already had sufficient example of the indomitable spirit of Anahareo to know that she would never stand tamely by and see me pack that load six miles alone. And so it proved. I ferried the goods across and had them neatly piled in a sheltered spot by night fall, cacheing the canoe on high land out of reach of any Spring flood. The next day I uncoiled my tump line and the fun commenced. A hundred or a hundred and fifty pounds, according to bulk, was the biggest load that could be juggled through that jungle of timber, slashed tops and almost impenetratable second growth, thus increasing the number of trips, and there was also the snow to contend with. And when I set down my load at the first stage,[1] I looked back and saw Anahareo behind me with a load of her own, following faithfully in my carefully chosen footsteps. On her arrival I looked pretty straitly at her, but she was so pleased with her achievement, and was so proud to

---

[1] A stage is a convenient stopping place at which loads are dumped, and they are generally about six or eight minutes apart, that being the length of time that a man can walk with a good load without fatigue. He recuperates on the way back for the next burden. This is the Indian system of packing and better time can be made by this method, carrying a maximum load, than by taking smaller loads and going right through.

find that she could be of assistance in this notorious jam, that I wisely decided to keep my mouth closed. Moreover she is a full-blood and can, as I have told her, be very obstinate at times. So she had her way, and I compromised by picking her loads, and shortening the stages, and but for her assistance I am certain that some of that load would still be on its way to Birch Lake.

We packed all that day, back and forth, load by load, without speech or rest save at noon for a drink of tea, climbing over piled up tree-trunks slippery with snow, forcing our way through tangled underbrush, plunging into snow-covered pitfalls—but never falling—until nearly dark, returning to camp wet with sweat, tired and hungry, but with that feeling of contentment and well-being that comes with a knowledge of useful work successfully accomplished.

We had moved the entire load of eight hundred pounds a half a mile.

The next day we did not do as well. The going became so rough owing to fallen timber that progress without a load would have been no easy matter. In some spots we were obliged to leave the bank altogether, and walk along the stream bed, stepping from one stone to another, or walking in the mixture of ice and water. It at last became necessary to take out a day and cut a trail, time that could be ill spared; but by the end of the third day the stream wandered away off our line of advance, and we had in its place an old tote-road that offered some fair travelling. We had progressed about a mile all told, and were now pretty well organized. We each had our own pile which we handled in our own way. Besides our main dumps, we had always one or two in-between loads scattered at strategic points ahead. These were the lighter stuff that could be carried perhaps twice as far as the heavier burdens, and on these advance trips we were able to spy out the lay of the land. These isolated loads eventually fell behind, so that instead of having to lose time resting after a stage was completed, we could cool off dropping back for them, again forging ahead with them, spotting out our route as we went, and so arrive back at the cache after a long easy walk, all rarin' to go.

Anahareo was getting hardened down to the job in the most remarkable way. She explained this by stating that she was so lightly built that she had little to carry but the load itself. The fourth day we moved camp, carrying the full outfit a mile beyond the last stage, thus being ahead of our work and not behind it so as to move less frequently.

That same night our load was sharply reduced. Two bags of potatoes out of less than three that we owned, as well as our fifty pound bag of onions, were frozen solid. Well, that was about two hundred pounds that we didn't have to carry any more. We got considerable consolation from figuring how this helped us. Allowing five more days to get in, at the rate of two hundred pounds a day saved, we had made a net gain of a thousand pounds. It was very encouraging; if we had had twice as far to go we could have saved a ton. Too bad though that it hadn't occurred to those stupid spuds to freeze at the river five days ago; we would now have been two thousand pounds ahead. In the woods a man has often to turn reverses to what good account he may, but this was the first time that I had ever figured myself out of trouble by means of arithmetic.

It could be seen that the country had once been well timbered, and this presaged well for what lay ahead of us in the un-cut areas, but we would have been better encouraged by the occasional sight of animal tracks. But there were none save those of deer which were exceedingly numerous, and rolling fat. We would at least live well this Winter, and a well fed hunter is likely to be a successful one. An old lumber camp stood beside the tote-road, and it had considerately been erected at the exact spot where a raging snow storm struck us, so that neither our goods nor ourselves were the worse for it. Here we discovered a twenty-five gallon barrel, empty and in good condition. This was a lucky find, as it would afford first-class sleeping quarters for the beaver, and would not be just dead weight, as on the trail it could conveniently be filled with the cookery and other odds and ends, and so pay for its transportation in the day time.

Since we had left the stream the beaver had made no attempt to wander away, and slept with us under the blankets. One would lie with each of us, snuggled up close, nearly always with their heads on our shoulders, or with their noses pushed tight to our throats, where they would puff and blow and sometimes snore, and grumble a little when we moved. Overtired as we often were during this rather trying period, there was some danger that in our heaviness we might roll over on them, or that they would become suffocated under the blankets. In the barrel they were safe and warm, and owing to its concave interior they were unable to get their teeth into it very effectively. Not being able to see over the top of it, and feeling no doubt left out of things they put up a violent protest at this new incarceration, signalling us with loud cries, and doing all within their power to attract attention. In response to this commotion, which at times was little short of terrific, we always lifted them out, but eventually they did succeed in carving out a large square hole about half way up. Here they would stand looking out and jabbering away, reaching with out-stretched hands and begging for pancakes, of which they were inordinately fond. And as they hung out over the edge of the aperture, with their droll gestures, and that queer language of theirs that it seemed we could almost understand, so human did it sound at times, they looked for all the world like the travellers to be seen leaning out of coach windows at a railroad depot. And on account of this resemblance we no longer called them Iroquois but named them Immigrants, which was all the name they had for quite some time.

They seemed quite satisfied with this arrangement, and soon came to look on the barrel as their home. When they wished to come out and spend the evening, generally about meal time, they shoved their bedding up close to the hole so they could climb out, and they re-entered at will by means of a box we placed for them. They were as mischievous as a couple of monkeys, and although they slept long hours, whilst awake they allowed no grass to grow under their feet. They were self-willed past all belief, and they were untiringly persevering in the prosecution of some purpose or other, whether it happened to be the investigation of a box of groceries, or the dismantling of our domestic arrangements. Opposition only promoted a more feverish determination to see the matter to the bitter end, and in the carrying out of the more really interesting projects, which the cluttered contents of the tent supplied without number, they exhibited, young as they were, an ingenuity and zeal that held out alarming prospects for the future. Had they ever been turned loose in a china shop, I'll guarantee they would have been remembered there for a long time to come.

These two irresponsibles were fast becoming a very material part of our existence, and with their clowning, their bickering and their loquacity, they invested the proceedings with an air of gaiety that would have been sadly wanting without them, and had they been suddenly taken from us they would have left a gap that would have been very hard to fill. We began to wonder how we had ever got along without them, and the shrill cries and ridiculous clumsy gambols with which they welcomed our return from the slavish labour of the pack-trail, did much to cheer and enliven us. And then too we had, on the way home, the exhilarating mental exercise of wondering what new form of devilment had been set afoot in our absence, as it was impossible for anyone not a magician to know what they would be liable to do next. But they gave us far greater pleasure than they ever did trouble, and the discovery on our arrival that the stove was down, or the dishes hidden in out of the way places, or that a fresh bannock carefully cooked against our homecoming, had been taken out of the grub-box and chewed and tramped into an unrecognisable pulp, did not, after all, seem to matter so much; that is, not after the first shock of discovery was over. The time never dragged while they were awake, for there was always something going on, and we never knew from one minute to another when some novel form of entertainment would be provided us.

There was something infinitely touching in their affection for each other, and their complete dependence on us, and there were moments when their gentleness and soft appealing ways were in marked contrast to their usual rather impetuous behaviour. They gave us the same recognition as if we had ourselves been of their own kind, and we were the haven of refuge to which they came in times of stress, which were frequent, as they were always getting minor injuries in their contacts with these unnatural surroundings. They were hostile to anything they deemed to be an intruder and became very angry at the continued visits to the tent of a weasel, one of them eventually making a pass at him, the agile weasel, of course being in two or three other places by the time the blow landed. And I once brought a small deer carcass into the tent to thaw out, and they both fought valiantly with the body all night.

They were the most adaptable creatures imaginable and were probably the only pets that could have been happy, or perhaps even have survived, under the severe conditions in which they were living. An amphibious animal, they were none the less undismayed by the lack of their natural element, and were content to drink water from a cup which we held for them; though the water pail had to be kept out of their reach, as they evidently mistook it for a plunge hole and continually tried to dive through it, with disastrous results. Being unable to collect bedding on account of the snow which was now nearly a foot deep, they took dry wood from beside the stove and converted it into shavings for the purpose.

As each new camping ground was reached they soon became busy with their small arrangements, exhibiting a workman-like ability to take advantage of whatever materials were to hand, building barricades, finding bedding and sometimes, if not too cold, cutting small poplar saplings outside and bringing them in for food. So that often we were all working together and at times got in each other's way, and on more than one occasion one of us had to stand waiting with perhaps an armful of wood, or a pail of water, while some busy little beast manoeuvered for position with a stick in front of the door. They adjusted themselves quite effectively to changing weather conditions. When it was warm they ran around in the tent, never leaving it without they had business outside, and when it was cold they stayed in their compartment and plugged the window, whilst we put a lid on top of it and thought no more about them.

It was now bitterly cold and bannock froze solid in the tent most nights. The snow was growing deeper every day, yet we were denied the use of snowshoes as packing on them with the loads we were carrying, will ruin the best shoe made. The packing was becoming increasingly arduous, and the work of breaking and making camp in the snow with bare hands was a recurrent hardship more to be dreaded than the actual moving, as the tent, continually damp with melting snow, froze stiff as a board the minute the stove was out and was as difficult to handle as if it had been made of iron. The constant grind was beginning to tell on us, and Anahareo was becoming exhausted. I at last prevailed on her to quit the pack-trail altogether and content herself taking care of camp. I was able to convince her, as at this time some one was needed to keep fire all night on account of the beaver. Fortunately the country was blessed with plenty of good wood.

It was getting late and the Fall hunt should have been well under way. I did set some traps in likely spots so as to have at least a few of them working, but they yielded nothing, nor had we seen a track or any other sign of a fur bearing animal since we had left the settlement at the forks.

This ill-advised trip began to look more and more hopeless as we progressed on it, but I reflected that we had not covered much territory since we had left the river ten days ago, and pinned my hopes on the country ahead. There were days when we made no more than a few hundred yards between the snow and the bad going, and working as I was, alone, progress was desperately slow. And I now began to be uncertain as to the exact location of Birch Lake, as the country did not pan out as described. A scouting trip ahead revealed no lake or any indications of one, and only a dreary, almost impenetrable slash was to be seen on every side. I later found we had been misinformed as to its location, but at this late date I determined to swing over to the creek, now some miles to the Eastward, follow it up to the lake and pick out a good route back to camp. As I proceeded, the country fell away a little to the North and lake formations were soon in evidence, and after fighting my way through one of the densest cedar swamps I had ever encountered, I worked across to a narrow body of water less than half a mile in length. The family of beaver, a small one, was there all right; in fact the lake would have been little better than a marsh, but for the presence of these animals who had dammed it at the outlet. The lumber-works extended no further than the foot of the lake; a most welcome discovery. A haul-way led back from it, a swamp road that lay in muskeg, which being snowed under, was not frozen and was about as treacherous a piece of going for a laden man as could be desired. Anyway it was a trail, and fairly clear of down timber, and my present passage over it would freeze it down a little and provide a certain amount of solid footing, so I carefully walked over it as though loaded so as to have my foot tracks in the right places. Every successive trip would improve this, so it would get better rather than worse. I followed the road as long as its direction served, and then switched off to a fairly clean ridge of hardwood, and was able to spot out as good a route through it as was possible by moonlight, coming out on the crest of a lofty hill that overlooked the valley we were camped in.

Here I stood awhile, leaning on my rifle and gazing out over the staring white silence. My mind was oppressed by a deep foreboding. Our problems might seem to some who read to have been of little account, but against the background of the simple life we led, they assumed momentous proportions. This expedition, entered on so blithely, began now to have all the appearance of a forlorn hope. I owned what was, considering the apparent chance of paying it, a heavy debt. The jealously guarded stack of provisions we had been so glad to get had now become an incubus under which, tired beyond measure, we now moved at the rate of a quarter of a mile a day, if that; and it hung, like an Old Man of the Sea about our necks, sleeping and waking, and was like to overpower us before we finally were rid of it.

Further, at the outlet of the lake there should have been mink and otter signs, but there were none; and no fisher, lynx, or marten roamed the hills. There were a few foxes and weasels but there was no price for them. True, I had discovered a family of beaver, a pitiful remnant of perhaps four individuals that instead of protecting, I might even yet have to destroy that we ourselves might live, and so break my covenant at the outset. And with my altered views this would be little short of murder. Was my change of heart after all only the unsubstantial vision of a dreamer, offspring of the folk-yarns of an imaginative and half-savage people, a chimerical, impractical piece of idealism that would wilt and wither under the pitiless searching glare of stark reality?

And far below I could see the tiny glow of the lighted tent that sheltered all I cared for in the world, a weary waiting woman, and two small orphaned creatures, sole living reminders of the halcyon days that had so suddenly slipped away from us. I looked down for a long time at the little spot of light, so small, so puny and inconsequential, giving out so bravely and perhaps so ineffectually, its feeble illumination in the midst of this vast and terrible desolation of a ruined and broken forest. And I visualised our return to that friendly town humbled, dishonoured, and destitute; a town no longer friendly. And on its streets I saw Anahareo pointed out as the wife of a man who could not pay his debts. Perhaps we would be forced to deliver our little friends into bondage, where there would be no more fun, no more pancakes—no more love. I went down with a heavy heart.

But all seemed bright and happy within, and we all of us ate, and the people smoked and relaxed in the warmth of the little tin stove that was put to such a number of uses, and served them all so well. And while it roared and crackled and grew cheerfully red I related my day's adventures; the finding of the lake, the discovery of the beaver house that was to mean so much, and told of the so-good trail we had, and how we were now all connected up with our winter home-to-be. And being started I told stories of the days before we met, of happenings and queer characters in the distant forests beyond the Height of Land, and of early Cobalt days; and Anahareo fell to laughing at the adventures of one Bungalow Bill, who had lived in a shack so small that he had to reach outside the door with his frying pan to toss a pancake. And told the story of how he had once gone out to pick blueberries, and how he had his two pails full and was on his way back to the canoe when he saw a cyclone coming. He made for the canoe, putting down his pails to run the faster, and got there just in time. Sure of his canoe he looked back to see how the berries were making out, and he saw them, sailing right up into the air in two spinning spirals, drawn up there by the suction of the "twister." And then the wind dropped, just like that—(a good sharp crack of the hand on the knee) and, would you believe it, the berries, finding themselves suddenly with no means of support, fell back down into the pails again, and not one was lost, no sir, not a one! And we laughed uproariously at the unbelievable tale, and the beavers, who responded to our moods with apt consistency, were greatly stirred by all the laughter and the fun, and came piling out from the window of their caboose and staged an hilarious wrestling match among the supper things, so that the tea pail was upset and the dishes flew in all directions, all of which caused a real scramble and more merriment.

And all this did much to dispel the fog of apprehension that was settling on me, but about which I said never a word.

CHAPTER SIX

How We Built the House of McGinnis

EVERYTHING MUST COME TO AN END, AND ONE NIGHT AT THE falling of dark, every last pound and parcel was stacked on the shores of Birch Lake where it would all have to stay until the ice improved. Having neither a sleigh nor a toboggan, we made a fire and constructed by its light a V-shaped rig that could be dragged, and loading our camp outfit on it, with the barrel, we hauled it in the darkness over some very tricky ice to the camping ground I had previously selected, and which was not far from the live beaver house.

And that night we slowly dozed to unconsciousness with the one all-pervading thought, the surpassing realization, that to-morrow there would be no trail to break, no more relentless pressure of a frozen tump line on numbed temples, no breaking of camp in the iron bitterness of a snow bound dawn, no more slavery, no more intolerable struggle. There had been real suffering this past two weeks, and much of the time the journey had been little but a hideous nightmare. But it was finished and was now become Experience; and much had been learned. Thinking thus, and unable to rest with these persistent and unsettling thoughts, I arose and threw open the door of the stove, and sitting by its light I smoked and pondered, while all my people slept. And the illumination from the narrow stove-door fell upon the weary sleeping face of Anahareo, this woman who had followed me through this grim ordeal with such uncomplaining courage and fidelity. And out of it there had been born a bond between us, deeper and more binding than any that marriage tie or duty could impose, the steel-tempered, unbreakable bond between comrades who, side by side, have fought a hard won victory over nameless tribulation.

And as I watched she stirred uneasily and half awaking said, "We're not away back there, packing in the snow, are we,—not any more? We're here now, eh?"

"Yes," I answered, from behind my smoke-cloud. "We are here." And then she smiled and fell asleep again.

We had arrived, yes—but where? And for a long time after, I sat and smoked and wondered.

There was now a cabin to be built. The site we had decided on for our Winter home was in a grove of dark majestic pine trees amongst which stood, decorous and graceful, a few slim white birches. The grandeur of these impressive surroundings rather dwarfed us and our efforts, and made us seem a little like pigmies, and the results of a day's work looked discouragingly infinitesimal in proportion. But the presence of big timber is always inspiring and this remnant of the primeval made us feel free and wild, and somehow exalted, and it helped us to forget that civilization was, so to speak, just around the corner, and that a scant mile or so away was a dreary ruination of stumps and slash.

But there was little time for philosophical reflection. It was the second week in November, and there was well over a foot of snow on the ground. The frost was in the timber, making for hard axe work. The size of trees required for building purposes were found to be far away, and most of them had to be hauled long distances with a tump line, on skids. It would of course have been easier to erect the camp near the most convenient timber, but the grove of pines and birches appealed to us, and we were willing to pay rather heavily for the privilege of living amongst them. Under these disadvantageous working conditions the shack went up very slowly and as it snowed nearly continuously, most mornings we had to shovel out the inside of the cabin before we could go to work. We were quite fussy about everything, the front exposure, the position of the door, and the way the windows faced; these latter were cut so as to give a view of the finest groups of trees.

Operations were being carried on across the lake from the tent, in which we lived meanwhile, and one evening we came back to it to find the barrel empty, and two winding and irresolute-looking trails leading in separate directions out on to the lake. The beaver had been gone some time. Our first thought was that, sensing the close proximity of their own kind, they had deserted us, as there was a patch of open water that the native beaver had kept open before their lodge. But the tracks led off erratically in another direction, down the lake. Beaver have a homing instinct that takes them unerringly back to a place they have taken a liking to. Though they have a remarkable sense of direction, young beaver appear to have no idea of distance, and I feared that they had set out for our last camping ground, where they had done a considerable amount of work. The weather had been soft all day but it was now freezing hard, which not only had formed a crust on which they would leave no further tracks, but if they were persisting in this attempt they would most certainly perish in their half furred state. But it transpired that they had no particular object in view except to wander, and they had left a maze of tracks along one shore that it was impossible to follow to any definite spot, save by the slow process of covering them all. Armed with a lantern we began the hunt. We worked as fast as possible, as they had been exposed to the cold a long time and would have to be found soon. We called continuously as we searched and were at length rewarded by hearing a feeble cry at a point nearly half way down the lake. When found the little beast was headed towards home but was lying there in the slush, having apparently given up hope. It was the male, in trouble again, and Anahareo hurried home with him while I continued the search. Very soon, however, I received a signal that we had agreed upon, given with a light, and returned to find that the other had already been back in the barrel on Anahareo's arrival. Before leaving on this hair-brained expedition, these enterprising adventurers had undermined and upset the stove, so it was some considerable time before all hands were restored to their normal good humour. From then on we took the barrel and its occupants over onto the job with us, having to keep a fire alongside of it.

Even with both of us working on the building, it was eleven days before it would be pronounced ready for occupation. Conditions were becoming a little disagreeable in the tent owing to the cramped quarters, the steadily increasing cold, and the fact that it snowed almost without ceasing. So one night we were mighty glad to move into the new cabin. It was at present much like an ice-house as the small stove had little effect on the frozen timber, and the apertures between the logs were not closed. The moss for this purpose, which I had had to chop out in solid blocks, would be some time thawing, and I arranged it around three sides of the stove, so as to accelerate matters as much as possible. On waking the next morning we found to our great astonishment, that the beaver had removed a quantity of the thawed out moss, and had made a very passable attempt to chink the crevices as high as they could reach, for a considerable distance along one of the walls. It is the nature of a beaver to plug any air leak or draught into his living quarters, and we were to find that this not only included cracks in walls, but extended to the apertures for doors and windows. But this taking over of a task that I had planned for myself that day was at first glance a little startling to say the least, especially to one just awakened. All that day I chinked and banked and made everything secure without, while Anahareo built racks and a table, and put up shelves and made all snug within. And it was quite a proud-looking place when it was all finished, with its smooth red spruce logs with green and yellow moss between them, and its white plume of smoke streaming up like a banner from the stove pipe, to spread in a blue shifting haze far overhead amongst the dark boughs of the pine trees. We both stood outside watching this column of smoke as it poured forth, which all bush people do when the first fire is kindled in a new cabin. The fire had been lighted the night before of course, but we had not been able to see the smoke. We enjoyed the spectacle. It had a very comfortable look, and gave an air of life and movement to the place. And inside, in spite of the moisture that formed on the walls and rafters as the logs thawed out, and dripped into everything, as it would do for a day or two, we held a small celebration, and if the neighbours had been closer we'd have had a dance. The stove pipe was a little narrow and sometimes when the wind was wrong the stove did not draw so well, and when on such days we inadvertently opened the draught too full, we had a smoke-storm. But that was easily dispersed by opening the door and waving it out with a blanket.

The cabin once completed, I hauled over the contents of the cache, procured a supply of wood, killed and brought in a deer, and then commenced to look over the country. It was by now early in December, and the mink hunt, if there was such a thing to be found here, was about over. So I must depend on foxes, fisher and lynx, if any, and these I went in search of. For days I tramped the surrounding hills, swinging wider and wider each day as I sought for signs, until I was no longer able to return nightly to the cabin. There were a few, very few fox tracks, but of other fur never a hair. With a sheet of canvas for shelter, half a blanket, some tea, flour, grease, and my rifle, I ranged far and wide over hill, valley, and ancient beaver meadow, traversing gullies, crossing small watersheds, and following streams to their head. I crawled through tangled swamps, swung across whole lines of ridges, and searched out every available spot where an animal might pass, killing my meat as I went, and sleeping out where night found me; but to no purpose.

Strangely, I was no longer discouraged. Somehow the matter had gone beyond that and was now become a joke. I became interested in a detached sort of way, to know just what this country would do to a man. The whole thing was preposterous. Anyway things couldn't very well get much worse, so any change there might be, must, I considered, be for the better.

In that I was wrong. It turned soft and the going got desperately bad. Wet, heavy, clammy days, such as I had not believed possible at that time of the year, settled down over the land, smothering it; days when the snow packed and sagged, clogging the snowshoes so as to reduce walking to little more than a struggle to successfully shift the weight from one unstaple foot-hold to the next before punching through to the bottom. This was followed by cold that covered the dripping trees with an icy coat, and crusted the snow with a brittle glassy shell that would not support the weight of a man. So that no matter how warily I walked I now broke through at each successive step, and with a crash that jarred my whole body, effectually breaking the steady rhythm so essential to the proper manipulation of snowshoes. The crust caught at the shoes with a jerk, throwing them out of control, and sometimes bringing me to my knees. This crust also precluded any chance of ascertaining the movements of possible animals, as they could leave no track on it. Whilst this shrinkage of snow might give satisfaction to some, with the large snow-shoes I was wearing it became only a handicap, and in any event mild weather and the conditions that follow it are no boon to a woodsman. These softening and debilitating conditions that made a mockery of efficiency and turned artifice to naught, were detestable in the extreme to one conditioned to the sterner but more appropriate circumstances of the High North, where a man passed smoothly, rhythmically, and sound-lessly over the surface of six feet of snow. It was as though the very elements themselves were in league against me, and had conspired to our undoing. The purging fires of adversity were not to my liking, and I cursed with exceeding bitterness the country that had brought me to such a pass. Thus will man ever rail against the rod that chastens him, though he may be driven thereby, and to his own profit, from a life-long lethargy of self-satisfaction. But it is hard to submit, give up the ship, pull down your flag. And that is what I now would have to do; strike my colours. I was thinking of my beaver colony.

I knew beyond any hope of repeal that they must go. I had made an undertaking to kill no more beaver and owing to a set of conditions arising directly from this vow, I must now break it. They were the only beaver left in the entire region; there were only four in the house. I would need them all. The cards were stacked, and had been from the outset.

Across the lake from the cabin stood the lodge that was to have been the foundation of my colony,—the substantiation of a dream, the fulfillment of a big idea. With the two young ones we had and this small family, I would have asked nothing more, and I well knew that once I had killed them the whole structure of my cherished purpose would topple down and never more be raised.

One evening I made my preparations. It seemed like getting ready for an execution. I took over an ice chisel, some bait, and traps. I made four sets. Every trap does not catch a beaver, but in two lifts I would have them all.

Anahareo stood by; she helped me, handed me the bait, passed me the dry sticks that were to guide the victims to the traps. She was, I knew, moved to the depths; but she said nothing, knowing from experience that when my mind was made up on such matters that it was useless to plead. Besides, it was not her way.

The sun was setting, and shone on the pitiful snow-covered home, the sun that was Life, the sun that these creatures would not be there to see when the spring came.

I dismissed these weak unmanly thoughts. It was done. In two days our debt would be secure. We turned to go.

Just then I heard a sound, a shrill treble voice; it issued from the beaver house, the voice, almost, of a child. Momentarily it startled me. Anahareo heard it too.

"Just like ours," she said.

"The very same." I listened. Another voice joined, raised in protest. Well did we know the details of this small domestic scene.

"He's eating. Some one is trying to steal his lunch." This from Anahareo. Placating sounds, then bleats and murmurs of satisfaction, the rattle of busy teeth.

"He's still got his stick." She elaborated, reading the story out. "He's eating it. Gee!" She laughed a little. "Gee! I'll bet you he's glad now."

Well he wouldn't have to worry about his stick after to-night and no amount of talk was going to change it.

"Pony!" I spoke harshly. "What is the use of this!"

Came a hollow plunge, and the water heaved in one of the newly cut holes: first out, that would be the old lady, the mother. I ran to the set and throwing myself down peered in, the ice chisel poised. With a quick stab I thrust the chisel down into the waiting trap, felt the jar as it snapped. I passed swiftly to the other three, sprung them.

There were no words. We avoided looking at one another. We collected our hardware and went home. The sun was still shining on the beaver house.

I had run my flag back up again.

When we entered the camp, the two rapscallions within stood a moment eyeing us, and then surged across the floor to our feet. Anahareo gathered them up in her arms and held them close, and her eyes were shiny. She is not usually demonstrative, but she is a woman and chicken-hearted; women are that way.

Perhaps too, she was thinking that across the way two other little creatures, just like these, had also something to be happy about, did they but know it.

CHAPTER SEVEN

How McGinty and McGinnis Opened a New Door

FROM THEN ON I GAVE UP TRAVELLING ENTIRELY. NOTHING IS more monotonous than time spent in objectless wanderings over a country you know to have been thoroughly explored, exploited, cut, dried, and laid out with scientific accuracy on a too correct map, especially if it be denuded of most forms of life. Any new features I might think I was discovering would be past history to a dozen, perhaps a hundred other men. Moreover, there was never sufficient snow for good travelling. Perhaps I am over particular, but I am something of an artist in my line, and take pride in good work on a trail.

To beings of our kind, cessation of travelling, the denial of that unappeasable urge to see what lays beyond the hills, meant stagnation, almost a cessation of living, and worse, long hours of idleness with their dark attendant introspection.

The beaver were our salvation. By now they had grown considerably, weighing in the neighbourhood of fifteen pounds apiece, and their fur had come in full, rich, and lustrous. Although they were growing up, they were as much attached to us as ever, and still cuddled up to us in bed. Our hours did not always coincide with theirs and they were often ready to rise before we were. We would sometimes lay perfectly still feigning sleep and hoping they would subside; but apparently they liked to see everybody getting around mornings, and would pick at our eyebrows and lips and otherwise aggravate us until, in self-defence, we were obliged to get up. We had to sleep on the floor on their account as they clamoured unceasingly to get into the bunk, and made it impossible for us to sleep there. We could, of course, have put them in their place as animals, but their perception of what went on around them was so extraordinarily clear that we felt that we would not be allowed to get away with it. And moreover their manner of expressing their desires was so explicit, and they were so sensitive to the least rebuff, that it seemed hardly the thing to do. That they were very responsive to our moods and extremely sensitive could be plainly seen. A bustle of preparation on our part induced them to like activity; as for instance when we were making our bed on the floor, they would run around us pulling at the blankets, and sometimes make off with the pillows. When we laughed a great deal, or held a more animated conversation than usual, they also became very animated. And I found a little self-reproach, and learned to better guard my tongue and temper, when I found that they kept out of sight, when I complained loudly and not too well concerning some pet grievance I might entertain.

The stalemate which had fallen upon us would have been well-nigh unbearable, with its prospect of a further three months of inactivity until the March hunt should commence, had it not been for these entertaining creatures, who kept us in a state of perpetual uncertainty and had our minds well exercised conjecturing as to their next move. They did the most unforeseen, un-heard of things and were at times incorrigibly mischievous. If variety is the spice of life, they supplied by their diverse and sometimes rather violent activities a condiment that certainly had a very enlivening effect on ours. It often took a good deal of forebearance to view with any approach to appreciation, the results of what they seemed to consider a fair day's work. In their spare time they were always demanding something, or moving some small object from place to place, or frolicking in amongst our feet, and we were never really rid of them save while they slept, and not always then. But they seemed so happy with everything, and their laughter-provoking antics so livened up the dull and dingy cabin, that we forgave them much of the inconvenience they put us to. Dave, the old Algonquin Indian, who had kept beaver himself in his younger days, had warned us of what we would be up against, and had told us some incredible yarns which we had hardly believed at the time, but I began to think that he had not told us the half of it.

And as these little elf-like creatures hopped and capered at their work, and ran back and forth or staggered around erect appearing and disappearing in the semi-darkness beneath the bunk, the table, or in corners, there appeared to be not two, but a number of them, so that the place had at last something the atmosphere of being inhabited by a whole crowd of small busy sprites. They were continually emitting queer cries and signals to one another in their shrill adolescent treble, and they made attempts to communicate with us in the same way, and were often astonishingly intelligible. Sometimes they squatted upright on the floor and performed their periodical and very meticulous toilet, or sat with their hands held tight to their breasts and their tails before them, looking like nothing so much as small mahogany-coloured idols.

There were moments in the midst of their most intense activity when they would stop concertedly, and in attitudes of arrested motion regard us with sudden, silent watchfulness; eyeing us searchingly, steadfastly, and so very wisely, as though, realizing all at once that we were not as themselves, they were trying to reach some decision concerning us; or as if to say, "Yes, big fellows, we know, we are small now, but just you wait awhile!" And their looks on these occasions seemed to be so full of meaning, as their actions were often so much to the purpose, that as they stood regarding us so strangely, they gave an eerie effect of being little dumb people with twilight minds who would some day, astoundingly, speak to us.

But towards the close of their hours of wakefulness, there would come a time when all this wisdom and alertness, all the skill and artful planning, all the business and contriving would be discarded and forgotten. And the aura of semi-human super-instinct would quite disappear and leave behind it nothing but two little animals who had become suddenly very weary, and who plodded soberly over to each his human friend to be lifted up, and then with long drawn sighs of vast content fall fast asleep.

These versatile guests of ours accepted camp life as a matter of course in spite of conditions that were so unnatural to their kind. They had no tank but lived precisely as any land animal would have done, getting along quite contentedly with only a wash dish nailed to the floor for drinking purposes. They were quite well satisfied with this arrangement, for though the door was open frequently during soft weather, they made no attempt to go down to the lake. Once we took them to the water hole but they refused to enter or drink out of it, but got off the ice as quickly as possible and scrambled up the snow path back to camp.

Their efforts to carry out their numerous plans resulted in the interior arrangements of the cabin being sometimes grotesque, and often exceedingly messy. The most notable of these was an attempt to build themselves a house. They had taken full possession of the space beneath the bunk with a proprietary air that was very droll to see in creatures so small. This spot they undertook to turn into a kind of private chamber, to which end they one night removed the entire contents of the wood box, and constructed with it a barricade all down the outside, between the bunk and the floor, leaving the end open as a means of egress. Inside the enclosure thus formed they next cut a hole in the flooring, and dug out a tunnel under the rear wall, which, when large enough served as a bed-room, though its present purpose was to provide material for plastering the skeleton rampart already erected.

We were not aware of the addition of this mud mine to the domestic arrangements, until one day we saw something coming up and over this rampart, to fall with a heavy "plunk" on the floor—a lump of mud. A stone followed, of fair size; a little later more dobs of mud, large dobs about the full of a quart measure apiece. Inspection revealed the tunnel, and also the fact that the inside of their partition was well and smoothly plastered. The odd consignments that had appeared on the floor were merely a little excess material that had slopped over. When they came out later they collected this and tamped the outside with it. They were really very economical. Moreover they were well organized, as the tunnel being as yet only big enough for one to pass at a time, they sometimes worked in shifts. When they both were on the job together one brought out the material, and the other took it and did the decorating.

All this explained the mysterious thumps and scrapings, and the sound of grunts and loud breathing that had been heard for some nights past issuing from under the bed. This barricade was eventually plastered completely, both inside and out, except at one end where a small aperture was left open, apparently for observation purposes as the window in the barrel had been. When soft weather occurred, the burrow being under the low side of the cabin, all the drippings poured off the roof down onto it and soaked through, transforming the stiff mud into a thin batter. At such times they would come out in the cabin so plastered with this gooey mess as to be almost unrecognizable, and would disport themselves all over the floor, or try to clamber onto our knees whilst in this condition.

We had read a book dealing with the building of the Union Pacific railroad in early days, and this construction work of theirs, with its wooden framework and earthen fill, reminded us a good deal of the description given, and the resolution and industry of the Irish workers engaged on it was well emulated by our own ambitious pioneers under the bed. So we now gave them Irish names, McGinnis and McGinty, to be as near alike as possible. These names suited them very well indeed, as they were as energetic and at times as peppery as any two gentlemen from Cork could well have been. Ever since the barrel had been discarded we had ceased to call them Immigrants but had named them separately, for the time being, also from characters in books. The male (now McGinnis) had a little game he used to play. Every day at noon when he arose, he would lay watchfully hiding behind the corner of his entrench-ment until one of us passed, when he would charge violently out and engage whoever it was in mock combat. This tournament took place each morning without fail, and was his one big moment of the day; so we made it a point to be sure of passing the appointed spot when we espied him. Then, soon after the assault, which was always made in silence and apparent deadly earnest, out would come McGinty to speak her morning monologue, declaiming in a loud voice with many different tones in it. And sometimes the two of them would sit there in the morning line-up as though for inspection and parade, and solemnly wag their heads in the way they have, and make the strangest sounds.

And the warrior became known as Ivanhoe, while the other, on account of her discoursing and long winded speeches, we had called Hawkeye, after a character we had read about who was always moralizing and laying down the law to those about him. But we liked the new industrious-sounding names the better, and they got to know them very well, but being so much alike, as they themselves were, when one of them was called they both would come. And this was the very last of all their christenings.

After the morning exercises we fed them tidbits which they retired into their house to eat, sitting as far apart as possible, and scolding under their breath to ward off possible attempts at piracy. The very audible smacking of lips as they ate often made us wish they could be induced to take some soup, to see just what effect would be produced. They were very choosy too and had individual tastes, being satisfied with no odds and ends or leavings, and if several pieces were offered them from the same bannock, they spent some time in their selection, like the hero in a novel who, in moments of stress, selects so carefully one cigarette out of a dozen, all identical in appearance. The lunch disposed of, they would emerge for the day's doings in great fettle, coming on deck all cleared for action, forging around the camp very alert and bustling in manner, as if to say "Well, here we are; what to do?" And almost always, it was not long before everyone was doing, ourselves included.

The fidelity with which their voices and actions registered their emotions was a constant source of interest to us, and they even seemed gifted with some kind of a sense of humour. I have seen one of them torment the other until the victim emitted a squawk of complaint, and then, having apparently accomplished his purpose, the aggressor would shake his head back and forth and twist his body as though in convulsions of mirth and then repeat the performance—so that an onlooker once said that he fully expected to hear the creature laugh.

There is no doubt that they possessed, in common with all their kind, capabilities not usually found in animals, though I much doubt that these could be any further developed in so self-willed and independent a nature; but, prepared as we constantly were for the unexpected, I think neither of us will quite forget the first time we saw them engaged in what is to a beaver, his national pastime. I had seen dogs, wolves, and foxes tussle and had watched most of the other beasts, from cougars to squirrels, tumble around and paw at one another like the animals they were. But these extraordinary creatures, not satisfied with the amusements that other beasts were contented with, stood up on their hind legs, put their short arms around each other as far as they would reach, and wrestled like men!

Back and forth, round and round,—but never sideways—forcing, shoving and stamping, grunting with the efforts put forth, using all the footwork they knew how, they would contest mightily for the supremacy. When one was, perhaps after some minutes, finally vanquished, with loud squeals, the bout was immediately terminated and they would make a few hops and turn their attention to their more sober occupations.

These strictly legal pursuits did not however supply the capricious and enterprising McGinty with quite all the excitement she craved. She developed a mild criminality complex, one of those "kinks" we hear so much about. Although she had free access to the few potatoes we had saved, and had helped herself to them at will quite openly, she suddenly seemed to get the idea that stealing them would be more fun. She took to going behind the bag and extracting them stealthily through a hole, and could be seen creeping along close to the wall with her booty, no doubt thoroughly enjoying the thrill. We allowed her to do this of course, and enjoyed watching her. Now opposition is the breath of life to a beaver; their whole life training is associated with the overcoming of obstacles, and the great incentive not being forthcoming in this instance, the pastime soon palled.

She next commenced purloining tobacco. We were apprised of this during the night by some very mournful wailing which we had come to recognize as meaning real trouble, and we discovered the bold buccaneer laid out in the middle of the floor not far from the stolen goods, which had been partly consumed. The poor little beast was evidently suffering and tried to crawl over to us but was unable to get her hind legs under her, as though paralysed. We picked her up carefully and laid her on the bunk. She was Anahareo's pet and clung to her, clutching at her clothes with paws, so like hands, that had lost their strength. She made no further utterance, but the look of dumb appeal, the weak attempts to get as close as possible to this well loved haven of refuge, spoke more eloquently than any sound she could have made. A beaver in serious trouble will sometimes grip you tightly, and look at you and seem to beg. I had not seen this before, and it moved me profoundly to search some past experience for a cure. I prepared an emetic, but she would not, or could not swallow it. She fell asleep or into a coma and her heart action nearly ceased, and I suddenly remembered a case of opium poisoning I had seen, or heard of, or read about somewhere. I told Anahareo to rub her, rub her hard over the whole body, to massage the hands and feet, to keep her awake at all costs. It seemed cruel, but it was a case of kill or cure. Meanwhile under Anahareo's direction I prepared a hot mustard bath. We put the beaver in it and her head fell forward into the mixture: we held it up. She was unconscious. The liquor did not penetrate the fur right away, but the feet and broad expanse of tail were exposed to it, and it had an almost immediate, though slight, effect. With her hand under the breast Anahareo announced an increasing heart action. The unconscious animal became alive enough to moan and hold up her head, but drooped again soon after being taken out, and soon the heart weakened so that its beat was almost imperceptible. Anahareo rubbed hard and continuously, and kept her awake while I prepared another bath. Placed in it she came to her senses again. We went at the thing systematically, and the camp soon had the appearance of a hospital ward, as we bathed the helpless little creature and tried to rub the life into her with towels. She was slipping away from under our hands, eyes closed, motionless, sinking. There seemed little hope. We worked over her for ten hours. We kept her heart going, but during that time she had three convulsions. Yet she still lived, and the time of dawn, so often fatal, was nearly past. I had seen more than one life go out on its grey receding tide. At daylight she had seemed to pass the crisis. She began to show signs of returning vigour. Her heart beat strongly; she stood up on her four legs. Then she took one last convulsion and straightened out. I dropped my towel; this must be the end.

"Well, Pony," I commenced, and then turned to put wood in the stove, and found other business in that direction. I didn't want to see. There would be a heart break in the death of this small dumb beast. Then I heard a cry behind me, not a wailing, not a lamentation as I had expected, but a declaiming, a discoursing with strange half-human sounds in it, a long loud monologue as of one laying down the law. And then I turned to see McGinty sitting bolt upright and making some attempt to comb her wet bedraggled coat. Truly, at the eleventh hour. And then I heard another sound from Anahareo.

It was the first time I had ever heard her cry.

Meanwhile McGinnis, either having become lonesome, or sensing in that undefinable way peculiar to animals that something was wrong, had been for some time trying to climb into the bunk, so we restored his partner to him and gave him some attention. For once he would have none of us, but flew to McGinty and smelled her carefully as though to be sure of her identity after so long an absence, and plucked at her and made small sounds, short mumbling little whimpers that we had never heard before, and ran beside her nose to nose, while she exclaimed in that strident voice of her, as was her fashion. And from under the bunk the whimpering sounds continued for quite some time; and later when we looked in to see if our patient was quite recovered, the two of them lay with their hands firmly embedded in each other's fur, as they had done so often when they were very, very small.

This dramatic episode put a period on McGinty's debut into the underworld, and for some time after she was quite exemplary. Any real misfortune seemed to have quite a chastening effect on them, and McGinnis, for his part, had been so good since his misadventure on the ice that Anahareo was quite convinced that he could not be long for this world.

They had contradictory, if not complex characters, with strongly marked individual traits. McGinnis, if reprimanded obeyed immediately and busied himself elsewhere, only to return to the forbidden act at a later date with an air of the most disarming innocence, to again retire when requested. McGinty had to be practically forced into compliance, and would seize the first opportunity to continue whatever depredation she had been engaged in. As soon as she saw that she had again attracted unwelcome attention, she would start to squeal in advance protest against the inevitable interference, meanwhile addressing herself to the matter in the most determined manner, sticking at it until the last possible moment. Yet it was all taken in good part and there were never any hard feelings, and this wilfulness, with resultant scoldings, in no way impaired their affection for us, and never was allowed to interfere with that hour of quiet and peaceful intimacy, which seemed to play such an important part in their daily lives, when bygones were bygones and we were all such good friends together. And when perhaps they missed, in some dim wistful way, the mother-love that was forever lost to them.

On one point however, they were strongly in accord, and that was in a determination to find out, by hook or by crook, what lay concealed beyond their reach up on the table. This table and its inaccessible contents had had an irresistible fascination for them from the time it was first set up. They seemed to think that they were missing something here. They were especially clamorous at meal times, and although we often gave them all the food they could dispose of, it did not assuage their burning desire to explore this piece of forbidden territory. They tried by every means possible to them to accomplish this object, and they once succeeded in pulling down the oilcloth cover. The resulting crash of tin dishes must have been very edifying, but this, apparently, was not enough. I had an idea they would eventually do something about it, but was not prepared for what actually did happen. We had never left them alone more than a few hours at a time on account of the cold, but one day, it being quite soft, we both took a trip to a lumber camp some miles away, and being invited to stay the night felt safe to do so. The cook, who had heard about the beaver, was very interested and expressed a desire to see them, so we suggested that he come over. As we were leaving he gave us a good sized parcel of treats for the beaver and said that he would be along to see us that day. As this was to be our first visitor here we wanted to give him a welcome, and hurried home to prepare it.

We found the door hard to open. That was because the blankets were piled against it. This however was the least of our troubles. Beaver can, under good direction, do a lot in a short space of time; in this instance the supervision had been adequate and the results sweeping.

The place was a wreck.

The beaver had at last got the table where they wanted it, having brought it down to their level by the simple expedient of cutting off the legs. We hadn't thought of that; there was always something you didn't think of with these hooligans. The long coveted contents of this piece of furniture must have been disappointing, consisting mostly of utensils, but these had been removed and most of them we found in the den later; some of them were never recovered and probably had been deposited in the far end of the tunnel. Our other fixtures were lying scattered over the floor in various stages of demolition. The wash stand also was down and the soap had disappeared. A five gallon can containing coal oil had fallen to the floor and had landed, luckily, right side up. The floor itself had escaped serious damage but was covered with chips, and slivers, and the dismembered trunks of our butchered belongings. The scene must have been very animated whilst in progress.

Since that time I have been subjected to similar and even more devastating visitations, but as an introduction to what might lay in store at a future date this was a little staggering, and certainly we were in no shape to receive a guest.

Meanwhile these whimsical playmates of ours, interrupted in their setting-up exercises by our arrival, were cautiously inspecting us through the loophole in their fortification, and identifying us now came out, two little capering gnomes that hopped over the piles of débris to welcome us home.

It was no use to punish them, as they would not have known what it was all about, being no longer in the act. We had thwarted their natural instincts and must pay for it.

So we fed them the dainties that the cook had sent while they sat amongst the wreckage and ate them—enjoying the finishing touch to what probably had been the most perfect day of their lives.

CHAPTER EIGHT

How We Made Christmas

APART FROM THEIR PURELY PHYSICAL ACTIVITIES, THE MENTAL and emotional capabilities displayed by these creatures, not yet fully developed, aroused in our minds a good deal of speculation as to where instinct ceased and conscious mental effort began.

I once saw in a newspaper a photograph of a Japanese railroad depot with the caption attached "Just like any other station!" as though the editor had been rather surprised to find that it was not built of bamboo and paper. My reaction towards any unusual demonstration of intelligence by an animal, had up till now been much the same. But since the coming of these small ambassadors from a hitherto unexplored realm, the existence of which had so far been only grudgingly acknowledged, this condescending point of view was no longer possible to either of us, and delving yet further into this remarkable new world offered fascinating possibilities. Other animals too might have qualities, which whilst not so spectacular perhaps, might be worth investigating.

The opportunities were unusually good. There was a good deal of soft weather that Winter, and creatures of all kinds were very active, and with the new angle on wild life which our experience with the beaver had given us, we thought it might be interesting to cultivate these others and see just how they responded. Anahareo had made friends with a muskrat that frequented the water hole and was something of a nuisance there, keeping it filled with grass and empty clam shells. He was a fat, jolly-looking fellow whom we called Falstaff on account of his paunchy look, and the fact that he was always eating when visible, and he used to sit at the edge of the ice and demolish the morsels she put down there for him. He eventually got so tame that she could feed him by hand, and I think he watched for her at last, as he would come bobbing out soon after she started down to feed him. He would trot a few feet out on the ice as if to meet her, and losing confidence go scurrying back through the hole, only to pop out again, and make another sortie and retreat. Day by day these runs got longer and longer, and the retirements less precipitate as his assurance increased, so that his education advanced by hops and runs if not by leaps and bounds. He had a small house of mud and weeds down at the shore, and had companions in there, but they could never be induced to put in an appearance.

We had besides, two squirrels who learned to come when called and jump on us, and take bits of bannock from our fingers. These two disagreed violently whenever they met, but in their dealings with us they displayed an ingratiating amiability that might or might not have been counterfeit, and was no doubt inspired by the ever present hope of a hand-out.

Whisky jacks to the number of perhaps a dozen, attracted by this distribution of free lunches, attached themselves to the place and were always on deck, sitting around unobtrusively and motionless on convenient limbs of trees, all fluffed up, and trying to look humble, and dignified, and indifferent all at the same time, as though any such vulgar thought as that of eating was furthest from their minds. But they had a weather eye on the door, and it had only to open when they all assumed a very wideawake appearance, and some of them would start to whistle a little song, hardly more than a whisper, which ceased immediately the door was closed again. There is, of course, no friendship amongst the wild folk that will stand up in the presence of food, it having on them something the effect that money has on not a few humans, and if a quantity of scraps were thrown to them, each would grab all he could and fly away with it. They were not, however, without some powers of discrimination as, if one happened to be alone at the time, he would stroll around amongst the bits and pieces looking for the biggest one. They too become very intimate, and some members of the flock would swoop down like attacking aeroplanes at any thing we held out for them, and lift it as they

passed. Yet others would light on extended fingers, and taking their portion, sit there for a few moments apparently enjoying the novel sensations they experienced, or perhaps warming their feet.

At first these birds were not distinguishable one from another, yet it
could soon be noticed that some of them had a kind of personality, an
individual manner or a look about them, that set them apart from their
fellows, so that they could be recognised quite readily. They are a light
built bird with no great strength or speed of flight, but they make up very
adequately in address what they lack in force. If sufficiently hungry they
could put on a most woebegone appearance which, while perhaps not
consciously assumed, had a highly desirable effect on the observer, but
which was exchanged for a very militant alertness on the appearance of
anything to eat. One of them carried this wheedling proclivity to the
point that when there was any altercation over some tidbit or other, he
would grovel in the snow with piteous cries, and exhibit all the symptoms
of apoplexy. This always caused a commotion, and under cover of it he
worked his way towards the coveted morsel, and suddenly recovering his
health would quickly seize it and decamp. Nearly all of what they took
was stowed away in nooks and crannies, from where it was most industriously retrieved and hidden by the squirrels; but as these caches were in
their turn consistently robbed by the whiskey jacks, things were pretty
well evened up, and everybody eventually got enough.

Yet in spite of their shameless solicitation, these feathered yes-men
were engaging skalawags, and had they been human, they would have
belonged in the category of those delightful rascals who can touch you
for your last cigarette, and make you feel that they are doing you a favour.

To have killed any or all of them would have been easy enough, but
the idea must have been repugnant to any thinking man. Yet I had caught
them yearly by dozens in sets intended for larger and more predatory
game, where, caught by the legs, they had struggled their harmless lives
out in helpless agony. And as these various creatures followed me, and
climbed my legs and bravely ran upon my hands and arms, to sit there in
all confidence, peering at me so bright-eyed and intelligent, bodies
vibrant with life and the joy of just being alive, the enormity of this
unthinking cruelty impressed itself upon me more and more.

Anahareo was very proud of having all these creatures around the house, and they somehow gave the place a lively appearance, and made us feel that we had been accepted as friends and fellow citizens by this company of furred and feathered folk. We attended to their wants quite as though we had been their custodians, which in a way we were, and at last our wild and ever-hungry family increased to the point that we were obliged to have rules and hours for them, while the beaver occupied the times between.

∾ ∾ ∾

YET IN SPITE OF ALL THESE DISTRACTIONS THE DAYS WERE often uneventful and very long. Fortunately, being both great readers, we had gone to the labour of packing in a number of magazines. They more than paid for their transportation by the pastime we got out of them, as we read and re-read them to ourselves and then aloud to each other. Among these was an English periodical which was evidently intended for readers coming under the denomination of "landed gentry." We were well landed, if no gentry, and this particular publication became a favourite with us, not only on account of the fine pictures it contained, but probably also because the conditions set forth in it were so utterly at variance with our own. So we ambled around amidst its precise and excellent pronouncements much in the manner of a man who circulates among courtiers attired in his shirt sleeves.

Fits of loneliness for the great free country we had left assailed us every so often, becoming at times almost intolerable, and while under their influence we were hard put to find means to combat them. Anahareo would take her snowshoes and wander in the woods or draw cartoons of people we had known, at which she was an adept. For my part, I often scribbled in a writing pad and along the blank edges of the magazine pages or on packing paper, running commentaries on the discrepancies in some of the nature stories we had read, skeleton descriptions of well-remembered scenes and short impressions of outstanding happenings or personalities we had met up with. By this same vicarious means I lived over small portions of my former life and got some solace from it.

Sometimes we extinguished the light, and opening the stove door wide, we would sit upon the floor before the fire, and the glow of the shifting embers threw red moving lances and shafts of crimson light out into the shadowy darksome cabin, and made strange patterns on the walls, and discovered in them secret new recesses that we had not known were there. And these beams came shining out on the tins and pots and other homely ware, so that they gleamed like burnished copper in some old baronial hall, and turned to rich rare tapestry the hanging blanket at the door. And behind the looming earthwork at our backs we could hear the intermittent murmur of the beaver, like subdued and distant voices from the past. So that the place seemed full of mystery, and we talked in whispers, and watched the embers glow and fade and break and fall apart, in the red and fiery cavern beneath the burning coals. And here faces formed, and little images and imaginary objects took their place and disappeared again as though upon a stage. And the shapes of some of them brought back to mind some half-forgotten story or an incident, or thought, and by them there nearly always hung a tale. And presently, as we remembered we recounted them while we sat within the small red circle of the fire-light.

Anahareo related, at these times, some of the innumerable exploits of Ninne-bojo, the conjurer, who was sometimes evil, sometimes good, at times a saint, more often a devil; a plausible rascal with a taste for the occult and having conveniently flexible notions of honesty, and who still survived in the folklore of the Iroquois, who are Anahareo's people.

And in my turn I told my tales of high adventure, and hunger and feasting in the great dim forests beyond the Height of Land, and sometimes talked of war, and old Bisco days. And in the cabin beside that little stove was brought to light much that had long lain buried in the past. And so intent did we become in our recountings, and so faithfully did we describe every act and every aspect of the actors in them, that they almost seemed to live again in the fiery amphitheatre, and I think they never slipped entirely back to where they came from, but the glamour of the stories seemed to hang about the place, like they had happened there. And sometimes I wonder if the spirits of the past that we conjured up, do not still gather in the old deserted cabin and tell their tales and play their parts again, while the cold moonbeams throw pale shafts of light through the crevices in the unchinked walls, and filter down through the empty stove pipe hole and make not a red circle but a white one, in which perhaps they sit before the ghostly stove.

Some of these chronicles I wrote down, getting a vast satisfaction out of the job, and I took at last to rolling these records up, and put them carefully away. Somehow they began to seem like old and honoured traditions that would otherwise be lost. Pretty soon there was quite a stack of them. I wrote little stories about our muskrats and squirrels and birds, and would read them aloud to Anahareo. She did not seem to be as deeply impressed by them as I thought she should have been, but we had a lot of fun out of it and she would tell them to the beavers afterwards. Of course they would listen awhile, and then shake their heads and roll on their backs as they always did when we made a fuss of them; and that was about all the appreciation I got. But I kept at it. I found that the English language did not have quite all the words I needed, and I was not above manufacturing the odd one. I stole freely out of the magazines, having no idea of the enormity of my offence at the time; but I was having a high old time, and was beginning to be, so I was informed, something of a nuisance around the house.

It occurred to me, experimentally, and with no idea of seriously accomplishing anything, to take the highlights of all these aimless scribblings and try to weld them into something. For I had noticed that, apart from the literary skill and carefully selected wording apparent in them, many of the narratives we read with such interest had very little meat on the bone, so to speak, when they were dissected. I had plenty of material, so decided to write an article with lots of meat on it. So I commenced the welding process. This took about a week, and resulted in a production about six thousand words in length, very meaty, and in which I covered the greater part of Northern Canada, and touched with no light hand on nearly every incident and animal common to that region. The beaver were in it, and all our other dependents that lived out in the yard and in the lake, so I felt I had done my duty by all of them.

I read it through repeatedly, each time with a more pronounced feeling of satisfaction, and made many alterations, and then rewrote it, working feverishly on it far into the night. I read it again, aloud this time, to

Anahareo and would have read it to the beaver if I had thought they would have listened. Anahareo listened dutifully and patiently, and we discovered several points on which I had not made myself quite clear. I easily overcame these ambiguities by adding lengthy and precise explanations. Anahareo worked with me on these troublesome parts and what one did not think of the other did, and the two of us racked our brains by the hour thinking up any fine points we might have missed. This story was going to be true to life if it took all Winter. These additions and interpolations brought this creation up into the neighbourhood of eight thousand words; no mean accomplishment for a maiden effort. Anahareo once suggested meekly that it might be too long, but I rejected the idea with some acerbity; I had read a similar article in which the author had only been able to squeeze about fifteen hundred words out of his subject. I intended to fall into no such error. Thoughts and ideas could come and go, to be used or discarded at will, but the moment one was recorded it became an acquisition. A story, once it was on paper, became a palace of dreams the structure of which was studded with rich gems, not one of which was to be on any account removed. Any suggestion that some of these be extracted for the general good, aroused a state of mind bordering on the mildly homicidal. I copied the effusion all out laboriously (I am not at all sure, at this distance, whether I used pen or pencil) parcelled it up with about fifty photographs intended to be used as illustrations, and made a special trip to town with it, a matter of forty miles. I was not particularly anxious to sell it, but wanted a whole lot of people to read this stuff, and if they paid me, why so much the better.

I mailed the parcel to a war-time address in England, which country, I had always understood, was the market for such material, giving special instructions to my agent that the serial, translation, moving picture, and book rights were to be retained, in accordance with something I had read on the subject. And some demon of perversity caused me to specify the very exclusive publication, already mentioned, which catered to the aristocracy.

Such a thing as a rejection slip was quite beyond my knowledge, and having estimated, by close figuring, that the cheque would not arrive for at least a month I started home at once, taking a few things for Christmas, which was close at hand. And as I marched along the trail in the driving snow storm, I pondered deeply on the days to come.

I had got some stuff off my chest where it had been fermenting for a long time, and somehow the writing of that manuscript had partially appeased the feeling of loneliness and home-sickness that had overcome me whenever I saw, smelled or heard anything that brought quick stabbing memories of the trails of yesterday. For now the North was not so far away. It was in my hand, ready at my call to leap to action in the jumble of words and disconnected phrases that flowed from my pencil, as I lived over again the joys and the triumphs, the struggles and the hardships that had made life so worth living, while my soul slipped back to wander once more, at will, in a land of wild romantic beauty and adventure that would soon, by all the signs, be gone beyond recall. Perhaps too, a man might live by writing about it; I had the practical experience but could I use it in this way?

A feeling of kinship for all the wild that had been growing on me for years, at this time seemed to have reached its culmination. My late experiences with the few creatures that were commencing to frequent the cabin, had caused me to have quite a feeling of responsibility towards them. Though they had not a tithe of the appeal that a beaver possessed, they were by no means the abysmal insensate creatures I had been wont to consider them, and they gave a remarkable response in return for a little kindness. Lately there had been an addition to our clientele. There was a half-grown fawn that used to feed across the lake from us. He was always alone, and probably had lost his mother. I had myself killed several does close in. This little creature, lacking perhaps an education on this account, had little fear of us and would sometimes cross the lake, and coming up the water trail would pass around the cabin on his way. This was always at about the same hour, every second day or so, and we took to standing outside and waiting for him and he would pass most unconcernedly and sometimes stopped and looked us over. He soon became quite tame, and we could move quite freely near him while he nibbled at the poplar tops that had been collected for the beaver. He was a mighty interesting thing to have around, and his confidence, or his ignorance, or whatever it might be, was the best guarantee of safety he could have. After his arrival on the scene, I used to go far back into the woods for our meat, so that the sound of shooting and the sight and smell of slaughter would not drive him away. Yet a short year ago I would have killed him with a club to save a bullet. And now I no longer wished to kill. I had beaten and abused the North that now I found I loved, and could I but live without this slaughter, this unnecessary brutalizing cruelty, I would be forever glad. A few clean kills for meat, that was the law of the Wild, and permissible. Perhaps this new idea, this writing would provide, but I had no notion how much a man would have to put out of this commodity. The thought of the possible unsaleability of my product never entered my head. A man may do a lot of thinking in forty miles, and the familiar setting of the whirling snow seemed somehow to clarify my mind, and as I plodded onward my aims began to take on shape and form.

My impulsive action in springing the beaver traps I had not regretted in the light of sober reflection. They were now safe. This decision was final and unchangeable. That I could tame these animals I was assured, nor was I wrong. Those other little beasts, the squirrels, the whiskey jacks, the muskrat, the little deer, they seemed to sense a sanctuary and trusted us, and the daily development of their confidence and the manifestations that accompanied it, were an absorbing study. They were more fun alive than dead, and perhaps if I could write about them they would provide many times over the value of their miserable little hides, beaver included, and still be there as good friends as ever. A man didn't need much of a hunting ground that way. I realized that these radical departures from my life training would require something more than the ordinary resourcefulness and physical courage of the woods to bring to a successful conclusion; but I did not know, at least so far as my new-born literary aspirations were concerned, that I was gaily disporting myself where an angel would have worn a life-buoy.

So I dreamed my dreams and builded my castles in Castile.

I had always felt that if a man believed himself capable of anything, put into his project all the best there was in him, and carried on in absolute sincerity of purpose, he could accomplish nearly any reasonable aim. I had seen it exemplified a hundred times. Perhaps the task I was setting myself was a little too much like trying to walk on the water, but the blustering fury of the storm exhilarated me, aroused in me a feeling that I marched in some wild parade or carnival and had a part in all this savage revelry, so that I felt that there was nothing that could not be overcome. And as I bore against it, and yet with all its howling frenzy it could not hold me back one step, I cried aloud that I was the better for its coming, that my faithful snowshoes could break a trail through any storm that was ever put across in this one horse lowland country.

Yet, did I but think of it, with all my shouting, all my boasted skill and cunning, I could not turn back from falling one single snow-flake of them all.

I arrived home in the thick of the blizzard and found the little cabin mighty snug to come into out of the tempest. Anahareo had busied herself crocheting bright wool borders on white sugar bags, split open and freshly laundered, and we now had these for window curtains, which gave everything a real cosy, homey appearance.

The beaver, so Anahareo said, had missed me, McGinnis especially had seemed to search for something, and had spent much time at the door, looking up at it. Neither of them was in evidence, but a nose was visible at the peep-hole in the redoubt and being at length satisfied as to my identity, they came bouncing out and capered around me in a great access of spirits, McGinnis repeatedly throwing himself at my feet until kneeling down, I offered them the sticks of candy I had for them, and which they sat and ate with loud and most unmannerly sounds of satisfaction.

I laid out my small purchases which the kindly store keeper had suggested that I make, saying as he did so, that it must be lonesome in the woods and that he liked to feel that we had Christmas back there too. And being now in a country where Christmas was recognized as a real festival, we decided that we ought to make all the good cheer we could and so forget our troubles for a while.

Personally I had always been too busy hunting to celebrate that festive Season, beyond submitting to a kind of hypocritical sentimentality that prevented me from taking life on that day; but never being quite sure which day it was, even this observance had fallen into disuse. But I was now a family man, and being, besides, sure of the date, we would now keep it in style.

I whittled out some boards of dry cedar, painted them with Indian designs and attached them to the sides and tops of the windows where they looked, if not too closely inspected, like plaques of beadwork. We painted hanging ornaments with tribal emblems and hung them in places where the light fell on them. We laid two rugs of deerskin; these were immediately seized as play toys by the two Macs, and had to be nailed down, when the beaver compromised by pulling handfuls of hair out of them; a pleasing pastime. Having killed a large eagle in my travels, I made a war-bonnet, a brave affair of paint and eagle feathers and imitation beadwork, that sat on a wooden block carved in the semblance of a warrior's face, and painted with the Friendship Sign in case we had a guest. It had quite an imposing effect as it stood on the table, at one end. We distributed coloured candles in prominent places, and hung a Japanese lantern from the rafter. Viewed from the outside, through a window, the interior exhibited a very pleasing appearance, though a little like the abode of some goblin whose tastes were torn between the pious and the savage.

On Christmas Eve all was ready. But there was one thing missing; Anahareo decided that the beavers were to have a Christmas Tree. So while I lit the lantern and arranged the candles so their light fell on the decorations to the best advantage, and put apples and oranges and nuts in dishes on the table, and tended the saddle of deer meat that sizzled alongside of the factory-made Christmas pudding that was boiling on top of the little stove, Anahareo took axe and snowshoes and went out into the starry Christmas night.

She was gone a little longer than I expected, and on looking out I saw her standing in rapt attention, listening. I asked her what she heard.

"Listen." She spoke softly. "Hear the Christmas Bells," and pointed upwards.

I listened. A light breeze had sprung up and was flowing, humming in the pine tops far above; whispering at first then swelling louder in low undulating waves of sound, and sinking to a murmur; ascending to a deep strong wavering note, fading again to a whisper. The Carrillons of the Pine Trees; our Christmas Bells.

Anahareo had got a fine balsam fir, a very picture of a Christmas tree, which she wedged upright in a crevice in the floor poles. On top of it she put a lighted candle, and on the limbs tied candies, and pieces of apple and small delicacies from the table, so they hung there by strings and could be reached.

The beaver viewed these preparations with no particular enthusiasm but before long, attracted by the odour of the tree, they found the hanging tidbits and sampled them, and soon were busy cutting the strings and pulling them down and eating them with great gusto. And we set our own feast on the table, and as we ate we watched them. They soon consumed all there was on the tree, and as these were replaced the now thoroughly aroused little creatures stood up on their hind legs and grabbed and pulled at their presents, and stole choice morsels from one another, pushing and shoving so that one would sometimes fall and scramble to his feet again as hastily as possible, for fear everything would be gone before he got up, while they screeched and chattered and squealed in their excitement. And we forget our supper, and laughed and called out at them, and they would run to us excitedly and back to the tree with little squawks as if to say "Looky! what we found!" And when they could eat no more they commenced to carry away provision against the morrow, sometimes between their teeth, on all fours, or staggering along erect with some prized tidbit clutched tightly in their arms, each apparently bent on getting all that could be got while it lasted. And when we thought they had enough and no longer made replacements, McGinty, the wise and the thrifty, pulled down the tree and started away with it, as though she figured on another crop appearing later and had decided to corner the source of supply.

It was the best fun of the evening, and instead of us making a festival for them, they made one for us, and provided us with a Christmas entertainment such as had never before been seen in any other home, I'm pretty sure. And Anahareo was so happy to see her tree well appreciated, and the beaver were so happy to patronize it, and everybody seemed to be so thoroughly enjoying themselves, that I perforce must be happy too just to see them so.

Stuffed to the ears, and having a goodly supply cached beyond the barricade, the revellers, tired now, or perhaps overcome by a pleasant fullness, soon went behind it too. Heavy sighs and mumbles of contentment came up from the hidden chamber beneath the bunk and soon, surrounded by all the Christmas Cheer they had collected, they fell asleep.

And after they were gone a silence fell upon us and all was quiet. And the stove began to be cold: and the place was suddenly so lonely, and the painted brave looked out so soberly at us from under his feathered bonnet, that I put on a rousing, crackling fire, and drew out from its hiding place a bottle of very good red wine that was to have been kept for New Year's.

And we drank a toast to the beaver in their silent house across the lake, and to the friendly muskrats in their little mud hut and all our birds and beasts, and to McGinnis and McGinty, who now lay snoring in the midst of plenty; and another to the solemn wooden Indian, and yet another to the good Frenchman who had supplied the wine.

And as we pledged each other with a last one, we declared that never was there such a Christmas anywhere in all the Province of Quebec. And certainly there never had been on this lake before.

CHAPTER NINE

How We Came to
the Depths

IN MARCH THERE BEING, IN THAT COUNTRY, NO LONGER ANY frost that could penetrate the stout walls of our shack, we decided to go out and collect our cheque. And sure enough there was one, and for a good substantial sum, from the British periodical I had selected as the rather unlikely target for my first shot at the authoring business. Under separate cover was a complimentary copy sent us, as was stated, on account of the unusual circumstances. In it was the article, reduced to about a quarter of its original length and illustrated by about five of my fifty photographs. I remember being a little hurt about this reduction at the time. When we turned to the page indicated and saw, in actual print in that royal-looking magazine, the words and phrases that had been produced under such difficulties and in such humble surroundings, and saw depicted there our cabin, the beaver dam, and McGinnis and McGinty themselves, we were so astonished that we could only grab the pages from one another and gaze unbelievingly at them, and sometimes bumped our heads as we tried to look at them together. Eventually, with a modesty more becoming to a newly hatched author, I allowed Anahareo to have it for herself, while I examined for the twentieth time the bright-tinted and beautifully engraved cheque. It certainly had a very comforting appearance and would take care of a large part of our indebtedness.

As I considered this pink slip of paper I was conscious of an indescribable feeling of freedom, of having stepped through some dark and long closed door into a new, unmapped territory that lay waiting with all its unknown and untried possibilities.

But there was more to it than that. The editor had written me a kind and personal letter, not at all in keeping with the austere magnificence of his product, and in it he stated that he was prepared to consider more work of this nature. What I had hardly dared hope for had actually come to pass, and with no fuss, no ceremony. Rather like stepping out in the dark, this first move, but it had been successful. And so, on account of what had seemed to be a foolish, idle pastime contrived in the heavy hours of despondency, the dawn had broken suddenly, bewilderingly bright and clear before us. And before I wrote accepting this new commission, I went out from the small hotel and bought me a fat yellow fountain pen, some ink and much paper, and a new kodak for Anahareo. And when he heard the news the generous store keeper, whom now we almost looked on as a patron saint, slapped me on the shoulder and gave his congratulations in the hearty fashion of a Frenchman, and said that he had known all along that something wonderful would come of it. My own feelings were not a little mixed. This correspondence was my first contact with a world that had been as far removed from my grasp as was the throne of Egypt, and while I hid my pride as best I could, and kept my light as dim as possible, you may be sure I did not go around with a bushel basket over my head to hide it.

On the forty mile journey home through the bright snow-bound forest, we walked lightly, Anahareo and I, lifted out of our sombre silent habits of the trail by the good fortune that had befallen us. And we travelled, not in single file as usually, but side by side as we talked and planned for the future, and figured how we would soon begin to tame whoever would remain at home of the beaver family that had been so providentially saved. We decided to build a kind of a beaver house on the lake for our two Irishmen, to give them a start. They, and the neighbourly muskrats, and the squirrels and birds, and the little fawn were to share in our new prosperity; and encouraged by our success with these smaller creatures we said that we must now also find a moose. And we would get together a few belongings, and improve the cabin, and cultivate our horned and furred and feathered friends and I would write about them, while Anahareo would supply the illustrations with her new camera. There were no trappers to encroach and destroy, and the beavers would mingle together and increase and fill the pond and spread, and populate the empty streams round about, and the house of McGinnis, as the lumberjacks for miles around now called our camp, would be the centre, and perhaps become a celebrated place. And I inwardly rejoiced that the bloodless happy hunting ground of my imagination was now within the bounds of possibility.

We had been five nights away from home, but the frost had been light and moreover we had protected the legs of the bunk, the washstand, and the table (on one stout centre leg now, and therefore harder to cut down, and also easier to repair) with spare stove piping, and had piled everything on these armoured retreats and on the shelves, so we felt no misgivings.

A few miles from camp we found strange snowshoe tracks turning in on our trail. It was black dark and we could not establish the identity of the shoes, but the indentations, made some time during the heat of these late March days and now frozen hard, could be easily detected beneath the feet. We had no idea who this might be, and always on the watch, we now dropped all discussion and fell into the loping trot we sometimes used. We had had many visitors from surrounding lumber camps on account of the beaver, but not from this particular direction, nor out of the solid bush as in this case, for your lumberjack sticks pretty closely to his roads. This man, as could be ascertained, did not straddle on his webs as does a white man but walked close-footed, like an Indian. This might prove interesting; we hurried. There was a light in the cabin, and not knowing who to expect we opened the door; and there standing before us, with the broadest of smiles and an outstretched hand was David White Stone, the old Algonquin. He had made the grade.

It was quite a reunion. I don't know when we had been quite so glad to see anyone. He still had the famous gun that could so unerringly pick one man out of a crowd, having been lucky enough to catch a short moose hunt with some sportsmen. He had been trapping all winter on the borders of New Brunswick, thirty odd miles away, and having found a pocket of beaver had done fairly well.

We had supper, and after everything had been talked over and conversation had died down a little, we began to call McGinty and McGinnis who had, for some reason, not showed up yet, although subdued sounds could be heard from them. Whereupon David looked at Anahareo and winked slyly with both eyes like an owl.

"They got business in there I guess," he said with a knowing grin and another double-barrelled wink. "I've not been idle since I came; here's a present for you."

And reaching behind the partition he pulled out one after the other two full grown beaver, still wet and—dead.

Anahareo let slip the spoon she was wiping and it fell with a little clatter on the floor. I pulled out my pipe; the tiny crack of the match was an explosion in the silence that suddenly had fallen on the place. Anahareo picked up her spoon and continued with the dishes. After what seemed a long time I remembered that this man was our friend.

"Thanks, Dave," I said, my mouth suddenly dry, "where are the others?"

"There's traps down there yet," he replied.

I lit the lantern.

"Let's go look at them now," I said.

When we were outside, Dave, sensing a discordance somewhere asked,

"What's the matter, Archie? Seems like I've done wrong or something."

He would never know from me.

"Why, no Dave," I answered, looking at him squarely, the lantern raised to see his face the better, and at the same time hide my own. "No, nothing like that—we've been a little unlucky this Winter, that's all."

Across at the lodge we pulled up five traps. David is an old beaver-man, one of the best. The two kittens were both caught.

"We got them all now," he offered uncertainly and added, "That's all there are." He gave me an oblique, keen glance.

"Yes," I agreed. "That's all there are," and looked down at the two half grown kittens that lay lifeless on the ice before their home that so lately had been filled with intelligent, pulsing life, and now was cold and empty in the starlight. There was nothing to be done. The ancient law of claw and fang had after all prevailed.

My palace of dreams had fallen and become a heap of ashes.

Sorrowfully I skinned the beaver next day, giving the hides to Dave. What was left I took back across the lake where they belonged. And as I placed the four poor naked bodies side by side beneath the ice before their door, I breathed a pagan prayer that the Spirit of the Wilderness, whose children they were, might see, and seeing understand.

The thaw commenced, and when Dave suggested that we all go out together and camp on the Touladi Lakes, we agreed. There was nothing to stay here for now save our few pets, who could live without us as they had done before we ever came. So the old man made a sleigh and a toboggan, and when they were finished, one morning at the crack of dawn we loaded up our equipment, with the beaver in the barrel, and the stove as well, and were ready to go.

And Anahareo went down to the small mud hut at the landing to feed our friendly muskrat for the last time, while the whisky jacks and squirrels perched and ran upon my hands and arms and took my final offerings; and what was left I scattered on the snow. The little deer we did not see again.

We left the warrior with his bonnet, standing stern and proudly at his post, the Sign of Welcome still upon his face; and left the paint work, and the emblems, and the gaily-bordered curtains in their places on the windows and the walls.

And we bid farewell to the House of McGinnis with its stories and its laughter, its hopes and its ambitions, its beasts and birds and spirits, left it standing there deserted in its grove of brooding pine trees, gazing out with its windows and its widely open door, at the empty lodge across the lonely silent lake.

And Dave saw that we were sad, and as he walked he shook his head and said he knew there was something wrong, but never asked. At the outlet he blazed a cedar tree and made on it the sign of the Duck, his patron bird, and in a notch below he wedged a piece of plug tobacco and said some words we did not understand.

Meanwhile, we looked in on the beaver, and McGinnis took this opportunity to make a flying leap out of the window of his coach and fell into the creek which was open. In the ensuing search and recovery the mists of sadness lifted for a while. With White Stone in the lead as chief, our little band plodded and wound its laborious way four days across the hills into the blue distance, on to Touladi.

We were overloaded and the going was bad, so that we travelled mostly at night while the frost was in the crust. Several times the toboggan, top-heavy with the barrel, upset, spilling its passengers out into the snow, which not liking very well they hastened back in again before the conveyance was righted, generally after a lively altercation as to who should get in first, or else climbed on the body of the load emitting querulous plaints of discomfort. They preferred to be in motion, and when the cavalcade was halted for any reason it was not long before the covering was pulled off the window of the caboose, and two brown heads with tiny black eyes would peer out in a most accusing silence. If a start was not soon made they became fractious, not ceasing their complaints until we got going again. I have exactly that feeling myself on a train ride so was able to sympathise with them, but Dave's point of view was that they were getting the ride for nothing with free meals thrown in, and that they should be more patient with us. Once the road was reached we had no further trouble, as Company teams soon picked us up, for in that country few vehicles will pass a wayfarer on foot without the offer of a lift. An official of the Company, not willing to see us camping out in tents, allotted to our use a small snug cabin on the shores of Lake Touladi. This camp, known as the "Half-way," became our home until we should choose to move.

Here we turned the beaver loose, and they spent their nights exploring the new waters, sleeping in the camp by day. We had many visitors, being now only five miles from Cabano, and were very contented, save for the cloud that hung heavy over the hearts of two of us. But this setback had somehow made me more determined than ever to carry on. The sacrifice at Birch Lake was not to be in vain, and never again would I desert my post and let those dependent on me foot the bill. That it should happen again was unthinkable. With set purpose and design I commenced again to write, and got away another article, though I doubted its acceptance for my new pen seemed somehow filled with a melancholy that flowed out of it into nearly every line.

Meanwhile we kept close watch on the beaver, as the region was full of travellers, river drivers and habitants. They were good company on their frequent visits and seemed very friendly towards us, but Dave, who spoke French fluently, overheard more than one scrap of conversation concerning the beaver that put us doubly on our guard. And the three of us took turns to patrol the neighbourhood, so that they were never beyond earshot at any hour. Our charges were not hard to keep track of, as they were always creating a commotion at some point or another. They built themselves a funny little beaver house a short distance away where the water was open and the soil clear of snow. They cut and slashed small poplars and willows in all directions, and their cries and slashings and other uproar could be heard at almost any time. Just about daybreak they would scratch and call out at the door, and being let in would come into our beds and go to sleep. They awoke about noon, and, without waiting to eat, scampered off to the big doings outside. They had made another partition for themselves of firewood, but they did not go behind it much, preferring our beds to rest in, and as beaver live twenty or thirty years it looked as though we would have to spend the rest of our lives sleeping on the floor.

At this time there came to live with us an old man who had for many years trapped muskrats on these lakes. This hunt was his by right and he depended on it. On account of the danger to the beaver his coming meant only one thing—we must move. So David went out to Cabano intending, with his knowledge of French, to seek a job, while Anahareo and I collected the beaver, loaded them into the barrel, and catching a passing team moved everything to a little lake that lay beside the road, still nearer to the town. Here, under some big elms, we made camp, while McGinnis and McGinty disported themselves around an old beaver house and dam that stood at the foot of the little pond. There was plenty of feed and water and these old works besides, and they would be well fixed here until I could locate another colony in which to introduce them. When our work was finished, we went down to the lake and called them. They came racing over and tumbled their black dumpy bodies all about our feet, labouring under some great excitement, doubtless on account of the old beaver works. They calmed down a little to eat some sticks of candy, still jabbering away in concert, telling us, no doubt, about their discoveries, and the new estate that had fallen to them with all its ready-made castle and appurtenances. They were hardly able to contain themselves, and after a few moments of gambolling with us, during which they pulled strongly at our legs and charged back and forth as if to have us join in the fun, they hurried off to their small properties like a pair of kids to a circus, two absurd but happy little creatures enjoying their new freedom to the utmost, and who from now on would live as they were intended to.

It was almost a year since we had found them, two tiny helpless orphans at the point of death, and this celebration seemed a fitting anniversary. And my heart warmed the more towards them as I reflected that in their new-found self-sufficiency and independence, they still retained that child-like attachment to ourselves that we had feared to lose.

Once during the evening they came bustling up to camp, and coming inside combed themselves and talked loudly and long, and roamed around the tent as of yore, evidently recognising it, which was not remarkable as it had been their only home for half their lives. They smelled at the stove in which they had so many adventures, and McGinnis burnt his nose on it, while McGinty upset the grub-box, disclosing the bannock of which they ate a goodly portion and altogether seemed very much at home in these familiar surroundings. They had their usual petting party and even slept a while, and it was all so like those eventful days on the Birch Lake trail that seemed now so far away, that we were glad to be back in the old tent again with the little stove going and our two small friends beside us in its glow. Soon they headed for their lake, two gnome-like capering little figures that alternately bounced and waddled side by side down the water trail, and we followed them to the landing as we always did, and somehow wished that they were small again.

We watched the two V's forging ahead towards the ancient beaver lodge until they disappeared into the dusk. And in the star-light, the wake of their passing made pale rippling bands of silver that spread wide behind them, and touched the shore at last, and so were lost. Once, in answer to a call, a long clear note came back to us, followed by another in a different key. And the two voices blended and intermingled like a part-song in the stillness of the little lonesome pond, and echoed back and forth in the surrounding hills and faded to a whisper, and died.

And that long wailing cry from out the darkness was the last sound we ever heard them make.

We never saw them any more.

∾ ∾ ∾

THIS KNOWLEDGE DID NOT COME TO US AT ONCE, BUT WAS slowly borne upon us with the slow immutable passage of the days. One evening passed with no ripple to break the glassy surface of the water, no eager response in answer to our calling. A second night passed, a third and yet a fourth, and there came no racket on the water, no cheerful chattering, no familiar small brown bodies trotted up the water trail on happy visits. The rain washed away their tracks; their sticks of candy wasted quite away. At the Half-way their small works had been removed, and the unfinished lodge had been submerged and soon was swept away. There was nothing left of them, nothing at all. It was as if they had never been.

That they should follow the Spring flood to the mouth of any stream was inevitable; but their return, in a country of this nature, was just as sure.

We followed the stream up to its source and down to the mouth, caving in through snow banks under mined by its flood, wallowing in slush on broken snowshoes, calling, calling— We scoured the whole neighbouring district. We covered the shores of Touladi foot by foot, and followed every creek. We did this until the possibilities were exhausted, while all around us shots resounded and tracks of men crisscrossed in all directions. Anything could have happened; once we found a deer half skinned, the hunters disturbed by our coming; here and there traps were laying set, regardless of season. I doubt if they ever reached the mouth. Tame as they were they would be easy victims, and one man with a club could have killed them anywhere, they who so much craved affection and needed so little to be happy. And we could only hope that they had passed together to the Great Beyond, side by side as they had lived, and that in their last moments they had known it was not we who took their lives away.

A good-natured and deeply religious people these, nonetheless more than one of them had intimated that little would be added to us in the hereafter for our consideration to creatures having neither speech nor a soul. Their principles would include no mercy to an animal. Some were sure the beaver had been killed, others were as certain they had not. We could not know and we carried on our ceaseless, hopeless quest.

The canoe was forty miles away and we needed to prosecute our search. We walked in and paddled back eighty miles in three days. On the river bank stood the tent poles of our camps. At one we saw a little pen of sticks, made before the days of the famous coach; a happy camp it had been. We passed the spot where they had so nearly drowned and had been saved, passed it swiftly, never speaking. That night we slept out on the beach of Temiscouata, too tired to walk the five miles to our camp. The next day we resumed our search. For many more days we ranged the countryside. We scarcely ate; our sleep was troubled and our waking hours full of sorrow. Often we made long trips to inspect some hide we heard of; McGinnis had a burnt nose and some grey hairs, McGinty was jet black. We found, mercifully, no such skins. We questioned travellers, followed some, one or two we searched. We went armed; we made enemies. A grim and silent search it had become. Constantly we got false leads, and momentarily buoyed up, followed them to inevitable disappointment. Sometimes, towards the last, we acted on the impulse of some foolish dream a vision conjured up by fatigue and hunger and restless haunted slumber. There was little that escaped us, and we found beaver that no one knew even existed.

And all the time we travelled we kept some dainties in the tent and on the landing; but no one ever ate them, ever came for them.

And Anahareo grew gaunt and pale and hollow cheeked; her eyes began to have a strained and hungry look. Once she said, "I wonder what we have done. Anything else in all the world could have happened to us—anything but this." And again "We thought we would always have them" and in her sleep she said, "They loved us."

And we hoped on long after we knew that there was nothing left to hope for. We sat at nights in the darkness by our unhappy camp beneath the elm trees, waiting, watching, listening for a well remembered cry of greeting, or the thump of clumsy plodding feet that never came, never would come. And we saw nothing save the still lake and the silent ring of trees, heard nothing but the tiny murmur of the brook. The leaves came, and grass grew undisturbed on the ancient beaver house; the pond dried to a marsh and only the stream remained, running slowly through it.

And at last we knew that they were gone forever, into the darkness from whence they came, two random spirits from the Land of Shadows that had wandered in and stayed a little time, and wandered back again, that had passed like the forgotten winds of yesterday, had vanished like the figment of a dream.

And they left behind them no sign, no trace, save an empty barrel with a hole in it that sat beside the lake, and dried and warped and fell apart, and became a heap of staves and rusty hoops.

And the aged trees whose great drooping crowns loomed high above our heads, standing omniscient in the wisdom of the ages, seemed to brood and to whisper, and look down upon our useless vigil, in a mighty and compassionate comprehension. And they stood about us in a serried dark array, as though to shield us and this spot from further spoilation by the civilization that could be at once so benignant and so ruthless. For they were of the Wild as we were, the Wild to which in our desolation we turned for a solace and a refuge, that ageless Wilderness that had ever been and would, somewhere, always be, long after we had followed our little lost companions and were gone.

And in the grove of stately elms the little tin stove was placed high in a hidden spot with its door open, faced towards the lake. So that the small wandering spirits that might sometimes be lonely would see, and remember, and sometimes enter in, as they had done in life when they were small. And so the stove that knew so many tales might learn another and a last one, a tale of which the end is lost forever, a story we could never, never know.

For we are Indian, and have perhaps some queer ideas; yet who among you having a faith of any kind, will deny us our own strange fancies and tell us we are wrong, or say us no.

The camp beneath the elms is far away. Yet memories linger on, and that last long haunting cry rings often in our ears.

We sometimes hear it in the storm, and in the still of evening; at dawn in the song of the birds, and in the melancholy calling of a loon, half-heard and distant in the night. It wails in the minor cadences of an Indian chant, and swells in the deep notes of an organ played softly by a master hand; it mutters in the sound of sleepy streams, and murmurs in the rumour of the river, in the endless tolling of the waves upon a lakeshore—each and everyone a note from the composite of Nature's harmony, chords struck at random from the mighty Symphony of the Infinite that echoes forever on, down the resounding halls of Time.

BOOK TWO

QUEEN OF THE BEAVER PEOPLE

I think I could turn and live with animals, they are so placid and self-
    contained.
I stand and look at them sometimes half the day long.
They do not sweat and whine about their condition.
They do not lay awake in the dark and weep for their sins.
They do not make me sick discussing their duty to God.
No one is dissatisfied, not one is demented with the mania of owning
    things,
Not one kneels to another, nor to his kind that lived thousands of
    years ago,
Not one is respectable or industrious over the whole earth.
So they show their relations to me, and I accept them,
They bring me tokens of myself, they evince them plainly in their
    possession.

—Walt Whitman

CHAPTER ONE

How Anahareo
Left Touladi

HAUNTED BY THE MEMORY OF OUR LITTLE BUDDIES THAT were lost and gone, I felt that the task of reclamation of the species to which I had set myself had become something in the nature of a duty. They had left behind them two souls that were the better for their coming, and had provided an inspiration and an impetus that, as though it were a mantle they had put upon us, had influenced the order of our lives. Without them it is certain I never would have put a pen to paper, and though my ability is, and always must be, very limited, the records I made of their short lives and the attitude towards Wild Life that they inspired, were instrumental in paving the way to the recognition which, unsought and unexpected, was to follow. I determined that they should live again, by hundreds, in their successors.

Dave, with his knowledge of French, had got himself a job, but often visited us.

"I'm sure now they are killed," he stated. "We can't get along without beaver now; we must get some more. I'll help you."

"What about your job?" asked Anahareo, with some concern. He had already lost ten days of his time searching for the lost ones, which fact he had not, until now, seen fit to let us know.

"To hell with the job," said Dave. "A man can always get a job. But them little fellas—they never meant to go away—we can't forget them like that." His eye took in the remains of the barrel. "Their old caboose," he said. He shook his head, and looking at Anahareo with one of his rare smiles, added, "You know, I kinda like to see beaver around here myself, some way."

An old shrapnel wound, rebelling against the rough treatment of the past month, came to life and put me temporarily out of commission. So Anahareo and Dave walked twenty-five miles through the bush into the Sugar Loaf Hills and took two more kittens. There were four young ones in the house, but the old man would take only one pair. He said that if he had to take them all that he would kill the mother and be done with it. She would, in his opinion, be better dead.

Anahareo carried them on her back, in a bag, the whole way and they arrived half starved and noisy, two bits of creatures that would have disappeared from sight in a pint measure, and that weighed perhaps three ounces apiece. They were very delicate and had but a tenuous hold on their tiny lives. By rights they were too young to have been taken.

Dave stayed on, giving us two weeks more of his time, to help us raise them but one, the little male that Anahareo called Sugar Loaf, after his home mountains, woke up one evening with all the power gone from his legs, and gasped out his puny life before the dawn. The other took sick, refusing to eat the decoction of canned milk and bread that had been their diet, and lay with her head in a corner of her box, a small huddle of misery and pain.

To the population, our attitude towards Nature was incomprehensible, savouring to them strongly of heathenism, which perhaps it was; but the townspeople were not long in finding out about this new development, and aroused by our now well broadcasted history some of them tried to help us. We received much advice, and had the sick beaver been a human being it could not have had much more attention. A woman offered to supply us with cow's milk, and two doctors, all there were in the town, came to our assistance. On their advice we accepted the milk, and thinning it down very weak under the direction of a motherly and very efficient old Irish lady, fed it to the invalid. A man and his wife who had decided to see this thing through between them, administered the doses, every two hours, with a glass syringe, one holding the beaver and the other pumping. The effect, after the third or fourth application, was magical. In two days the kitten was as well as ever, and soon began to evince that assurance and independence of disposition that has since helped to make her one of the best known wild animals in North America. For this inauspicious beginning was the first entry into public life of the now famous Jelly Roll, screen star, public pet Number One, proprietor of Beaver Lodge, and a personage, moreover, with something to say at the seat of Government in Ottawa.

We moved our camp to Big Temiscouata, and erected it at the mouth of the creek on which McGinnis and McGinty had had their last adventure, in case they should ever return. And in the slack water at the foot of it Jelly Roll disported herself, made tiny bank dens and queer erections of sticks, what time she was not engaged in galloping up and down the path to the tents. She grew apace, and as soon as she was big enough she commenced removing magazines, vegetables, wood or anything that took her fancy, and acted generally in a manner which plainly indicated a personality that was well prepared to cope with whatever vicissitudes life might hold in store. She refused to live in the tent, preferring domiciles of her own manufacture, of which she had four or five scattered around in the pool below.

Aside from fits of affection which attacked her in spontaneous and rather overwhelming outbursts, she was totally different in character to her predecessors. She had little of their clinging dependence, and having lost her small companion whilst yet too young to realize it, she came speedily to look on us and our belongings as a natural part of her environment.

Our devotion to our animal friends seemed to have impressed the townspeople much in our favour, and despite differences in creed, colour, and language, we were accorded a friendly recognition as citizens of the town. On holidays picnic parties were made up, and landing at our beach spent hours enjoying themselves in the shade of our birchen grove. Jelly always inspected each member of these gatherings, a habit she has retained to this day, and never registering any great approval of any of them, would amble towards one of her numerous domiciles with such a look of disdain about her rear exposure that her departure was always a source of great merriment, and perhaps some little relief. The priest, a learned gentleman, proficient in languages and a keen student of human nature, took a scholarly and benevolent interest in us and our manner of living, and visited us on more than one occasion.

We ourselves were at first a little awkward with our guests, but their tactful and considerate behaviour soon aroused in us a desire to look and act our best before them, so that we went to some pains to bestir ourselves and meet them on the common ground of good fellowship.

It was no doubt this innate courtesy and instinctive regard for the feelings of others that enabled the French settlers of an earlier date to get along with the Indians, so that they were often spared whilst people of other nationalities were massacred without mercy all around them. It was this same spirit that, on our infrequent visits to town, was to be seen even in small boys, who politely raised their caps to a buckskin clad *sauvage*, and in little girls that shyly bowed and blushed on meeting a woman of a conquered race. On our progress through the streets, women smiled and bade the time of day, while men stopped and chatted; should we be loaded, as was often the case, people stepped off the sidewalk to give us place. This community spirit permeated the lives of these people, and was no insincere pretension or false veneer assumed for purposes of expediency, and was observable especially in times of stress. When a fire took place everyone who was able to be present helped subdue the flames, and the family, if rendered homeless, found shelter in any one of a dozen neighbours' homes. When a death occurred the bereavement was everyone's, and it was a matter of civic pride that as the funeral cortège passed through the streets the small traffic was held up, pedestrians halted, and store keepers came out of their establishments, while all stood bareheaded in attitudes of respect until the solemn procession had gone by; and no matter what may have been the record of the deceased while living, now that he was passing from among them, it was remembered only that he had been a brother citizen.

In such a place, any bleakness or angularity of character a person might possess could not but become mellowed and suppressed. Dave had lost his job owing to his frequent and lengthy absences on our account, and being unable to get another, we were glad to have him with us again, share and share alike in the Indian way.

The proceeds of my second article had arrived and with all bills paid and a well-filled cache beside the tent, we had no immediate worries. We pooled our resources, and while I supplied the groceries David procured the meat and fish of which there were plenty in the adjoining woods and lakes. As an interdependent and self-sustaining community we could have existed here indefinitely, but I think we all began to pine for our North country, and most of our conversations drifted around to reminiscences of it and the making of plans to get back there. I could see no possibility of undertaking my own project in this region, and Dave began to be restless, and was getting anxious about his gold mine. This mine was apparently the only hope there was for any of us to carry out our ambitions—Dave's to retire, Anahareo's to prospect, and mine to create a beaver sanctuary. But there were no resources available that would finance such a trip as Dave contemplated. It was now July, and Winter supplies and all expenses for three had to be taken care of before Fall, with time allowed to make a heavily loaded trip, with many portages, over a distance of more than two hundred miles. We were all to be partners, and as the mine was Dave's and I had nothing to offer, it seemed to me to be up to Jelly and I to supply the sinews of war. So I watched closely her activities and wrote stories about her, and penned long articles on Wild Life from the new angle of my changed attitude towards it.

I read these to a couple of English speaking acquaintances, who were much amused by them, so they said, and one of them who had been something of a public speaker, persuaded me that they were good lecturing material. But I could not yet speak French sufficiently well to use them in that way. The only place of any account where English was universally spoken, was a resort on the south shore of the St. Lawrence, known as Metis Beach, and it was far away. But I resolved to try my luck, and we wanted badly for other people to know how we felt about things in general, so Anahareo being willing to take a chance with me, we turned over everything to Dave, packed up Jelly Roll, some provisions and a camping outfit, and took the train for Metis.

We arrived there with the usual dollar sixty-nine in pocket, and soon found that a lecturing tour that was lacking in a few accessories such as advertising expenses, a manager and so forth, and for which the only

stock in trade was a writing pad full of notes, was not likely to be a paying proposition.

In the first place we had difficulty in getting permission to camp, as
people of our kind were apparently not common here. A Frenchman
allowed us to make camp on his property, and I then made a personal can-
vass of the possibilities, at great injury to my pride, and was told that we
would have to publicize ourselves. At this we shrunk up like two worms
that had fallen into a dish of salt. To give a lecture was one thing: to vulgarly
advertise was another. Meanwhile we were getting nowhere. Jelly, always
used to plenty of water, was frantic in her box and cried continuously.

Two weeks passed, and so sensitive had we become at the bare thought
of the whole idea, that we cringed in our tent alongside the unfriendly
Atlantic Ocean, while Jelly clamoured and grew thin for this salt water that
we dare not let her into. We had a letter from Dave in which he hoped we
were getting along well. And so we were, getting along well towards the
end of our provisions. I considered wiring our store keeper, for tickets
back to Cabano, which he had guaranteed in case of failure. But this
seemed like rank cowardice, and besides, too much was at stake. I decided
at last to make a move of some kind, so retired into a remnant of bushland
and wrote out a lecture of about five thousand words.

Meanwhile word had gone around the resort concerning our aims,
and a member of the family who originally settled there, and who owned
most of the place, appointed us a camping ground on their property,
where there was a small pond. Here Jelly Roll was in clover again. One
of the leaders of the summer colony became interested in our project, read
the lecture, and approved the sentiments expressed in it. She gave the idea
the stamp of her approval, and graciously constituting herself secretary,
advertising manager, and treasurer, went to work to launch the enterprise.
Her young sons and their friends sold tickets, while she herself, an artist of
no small ability, made and issued a number of beautifully illustrated plac-
ards. She informed me of the date and place of the lecture, which was to
be in a ballroom, and gave me some sound advice on elocution.

I touched up my material, and on the evening set for the encounter,
we slipped unobtrusively into the building by a rear entrance. In a back
room we sat awaiting our call, paralysed with fright and wondering if

Jelly had upset the milk back at camp, or had got run over by one of the numerous automobiles that infested the country. In either event I would, at this moment, have cheerfully traded places with her. We received our summons, and the march to the chamber of execution was one of the bravest acts of my life. Anahareo trailed along with me as moral support, but it was a case of the blind leading the blind, and when I faced all those people, hundreds of them, gathered in a compact mass in the auditorium, I felt a good deal like a snake that has swallowed an icicle, chilled from one end to the other.

But rescue was at hand. The lady who sponsored us now came forward and spoke a few well chosen words of introduction. The audience applauded her. Silence fell. Zero hour had arrived. I fixed my eyes on a kind-looking face in the front row, and suddenly found myself speaking. I heard murmurs; people looked at one another and nodded, seemed interested; gaining confidence I warmed to my subject, and pursued my theme to the end. A moment of pause and then came applause loud, steady, long. My head swam momentarily; all this noise—and for us! A British army colonel arose and spoke words of appreciation he—I could hardly believe my ears—said that it was not a lecture, but a poem; more applause. Then these people crowded around us, shook our hands, congratulated us.

Other lectures followed. I was called on to speak at parties, in other halls, in the hotels. Always Anahareo stood by. I often think she had the hardest part, to sit there, in an agony of shyness, trying to look composed and at ease, and valiantly succeeding. Some parents brought their children to us, commissioning us to instruct them in a few of the simpler devices used by the Indians in the woods. Some of the small grains of knowledge that we dispensed no doubt found lodgment in enquiring young minds, but much of it, I fear, fell on stony soil. Anahareo, with her shrewder woman's instinct, told them tales of the likable but somewhat villainous Ninne-bojo, as well as other folk-yarns of her people, the Iroquois. But for my part I forgot that children of a certain age are sometimes inclined to be a little blood-thirsty in their choice of stories, and harped perhaps a little too insistently on kindness to the weaker brethren of the forest. That some of these lectures were not producing quite the desired effect on all present, I was very well aware, but I was a little startled when, in answer to my request for questions, a sturdy young fellow of about thirteen summers rose in his place and demanded:

"Did you ever kill anybody?"

"No," I confessed to the omission a trifle guiltily.

"Didn't you ever scalp anyone?" continued this embryo prosecuting attorney. I admitted that I had not, hoping at the same time that my forbearance would gain his juvenile respect. He gave me a long, level look.

"Well, I think you're a dumb guy," said he, and sat down with an air of great decision.

Jelly, at one of these talks, provided the illustrations, and her lively expressions of disapproval of the lecturing business, contributed as much to the interest of this particular audience as anything that I had to say.

We opened a bank account. Our camp ground was crowded with children, and Jelly became the most popular person at Metis Beach, and was badly spoiled. I have good reason to believe that she never rightly got over it. On our last night, a missionary of the Canadian Bible Society, an old acquaintance whom I had not known was present, rose at the close of my farewell speech, and told how he had known us in the far North, and established without doubt our identity.

To these people, each and every one of them, who so accepted us without endorsement of any kind, mountebanks as we must at first have seemed to them, I owe a debt of gratitude that no words written or spoken, could convey. I had not known that people could be so kind. And when one courtly, gracious lady, high in the society of a large city, said to us in parting that we had taught the people something, I remembered the words of an Eastern prophet of whom I once had read and replied, tritely perhaps, but none the less sincerely, "Have I taught?—then have I also learned."

And there was more meaning in my answer than perhaps she ever guessed.

And to our patron, to whom we owed it all, we gave a name; we called her Sha-san-oquet which means Opens-the-Clouds. For that is what she did for us.

Dave met us with open arms on our return, and would hardly credit our story. But he had to credit the bank roll and the two tickets to Abitibi provided us by our good friend the English colonel. And we could scarcely realise that now we were free, free to fulfil our chosen plans, free to return to our harsh, untamed, beloved North with its romance, its wild freedom and its gold; free at last to leave this sad disfigured country with its tortured ravaged forests and its memories and grief and tribulation.

Time was getting short and there was far to go, so the next day we broke camp and crossed over to the station. We loaded the canoe and all our dunnage on the baggage car, and put Jelly on the day coach in a well-made ventilated box.

As we sat on the waiting train I looked across Temiscouata, looked at the dark Elephant Mountain that stood so still, so silently on guard at the portals of Touladi. Anahareo was looking there too. Each knew what the other was thinking—back of that towering pine-crowned granite cliff, somewhere, living or dead, were the two little creatures that had loved us; and we were abandoning them—for a gold mine. Quitters!

Anahareo choked back a sob. Rising she took her bundles from the rack. "I'm getting off," she said in a husky voice. "They might come back and us not there—"

My thoughts to the letter. I knew she meant it. There was not time to discuss the matter anyway—just the break that was needed; now somebody would have to stay. I picked up my guns, carefully wrapped for the trip.

"You're right," I concurred, "we can't quit like this. But one is all that is needed here. I am staying." This was no self-sacrifice; now that the words were said I was conscious of a feeling of relief, as though some crime, in which we were to be unwilling accomplices, need not now be committed. Anahareo couldn't see it that way but there wasn't much time and my facts were unassailable; I didn't care for prospecting, I had my writing to do; the fate of McGinnis and McGinty was as yet undecided, and Jelly didn't like train rides and might even die on the trip; all of which was true and therefore unanswerable. So we got off the train, Jelly and me, after saying our farewells, and I got out from amongst the baggage one tent, some cookery, and my dunnage, and I said goodbye to my old canoe and whispered to it to carry my people staunchly.

I knew how much they wanted to go.

Dave disembarked, his face set very stern and hard, his eyes troubled, for Indian people do not take partings casually.

"Take care of her, old-timer," I said, and looked him squarely in the face. Sixty-seven years on the trail—I knew she was in good hands, perhaps better than my own.

"Yes, I will," he said simply, and stood silently holding my hand for the few moments before the warning cry of "All Aboard," and with a last strong clasp he winked prodigiously with both eyes together, and cried out as he ran for the now rapidly moving step, "We'll come back with a bag of gold and paint this old town red!" and gave his old time Indian yell,

"Hey—ey—ey——Yah!"

And that was the last I ever saw of Dave.

The train was gathering speed, and I watched with stinging eyes two brown faces with black hair streaming in the wind of their going, and two arms that waved and waved, and grew smaller and smaller as they receded into the distance, until the train rounded a curve and they were no longer to be seen.

I loaded my belongings on a wagon, and hugging Jelly tightly under one arm I went back through the blurred and empty streets to the ferry, back to Touladi.

CHAPTER TWO

How the Queen and I Spent the Winter

I FOUND IT HARD TO ADJUST MYSELF. AT ONE BLOW I AS BEREFT of all my little community. Anahareo, my brave and faithful Anahareo, who had been through so much with me; Dave, with his troubled eyes at parting, his impenetrable self-possession quite gone; my canoe—I felt stripped, empty, kind of weary, famished and lost, with a fierce gnawing at my heart that would not be allayed.

I was now, my period of war service excepted, without a canoe for the first time in twenty-five years, and felt as must a rider who finds himself suddenly afoot in a desert; and the circumstance affected my morale nearly as much. This one, in particular, had been a tried and true companion of many toilsome journeys, and I missed it as though it had been a living thing. And while it was a gift to Dave, one that I had been proud to make and he to receive, when I touched for the last time the worn spot on the gunnell where the paddle had worked so long, I experienced some of the sensations of a sea-captain who sees a well-beloved vessel sink beneath the waves. But I consoled myself with the thought that it was gone to some good purpose, and was in the hands of a man who was, if anything, more meticulous in the care of equipment than I was myself, and whose skill would never bring discredit to a good canoe. And in the same good hands was the welfare of Anahareo, who, full of ambition and hopes for the future, was faring forth to do her share in the seeking of our fortune, neither knowing nor caring what she might be called upon to face—going far into a country that lay no great distance from Labrador and having, as I had good reason to remember, a similar climate. But cold weather and storms mean but little to our kind of people, and she came of a nation that had made a considerable mark in history, so I had no real fear as to the outcome.

But I was lonesome for the first time in my life. Yet I had, for a solace, a very cheerful and entertaining companion, the little beaver who, if she was ever lonely, never showed it. No longer a kitten, she had developed into a beautiful specimen of her kind, was always bright and very much alive, and had a rich, full-furred coat, dark and glistening, which it had been Anahareo's pride to carefully groom each day.

It became necessary to get ready for the Winter, and I, on advice, located a small camp, well built and in good shape, situated on the shores of a little lake that lay about five miles back of the Elephant mountain. A bush road led to it, mostly swamp, and hiring a team to bring in our supplies we, Jelly 'n' me, moved to it for a permanent abode, she being carried in a packsack with her head and arms free, viewing the scenery round about on the way in.

What had passed now seemed to be an epoch, a line of demarcation in our lives, dividing the new from the old. And symbolical of the new was this tiny squalling brat upon my back. Little did I think as she sat in the packsack and chittered and mumbled and upbraided and pulled my hair, that she was to become a very noted lady, and was to make a name for both herself and me. Her whole short life of five months had been turned topsy-turvy, inside out, hell, west and sideways. She had been transported hither and thither on trains and wagons, carried long distances in a variety of boxes, had been Exhibit "A" on a lecture tour, and had finally spent two entire days in a stable. In the latter place, for a swimming pool she had a dish pan, and instead of poplar had been fed pancakes.

And now came the end of this last short, but very eventful journey, to where all was peace and quietness and contentment, to this little lake set high in the mountains where there was plenty of deep water for birling like a spinning log and diving to her heart's content. Here was any amount of mud in which to play and build any number of little imitation beaver houses on the shore, and there was even a long burrow with a

roomy sleeping apartment at the end of it, left by some long departed
family of her kind. All this spelled a happiness she had never before
known, and she had a delirious time for the first few days. She slept in the
burrow, which was up the creek about half a mile from the cabin, but
every evening about sunset she was at the cabin door, scratching to be let
in. She came in several times a night and spent an hour with me, and
took a great interest in my doings. She was particularly attracted by the
bunk, recognizing perhaps the scent of the blankets on which she had
been in the habit of drying herself off. I made a kind of chute for her, and
she would climb into the bed by means of this, getting out by the very
simple process of falling over the side, and as I left the door ajar on her
account, I often awoke in the morning to find her fast asleep beside me.

Meanwhile I found plenty of outlet for my desire to write. During a
visit to town I picked up a sporting magazine and I was strongly attracted
by the conservation ideas expressed all through it, and read in it an article by a man I had known well in Ontario. He was pretty much of a the-
orist who wrote greatly from second hand experience, and while part of
his information was correct, a good deal of it was misleading. Sitting
down in the house of a friend I wrote an article on the subject, taking
those of his statements which in my opinion were incorrect as a theme,
and discussing them from a point of view of personal observation. It was
called "The Vanishing Life of the Wild," and the periodical was Canadian
Forest and Outdoors, the official organ of the Canadian Forestry
Association of which I was later to become a life member. This was my
first appearance in print in this country. They asked me for more, and I
wrote intermittently for them for three years.

Country Life, in England, who had had two articles from me and a
series of long rambling personal letters written to the editor during fits of
loneliness, now sent me a request to write a book. Nothing loath I accepted,
at the time not having the remotest idea of how I was going to set about it.
On giving the matter thought, one difficulty appeared to be insurmount-
able, and that was how, with my entire lack of technical knowledge, to give
an account of happenings in which I acted in the role not only of an
observer but of an active participant, and yet to avoid an offensive use of
the first personal pronoun. I knew of two devices; the employment of

coldly formal references to the writer himself in the third person, and the substitution of the foremost numeral, one for the foremost pronoun. This looked to me like merely juggling with words. The undue use of these pretexts seemed only to impart to the narrative an air of portentous hypocrisy that was unworthy of so simple and noble a theme as my beloved wilderness; and I have since discovered that these sometimes convenient forms can be little more than subterfuges, under cover of which your true egoist often does his stuff. So I decided to write, not a personal biography, as requested, but a series of essays on the North itself. In this present work, however, it seemed that a few good healthy unequivocating "I's" standing up honestly on their own hind legs, would do no harm whatever. It feels a lot better, this time, to be more of a humanist.

Every once in so often, attempts were made to buy Jelly Roll, who had become to me more than just a pet and was not to be purchased at any price. One of these offers came from a man living in the near-by village of Notre Dame-du-lac. On his invitation, though with no idea of selling the beaver, I paid him a visit. He was a hunchback, and had a kind of a little exhibition by means of which he lived, consisting of different kinds of dogs, some of which danced, and one could walk a tight wire. He had a good sized bear that turned the handle of a hurdy-gurdy and rode a three wheeled bicycle, and it was strange to see the means this beast had evolved to perform his act with as little labour as possible. He (the bear) also had learned to carry a gun on his shoulder, fall supposedly dead at the report of a cap pistol, and rise at a word. Bear and dogs, as a finale, danced to the tune of a gramophone, all in an erect position. To keep control the hunchback joined the slowly revolving circle, likewise moving his feet in time to the music, quite oblivious of the appearance he gave of dancing with his animals. He was not quite as tall as the bear who on that account appeared to lead this weird dance, and in the shadowy, ill lighted gallery the whole effect was a little eerie. He was popularly and aptly known as the Hunchback of Notre Dame, and was, to some, a rather sinister figure, but on closer acquaintance he revealed a character of great benevolence and gentleness, and I could well believe his statement that he obtained his results with animals by kindness and patience. The most remarkable feature of his performance was the casual, almost inaudible voice in which he issued his suggestions—they could hardly be called commands—and the implicit obedience, amounting almost to co-operation that he was given. This man died later, and his one fear expressed before his passing was verified; the show was disbanded and these animals were dispersed, and the bear, turned loose and refusing to stay in the bush, haunted the scene of his old home and was shot to death by timorous villagers.

At this time a letter arrived from Anahareo reporting progress. All had gone well, save that they were lonesome, seemingly a chronic condition with all of us, and they had been, at the time of writing, ready to leave with a canoe load of supplies for Chibougamou Lake, two hundred odd miles North from the steel.

There had, she related, been adventures in Quebec City. David, bewildered by the number of taverns that were to be found everywhere, had gotten lost. Anahareo, after two days of waiting started to trail him down, inquiring at all beer parlours. Yes, he was well known at several taverns, and had been feeling, oh, just so-so, when last seen. His ecclesiastical leanings when in this condition prompted her to consider searching all the churches, beginning with the largest and working down. She compromised by making the rounds of the police stations, but none of them had any record of him. She found him in the railroad depot, tired and very hungry. I have it on the word of witnesses that they almost embraced. Dave, it appeared, having lost all track of time, and supposing he had missed his train and that Anahareo had gone on without him, had boarded the first one he saw, and without ticket, money, equipment or anything else except the clothes he stood up in, and a headache, had proceeded sixty miles or so in the wrong direction. Apprised of this fact by the conductor he got off and had walked back. I kind of sweated as I read all this, but by now they were safely away on the lakes. They wanted for nothing, and I knew that once in the bush few men were David's peer.

Meanwhile I myself was busy. Hunting season was open and hunters swarmed in the woods. This made it necessary for me to patrol the scene of Jelly's activities all night, and I slept beside her burrow in the day time. I much doubted if there were many of the Cabano men who would have deliberately killed her, but as with McGinnis and McGinty, it would only take one man to turn the trick and I was resolved to take no chances.

I was greatly assisted in this by the trapper who claimed the hunting ground I was occupying. Instead of trying to oust me from his holdings, on finding that I was without a canoe he lent me one, and drew me a map of the district so I could patrol the more effectively.

Hunting season passed and the woods became again deserted and we, this beaver and I, carried on our preparations for the Winter each at his own end of the lake. The outlet, near which my cabin was situated, passed through a muskeg, and the immediate neighbourhood was covered with spindling birch which I was rapidly using up for wood. Jelly had by far the best part of it so far as scenery was concerned, being picturesquely established at the mouth of a small stream that wandered down from the uplands through a well timbered gully. Here she lived in state. She fortified her burrow on the top with mud, sticks and moss, and inside it had a fine clean bed of shavings (taken from stolen boards), and had a little feed raft she had collected with highly unskilled labour, and that had a very amateurish look about it. But she was socially inclined, and often came down and spent long hours in the camp. When it snowed she failed to show up and I would visit her, and hearing my approach while still at some distance, she would come running to meet me with squeals and wiggles of welcome. We had great company together visiting back and forth this way, and I often sat and smoked and watched her working, and helped in any difficulties that arose. After the ice took her visits ceased altogether, and becoming lonesome for her I sometimes carried her to the cabin on my back in a box. She did not seem to mind these trips, and carried on a conversation with me and made long speeches on the way; I used to tell her she was talking behind my back. She made her own way home under the ice in some mysterious manner and always arrived safely, though I made a practice of following her progress along the shore with a flashlight, to make sure she did. This distance was over half a mile and I much admired the skill with which she negotiated it, though she cheated a little and ran her nose into muskrat burrows here and there to replenish her air supply. One night, however, after going home, she returned again unknown to me, and in the morning I found the door wide open and her lying fast asleep across the pillow. Nor did she ever go outside again, evidently having decided to spend the Winter with me;

which she did. So I bought a small galvanised tank for her and sunk it in the floor, and dug out under one of the walls what I considered to be a pretty good imitation of a beaver house interior.

Almost immediately on her entry, a certain independence of spirit began to manifest itself. The tank, after a lengthy inspection was accepted by her as being all right, what there was of it; but the alleged beaver house, on being weighed in the balance was found to be wanting, and was resolutely and efficiently blocked up with some bagging and an old deer skin. She then dug out at great labour, a long tunnel under one corner of the shack, bringing up the dirt in heaps which she pushed ahead of her and painstakingly spread over the floor. This I removed, upon which it was promptly renewed. On my further attempt to clean up, she worked feverishly until a section of the floor within a radius of about six feet was again covered. I removed this several different times with the same results, and at last wag obliged to desist for fear that in her continued excavations she would undermine the camp. Eventually she constructed a smooth solid side walk of pounded earth clear from her tunnel to the water supply, and she had a well beaten play ground tramped down all around her door. Having thus gained her point, and having established the fact that I was not going to have everything my own way, she let the matter drop, and we were apparently all set for the Winter. But these pro-ceedings were merely preliminaries. She now embarked on a campaign of constructive activities that made necessary the alteration of almost the entire interior arrangements of the camp. Nights of earnest endeavours to empty the woodbox, (to supply materials for scaffolds which would afford ready access to the table or windows), alternated with orgies of destruction, during which anything not made of steel or iron was sub-jected to a trial by ordeal out of which it always came off second best. The bottom of the door which, owing to the slight draught entering there, was a point that attracted much attention, was always kept well banked up with any materials that could be collected, and in more than one instance the blankets were taken from the bunk and utilised for this purpose. Reprimands induced only a temporary cessation of these depredations, and slaps and switchings produced little squeals accompanied by the vio-lent twisting and shaking of the head, and other curious contortions by which these animals evince the spirit of fun by which they seem to be consumed during the first year of their life. On the few occasions I found it necessary to punish her, she would stand up on her hind feet, look me square in the face, and argue the point with me in her querulous treble of annoyance and outrage, slapping back at me right manfully on more than one occasion; yet she never on any account attempted to make use of her terrible teeth. Being in disgrace, she would climb on her box alongside me at the table, and rest her head on my knee, eyeing me and talking meanwhile in her uncanny language, as though to say, "What are a few table legs and axe handles between men?" And she always got forgiven; for after all she was a High Beaver, Highest of All The Beavers, and could get away with things no common beaver could, things that no common beaver would ever even think of.

When I sat on the deer skin rug before the stove, which was often, this chummy creature would come and lie with her head in my lap, and looking up at me, make a series of prolonged wavering sounds in different keys, that could have been construed as some bizarre attempt at singing. She would keep her eyes fixed steadily on my face all during this performance, so that I felt obliged to listen to her with the utmost gravity. This pastime soon became a regular feature of her day, and the not unmelodious notes she emitted on these occasions were among the strangest sounds I have ever heard an animal make.

In spite of our difference in point of view on some subjects, we, this beast with the ways of a man and the voice of a child, and I, grew very close during that Winter for we were both, of our kind, alone. More and more as time went on she timed her movements, such as rising and retiring and her mealtimes, by mine. The camp, the fixtures, the bed, the tank, her little den and myself, these were her whole world. She took me as much for granted as if I had also been a beaver, and it is possible that she thought that I belonged to her, with the rest of the stuff, or figured that she would grow up to be like me and perhaps eat at the table when she got big, or else that I would later have a tail and become like her.

Did I leave the camp on a two day trip for supplies, my entry was the signal for a swift exit from her chamber, and a violent assault on my legs, calculated to upset me. And on my squatting down to ask her how the thing had been going in my absence, she would sit up and wag her head slowly back and forth and roll on her back and gambol clumsily around me. As soon as I unlashed the toboggan, every article and package was minutely examined until the one containing the never-failing apples was discovered. This was immediately torn open, and gathering all the apples she could in her teeth and arms, she would stagger away erect to the edge of her tank, where she would eat one and put the rest in the water. She entered the water but rarely, and after emerging from a bath she had one certain spot where she sat and squeezed all the moisture out of her fur with her forepaws, very hands in function. She did not like to sit in the pool which collected under her at such times, so she took possession of a large square of birch bark for a bath-mat, intended to shed the water, which it sometimes did. It was not long before she discovered that the bed was a very good place for these exercises, as the blankets soaked up the moisture. After considerable inducement, and not without some heartburnings, she later compromised by shredding up the birch bark and spreading on it a layer of moss taken from the chinking in the walls. Her bed, which consisted of long, very fine shavings cut from the flooring and portions of bagging which she unravelled, was pushed out at intervals and spread on the floor to air, being later returned to the sleeping quarters. Both these procedures, induced by the requirements of an unnatural environment, were remarkable examples of adaptability on the part of an animal, especially the latter, as in the natural state the bedding is taken out and discarded entirely, fresh material being sought. The dish out of which she ate, on being emptied she would shove into a corner, and was not satisfied until it was standing up against the wall. This trick seems to be instinctive with all beaver, and can be attributed to their desire to preserve the interior of their habitation clear of any form of débris in the shape of peeled sticks, which are likewise set aside in the angle of the wall until the owner is ready to remove them.

Any branches brought in for feed, if thrown down in an unaccustomed place, were drawn over and neatly piled near the water supply, nor would she suffer any sticks or loose materials to be scattered on the floor; these she always removed and relegated to a junk pile she kept under one of the windows. This I found applied to socks, moccasins, the wash board and the broom, etc., as well as to sticks. This broom was to her a kind of staff of office which she, as self-appointed janitor, was forever carrying around with her on her tours of inspection, and it also served, when turned end for end, as a quick, if rather dry lunch, or something in the nature of a breakfast food. She would delicately snip the straws off it, one at a time, and holding them with one end in her mouth would push them slowly in, while the teeth, working at great speed, chopped it into tiny portions. This operation resembled the performance of a sword swallower as much as it did anything else, and the sound produced was similar to that of a sewing machine running a little out of control. A considerable dispute raged over this broom, but in the end I found it easier to buy new brooms and keep my mouth shut.

Occasionally she would be indisposed to come out of her apartment, and would hold long-winded conversations with me through the aperture in a sleepy voice, and this with rising and falling inflections, and a rhythm, that made it seem as though she was actually saying something, which perhaps she was. In fact her conversational proclivities were one of the highlights of this association, and her efforts to communicate with me in this manner were most expressive, and any remark addressed to my furry companion seldom failed to elicit a reply of some kind, when she was awake, and sometimes when she was asleep.

To fill her tank required daily five trips of water, and she got to know by the rattle of the pails when her water was to be changed. She would emerge from her seclusion and try to take an active part in the work, getting pretty generally in the way, and she insisted on pushing the door to between my trips, with a view to excluding the much dreaded current of cold air. This was highly inconvenient at times, but she seemed so mightily pleased with her attempts at co-operation that I made no attempt to interfere. Certain things she knew to be forbidden she took a delight in doing, and on my approach her eyes would seem to kindle with a spark of unholy glee and she would scamper off squealing with trepidation, and no doubt well pleased at having put something over on me. Her self-assertive tendencies now began to be very noticeable. She commenced to take charge of the camp. She, so to speak, held the floor, also anything above it that was within her reach, by now a matter of perhaps two feet and more. This, as can be readily seen, included most of the ordinary fix-tures. Fortunately, at this late season she had ceased her cutting opera-tions, and was contented with pulling down anything she could lay her hands on, or climb up and get, upon which the article in question was subjected to a critical inspection as to its possibilities for inclusion into the rampart of heterogeneous objects that had been erected across her end of the camp, and behind which she passed from the entrance of her dwelling to the bathing pool. Certain objects such as the poker, a tin can, and a trap she disposed in special places, and if they were moved she would set them back in the positions she originally had for them, and would do this as often as they were removed. When working on some project she laboured with an almost fanatical zeal to the exclusion of all else, laying off at intervals to eat and comb her coat with the flexible dou-ble claw provided for that purpose.

She had the mischievous proclivities of a monkey combined with much of the artless whimsicality of a child, and she brightened many a dreary homecoming with her clumsy and frolicsome attempts at wel-come. Headstrong past all belief, she had also the proprietary instinct natural to an animal, or a man, that builds houses and surrounds himself with works produced by his own labour. Considering the camp no doubt as her own personal property, she examined closely all visitors that entered it, some of whom on her account had journeyed from afar. Some passed muster, after being looked over in the most arrogant fashion, and were not molested; if not approved of, she would rear up against the legs of others, and try to push them over. This performance sometimes cre-ated a mild sensation, and gained for her the title of The Boss. Some ladies thought she should be called The Lady of the Lake, others The Queen. Jelly the Tub I called her, but the royal title stuck and a Queen she was, and ruled her little kingdom with no gentle hand.

There was one change that this lowly animal wrought in my habit of mind that was notable. Human companionship, in spite of, or perhaps on account of my solitary habits, had always meant a lot to me. But before the coming of Anahareo I had enjoyed it only intermittently. Its place had been taken by those familiar objects with which I surrounded myself, which were a part of my life,—a canoe that had been well-tried in calm and storm and had carried me faithfully in good water and bad, a pair of snowshoes that handled especially well, a thin-bladed, well-tempered hunting axe, an extra serviceable tump-line, my guns, a shrewdly balanced throwing knife. All these belongings had seemed like living things, almost, that could be depended on and that I carefully tended, that kept me company and that I was not above addressing on occasion. Now there was this supposedly dumb beast who had, if not entirely supplanted them, at least had relegated them to their normal sphere as useful pieces of equipment only. In this creature there was life and understanding; she moved and talked and did things, and gave me a response of which I had not thought an animal capable. She seemed to supply some need in my life of which I had been only dimly conscious heretofore, which had been growing with the years, and which marriage had for a time provided. And now that I was alone again it had returned, redoubled in intensity, and this sociable and home-loving beast, playful, industrious and articulate, fulfilled my yearning for companionship as no other creature save man, of my own kind especially, could ever have done. A dog, for all his affection and fidelity, had little power of self-expression, and his activities differed greatly from those of a human being; a dog was sometimes too utterly submissive. This creature comported itself as a person, of a kind, and she busied herself at tasks that I could, without loss of dignity, have occupied myself at; she made camp, procured and carried in supplies, could lay plans and carry them out and stood robustly and resolutely on her own hind legs, metaphorically and actually, and had an independence of spirit that measured up well with my own, seeming to look on me as a contemporary, accepting me as an equal and no more. I could in no way see where I was the loser from this association, and would not, if I could, have asserted my superiority, save as was sometimes necessary to avert wilful destruction.

Her attempts at communication with me, sometimes ludicrous, often pitiful, and frequently quite understandable, as I got to know them, placed her, to my mind, high above the plane of ordinary beasts. This, and the community of interest we had of keeping things in shape, of keeping up the home so to speak, strengthened indissolubly the bond between the two of us, both creatures that were never meant to live alone.

Soon the snow was deep enough for good snowshoeing, setting me free to cover the country easily and systematically, in an effort to establish definitely whether McGinnis and McGinty lived or not. All beaver found (to a hunter, even in the dead of Winter, with three feet of snow on the ground, this is not so difficult as it would seem) could be easily re-located in the Summer without waste of time, and their identity then ascertained. I found three more families, one of them within a few miles of the cabin and on the same waters. This latter discovery gave me no particular joy, as I had given up all idea of attempting any conservation project in a region where the inhabitants, on whose good will the safety of my proteges would depend, held animal life so cheaply. Anyone of the several colonies could have been the retreat of the lost yearlings, but nothing could be determined about them till late Summer, a beaver's habits being what they are.

I commenced to plan my book, but somehow was not able to get started. I had no idea how to put a book together. I bethought me of the "Writing System" that Anahareo had brought away from her home thinking they were cookery books. I dug them out of the oblivion in which they had so long lain forgotten and soon became deeply absorbed in matters of "Setting," "Dialogue," "Point of View," "Unity of Impression," and "Style." And while I could not put any of these instructions to their fullest use, having no very clear notion of what form, if any, my narrative would take, this "Unity of Impression" that was so urgently recommended seemed to be of the first importance, and is the one point that since has kept my pen, a little inclined to wander into irrelevant bypaths of reminiscence, more or less within the limits of my subject. My stories seemed to have the peculiar faculty of writing themselves, quite against any previous plans I made for them, and they generally ended up in an entirely different direction from what they started in, so that the forepart had to be completely re-arranged to satisfy this exacting and at times exceedingly troublesome rule.

Meantime, I could not but worry about Anahareo, although she was well equipped and under the care of a man whose equal as a woodsman was seldom to be met, for I knew the country they had gone into, a region of very large lakes and severe storms, and having a climate that made Winter in Temiscouata seem like late Fall weather by comparison.

With these thoughts on my mind I found it impossible to

concentrate. Thinking that a visit to the scene of our earlier struggles, and that the atmosphere of the place where my first literary aspirations had been born, might be something in the nature of an inspiration, I gave my camp into the care of a friend, and loading my toboggan with a light out-fit made the long pilgrimage to Birch Lake.

On arrival I made camp at the same old tenting ground, using even the same poles, that had been so carefully laid by for future use.

The place was sadly changed. Though the roofing was torn and the chinking had mostly fallen out, the camp was otherwise much as we had left it. But the beaver dam had gone out of repair and the lake, once the snow was off it, would be little better than a rock-studded swamp. The beaver house, untenanted, stood high above the empty basin, the entrance plainly visible. Even the muskrats must have left there long ago. The birds were all gone and a stranger squirrel scurried away at my approach. But the great pines still stood towering, mighty in their silence; and standing there immovable in their impenetrable reticence, they seemed to meditate, and brood upon the past.

My feelings as I entered the cabin were those of one who visits a shrine. The relics were all there, though the now leaky roof had afforded small protection to them. The famous war-bonnet hung limp and lifeless, its gay feathers bedraggled, and the warrior, the Sign of Welcome gone from off his face, was but a wooden block. The homely paintings, that had looked so like beadwork if you stood away from them a little were marred and disfigured, and partly washed away. The Christmas tree leaned dry and withered where we had left it, in its corner. The cut table-legs, the chewed deerskins, and drinking dish upon the floor, the very tooth marks—Anahareo's curtains on the windows, all were there. The redoubt built with such pathetic industry remained intact, but no small black eyes peered wisely through the peep-hole in the end of it, no gam-bolling elfin figures raced from behind it in mock battle, no small wail-ing voices declaimed aloud—no Ivanhoe, no Hawkeye.

And I took my old place sadly on the bench and wished I had not come. And as I sat in reverie it fell to dusk. But outside the sky was still crimson from the sunset, and the glow from it shone redly through the gaping crevices and was reflected down the vacant stove pipe hole, so that the floor and walls were coloured with it. And the dingy, empty cabin was transformed, and took on again something of the glamour of its former days, and seemed once more an enchanted hall of dreams. So that it was no more an abandoned heap of logs and relics, but was once again the House of McGinnis in all its former glory.

And quite suddenly the place that had seemed to be so lonely and deserted was now no longer empty, but all at once was filled with living memories and ghosts from out the past. And then I made a light, and here amongst the wraiths began to write.

In two nights, two chapters of "The Vanishing Frontier" were finished, "The Tale of the Beaver People," and "The House of McGinnis." I made out in my writing that our lost friends still were living, and hoped my readers would forgive me the deception, if it was one, which neither they nor I will ever know.

And they lived again in those few pages if no where else.

For a week I wrote furiously, while ever in my ears was the soft laughter of a woman, and the sound of small voices that were so much like the voices of little children. And the phantoms sat with me and moved and played, and the characters in my stories lived again. And they were not sad, these wraiths of yesterday, but happy ones, and walked in gladness before me as I wrote. And I found myself able, at last, to capture thoughts that had hitherto been beyond expression. And here it was borne upon me why they had so much impressed themselves upon us, these little beasts. They had been like little Indians in their ways, and had seemed emblematic of the race, a living link with our environment, a living breathing manifestation of that elusive Something, that Spirit of the Waste Lands that so permeated our own lives, that had existed always just beyond our reach, and could never before be grasped in its entirety. In some tangible way they and their kind typified the principle that is inherent in all Nature. The animal supreme of all the forest, they were the Wilderness personified, the Wild articulate, the Wild that was our home, and still lived embodied in the warp and woof of it. Through them I had a new conception of Nature. Although I had not hitherto given the matter much consideration, it was not inconceivable that every other creature, and perhaps every other thing was, according to its place and use, as well provided to fulfil its special purpose as were they, though not perhaps so obviously. I had lived with Nature all my life, yet had never felt so close to it before, as I better understood the Spirit that had fashioned it—nor yet so far a part from it, in the sudden knowledge of my own unfitness to interpret or describe it. As well now attempt a history of the Creation.

So I kept my theme well within the limits of personal observation and experience, and left interpretation to those of greater skill in writing.

The swing of an Indian on snowshoes, the rolling, easy gait of a bear, the lightly undulating progress of a swift canoe, the black sweeping rush of water at the head of a falls, the slow swaying of the tree-tops, were all words from the same script, strokes from the same brush, each a resonance from the changeless rhythm that rocks the Universe. We were more kin to those creatures than we had known. Not the exaggerated veneration of a pagan mythology this, nor any doctrine of animal or Nature worship, but the same realization of the great Original Plan that caused a Christian minister to say, as he stood rapt in the contemplation of a mountain lake,

"An Indian, an animal, and a *mountain* move as to some rhythm of music. All the works of the Creator are cast from the one mould, but on some the imprint of His finger is more manifest."

My writing even had sprung from these things, they ran all through it. And I sorrowed no more. The tree falls and nourishes another. From death springs life; it is the Law. And these writings that were no longer mine, but which I now saw only as recorded echoes and not creations of my own, had captured, in their poor way, the essentials of what had eluded me so long.

And I felt at last that I had been made to understand. And the House of McGinnis, as I left it in the starlight, seemed no longer a headstone at the grave of lost hopes, was no more an end, but a beginning. And before leaving I took one or two peeled sticks and some chips, a few brown hairs, and a dried sprig from off the Christmas tree, and rolled them tightly in a piece of buckskin, to be my medicine, my luck, and for a token.

And I bid the cheerful ghosts farewell and left them there behind me; yet as I journeyed onward down the well-remembered trail, whereon no tracks showed in the starlight save my own, I felt that in the darkness there behind me was a woman, and with her two little beavers in a stove.

CHAPTER THREE

The Coming
of Rawhide

ON ARRIVING HOME I WAS PRESENTED BY MY FRIEND WITH another letter from Anahareo. The possibility of hearing from her by air mail never had occurred to me. They were safe and well, but Dave's claim had been staked just twenty-eight days before their arrival, and was rated the richest property in the whole area. They had both had to go work for wages on what was to have been their gold mine. Dave's last Eldorado was gone; and he was old. Broken and embittered, he had gone out, back to his own land to lay his bones with those of his fathers, beneath the singing pine trees on the Ottawa. Anahareo was waiting for the break-up in order to return. This would not be till early June. So now the book was no longer a pastime but a serious undertaking; on the proceeds of this venture we must depend to make a move, and we got right busy, Jelly and me. From then on I worked unremittingly on my script, writing at night and going out only to replenish the wood supply. I did not, and do not, aim at literary excellence, it being beyond me, sacrificing what might be correct usage to paint a picture in words. I felt, and still feel that if I had, in my little knowledge, to pay too much attention to technical niceties, my thoughts might be dressed in a coat of mail, rather than in the softer habiliments with which Nature clothes even her grimmest realities. If I considered that by putting a word in front that should be behind, and vice versa, I could better express some thought, I would do so, on the same principle whereby a snowshoe is often handier to dig snow with than a shovel, and the handle of an axe is sometimes better suited to breaking a way through snow encumbered undergrowth than is the blade. My factory-made English on which I had looked with something approaching contempt, could now be put to some use. It was brought out of cold storage where it had languished for the better part of three decades, and on inspection, in the light of modern requirements, was found to be woefully short on words. This had to be mended, and I wrestled for hours with books of reference on the English language. From a book of English poems, Longfellow's Hiawatha, and Service's Songs of a Sourdough I unearthed verses suggestive of the chapters they introduced, a fashion long out of date, it was said, but it appealed to me and I was not interested in fashions; I was getting something off my chest.

The pile of MS. increased to imposing and rather alarming proportions. I often awoke from sleep to make alterations, made constant notes, and to get the proper effect of difficult passages, I read them aloud to Jelly, who, pleased with the attention and the sound of rattling papers, would twist and turn in queer contortions of delight. I erected a table alongside the bunk, so that I could sit there and reach out at any moment and jot down any notions that came along.

And while I wrote Jelly pursued her own studies, and carried on with her highly important jobs such as moving and placing objects, and took care of little household chores such as banking up the bottom of the door, or the re-arrangement of the wood pile. Often she would sit bolt upright beside me on the bed, looking up in a most intent manner at my face, as though trying to fathom what my purpose could be with that queer scratching noise. She was a paper addict and was much attracted by the rustle of the stationery, and constantly stole wrapping paper and magazines and books, taking them home with her, and when she was on the bunk with me she would reach out very often at my note book and other papers, and we sometimes had lively discussions on this matter in which I was not always the winner. One day however she succeeded, quite, I think, beyond her expectations or mine. Forgetting to erect the barrier between the bunk and the table, I returned from cutting wood one day to find everything pushed off it, including a camera, a lamp, and a row of books; and she had registered her entire approval of my literary efforts by removing the MS. bodily. A few sheets of my work were scattered on the floor, but the rest were not to be seen. A visit of investigation to the abode of the culprit was received with squeals of mingled trepidation and protest, but I routed her out and raked up the manuscript with the blackened wooden poker and a piece of wire, the paper fiend meanwhile trying desperately to maintain her rights of ownership. Luckily all of it but one page was recovered, and as she had no doubt scooped up the entire pile with that steam shovel of a bottom jaw of hers, it was little damaged. But the resulting mix-up was very little short of cataclysmic. Imagine about four hundred loose sheets closely written on both sides, in pencil, with interpolations, alterations, and notes wedged in here and there, with lines and arrows and other cabalistic indications of what went where, and *unnumbered*, and you may get the idea. It took me the best part of three days to reassemble, and in some instances, re-write the script. This time I painstakingly numbered the pages.

So we kept on with our book, Jelly and I, and it began to draw to a close. And ever there passed before me as I wrote, the pageant of the far-off Height of Land—the trooping forest swaying, swinging ever to the Northward, rows of shrouded trees, like spectres standing on parade, that loomed beside the trail in the light of the Aurora, where caravans of snowshoe-men marched as in an avenue of ghosts, their toboggans singing shrilly on the frozen trail behind them; or where single silent hunters stalked grimly on, alone. And I wrote not so much of men, whose comings and goings, whose very existence, was of such small significance in the vastness of The Great White Silence, but of the Frontier in all its aspects and its phases, the Frontier that even now was vanishing, seemed indeed to be already gone; for the ruins amongst which I now was living showed only too plainly what its fate was soon to be. And so I called my book "The Vanishing Frontier."[1]

And ever my mind turned back to Mississauga, roaring between its looming maple-crested mountains—the wild Forty Mile rapids, the swift rush of the Three Mile, the flashing mane of the White Horse, the Cheneaux with its toll of human lives, the heavy thunderous roar of Aubrey

[1] This title was changed by the publishers to *Men of the Last Frontier*, the only alteration of any account in it.

Falls over its redstone cliffs, the Gros Cap with its sheer towering walls of granite and gnarled distorted jack-pines jutting out from precarious ledges, the dark, cavernous pine forests, the smell of drying leaves of birch and ash and poplar, the rhythmic, muffled thud of paddles on hardwood gunnells, blue smoke trailing up from the embers of slow fires, quiet, observant Indians camped beneath the red pines, beside its racing flood—

And ever in my heart there was an acheing loneliness for the simple kindly people, companions and mentors of my younger days, whose ways had become my ways, and their gods my gods; a people now starving patiently, quietly and hopelessly in their smoky lodges on the wind-swept, ravished barrens that Progress had decreed that they should dwell in. I thought of the young children who died so pitifully, while the parents with stony faces kept vigil turn about to keep the flies away, till, like little beavers, they slipped silently and stoically away on the grey wings of dawn that carries so many souls into the Great Unknown. And I remembered that with all my repining their case was infinitely worse than my own, and felt somehow that my place was with them, to suffer as they were suffering, that I should share their misery as I had shared their happier times.

Came Christmas, which we two spent together. I think Jelly enjoyed it, as she ate so much that she was in visible discomfort all the next day, but my own lone festivities were rather futile and a little unhappy. However, I hung up a paper lantern from a rafter and after the candle in it was lighted Jelly did happen to look up at it a couple of times, so I didn't feel so flat and ridiculous about it after all. I had several invitations for New Year's, and leaving Jelly well fixed for water and feed, and the camp well warmed, I spent that afternoon and night in Cabano.

On this holiday the French Canadian throws himself into the spirit of joyous conviviality of the Season with a carefree abandon that throws wide all doors, opens all hearts, and puts a period to all feuds; and he allows, on this Day of all the year, this Jour De L'An, his robust love of merriment to have full sway.

In town everything had a festive air that could not but have its effect on the dourest onlooker. The streets were full of people dressed in all their best. Church bells were ringing, men arrived hourly from the woods in strings, singing as they passed along the streets, and the whole village had such an atmosphere of good will and bonhomie bubbling up from it, that no weather however stormy or evil could possibly have penetrated or subdued it, if indeed it would ever have been noticed. Music could be heard resounding in every direction, from the organised revelry of the radio, to the blare of a gramophone, and there issued out upon the frosty air the skirl of fiddles, playing the wild rhythms of the jigs and reels and the clever and intricate step dances in which these people find a self-expression and an outlet for their feelings which is peculiarly their own.

There seemed something so very reminiscent of the intimate community spirit of an Indian village in all of it, that a wave of homesickness swept over me as I passed down the narrow tree lined streets. But this was soon driven entirely from my mind as I was saluted on all sides, shaken by the hand, and called into houses that I had never before entered, and made to partake of whatever cheer they were all enjoying. And it was all done in such an unpretentious, genuine, and simple way that I clean forgot that I was a gloomy half-breed, and gave my best in entertainment in return.

Every house was full of music and play and laughter. Here were no funereal, stupefying "rhythms" or erotic, maudlin inanities, but gay quadrilles, fine old waltzes, snappy fox-trots, and whatever the circumstances of the host, whether he laid a ceremonious feast, or could afford no more than fried pork or venison or good French bread, the parting guest was sped with a full belly and good wishes, and perhaps a few glasses of red wine to fortify him against his journey home. Here the sophisticates, had there been any, would have had no need to pose or attitudinize, for no eye would have rested long upon them in all this healthy, hearty fun, and many a solid citizen lost his dignity that night and got it back just as good as ever in the morning.

At one of these entertainments was an old gentleman of some account in the place, who had on this occasion at least, so far forgotten his age as to proclaim for all to hear, that he was positive he could leap over a house—not too big a one of course—and told me of his prowess in his younger days. He related how, when once waylaid by a crowd of hoodlums, he had torn up a whole picket fence and advanced to the attack behind its cover, and had swung it right and left with such vigour and address (during this part of the recital it was necessary to duck quickly once or twice), that he had driven the enemy away in terror and confusion, leaving their fallen behind them. And so elevated did he become as he re-enacted the glories of those palmy days, that when he left the house he took the wrong overcoat, and being a small man, walked gravely down the street enveloped in a garment several sizes too large for him, with sleeves reaching nearly to his knees and skirts that trailed upon the snow behind him.

At another house was a guest who was a stranger, like myself. He had a little Ford truck and travelled from place to place without any settled abode, and passed amongst the villages selling sewing machines, or cigars, or cook-books, or even a good recipe for moonshine. He had a scarred face and was nearsighted, and wore thick enormous spectacles and a cowboy hat, and had only one finger remaining on his right hand. But he made no effort to disguise these infirmities, or belittle them, as most of us would have done, but paraded them, just now, as fortunate endowments of Fate that enabled him to contribute to the pleasure of others not so gifted, and made impersonations by means of them and sang comic songs, and played the piano with his six fingers in imitation of a great musician, and danced with nimble feet. So that the ladies were glad to plant a New Year's kiss on the poor distorted face, and men took the crippled hand of this noble, gallant clown and were sorry to see him go, and wished him Godspeed on his wanderings.

And at midnight a fusillade of shots was fired from every kind of firearm, and timed by every kind of clock, so that volleys were being fired from time to time for several minutes, according to whether clocks were fast or slow. And as long as the bullets were sent up and out in the general direction of the lake no one cared a great deal where they fell, as no good citizen had any business to be outside the town on such a night.

And in the midst of all the celebration and the merriment I thought suddenly of my little brown buddy, waiting up there alone in the dark and empty cabin in the hills. So I slipped away on my snowshoes through the midnight forest to my home behind the Mountain of the Elephant; and with a parcel of peanuts and apples and candies, Jelly had her New Year's too, and enjoyed it every bit as much as I had done—better perhaps, because she had no memories behind her. For no matter where, or under what happy circumstances I ever found myself, I never once forgot my mission, and, should I be successful, its probable results. I never ceased to listen quietly, studying the language, asking guarded questions; ever on the watch. For my search was not only for living beaver, or for perhaps some hides or even bones, but might even yet be for a man. And sometimes I walked in hate amongst these people who would be my friends.

Late in February I sent the completed MS. away, and being now free I commenced the study of words, with the assistance of my book of synonyms and a dictionary. I found words elusive and hard to trap. But each one as it was cornered up in a book or magazine was caught, and went down into a note book and was brought home and given a thorough and exhaustive going over. Often it would have little to recommend it save that I liked the sound of it. I sought words that suggested in their pronunciation the idea I would try to express by means of them. I was much preoccupied with this note book and the still-hunts in the trackless jungles of the book of synonyms, and at times forgot to eat. I became vocabulary-conscious, began to use four and five dollar words, and often my conversation was unintelligible even to my English-speaking friends. I had attacks of absent mindedness, and eventually got to the stage where I once reached for the ink bottle to fill my pipe, and another time caught myself on the point of attempting to fill my pen out of the tobacco can. Progress by any other name could have been no worse.

There was a lawyer who often visited me, always bringing cheer with him, and sometimes a merry crowd of friends. He seldom came without some gift for me and once showed up in the middle of the night, having lost his way, and announced that he had left a radio down the trail a piece. It was a portable model, and the next day we packed it in, with its appurtenances. This machine was a complete mystery to me, but he installed it and rigged the aerial, and that night the camp, usually so quiet, was filled with music.

I overcame my aversion to any form of machinery from ploughs to railroads, sufficiently well to listen in on this set. Here, I soon discovered, was a word-mine all by itself. From then on radio announcers, authors, book reviewers, news reporters, politicians, and others whose trade is words, became my nightly company. These people and the works of Emerson and

Shakespeare, and the Bible, each made their unwitting contribution to my omnivorous appetite for the means wherewith to express myself.

Always, night travelling had had an irresistible fascination for me, to which predilection I owed my name. This familiarity with darkness and the development of certain faculties that went with it, stood me in good stead in my work of patrolling and in locating Jelly at any and all hours; and between tours on the rounds of my self imposed duties, and at intervals between sleeps, I studied the English language from dark to sunrise. My coal oil bill went up, and the books I bought cut deeply into my eating money; but there were lots of deer and for clothes I wore buckskin, taking time out to tan the hides. This latter practice attracted the attention of the local game warden, who came in armed with written orders to impose a fine on me. I had to talk pretty fast to him to get him to see things my way, and saying that he felt there had been a mistake he advised me to write to Quebec City. This I did, and later received from the head Warden of the district, a letter expressing regret for the trouble I had been put to, and a hunting and trapping licence was awarded me free of charge. Again the noblesse of Old Quebec.

During the New Year's festivities I had become acquainted with an Irish family who all but adopted me using me as though I had been son and brother, giving me the freedom of their home, and who entered into all my joys and woes, laughed when I laughed, and danced and sang for me when I was low in spirits. A carefree happy-go-lucky group of people they were, who cared little whether I wore my hat backwards, sideways, or at all, and who made my coming the signal for a gay party of music and singing. And with them I formed a friendship that exists today, and at this distance, as strong as ever it was then. It was after one of these visits that I returned on a day late in March, to find the camp door open and my little companion of a lonely Winter gone.

I stared stupidly at the open door: my head swam for a moment with the sudden, devastating feeling of bereavement, and I remember that I shouted once aloud, made some meaningless sounds. Then I got busy. At first I thought she had been taken, but evidently she had at last solved the problem of opening the door from the inside, having long learned the trick of shutting it. The warm sun of an early Spring afternoon had lured her out to a not improbable death by freezing, as there was as yet no open water and there was easily four feet of snow in the bush. Her tracks revealed that she had been gone a full day, and her trail led up the lake to her playhouse of the Fall before.

Unable to find an opening in the ice she had followed the course of the creek up stream, and at no place did it offer a chance of entry. The stream eventually petered out in a maze of alders and cedar swamp in which she had wandered in all directions. She penetrated this swamp for a distance of about a mile and then became lost entirely, digging deeply into the snow in spots, in a futile endeavour to find water. Her steps were becoming short, and in many places she had lain down for long periods thawing out a bed for herself. It was easy to see where night had caught her, as a crust had then commenced to form, on which she left less and less impression as it hardened; and the poor ugly in-toed tracks became indistinct and finally disappeared altogether—and still headed away from home and safety. The temperature had abruptly dropped and a beaver's feet and tail freeze easily, completely disabling him.

I did not return to camp that night but hunted the swamp till daylight, calling every few minutes. I searched it and the surrounding gullies and ravines in all directions, that day and many succeeding days, and there being a moon, for as many nights as it lasted. Came a spell of almost zero weather, not infrequent during early Spring. I then knew that if my little chum had by any series of accidents escaped the foxes and was still without sufficient water, she would be by now almost certainly frozen to death; and in support of this theory I one day found a porcupine in that condition. The weather later became soft and I travelled day after day combing the country for signs of the wanderer, even visiting lakes to which she probably could never have got. At the end of twenty days I sat dispirited and well nigh worn out from dragging heavy snowshoes over wet snow at a time of year when bush travelling is considered virtually impossible. My injured foot had given out and my snowshoes were so worn as to be almost useless, but as there had been a couple of days of heavy rain followed by a sharp frost, I decided to take advantage of the crust that formed and make one more attempt. I repaired my snowshoes as best I could and was starting out, when I saw a black object working its way along the shore line, about fifty yards away and headed for the cabin. For a moment I watched it, and then, the certainty entering my mind that my search was ended I went forward and met it and there, plodding slowly but persistently ahead, poor as a rake and otherwise the worse for wear, came my long lost friend the Boss.

It was a great reunion. For her part, she took up camp life about where she had laid it down, had a good feed, slept for twenty-four hours, and said no more about it. I later found where her unerring instinct had located water in the nearly dry bed of the stream, and she had holed up there for nearly three weeks, under the snow, until the rain had created a freshet on which she had descended to the lake, and there being by then a strip of open water she had been released.

Come open water she left the camp, and I much feared that she would leave on some rambling excursion to look for a partner, and finding one, not return. But she waived her privilege and proceeded up the lake, where she formally took up her abode in her burrow, visiting me regularly several times a night. She followed the canoe around the lake and surprised me one day by scrambling over the side and flopping into it. This seemed at the time a little extraordinary, and especially remarkable was her manner of doing this, as she had a nice sense of equilibrium, canting the canoe only a few inches. She continued this practice, and varied the performance by climbing onto the stern seat and taking a high dive into the lake, slipping smoothly into the water as though oiled. On what I took to be special occasions she played a kind of a game with me, giving me a false lead as to her intended direction, and then diving. I would attempt to follow her, and she would suddenly appear in a totally unexpected spot some distance away, and on my approach she would birl around and around like a log, or spin in an erect position, partly out of the water, and throw herself backwards with a mighty splash in very evident pleasure, perhaps at having fooled me. This she would do for perhaps half an hour at a time. She would sometimes dive alongside the canoe, and I could see her straining every muscle to gain on me whilst supposedly out of sight, and on coming to the surface ahead of the canoe, which of course I always made sure to allow for, she would wait for me to catch up and then repeat. She often signalled me by calling, giving a clear penetrating note capable of being heard for half a mile, and should I call her with a similar sound she seldom failed to answer me, if within earshot. Her favourite amusement was to place her two front legs around my wrist, gripping hard, and standing erect with my hand pressing against her breast, she would push and strain in a sustained effort to upset me. Sometimes in the course of this pastime she would back up, trying to drag me forward until I was off balance and then attempt to rush me off my feet. She now weighed all of twenty pounds and was solid bone and muscle, and was surprisingly strong. I have since found that there was nothing very out of the ordinary in these activities as they are all customary amusements of any beaver; the remarkable part is, that she should elect to remain with me and so employ herself, instead of seeking her own kind of which there was a colony less than three miles away, and easily accessible to her.

Just before the leaves came I set a trap for a marauding otter, on a stream some distance away, as I had found beaver hair in his droppings; Jelly, on account of her optimistic outlook on life, would fall an easy victim. One morning on visiting the trap I found it gone, and projecting from under a submerged log saw the tail of a beaver. On pulling the chain I found resistance, and hauled out a living beaver, an adult. He had a piece of his scalp hanging loose, and half-drowned and scared almost to death, he made little attempt to defend himself. I removed the trap and took him home with me, tied up in a gunny sack. His foot was badly injured, and being one of the all-important hind, or swimming feet, I decided to try and repair the damage before I liberated him. For the first twenty-four hours he hid himself in the Boss's late apartment, emerging only to drink, and he ate not at all. At the end of that time he came out into the centre of the camp with every appearance of fear, but I was able to pick him up and speaking kindly to him, offered him an apple which he took. I worked on him all night doing my best to inspire confidence, and succeeded to the extent that, crippled as he was, he commenced a tour of the camp, examining everything including the door, which he made no attempt to bite through. In the course of his explorations he discovered the bunk, climbed into it up Jelly's chute, found it to his liking, and from then on ate and slept there, occasionally leaving it for purposes of his own, such as to dispose of his peeled sticks or to take a bath. He slept between my pillow and the wall, and nearly every night he became lonesome and came around to sleep in the crook of my arm till daylight, when he went back behind the pillow. I might add here that I was under no hardship, as a beaver is perhaps one of the cleanest animals in existence. After all I was responsible for his condition, and any small sacrifices that I had to make were cheerfully submitted to.

Although the weather was still cold I dared light no fire in the camp, as the noise of the stove drove him frantic; tobacco smoke caused him to hide away for hours. The operation of dressing his foot single handed was an undertaking of no mean proportions. It was swollen to an immense size, and two of the metatarsal bones projected through the skin. His teeth were badly shattered from his attempts to break the trap, and it would be weeks before they were again serviceable. The loose portion of his scalp had dried, and hung from his head like a piece of wrinkled hide, so I severed it and named him after it, calling him Rawhide, a name he still retains and knows.

For two weeks I worked hard to save the injured foot, and to a certain extent succeeded, although I believe the antiseptic effect of the leeches which clustered in the wound on his subsequent return to natural conditions, completed a task that taxed my ingenuity to the utmost. Whether on account of the attention he received, or because labouring under the impression that I had saved his life, or from very lonesomeness, I cannot say, but the poor creature took a liking to me, hobbling around the camp at my heels, and crying out loudly in the most mournful fashion when I went out. These sounds on one occasion attracted the attention of the Boss who forthwith raced up into the camp to ascertain the cause. On seeing a strange beaver she nearly broke her neck trying to get out of the camp, running in her haste full tilt into the door, which I had closed. She then reconsidered the matter, and returned to give the newcomer the once over. She at once decided that here was somebody who, being disabled, would be perfectly easy to beat up, which kind and chivalrous thought she immediately proceeded to put into execution. After a considerable scramble which ended in my having to carry the would-be warrior bodily down to the lake, objecting loudly, quiet was restored. She apparently resented the presence of a stranger in the home, no matter whose home; she ruled here as queen and had no intention of sharing her throne with anybody, it seemed, and I had to fasten the door from then on to keep her out.

On my patient becoming convalescent I bid him good luck and turned him loose, not without some feelings of regret, as he had become very likeable and affectionate. The next day, on visiting the domicile of the so-militant Queen, I saw a beaver and called it over. The animal answered and swam towards me, and my surprise can be well imagined, when I recognised the now well known voice and lines of the cripple. He came to the canoe with every sign of recognition, followed me down the full length of the lake, and crept behind me into the camp. While there he lay for a time on a deerskin rug, and whimpered a little and nibbled gently at my hands, and presently slipped away to the lake again. And this practice he continued, sometimes climbing, with assistance, onto my knees and there conducting an assiduous and very damp toilet. He had nothing to gain by these manoeuvres, and could have left at any time for parts unknown, had he been so minded. While I can not go so far as to say that he was grateful, there is little doubt but that the treatment he had received while sick and confined to the cabin had had its effect on him, for he haunted me and the camp environs, unless driven away by the Boss, whose treatment of him was little short of brutal. She was insanely jealous and drove him away from the camp repeatedly, and would not allow him to approach me if she were present. On more than one occasion she chased him far down the stream below the outlet, where I could hear him crying out; but he always stuck to his guns and came back. In spite of her hostility he followed her around and did every thing she did, hobbling on his injured foot emitting plaintive little sounds, and seeming almost pitifully anxious to fit into the picture and be one of the boys. He even succeeded, after several failures, in climbing into the canoe, only to be thrown out by the Boss, on which I interfered. He somehow gave the impression that he was starving for companionship, and Jelly refusing his advances he turned to me. He did all these unaccustomed things in such a dumb and humble way, yet with such an air of quiet resolution about him, that I always took his part against the more flamboyant and self-sufficient Jelly Roll. And by this very quiet insistence, this inflexible yet calm determination, this exercise of some unexpected latent power within him, he overcame one by one the obstacles imposed on him by his new environment and found his place at last, and eventually took control and became no more a suppliant but a leader.

The Boss had for me the friendship that exists between equals; we were rough and tumble playfellows, old-timers together who could take liberties with one another and get away with it. But the stranger, for all his harsh sounding and rather unsuitable name of Rawhide, seemed to want only a little kindness to make him happy, and was as gentle as the touch of the night wind on the leaves; yet I once saw him, driven to passion by too much persecution, shake the Boss like she had been a paper bag.

And I think she owes it to him that she lives today.

A rogue beaver, old and watchful and wise, his colony no doubt destroyed by hunters, now gone bad and ranging far and wide, descended on these two while I was away and tried to take possession. On my return I found Jelly laid out on the landing before the camp. A thin trail of blood led to the door but she must have been too weak to enter, and had dragged herself back to the water's edge to wait. Her throat was torn open, some of the parts protruding; her bottom lip was nearly severed, both arms were punctured and swollen and nearly useless, and her tail had been cut completely through at the root for over an inch of its width and there were besides a number of ugly gashes on the head and body. There was nothing I could do save to disinfect the wounds. Meanwhile she lay inert, her eyes closed, moaning faintly, while her blood oozed away into the mud of the landing she had so stoutly maintained as her own; and in her extremity she had come to me, her friend, who could only sit helplessly by, resolving to let her quietly die beside her pond, where she had once been a small lonesome waif, before she was a queen.

I sat beside her all night, and at intervals fed her milk with the old glass syringe that once before had brought her back from the edge of the Valley of Shadows. Towards morning she seemed to draw on some hidden resources of vitality and bestirred herself, and slowly, painfully, crawled up into the cabin; for I did not dare to pick her up for fear of opening up her now clotted wounds afresh. She stayed with me all that day, leaving again at night, in bad shape but with the best part of two cans of milk inside her, and apparently on the mend. Only the marvellous recuperative powers possessed by wild animals and man in a state of nature, brought her around. I did not see her again for a week, but often passed the time of day with her through the walls of her abode, and heard her answer me. By the signs I discovered around the lake and from what I saw of him another time, the visitor must have been of enormous size, and there is no doubt that had she been alone she would have been killed. Rawhide also bore marks of the encounter but to a less degree, and I am sure by what I have since seen of his other abilities, that his assistance must have turned the tide of battle.

From then on the two of them lived in perfect harmony, and have done ever since. But with the knowledge that the presence of an intruder may result in pain and suffering, to her all strangers, human or animal, from then on were anathema. Guests who wished to view the beavers might no longer stand on the recognised landing places or trails and admire the beauty of the fur, the intelligence of the eye, the noble lines of the head, and so forth. They, the guests, were firmly and none too politely pushed off the said trail or landing. They were very definitely put in their places, and resistance stirred up trouble. The shore, the lake itself, the canoe, she claimed them all. Even the camp, it appeared, was hers, as she chased people out of it and ran them up the road, and it was highly probable that she even thought she built it.

They both acted much as if they owned the pond and environs, and certainly without them it would have been just a shallow, lifeless, muddy sheet of water. Their presence there gave life to it, and imparted to the valley an indefinable air of being occupied that no other creature save man could give to it. Many came to this hitherto deserted spot because of them, and it became something of a metropolis, in a mild way of speaking. And some of those who came, with the poetic instinct of the Frenchman, thought it should be named for them, and so the hills that trooped down from the crest of high Elephant Mountain and stood gathered around the lake, became the Jelly Roll Hills and the pond was Rawhide Lake; and knowing well the history of the camp they named it Beaver's Home.

So we were all officially designated on the local records, and all three of us proved up on our possession by improving the estate. The beavers cleaned out runways and landings in convenient places, and built a lodge and kept the dam ship-shape and up to date, while I banked my own cabin and re-chinked it, and brightened up the interior a little and raked the yard.

Near their house the beavers cleared themselves a playground, on which no human being but myself might set a foot, and Jelly once chased a party of three people off this place, two of whom retired to high ground and another climbed a tree.

And the Queen deliberately stood up in the centre of her plaza, and shook and twisted her head and body in the irresistibly mirth provoking contortions with which a beaver shows his appreciation of what he considers to be a very good joke.

A beaver's memory is long, and I think she has never quite forgotten that adventure that so nearly cost her life, and even to-day, if I be absent, the Queen will tolerate no stranger on the place.

CHAPTER FOUR

The Dark Hour
and the Dawn

IN EARLY AUGUST, AT WHICH TIME BEAVER ARE LOCALIZED IN
their permanent works, I took up again my quest, the only thing that was
keeping me in this cut and tortured remnant of a wilderness with its ever
present menace to the lives of my two dependents. There was little food
for them on the shores of the pond and once it was exhausted they might
leave me; one more year in this locality would make a move imperative,
though I was well aware that no matter where I went every man's hand
would be against them, and that I might some day be forced into serious
trouble on their account. Every time I received a cheque for an article I
was sorely tempted to abandon my hopeless search, leave someone in
charge of the beaver, and make a journey back to Ontario and find some
point where we would all have a safer and more congenial environment.
But I quenched these disloyal thoughts and thought only of the lost ones,
feeling as a man who plots against absent friends. I quit writing entirely
having run out of material and unable, between trips, to apply the concentration necessary to the elaboration of new themes. So I gave up all
thoughts of literary work in the prosecution of my hunt. A month's travel
proved beyond any doubt, that none of the few scattered lodges and bank
dens previously located were occupied by McGinnis and McGinty. Some
of the townspeople took a lively interest in the affair, and I received much
well-meant information. But it takes a hunter to read the signs with any
accuracy, and these clues rarely amounted to anything. But I followed

them every one to the end, travelling through swamps and slash, sleeping out in any weather only to find, after days of wandering, an old lodge that had been deserted for years, or more frequently the cuttings of a porcupine instead of those of beaver.

This search had lost its reality to me, and had become an uncompleted mission which must be adhered to from a sense of duty, until every chance had been eliminated, in the possibility, but no longer the expectation, of its fulfillment. Often it seemed little but a useless struggle against the unalterable laws of fate, that I sought to change from their invincible decrees by the very doggedness and persistence of my efforts. And when with an empty belly, sometimes in the darkness, often in the rain, perhaps after dragging for miles through tangled, mosquito-infested cedar swamps in which it was at times necessary to crawl, I pursued some phantom clue to its inevitable failure, it assumed the proportions of a nightmare in which one struggles hopelessly to gain some vital but unattainable goal. Yet in the bush nothing can be taken for granted, and I intended to stick until the last dog was hung. The all-too-evident hopelessness of my object, now no longer to be disguised, together with a number of other things, weighed heavily on my mind. It was long since I had heard from Anahareo; not only was she far removed from any means of communication, but she herself would not return for months. The mine on which we had so depended had failed us, and unable to get out of the country she might become destitute among strangers. Our sole income was my small pension; there was no work to be had here, and if there had been I could not have taken it without leaving the beaver unprotected. I was alone in what amounted to a foreign land, and there was moreover the depressing influence, exceedingly potent, of the country itself, this terrible graveyard of a blasted ruined forest, slashed, racked and slaughtered, a wilderness with the soul torn out of it. These factors and the ever present danger to the beaver, liable to be consummated at any moment were ever before me. There seemed to be no way out, and I knew not what the end might be, save that in the event of the beaver being butchered, I would exact retribution that, in its results, would drive me forever from the haunts of man. I felt as one caught in the slow drag of some dark sinister stream that was drawing me in its flood, irresistibly down to some vortex of destruction and despair.

Added to this, Mons. Duchene, my lawyer friend, had died, leaving behind him a sense of deprivation and a real regret. Even the beaver had taken to him. During the summer when both beaver were frequenting the camp, he had stayed several nights. He slept in the bunk alone while I lay on the floor, as I frequently did. The first morning, on waking, I asked him how he had slept and he said not too well. On being asked the reason, he said that he had no room in the bed. "Look," he told me; and there in the bunk with him, stretched out on their backs and occupying most of the bed, lay the two beaver fast asleep!

Had these animals, to whom strangers were always an object of indifference, if not actual suspicion, been able to so decipher the generous character of this man? I wondered. He never knew just what his gift had meant to me, and for a long time I left it silent on its box.

On the shores of one pond on which lived two beavers whose identity I had not yet established, I once found a bed of brush; beside it were some empty rifle shells, and carefully wrapped up and concealed, a powerful jack-light. The hunters would evidently return. Taking a position directly across the narrow sheet of water, just behind the low ridge that bordered it, I lay in waiting four days and five nights, living on snared rabbits broiled before the embers of careful smokeless fires. On the fifth afternoon the hunters came. I appeared suddenly and without sound behind them, armed. The moral effect was quite good. However, it transpired that I knew these men and believed they were what they claimed themselves to be—poor devils out of a job, trying to get some meat for their families. Pot-hunters, if you will, but who had a better right than they? They were even unaware of the presence here of beaver. But I requested them to move, making no mention of the illegal jack-light which was none of my business, unless they had been obstinate. I took them to a good deer-lick; perhaps they had some luck there. But things were not always so smooth. Nevertheless I had my way, always, as fortune had it, by fair means; in emergency I would have not been particular as to the means. I could understand better the old-time Indian's point of view, the atrocities they committed in defence of their families and homes, or to safeguard a piece of territory, an individual tree, a shrine, or a rock. Some hostility was aroused. It was said by some that I did not, according to law, possess any beaver, that they belonged to the province; to them it was a question of ownership, chattels, law. We own no lives but our own and I sought only to save, if possible, two that I valued.

That I should make enemies was inevitable, and incidents occurred that are best not recorded. And many miles from home, sometimes with camp made or even waking from sleep, I would suddenly become obsessed by the thought that the volunteer assistant who took charge of my little community in my absence had become tired of his thankless task, and had left Jelly and Rawhide open to attack from some ill-wisher; and I would hurry homeward day and night through the tangled slash. But my faithful friend was always at his post, nor did he ever give any sign of impatience, although the pickings were often pretty thin at Rawhide Lake, as I was now living on my infinitesimal army pension. Eggs, caviare and champagne entered the cabin only by way of the loud speaker, and the beaver too went pretty short on treats. They always begged for them, and when after buying only absolute necessaries for myself there remained a few dimes and nickels, these were always invested in a parcel of apples. And the little beasts were so overjoyed to have them, and it was so much pleasure to witness their enjoyment, that I found it no hardship to stint myself the least bit in tobacco and some other things that were not real necessities, so as not to disappoint them too often.[1]

I received another letter from Anahareo. With the wages she had earned driving a dog team all the previous Winter for a company, she had bought herself a grubstake, and was on the trail of another fortune. This

[1] During this period the writer was in actual want, though frequent and highly attractive offers were made to buy this pair of Beaver. To illustrate the feeling inspired by the disposition of these animals an extract is appended from an unpublished article, written by the Author as a kind of soliloquy, during an especially trying time.

"...But be times ever so hard, let the pot be empty and the belt somewhat tightened on occasion, they will never die to provide the wherewithal for me. A thousand times the value of their coats so proudly scrubbed and combed would not pay for the loss of my ever-happy playfellows; for they trust and seem to love me. And did I so betray them or sell them into bondage, methinks there are nights when I would awake and listen in the darkness to the fancied sound of childlike voices, the pleading voices of my Little Brethren, and see looking reproachfully at me the wise, sad eyes of my Beaver People."

was probably for the best, as although her presence here on patrol in my stead would have set me free to go to work, if any such was to be had here, yet the deadly monotony of the place would in time have been very depressing, and perhaps have driven her away again. If only I could present her with McGinnis and McGinty on her return, the loss of the gold mine would be of small account!

Meanwhile, with the intensive observations I took, and experiments I conducted to ascertain the movements and identity of any beaver that came within the wide orbit of my reconnoitring, I was accumulating more and more data concerning these animals than I had, in my supposedly complete education in them, considered possible; and my previous knowledge, hitherto confined to the requirements of the hunt, was as nothing compared with what I now commenced to learn. I found that by the exercise of a little patience and judgment I could, in course of time, get to see different members of a family within a measurable distance, provided they were house beaver and not individuals living in a bank. After my familiarity with my own animals, it seemed to be somehow only natural that I should be able to confidently approach any and all of them, even if wild, and it is probable that three years of living on the closest terms with these creatures must have had its unconscious influence on my conduct and manner of approach. Even my very attitude of mind may have communicated itself to them, as animals seem gifted that way. I found that, after some days of quiet watchfulness, I could inspire these elusive creatures with some measure of confidence, and that at the sound of my voice, not in imitation of their own calls but in tones of a certain pitch, they would sometimes leave their house and swim back and forth or lay quietly on the water, observing me, at a distance of a few yards. One, a young fellow, actually came ashore and peeled a stick, disregarding me utterly, and could have been no more than six feet away. There was nothing supernatural in all this, and I think that any other person who had had the same acquaintance with them, and who felt about them as I did, could have had the same experience, and I have since discovered that these results were greatly attributable to the disposition of the animals themselves. I believe today that animals having a high mentality, and that have not yet suffered at the hands of man will, if given an opportunity, come to a conclusion regarding his intention towards them and act accordingly. Interesting as these experiments were, I eventually desisted from them, as the beaver would fall a prey to the hunters soon enough, without my dulling their instincts of self-protection for my own gratification.

The two that were now my sole company were, in the fearless intimacy of their relations with me, adding to my store of information daily. I saw them continuously, and within touching distance, occupied in all the arts of their profession, adding their quota of interest to what was to be the most eventful Summer of my career. These two were completing a house and dam. And never before having had the same opportunity of seeing these erections in process of actual construction to such advantage, I spent hours watching them. My advent was always a signal to knock off work for the purpose of playing a wet, splashy kind of game, and this occurred at intervals all night; but the greater part of the time was spent in labour that was never abandoned till after daylight.

The interest inspired by their activities would alone have caused me to spend the night watches in this manner, but this was also made advisable by the presence of the numbers of poachers and would-be hunters that ranged the woods, and these would be a menace from now until the beaver were safely ensconced in the camp. For I did not intend them to pass the Winter in their new house half a mile away, owing to the danger of their being trapped some day while I slept. But they had made elaborate preparations and were every day adding to them, and in their search for material they stole every movable article they could find and utilized it in some manner or another. One night the paddles were removed from the canoe, to be found later firmly enmeshed in the structure of the house. This edifice, besides the usual material of sticks and mud, had sometimes a weird assortment of household articles embedded in its surface like raisins in a pudding, all of which had to be surreptitiously extracted. Bones, bottles, firewood and old bags were taken and utilized in the building of the dam, and I returned once from town to be greeted at the landing by a pile of objects of a very varied description, including a shovel, a bag containing potatoes, a box of foolscap, a pair of pants and an Eaton's catalogue, and interspersed through this collection were numerous blocks of stove wood. Other materials lay scattered along the trail in various stages of transportation, all destined for the lodge and dam. I had left the camp door secured against them, but these ambulating saw-mills had easily gained entrance by simply carving away a portion of the door. The good work was still going on when I arrived, and I was met with great acclaim and much excited rolling and falling on backs, and they seemed mightily pleased with themselves. On yet another occasion I entered the cabin to find Jelly on the bunk busily engaged in ripping up and pushing overboard my carefully laid bed of balsam brush, while below her on the floor stood Rawhide, who received it and stowed it away under the bed, for what purpose was not apparent. Most of the damage being now done, I sat down and watched the exhibition with some interest until, it suddenly occurring to me that the blankets were missing I interfered, and found them tangled up with the brush in under the bunk, and liberally salted with needles off the boughs.

At the height of the poaching season I received some information that caused me to pick up the beavers and keep them in the safety of the cabin for the matter of a week. They were now three parts grown and powerful for their size. The first night in camp they cut down a table, tore up part of the floor, upset a pail of water and broke a window. Their manner of accomplishing this last feat is worth recording. On the floor beside one wall was an eight foot canoe-pole with an iron socket on one end of it. I had noticed that they were fooling with this and had thought little of it, until they suddenly rushed the pole, heavy end foremost, across the floor together. When near the opposite wall Jelly Roll, who was ahead, reared up and held the end above her head with both hands, while Rawhide, at the other end, kept going and drove the iron socket crashing through the window. It is not to be supposed that they had any intention of deliberately breaking the glass, having no knowledge of its nature, their purpose being no doubt to commence the erection of a scaffold on which they could climb to close the aperture they thought existed there. But this notable instance is the only example that I have so far been a witness to, of actual team work on the part of beaver, in the carrying out of a plan of action conceived on the spur of the moment.

I wrote casual articles on all these doings, and the editor who was taking my work, wrote me to the effect that the interest aroused by these descriptions had prompted him to notify the National Parks Service of the Department of the Interior at Ottawa concerning them, with a view to the possibility of having the beavers' activities placed on record in the form of moving pictures. Almost immediately I received a visit from an official of the National Parks Service, a gentleman with a wealth of iron grey hair, a shrewd but kindly face, and a pair of penetrating blue eyes that looked out at one, rather disconcertingly at times, from under his shaggy Scotch eyebrows. At the railroad station he informed me that although he himself was convinced that my tale bore the stamp of authenticity, before any expensive operations could be undertaken, the lay-out would have to be looked over. He expressed himself as being prepared to see something a little unusual, but I will never quite forget the look on his face when, on arriving at the lake I called the beaver out, and swimming beneath the surface and unobserved by him, they suddenly popped out of the water beside him, climbed into the canoe, and gave him a very thorough examination. They mussed up his clothes but he cared little. The beaver were as represented, and that was that.

He stayed two days, and during that time the beaver were constantly in and out of the cabin. The beavers' actions had seemed very matter of fact to me having, during nearly three years, gotten over the novelty of the situation, but this official told me frankly that there was nothing to parallel it anywhere, and that something must be done about it immediately before anything happened to the beaver. I told him the story of McGinnis and McGinty and how they had been the moving spirit behind this endeavour. He was quite moved by the recital and said that such a thing must not be allowed to happen again. However nothing was decided, save that when he left, he told me to expect a moving picture outfit to arrive within a few days.

In less than a week the cameras were grinding away while Jelly and Rawhide swam, dived, walked, ran, hauled sticks around, climbed in and out of a canoe, and did besides a hundred and one other things that no one had ever seen a beaver do before, and which formed the subject of the first beaver film of any account ever taken, "The Beaver People."

The difficulties connected with the filming of this first beaver picture were numerous. The operator who, in his enthusiasm, spent much of his time standing ankle deep in mud and water, and once slid waist deep into the creek, had little knowledge of beaver, and I had considerably less of picture taking, still or otherwise. The beaver were, however, very helpful, staying on deck all afternoon and acting very polite and interested, the main difficulty being to keep them far enough away from the cameras.

The picture was released and later in the year the official who had first approached me paid us another visit, and stated that he was now in a position to offer me the protection I so much desired for the beaver. The picture, he said, had been received with acclamation all over the Dominion, and was to be shown in all civilized countries. And you can bet us beaver people were a proud bunch.

The history of this endeavour, apart from the results achieved, had been considered to be deserving of recognition, and it had been arranged, pursued my visitor, that I might continue with the work I was now engaged in, under the auspices of the Dominion Government, and at a regular salary. The safety of the beaver would be guaranteed as long as they should live, and they would never be taken from me; they would never be made the object of political issues or of any form of experimentation, and the administration and their increase, if any, would be left entirely in my hands. Further, I would be given every opportunity to carry out my conservation ideas in a dignified and constructive manner, without the necessity for anxiety as to the means. A house would be built for Anahareo, to be designed according to our own plans. The beaver would be supplied with all the apples they could eat, and in return certain duties would be expected of them. They were to afford opportunities for research to students of wild life and natural history, and for scientific observation, and it was considered that the contribution they would make to a more general public knowledge of our national animal, would constitute them a valuable educational exhibit of national importance and would provide a living argument for conservation. I myself would become a servant of the Government of Canada.

He skilfully drew me out, this earnest grey haired gentleman, and influenced by his utter friendliness and his attitude towards Indians, animals and all of nature, I told him of my ideas and aims, and of the bitter struggle it had been to keep on with them after such devastating failures. He listened in grave silence and when I had finished said, "You're the man we want." And from his further conversation I gathered that my activities had been under observation for some time past. And with his infinite tact and consideration he somehow made it appear that the gain would be his, that he was the petitioner, when my anxiety on behalf of my dependents must have been so very plain to see. But he did not hurry me, and went away leaving it in my hands to decide. And after I saw him off at the station, I went back behind the Elephant Mountain and thought it over.

It was the chance of a lifetime; yet the decision was a momentous one to make, and I gave the matter long and deep consideration.

Outside of forest ranging and guiding I had never had a job of any kind. If I embraced this opportunity, with all its multitudinous advantages, it would seem to mean the absolute surrendering of my freedom, might put an end to all my wanderings in the wilderness. It all seemed very final and a little frightening and unexpected. Yet did I remain true to what I deemed to be my obligations, all thought of liberty must be given up. And two things stood out compellingly and clear as light; my object, which had seemed at last so unattainable, was now within my grasp, and my two small friends would be forever beyond the power of any one to harm, free for all time from the haunting fear of death, that is the inescapable heritage of the beaver folk. These were the main issues; all others dwarfed beside them.

And so I chose aright for once, and today am freer than perhaps I ever was before, and have a little kingdom all my own, so far as any one is here to tell me different.

And when I penned my letter of acceptance, turning over the beaver and myself to National Parks of Canada to do with as they would, I asked that we, the beaver and I, should never be parted, and that if I should ever find McGinnis and McGinty that I would be allowed to take them too; for here was one door that I could never bring myself to close.

Both these requests were granted.

And thus I attained the consummation of my long thwarted desires and in a way I never dreamed of; not owing to any act of mine, not through any startling demonstration of ability on my part, not altogether on account of anything I said or wrote, save as might have sprung from the natural and orderly process of forces that are always greater than we, or than anything of our devising, but by reason of the vision and fore-sight of others.

Long months, years of privation in pursuance of a principle, of futile tilting at lifeless and unimpressionable windmills, were bearing rather unexpected fruit. The tide of my affairs, that had ebbed so steadily, had turned to some effect; for there were other matters, of which later. I had read that the law of averages was invincible. I could now believe it. Emerson wrote that the effect blooms in the cause, that no sustained effort, good or bad, but had its inevitable complement of reward or pun-ishment—an interesting but debatable theory that had no place in real life, apparently, and was only to be accepted by anyone in a philosophical frame of mind. But it had worked out, in this instance, and at a time when I had been ready to brand it, in my own mind, as a lie. The dark cloud that lurked behind every silver lining, I could always detect with great precision. Today, Emerson's "Compensation" is one of my favourite and most consoling pieces of literature in times of stress, and although much of it is yet beyond my comprehension, I read it with increased profit at every sitting.

ᔕᔕᔕ

AND NONE OF IT COULD HAVE BEEN MADE POSSIBLE without the whole-hearted and vigorous, if unwitting co-operation of two homely, clumsy-looking, wilful and mischievous, yet lovable beasts.

Less than a week after the arrangements were concluded and I was to prepare myself to move, these contrary creatures suddenly absented themselves from me and all my works, and were, with no warning at all, frozen into their lodge for the Winter.

They were now as far out of my reach as if they had been in China.

CHAPTER FIVE

How We Left Rawhide Lake

IT WAS A DREARY WINTER. AFTER THE BEAVER PEOPLE HAD paid me their last visit and danced for the last time their bizarre Pleasure Dance upon the landing, and had retired to their skillfully constructed hut at the head of lake, I found it none too easy to adjust myself. The companionship of these fun-loving, bustling little workers had become more or less indispensable to me in and around the lonely camp at the outlet, and the knowledge that they would spend the Winter in comfort and security on the fruits of a Summer of intense industry, did little to lift the pall of solitude that immediately fell upon the landscape. The den that I had so carefully improved and lined with marsh hay remained untenanted, and the big new tank, especially made for them, sat in gloomy and resounding emptiness in a corner. The constantly recurring thought that my two retainers, now full grown and entirely beyond my influence, would revert to the wild state, and that answering neither call nor entreaty would go sailing by on the Spring flood to the same fate that had befallen the other small adventurers, cast a gloom over the sunshiny days of early Winter.

Many were the pilgrimages made to the tall snow-shrouded house at the far end of the lake, and often I carefully opened up the white coverlet and spoke through the hollow air-space beneath it, the well-known words and phrases that so far had never failed to provoke weird contortions and sounds of joy. But now no sound rewarded me save the echo of my own voice across the empty solitude. Yet beneath that conical white

395

mound that stood high above the level of the wind-swept muskeg was life, and two plump furry bodies lay sleeping soundly and pitifully in fancied security, little knowing that the very defences on which they so depended, served but to advertise their presence to every passing vandal. Well I knew that did I betray my trust and neglect to guard these living creatures committed to my charge, they would never see the Spring. And I swore that if any power on earth could save them I would invoke it, if I mortgaged my entire future to do so.

And then one never-to-be-forgotten day I found a hole, cut with an axe, in the thin ice beside the beaver house. A heavy storm was on, effectively obliterating all tracks in the open muskeg. Scraping away the accumulated snow from around the opening, I found a crimson stain—blood!

In five swift seconds I reverted to the savagery of forgotten ancestors and turned my faculties loose on that hunt supreme, the man-hunt. Out in the open the tempest baffled me, but in the shelter of the timber I found the indications I was looking for, undoubtedly left in such a manner as to be confusing to one who followed. This man knew his business well, but not quite well enough. A fugitive who once sets his snowshoe, or his foot, into the high and narrow coping of piled up snow that covers a fallen tree at any elevation, has made an impression, a slot that no snowstorm, or any number of snowstorms, can ever quite fill in. And even if he undertake to do this himself, he can by no means reproduce the strata of the successive storms that made it.

Fortunately for all concerned he had at least two hours the start of me and was now at home, safe for the moment. I spun a web of evidence from odd tracks, and later by careful questioning in the village, spotted out my man. As to my intentions, had I finally proven the case to my own satisfaction, the less said the better. Suffice it that a timely thaw revealed, at some distance from the lodge, the mangled body of a muskrat, evidently killed by an owl, as the head was missing and the body roughly skinned. Hearing of this the suspected hunter sought me out and told me how he had cut open a rat hole near the beaver house to get a drink, and had then noticed the nearby bloodstain. Realizing the construction that might be placed on this, he had feared to carry out his intention of paying me a visit, and depending on the storm, had tried to mask his trail.

But for two weeks I had suffered the mental tortures of the damned, while I laid plans, carefully and cold-bloodedly conceived, that could have ruined three lives, if no worse, and have sealed the beavers' fate in reality. And my dreams have often since been troubled with the picture of it.

And so ended the Mystery of the Murdered Muskrat, in which, for once, I rather out-sherlocked myself.

From then on I worked systematically; and around the little valley I drew a circle on my snowshoes, with the lake for its hub, which none could cross without discovery and within it kept a hard packed trail between the cabin and the lodge, on which a flying trip could be quickly made; the trail of the Beaver Patrol.

The small receiving set had now become an important factor in my life, for here was an inexhaustible supply of company and music on tap, and I went to much trouble to keep the batteries replenished, drawing them in and out on the sleigh at frequent intervals.

When Christmas came I went out, but my heart was not in the festivities of the generous family that had me for a guest, so I spent New Year's at the cabin, listening to the celebrations on the radio. I had by now got into the way of keeping these festivals in some kind of a way, and at midnight, aroused by the announcements that came to me from out this blind man's theatre, and stirred by the knowledge that the whole world was enjoying itself, I did not see why Rawhide Lake should be left out of it. So I turned on the electric torch and let it stream through the window, down on to the frozen lake, and in the spotlight of its beam I stood at the water hole and fired a few shots in the air, and yelled a little. And I fired one shot straight and true to the Eastward, towards the far off House of McGinnis and its helpful happy ghosts, and another over the beaver house, and yet another into the North, towards Chibougamou, where my prospector was. And on each bullet I breathed a message, and sent it out into the vast emptiness of the New Year's night.

Meanwhile, between patrols, I wandered through the uplands and followed the old disused lumber roads to see what lay at the end of them; but it was like wandering through an empty haunted house. There was never anything but an old deserted camp surrounded by stumps and stark dead trees, ghosts of a forest that was gone. There were small blocks of timber, and here and there a lone pine tree, diseased perhaps and spared on that account. I always made my dinner fire near one of these and tried to feel at home. But it was beyond my imagination; they were destined for the axe in any case and I could only pity them. And on leaving I would look back a dozen times at the moving smoke of my lunch fire, as though it were something there that was alive and kept the old tree company when I was gone. All Northern people loved the pine trees, perhaps because those of us of any age at all, had lived the forepart of our lives amongst them. Now, as we followed the receding waves of this vanishing frontier further and further North to where pine no longer grew, we found them to be rare, and missed them. Even David, with his stern repressions, allowed this feeling to escape him once. We had come across a giant pine, four feet across the stump maybe, towering in dignified aloofness high above the trashy second growth of popple and willow by which it was surrounded, standing there mighty in its loneliness, like to some ancient warrior who has awakened from centuries of sleep, to find his comrades gone and his course beset by an innumerable horde of weaklings. And Dave took his light axe from his belt and cut away from the roots of the great conifer, and for a space all around the foot of it, the parasitic growth of rubbish that had accumulated there.

"Dam' things," he mumbled, half ashamed. "They'll kill 'um; only decent tree in the country."

There were not even any wolves here, and a country without them seemed lacking in some strong ingredient. I missed their wild cantatas, and the lazy inbred deer, lacking any incentive to move around and improve themselves, died like rabbits all through the woods.

In town I met one Indian. Civilization had surely gotten in its work on him. He had a broad Cockney accent, and a large repertoire of shanty songs which he rendered most entertainingly. He was more or less of a hobo and was well versed in his art. He could size up a store full of people and pick his prospect unerringly, extracting from him a nickel, a dime, or a quarter, or whatever he appeared to be good for, before the astonished victim quite realized what it was all about. He was a great thief, so he told me with some pride, but as he was on his uppers and his company might be entertaining, I had him stay with me a while. He practised none of his accomplishments on me, and was a good worker around the place, and weaved some very fine baskets from strips he skilfully pounded out of ash timber, and dyed. But he was afflicted with what he termed "itchy feet," a malady which could only be alleviated by the soothing contact of long stretches of railroad ties, applied at regular intervals. So one morning, with one of his small baskets filled with supplies he set out, bound for no particular place, singing happily as he went, a piece of drift flung from the spinning flywheel of Modernity, a shred of waste material spewed from the bowels of the Machine that would some day engulf us all. And as he disappeared, this cheerful vagabond, amongst the trees along the out-bound trail, his song echoing back behind him, I remembered that he belonged to the oldest civilized of all the tribes. The wild freedom of his ancestors that had made them something noble, perverted, was come to this.

No son should ever be mine to rear to such a heritage.

And then one day I returned from patrol to find sitting in the cabin waiting for me, Anahareo! She had come out to civilization by plane. We had much to talk about, and we talked about it,—plenty. Although she was prepared, by my few letters, to hear that my attempts to recover McGinnis and McGinty had been unsuccessful, when I told her that there had been no trace of them, no sign, nothing—and when, to prove to her how thorough had been the search, I described the history of the past year and a half, and told her straight that there could be no longer any hope,—she did not trust herself to speak, just held the relics in her hand and looked at them. And she stayed so for a long time, turning the dry, dead keepsakes over and over on their buckskin wrapper, and at last said softly:

"Don't let's ever forget, will we, eh? Never?"

Her greatest wish could now never be accomplished, and save at Christmas, in commemoration of that one unforgettable Christmas Eve on faraway Birch Lake, she never mentions our little old companions that are gone. Nor do I ever trespass on this silent remembrance which is hers.

As to her own affairs, her tale was quickly told. The Depression, so soon to make itself felt the world over, was already on its way. The mining business had not been what it was cracked up to be; her claims, any claims in fact, were unsaleable, and had become something in the nature of a whole herd of white elephants. They were eating up money faster than she could earn it, so she had relinquished them, and had got out of the country while she still had the price to do so. But her joy at all the good news I had for her made these matters of small moment, in her estimation. She had had what she called her "fling" and was satisfied. But there was a note of sadness in her triumph when she spoke of Dave. Some busy-body, full of ideas of uplift and education of the savage mind, had painstakingly explained to him that his long cherished belief that somewhere beyond the Northern horizon there existed a vast unexplored hunting ground, was a delusion; that the white people had penetrated to the furthermost recesses of the wilderness, and that the end had been reached, that there were no more beaver, no more pine trees; it was all a myth. No one cares to break the faith of a simple man, but this reformer had gone to some trouble to convince his victim, and had succeeded only too well in administering, over a course of months, doses of poison from the tree of knowledge. Although there existed, and still exists, some foundation for his ideas, Dave had only half believed in those things; but this stark and utter disillusionment, together with the loss of his fortune so nearly won, had ruthlessly tumbled his house of cards about his ears. His dream shattered, his last hope gone, he had brooded and fallen into a melancholy from which he could not be aroused. The spring of his vitality had dried within him and he had seemed to wilt and wither; his age had come upon him all at once, and left him a weary, unhappy old man.

And one night, not long before the falling of the leaves, he had come to bid Anahareo good-bye. He was going home. And with his canoe—my last gift to him, a tiny outfit, his beloved gun, and his recollections, he had paddled away into the calm moonlight night, on his way back to the scenes of his childhood, broken, hopeless, and alone.

The Winter was not without event. The book was accepted, and it had been published practically verbatim, except the title, which had been altered. The results were numerous and interesting. Small amounts began to percolate into the bank. The workings of a bank account were, and are yet, a puzzle to me, and although these amounts were quite small and continue to remain so, I found writing cheques on the brilliantly printed slips provided, an exciting and adventurous pastime. We both got a great kick out of having the people at the other end accept them. Moreover there was the delightfully informal correspondence entered into on occasions when the sums indicated on these gay coloured tokens were in excess of the funds. I have since, however, succeeded in working out a system whereby I can forecast this contingency quite accurately. My writings began to appear in different publications. Some editors, and kindly, wished to make changes in my work, substituting for my faulty phrasing, constructions more in accordance with correct usage. But these alterations seemed somehow to destroy the effect I attempted to produce, and unable to adjust myself to the higher standards so set up, I objected strenuously. After some lively discussions back and forth, by mail (exhilarating and quite safe) my requests were acceded to, probably more to put an end to the correspondence than anything else. I imagine that some of my letters on the subject must have been carried out of the office by means of a pair of tongs and dropped, with some relief, into the incinerator. My obvious amateur standing no doubt protected me, and editors, it seems, can be not such bad fellows after all.

I received numbers of press notices. Most reviewers, realising perhaps my lack of technical knowledge, were kind and let me down easy, even praised me. Some of them, perhaps to see how far I would go, encouraged me to try again, and in some American and English newspapers my work was given several columns of favourable comment. Letters came from Germany, Australia, London and New York; a Canadian college in Ontario—my home Province—gave it recognition. I felt elated, yet somehow apprehensive—I had started something; I had fired an arrow, wildly, in the air and it had come home to roost, and in great feather. One or two critics, (or perhaps I should be more precise and say, one critic), mildly scandalized apparently, that an uncultured bushwhacker of acknowledged native blood should so step out of character and become articulate, were more severe. They seemed to take it as a personal affront that there were in existence beings who, without benefit of education, had common knowledge of many things not taught in halls of learning, casting, by implication, some doubt on my knowledge of a subject with which they themselves could have had but little acquaintance; quite as though they were, by some divine right, omniscient. They probably did not realize that the rather standardizing influence of an intensive education militates

somewhat against the development of an ability to grasp the more subtle
and elusive nuances of a culture peculiar to the Wilderness.

And then, unkindest cut of all, came an accusation that most of the
text had been the work of a ghost writer. On discovering the meaning of
this, and not having the poise of those who affect to be "rather amused"
when unjustly censured, I had a few strait moments with myself; so it was
not I that wrote the book, but two other fellows from Utica N.Y., or perhaps a man from Aberdeen—after all my sweating, conniving, contriving, and conspirating with that dictionary, the synonyms and the
"System"! I love the simpler things of life; homely useless dogs, cheap cigars, clothes and music that are a little out of date, and men that sometimes forget to remember that they are God's greatest feat of creation. A
menu written in a foreign language adds nothing to the elegance or
flavour of a repast, to me, nor does the shape of the dishes or the colour
of the food. Therefore it can be easily seen that this broadside, delivered
by such a connoisseur, struck well below the water-line. However,
Shakespeare had, it appeared, something the same trouble with a man of
the name of Bacon, yet he had done quite well at the writing business.
And as to the imputation, made a trifle scornfully, that I must be possessed of some high form of erudition to have accomplished anything,
that I somehow must be cheating, that I was, in fact, stepping rather out
of my class as one of the unchosen,—Emerson was again good enough to
come to my rescue with a passage, taken from his "Self-Reliance":

"They cannot imagine how you aliens have any right to see—how you
can see. 'It must be somehow that you stole the light from us.' They do
not yet perceive that light, unsystematic, indomitable, will break into any
cabin, even into theirs."

Moreover, I was much comforted by the reflection that there is always
the odd one who would not have us see the light save through his own
particular knot hole, and who would undertake to categorize us all, and
put us in our little box and lock us in there.

In other words, I was having the time of my life.

There were other developments; my mail increased to alarming proportions. The world, I found, had a number of very wonderful people in
it, and some of these letters made me feel that I was at last emerging

from the role of despoiler and had joined, even if in a very minor capacity, the ranks of the producers. These acknowledgments of appreciation made us both very happy. It was not now so much like shouting blindly out into the darkness. Our aims were actually considered sane and reasonable. Some of this correspondence was a little unmanageable; a lady from Chicago whose husband was in gaol, suggested that we spend less of our energies on animals, and offered as an alternative that we shelter her until her erring spouse should be released; this would, in her opinion, constitute a worthy effort on behalf of suffering humanity.

Representatives of various sects addressed to me a voluminous correspondence, each suggesting that I adopt his particular faith. These communications left me in something of a quandary, as the only way in which I could have accommodated them all was to have divided myself up amongst them; and as each was so sure he was the only one that was on the right trail, it was all a little bewildering. It perhaps did not occur to these good people that I might have a creed of my own that made for honesty of purpose, reverence, and the love of my fellow man, as much as any one of theirs did. Some of these condemned me for my love for animals, telling me to look to my own soul. I do not venture to drive a bargain with God, and feel that if I do the right thing by my fellows, human and animal, my soul will be adequately cared for. I think that God must sometimes feel sorrowful and perhaps a little hurt to find himself so misunderstood that countless numbers of good people, whilst scrambling fervidly to provide themselves with safe conduct to the hereafter, look with a kind of self-complacent disdain on the rest of His works that they, not God, have pronounced to be soulless, and even look with distaste, if not with actual hostility, on any form of worship which differs from their own which they, not God, have devised. These people could not divine that this devotion sprang from a reverence for all the works of Him whom they themselves worshipped, though perhaps in a little different way—He, who to us was not the awful unapproachable Presence of more than one of their theologies, but was the Unseen Musician whose melodies whispered in the singing of the pine trees, or resounded in the mighty symphony of the tempest; Whose purpose was made manifest in the falling of the leaves and in their budding, and in the ceaseless running of the waters, and in the rising and the setting of the sun—Who could point a lesson in the actions of a lowly animal. Religion has always seemed to me to be simple and spontaneous, and any involved or mechanical, stereotyped creed a travesty of truth; while, to some, prayer can become little more than servile solicitation.

Interviewers appeared who put us gently through our paces. We were invited to a convention in Montreal; I was supposed to speak. Having, with great difficulty, though with no great certainty, persuaded Anahareo that she would not be called on, I finally persuaded her to accept her end of the invitation, and come along to supply the well known moral support. We arranged for a couple of friends to undertake the beaver patrol and went down together. The train drew into the city by some back entrance or other, and the portentious and over-powering gloom of huge industrial buildings just about had me buffaloed, as I realized that this appalling pile of stone and iron was the city that I was to electrify with my remarks. However, as with a war-bonnet, the front view of it was better than the back, and Mr. Dallyn, the editor who had done so much for us and who was now our host, was seated in the audience with Anahareo, and as he had suggested, I addressed my speech to them, the rest listening in at their own risk. Here we saw the beaver picture for the first time.

From now on I met and conferred with many conservationists, professed and real. The genuine conservationist was unmistakeable, and I made a number of worth while and highly instructive contacts, not a few of which still continue. But some of these gentlemen, while enthusiastic, were faintly ridiculous in their insistence on getting full credit for every word said or written by them for their cause, while we could not see that it mattered a great deal who said or wrote what, so long as we got results. On the whole, the attitude of these individuals was rather suggestive of the peculiar egoism of some actors that we hear about, who stoop to petty subterfuges to draw attention to themselves, losing sight of the production as a whole. It seemed to be a custom, none the less, to introduce a speech, and sometimes an article, with a few disclaimers of a self-deprecatory nature with the obvious intention of enlisting the sympathy of an audience or a reader; a kind of crafty modesty which detracted greatly from the force and dignity of an otherwise well-turned argument.

There was a rather depressing suspicion that others were interested in no measures in which the subdued rustle of currency was not somewhere audible; and there is a melancholy fear that the left hands of a good many of these gentlemen were well advised of what their right hand was about to do, a couple of good jumps in advance. Listening to their conversation I began to see the difference between a line of credit and a credit line, and came to realize that, in the words of a famous comedian, the dollar will never go so low as the means some people will adopt to get it.

But by far the greatest part of my contacts were with sincere and earnest men who had the situation with regard to wild life very much to heart, and I formed many associations that were an inspiration and that formed the basis of more than one friendship. I was approached by groups who, honest enough in their intentions, wanted to get in on this venture, supposing me to be a prosperous fur farmer, and they smiled knowingly when I said that I did not intend to use commercially whatever knowledge I might in time accumulate.

With regard to an issue so new and having as yet no definite policy, arguments were inevitable. Some thought that all remaining timber should be turned over to commercial interest, the practice of reforestation being their platform. I gave as my views that reforestation, whilst it should be carried on intensively was not preservation but substitution, and that in face of the fact that it took a hundred years to grow a respectable tree, its undue propagation as a sole means of restitution, amounted to an attempt to run a bill with the nation which would not be payable for a century or so, by which time, it seemed to me, the debtors would be safely out of it, and would care little who was to foot the bill. These kitchen garden forests, I urged, whilst as necessary to the development of the country as were fields of grain, could never replace the magnificent forests of great trees that they supplanted, citing, in support of my contention, the notorious example of Green Timbers on the Pacific Highway. Others thought that fur farming solved the wild life problem, which I was persuaded it never could do, save commercially, and added a statement I had heard on the radio, to the effect that the value of wild life as a tourist attraction in the United States, was worth some hundreds of millions of dollars yearly, asking my opponents what they thought of that for a commercial enterprise. It was all a matter of opinion and these discussions were very stimulating, and while my opponents could not always agree with my rather radical views, they broadened my perspective considerably, and enabled me to grasp other points of view besides my own.

I had offers, highly remunerative some of them, but none that could afford the beaver the same protection that National Parks had guaranteed. Other lectures were awaiting my acceptance but I dared not leave my wards too long in the care of a substitute, and was obliged to refuse them all.

Meanwhile, in advices received from Ottawa, we learned that Jelly and her leading man had attracted wide attention, not only at home, but overseas and across the border, of which they were supremely unconscious as they lay snoring together in their castle of frozen mud.

In March we commenced our campaign for their recovery, for we had no idea what would be their attitude towards us after five months spent in seclusion and entirely beyond our influence. We commenced by cutting a hole in the ice near the feed raft, and found it to have been nearly consumed, and this we replaced at intervals with fresh birch, poplar, and willow, which was always taken away piecemeal, though we never saw a beaver.

April came and with it warm days, melting snows and shaky ice. It now became necessary to, if possible, re-establish communication with our long absent friends. Being now two years old, and having been completely out of contact with human beings for five and a half months, and at a phase in their lives during which they usually desert their own home and parents and branch out to establish for themselves, I doubted much but that their spirit of independence might be stronger than memory or affection. My experience with beaver, although wide and life-long, had not hitherto included any such situation as now presented itself. None the less I designed and filled in the specifications for transportation tanks and boxes, and carried on my preparations for the removal with all confidence. I have found that a vacillating and uncertain attitude of mind in dealing with animals appears to communicate itself to them, especially the highly perceptive wild creatures who seem to possess a sixth sense, of which I had already had sufficient demonstration to cause me to take it into some account.

We transported our entire equipment, save a few necessaries, to the railroad ready for shipment, and gave away all but a little of our remaining provisions. Having now burnt our bridges behind us, we went to work. We cut two holes in the ice opposite the lodge and placed in them a choice assortment of poplar and willow, already budding and succulent with sap commencing to rise in the warmth of the early Spring sun. This provision was persistently destroyed by the constant nibbling of the hungry muskrats, whom we frequently saw, and we as regularly replaced it.

At these holes we watched, turn about, from sunset till daylight, and one evening after about a week of this, during my turn of duty at this listening post, I saw the swirl and larger bubbles of the passage there of a beaver, and noted that although he eventually took away a stick, he passed around the hole several times, far enough back to be out of sight, apparently searching systematically for one that might protrude beyond the open water, in under the ice. I set the next bait further into the centre of the hole so as to be in plain view, but nothing was then taken till after dark. The reason for these manoeuvres was, I believe, greatly owing to the extreme sensitiveness of the eyes to light after a long period spent in darkness and much sleeping.

The weather turned soft and the ice began to give out along the shore line, and we took turns or sat hours together motionless, a little distance from the holes, calling softly with the inflections that had in the past always elicited a response, until on the third evening, after a preliminary and very lengthy inspection from under a hollow shelf of ice, a beaver broke water, emitted a long low call and disappeared with a mighty splurge. After perhaps a half an hour, during which we sat tensely waiting, calling at intervals, the beaver reappeared, swam uncertainly around for a few minutes, and being at last satisfied with our appearance, climbed out on the ice beside us and commenced the well-known and oft-repeated toilet—Jelly Roll, the Boss, in person; the same voice, the same clumsy waddle, and the same air of arrogant self-sufficiency as she took an apple, and shaking it back and forth with little squeals, ate it with evident enjoyment within reach of our hand.

Triumph! after nearly six months in the wild state she had returned to us, faithful as the seasons themselves. But I was dubious about my little wild fellow, who had stayed with me unasked and of his own accord, and whose gentle trusting ways had made his short stay with me so pleasant.

However we continued calling over two more nights, and once by the light of the young moon saw a dark object laying motionless on the water in the most distant of the holes. Jelly was beside us, fussing around our feet, and the shape of the floating object was unmistakably that of another beaver. That he was very much alive was evidenced by his abrupt disappearance at some movement. The next night he took an apple with every sign of confidence, and the following evening spent a considerable time out on the ice in company with the Boss and ourselves.

Again triumph; a wild beaver tamed by hand but never captive, he had come back to us from his natural state after nearly half a year of absence. Almost unbelievable it seemed, but there he was and not to be denied. The atmosphere brightened considerably after this, and I had no further doubt as to the outcome.

I went out to town and wired the National Parks Service that the beaver had surrendered themselves.

Now to capture them, remove them from a home to which they must have become attached, and to inflict on them the terrifying alarms and hardships of a journey of a thousand miles or more, without impairing this wonderful confidence and fidelity in the simple mind of a wild animal. You have but to fool them once or twice and the work of years becomes null and void; and only by the most delicate tact and diplomacy can the lost ground be recovered, if at all, especially with the more intelligent species.

I attempted to secure Jelly Roll the following evening, but she had so increased in size and strength that I found it impossible to lift her from the ground without a struggle, the very thing I wished to avoid. We both tried it without success; we could pull her ears, open her mouth, yank her tail and roll her on her back, do anything in fact that we pleased, but this lifting business was now strictly against the rules. So a wooden box was constructed and laid on its back, with the lid lying flat and facing the water, and into this, all unsuspicious, walked the Boss. With the guilty feelings of those who betray a friend, even if only for his own good, we promptly stood up the box and clapped down the lid. Swiftly adjusting the tump line we were quickly away with our load. Voiceless, motionless, the Boss stood the gaff until liberated in the camp, when the first dumb bewilderment gave way to wild clutchings and wailings as she seized hold of parts of my apparel. Her fright was quite pathetic, and she had to be pacified and reassured almost as much as a child would have been, and nothing would now do her but that I should pick her up like the big tub she was, while she buried her head in my clothing. Gradually she commenced to look around, and finding herself in familiar surroundings eventually recovered her composure.

Rawhide was a good deal harder to capture as he would not enter the box, and on this particular night had decided not to leave the water. But I eventually got my hands on him and he submitted quite docilely to being carried away, and was a good deal easier to handle than Jelly had been. The beaver made no attempt to escape during the night and slept soundly with us in the blankets, and the next morning they submitted quietly to being placed in a ventilated tin box provided for the purpose, and all hands hit the trail for town.

We said good-bye to the empty cabin and the now deserted lake that had been our home for almost two years, and we were not a little lonesome as we trudged over the snowshoe trail drawing our living freight behind us, leaving behind us forever, somewhere, those that I had stayed here so long to seek. My search, carried on hopelessly for two years, was over; and yet the thought persisted that they were not dead, that we were deserting them, leaving our task undone. So it was in silence and with dragging feet, that we followed the trail that we had come to know so well, and even the stern mountains seemed to look down on us in sorrowful reproach at our desertion.

The Quebec Government had waived all rights in any of our pets, and the permit, as promised, called for four beavers. But in the big tank so carefully designed, there were two extra places that were empty.

A deputation of citizens came to see us off and we left real friends behind us in that town. And as the train pulled out at last, we stood hand in hand on the step of the hindmost car, never moving, never speaking, watching Temiscouata and its mountains slowly fade from view.

෴ ෴ ෴

AU REVOIR NOS AMIS, GAY, HOSPITABLE, EVER HAPPY, SINGING French Canadians.... *Bon voyage.*

Good-bye Elephant Mountain, farewell House of McGinnis; sleep on little friends, Nitche-keewense,—Little Brothers, sleep on——

CHAPTER SIX

How the Pilgrimage was Ended

IT IS NOW FALL, THE TIME OF HARVEST, AND THE QUEEN AND her little band are busy gathering in supplies against the long Winter, as are the more responsible and useful members of society everywhere.

Landings have been reopened and runways cleaned out, and into them with uncanny accuracy trees fall crashing at almost any hour from four in the afternoon till daylight. The feed raft that floats before the cabin[1] is getting daily heavier, wider, and more solid. Heavy logs are piled on it to sink it deeper, whilst on the under side the limbs and branches of the fallen trees and all the choicest portions, many of them

---

[1] These beaver are so attached to their human associates that they have taken advantage of a tunnel that was bored for their convenience when the cabin was built, and have constructed over the mouth of it, inside the residence, a large beaver house which occupies nearly one third of the floor space, is about twelve feet across, and would weigh not less than a ton. The beaver bring the building materials in through the door, which they are able to open from either side, and the entire family uses this erection as a permanent abode, summer and winter. From it they have egress into deep water through the tunnel, and they attach their feed raft to the front of the cabin, which abuts onto the lake. Having successfully adjusted their arrangements to suit these unusual conditions, they live and carry on their normal activities precisely as do their wild brethren. The adults have never been known to leave the body of water on which they are domiciled, though no restraint has ever been placed on their movements. The young, on attaining maturity, follow their natural course and spread out through the surrounding lakes and streams to mingle with the native beaver, and are frequently seen.

with a short projection used as a retaining hook, are secured below the reach of ice.

Heavily laden beaver swim slowly by separately, in groups, or all in line as on parade, their loads gaily caparisoned with sprays of coloured leaves like trappings—the Pageant of the Workers of the Wild. Sometimes I tune in on some symphonic orchestra, and they go sailing by in their steady slow procession to the martial strains of Zampa or the Polonaise, or slip silently along the shadowy surface of the water while the Moonlight Sonata weaves a spell about them—pictures in sound I wish that half the world were here to see.

At this season young beaver commence to perform some useful work, but up to this time few of the rules which govern adult beaver behaviour seem to apply to the kittens. They lead a happy carefree existence of playing, wrestling, and exploring. They roam the waters of the home-pond in pairs or groups, forming attachments amongst themselves, signalling with shrill cries when separated. They pester the older beaver at their work, and although this must be very exasperating, the adults show no sign of irritation, and will go to a great deal of trouble to avoid injuring them accidently. This is difficult as the little fellows seem to be always in the way of a heavy log or under a pile of limbs, or crowded together at the foot of a runway. They seem to be protected by the good luck that favours irresponsibles, and come out of every jam unhurt and looking for more excitement.

The passage near any group of them of a large beaver with a tow, is a heaven sent opportunity for excitement. With a concerted rush they attack the convoy, attaching themselves to the load, pulling at it, cutting pieces off it, climbing on the laden animal's back, or vainly trying to engage him in a wrestling match or some other aquatic sport. Such diversions serve to break the monotony of life on a small pond, but are a serious matter for the harassed object of this persecution, who takes it all in good part. The adults are not above resorting to such subterfuges as waiting motionless until the band of marauders disperses, or diving suddenly with the tow and swimming beneath the surface to dislodge them from it; but these stratagems seldom succeed, as at the first movement, or in the latter case on their reappearance from the depths, the parasitic little demons descend upon them, and pursue them until they have disposed of their load. A procession of this description, with its varied and tumultuous movement and attendant uproar, adds a gay and carnival-like air to the otherwise somewhat sober proceedings, but must take a considerable toll in energy and patience. However, as the season advances these corsairs cease their piratical activities, and direct their abounding energies into more productive channels, and can be seen hauling in their own small loads regularly and with great diligence.

The lively scuffling and tussling in which the kittens engage amongst themselves is often quite rough, though harmless. There is always one of their number who considers himself a match for two or three others, and some day he inevitably gets himself set upon by the entire crowd of youngsters. If this occurs on land where escape is difficult, he is quickly disillusioned of his vaunted prowess. Unable to stand the pressure, he will eventually make a dash for the water, throw himself in on head, back, side or whichever part arrives first, and sink like a stone out of sight. The incident seems to be soon forgotten, as these little animals take nothing very seriously and the deposed champion, on his return, is not further molested.

Most all day a complete and utter silence reigns upon the pond. But about an hour before sundown, first one then another black head breaks water, loud cries and signals echo back and forth, and soon the hitherto calm water and the deserted lake shore near the cabin becomes a scene of activity reminiscent of that to be seen around the old red school house at four o'clock.

It would seem that the task of identifying each and every beaver, all so similar in appearance, were well nigh impossible. It can, however, be done. Before two months of age they stick pretty closely to the house, during which period I put in my more intensive taming operations; after that time they develop individual characteristics of voice and action, or slight variations in shape which, if studied closely, make them recognizable. They seem to run in types, each brood exhibiting distinct personalities similar to those of the last one; so that there is always the Loud Talker, the Independent, the Mad Hatter, the Busy Appearing One, or the Lazy Bones, or the One That Stays Out Late. Before I got on to this I used to count as high as twenty beaver, as alike as peas or houseflies, when there were only four or six. Fortunately, although they are constantly on the move, they go in groups of two or three together, and there being only a limited number of them, I do not have to be in more than two or three widely separated places at the one time, in order to count heads before they switch places and intermingle.

We used to name all the new arrivals as soon as they began to be distinguishable, so we had Happy and Hooligan, Wakinee and Wakinoo, Silver Heels and Buckshot, Sugar Loaf and Jelly Roll Number Two, and a host of others, but eventually we ran out of names. They never answered to them anyway, but would always come to one particular call, a plaintive wailing note pitched in a close resemblance to a common signal of their own, though different enough for them to recognize its origin. This cry was a prolonged, "Mah—— W—e—e—e—e—e," given with a wavering inflexion, and its sound, repeated a few times, rarely failed to attract one or other of them, or at least elicit an answering hail. It became at last, by long usage, a kind of community name for them, and we came to call them, each and every one Mah-Wee; so if one was called they all came, a very convenient arrangement. This name was very suitable in more ways than one, as it is similar in sound to the Ojibway word signifying "to cry," a vocal expedient they made use of on the slightest pretext. Such, however, is their independence of character that once having put in an appearance, or given some more or less heedful answer to the summons, it would be some hours before they would again respond to it. They could, however, be depended on to appear at least three times a night and also for the usual morning check up when they returned to retire for the day.

The depredations continue as of yore. Often I enter the cabin after some lengthy absence on patrol to find my quarters have been invaded, and almost invariably some burglary has been committed. Perhaps a pot of potatoes has had the lid picked neatly off and every last potato taken out of it. Once these potatoes were in a stew and had had to be fished for. A beaver's hands are not made for fishing, but this difficulty was easily overcome by upsetting the stew-pot, with more or less gratifying results. Sometimes the woodbox has been emptied, a box of apples opened, or a chair hauled down into the lake, and being useless for any purpose, abandoned there. Dishes, apparently, are trophies of high value; unless fastened down, their rice dish is removed as soon as it is empty and is never seen again. Several have been lost that way, though one of them was, after three months, very politely returned one evening and was found, high and dry and very clean, up on the bank beside the house.

I returned from a perhaps too lengthy visit to a neighbouring Ranger's camp, and on going behind the cabin to collect some wood I had split for the night, found it to be all gone; also, some green poles collected for fuel were not to be seen. The interest aroused by these features prevented me from noting further and far more interesting developments till, finding the place kind of bare, I suddenly missed the store tent. Investigation revealed that it was down, and that most of the poles that had held it up had disappeared. Fortunately it had been empty. The stationary saw-horse, being made of green poplar, had been cut off close to the ground and spirited away bodily and never was seen again. This, of course, was the work of the Queen, levying taxes on the estate. There was nothing so unusual about this, except that it had been the only time that I had ever permitted myself to overstay.

I receive numbers of communications in regard to conservation and kindred subjects, and I have several bags filled with them, sorted into lots. Wishing once to look through one of these bags, I brought it into the camp and thoughtlessly left it standing in a corner. Being busy outside, I paid it no further attention for the time being until, looking for the letters, I found them gone, bag and all. A disturbance in the beaver house, which I had been wondering about in a detached sort of way, indicated that the booty had been brought in and was being forcibly divided. Screams and squeals of outrage in a well known voice apprised me of the identity of the thief, as Jelly struggled against hopeless odds to maintain her rights. The resultant uproar was little short of appalling, and the scene must have been ludicrous in the extreme as she tussled valiantly and vainly for the possession of her prize which, consisting of some hundreds of letters, was entirely beyond her control.

Perhaps she thought that having been for a long time now a Star of no mean magnitude, it was about time she had some fan mail of her own. Anyway that mail remains unanswered to this day but, as it was all used for bedding for the entire beaver family, it was utilized in a way that the writers never imagined in their wildest dreams. So these epistles are serving the purpose of Conservation after all, which is what they were originally intended to do in any case.

While the ice is making, the beaver succeed in keeping open a channel to their accessible cuttings, in which they tow supplies up to the last minute. The whole family breaks ice for several hours each day to accomplish this, succeeding in keeping it open for perhaps a week, but this watery highway eventually freezes over. Jelly then takes to frequenting the water hole, after one has been opened for our own purposes, and through it I give her quantities of apples, sometimes till nearly Christmas. She takes them all away, by relays, and on her return home the sounds of strife, followed by a steady and contented munching mingled with grunts of satisfaction in different keys, give evidence of her generosity to those who make up in appetite what they lack in enterprise. I surmise that air that is very frosty must cause discomfort to lungs acclimatized to soft weather and the humid atmosphere of a beaver house. I was led to believe this by the fact that in cold weather she never emitted any of her usual sounds of greeting when her head appeared, and closer inspection showed that on cold nights she never drew breath while in the open, which accounted for her hurried withdrawals. I now allow a scum of ice to form, and shove the apples under it. So I do not see her, but the apples disappear with monotonous regularity, until the arrival of more severe weather makes this practice inadvisable.

About a year and a half ago another subject was added to Jelly's fast spreading kingdom. A little daughter came to us. She and the Queen get along well together, but we do not leave her in accessible places, as Jelly's habit of appropriating articles which she takes a fancy to, might result in us having to open the beaver house and rescue a very wet and outraged young woman from the ministrations of her triumphant abductor.

Although Jelly is by about ten pounds the heavier, they are much of a size, and stand boldly up to one another and sometimes talk together. And as neither one of them can, as yet, speak any English, a conversation is held the like of which has not, I think, been ever heard before. The little girl is delighted when this big, dark furry toy, this good natured teddy-bear with the so pretty coloured teeth[1] takes an apple from her hand.

[1] The incisor teeth of a mature beaver are a dark orange in colour.

Gently the beaver takes the offering, with none of the tom-boy gambols she indulges in with us, and yet never so gently as Rawhide, humble, tireless, patient Rawhide, changeless and unchangeable as the courses of the Wilderness whose son he is, faithful as the rising and the setting of the sun. He never seems to mind his crippled foot that looks so odd beside the good one, and has perhaps forgotten how I nearly took his life. These matters are of small moment to him now; he has his work, his babies that he loves so unselfishly and, in his simple, wistful way he is happy. Sometimes, as he sits regarding me so quietly, so attentively and so inscrutably, I would give much to know what deliberations are going on behind that impassive mask, back of those grave, observing eyes.

For he is the silent power behind the Throne at Beaver Lodge, and should he some day decide to move his people away from here, no power on earth short of confinement or death could ever stop him. So it behoves me well that I should not offend.

He and Jelly are known, in some small way, in many countries, but they sleep on in unconscious innocence of their celebrity. And as they lie there snoring in contentment, I wonder if the Queen remembers the dingy camp in far off Temiscouata, the bed, the table, the deerskin rugs on which she used to sleep before the stove, the welcomes home she used to have for me. Or if she has ever a passing thought for the long lonely days before the coming of Rawhide, when we were such good company and often slept together, and how she used to "help" me get water, and would shut the door in my face; and how we wrote our book, and how she got lost and must have nearly died—and how Anahareo came back to us again.

Perhaps these matters are only a dim recollection now, and meanwhile she lords it over Rawhide and Anahareo and little Dawn and all the rest of us, and is content.

Epilogue

IT IS NOW THE MOON OF SNOWSHOES. ANAHAREO AND the small new daughter are spending the Winter out in town. The beaver are safely stowed away within their fortress. The visits and the begging and the frolics, the apple raids, the shoutings and the stealing are all over for the time, and all the queerities and oddities and individualities are laid away securely for the Winter. And I am lonesome for them all, and so I spend my time with them on paper. And as I re-read these badly jangled themes and disjointed phrases with which I try to write my recollections, I sometimes feel that I am only another good bushwhacker gone wrong. And then I call to mind the House of McGinnis, and its one time occupants and what we owe to them, and how through them our object was achieved. And so I must persevere.

And as I pen some dry precise report, in which I weigh my words and balance supposition with proven fact, and perhaps speak dubitatively of some things that I feel are true but have not yet established, I feel that I am giving all the best I have to this labour that has fallen to my lot—that I am keeping faith.

And I know, too, that my work which I had thought had reached its consummation, has only now begun.

Out on the frozen frontage of my cabin stands another lodge, a replica of the one indoors. It is at present empty. No doubt it will be put to some use, according to some plan the owners have, of which I anxiously await the fulfilment. This house-to-let is a pretty bleak and lonesome-looking erection, and emanates all the cold hostility that surrounds a residence whose tenants have decided to be not at home; and at times I feel rebuffed as I look at it in the pale glow of the Northern lights.

But on entering the cabin and hailing the invisible company who occupy the lodge that stands within it, I get a lazy mumbled answer to my call. I hear also a few whimpers of protest from bed fellows who enter sleepily into the age-old discussion as to who has all the bed.

Sounds of slumber issue from the bowels of the thick-walled lodge, as some tired worker rolls over on his back and snores prodigiously in the security he has worked so hard to earn, whilst he dreams, perhaps, of rows of shining poplar trees, of new, undiscovered streams, or of lake shores lined with apples.

And I know that all is well with my little company of fellow pilgrims, and that I also may now call it the end of a day.

And here they will always be, in the peace and quietness of their silent lake amongst the hills, till they pass on in the fullness of time to join the hosts of their brethren who have gone before them, leaving behind them others in their stead who may perpetuate, in each their turn and for all time to come, the ancient and honourable traditions of the Beaver People.

ᕗ ᕗ ᕗ

THE ROCK-BOUND MISSISSAUGA ROARS ON BETWEEN ITS palisades of pine trees. The Elephant Mountain still stands at the portals of Touladi. Somewhere in the wild Laurentian uplands are little mountain lakes on whose shores the ashes of my camp-fires still remain.

Some day I hope to see them all again.

And there are those with whom I must smell smoke once more and talk and reminisce of days gone by, of old landmarks and long remembered trails. I must speak again the language of the Ojibways, my adopted people, lest it be thought that I have forgotten. Once again I must hear the Mississauga Dance and tread a measure to the drum of Mato-gense, called Little Child, the Conjuror. For the call of the River comes often upon me, in the evenings, at dawn and when I am alone.

Some time, when the leaves are turning and the moose maples are flaring redly on the granite hills, I want to enter Bisco as I left it, in the night-time by canoe, and give the loud long whoop of the Laughing Owls, and hear it answered from the dwellings of a dozen Bisco men.

All these things will I do in the fullness of time, but it cannot be for very long.

My duty lies beneath these Western skies.

On all sides from the cabin where I write extends an uninterrupted wilderness, flowing onward in a dark billowing flood Northward to the Arctic Sea. No railroad passes through it to burn and destroy, no settler lays waste with fire and axe. Here from any eminence a man may gaze on unnumbered leagues of forest that will never feed the hungry maw of commerce.

This is a different place, a different day.

Nowhere does the sight of stumps and slashed tops of noble trees offend the eye or depress the soul, and the strange, wild, unimaginable beauty of these Northern sunsets is not defaced by jagged rows of stark and ghastly rampikes.

The camp is known as Beaver Lodge; yet to us it will always be a replica of that House, the Empty Cabin, that is so far away—a little richer perhaps, a little better built, but the spirit is the same. Save for the radio, the kitchen range, the shape of the roof, it is as near to it as maybe. It is built of logs; the windows face out on the groves of trees. A painted warrior stands post in his appointed place, his eagle bonnet spread in brave array; the paint work, the emblems, they have all been reproduced. The tokens are all here.

Atavistic? Perhaps it is; but good has come of it.

Every wish has been fulfilled, and more. Gone is the haunting fear of a vandal hand. Wild life in all its rich variety, creatures deemed furtive and elusive, now pass almost within our reach, and sometimes stand beside the camp and watch. And birds, and little beasts and big ones, and things both great and small have gathered round the place, and frequent it, and come and go their courses as they will, and fly or swim or walk or run according to their kind.

Death falls, as at times it must, and Life springs in its place. Nature lives and journeys on and passes all about in well balanced, orderly array.

The scars of ancient fires are slowly healing over; big trees are growing larger. The beaver towns are filling up again.

The cycle goes on.

The Pilgrimage is over.

Sajo and
the Beaver People

To
Children Everywhere
and to All
Who Love the Silent Places

Contents

I. The Land of the North-west Wind / 424

II. Gitchie Mee-Gwon, the Big Feather / 429

III. The Home of the Beaver People / 435

IV. The First Adventure / 442

V. Sajo's Birthday / 450

VI. Big Small and Little Small / 457

VII. The Trader / 465

VIII. Sajo Hears the Talking Waters / 471

IX. The Red Enemy / 477

X. The Empty Basket / 485

XI. White Brother to the Indians / 491

XII. The Big Knives / 500

XIII. The Little Prisoner / 507

XIV. Patrick the Policeman / 516

XV. Unto the Least of These / 524

XVI. Mino-ta-kiyah! / 535

XVII. In the Moon of Falling Leaves / 544

Glossary of Ojibway Indian Words / 553

CHAPTER ONE

The Land of the
North-west Wind

FAR, FAR AWAY BEYOND THE CITIES, THE TOWNS AND THE
farmlands that you are so used to seeing all about you, away beyond the
settlements of Northern Canada, lies a wild, almost unknown country. If
you wished to see it you would have to journey over the hills and far away,
to where there are neither railways nor roads, nor houses nor even paths,
and at last you would have to travel in a canoe with your Indian guides,
through a great, lonely land of forest, lake and river, where moose, deer,
bears and wolves roam free, and where sometimes great herds of caribou
wander across the country in such vast numbers that no one could possibly count them, even if he were there to do so.

Here, in this great Northland, you would see a part of North America
as it was before the white man discovered it, and as it will remain, I hope,
for many, many years to come. You would not see very many white people there, even today, for besides the few trappers and traders, the only
human beings that live there are the scattered bands of Ojibway* Indians
that have made this land their home, calling it the Land of Keewaydin,†
the North-west wind. They are a race of people so ancient, and they have
been there so long, that no one, not even they themselves, know where
they came from or how they ever got there. Far beyond the reach of civilization, they live very much as their forefathers did when Jacques

* Pronounced *O-jib-way.*
† Pronounced Kee-*way*-din.

Cartier landed on these shores over four hundred years ago. Their villages of teepees,‡ tents and sometimes log cabins, are still to be found, often a hundred miles apart, in sheltered groves and sunny openings in the woods, or beside the sandy beaches on some pleasant lake shore. In these small towns the Indian families live, each in its own dwelling, in happiness and contentment, well-fed in good times, going a little hungry when times are bad, as is the case with more civilized people.

Everybody in these villages has work to do; even the young people must do their share. Nearly all this work has to do with travelling, as Indians are constantly on the move. Some seasons, the animals on which the Indians depend for a living disappear out of a district, and the people must follow them or find new hunting-grounds, so that whole villages have to be pulled down, and everything (except the log cabins, of course,) must be loaded in canoes or on toboggans, according to the time of year, and moved for many miles. On these Winter trips little boys and girls take their turn at breaking trail on snow-shoes, feeling very proud as they lead the long procession of dog-teams and toboggans and people, for a mile or two at a time. In Summer they paddle all day in the canoes with the older people, and each has his or her small load to carry on the portages. They really enjoy their work, and they are just as serious and business-like about their tasks as are their parents.

Those of the Indian children who spend their summers near a fur-post or on a reservation, have an opportunity to go to school, and often make good scholars; some, indeed, become lawyers, others doctors, writers, or artists, and are very successful. But those of them who live the year round in the wild country have an education of another kind. The forest is their school, and in it they study the lessons so necessary to their way of life. Geography, history, or arithmetic or English would be of no use to them; their studies are plant and tree life, the ways and habits of animals and how to track them; how to catch fish at all times of the year and, most important of all, how to make fire in any kind of weather, such as rain, wind or snow. They learn the calls of all the birds and beasts, and can imitate some of them very well. They are trained to observe the movements of water in the rivers and lakes, so as to become skilful in the handling of

‡ Pronounced *tee*-pee.

canoes, and they learn the proper use of snow-shoes, guns and axes, and how to drive a dog-team besides such every-day tasks as sewing moccasins, tanning hides, and finding firewood in places where there looks to be none at all; and they must be able to cook. Such a thing as a compass is unknown to them, and they can travel anywhere they wish in the forest by means of the sun, stars, moon, shapes of trees, formation of the hills, movements of animals and many other signs far too numerous to mention here. Their knowledge of woodcraft is so great that they become very self-reliant, and are able to make long trips alone and face without fear many dangers, as did the Indian boy and girl in this story.

The Indian life is so hard and toilsome that no one in these villages can be lazy very long without quickly running short of food, clothing or shelter; and while the people will help one another and divide up whatever they may have, a lazy person is very much looked down on. Yet in spite of all this hard work, the younger people find much time to play their simple and very active games. Sometimes, after the day is done and darkness falls, they will sit out beneath the glittering northern stars, around the blazing camp-fires, and listen to the tales of their elders. Some of these tales are about hunting trips, or far-off tribes of Indians, or about great men of long ago; others are about strange adventures in the forest. But the strangest tales of all, to them, are told by those of the grown-ups who have visited that wonderful country so far away to the south, where the white people come from; where are great sleighs on wheels that run with the speed of wind over an iron trail, by which they mean the railroad, and where smoke-canoes, as they call steamboats, go nearly as fast on the water; where there are no Indians and not many trees, only rows of tall stone houses between which people walk in crowds, rushing, hurrying along, seeming to go nowhere and come from nowhere. A country, they are told, where if you have no money you cannot sleep or eat. And they find this last to be the very strangest thing of all, because in the woods travellers are always welcome to rest and eat in the camps of white trappers or in an Indian village, free of any charge. For these children, and most of the older people too, know as little about the necessities of city life as perhaps you do about their wilderness.

And now, as chance travellers from the distant settlements tell to these black-eyed, smiling Indian children stories of a land they have never seen, so I, who once was one of them, will tell to you a tale from that great wilderness that is so far away.

First, though, you must know that all through this forest that is so dark and mysterious, with its strange animals and people, there run a great many rivers, which are used as highways not only by the Indians in their swift canoes, but by many water beasts such as beaver, otter, mink and muskrats. And in the woods are countless trails, although perhaps you could never find them, on which the animals that live on land travel as though upon a road. For all these creatures are continually on the move. They, as well as the humans in this land, are always busy. They have their living to find or make, and their young ones to take care of and feed. Some live alone, with no settled home, and others keep together in large numbers, having good-sized towns tunnelled out beneath the ground, the different houses of each family joined, in groups, by passages. The very wisest among them, such as beaver, build themselves warm houses, store up water in which to swim, and put up large supplies of food for the winter months, working almost like men, often talking together when resting from their labours; and they all have, each in their own way, a great deal to attend to.

And on account of their cleverness and industry, the Indians, even though they must kill some of them in order to make a living, cannot help but respect these animals and take a great interest in all they do, looking on them almost as separate tribes of people, of a kind little different from themselves. Beavers are especially respected, and some Indians can understand to a certain extent what they are saying to one another, as their voices are not unlike those of human beings. All animals, however small or apparently useless, have their own proper place, and the Indians know this, and never bother them without good reason; and because they share with them the hardships of this forest life, they call them Little Brothers. Frequently they keep them as pets, and you will often see bear cubs, young beavers or perhaps an otter, or sometimes a calf moose or a deer running loose in an Indian encampment, free to go wherever they want, but staying around just because they feel at home and seem to enjoy the bustle and excitement of camp life. As they become full-grown, so they eventually wander away, but it is not for long that the village will be without pets of some kind or another.

And now that you know what the country is like and how the Indians live, and have heard a little about some of the animals, I will tell you a tale of the Little People of the Forest, a tale that is real, and has its beginning on one of those waterways I told you of, where lived a happy family of the Beaver People.

I will tell you about an Indian hunter and his young son and daughter, and of two small kitten beavers that were their friends. And you shall hear of their adventures in the great forests of the North, and in the city too; of what good chums they were, and how one of them was lost and found again, and about the dangers they were in and all the fun they had, and what came of it all.

And now we will clean forget the motor-cars, the radio and the movies and all the things we thought we could not do without, and we'll think instead of dog-teams, of canoes and tents and snow-shoes, and we'll journey to that far-off, magic land.

And there you'll see great rivers, and lakes and whispering forests, and strange animals that talk and work, and live in towns; where the tall trees seem to nod to you and beckon as you pass them, and you hear soft singing voices in the streams.

And we'll sit beside a flickering camp-fire in a smoky, dark-brown wigwam, while you listen to this tale of Long Ago.

CHAPTER TWO

Gitchie Mee-Gwon, the Big Feather

UP THE BROAD, SWIFT CURRENT OF THE YELLOW BIRCH RIVER, in the days before the eyes of a white man had ever looked on its cool, clear waters, there paddled one early September morning a lone Indian in a birch-bark canoe. He was a tall, gracefully built man with keen dark eyes, and long black hair that fell in two braids over his shoulders. He was dressed in a suit of fringed buckskin that had been smoked to a rich brown, and altogether he looked a good deal like those Indians you see in pictures, or read about.

His canoe was bright yellow, dyed with the juice of alders to the same colour as the stout, golden-tinted trunks of the yellow birch trees that covered the surrounding hills, and the seams along its sides were sealed with narrow strips of shiny, black spruce gum, to keep the water out. This canoe had a large eye, like that of some enormous bird, painted on the front of it, and behind, at the very end, was fastened the tail of a fox, which swayed gently back and forth in the breeze. For the Indian liked to feel that his canoe was actually alive and had a head and a tail like all the other creatures, and was sharp-eyed like a bird, and swift and light like a fox. In it there was a neatly folded tent, a small bag of provisions, an axe, a tea-pail, and a long, old-fashioned rifle.

From the tops of the birches on the hillsides there came a low whispering, a sound of rustling that never seemed to cease, as the wind played amongst the leaves, so that the Indians had named these highlands the

429

Hills of the Whispering Leaves. The river banks were lined by a forest of tall, dark pine trees, and their huge limbs hung out over the water, far above it; and along the shore beneath them robins, blackbirds, and canaries flew and fluttered, searching for their breakfast among the new grasses and the budding leaves of the pussy willows. The air was heavy with the sweet smell of sage and wild roses, and here and there a hummingbird shot like a brilliant purple arrow from one blossom to another. For this was May, called by the Indians the Month of Flowers.

Gitchie Meegwon,* the Big Feather, for such was the Indian's name, belonged to the Ojibway† nation. He had paddled against the strong current of the Yellow Birch river for many days, and was now far from his village. Steadily, day after day, he had forged ahead, sometimes moving along easily on smooth water as he was doing now, at other times poling up rough rapids, forcing his frail canoe up the rushing, foaming water and between jagged, dangerous rocks with a skill that few white men and not all Indians learn. This morning his way was barred by a waterfall, wild and beautiful, higher than the tallest pine trees, where the sun made a rainbow in the dashing white spray at the foot of it. Here he landed, just beyond the reach of the angry, hungry-looking whirlpool that tried very hard to pull his canoe in under the thundering falls. Picking up the canoe he carried it, upside down on his shoulders, over a dim portage trail between the giant whispering trees, a trail hundreds of years old, and on which the sun never shone, so shaded was it. He made a second trip with his light outfit, loaded his canoe, and out in the brightness and the calm water above the falls, continued his journey.

He glanced sharply about, as the bends in the river opened up before him, and saw many things that would have escaped the eyes of any one but a hunter; an exciting glimpse of a pair of furry ears pointed his way, the rest of the creature hidden; or of bright eyes that gleamed out at him from the shadows. Once he saw a silver-coated lynx fade like a grey shadow into the underbrush. Here and there deer leaped hastily away towards the woods, whistling loudly through their nostrils as they bounded like red rocking-horses through the forest, their tails flashing

* Pronounced *Git*-chie *Mee*-gwon.
† Pronounced O-*jib*-way.

like white, swaying banners between the trees. Once he came upon a great moose, as big as any horse, who stood chest-deep in the river, his head buried under the surface while he dug for lily roots on the bottom. As Big Feather paused to look at the moose who, busy with his task, had not heard him, the huge creature raised his head with a mighty splurge and stood there staring in surprise, while the water poured in streams from his face and neck. Then he turned and plunged ashore and soon was gone, though the heavy thudding of his hoofs and the sharp crack of breaking limbs and small trees could still be heard for a minute or two as he galloped crashing through the woods.

Even with all this company, Gitchie Meegwon was a little lonely, for back at the village, now so far away, he had left his two young children, a girl and a boy. Their mother had died, and while the women of the village were kind to them, they missed their mother very much, and he knew they must be lonesome too, as he was. The three of them were great friends and were seldom parted, and every place he went their father always took them. But this time he was alone, as this was likely to be a dangerous journey, for he expected to have trouble with some poachers before it was finished. Gitchie Meegwon had built a fine log cabin for his small family, for a Summer home, and there they had been happy and comfortable together, resting after the hard Winter's hunt, when word had been brought in by a friendly Cree Indian that a band of half-breeds from down near the settled country had invaded the region, and were killing all the beaver as they went through it in large parties. The real bush Indians do not hunt on each other's trapping grounds, considering such behaviour to be stealing, but these town-bred half-breeds had given up or forgotten the old ways, and were likely to clean out every trapping ground as they came to it. And without fur with which to buy provisions at the trading post, Big Feather's family would go hungry. So now he was up here, deep into his Winter hunting ground, to protect it from these strangers. But he had seen none of them nor any sign of them, and the weather being now warm, and fur-animals no longer worth stealing, he felt that his work was done, and tomorrow he intended to turn back for home.

With these pleasant thoughts in mind, he was passing along close to the river bank, watching for any tracks there might be left by the careless half-breeds, when all at once he smelt a strong, sharp scent upon the air— some beast, or perhaps a man, had passed nearby and crushed the spicy-smelling leaves of a mint plant. Instantly on the alert, he glanced quickly at the bank, when suddenly a short, dark, heavily built animal sprang out into the river right in front of his canoe and sank like a stone, out of sight. Almost immediately a black head and a brown, furry back came floating up a short distance away, and the creature swam rapidly round the canoe until, cleverly getting to a spot where the wind was from the Indian to himself, he caught the man-scent, that all the Forest People fear so much. Down came his wide, flat tail on the water with a terrific splash, the water flying in all directions as he dived like a flash, this time for good.

Big Feather shook a few drops from the sleeve of his leather shirt, and smiled; this was very much what he had wanted to see. It had been a beaver. And before the echo of the beaver's alarm signal had died away, there came another from around the next bend, sharp and loud, almost like a gun-shot. There were two of them.

The Indian smiled again, for now he began to feel sure that no one had hunted here. These beaver would have been only too easy to catch; if these careless fellows, who allowed him to get so close to them, right on a main highway so to speak, had not been captured, the rest of them must all be safe. Still, to make certain, he decided to visit their home, where there should be others. Their house would not be hard to find as beaver, when on their travels, cut small green saplings of alder, poplar, and willow here and there, eating the bark off them, and these peeled sticks show white and shiny every place they land, so a person has only to follow from one to another of these feeding places, to discover where they live. Very soon the Indian came to where a little stream ran down into the river, and at its mouth he found what he expected, a number of these slim, shining sticks, remains of a beaver's meal. No doubt their house would be somewhere up the little stream, in some quiet spot such as beavers love.

The beavers had eaten at the edge of a nice open point where a few giant pine trees stood about, as though they had wandered out from the forest and could not get back again. Here Gitchie Meegwon made a small fire and had his own noon meal. Indians drink a good deal of tea on their travels, so leaning a slim pole over the cheerful blaze he hung his tea-pail on one end of it to boil, the other end being stuck firmly into the ground to hold it in position; he arranged strips of deer-meat on sharp forked sticks, before the hot coals, and under them placed slices of Indian bread, or bannock as it is called, to catch the delicious gravy that fell from the meat as it cooked. After he had eaten he smoked quietly for a little time, listening to the humming of the breeze in the wide, fan-shaped boughs of the pines. Very like music it sounded to him, as he leaned back contentedly and watched the lazy smoke wafting this way and that, as it made strange patterns in the air. For these things were his pictures and his music, all he ever had, and he enjoyed them perhaps as much as you do your movies and your radio.

Soon, after covering his small outfit with the overturned canoe, he took his long-barrelled trade-gun and started up beside the brook, on his way to the beaver pond that he knew must be at the head of it. His moccasins made no sound, and left no track, as he walked softly in the quietness and calm of the sleepy forest, while squirrels shrilled and chattered at him from the boughs, and whiskey jacks, those knowing, cheerful camp birds to be seen nearly everywhere in the woods, followed him from tree to tree, sometimes getting ahead of him to peer wisely and whistle at him as he passed. He enjoyed the company these small creatures gave to him, and took his time and walked quite leisurely along. Suddenly he stopped, listening. His keen ears had caught a strange, unexpected sound, which quickly became louder and louder and was all at once a roar—and then he saw, coming swiftly down the creek bed towards him, a rush of yellow, muddy water, bringing with it a mass of sticks and litter which filled the banks to the very top and went pouring by in a wild, swirling torrent. Something terrible was happening up at the beaver pond! It could be only one thing; some man or beast, something, must have torn out the beaver dam, and this rushing torrent was the beavers' so carefully saved up water, without which they would be helpless.

In a moment, rifle in hand, Big Feather was leaping and tearing his way through the forest that had but a moment before been so pleasant, and seemed now so dark and threatening. Forward he raced at top speed, running on swift-moccasined feet to save his beaver colony from destruction, springing high over logs, smashing his way through wind-falls and branches and tangled underbrush, leaving the squirrels and the camp birds far behind him, bounding like a deer through the shadowy woods towards the pond, hoping he would be in time. Well did he know what had happened.

Negik, the otter, bitter and deadly enemy of all the Beaver People, was on the war-path and the beavers, their water gone, must even now be fighting for their lives.

CHAPTER THREE

The Home of the Beaver People

HAD WE WALKED UP BESIDE THAT BUSTLING LITTLE CREEK while Gitchie Meegwon was making his dinner, instead of waiting to watch him as we did, we would have arrived at the beavers' home before the otter broke the dam, and have seen what it was like up there and how the beavers lived. We would, after a rather long walk, have come out quite suddenly on the shore of a small, deep pond. Right across the front of this pond, and blocking the bed of the stream that came out of it, was a thick, high wall of sticks and brush. It was all very tightly woven, and the chinks were filled with moss and the whole business well cemented with mud. Along the top of it a number of heavy stones had been placed to keep it solid. It was nearly one hundred feet long and more than four feet high, and the water flowed over the top of it through a narrow trough of sticks, so that the stream was wearing away at it in only this one spot, where it could be easily controlled. So well had it been made that it looked exactly as if a gang of men had been working at it—but it was animals, not men, that had built it.

This wall, which was really a dam, seemed as if it were holding the lake in place: which is really what it was doing, for without it there would have been no lake at all, only the stream running through.

The pond was bright with sunshine; very silent and peaceful it was, back there among the Hills of the Whispering Leaves, and so calm that the few ducks dozing quietly upon its waters seemed almost to be float-ing on air, and the slim white poplar trees that stood upon its banks were reflected so plainly on its smooth surface, that it was hard to tell where the water stopped and the trees began. It was very beautiful, like a fairy-land, with its silver poplars and Mayflowers and blue water. And it was very still, for nothing moved there, and it seemed quite lifeless except for the sleeping ducks. Yet, had you watched patiently for a little while, being careful not to move or talk, or even whisper, you would have seen, before very long, a ripple on the water near the shore as a dark brown head, with round ears that showed very plainly, peered cautiously out from the rushes at the water's edge, and watched and listened and sniffed. The head was followed by a furry body, as its owner now came out in full sight and swam rapidly, but without a sound, to another place on the far shore, there to disappear among the reeds. The tall reeds swayed and shook for a minute as he worked there, and then he reappeared, this time holding before him a large bundle of grass, and swam over towards an enormous black mound of earth that we had been wondering about all this time, and dived, bundle and all, right in front of it. He had scarcely disap-peared before another head, with another bundle, could be seen swim-ming from a different direction when—somebody moved, and with no warning at all, a huge flat tail came down on the water with a heavy smack, and with a mighty splash and a plunge the head and its bundle were gone. Now this was exactly what had happened to Big Feather, down on the river that morning, and for the same reason. For that great mound, taller than any of us, before which the swimmers had dived, was a beaver house, and the dark-brown, furry heads were those of the Beaver People themselves. And they had been very busy.

The lodge had been built up to more than six feet in height, and was a good ten feet across. It had lately been well plastered with wet mud, and heavy billets of wood had been laid on the slopes of it to hold everything firmly in place. It all looked very strong and safe, like a fortress, and even a moose could have walked around on top of it without doing it a bit of harm. Up the side of it there was a wide pathway, on which the building materials were carried, and had you been more patient or careful a while ago, or perhaps had the wind not played a trick on you and given you away to those keen noses, you might have seen old father beaver dig out a load of earth from the shore, go with it to the house, swimming slowly and carefully so as not to lose any, and then standing upright like a man, walk to the top of the roof with the load in his arms and there dump it, pushing it into nooks and crannies with his hands, and shoving a good-sized stick in after it to keep it there.

And all this work had been done with a purpose. It was a very important time, this Month of Flowers, for inside that queer-looking home, hidden away from the eyes of all the world, were four tiny kitten beavers. Woolly little fellows they were, perfectly formed, with bright black eyes, big webbed hind feet, little hand-like fore-paws and tiny, flat, rubbery-looking tails. They had marvellous appetites, and their lungs must have been very good too, for they were the noisiest little creatures imaginable and cried continuously in long, loud wails that were very much like the cries of small human babies. Like any other babies, they needed a great deal of attention—and you may be sure that they were getting a lot of it too.

The living room, or chamber, inside the lodge, was large enough for a person to have curled up in it with ease, and was very clean and sweet smelling with its floor of willow bark and bed of scented grasses. The entrance was through a short, slanting tunnel one end of which, called the plunge-hole, was in the floor, and the other end came out below, near the bottom of the lake. The dam held the pond up to a level nearly even with the floor, keeping the plunge-hole always full, so that the tiny kittens, who were a little wobbly on their legs as yet, could drink there without falling into it; or if they did (which happened rather regularly), they could climb out again quite easily. The whole tunnel and the outer door-way were under water, so that no land animals could enter, or even see it, unless they were first-class divers, which most of them are not. But if the dam should break and let the saved-up water out, the beaver would be in grave danger, as not only could their enemies, such as wolves and foxes, find their way into the house, but the beaver would be unable to protect or hide themselves by diving suddenly out of sight, as you saw them do a little while ago.

ཀྱུ ཀྱུ ཀྱུ

THE FATHER HAD, TOO, A PRETTY STEADY JOB KEEPING THE trough, which you might call a regulator, clear of rubbish, so that the water could flow freely and not become too high, and so flood the house, but was always at exactly the right level. Between whiles, both he and the mother attended to their babies' every want, changing their bedding every so often, bringing in small sprays of tender leaves for them to eat, combing and brushing their wool (you could hardly call it fur), while they made queer, soft sounds of affection and talked to them in that strange beaver language that, at a little distance, sounds almost as though human people were speaking together in low voices. And the shrill wailing cries of the little ones, and their chattering, and their little squawks and squeals, could be heard even through the thick walls of the lodge, so noisy were they when they were hungry, or pleased, or in some small trouble, which, one way and another, was pretty nearly all the time. And when either their father or their mother returned (they were never away together; one or the other was always on guard) from a trip to the so-important dam, or brought in new bedding of sweet-grass, he or she would give a low, crooning sound of greeting, to be immediately answered by a very bedlam of loud shouts of welcome from the young-sters, that went on long after it was at all necessary. They were never still unless they were asleep, and were continually scrambling around, and tussling together, and clambering over everything, and by the noise they made, seemed to be enjoying themselves immensely. And altogether they were pretty much like any other family, and were very snug and happy in their home.

The little ones were now old enough to try their hand at swimming in the plunge-hole, though at present this exercise consisted mostly in lying on top of the water, not always right side up, and going round and round in circles, screeching with excitement. And being so very light, and their fluffy coats containing so much air, they could not seem to sink deep enough for their webbed hind feet to both get a grip on the water at the same time, so they swam with first one foot and then the other, rolling from side to side and bobbing up and down, squirming and squealing and wiggling, while their parents passed anxiously around amongst them, giving them encouragement, or perhaps advice, in their deep, strong voices. From what I have seen of such goings on, it must have been rather a troublesome time for the old folks, this business of learning to swim, but the youngsters seemed to be having a good time which, as you will agree, is, after all, something to be considered.

But they would soon become tired, and climbing out onto the drying-off place (a little lower than the rest of the floor, so the water would soak away and not run all over the beds), every little beaver carefully squeezed, rubbed and scrubbed the water from his coat on the front, sides, back, every place he could reach, sitting upright and working very industriously, puffing and blowing as most of us do after a swim. Then, when this was all over and everybody was dry, or thought he was (some of them would topple over once in a while and made rather a poor job of it), the call for lunch would go up in a loud chorus, and the new green leaflets and water plants that had been provided ahead of time, with the idea, no doubt, of putting a stop to the uproar as soon as possible, would be divided up, and pretty soon all the busy little jaws would be munching away, and the piercing cries died down to mumbles and little mutterings of contentment. And soon the little voices became quiet and the small black eyes closed, while they lay cuddled together on their sweet-smelling, grassy bed, with their tiny fore-paws so much like hands, clutched tightly in each other's fur.

And this would be their daily program until, after perhaps three weeks, would come that glorious day when they would venture down the long, dim tunnel out into the brightness of the great unknown world that was all about them, but which they had never seen. And while they slept the old ones stood watch and guard, turn about, and took turns to inspect the defences of their castle and the dam on which their very lives depended, and kept a weather eye out for enemies, and collected food and bedding for when the babies should awaken, and carried on at the hundred and one jobs that make father and mother beaver a very busy pair of people during the latter part of May, the Moon of Flowers.

Our four young heroes, or heroines, or both, had just arrived at that thrilling stage of the proceedings when they could at last dive without bobbing up immediately, tail first, like a rubber ball, and could swim around on the surface for quite a respectable distance without calling loudly for help, when one day at noon, at the very time when we had been watching Gitchie Meegwon at his dinner, the father noticed that the water in the entrance was sinking. He watched it for a moment; the mother heard it too, heard it gurgling and came to look—the water was going down, swirling down into the tunnel—was gone!

Some one had broken the dam!

Into the empty plunge-hole, one after another tumbled the two big beavers. There was no time to be lost. They were losing their precious water, the water upon which the lives of their little ones so much depended! Their home was open now to all the world; it might mean the death of all of them. The four kittens terrified, realizing that something terrible was wrong but too young to know just what it might be, crept close together, whimpering, while their alarmed parents tore through what was left of the water, towards the dam.

They found a hole, nearly as big as a barrel, right at the deepest part of it, where it would quickly drain the lake to the very bottom. Madly the beavers began to work, pulling down sticks from anywhere, tearing out great armfuls of earth from the marshy shore, slashing off limbs from fallen trees with their razor-sharp teeth, rolling stones into the hole and shoving grass and brush in between them, digging up mud and pushing it before them into the break, where the suction of the now rapidly falling water held it plastered tight against the sticks and stones and brush. But the pond had been too small for so big a leak, and water was not coming from the tiny stream that fed it, nearly as fast as it was going out.

And now that the dam was almost repaired, the pond was empty!

Despair seized on the beavers (don't let any one ever tell you that animals cannot feel despair!) as they worked, but they never gave up until the very last load was in its place, and then, their task finished, they turned and plodded wearily and unhappily back towards their four little babies in the house, useless now as a protection—the house they had worked so hard to build, the babies that they loved so very much. Beavers are slow walkers, and what had once been a short, easy swim had now become a slow, awkward scramble through slippery mud and over rocks and tangled, fallen water plants and weeds. Precious minutes would pass before they would have staggered, and crawled, and dragged their way to that dark mound that now seemed so far away. Anything could catch them. If a bear or a wolf should pass and see them they would have no chance; the Beaver People were defenceless now, for they were never made to fight, only to work.

Hurry! Hurry! Gitchie Meegwon, run your fastest; your Little Brothers need you badly, need you now! Soon, any minute, he should be here——

Across the muddy bottom of the pond the two big beavers struggled slowly, painfully, and pitifully on their short and weary legs towards their unprotected home and babies, while, within the lodge, huddled together, their tiny hands clutched tightly in each other's woolly fur, four helpless little kitten beavers stared in terror at a sleek, black monster with a flat, evil head, that crept slowly through the entrance towards them, his teeth bared, hissing like a snake as he came. Negik[*] the Otter, the hungry, the cruel, and the sly, having broken the dam and so drained the pond, could now get what he had come for—kitten beaver meat! Now was his time. His snaky body blocked the plunge-hole; there seemed to be no escape. He gathered his legs beneath him, ready to spring.

Just then Gitchie Meegwon, breathless, his shirt off, his gun ready, burst through the reeds beside the dam, and leaping from rock to rock, made for the beaver house.

---

[*] Pronounced Nee-*gik* with the "g" hard as in "go."

CHAPTER FOUR

The First Adventure

THE OTTER SPRANG. BUT IN HIS EAGERNESS HE TRIED TO SEIZE the little beavers all at once, and they, quick as so many coiled springs, threw themselves sideways in the way that beavers have, and scattered before him as he came. Aiming at no particular one, he missed them all, nearly stunning himself against the wall of the lodge with the force of his leap. This confused him for a second, and the kittens rushed past him through the entrance, now no longer blocked by his body. The otter, roused to ferocious anger by his failure, and knowing very well that he could catch them one by one outside, was about to turn in pursuit, when the doorway was again darkened. That was all the warning he had. The next moment he was fighting for his life with the two big beavers. They had arrived only just in time; and they, usually so playful and good-natured, would fight to the death in defence of their young ones.

The otter was quicker on his feet and fiercer than they were, and could lock his jaws like a vise once he had bitten in, like a bull-dog; but a beaver's hide is tough, and the chisel-shaped teeth, that could hew down big trees and had never before been used to do harm to any one, now slashed through skin and muscle, inches deep. They held on with their hands and drove their razor-edged cutting-teeth in deeper and deeper. The otter fought hard, for he was no coward, trying for his favourite hold on a beaver's nose and mouth, so as to prevent at least one of them from using its teeth. But he had all he could do to defend his own throat, at which the beavers were aiming. He twisted and turned like a great hairy lizard, lashing out right and left with his snaky head, hissing, snapping, and snarling. The beavers held on in deadly silence, while he dragged them from place to place, and they drove their teeth in again and again. For here was an enemy, the worst one of them all, who must be got rid of somehow—anyhow. Fighting fair with this evil beast was only a waste of time; the matter must be settled once and for all. Over and over they fought and wrestled and rolled, until they rolled right out through the plunge-hole, a squirming tangled mixture of legs, tails and glistening teeth, almost at the feet of Gitchie Meegwon, whose last flying jump from one rock to another had brought him close beside the beaver house. The sight of this new foe discouraged the otter completely, and with a violent effort he broke loose and in one leap was beyond the beavers' reach. Paying no attention to the Indian, they scrambled after the fleeing otter, but the slimy mud that held them back gave the otter just the kind of going that he needed, and he threw himself forward in the slippery ooze and slid twenty feet at one shot, took two or three jumps and another slide, and kept this up until he was at the dam, and over it, and away—forever.

Never again would he make war on the Beaver People!

Big Feather, standing on a nearby rock, saw his retreat. Once he aimed his rifle at the otter, but thinking he had punishment enough he let him go. Anyway, everything was all right now, and water was beginning to collect again. A good-sized pool had already formed in the basin of the pond, getting larger all the time and held there by the dam, which, as you remember, the beaver had repaired; and Big Feather was obliged to hurry back to shore before his rocks became covered again. However, he was still a little anxious, as he had seen the young ones rush out, but had not seen them go in. So he sat down on the shore, in a spot where he could be neither seen nor smelled, and watched the goings on. Soon he saw the mother beaver commencing to collect her little ones, one at a time. Two of them had come out of hiding, and as she came for them in turn, each would mount upon her broad, flat tail which trailed behind her like a short toboggan, and standing upright on it and holding onto his mother's fur with his hands to steady himself, would be dragged across the mud to the doorway. And the little fellows would look around them as they rode on this queer conveyance, taking in all the sights, no doubt feeling mighty pleased with themselves. I think Big Feather got as much fun out of it as they did; he saw two of them taken home this way and laughed to himself at the comical sight. And as he watched, he could not help feeling, somehow, that it was a great shame ever to kill such creatures, that worked so hard to protect their babies and their humble home, and seemed to have such real affection for each other—almost like killing little people, he thought. He had never before seen such things as had happened here today, and he began to realize why some of the older Indians called the beavers Little Talking Brothers, and Beaver People.

Although he had neither food nor blanket, he made up his mind to stay all night in case the otter should return, or another one come, for they often travel in pairs. But none did, and when Gitchie Meegwon left next morning he saw that the pond had filled up completely, and was running over as before; the secret doorway was again hidden and everything was in good order, and the same as it had ever been.

That is, nearly everything. What he did not know was, that two of the kittens, scared almost out of their wits, had scrambled on and on through one of the long passageways that beavers often dig for various purposes under the muskeg,* and coming to the end of it had found themselves near the dam. Trying to get as far away as they possibly could from that fierce monster, and hardly knowing or caring where they went, they had slipped over the dam unobserved. They had gone on down the now dry and empty stream-bed, hearing in their excited imagination the hissing breath of Negik close behind them. So real did this become to them, and so near did it seem to be at last that they scrambled hastily under a hollow in the bank—and not a moment too soon. For they were scarcely out of sight before the otter went hurrying by; they really had heard him. Fortunately, baby beavers, like the very young of many other animals, give out no scent, so that not even a fox, for all his sharp, inquisitive nose, could ever have found them except by accident. So Negik never knew they were there, and kept on putting as much ground between himself and the beaver pond as he could.

* A quaking bog, often partly afloat.

Too terrified now to move lest their enemy should return, the two mites clung together in their shelter, afraid to go ahead, afraid to turn back. So they waited for their mother, who would be sure to look for them. But that lack of scent that had just now saved them from the otter, was to be their undoing. For their parents, searching frantically everywhere, could not trace them and never knew they had even left the pond; and in their excitement and fear the kittens had never noticed how short a distance they had really come. So, like two tiny lost children, they sat miserable and lonely in their little cave, listening for a deep, crooning voice that they loved, waiting, waiting for the big kind mother who had always comforted them in their small troubles and kept them warm with her brown, furry body and had combed and scrubbed them so carefully every day. Surely she, or their father, who had played so gently with them and taught them how to swim, and had always brought them sweet-grass for their beds and sprays of tender leaves for them to eat, would soon come for them! But now there were no sweet-grasses, no juicy tender leaflets, only hard rocks and gritty sand; and no father, no mother ever came for them. And so they crouched together all the long night, shivering, hungry, and afraid.

Once a slim, dark creature, the shape of a weasel but much larger, peered in at them, and they waited, still as two mice, scarcely daring to breathe, while he sniffed loudly at the opening where they were hidden, and then passed on. It had been a mink who, seeing two of them together, had feared to attack them. Later on they peered out cautiously from under the bank, but ducked back just in time to escape a great, grey shape that swooped down at them from above, an awful, ghostly creature with huge, staring yellow eyes, that missed them only by an inch or two and swooped up again, to sit on an overhanging branch. From the branch it stared and stared, and snapped its beak and gave loud, long screeches, and made a horrible chuckling sound.

Wap-aho,* the Laughing Owl of the woods, had spotted them and was waiting patiently for his chance. And every time they peered out from their hiding-place, the dreadful yellow eyes were there, staring down at them.

* Pronounced *Wop*-a-*ho*.

At daylight the owl was gone, and as the dam was full again and spilling over by now, the stream was running freely. And on its flow the beavers now set out to find their home. If they had only known how close it was! But the poor little heads were badly muddled now, and they were entirely lost. And, too small to swim against the current, they went the easiest way and floated with it, slipping down, down the stream, farther and farther away from their home, their parents, and the tiny sisters[†] they had romped and played with so happily all their short lives.

On they floated, weak and hungry for want of the leaves and plants they did not know how to look for; yet they felt a little safer now that they were in the water once again—drifting along on this fruitless journey that could have only one ending. As the little stream began to reach the level of the Yellow Birch it flowed more slowly and became quieter and quieter, and they floated easily and smoothly upon its lazy waters. Once a deer, feeding in a shallows, looked up and saw them, watched them with his gentle eyes, his long ears pointed forward. Further on they met a hurrying muskrat, who gave them a sharp chitter of greeting and passed them by. Birds looked down on them and called to them from the tree tops, far above; and the sun was warm and pleasant, and the world was very beautiful as they floated sleepily, dreamily along—to nowhere. And so they would go on, dreamy with hunger and weakness until, as sick little beavers do, they would fall asleep at last and never wake.

Then, as they floated out onto the broad, calm waters of the Yellow Birch, Gitchie Meegwon saw them.

He had been back at his dinner place again, at the foot of the stream, and quietly launching his canoe he paddled softly over to them. They heard him, opened their eyes a little and saw him. Somehow they were not afraid, as he lifted them into the canoe by their tiny black tails. Perhaps they didn't care any more, or maybe the big watchful eye painted on the front of the canoe didn't look so sharp and fierce as it was intended to. Perhaps, too, they knew he wouldn't harm them; for animals, even very young ones, seem to know who is their friend.

He handled them very gently, for they were very small and pitiful as he held them cupped in the hollow of his two hands. Their wee front

[†] Only the little males would have been so venturesome.

paws were tucked up in feeble little fists,[*] as though to put up some kind of fight for their tiny lives; but the chubby heads were too heavy and drooped down, and their eyes were closed. Big Feather knew they must be dying, and was sorry for them. For he was a kindly man, as hunters so often are, when they stop to think.

He would try to save them. After all, he thought, he had made his living killing beavers for their fur, and it seemed only fair that in return he should do something for these two lost waifs that had drifted almost into his hands. On shore, he took from his provisions a can of milk, and making a thin mixture of some of it with water, poured a little in their mouths. And as he held the small woolly bodies gently in his big brown hands, he could feel how flat and empty their little stomachs were, and how feebly the little hearts were beating. And as he fed them they clutched tightly at his fingers with their tiny hands. And his heart softened more and more towards them as he fed them, though he hardly knew what he was going to do with them. He had little time to spare, as he had promised Sajo[†] and Shapian,[‡] his children, that he would be back on a certain day, and he did not want to disappoint them. If he carried the kittens back to the pond they might never find their way across, and if he let them go here they would certainly starve, or else the hawks, or an eagle, or even a hungry fish would get them. But he had far to go, and they would be a nuisance; after all they were only little animals—yet, they were in great trouble and needed help, and he felt that it would be wicked to abandon them; for some of the old-time Indians had very strict rules about such things.

Their mother had thought them very beautiful; but the Indian found them to be very homely indeed, with their big hind feet, short, round little bodies, and little pug noses, rather like Pukwajees,[**] or Indian fairies.

[*] A beaver's attitude of defence. They are capable of striking quick, sharp blows, using the strong, heavy finger-nails, or with the hand balled into a fist. The latter device is used when it is desired to avoid inflicting injury with the nails, as among themselves. Note that the little beavers, even though at the last extremity, instinctively chose the gentler method. Such is their disposition.

[†] Pronounced *Say*-jo.

[‡] Pronounced *Shap*-ee-an.

[**] Pronounced *Puk*-wajees.

In fact, they were so homely that really they were cute, he finally decided, just the thing for pets! Sajo, his little daughter, was nearly eleven years old, and was soon to have a birthday. They would make a fine present— the very thing! And when they became too big to have for pets, they could be brought back to their old home again. And just then, feeling the effects of the milk, they began to cry for more—those voices! They quite finished Gitchie Meegwon—how could a man desert two creatures that were able to cry so much like children, he asked himself, at the same time pouring some more milk down the hungry little throats.

And so he cut a large sheet of tough, leathery bark from a fine birch tree that stood close by among the pines, and with it made a strong, light box, or basket, with strips of cedar wood to hold it in its shape, made a close-fitting lid that fitted neatly down over the top of it, and punched it full of holes for air, and made a handle of braided cedar bark to carry it by. And inside it he put some bedding of grass and rushes, and green foodstuffs such as he knew that beavers loved. And when he lifted them in by their little flat tails (they made a first-class handle!), and they smelt the nice clean bed of sweet-grass, the very same as they had always had at home, and found the tender buds and leaves that they had been unable to find for themselves and that they had wanted so badly; and what with the kind, soothing voice of their new friend, and the way their little bellies were all filled up, and what with—oh, one thing and another, they suddenly felt very much better.

And they forgot the otter with his hissing, fishy breath, clean forgot the owl with his staring yellow eyes and fiercely snapping beak, who had laughed at them so grimly in the darkness. And they jabbered together with little bleats and squeals, as they had not done this long time past, and ate and ate until they could hold no more.

Big Feather, as he dipped and swung his paddle in his swift canoe, on his way back to his home and loved ones, was very pleased with the gift that he would bring his children (of course the boy, who was three years older than his sister, would have to share in the fun too, even though it was not his birthday); and he was glad because he had helped two suffering forest creatures. And speaking to the canoe, or his gun, or maybe to the little beavers, or perhaps just talking to himself, he said:

"Mino-ta-kiyah,* it is well! Kae-get mino-ta-kiyah, it is well indeed!"

And the two small adventurers must have found things to be going very well with them, too, as they had become very quiet. Indeed, they were very comfortable on their nest; and they could hear, through the air holes in their birch-bark chamber, the song of the blackbirds and the thrushes, and the cheerful gurgling of the water all around; the drowsy humming of the insects and all the other pleasant woodsy sounds. Yet, even in this new-found happiness, they did not quite forget, never would quite forget, the kind father and mother, and the old home and small companions they had lost; and they were lonely for them all at once, so they whimpered a little and crept together and held each other tight. Then the loneliness would go away again, when they were close together, and the tired little heads nodded, and the little voices were quiet, and the round black eyes just would *not* stay open any more, and then the pleasant sounds outside faded quite away, and their troubles, at last, were altogether gone. And so they fell asleep.

And that is how two small, lost kitten beavers, so small that both of them could have sat together very comfortably in a pint-pot, went on their way to a new home and friends, and saw many strange and wonderful things that the wisest of beavers had never even heard about, and had adventures such as no beavers ever had before, I'm pretty sure.

It was indeed, as Big Feather had said, mino-ta-kiyah—really quite first class, in fact!

---

* Pronounced Mee-*no*-ta-*kiy*-ah.

CHAPTER FIVE

Sajo's Birthday

ONE DAY, ALMOST A WEEK LATER, SAJO AND SHAPIAN WERE busy preparing for their father's homecoming. Gitchie Meegwon's home was a short distance away from the Indian village of O-pee-pee-soway,[*] which means The Place of Talking Waters. The Indians had so named the village on account of a little low waterfall that was near by, where the bubbling and the murmuring of the water made a sound like that of low, dreamy voices, so that the people said that there were spirits in the falls.

The cabin in which they lived was built of pine logs, and stood not far from the lake shore, on a grassy knoll. The forest started right behind it, but all around the camp the ground had been cleared of underbrush and fallen timber, leaving only the finest trees, which formed a lovely glade through which there could be had a splendid view of the lake. This lake was a large one, and the farther shore showed only as a range of tumbled, forest-covered hills that seemed to be rolling forever on into the blue distance, like the waves of some great, dark ocean. A narrow footpath, or water-trail, led down the slope from the cabin to the landing, where stood a grove of tall and graceful poplar trees, in whose leafy shade Gitchie Meegwon and his young son and daughter spent many a happy Summer day beside the water, and often took their meals there.

The cabin was not large, but it made a handsome appearance from the outside, with its walls of red-brown logs and rows of green and yel-

[*] Pronounced O-Pee-*pee*-soway.

low moss between them. Though it had only one room, it was even more pleasant to look at on the inside. The floor, of solid logs hewed flat and fitted tight together, had been scrubbed until it was as clean and bright as any floor you ever saw, and on the three bunks that stood in a row along one wall, rich-looking Hudson Bay blankets were neatly folded. Some of them were red, some were white, and others green, each with wide black stripes at either end, and they made the place look very gay and cheerful. The three windows, a single large pane of glass in each, were as spotless and shining as windows ought to be, as shiny as the inside of a rifle barrel, so Shapian put it; for that was his idea of something that was very clean indeed. That was the way he kept his own rifle, and today it had been oiled and rubbed, inside and out, till it fairly glittered in its corner, opposite the door where any one who entered could not help but see it. For this rifle, which had cost him four good mink skins at the Trading Post, was the proudest of all his possessions, which, I may tell you, were not very many.

Sajo had gathered the stems of bulrushes and dried them, and then cut them into short lengths and dyed them blue, and red, and yellow, and threaded them, like long, narrow wooden beads, on strings, and these hung down in rows beside the windows. She had arranged the different colours to make a kind of pattern, and they had quite an expensive look about them—rather like curtains she thought, as she glanced at them for about the hundredth time.

On the table, all the tin dishes and knives and forks had been arranged in their proper places, and in the center was a large loaf of Indian bread, or bannock, as it is called, freshly baked and still steaming hot, and stuck upright in the top of it was a very small spruce tree, no higher than your hand. It was really a tiny Christmas tree, and although it was not Christmas time, Sajo was nearly as happy as if it had been, and that was her way of showing how she felt about everything. The little iron stove that had been polished until it looked like a new one, had no oven and no legs, and was raised some distance from the floor on flat stones, which was a very convenient arrangement, as, to bake bread, all one had to do was to cook the dough for a while on top of the stove, and then put it underneath, between the warm stones, where it got finished off and nicely browned by the heat from the fire above. Otherwise the loaf would have had to be turned over in the pan when it was half baked, which would have made matters a little uncertain. And Sajo made good bread, I can tell you that, for I have eaten it many's the time.

Shapian had done his part too, as could be seen by the large pile of wood in a box behind the stove, and the rug of deerskin, newly stretched and dried, that lay in the center of the floor; while in a huge pot upon the stove, were cooking all the choicest portions of the meat—obtained with that so much-prized rifle in the corner. Shapian was a manly-looking boy, tall for his age, with the copper-coloured skin and dark eyes of his people, the Ojibways. He sat quietly waiting; his father had set this day for his return, and when he promised something he always kept his word, as nearly as the uncertainties of forest life would allow. But his sister, younger than he, her brown eyes aglow and her jet black hair, in two long braids, flying behind her, ran and hopped and skipped from place to place, tending to the cooking, placing around the table the rough wooden blocks they used for chairs, and putting the finishing touches to the wooden curtains.

Shapian had seated himself where he could get a good view out across the lake, through one of the windows, and was watching for the first sight of Big Feather's canoe—though he pretended not to be, and had picked a window on the far side of the room, through which he could keep an eye without appearing to do so. It would never do, he thought, to show how anxious he was. He was only fourteen, but he was feeling quite grown-up just now, as he had been the head of the household for well over a month. Sajo sang a little song as she worked, and was all aflutter with a many-coloured tartan dress, and on her dancing feet was a beautiful pair of beaded moccasins, worn only on special occasions. For this was to be a big day for her; not only was her so-loved father coming home, but it was her birthday. Poor Sajo, she did not often get a birthday gift since her mother had been laid to rest beneath the wild-flowers, but she still had two wooden dolls her father had made for her on two different birthdays. This year he had been away and would have had no time to make her anything. So the two dolls, Chilawee and Chikanee by name, had been brought out and were sitting on the edge of one of the bunks, not looking particularly cheerful, though they too were all dressed up in tartan plaid, as Sajo was, and their complexions, which had either soaked in or run off, had been renewed with a paint brush, and they each had a little head shawl round their wooden faces. They *did* look rather dumb, come to look at them; they had neither fingers nor noses nor mouths, but it is very likely that they didn't know the difference, and they would have to do for this time. At least, so Sajo thought, but we know differently, you and I, and she never guessed, as she went so happily about her tasks, the big surprise she was going to have.

Meanwhile Shapian sat very still and watched across the room, through his window, wishing that his sister would act a little more dignified and not be so wild and excited—still, two such big events as these coming both together on the same day, must be rather unsettling to a woman, he supposed. And then his own heart began to beat a good deal faster and he had all he could do to keep from rushing to the window; for out on the lake far, far away, he saw a tiny speck.

"Sister," he said, speaking slowly and distinctly, as was his fashion, "our father is coming."

"Where? Where?" cried Sajo, and without waiting for an answer she snatched up her head shawl and ran out through the door, looking eagerly in every direction. "Where, show me, quick!" Shapian pointed out over the water, to the speck.

"There," he said. "That little spot."

"Oh," said Sajo, and her voice fell a little; that spot could be anything. "Maybe it's a bear or a moose swimming," she suggested, hoping he would say it wasn't. But an answer came before he had time to speak.

Far off, faintly, they heard a sound, a faint, sharp crack—a rifle shot; and then, right away, another. They listened; there was a pause while you could count three, and then another shot.

"The signal! The signal!" cried Sajo, and Shapian replied quietly: "Yes, it is our father's signal," and then, quite forgetting himself, turned and rushed into the cabin with her, saying:

"Let us get ready quickly," and although the canoe was still some miles away and would not be in for at least an hour, there then commenced a great bustle as they went to work. They ran to the shelves for the jars of preserved blueberries and wild strawberries that Sajo put by every year though these were really the first she had ever done all by herself, but she had made a good job of them, and liked to feel that this had been going on for years and years. And they put on the big tea-pail to boil and stuck a long iron fork into the meat to see if it was cooked, and ran from table to stove and from stove to table and back again, and altogether acted a good deal like any other children would have done on such an occasion, whether they were rich or poor, or royalty, or just a couple of little Indians.

And when at last there came that long-looked-for moment when the yellow bark canoe, with its watchful eye and swaying tail, slid to a stop upon the sandy beach, everybody began to talk at once and Gitchie Meegwon stepped out on the shore and took their hands, or as many of them as he could hold in one of his, while he held the other, for some reason, behind him, and tried to answer all the questions at once, while his face, that could look so stern, was full of smiles and laughter as he cried:

"Children, children, let me speak, give me a chance to speak—yes, I am safe, no, I didn't see any half-breeds, and yes, our hunting ground is not disturbed—or no, I should have said, and yes, I was lonesome, but not now, and—Happy Birthday to you my Sajo, Happy Birthday, my little daughter" and not till then did he bring out from behind his back the other hand. In it there was, just as we had guessed, the birch-bark basket, which he held by its braided handle up beyond their reach, and said:

"Gently, gently; see! I have brought you a gift for your birthday, Sajo," and gave it to her and told her to carry it with great care, while he turned to Shapian and added: "For you too, my son; there are two of them."

"Two of what, father?" asked the boy, looking after his sister, who had started away. "What is in the basket?"

But Big Feather said for him to wait and see. And they followed Sajo to the cabin as she went up the pathway at a funny little gliding run, supposed to be jolt-proof, so that while the small beaded moccasins twinkled in and out from under the tartan dress at a great rate, her body was held as stiff as possible from the knees up, so as not to jar the basket, which she held out in front of her as though it were a large and very delicate egg that would break into a thousand fragments at the slightest shock. Very carefully indeed she went, for out of this mysterious box there came the strangest sounds. A baby, she thought, no, two babies—though it seemed they must be very little ones to be in so small a space. Once inside, she set the basket very gently down upon the floor, and while Shapian (he had lost no time on the way either) held the sides, she took off the lid, and looking inside saw what you and I knew all the time were there—two small, round woolly bodies and four little paws that reached for the edge of the box like tiny hands, and two pairs of bright black eyes, like shoe-buttons, that looked up at her so knowingly.

"Oooh!" she breathed, a kind of a gasp it was. "Oh! Oh!" And that's all she could say, and could think of nothing else to say and so said "Oh!" again; and at last:

"Teddy bears, live teddy bears," she cried, and then she turned the basket gently on its side and out they came; and she saw their tails and knew then what they were! Better than Teddy bears——

"Little beavers, it's little beavers," burst out Shapian, pale with excitement, his youthful dignity gone to the four winds, "real ones, alive!" while the tall Big Feather stood smiling down at the two delighted youngsters, very pleased indeed to see how well his present was received. Sajo sat beside them in wonder on the floor, her mouth still an "O," but no sound was coming out of it any more. And now she was too busy to draw her father's attention to the curtains she had been so proud of, although you may be sure his sharp eyes did not miss them; and the dinner was kept waiting and the famous gun, so clean and shiny, stood forgotten in its corner.

Gitchie Meegwon had looked after the kittens very carefully on the long journey, and had fed them well and they were round, and fat, and cuddly-looking, and Sajo thought they were the cutest things she had ever seen. And when they clambered onto her knees with little shaky whimpers, she bent down over them, and rubbed her face on their soft wool, that smelled so sweet from their bed of scented grass and willow bark. Soon Big Feather and Shapian went out to find fresh leaves and bedding for their small guests; but Sajo stayed behind. And while these two were away, she picked the little beavers up and held their dumpy little bodies, one at a time, in her two small hands, where they fitted very comfortably, and whispered softly to them—and, wonder of wonders, they answered her in little childish voices, and held onto her fingers with their wee hands (you could call them nothing else), and looked at her very attentively out of their bright black eyes that seemed somehow to look so very wise. And when she held them both together in her arms they made funny little sounds, and pushed their warm, damp noses tight against her neck, and blew and puffed, as little babies do.

And she knew that she was going to love them very much.

And at that, Chilawee and Chikanee, the dolls, who had been looking on rather gloomily up till now, seemed more disconsolate than ever, so to spare the poor creatures any further pain, Sajo put them with their faces to the wall, back on the shelf where they belonged.

And in that plain log cabin, far back in the forests of the Northland, there were that day three very happy people: Gitchie Meegwon, because his homecoming had been so glad a one; Shapian, because his father had given him, too, a share in the beavers and had praised his work besides; and Sajo, because of the most wonderful birthday gift that she had ever had.

CHAPTER SIX
Big Small and Little Small

THE KITTENS QUICKLY TOOK A LIKING TO THEIR NEW WAY OF living, and although no human beings could ever quite take the place of their own parents, everything possible was done to make them feel at ease.

Shapian partitioned off the under part of his bunk with sheets of birch bark, leaving one end open; and this was their house, in which they at once made themselves very much at home. Gitchie Meegwon cut a hole in the floor and fitted down into it a wash-tub, for a pond—not much of a one perhaps, but it was as large as the plunge-hole had been, and they spent nearly half their time in it, and would lie on top of the water eating their twigs and leaves. Whenever they left the tub, they always squatted their plump little personalities upright beside it, and scrubbed their coats, first squeezing the hair in bunches with their little fists to get the water out. That done, the whole coat was carefully combed with a double claw that all beavers are provided with, one on each hind foot, for this purpose. All this took quite a while, and they were so businesslike and serious about it that Sajo would become as interested as they were, and would sometimes help them, rubbing their fur this way and that with the tips of her fingers, and then they would scrub away so much the harder.

It was their fashion, when drying themselves off this way, to raise one arm high above their heads, as far as it would go, and rub that side with the other hand, and being upright as they were, it looked as if they were about to dance the Highland Fling. They often sat up in this manner while eating the bark off small sticks, and as one or other of them held a stick crossways in his hands, rolling it round and round whilst the busy teeth whittled off the bark, he looked for all the world like some little old man playing on a flute. Sometimes they varied the show, and when the sticks were very slim they ate the whole business, putting one end in their mouths and pushing it on in with their hands, while the sharp front teeth, working very fast, chopped it into tiny pieces. The rattle of their cutting machinery sounded much the same as would a couple of sewing machines running a little wild, and as they held up their heads and shoved the sticks, to all appearances, slowly down their throats, they looked a good deal like a pair of sword swallowers who found a meal of swords very much to their taste.

They had to have milk for the first two weeks or so, and Sajo borrowed a bottle and a baby's nipple from a neighbour in the village, and fed them with it turn about. But while one would be getting his meal (both hands squeezed tight around the neck of the bottle!), the other would scramble around and make a loud outcry and a hubbub, and try to get hold of the bottle, and there would be a squabbling and a great confusion and the can of milk was sometimes upset and spilled all over; so that at last there had to be another bottle and nipple found, and Shapian fed one kitten while Sajo fed the other. Later on they were fed bannock and milk, which made things a little easier, as each had his own small dish which the children held for him. The beavers would pick up the mixture with one hand, shoving it into their mouths at a great rate; and I am afraid their table manners were not very good, as there was a good deal of rather loud smacking of lips, and hard breathing to be heard and they often talked with their mouths full. But they had one very good point, which not all of us have, and liked to put away their dishes when they were through, pushing them along the floor into a corner or under the stove; of course if there was a certain amount of milk-soaked bannock left in them, that was quite all right, so far as the beavers were concerned, and by the time the dishes had arrived at their destinations these remains had been well squashed and trampled on the line of march, and the floor would be nicely marked up with small, sticky beaver tracks, having sometimes to be partly scrubbed. Sajo always collected the little dishes and washed them up, as she did those of the "big people." Being fed separately, each of them came to look on one of the children as his special friend, and one of them would go to each when they were called. At first they had no names, and the children just called, "Undaas, undaas, Amik, Amik,"* which means "Come here, come here, Beaver, Beaver." But a little later on Sajo remembered the day that the two wooden dolls had seemed to be looking on when the kittens first had come, and how these new arrivals had so quickly taken their place. Well, she thought, they may as well take their names too, and so she called the beavers Chilawee and Chikanee,† which means Big Small and Little Small. The larger one of the two was called Chilawee, or Big Small, and the not-so-large one was called Chikanee, or Little Small. And so they were all named; and the names suited them very well too, because after all, they *were* very small and they *did* look a lot like a pair of woolly toys that had come to life and stepped down off a shelf. It was not long before they got to know these names, and would always come out from the house under Shapian's bunk when called on; but the names sounded so much alike, that when one was called they both would come, and as they themselves were as much alike as two peas, the difference in size being not very great, it was often pretty hard to tell which was which. To make matters worse, they did not grow evenly; that is, one would grow a little faster than the other for a while, and then he would slacken down and the other would catch up, and get ahead of him. First one was bigger than the other, then the other was bigger than the one! And it would be discovered that Little Small had been Big Small for quite some time, whilst Big Small had been going around disguised as Little Small. No sooner would that be fixed up than they would change sizes again, and when they evened up, in the middle stages as it were, they could not by any means be told apart.

It was all very confusing, and Sajo had just about decided to give them one name between them and call them just "The Smalls," when Chilawee settled matters after a manner all his own. He had a habit of falling asleep in the warm cave under the stove, between the stones, and one day there

* Pronounced Am-*mick.*
† Pronounced *Chill*-a-wee and Chik-a-*nee.*

was a great smell of burning hair, and no one could imagine where it came from. The stove was opened and examined, and swept off, and the stove-pipes were tapped and rapped, but the smell of burning hair was getting stronger all the time; until some one thought of looking *under* the stove, to discover Chilawee sleeping there unconcernedly while the hair on his back scorched to a crisp, and he was routed out of there with a large patch of his coat badly singed. This made a very good brand, something like those that cattle are marked with on a ranch, and it stayed there all Summer, making it very easy to tell who was who; and by calling one of them (the burnt one) *Chila*wee, and the other Chika*nee*, so as to be a little different, they got to know each his name, and everything was straightened out at last.

They were a great pair of little talkers, Chilawee and Chikanee, and were always jabbering together and sometimes made the strangest sounds. And whenever either of the children spoke to them, which was often, they nearly always answered in a chorus of little bleats and squeals. When there was any work going on, such as the carrying in of water, or wood, or the floor was being swept, or if the people laughed and talked more than usual, or there were any visitors, the two of them would come bouncing out to see what it was all about and try to join in, and they would cut all kinds of capers, and get pretty generally in the way. It had been found that if given any tidbits from the table, they always took them into their house to eat or store them. So when they, like bad children, got to be something of a nuisance to the visitors, they had to be bribed with bits of bannock to make them go back in again; but before long, out they would come for some more bannock, and take that in with them, and out again and so on. Very soon they got to know that visiting time was bannock time as well, and when mealtimes came around they knew all about that too, and would be right there, pulling and tugging at the people's clothes and crying out for bannock, and trying to climb up people's legs to get it. And of course they always got what they wanted, and would run off with it to their cabin under the bunk, shaking their heads and hopping along in great style.

They followed the children around continuously, trotting patiently along behind them; and their legs were so very short and they ran so low to the floor on them that their feet could hardly be seen, so that they looked like two little clockwork animals out of a toy-shop, that went on wheels and had been wound up and never *would* stop. Anything they found on the floor, such as moccasins, kindling wood, and so forth, they dragged from place to place, and later, when they got bigger and stronger, they even stole sticks of firewood from the wood-box and took them away to their private chamber, where they sliced them up into shavings with their keen-edged teeth and made their beds with them; and nice, clean-looking beds they were too. Any small articles of clothing that might happen to fall to the floor, if not picked up at once, quickly disappeared into the beaver house. The broom would be pulled down and hauled around, and this broom and the firewood seemed to be their favourite playthings; greatly, I suspect, on account of the noise they could make with them, which they seemed very much to enjoy.

But their greatest amusement was wrestling. Standing up on their hind legs they would put their short arms around each other as far as they would go, and with their heads on each other's shoulders, they would try to put each other down. Now this was hard to do, as the wide tails and the big, webbed hind feet made a very solid support, and they would strain, and push, and grunt, and blow until one of them, feeling himself slipping, would begin to back up in order to keep his balance, with the other coming along pushing all he could. Sometimes the loser would recover sufficiently to begin pushing the other way and then the walk would commence to go in the opposite direction; and so, back and forth, round and round, for minutes at a time, they would carry on this strange game of theirs, which looked as much like two people waltzing as it did anything else. All the while it was going on there would be, between the grunts and gasps, loud squeals and cries from whoever was getting pushed, and much stamping of feet and flopping of tails, trying to hold their owners up, until one of them, on the backward march, would allow his tail to double under him, and fall on his back, when they would immediately quit and scamper around like two madcaps. It was all done in the greatest good humour, and the two children never grew tired of watching them.

Between this uproarious exhibition, and the flute-playing, and the sword-swallowing, and the begging, the trundling around of wood and all the other racket and commotion that, on some days, only ceased when they went to sleep, the beavers were about as busy, and noisy, and amusing a pair of little people as you could wish to live with.

But they were not always so lively. There came times when they were very quiet, when they would sit solemnly down together with their hands held tight to their chests and their tails before them, watching whatever was going on, still as two mice, looking, listening without a word, as though they were trying to make out what everything was all about. And sometimes, as they squatted there one beside the other, like two chocolate-coloured kewpies or little mannikins, Sajo would kneel in front of them and tell them a story, marking time to the words with her finger before their noses, as though she were conducting an orchestra. And they would sit there and listen, and watch her finger very closely, and soon they would commence to shake their heads up and down and from side to side, as beavers always do when they are pleased, and at last they would shake their whole bodies and their heads so hard that they would topple over and roll on the floor, exactly as if they had understood every word and just couldn't help laughing themselves to pieces over the story.*
Shapian would stand by taking it all in, and finding it rather ridiculous; but at the same time he wished, very privately of course, that he was not quite such a man, so he could join in this story-telling business himself. There were times when this thing of being grown up rather interfered with the fun!

Sometimes the little fellows were lonely and would whimper together with small voices in their dark little chamber, and Sajo, who had never forgotten her own mother and knew why they were lonesome, would take them in her arms and croon softly to them, and try to comfort them. And they would snuggle up close to her, holding tight to each other's fur all the while as though afraid to lose one another, and would bury their wee noses in the warm, soft spot in her neck where they so loved to be;

* This is actual fact, as are all the animal actions described in the story. Young beavers, raised by hand, will often respond in this manner to the advances of a person they know well. Wild beavers communicate their emotions to one another in this and other very striking ways.

and after a while the whimpering would cease and they would perhaps forget, for this time, and they would give big, long sighs and little moans of happiness, and fall asleep. For after all, with all their mischief and their shouting and their fun, they were just two small lost waifs, and they gave to these two human children, in their own humble way, the same love they had given to the father and the mother they had lost, and whom they never would forget.

And especially Chikanee loved Sajo. Chikanee was not as strong as Chilawee, was quieter and more gentle. Chilawee had a rather jolly way about him and was more of a roisterer, one of those "all for fun and fun for all" kind of lads to whom life is just one big joke; but Chikanee often had lonesome spells by himself, in corners, and had to be picked up and petted and made much of. Often he came out in the night and cried beside Sajo's bed to be taken up and allowed to sleep there beside her— while Chilawee lay on his back in the hut, snoring away like a good fellow. When Chikanee was in some small trouble, such as bumping his nose on the stove, or getting the worst of a wrestling match, he came to Sajo for comfort, and Sajo, always ready to sympathize with him because he was the weaker of the two, would kneel down beside him on the floor; and then Chikanee would climb onto her lap and lie there, happy and contented. Chilawee, when his badness was all done for the day, and he was feeling perhaps a little left out of things, would come over to get *his* share of the petting, squeezing in tight beside Chikanee, where he would settle down after giving a few deep sighs, vastly pleased, no doubt, with his day's work. And Sajo, not wishing to disturb them, would stay there until they were ready to go.

It was very easy to tell them apart by now, as they had become quite different in their ways. Chilawee was stronger, bolder, and more adventurous than his chum, a kind of comical fellow who seemed to enjoy bumping his head on the table legs, or dropping things on his toes, or falling into the wood-box. He was as inquisitive as a parrot and wanted to be into everything, which he generally was, if he could reach it. Once he climbed up onto the edge of a pail of water that some one had left on the floor for a moment, and perhaps mistaking it for a plunge-hole, dived right into it. The pail, of course, upset with a bang, splashing the water in all directions. Chilawee was most surprised; and so was everybody else. But in spite of all this wilful behaviour, he was just as affectionate as Chikanee, and dogged Shapian's footsteps (when not otherwise engaged!) nearly as much as the other one did Sajo's. And he could not bear to be away from Chikanee very long. Everywhere they went they were together, trotting along one behind the other, or side by side, and if they should become parted on their wanderings in the camp, they would start out to look for each other, and call to one another. When they met they would sit quite still for a little time, with their heads together, holding each other by the fur—though this wistful mood soon passed off, and it was not long before it all ended up in one of those queer wrestling matches, which seemed to be their way of celebrating.

And Sajo often thought how cruel it would be ever to part them.

CHAPTER SEVEN

The Trader

THERE CAME A TIME WHEN BIG FEATHER SAID THAT THE kittens should be allowed their freedom. They were now quite a size, and very active and strong, and the children were a little afraid that they would wander off and be forever lost. But their father told them how little beavers will not leave their home, if kindly treated, but would always return to the cabin as if it were a beaver house. He said they got lonely very quickly and would only stay away an hour or two.

So, one great, glorious, and very exciting day, the barricade that had been kept across the bottom of the doorway was taken away, and out they went. Not all at once though, as they did a lot of peeping and spying around corners, and sniffed and listened to a whole host of smells and sounds that were not really there at all. They made two or three attempts before they finally ventured down to the lake, with Sajo and Shapian on either side for a bodyguard. They started off at a very slow and careful walk, sitting up every so often to look around for wolves and bears; of course there weren't any, but it was lots of fun pretending. And as they came closer to the lake the walk became faster and broke into a trot, which soon became a gallop and into the water they rushed—and then dashed out again, hardly knowing what to make of so large a wash-tub as this. However, they soon went in again, and before very long were swimming, and diving, and screeching, and splashing their tails and having a glorious time "Just like real beavers," said Sajo.

It wasn't long before they commenced to chew down small poplar saplings. These they cut into short lengths, and peeled the bark off them in great enjoyment, while they sat amongst the tall grass and the rushes at the water's edge. They played and wrestled, and ran up and down the shore, and romped with their young human friends, and tore in and out of the water in a great state of mind. They stuck their inquisitive noses into every opening they saw, and found in the bank an empty muskrat hole. As they were just about the same size as the late owner of the hole, this suited them exactly, and they started to dig. The opening was under water, and as they worked away there the mud began to come out in thick clouds, so that nothing in the water could be seen. And for a long time the beavers disappeared until, becoming alarmed, Shapian waded into the water and pushed his arm inside the hole and felt around. The beavers were not there! "Sajo" he called excitedly, "they are gone!" And the two of them commenced hurriedly to search among the reeds and brush along the shore, when they heard behind them a most forlorn wailing and cry-ing, and there, following them, running as fast as their stumpy little legs would carry them, came Chilawee and Chikanee, scared half to death for fear that they were being left behind. They had left their work, and, swim-ming away under the muddy water, they had slipped away, and had landed further down the shore without being seen.

And now they were tired. So, sitting down like two little furry elves, they scrubbed, and rubbed, and combed their coats, and when that was done and they were quite dry, they turned and walked slowly and solemnly, side by side, up the pathway to the house. And there, with a big chunk of bannock apiece, they slipped quietly away into their birch-bark bedroom and ate their lunch; and then squeezing as tightly together as they could get on their nice, dry bed of shavings, fell fast asleep. And that was the end of their first, great day of freedom.

At last they were, as Sajo had said, Real Beavers.

Every day after that, as soon as the door was opened, they trotted down to the lake and had their daily swim. They spent hours at a time digging out the burrow they had found, and when it was far enough back to be safe, as they considered (you would have thought from the way they sometimes watched and snooped around, that the country was full of dragons), it was turned upwards and made to come out on top of the ground, and so became a plunge-hole, and over it, to the intense delight of Sajo and Shapian, they built a funny little beaver house! So now they had a real lodge, with a small chamber in it and an under-water entrance, a tunnel and a plunge-hole, all complete. The lodge was a little shaky about the walls, and was not very well plastered, but it was really quite a serviceable piece of work, considering.

Then they collected a quantity of saplings, and poplar and willow shoots, and made a tiny feed raft with them in front of their water-door-way, as grown-up beavers do, although it was ever so much smaller. Of course, all this feed would become sour in the water long before it could be used, and the Summer was no time for feed rafts anyway, and the wobbly house could never keep out the rain; but little they cared! They had a warm bed of their own up in the cabin, and there was always plenty of bannock, and, on certain occasions, even a taste or two of preserves, and each had his own little dish to eat it out of, so that counting everything, they owned a considerable amount of property for the size of them and were really quite well-to-do. So they didn't need either the crazy-looking lodge or the feed raft, but it was great fun fixing things up and cutting little trees, and digging, and playing with mud (mud houses must be so much more interesting to make than mud pies!) and doing all those things that beavers like so much to do, and cannot live contentedly without.

Sajo and Shapian, who spent nearly all their time down there, were having just as good a time looking on, often helped as well, and any building materials such as sticks, brush, earth, or the odd stone that they brought down, was immediately pounced on by the two little beavers and carried away. And sometimes these young scallawags would come ashore covered with mud from head to foot, and try to climb all over their friends, and then there would be a regular scramble, and a great deal of laughter.

Shapian built a play-house by the water-side, and they were often all in there together, while they rested in the shade of it, and this was Chikanee's favourite spot, and he often went there to look for Sajo, and would always come there when she called him. But Chilawee, the adventurer, who was more of a rover, and something of a pirate I'm inclined to think, could not stay still anywhere very long, would soon ramble away, and was continually getting lost. Of course *he* knew he wasn't lost, but the others thought he was, which amounted to the same thing so far as they were concerned; and then of course there would be a hunt. And he would turn up in the most unexpected places, and would be found in the play-house when it was supposed to be empty, or in the cabin when he was supposed to be in the play-house, or hidden away in the beaver wigwam, or under the canoe, where he would be asleep as likely as not. And when found, he would sit upright with his tail up in front of him, and would teeter-totter and wiggle his body and shake his head, as if he were either dancing or laughing at the trick he had played on the rest of them. If there was a sudden and unreasonable commotion anywhere, it was nearly always safe to say that this scapegrace was at the bottom of it, and when there was any shouting, or squealing, or any kind of an uproar going on, Chilawee was always at his best—or his worst, whichever way you happened to look at it, and his voice could be heard calling from all kinds of places at all kinds of times.

Nor was Chikanee quite the saint you may begin to think he was; he had as much fun as any of them. But there were times when he would break off quite suddenly, as though some thought had come into his little head, perhaps some dim memory of his home-pond that was so far away among the Hills of the Whispering Leaves. And then, if Sajo were not there to comfort him, he would waddle on his squat little legs, up to the play-house to look for her. If he found her there, he would sit beside her and do his careful toilet; and after he was all tidied up, he would nestle close to this so well-loved companion, and with his head on her knee, try to talk to her in his queer beaver language and tell her what the trouble was; or else lie there with his eyes half closed and dreamy, making small sounds of happiness, or perhaps of lonesomeness, or love—we cannot know. Very, very good friends indeed were these two, and where one was, there would be the other, before very long.

And what with all the lively antics, and the skylarking, and the work (not too much of it of course) and all the play, it would be hard for me to tell you just who were the happiest among these youngsters of the Wild, those with four legs, or those with two. But this I *do* know, that they were a very merry crew, in those happy, happy days at O-pee-pee-soway, The Place of Talking Waters.

꩜ ꩜ ꩜

THE TIDBITS OF BANNOCK HAD BEEN GETTING SMALLER AND smaller. Big Feather had been away some days now for more provisions and had not yet returned, and now there was hardly any flour. Nobody, children or beavers, had very much to eat, until one day the four playfellows arrived back at the cabin to find Gitchie Meegwon there.

He looked very grave and troubled about something. But the provisions were there; a bag of flour and some other goods lay on the floor, and beside them stood a white man, a stranger. This man had with him a large box. Big Feather spoke kindly to his children, but without smiling as he generally did, and they wondered why. The white man, too, stood there without speaking. Somehow things didn't look right. Even the little beavers seemed to feel that there was something amiss, for animals are often quick to feel such things, and they too, stood there quietly, watching.

Shapian, who had been to Mission school and understood English fairly well, heard his father say to the man:

"There they are; which one are you going to take?"

What was that? What could he mean? With a sudden sick feeling Shapian looked at his sister; but of course she had not understood.

"Wait till I have a look at them," said the stranger, answering Big Feather's question: "Let them move around a bit." He was a stout, red-faced man with hard blue eyes—like glass, or ice, thought Shapian. But Big Feather's eyes were sad, as he looked at his boy and girl. He asked the white man to wait a moment while he spoke to his children.

"Sajo, Shapian; my daughter, my son," he said in Indian, "I have something to tell you."

Sajo knew then that some trouble had come to them. She came close to Shapian, and looked timidly at the stranger—why! oh why, was he looking so hard at the beavers!

"Children," continued their father. "This is the new trader from the fur-post at Rabbit Portage; the old one, our good friend, has gone. A new

Company has taken over the post, and they ask me to pay my debt. It is a big debt, and cannot be paid until we make our hunt, next Winter. The other Company always dealt that way with the Indians, but the new Company say they cannot wait. We now have no provision, as you know, and this Company will give me nothing until the debt is paid. So I must go on a long journey for them, with the other men of the village, moving supplies to the new post at Meadow Lake, which is far from here. My work will pay the debt, and more, but I will receive no money until I return. In the meantime you, my children, must live. I cannot see you go hungry. This trader will give us these provisions"—here he pointed at the bags and parcels lying on the floor—"and in exchange he wants—he wants one of the beavers." He stopped, and no one so much as moved, not even the beavers, and he continued, "Live beavers are very valuable, and whichever one he takes will not be killed. But my heart is heavy for you, my children, and"—he looked at Chilawee and Chikanee—"and for the little beaver that must go."

Shapian stood very still and straight, his black eyes looking hard at the trader, while Sajo, hardly believing, whispered, "It isn't true. Oh, it isn't true!"

But Shapian never spoke, only put his arm around his sister's shoulder and stared hard at this man, this stranger who had come to spoil their happiness. He thought of his loaded gun, so close behind him in the corner; but his father must be obeyed, and he never moved. And he looked so fiercely at the trader that, although Shapian was only a four-teen-year-old boy, the man began to feel a little uneasy; so he opened his box, and reaching out for one of the beavers, picked the little fellow up, put him in it, and shut the lid. He nodded to Gitchie Meegwon:

"Well, I'll be seeing you down at the post in a couple of days," he said, and walked out with the box under his arm, shutting the door behind him.

Then Sajo, without a sound, fell to her knees beside her brother and buried her face in his sleeve.

The trader had chosen Chikanee.

And Chilawee, not knowing what to think, suddenly afraid, went into his little cabin, alone.

CHAPTER EIGHT

Sajo Hears the
Talking Waters

THE NEXT DAY BIG FEATHER STARTED AWAY FOR THE FUR-post, on his way to work out his debt to the Company. With him were seventeen other men from the village, in three big bark canoes. At Rabbit Portage they would load up the canoes with supplies for Meadow Lake, or Muskodasing,[*] another of the Company's posts, far to the North. The brigade, as such canoe caravans are called, would be gone a month or more. And Sajo, Shapian, and Chilawee were left alone at O-pee-pee-soway.

When the trader had so sharply shut the door between her and the one thing, next to her father and her brother, that she loved most in all the world, it had seemed to Sajo as if the door had closed on her heart as well, and that it too had gone out with Chikanee, in the box.

After this, a big change had come over all three of them. The happy circle had been broken up. There were no more merry parties in the play-house, no more fun or laughter on the lake shore. Chilawee cut no capers any more, and his voice, that used to be heard at all times and everywhere, was still. He never did his funny, jolly dance and never played, but wandered miserably up and down the water-trail all the day long, searching for Chikanee. He couldn't seem to get it into his little head that his playmate was gone. He would start out fresh and hopeful every morning, at a little trot, feeling sure that he would find him somewhere, looking in every corner of the play-house, and running from one to another of the

[*] Pronounced Mus-ko-*day*-sing.

trampled places in the grass and reeds, where they had so often sat together and combed themselves, and wrestled, and basked in the sunlight. He swam up and down along the shore, searching at all their old landing places, and dived in and out of the shaky little lodge that it had been such fun to build.

So he hunted all day, until at last he would give up, and his eager, shuffling trot would become a slow and weary walk, and he plodded on his tired little legs, up the pathway to the camp and lay, without a sound, in his empty, silent hut—no longer a rollicking pirate, no more a mischievous scapegrace, but just a lonely, sorrowful little beaver. He was not Big Small any more, just Small, because now he was all the Small there was. The two children followed him on his rounds, and pretended they were looking too, though they know his search was useless; for they could not bear to see him hunting around all by himself, like an unhappy little ghost. And when he ate from his dish, they both sat down beside him and held it for him; sometimes there would be one or two big tears fall into the bread and milk when Sajo thought of Chikanee, who should have been there too— poor Chikanee, poor Little Small who had been so soft and gentle and who had often been so lonesome, now away somewhere in the great city, where there was no more romping, no more bannock, no more fun.

Somehow it seemed that he couldn't be really gone. You more than half expected to find the squat little figure sitting somewhere in the playhouse, or see a short-legged dumpy little body come bouncing out beside Chilawee from the birch-bark cabin for his daily feast of bannock, and almost any minute you were ready to declare that you had heard his voice down at the landing. Even his little tracks, much smaller than Chilawee's, ugly, intoed, and pathetic, were still there in the mud beside the water. Sajo would go very often to look at them, and when no one was near she knelt down and touched them gently with her fingers and whispered to them; until at last they were washed away and disappeared. Over the very last one that was left she laid a sheet of birch bark, and every day made a visit to it alone; but even it gradually dried out and faded to dust, and was soon quite gone.

And then there was nothing left of him at all.

Though Chilawee's voice was seldom heard these days, yet sometimes in the night he awoke and, whimpering in utter loneliness, groped in the darkness for another small, round body that he could never find. And Sajo would hear him and awaken, and would creep into his chamber with him, and lie beside him on his little bed of shavings and hold him close to her, sobbing, until they both would fall asleep again.

Shapian sat for hours looking out over the lake, staring across at the far-away, forever marching hills, saying nothing, his heart aching for his sister, who never sang or laughed around the cabin any more. And a lump would come in his throat—and then he would look around very fiercely; for no one must ever know how hard it was to keep back the tears. How he hated those bags and parcels the trader had exchanged for Chikanee! The bannock nearly choked him when he ate it. If only he had thought to offer the trader his gun; four mink skins it had cost, and surely it was worth as much as one small, very small kitten beaver!

Although they had shared their pets, and Chilawee was really his, Shapian gave him up entirely to his sister. And she would sometimes take the little beaver, and carry him quite a distance up a creek that came tumbling down from out the hills behind the village, to where there was a low waterfall. Beside the fall there was a great, whispering pine tree and here, beneath the tree, she would sit and try to think of some way to get Chikanee back, while Chilawee swam, and dived, and even played a little by himself, in the quiet, deep pool below. He seemed happier there, Sajo thought, because the pool was small, and did not seem so wide and empty as did the lake, with its miles and miles of distance all around and only one small beaver there to fill it up.

And while her small companion swam around, or peeled his willow sticks, and sometimes sat upon her lap and combed himself, Sajo would listen to the voices in the falls. For, if you wait very patiently beside rapids or a waterfall you seem to hear, after a time, the sound of low murmuring voices, voices that come and go, now louder, now softer, sometimes seeming quite distinct, then fading away to be lost again in the muttering of the water. All the Indians have heard these sounds, and white people who have listened say they too can hear them, soft and singing in the brook. The Indians say that these are the voices of people from the Spirit Land, come back to speak to those they love. And here Sajo would sit until the voices came, and try to make out what they were saying. She was sure that some day she would be able to understand them, which was indeed likely, because Indian language so much resembles the sound of running water, the sighing of the wind, and the whispering of the trees. And Chilawee often sat beside her very quietly, as if he were listening, and perhaps he heard them too, better even than Sajo did, for a beaver's ears are much sharper than a person's.

This was the spot that the Indians called O-pee-pee-soway, The Place of Talking Waters, for which the village and the country round about were named. It had been Sajo's favourite place ever since she had been a very little girl, whenever she was lonesome, or wanted to think, or make up her mind about something. Often she would lie in the shade of the great pine, looking up into the dark, shadowy caverns between the giant branches; and when the sunbeams glanced through them and shone into those darksome caves, it looked very beautiful up in there, like some far-off, undiscovered country where there were fairies and other strange beings, and she sometimes wondered if that was where the spirits lived who spoke to people from the Talking Water. And as she lay gazing up into the gently swaying pine-top, listening to the stream, she used to feel somehow that her mother was near, speaking to her; and this made her very happy.

One day, as she sat there with Chilawee in her lap, listening to the drowsy murmur of the little fall, the sounds seemed to become very clear and plain, and she leaned back against the tree and shut her eyes, so as to hear them better. And after a while the sound of the water became less and less, and soon died quite away; and she thought that she could hear in place of it, some one speaking very softly, very plainly there beside her. Soon she began to make out the words, and the words were in the Indian language, that sounds so much like running water: "Sajo, Sajo, mah-jahn, mah-jahn. Sajo, Sajo, 'den-na jah-dahn," repeated over and over again, like a rhyme of poetry, or a song:

Sájo, Sájo,
Máh-jahn, máh-jahn.

---

* The J's are all pronounced soft, as in "zh" or "zsh" except in the name Sajo, where the J is hard as in "John." Accent on all first syllables.

Sájo, Sájo,
'Den-na jah-dahn.*
Sajo, Sajo,
You must go.
To the city
You must go.

On and on the voice seemed to chant these words, now louder, now softer, the sound coming and going as the murmur of the water in the falls had done. And it became so plain at last, that she seemed even to recognize the voice, a voice she had not heard for so long, her mother's voice. And she cried:

"O my mother, here is Sajo; O my mother, tell me more. I will listen to the words you tell me." And she reached out towards the sound and touched something soft and warm, and she opened her eyes rather suddenly to find her hand on the warm, damp nose of Chilawee, who was sitting up on her lap, pulling at her head shawl. She knew then that she had, for a moment, been asleep; and the words were lost again in the singing of the water, and the falls murmured on and on as they had always done.

Then Sajo jumped to her feet and took Chilawee up, and said to him:

"Chilawee, Chilawee, we are going to get Chikanee; we must go to the City for Chikanee. My mother has told me. I *know*."

So carrying the little beaver in her arms she started to run home, and as she ran she said to herself, yes, it was the voice of my mother. The Great Spirit let her come to the waterfall and speak to me; and she told me to go to the City—just wait till I tell Shapian!

❧❧❧

AND WHO CAN SAY THAT THE GREAT SPIRIT OF THE WILD lands, who watches over all the Little People, did *not* guide the waters while she slept, so they should seem to speak?

Meanwhile Chilawee got all shaken up with the running and didn't like it a bit, and he struggled to get down and began to cry out at the top of his voice, as he had not done for many a long day. Sajo thought, "He's got his voice back again, as before Chikanee went away, and that means my dream will come true. I *know* it will"; and she ran so much the harder. And between the running of one, and the calling out of the other, both of them were pretty well out of breath when they arrived at the cabin. And Shapian, seeing them in this state, came quickly out of the door and asked what the matter was; and Sajo told him of her dream, and how they must certainly go to the City.

But Shapian was not so ready to agree; he hadn't yet had time to think it over, and besides he hadn't had any dream. So he said:

"This is foolish, my sister; the City is far, we don't know the way, we have no money, and without money we can get neither bed nor food there; besides we would have to take Chilawee; and what would our father say?"

This all sounded very discouraging, but Sajo was not to be so easily turned aside, once she had made up her mind, and she answered:

"Our father is as sorry as we are, and would be glad if we found Chikanee again; for none of us have been happy since he was taken away."

But she said nothing about how she thought they were going to get to the City, or about what they would do if they did get there. For she believed very firmly in the message she had heard, and was quite positive that something wonderful was bound to come of it.[*] And Shapian looked at his sister and saw how her eyes were shining with hope, and how suddenly joyful she had become. To do as she asked would be hard, he knew, the hardest thing he had ever tried; but to refuse, without even trying, and then to see her more broken-hearted than ever, would be harder yet. And his father had said, before he left, for him to do all he could to make her happy once again. So there was only one thing to be done.

"Yes," he said, "we will go." And he stood up very straight, in the way he had, and looked very firm and manly. "Yes. I will take you to the City. Tomorrow."

But for all he looked so stern and proud, Shapian had not the faintest idea of how he was going to set about it, nor did he ever guess what a desperate adventure this would turn out to be.

[*] It is customary among the more primitive Indians to decide on a course of action in accordance with a particularly vivid dream.

CHAPTER NINE

The Red Enemy

LATE THE SAME NIGHT, EVERYTHING WAS IN READINESS FOR the journey. It would take Sajo and Shapian nearly a week to get to the trading post at Rabbit Portage, the first step of their long journey to the city; and they had no idea what lay beyond the post. So they took plenty of everything that was needed for a long trip. Sajo had made several large bannocks, and filled different-sized canvas bags with flour, tea, and salt, and she made up a parcel of dried deer meat and set aside a small pail of lard, and put matches in a tight-topped can where they would remain dry; while Shapian rolled up a tent and blankets, fixed up a fish-line, sharpened his belt-axe and his hunting knife, whittled a thin edge on the blades of the paddles, and boxed up whatever pots and dishes and other small items of cookery they would have need of.

The sun had not yet arisen on the following morning, when breakfast was over and the full outfit was loaded in the canoe, along with Shapian's rifle; for much as he prized this gun, he intended to sell it if he could, hoping that it would bring at least enough to pay their way to the city. What was to happen after that he didn't dare even to think about. Chilawee went in the same birch-bark basket in which he and Chikanee had first come to O-pee-pee-soway, and in the cookery-box Sajo had put *both* the little beaver dishes, as this helped her to feel more certain that they were going to bring back Chikanee and Chilawee together.

"We will need them both," she said aloud, "for," and here her voice dropped a little, "we *are* going to get him, I think," and then louder, as she nodded her head and pursed her lips, "I just *know* we are." And to make her belief the stronger she added, "My mother said so. In the sound of Mudway-oshkay.* I heard her, in the sounding of the water she has told me!"

You see her dream seemed so very real, and meant so much to her.

The village was some distance away from their cabin, and they had told no one about their plans, for fear the older people might try to stop them. The old Chief especially might forbid them. So they slipped away into the mists of early morning without any one being the wiser. And as they floated out from the landing, Sajo shook her paddle above her head, as she had seen the men do when they started on a journey, shouting the name of the place they were bound for; and so she held her paddle up and cried out "Chik-a-*nee*! Chik-a-*nee*!" You could hardly call Chikanee a place but, she thought, wherever he is, that's where we are going. But Shapian did not wave his paddle, nor did he shout; for he was not so sure where they would end up.

And so they left the Place of Talking Waters, and started out on what was to be, for all three of them, their Great Adventure.

The canoe was the one with the eye and the tail, the same canoe in which we first saw Gitchie Meegwon on the River of Yellow Birches, and in it they paddled swiftly all that day, the great eye staring eagerly ahead and the fox's tail fluttering gaily out behind, as the canoe fairly leaped forward at every stroke of the paddles. They stopped occasionally in order to put Chilawee over the side to have a drink, and to swim around for a minute or two so as to get cooled off, for the weather was very hot. That night they put up their tent in the woods along the shore, and spent the night there. The next morning at daybreak they were away again, and paddled steadily till dark, stopping only to eat and to exercise their furry chum. Each morning they were on their way before the sun rose, and every evening they made camp in some sheltered spot beside the water, where Chilawee swam around all night, always returning to the tent at daylight to fall asleep in his basket, where he remained quietly all day. Both children worked on the portages, of which there were a number, each carrying his share of the

* Pronounced Muh-*dway-oshe*-kay.

load. There were two trips apiece, including the canoe, which Shapian carried alone. Neither of them found this to be particularly hard work; in fact, they thought nothing at all about it one way or the other, for that kind of a journey was nothing new to either of them.

And so, day after day they forged ahead, onward, onward, ever onward; and two small backs bent and swayed like clockwork and two paddles swished and dipped all the long day, as regularly and evenly as the step of marching soldiers, while the burning sun rose on one side of them, passed overhead, and sank again like a great red ball behind the dark wall of the forest. Day after day the faithful bark canoe carried them staunchly and steadily forward, outward bound on the long search for the absent Chikanee.

And in all that great wilderness they were just a little moving speck that crawled across the silver surface of wide, boundless lakes, alone on the face of all the world; but it was a speck that held two young hearts that were full of courage and one, at least, that was high with hope—and another whose owner was full of bannock, and who lay snoring content-edly, even if not too happily, in his basket.

One morning they awoke to find a faint smell of wood-smoke in the air, a smell of burning moss and scorching brush and leaves, and they knew that somewhere, seemingly far away, there was a forest fire. But it was closer than they had at first supposed, for as soon as they were well out on the lake and were able to look about them, they could see an immense pillar of smoke billowing up from behind the distant hills; and they did not paddle very far before they found that their route would bring them more and more in its direction. The lake was getting very nar-row, and farther on it ended and became a river, across which the fire could easily jump. Shapian determined to get through this narrow place as quickly as possible, to a large lake that lay beyond, where they would be safe. So they hurried on, and as they went the smoke spread higher and wider, so that it was no longer a pillar, but a white wall that seemed to reach the sky, and rolled outwards and down in all directions, becoming thicker and thicker until the sun was hidden, and the air became heavy and stifling, and very still. The whole country to the Eastward seemed to be on fire, and although the blaze itself was hidden by the hills, even at that distance there could be heard a low moaning sound, that never ceased and was, minute by minute, becoming closer, and headed almost straight towards them—they were right in the path of the fire. The big lake was some distance away, across a portage, and there was no time to be lost if they were to cross over to it before the fire rushed down upon them; for, while some forest fires move slowly, others have been known to travel as fast as thirty miles an hour.

As the hot smoke cooled off, it began to come down, settling in a dark, blue haze over all the land, making far-off points invisible and near ones look dim, so that soon nothing could be seen but the row of trees nearest the shore-line, and the children were only able to keep their right direction by watching this, and by the sound of the rapids that lay ahead of them. Very soon they arrived at the head of this steep place in the river, where the water rushed and foamed wildly between, and over, dark jagged rocks for several hundred yards. It was a dangerous place, but Shapian dared not take time, with the double trip they had, to cross the portage that went round it, and he decided to take the quicker route and run the rapids.

For the fire was now not far away, and the sharp turn that he knew to be at the end of the swift water, would head them straight for it. The roar of the fire was now so loud as to almost drown the sound of the noisy rapids, and Shapian soon saw that it was to be a hard race, and a swift one, to gain the lake—and then there was the portage, and it was a long one.

The smoke was now so thick that when they neared the rapids they could not see fifty feet ahead of them, and Shapian had all he could do to find the place to enter it. Standing up in the canoe to get a better view, he at length found the starting point; and then with a swift rush they were into the dashing, boiling white water. Although he was hardly able to see through the smoke, Shapian skilfully picked his way down the crooked, difficult channel between the rocks. Great curling, hissing waves lashed out at the frail canoe, throwing it violently from one white-cap to another; dark, oily-looking swells gripped its underside like evil monsters seeking to pour in over the sides and sink it. Spinning eddies snatched wickedly at the paddles as the little craft leaped like a madly charging horse between the black, savage-looking rocks that lay in wait to rip and tear the light canoe to pieces.

And above the thunderous roar of the tumbling waters there came the duller, deeper, and terribly frightening sound of the oncoming fire. Smoke poured across the river in dense, whirling clouds, and through it sped the leaping canoe with its crew of three. And the sleeping passenger in the basket woke up, and excited by all the noise, and quite aware that something unusual was happening, began to take a part in the proceedings, and added his little thin voice to the uproar, though it could hardly be heard, and he rocked and shook his house of bark so violently that a moment had to be spared to lay a heavy bundle on it to keep it right side up.

Shapian strained and fought with his paddle and all of his young strength against the mighty power of the racing torrent, turning the canoe cleverly this way and that, swinging, sidling, and slipping from one piece of clear water to the next, checking the canoe in the quieter places while he stood up to get a better view of what lay ahead—and then away into the white water again. Meanwhile Sajo pulled and pushed and pried on her paddle with might and main, as Shapian shouted to her above the rattle and the din, "Gyuk-anik" (to the right hand), or "Mashk-anik" (to the left hand), or "Weebetch" (hurry), and sometimes "Pae-ketch" (easy there). Sheets of spray flew from the sides of the canoe as it heaved and bounced and jerked. Some of it came in and Sajo, who was in front, soon became soaked. Except that the smoke made the safe channel so hard to find, they were in no real danger from the rapids itself, for Shapian, like all his people, both young and old, was very skilful in a canoe and understood, even at his age, a great deal about the movements of water; and he had often run this rapids with his father. And Sajo, trusting in him completely, laughed and cried out in her excitement, for this was like a show to her, and she let out little yelps as she had heard her father and the other Indians do, with their louder whoops and yells as they ran a dangerous piece of water—though she had always been left safely on the shore to watch. But Shapian, who knew how serious things really were, never made a sound besides his loud commands as captain of their little ship, and when he could spare an eye from the turmoil of madly boiling water all about him, gave anxious glances to the side from which the fire was coming. And coming it was, with the speed of a train it seemed, rushing down the hills towards them like a crimson sea, with great roaring streamers of flame flying high above the burning forest. Once he looked back, to find that the fire had crossed the narrow lake behind them; now there was only one way to go—forward, though he said never a word to Sajo about it. The air, that had been thick with heavy rolls and banks of smoke, now commenced to turn darker and darker, and the light was dimmed until it appeared almost as though twilight had fallen, so early in the day, and hardly anything could be seen around them; and nothing seemed real any more and they moved like people in a dream.

Desperately Shapian drove the canoe ahead, for well he knew that if they were caught in this place they would be either burnt alive or suffocated. By now the portage was not very far, and beyond it lay the lake that they must get to—and get to fast!

They shot out from the foot of the rapids into a deep, still pool, and here they found themselves surrounded by strange moving shapes, dimly seen through the smoke-clouds, as on all sides all manner of animals were passing, tearing along the shore, or swimming through the pool, or splashing noisily along the shallows, by ones and twos, separately or in small groups, all headed for the big lake, the same one our own travellers were aiming for, each and every one making for the safety he knew that he would find there. Animals that seldom wetted their feet were swimming in the pool—squirrels, rabbits, woodchucks, and even porcupines. Deer leaped through or over the underbrush, their white tails flashing, eyes wide with terror. A bear lumbered by at a swift, clumsy gallop, and a pair of wolves ran, easily and gracefully, beside a deer—their natural prey; but they never even looked at him. For none were enemies now; no one was hungry, or fierce, or afraid of another. And all the people of the woods, those that went on two legs and others that had four, and those with wings and some that swam, animals and birds and creeping things, creatures, some of them, that dared not meet at any other time, were now fleeing, side by side, from that most merciless of all their foes, dangerous and deadly alike to every one of them from the smallest to the greatest—the Red Enemy of the Wilderness, a forest fire.

Right before the canoe, deep in the water, stood a giant bull moose, largest of all the forest folk, his hair scorched from his back, one of his half-grown horns gone,[*] his sides heaving as he sucked in great, deep

[*] At the time of this incident, during July, a moose's antlers would be only partially developed.

breaths of air; he must have been nearly caught, and perhaps had run many miles with the fire close behind him, and had only escaped because of his enormous strength and speed. Shapian could have touched him with his paddle had he wished, but the huge beast paid them no attention, and getting his wind again, plunged ashore and joined the other creatures of all shapes and sizes that, all brothers now in this great calamity, were hurrying together to the safety of the lake.

And with them, in this wild and queer procession, were our two little Indians and their tiny pet.

Sajo, now realizing what all this meant, became terror-stricken, so Shapian, almost in despair himself, yet knowing that their lives depended on him, kept his courage up and soothed her as best he could, and she paddled bravely on. But the forest that had always been their home, and had always seemed so friendly, had suddenly become a very terrible place to be in. It would have been so to any grown-up; yet these two children, one of them eleven and the other fourteen years of age, remember, kept their heads and fought like good soldiers for their lives, and for Chilawee's. And this same Chilawee was no great help, as you can well believe; on the contrary, he showed every sign of causing trouble and delay. Sensing real danger, as all animals do, and scared out of his wits by the sounds and scent of the other creatures that passed on every side, he was screeching at the top of his lungs and pounding and tearing at the lid of his prison, as it must now have seemed to him, and if some way were not found to quiet him, he would soon be out of it; and once in the water he could never again be found in all this hurry and confusion.

A few short minutes and they were at the portage. The trail was nearly hidden by the blinding smoke, and down the slopes of the nearby ridge the hoarse roar of the fire was coming swiftly. The darkness that had fallen as the smoke poured over the forest, was now lighted up by a terrible red glow, and the heat from it could be plainly felt. Quickly they threw their stuff ashore. Chilawee was now in such a state that he could never be carried in any other way except as a separate load. This landing being safe for the minute, and not knowing what shape things were in at the other end, they at once decided to leave him here. It was but the work of a moment to turn the canoe over on top of the basket, so as to hold down the lid (like all his kind when very frightened, Chilawee forgot to use his teeth), and taking each a load the children started across, running at a dog-trot.[*] On all sides thick moving coils of black and yellow smoke wound and billowed around them as they ran, took strange shapes and forms and seemed to reach out with pale waving hands to hold them back. Through the whirling smoke-clouds the trees beside the trail loomed indistinct like tall, dark, silent ghosts; while here and there red eyes of flame glowed at them through the haze.

But Sajo and Shapian kept right on at their steady trot. At the far side there was a breeze from off the lake, and the end of the portage was clear. Gulping a few breaths of fresh air, they left their loads beside the waters' edge and raced back for Chilawee and the canoe. The race was often little but a scramble as, gasping and half-blinded, they staggered down the trail, half the time with their eyes closed to relieve the pain in them, and to shut out the stinging, burning smoke, while they groped their way along, their hearts filled with a fear such as they had never before known. By the time they were back at the canoe, sparks and burning brands were falling everywhere, and the angry glow had deepened so that everything, trees, smoke, and water, were red with it. And now, close at hand, could be heard a dreadful, low, rushing sound.

The fire was almost upon them.

And at the same time Chilawee, having made up his mind to save his own little life as best he could, was gnawing steadily away at the thin bark sides of his box; in no time at all he would be through. If only it would hold together for just five more minutes!

In a moment Shapian tore off his sister's head shawl, and quickly soaking it in water, with swift movements wrapped it about her head and face, leaving only her eyes and nose showing. Then splashing water over her clothes, he said:

"Do not wait. I will come quickly. Go!"

And hugging Chilawee's basket tight to her body with both arms, Sajo disappeared into that awful, glowing tunnel of a trail.

---

[*] This is not an unusual pace with Indians when carrying a load, and on level ground is easier than walking.

CHAPTER TEN

The Empty Basket

AFTER HE HAD SEEN HIS SISTER PASS FROM SIGHT, SHAPIAN was delayed perhaps a full minute while he wetted his own clothes and slipped the paddles into the carrying-thongs. How he wished now for his father's guiding hand! He was doing the best he knew, with his small experience, to save the lives of all three of them (for he looked on the little beaver almost as though he, too, were a person, a little brother who must be saved as well) and he hoped he had chosen aright. And now Sajo was in there ahead of him, alone; he must hurry!

Throwing the canoe up, and over, with his head inside between the paddles, which formed a kind of yoke, he was quickly on his way. But in that short minute that he had been detained, the fire had gained on him, and while he ran as swiftly as a boy of fourteen could well do with a twelve-foot canoe on his shoulders, he saw, not far away to one side, a solid, crackling wall of flame. Trees fell crashing in the midst of it, and others burst with loud reports like gun-fire. Onward he tore through what had now become a cave of crimson smoke, half-choked, his eyes stinging, his head throbbing with the heat. But he clenched his teeth and kept on, while close beside him the blazing forest crackled, and thundered, and roared. Whole tree-tops caught fire with a rush and a horrible screeching, tearing sound, and flames leaped from tree to tree like fiery banners, ever nearer and nearer to the trail.

Beneath the canoe some clear air remained, which helped him a little, but the heat was all he could stand. Once a burning spruce tree came crashing down so near the portage that its flaming top fell across the trail ahead of him in a flurry of sparks and licking tongues of flame, and he was obliged to wait precious moments while the first fury of the burning brush died down. Then he jumped, with the canoe still on his shoulders, over the glowing trunk. The hot breath of it fanned his body and nearly strangled him, and he stumbled to his knees as he landed. Righting himself he cleared the canoe before the fire had harmed it, but the bravely flying fox tail had caught on fire, and in a moment was scorched to a crisp. But he went on.

On the upturned canoe fell large flakes of burning bark and red-hot ashes, that lay there and smoked and smouldered, so that to any one who might have followed him, it must have seemed to be already burning, which for very truth, it was not far from doing. And now he should have caught up to his sister; she would be slower than he, for the basket was an awkward affair to run with, whereas a bark canoe, though very much heavier, was a steady, well-balanced load, even for a boy. And he suddenly became terrified lest Chilawee had cut open his box and escaped on the way, and that Sajo having delayed somewhere to capture him, he had passed them. But just ahead, the smoke was clearing and he felt the wind from the lake. Then, sick and dizzy, his sight blurred by the water that streamed from his eyes, he stumbled again, and this time fell heavily, canoe and all, over something soft that lay in the pathway—there, face down across the trail, lay Sajo! And clutched tightly in one of her hands was the basket—empty. Chilawee had at last cut his way out, and was gone!

Hardly knowing what he was doing, Shapian crawled from under the canoe, lifted Sajo across his knees, scrambled, somehow, to his feet and then, his breath coming in choking sobs, his knees bending under him and a great ringing in his ears, he staggered with her in his arms to the lake shore.

Here he laid her down and threw water over her face, and rubbed her hands, and cried out, "Sajo, Sajo, speak to me, speak!" And she opened her eyes and said faintly, "Chilawee." And he dared not tell her there was no Chilawee any more, only an empty basket.

And now the smoke was rolling out over them even here; the whole portage was aflame, and waiting only to wet Sajo's shawl and throw it over her face, Shapian went back for the canoe. Fortunately it was not far, as, unable to lift it any more, he seized it by one end and dragged it to the water, stern out and bow inshore so as to load the quicker. Quickly he threw in the bundles, and lifted Sajo into the bow, while she held tightly to the basket and cried weakly, "Chilawee, Chilawee, Chilawee," and moaned, and kept repeating, "Chilawee."

All this took but a short time, and running lightly over the load to the other end, Shapian commenced to back the canoe out stern first, as fast as he was able and a big sob came in his throat as he thought of their little furry friend who was now past all help. Yet surely, he thought, the little creature, gifted to find water easily, might have reached the lake, and even if lost might still be living—when, behind him, from out on the lake, came the sound of a smart slap, and a splash upon the water, and there was the lost Chilawee, alive and quite well, thank you, giving out, by means of his tail, his private and personal opinion of this Red Enemy that he had so narrowly escaped. And Shapian shouted out in a great voice, "Sajo! Sajo! Chilawee is safe, Chilawee is out on the lake—look!"

And at that Sajo, lying there in the bow of the canoe, burst into tears and sobbed as if her heart would break; she would not cry before, when she believed her little friend was dead, but now he was known to be safe she was free to cry all she wanted, to cry as loud and as long as she liked—with joy!

Chilawee was quite far out, and in no danger, but a canoe does not start very quickly when paddled backwards, and being still in shallow water, was too close to shore for safety; and at the edge of the forest, leaning out over the water, was a huge pine tree that was hollow, and had been burning fiercely all this time. Shapian was still struggling to get the canoe backed away far enough to turn it (and it did not take nearly as long for all this to happen as it does to tell about it), when the bark of the pine, dried out by the intense heat, cracked wide open, and the hurrying tongues of fire rushed up this channel as if it had been a stove-pipe, to the top of it. The great fan-shaped head of the towering tree, that had looked proudly out over the wilderness for many a hundred years, burst into a mass of flame that leaped into the air above it, the height again of the tree itself. And then the burnt-out butt, unable to stand against the force of the soaring flames, gave way, and the mighty trunk tottered and began to fall, outwards towards the lake, swayed a little sideways, and then started on its fiery path, straight for the canoe. Slowly at first, then faster and faster the hundred-foot giant overbalanced, and the terrible fan of flame rushed downwards. Real terror, for the first time, seized on Shapian, and with desperate strength he stopped the canoe and drove it smashing into the shore, while just behind him the burning tree plunged into the lake with a deafening crash, and a hissing and a screeching that could have been heard for a mile or more as the fire and water met. Smoke and steam poured up and smothered everything as the flames went out, so that Shapian could see nothing, and the waves from this terrific splash rocked the canoe violently and Sajo, beside herself with fright, jumped to her feet in the dangerously rolling canoe and screamed, and screamed, and Shapian sprang over the side and ran through the water to her, and held her in his arms, and comforted her, and told her that there was nothing more to fear.

And out on the lake Master Chilawee slapped his little tail in small defiance; or perhaps it was intended for an imitation of the falling tree— in which case, I can tell you that it was a pretty feeble imitation.

In a few short moments the canoe was away, this time without any accident, and the little beaver, seeming mighty glad that he was found again, gave himself up quite cheerfully and was lifted by this so impudent tail of his and dropped aboard, where he clambered around on the load, and smelled at the children, and ran about, and altogether showed signs of the greatest pleasure and excitement. He did not seem to have lost one single hair, no doubt because he ran so low to the ground on his short legs, so that everything passed over him; and so now he was celebrating, and they all had quite a reunion out there on the lake.

Before they had gone very far, Sajo began to feel better, and soon was well enough to sit up. Shapian would not let her paddle, and had her sit facing him, while she told her story, and related how, choked by the hot, burning smoke, and not being able to see, she had been unable to catch Chilawee when he fell from the basket, and had become confused and fallen, where, she did not know, and had then been unable to get up again. And that was all she knew about it until she found Shapian pouring water over her face. She did not remember calling Chilawee, though she knew he had run away, having seen him, as in a dream, disappear into the clouds of smoke. And when she was done her story she began to look hard at her brother's face, and then to laugh! And the more she looked the louder she laughed, and Shapian was a little frightened, and began to wonder if the dangers she had been through had touched her mind, until she exclaimed:

"Shapian!—your face—you should see it, why—you have no eyebrows!" And then suddenly she stopped laughing and felt for her own eyebrows, and asked anxiously: "How are mine, are they all right?" and looked over the side of the canoe at the water to see the reflection of her face. But the canoe was moving, and ruffling the water and she could, of course, see nothing, and now very alarmed, she cried:

"Oh, stop the canoe so I can see—tell me, are my eyebrows there?" And she got into a great way about it, and Shapian laughed at her, in his turn, and would not say; until at last he told her they were there all right, yes, both of them; which indeed they were, as her face had been covered most of the time. But it was just like a girl, said Shapian to himself, to worry about a little thing like eyebrows when they had all so nearly lost their lives. And truly, a little more, and there would have been no happy ending to *this* story.

The canoe had suffered most and was leaking rather badly, but otherwise everything was going quite smoothly again. But behind them the fire swept over the portage and on beyond it, like a conquering army, leaving everything in its path a blackened, smoking ruin. Well, they were safe now, and except for two aching heads and two pairs of smarting eyes, were in the best of spirits. Shapian, for once, felt quite encouraged at having beaten the fire, because, as Sajo put it, there was hardly *anything* worse to be met with than a forest fire, and they had come right *through* it (as she imagined), so nothing in the world could *ever* keep them now from Chikanee. And as for Chilawee, he appeared to have come through the affair the best of any of them, and evidently gave the matter no further thought, and stretching himself out on the bottom of the canoe, with his head comfortably pillowed on Sajo's knee, he promptly went to sleep.

That afternoon they made an early camp, in a good safe place, on an island far out on the lake, and here they looked over the damage. Shapian could not very well repair his eyebrows, which would grow out later of their own accord, but he had plenty to do with the canoe. The gay and gallant tail was just a blackened, shrivelled piece of skin, and the once keen and watchful eye was nearly gone, most of the paint having blistered, and cracked, and fallen off. The hard smash the bow had got against the shore when they had dodged the falling tree, had torn off a good-sized strip of bark; the spruce gum at the seams had melted, and the burning embers that had fallen on it had smouldered long enough to scorch a number of thin places in the sides and bottom. Also their tent and blankets had a few holes burnt in them by flying sparks. But the loss was quite small, considering, and they could easily have fared a great deal worse. The top was gone from Chilawee's box, and in the side of it was a hole the size of a quart measure, Chilawee's part in the battle! But there were plenty of birch trees around, and Shapian cut sheets of bark from them, and sewed a patch on the hole and made another lid that fitted nearly as well as the old one, and he fixed up the canoe with a few patches and some fresh gum. The eye and the tail would have to wait until later. Sajo, meanwhile, busied herself with needle and thread, which no Indian girl or woman will travel very far without, and soon had the tent and blankets serviceable again, and by the time darkness fell, everything was in readiness for a new start in the morning.

And that night, as the two of them sat side by side, looking across to the mainland, they were thinking how nearly they had come to never seeing their father again, and they were lonesome for him. And they could hear, even yet, faintly in the distance, the low moaning of the fire, while the sky shone red for many miles, lit up by the beautiful, but terrible glow from that greatest of all dangers of the wilderness, before whom all alike are helpless, and which can be brought about so easily so that great forests, and thousands of animals, and often whole townsful of people, have been destroyed by a single match in the hands of one careless man.

And later, as Shapian lay on his bed of brush, watching the slow fading of the red glow on the canvas walls of the tent, as the fire died down amongst the swamps and bare rocks that it finally had a run into, he came to the very pleasing conclusion, that even if he were not really yet a man, at this rate of going, it would not be very long before he was one.

And looking over at Sajo, who lay fast asleep with Chilawee cuddled in her arms, he heaved a big sigh, and closing his eyes, was soon with them in the Land of Dreams.

White Brother
to the Indians

AFTER TWO MORE DAYS OF TRAVEL, SAJO AND SHAPIAN arrived at Rabbit Portage. Its full name was Wapoose-ka-neemeech,[*] or in English, The Place of Dancing Rabbits. It had been so named because rabbits were very thick at this place some years, and these animals have a way of thumping their hind feet rapidly on the ground, so that by moonlight, when there are a number of them doing this, it appears and sounds very much as if they were dancing. However, I think we will call it Rabbit Portage, as the white people do.

The youngsters pitched their camp in a little bay near the post, where Chilawee could swim in safety, as the regular Indian camping ground, though empty just now, would be swarming with hungry sleigh dogs that had to find their living as best they could in the Summer time, and would kill anything that was small enough, and eat anything that was not made of wood or iron; even very young children had to be kept out of their way. After the tent was up, and a good thick, springy floor of brush laid down, and wood had been collected and everything comfortably stowed in its place, Shapian took the canoe and went to visit the fur-post.

Here he found the trader, the same trader who had been to their home on that fateful day, earlier in the Summer. He was new to the country and could talk only a little Indian, and Shapian's English was not any too good. So the trader took him into his little private office behind the store, where

[*] Pronounced *Wah*-poose-kah-*nee*-meech.

they would not be interrupted, and here they managed somehow to understand one another. Shapian, standing before the trader upright as an arrow, explained everything as best he could. He told how everything had seemed to go wrong since Chikanee had been sold, and how his sister was all the time downhearted, and how lonesome was Chilawee, and how unhappy they all were. And the trader, sitting there behind his desk, looking more like a judge than a trader, listened very closely to all that Shapian said, and when he had finished the white man said:

"So Chila—who—?"

"Chilawee," corrected Shapian.

"Oh, yes," continued the trader, looking very severe, "so Chikalee, he's lonesome, eh? And your sister too; and you want Chik—what's his name again?—Chinawee back, eh?"

"Yes," answered Shapian patiently. "Want Chikanee back."

And the trader cleared his throat rather gruffly, and gave a little snort—what nonsense, he thought, so much fuss over a little whining beast no bigger than a puppy! But Shapian kept on in a low, even voice, picking his words slowly and carefully in the trader's language, of which he knew so little:

"Me, I will work. I will make wood [he meant "cut wood"] for your Winter. I work all Summer for you; also I sell you my gun. So I trade now, the wood and my gun for Chikanee. Those are my words, me." But they were words that trembled a little at the last, for this gun was very dear to him.

"I don't want your gun," said the trader sharply. "This post sold it to you, and we most certainly won't buy it back. This is no pawnshop!" And his hard blue eyes looked very fierce indeed. Poor Shapian, who didn't even know what a pawnshop was, looked down at his moccasins to hide the trembling of his lips, and then proudly raised his head again, and said in his low voice:

"Then I work all Winter as well, me: all one year I work for you. One year for Chikanee."

Fiddlesticks! thought the trader, was the boy crazy? It was plain to be seen that this man knew very little about Indians. Suddenly he asked:

"Did you see the fire?"

"Yes," replied Shapian. "Me, Sajo, Chilawee, pass through fire; one portage burning up. Pretty near finish us."

The white man stared hard at him—through the fire! "Preposterous," he was about to say, and was going to speak roughly again; but he thought the better of it, and made only another gruff sound in his throat. For even he could not help seeing how much in earnest the little fellow was; and then, seeing this, he was really sorry, for he knew that he could do nothing. Chikanee had been sold again, this time to some city people who had a park where wild beasts were kept in cages (Chikanee a wild beast!), and a live beaver was a rare and valuable animal. He explained all this to Shapian, still speaking roughly because he was new to trading and thought that it was the right way to speak to Indians, though in spite of his red, angry face and hard blue eyes, he was not quite the ogre he made himself out to be, and he finished by feeling the least bit uncomfortable. And he talked in as kindly a tone as he was able to, when he told Shapian that Chikanee (Chikaroo this time!) had been gone a month now, and had been sold for fifty dollars.

Fifty dollars! The boy's heart sank—fifty dollars, he had never seen such a sum. Traders hardly ever gave money; they gave only goods in exchange for fur, because the Indians would only have to spend the money in the same store they got it from in the first place, at the post, so it was hardly worth the trouble of carrying around. Fifty dollars—his offer of work, and his precious gun, both refused! And he had nothing else to give. But it was not his way to give up quickly, and he went back to camp and told Sajo that he had found out just where Chikanee was. And she was very glad at this piece of news; for he never told her how hard-hearted the trader had been, nor about the large sum of money that they would never be able to get. So Sajo thought that there was nothing to do now but wait until Shapian had cut a little wood, and earned their fare to the city and back (it couldn't be very much, people came and went every few days!), and a little besides to buy back Chikanee with. And in a way she was right, that was all there was to do. But she didn't know how hopeless it all really was.

So Shapian bore his load of misery alone, and racked his young brains to think of a way to earn fifty dollars. And as for the railroad fare, he had been afraid to even ask about it, and sometimes, too, he wondered what his father was going to say about all this, though he was pretty sure that anything he did to make Sajo happy, would be very easily forgiven, even if it were not quite what had been expected of him. All night he tossed and turned in his blanket while he planned and planned. If only they could get to the city somehow! He had heard that some of these white people were kind, especially the city people; not at all like the traders. If he could get down there and tell the folks who owned Chikanee, how things were and how miserable everybody was, perhaps they would let Chikanee go home with Sajo, while he stayed behind and worked for them till the little prisoner's freedom had been paid for. Otherwise, he was sure, the whole expense would come to a hundred dollars. Poor Shapian, he could think of no greater amount of money than a hundred dollars. He had heard spoken of as rich, an Indian who had earned a hundred dollars real money; this man had been out as a forest guide with a party of Americans. These Gitchie Mokoman—Big Knives, as the Indians called the Americans, were not hard to work for; they expected their guides to be friends, not servants, so the men of the village said, and they paid very high wages and often gave away their tents, or blankets, or guns, even whole camping outfits, after the trip was over. And at that thought a new idea came to him; and it was this:

Every second or third day, there came up river to Rabbit Portage a big, clumsy-looking steamboat, a wood burner with two decks and huge wheels on its sides, in boxes. This unlikely-looking craft made the journey back and forth to the railroad. But no one could go aboard without money—always money, thought Shapian, and wondered how much the captain wanted for the trip; more money than he had, anyway, for he had none at all. But numbers of Americans came up on the boat from time to time. It was quite likely that some of them would need a guide, and this was work that he was well able to do.* Full of this fresh plan, he hurried over to the post as soon as he had had his breakfast; but there was no one

---

* The hunting, fishing and scenic beauties of Northern Canada have attracted to the more accessible outposts large numbers of sportsmen, largely Americans, who employ the Indians as guides, or scouts, and some of the villages derive their sole revenue from this source.

there except the trader until nearly noon, when the steamer was expected. Shortly before mid-day this cumbersome affair chugged its way up the river and came in to the dock in a grand sweeping half circle with a great splashing of paddle-wheels, and shouting of orders, and bell-ringing, and all the pomp and circumstance to be expected of the one and only real, live steamboat in the entire country. Sure enough, a crowd of tourists came ashore with their camping outfits, each having enough, to Shapian's notion, to supply at least forty people. They looked curiously at the Indian boy, with his buckskin moccasins and long braided hair, the first real Indian that some of them had ever seen, and they whispered and passed remarks amongst themselves, and one or two pointed black boxes towards him and clicked them at him. And he was ashamed and shy in front of all these people, who were so noisy, who dressed so strangely, and whose faces were either so very red or very pale. And suddenly he felt very small and very much alone before them all, and he knew that never could he be brave enough to guide even one of them; and he turned and commenced to walk away as fast as he possibly could, without actually running, when he heard a voice calling out in Indian,

"Wait, my son, wait. I want to speak with you."

He had seen no Indians there, but he stopped, and looking back, saw coming towards him some one who was speaking in the Ojibway language quite as well as he did himself, yet who was not an Indian at all, but a white man, tall and strong looking, with bright yellow hair and blue eyes—not hard blue eyes such as the post manager had, but smiling, kind blue eyes. His white shirt was open at the throat, and his sleeves were rolled up above his elbows, all of his skin that showed was tanned by the sun, almost to the same colour as an Indian's. And he wore moccasins; though Shapian, in spite of his nervousness, noticed that he walked a little carefully in them,* as though he was not very well used to them. And the stranger came close to him and put his hand on the boy's shoulder, and somehow, Shapian was no more shy or awkward, and he paid no more attention to the loudly talking tourists who were watching, and saw only the smiling brown face, and heard only the words of this fair-haired

---

* The word "tenderfoot" arose from the inability of newcomers in the wilderness to wear moccasins until their feet became hardened to their use.

man who spoke his language so well, using all the soft tones that Shapian was so accustomed to.

"Do not be afraid," said the yellow-haired man. (Shapian had already named him Yellow Hair, in his own mind.) "These are all good people, Gitchie Mokoman—Americans. They like Indians, and only want to take your picture." Just the same he drew Shapian away, as he went on: "But let us go to your camp and talk. I want to hear about your adventure in the fire, and besides, I have wished to see the children of Gitchie Meegwon this long time." He said that he knew Big Feather very well, calling him Quill, as all the white people did.

Shapian felt right away that this was a friend, and his heart warmed toward the man, and although he had known him only so short a time, he felt that here, at last, was some one he could trust. And so he led his new friend through the woods to the camp, not taking him in the canoe, as he had always heard that a white man would upset you in so small a canoe—though he afterwards found out that this brown young man could handle a canoe very well indeed.

Sajo had been getting dinner ready, but when she saw them coming she ran and hid herself in the tent, for, besides the trader, whom she hated, she had never seen a white man so close before, and Shapian found that he was going to have quite a job to coax her out of there. But when she heard the visitor talking Indian so well, and heard his merry laugh, she peeped out, and found herself looking fair and square into the kindest and merriest pair of eyes, next to her father's, she had ever seen—and then she knew she was caught, and so came out, and sat by the fire and pretended to be extremely busy with the pots and dishes. Just the same, she wanted very much to look at this so very pleasant stranger, and so she pulled her head shawl well over her face, and peeped out at him from under it. And every so often he would catch her at it, and she would blush and bob her head down, so the shawl hid her face again, and would get so busy around the fire that at last there really was some cooking done. And so they all had dinner together. And Shapian felt for this white man even more respect, when he found that he could seat himself on the ground as comfortably as any Indian, something that Shapian had so far never seen any white man able to do, except the trappers, who are often, themselves, very like Indians in their ways.

And the yellow-haired man praised the cooking, and said he had not enjoyed such a meal for a long time; and I don't really think he had, for it had only been bannock, with lard instead of butter, and some strips of dried deer meat, and tea without any sugar. From the way he acted, you would never have known but that it was a feast.

After dinner, their guest lit a cigarette and smoked a while. Sajo found this to be a very strange way of smoking. All the Indians, including a good many of the old women, used pipes, and she had never seen a cigarette used before; but she supposed it was another strange idea of this strange man, who talked such good Indian and yet had such queer ways about him—but mighty pleasant ways, they agreed together in whispers.

And while he smoked the stranger told them about himself. He was a missionary, not—he put in hastily—one of the interfering kind that wanted to change *all* the Indian customs and simple beliefs, some of which he thought were very beautiful; nor did he want to force his own particular way upon them, but he was one who felt towards them as a brother. He had learned the Indian language from books, and moved from place to place amongst the Bush Crees, the Salteaux,[*] the Algonquins and Ojibways (all of whom talk a similar language), working amongst them, teaching school, taking care of the sick, and trying to bring happiness wherever he could. And all because he felt that all the people of the world belonged to one great family, and believed that the Great Spirit loved and cared equally well for both red men and white, and he wanted to work for Him. And he told them how there were good people in the cities who paid all his expenses so that he was able to give his full time to this work, without having to ask the Indians for anything.

And this Indian boy and girl listened in wonder to hear such things, for they had always supposed that the Indians had been forgotten, and that no one cared any more about what happened to them, now that their land had been gotten away from them. But they could not help but believe that this man was what he said, a brother to them, even though his skin did show to be so very white wherever the sun had not touched it, and though his eyes were not black like theirs, but blue as the sky itself at noon-day.

[*] Pronounced Soto.

About this time Chilawee, who had been drying himself off after his latest bath and combing himself in the tent, hearing all the talking, and having, I suspect, more than an inkling that something was going on in the way of dinner, now came tumbling out to see what it was all about. Seeing the stranger, he at once decided that he must be examined. On his way over he came to the dinner table, which was nothing but a clean, white sheet of canvas laid upon the ground, with the dinner things still on it, and he walked right across this, tramping among the dishes, until he arrived in front of the visitor, and he then sat up on his hind legs and took a good close look at him. Perhaps he thought that such a large visitor ought to be good for quite a lot of bannock, if properly handled— anyhow, what he saw seemed to please him very much, for he commenced to shake his head back and forth, and from side to side and shook his body, quite in his old way of dancing, and presently fell on his back among the dishes where he continued to squirm and wiggle. And there was a magnificent clatter, and a great upsetting, and a spilling, and a scatteration of cups and plates, so, to quiet things down Sajo hurriedly gave him a big chunk of bannock, expecting him to go back in the tent to eat it. But this time he was not to be so easily bribed to leave the company, and he squatted right there on the tablecloth, and taking his bannock in both hands, commenced to enjoy himself thoroughly—keeping one bright black eye on the visitor.

And this was the first time since Chikanee had gone away that he had done his funny dance; so that Sajo took it for a sign, and was more sure than ever that things were going to work out for the best. Yellow Hair, for his part, thought this performance was about the funniest thing he had ever seen, and laughed so heartily that Sajo, quite forgetting to be bashful, joined in, for it certainly was a most comical sight, and even Shapian, for all his heavy heart, could not help but laugh a little too.

Then Yellow Hair asked them how they came to have a beaver, which is the shyest of all animals, so tame, though he already knew quite a lot about it from the trader; and he asked them many more questions. And although they were not, at first, very willing to tell him, he at last got all the story (for he was very clever at questions, this young man), how the two little beavers had been saved when they were nearly ready to die, and how they had been a birthday gift to Sajo from her father, and how they came to be named Chilawee and Chikanee—Big Small and Little Small. And he heard how sad they all had been since Little Small had been taken away from them, and how unhappy and lonesome poor Chilawee had become, and he listened (he was a very good listener too) while they told how they had started out to search for their little friend, and on the way had nearly lost their lives in the forest fire. And Shapian, at the end, said that he must now find work so as to have money to go to the city and bring Chikanee home again.

And after he had heard it all, the young man looked grave and became very quiet, and the laughter was quite gone from off his face; for he knew that there was no work for Shapian, though he kept it to himself. And he reached out thoughtfully and stroked the soft, silky fur of the little beaver and said, half to himself, in English,

"So this is Big Small; and Little Small is far away, alone in the city. And these children—this must not be!"

And he stole a glance at Sajo, for he had noticed her pull her shawl, which had fallen across her shoulders, back over her head again; and he could see beneath it, two big tears rolling slowly down her cheeks, though she had tried very hard to keep them back.

So he arose, and went away. But before he left he said to them:

"I am your friend, and your father's friend. Tomorrow I will return, and we will have dinner together again. Perhaps I can take away this cloud that lies so dark across your trail. I do not know, but I will try very hard. That is my work, to help clear away the mists from the face of the sun, that it may shine upon us all."

And with a wave of his hand he was gone.

CHAPTER TWELVE

The Big Knives

IMMEDIATELY AFTER HIS RETURN TO THE POST, THE MISSION-
ary had a long talk with the trader in his office. Soon he came out with a
sheet of paper marked "NOTICE," which he tacked on the door of the
building. The tourists were still around at that time of the day, and several of them saw him doing this, and right away they all had to see what
was on the notice. It called every one to a meeting that was to be held, at
four o'clock, in the Indian schoolhouse on the hill behind the store, on a
matter of great importance. In so small a place the news quickly spread,
and, having nothing better to do, and rather wondering what this busy-
appearing fellow might have to say, everybody that could go, went.

The room was small, and some had to stand outside, listening in at the
windows and the door. The young man with the yellow hair stood upon
the teacher's platform, and when every one was settled he commenced to
speak. At first you could hear a little whispering, and coughing, and shuffling of feet, but this soon died down as he went on, and soon everybody
was listening, listening very hard. For he was telling the people a tale;
something very different from what they had expected, something such as
they had never heard before. He was as good at tales as he was at questions, this White Brother to the Indians. And the place became very quiet;
and there was no sound but that of the young man's voice.

And the tale he told was the story of Sajo and Shapian, of Big Small
and Little Small.

And at the last he said:

"... for we are still our brother's keeper. And let us remember that these young people who have braved the dangers of the Wilderness as perhaps you and I could not have done, whose colour is perhaps different to ours, whose language is not our language, and whose ways are not our ways, are our responsibility, yours and mine; they are not just a couple of Indian kids, but two very unhappy children. And who knows but what they may be right in what they think, and that those small beasts that are their friends may have, after all, feelings that are very like our own.

"And let me say, before you go, that as you pass out through the door you will find, on the right, a large, empty Hudson's Bay tea-can; it will hold about a quart. How about it, folks?"

When he had finished, the place broke out into a kind of a mild uproar, and everybody seemed to want to speak at once, and the ladies were saying: "Oh! Did you ever hear—" and "Imagine, all that way alone!" and "—poor dears, through that dreadful fire!" And gentlemen stood up and reached into their pockets, and talked loudly to one another, and made such remarks as, "Why, I wouldn't have missed this for anything," and "Where are they; we've got to do something about it." And one of them asked· "Where did he say the can was?"

And as the people commenced to file out through the door there came, from the direction of the tea-can, cheerful clinking sounds, and the crackle of crisp new bills and the rustle of old ones; and not all one-dollar bills either, let me tell you, but twos, and fives, and the odd ten as well. And there were, besides, young people who wanted to help, and these too put in whatever they could spare from their holiday allowances.

And last of all the trader went out; and when he came to the door he looked carefully around to make sure that no one was looking, winked one eye (the one farthest from the tea-can), and reaching out quickly as though he were afraid of being seen, dropped into the can a tightly folded little wad of bills, and was heard to mutter to himself:

"Well, Chikawee, or Chilakee, or Chikalee, or whatever you call yourself, here's good luck to you!"

But this brown young man, who was still on the platform, was not only good at questions and answers, and at telling stories; he also had remarkably good eyesight. And he saw.

Later in the day Yellow Hair went over to the children's camp, and when Shapian saw all that money, he could hardly believe it was for him. He was even a little frightened, and asked:

"What must I do—what work do they want me to do?"

"Nothing," answered Yellow Hair. "There is no time to work. You must go at once, or perhaps your little friend will be gone—animals get so lonely they sometimes die. These Gitchie Mokoman, they say for me to tell you that it is a gift. Long ago, the nation to which they belong was very cruel to the Indians, and they know now that wrong was done, and they are sorry; now they want to help. They are a great and generous people. All they ask is, that sometime, when you meet some one in trouble, help them if you can."

"Oh! I will, I will," said Shapian earnestly. "Tell them I will, and that I thank them." The tears stood in his eyes, where all his troubles had never been able to bring them. And so the roll of money was placed carefully in an envelope, while Sajo looked on, her eyes big and round with joy, and excitement, and about half a dozen other feelings that she would never have been able to tell you about; she knew nothing whatever about money, but now, she thought, there was nothing between them and Chikanee, nothing at all. She was glad, but not a bit surprised, and she said she had just *known* that everything was going to be all right, and that the white people were not *nearly* as bad as they were made out to be, and that it only went to show how true her dream had been!

In the envelope the Yellow Hair enclosed a note to the station agent at the railroad station, asking for two return tickets to the city. And although this looked like nearly all the money in the world to Shapian, after the railroad fares were paid there would be very little left; for, although the tourists had been generous, there had not been, after all, very many of them. The missionary thought to himself that perhaps Shapian might have to stay behind and work out the price of Chikanee's liberty, if the park owners would consider such a thing. Anyhow, the only thing to do was to try. Yellow Hair also gave Shapian a letter addressed to the head man of the group of workers to which he belonged, who would find lodgings for them, and told him that as soon as he arrived in the city he should ask to be taken to a policeman, and then show him the address on the envelope. The missionary explained very carefully what a police-man looked like and how he would be dressed, and made Shapian prac-tise saying the word. The nearest he got to it was "poliss-man"; but this was considered to be quite plain enough to be understood. Chikanee, he told them, had been sold to the owner of an amusement park in the city, and any policeman could take them there.

And now, thought Shapian, with any luck at all, they should be back in time to welcome their father home, as the brigade was expected to return soon; and, he reflected, it was a lot easier to explain things when something you did, that was a little against the rules, turned out to be all to the good.

Their friend helped them to collect a bundle of poplar feed for Chilawee, besides the bannock that Sajo had made, and he promised to take care of their canoe and camping outfit until they should return. And when, on the following day, the boat was ready to leave, everybody in the whole place was on the dock to see them off. Some of the American ladies had fallen right in love with little Sajo, calling her Brown Eyes, and Little Moccasins, and one of them named her Madame Butterfly. And the men shook hands with Shapian all around, and called him a brave fellow, and said they were proud to know him. Even Chilawee came in for his share of the attention, though I don't believe he liked it very well, for he turned his back on folks in a manner that was decidedly impolite, and carried on with his own small affairs. The trader was there, looking around very severely, as if he heartily disapproved of the whole business; for he was determined that no one should ever know that he had put any money into this ridiculous affair.

At the very last, the missionary, who had been standing apart from the crowd looking at the trader, smiling to himself about something or another, came to the gangplank just as Sajo and Shapian walked aboard, and took the hand of each of them, and patted the little beaver on the nose, and said:

"Good luck to you, children of Gitchie Meegwon. I will tell your father everything. May you be successful, and all four of you come safely home again. We will be waiting."

∾∾∾

THAT VERY DAY, THREE CANOES COULD BE SEEN APPROACHING the burnt portage on which Sajo, Shapian, and Chilawee had had their desperate adventure. The canoes came onward at terrific speed. In them were Indians, stripped to the waist, their long hair tied out of the way in knots on top of their heads. Silent, grim-looking men they were, their naked shoulders glistening with the sweat of hard paddling. The brown bodies bent and swayed and paddles flashed in the sunlight as the canoes drove down swiftly upon the portage. The first one had no more than touched land, when a man leaped ashore. It was Big Feather. The brigade had returned and Big Feather had found his cabin empty!

Throwing himself on his knees beside the water he scraped away the litter of the fire, now cold, and found there the sharp V made by the bow of a canoe; and he saw, too, a small moccasin track, half washed away. Springing to his feet he shouted:

"They have passed here. Quickly! Take axes, clean out the portage, I will search the trail for—" He stopped as an old man with white hair and a wise, wrinkled face, said:

"Stay, my son. My old eyes have seen many things. Stay and rest yourself. *I* will first cross the trail. Perhaps I may read——"

And Gitchie Meegwon bowed his head to the words of his Chief, and waited, patiently. The trail was piled high with blackened, twisted trees, criss-crossed in every direction. The men chopped furiously amongst the fallen timber to open a passage for the canoes, while Gitchie Meegwon, unable to rest, busied himself cooking for the others, for the work would take no little time.

The old man went on across the portage, and searched very carefully amongst the wreckage of the fire, for whatever there might be of tracks or other traces of the children. As we know, he found no little bodies, but any logs that lay flat on the ground, and that he was able to move, he lifted aside, and looked beneath them very closely for tracks or any other signs. For fire sometimes moves so quickly that it leaves its work half done in places; and under one of these fallen logs, crushed but only partly burnt, he found the top of Chilawee's basket. He found, too, at the far end, a deep cut in the soft soil of the landing, where a canoe must have been driven very violently ashore—why? he asked himself, when it was going the other way! And then, looking out shrewdly at the huge tree, half burnt, that lay in the water no more than the length of two canoes away, he read the story to himself. For he was a very wise old man, and had been a warrior once, in days gone by, and could read the Wilderness as we read a book. And for this he had been named Ne-Ganik-Abo,[*] Man That Stands Ahead, or Stands First, by his people.

So he returned across the portage and told the unhappy father that he need sorrow no more. And he stood among the assembled Indians and told them what he had found, and that he was sure that the children had escaped the Red Enemy. Gitchie Meegwon, holding in his hands the scorched and blackened top of the basket, only wished he knew.

That night, after camp had been made and it had fallen dark, Big Feather climbed a great, bare, rocky hill that stood high above the face of the Wilderness, and there, with the wrecked and ruined forest stretching out on every side below him, his face painted in dark lines of sorrow, he raised his arms towards the sky and prayed aloud to the Great Spirit of the Wild Lands:

"O-way! O-way! Manitou, O Spirit that watches over all the Forest People, keep my little ones from harm. Keep my children safe.

Since they have gone my days lie dead around my feet, as do the ashes of this burnt and broken Wilderness.

The Sun does not shine any more, and I cannot hear the Singing Birds. I hear only the laughing voice of Sajo; all I see is the face of my Shapian with his brave eyes, facing the flaming forest.

Manitou, I have done wrong. The fault is mine. I, who brought sorrow to the heart of Sajo, cast a shadow across the smiling face of Sajo.

O Gitchie Manitou, bring them safely back to O-pee-pee-soway, The Place of Talking Waters. Great Spirit of our people, keep my children safe.

O-way-soam! O-way!"

[*] Pronounced Nee-*gan*-ik-*ab*-o.

And while his voice rang out across the empty, silent burnt lands, there sat behind him in the moonlight, the old white-haired Chief, with his wrinkled face and his eyes so full of wisdom, who tapped slowly, and softly, on a painted drum.

Meanwhile Sajo and Shapian, all unknown to their anxious father, were hastening, farther and farther away from the Land of Talking Waters, speeding onwards through the darkness towards the distant city, as fast as the hurrying wheels of a train could take them.

CHAPTER THIRTEEN

The Little Prisoner

AND MEANWHILE WHAT OF CHIKANEE?

We must go back to the day the trader walked out of Gitchie Meegwon's camp with him, right out of the lives of his friends, it seemed, for ever.

During the four or five days it took the trader, with his Ojibway canoe-man, to make the journey back to Rabbit Portage, Chikanee did not fare so badly, as one of the Indians took good care of him, keeping him well supplied with feed and water. But he could not understand why Chilawee was not with him, and wondered where Sajo and Shapian had disappeared to. And he began to be lonesome for them all, and often cried out for Sajo to come to him, as she had always done when she heard the little beaver calling. But no one came except the strange Indian, and then only to change his water and to give him food. This man, by the trader's orders, accompanied Chikanee on the steamboat to see that he arrived safely at the railroad, and there left him; the money for him was paid over to the Indian, and what happened to him now did not greatly matter.

Having now come to a stop, and thinking that he must be home again, he wailed loudly for liberty and recognition, expecting his play-mates to come and take him out of this stuffy and uncomfortable box. But none came. So he started to chew at the box, and strange, harsh voices spoke angrily to him. He next tried to climb the walls of his prison, but they were too high, and these strangers shouted at him, and pounded

507

on the box to keep him quiet, and now, thoroughly frightened, he lay still, whimpering and lonely. Where, oh, where was Sajo, who had always comforted him in his small troubles, and in whose arms he had so often found such happiness? Where was Chilawee, from whom he had never before been separated for so much as an hour?

A little later he was loaded onto a train that thundered and roared its way for many hours. When the train first started, he forgot to close his ears, as a beaver can do to keep out water and unpleasant sounds. The noise drove him nearly crazy, and in his terror he tried to dive to freedom through his tiny dish of water, and upset it; so that besides his other misery he soon began to suffer from thirst. He had been snatched away from home too hurriedly for Sajo to have time to drop a bannock in the box, which would have lasted him several days, and no one thought of providing him with anything to eat, and now, sick, hungry, lonesome, and wild with fear, he started desperately to cut his way out of the crate. In this he would have quickly succeeded, but striking a nail he broke one of his four cutting teeth, which made gnawing too painful to continue. His bedding, what little there was of it, became dirty, and the motion of the train thumped and bumped him against the hard sides of the box, so that he became bruised and sore. He tried hard to stay in the center, away from the walls of his prison, but never could. One of the trainmen, intending to be kind, threw to him some crusts of bread from his own lunch, but he thought that the little beaver's frantic clutchings at his hands was a sign of ill-temper. Chikanee was just a wild animal to these people, who did not know that he only wanted to be helped, and from then on they were afraid of him—so small a creature to be afraid of!— and no one attempted to give him any more bedding or food, and his water dish remained empty for the same reason.

And he raised his voice in cries of misery and called and called for his small companions, who now could never hear him, wailed in his childlike voice for them to come and take away this great trouble that had befallen him. But no one paid any attention, if they ever even heard him, drowned as was his feeble outcry by the uproar of the train.

At length, after many stops and starts, each of which jolted and slammed him from one hard side of his prison to the other, and a last, and

cruelly rough ride in a delivery bus, there came a sudden quietness. The
cleats were taken from across the top of the box with a frightful screeching as the nails were drawn, and he was lifted out by a hand that held him
very firmly by the tail; a large, strong hand, yet somehow a very gentle one.
Then the other hand came up and was held against his chest as he hung
head down, bringing him right end up, and a finger rubbed gently on one
hot, tired little paw, and a deep voice spoke soothing words; so that suddenly he felt rather comfortable. For this man was a keeper of animals,
and attendant in the park where Chikanee was to stay, and he knew his
business very well. And when he examined his small captive, and saw how
miserable, and bedraggled, and covered with dirt the little creature was—
he who had been so proud and careful of his coat!—the keeper said
angrily to the delivery man, who, poor fellow, was not to blame at all:

"No water, nothing to eat, dry feet, dry tail, dry nose, teeth all broken
up; if that isn't a shame, nothing ever was! Some way to ship a beaver, I'll
say! But we'll soon fix you up, old-timer." For the man had been expecting his little guest, having had a letter about him, and had everything
ready to receive him. Chikanee soon found himself in an enclosure built
of something like stone, but not nearly as friendly as stone, and surrounded by a rail of iron bars.

And in this jail of iron and concrete Chikanee, for no crime at all, was
to spend the rest of his days. Chikanee, gentle, lovable Chikanee, was
now supposed to be a wild and probably dangerous beast!

It was not a very large place, a mere hutch after the freedom of the big
lake beside which he had spent most of his short life, but that did not matter for the moment—he smelled water! And then he saw, right in front of
him, a deep, clear pool; not a very big one, to be sure, but at least it was
water. Into this he immediately threw himself and drank thirstily, floating
on the surface, while the cracked and dried-out tail and feet soaked up the
life-giving moisture, and the cakes of dirt loosened and washed from off
him as he swam slowly back and forth. This seemed like the beaver's heaven
itself, after more than three days of noise, starvation, dirt, and utter misery,
and the hot, fevered little body cooled off and all the bumps and bruises
ceased to throb, as the cool water slowly got in its good work on him.

And now, he thought, this must be just the plunge-hole. Down there, somewhere, lay the entrance, and through this he would set out and would, no doubt, come to his home-lake, there to find his playmates on the shore; and then Chilawee would run to welcome him and roll on his woolly back with joy, and Sajo would come and pick him up, and hug him and make much of him, and whisper in his ear, and tickle him in that funny place under his chin, and all these hard times would be forgotten.

So, with a great splurge he dived straight down—to strike his head on the hard bottom of the pool, almost stunning himself. Again he tried, with the same result. He scratched and bit at the concrete, thinking to tear his way through it to the tunnel that must, somewhere, lead out of it. But he only cracked and split his claws and took more chips out of his remaining teeth. Then he scrambled out of the pool and over to the bars, and tried to squeeze through them; but they were too close together. He tried to gnaw at them, but his broken teeth never even scratched them. So he ran round and round inside the enclosure, stopping here and there to dig, but to no purpose. For a long time he worked, running back to the pool and out again to the bars, trying to gnaw, trying to dig; but it was useless. At last he realized that there was no opening anywhere, no plunge-hole, no escape; and weary, wretched and hopeless, he lay flat on the hard, hot floor of the pen and moaned, moaned as he had done when Sajo had nursed him to sleep whenever he had been lonesome—only then he had moaned with joy, and now it was from misery. And his little paws ached for just one touch of Chilawee's soft, silky fur. And now there was no Sajo, no Chilawee, only one unhappy Little Small in prison, all alone.

The attendant stood by for a long time, and watched and shook his head, and said, "Too bad, little fellow, too bad." This was his job, taming these wild creatures that were sent to him from time to time; yet, liking animals as he did, he sometimes hated the work. To him they often seemed to be, not wild things at all, but hopeless, unfortunate little people who could not speak, and who sometimes were so pitifully in need of the kindness for which they could not ask; and he had always felt that a man, who was so much bigger and stronger, and knew so many things that they did not, should be good to them and help them all he could. He pitied the little beaver that was struggling so helplessly to be free, for this was not the first one that had come under his care, and he knew their gentle nature. And stepping in through the gate of the pen, he picked up Chikanee carefully and cleverly, so that, as in the first place, he was not scared or excited, but was actually comfortable in his hands—they were so much more friendly than the concrete!

The keeper carried Chikanee to his cottage, which was close by, inside the park. He had three young children, and when they saw their father bringing in a little beaver, they crowded round to see, and they shouted and clapped their hands with glee, so that Chikanee was afraid again, and tried to burrow into the man's coat; for already he had begun to trust him. And their father quieted the young ones and set the little creature on the floor where, finding himself once more in a house, he felt a little more at home than in the cage. They all stood watching to see what he would do, and the keeper's wife said:

"The wee mite! Look how thin he is. Joey,"—to one of the youngsters—"go get an apple; those other beavers we used to have were just crazy for apples."

So this Joey fellow went and got one right away, and put it down on the floor in front of Chikanee. He had never seen an apple before, but he sniffed at it and oh, what a wonderful smell came from it! And so he cut into it as best he could with his poor broken teeth and then, what a taste!— the most delicious taste in all the world! And seizing hold of this so wonderful tidbit with both hands, he demolished nearly the half of it. At this the keeper was very pleased, for some of his prisoners refused all food and died, but now he knew that this one would recover; something he had been none too sure about. And the delighted children laughed to see him sitting up there like a little man while he ate, and the keeper's wife exclaimed:

"There, didn't I tell you? He'll be all right in no time."

Then the man brought in the sprays of fresh, juicy poplar leaves he had placed in the pen for Chikanee, but which he had not touched. But now he ate them, and the children wondered to see him holding the leaves in little bunches in his hands while he put them in his mouth. Feeling a good deal better, by now, he made small sounds of pleasure while he ate, and at that the young ones marvelled even more, and one, a little girl with golden hair and a round, rosy face, said:

"Listen, listen to him talk, just like a little, wee baby. Oh, daddy, do let's keep him in the kitchen!" And their mother spoke up, too: "Yes, Alec, let's keep him here for a spell; there's no one in the park—it's almost like putting a child in prison." And Alec answered:

"Perhaps you're right. We'll fix him a place in here for tonight."

So they made a place for our Chikanee in the kitchen, and Alec the keeper fastened a low, wide pan of water to the floor, and set a large box down on its side, with plenty of clean straw in it for a bed for him. And there the little beaver spent the night, not happily, perhaps, but very comfortably.

The next morning Alec returned him to the pen, so that any of the public who came to the park could see him; but when evening came round again and the grounds were empty, the keeper brought him back to the cottage. And from then on he did this every day, and Chikanee spent all the hours when he was not "working," in the keeper's house, and in the kitchen had his bed, and his big pan of water, and ate his leaves and twigs there. Each day he had a nice, juicy apple, which quite made up for a lot of his troubles, though not for all of them; for never would he be anything but lonesome, so long as he lived.[*] Every morning there was a considerable mess to clean up, of peeled sticks, and cut branches, and left-over leaves, and the floor was all slopped up with water, but the children willingly turned to and cleaned up, after the beaver was carried away to his daily task of being stared at in the cage. Nobody seemed to mind the little trouble he was. He got along famously with the family and, in his own small way, soon became quite a part of the household.

As time went on he got to know them all. He would romp clumsily with the youngsters; and to them he was a kind of tumbling, good-natured toy, a good deal like one of those roguish wool puppies to be found on Christmas trees. But to Chikanee, it could never be the same as it had been at O-pee-pee-soway, and often he didn't want to play, but lay quietly in his box, his little heart filled with a great, empty longing for his old playmates.

Before very long his teeth had grown in, and he spent a lot of time sharpening them against one another, grinding and rattling them together at a great rate. A beaver's teeth grow continuously and he grinds

---

[*] Beavers possess probably the longest memory of any North American animal, much resembling the elephant in this respect.

and sharpens them constantly. His coat, which he had sadly neglected for a time, so that it had become all tangled and awry, now got its daily scrubbing and combing, and his small frame, that had for a while been little more than a bag of bones, soon filled out, and he began to look like the old Chikanee again. In a way he was happy; but never quite.

While in the cage he was really miserable, and the keeper knew this, and always felt badly when he put the little fellow in there each morning, and looked back at this pitiful little creature that gazed after him so wistfully as he walked away, sitting there alone on the bare cement floor, surrounded by bars that would have held a grizzly bear. He remembered that a beaver may live more than twenty years—twenty years in that prison of iron and concrete! In twenty years his own family would be grown up and away from there; he himself might be gone. The town would have become a great city (it was not really a very big place); people would come and go—free people, happy people—and through it all, this unhappy little beast, who had done no harm to any one, and seemed only to want some one to be kind to him, would, for twenty long and lonely years, look out through the bars of that wretched pen as though he had been some violent criminal; waiting for the freedom that would never be his, waiting only to die at last. And, thought the keeper, for no good reason at all, except that a few thoughtless people, who did not really care if they ever saw a beaver, might stare for a minute or two at the disconsolate little prisoner, and then go away and forget they had ever seen him. Somehow it did not seem fair, to this kind-hearted man, and when he watched the little creature rollicking with the children in his funny, clumsy way, he wished very much that there was something that he could do about it, and decided to make his small prisoner as happy as he could, and give him the freedom of the cottage as long as it was at all possible.

But Chikanee had not quite given up; he had one hope that for a long time he never lost. He quite expected that, in some mysterious way, Chilawee would come to join him; for in the old days, no matter where he had happened to be, it had not been long before Chilawee had turned up, looking for him. And so, every so often he searched for him very carefully, looking in the wooden hut that stood in the enclosure, going patiently all through the downstairs rooms of the cottage, sometimes taking a run outside and examining the woodshed very thoroughly, very sure that some day he would find him. But after a whole month of daily disappointments he began to lose courage, and at last gave up his search that always turned out to be such a failure.

And hundreds of miles away, Chilawee was doing the very same thing, and all for nothing.

Chikanee was just beginning to get over this, when something took place that was the very worst of all—and yet something that was very near to his dearest wish. One day an Indian woman, with a bright shawl on her head, passed by the pen. The moment he saw her, Chikanee dashed wildly at the bars, reached through them with clutching paws, and let out a piercing cry, for fear she would pass him by. At this the woman stopped and spoke to him, and the sounds she made were the same as he had heard so often in the Indian country, at home! But not the voice. And seeing her face, and catching the scent of her, he turned and plodded slowly back to the bare wooden hut again, more dejected and downcast than he had ever been. He had thought it was Sajo.

But this experience stirred him, and brought new hopes to him; he got the idea that some day Sajo *would* come. And from then on he watched for her. Crowds of people visited the park in the afternoons, and most of them paused by his cage to see what a beaver was like. But his "customers" never stayed long, and soon passed on; to most of them he looked to be just a scrubby little pup with a flat tail. Some just gazed carelessly, others curiously, a few poked sticks at him and made harsh and, as he thought, threatening sounds; a few, a very few pitied him, and one or two were friendly and gave him peanuts and candy—but none of them was Sajo. But he continued to hope, and spent his time watching closely every face he saw, sniffing every hand he could get near to. But he never saw the face he looked for, never caught the scent of that so-beloved little hand. Yet he was sure that some day a well-remembered voice would call out, "Chik-a-*nee!*" that the small brown hands whose touch had so often thrilled his little body, would again pick him up, and then—oh! the joy of once more pushing his nose close into that special spot in a certain warm, soft neck, there to puff and blow a little while and then to slumber, and forget!

Hours at a time he spent this way, watching, waiting, hoping; and later, on his little pallet in the kitchen, he would think, in some dim and misty way, of the happy days that seemed now to have been so long ago, and thought of the little chamber under Shapian's bed, that Chilawee and he had had between them for their very own, and of the crazy, tiny beaver house, and all the other arrangements that they had worked so bravely at together. And at last he became listless, and kept to himself, even when he was supposed to be happy in the kitchen; and he never played with the children any more. He neglected his coat, so that it became matted and unkempt. And he began to refuse his food, and would sit with his apple untouched in his hands, his little head drooping, eyes closed, breathing fast and heavily.

And the keeper, looking at him sorrowfully, knew that there was no longer any need to worry about the twenty years; or any years.

Chikanee wasn't going to live.

And the wee brain grew hot and feverish with longing, and he seemed sometimes almost to see his old playfellows there before him, and thinking of them fell asleep, and sleeping dreamed of them. For animals *do* dream, as perhaps you know, and often wake up half scared to pieces from a nightmare, just as you or I do, and from the sounds they sometimes make, some of their dreams must be quite pleasant, too.

One evening he awoke from a dream that was so real, that he thought himself once more at home with his friends, so he got up and ran whimpering about the kitchen, looking for them, and not finding them cried out again and again in loud sobbing wads, from very lonesomeness and misery. And as he cried, his voice was like the voice of a small, lost child.

For he did not, could not know, that less than a mile away, in another and similar room, was another and similar little beaver, and that there with him, waiting for morning, too excited to even think of sleeping, were two little Indians—a boy that stood straight and proudly, like an arrow, and a little girl who wore a brightly coloured head-shawl.

And in one corner of the room there stood an old familiar, well-worn, birch-bark basket.

Yes, you guessed it. Sajo and Shapian had really come, at last.

Patrick the Policeman

WHEN THE TRAIN ON WHICH SAJO, SHAPIAN, AND THEIR small fellow-traveller Chilawee, were riding, made the last of its many stops and came to a standstill in the city station, the children were almost too scared to get off. The conductor, who had had his eye on them all the way, helped them out, spoke a few words of encouragement, and left them to attend to his other duties.

They found themselves in a world of noise. The hurrying throngs of people, the hiss of escaping steam, the clang of engine bells, the shriek of whistles and the thunderous bellowing of starting and stopping locomotives, deafened and terrified them, and they stood hand in hand on the platform, not knowing which way to turn and not daring to move. Before, behind, and on every side of them was a terrific confusion and a ceaseless din. Lorries piled high with baggage of every kind rumbled by, and one of these came straight for them and Shapian pulled his sister aside only just in time to escape being run over by it. The depot was, to them, a vast, echoing cave filled with terrifying sights and sounds, and never before had they felt so small and defenceless. They felt more alone here, in the midst of all these people, than they had ever done in the forest, with its silence and its quiet, peaceful trees. People looked at them curiously as they passed, but every one seemed to be too busy rushing this way and that to pay much attention to them.

So there they stood, in all that deafening uproar, two little people from the Silent Places, as scared and bewildered, and nearly as helpless, as the two tiny kitten beavers had been when Gitchie Meegwon found them floating on the Yellow Birch river. Yet Sajo, with all her fear, had only one thought—Chikanee had come through all this *alone*! While Shapian began to wish himself back in the forest fire again, amongst the friendly animals. Chilawee, for his part, closed his ears as tightly as two tiny black purses and lay perfectly still, jammed into a corner of his basket.

They had been standing there for what seemed to them an hour (though it had really been only a few moments), and Shapian was thinking of making *some* kind of a move towards a huge door through which crowds of people were flowing like a swift, rushing river, when there stopped in front of them a young boy. He was about Shapian's own age, and was dressed in a neat, red uniform with bright buttons all down the front of his short, tightly fitting coat. On the side of his head there was a little hat that looked more like a very small, round box than anything else.

"Hullo, you kids," he said cheerfully, "are you lost? Who are you looking for?"

Poor Shapian, confronted by this self-possessed and magnificent-looking personage, and never before having seen a page boy, found that he had completely forgotten any English he ever knew. He could remember only one word; so he said it.

"Poliss-man," he stammered nervously.

"You want a policeman, eh?" said the page, who was a smart lad and got to the point at once. "Come along with me." And beckoning to them he set off at a great pace, his shiny boot-heels tapping sharply on the hard platform. The little Indians, silent-footed in their moccasins, slipped softly along behind him, though they nearly had to trot to keep up, Shapian carrying Chilawee's basket in one hand and holding tightly to his sister with the other. It must have been a queer-looking procession! Their guide steered them through the crowds, over to the entrance and down a great hall filled with more people, nearly all the people in the world, thought Shapian, and brought them over to a big, stout man who stood beside a door at the far end. He also had a number of bright buttons on his coat.

"Hey, Pat," the page called to him, "here's a couple of kids want to see a policeman," and pushed them forward, continuing, rather disrespectfully, I fear, "You shouldn't be hard to see, you're big enough. Look like Indians to me—better watch your scalp!" And with an impudent grin at the police officer and a wink at the children, he dodged into the crowd and disappeared.

"Oho," exclaimed the policeman loudly, looking down on the two youngsters, with his hands behind his back, "Oho, so it's scalps, is it?" said he, looking very fiercely at them, as though he were about to take them prisoner—though his eyes had an odd twinkle about them and were pleasantly crinkled at the corners. "'Tis young Injuns yez are, eh? The little craytures! Well, 'tis a mighty poor scalp ye'll get from me, that's been bald as an egg this twenty years; and well did the little imp know it that brought ye here!"

He was built something on the lines of Father Christmas, and although he talked so fiercely his face was round and jolly, and he wore his helmet a little to one side of his head in rather a jaunty sort of fashion, as though being a policeman was the most entertaining business imaginable. But seeing that the "little craytures" were becoming alarmed, he asked, in what he considered to be a lower voice (I don't think he had any low voice, myself):

"And what can I be doin' for ye?"

"You—poliss-man?" asked Shapian timidly.

"Yes, me lad," answered the constable, putting his helmet just a trifle more to one side, "I'm a policeman, and a good one—the O'Reillys have iver been of the best—Hullo! what's in the basket?" For Chilawee had now commenced to wail.

"A-mik," answered Shapian, taking off the lid for him to see and repeated "A-mik," at which, to his great astonishment, the policeman began to laugh very loud indeed, "Ho-hoho-hoho! so it's a Mick he calls me, knew I was Irish right away—sharp as a di'mond, the little haythen. Ye said it me boy, I'm a Mick, sure I'm a Mick." For he was very proud indeed of being Irish, and imagined that Shapian had known it when he used the Indian word "A-mik," which means, of course, "Beaver." He thought this Indian lad very smart to have discovered it; and Shapian, hearing him say so often that he was "a Mick," came to the conclusion that he belonged to some strange race of white men who called themselves "Beavers," a very honourable title indeed! And so, finding such extremely good points in one another, each of them found the other to be a rather clever fellow, which put them at once on the very best of terms.

"And where would ye be wantin' to go?" now asked the policeman.

Shapian, along with his English, had quite forgotten the letter Yellow Hair had given him, but now remembering one, he thought of the other, and pulling it out gave it to the officer, who read the address on the envelope and said,

"I see. I'm on dooty and cannot leave; but set ye down and wait, and I'll take ye there. And it's Patrick O'Reilly himself will see that no harm comes to yez." And he patted Sajo kindly on the head, and Shapian having at last been able to tell him in English what Chilawee really was, he asked to see him, and pronounced him to be a "fine little baste, what there was of him," as he didn't see a great deal, for our bold Chilawee had become very meek indeed, probably thinking by the way things were going that the end of the world had come, and he hid his head, and his tail, and all his legs and feet and made himself as small, and as he thought, as invisible as possible, and certainly he was not much to look at, for the time being at least.

And so our two young wanderers, feeling a good deal more at their ease, sat on the end of a long row of seats and waited. And the big policeman, who seemed to be in such continual good humour over nothing at all, asked them a number of questions, and Shapian, having got his English into pretty fair working order by now, told him most of the story. And the jolly Irishman became quite depressed about it, and said that he—Patrick O'Reilly himself, mind you—would take them to the people who owned the park, "And it's meself as will tell them the plain truth, with both hands, so I will," he said aloud, and so disturbed did the worthy officer become as he thought the matter over, that he got a little mixed in his speech. "'Twould bring tears to the eyes of a heart of stone," he declared. "Melt the candles off a Christmas tree, so it would!"

A little later he was relieved by another constable, who joked good-naturedly with him about the "family" he had got for himself, and they then went out together onto the street, where there were fewer people, and there was not so much bustle and noise. Their new friend talked nearly the whole time, for he was doing his very best to make them feel at home, and Shapian talked too, in his queer, broken English. Sajo listened meanwhile, all eyes and ears, though she could not understand anything; but she felt that they were safe with this big, blue-coated man beside them and now no longer afraid, she felt like crying out with happiness; for was not Chikanee right here, in this very city, perhaps on this self-same street? And she began to enjoy looking around at the wonders that were to be seen on every side—horses, which she had heard about but never seen before, the street-cars that sailed along so nicely without even a horse to draw them, beauti-ful ladies in beautiful clothes, and best of all, the gay shop windows. Once they passed a restaurant, and the smell of food and the sight of the deli-cious-looking pies and cakes in the window brought their weary little faces round so sharply in that direction, that the policeman, noticing it, and hearing them whisper together in Indian, guessed that they were hungry.

"Well, now," he exclaimed, "and it's hungry yez are, and me blatherin' away like some ould gossip, with the two of yez near ready to drop, belike. 'Tis not the way of the O'Reillys to l'ave a friend shtarvin' to death on the doorstep, so to spake. We'll in and have a bite."

"Yessplease," said Shapian. "My sister, that's hungry long time now," though it would have been hard to say which of them was the hungrier. So Patrick herded them into the place ahead of him, and after they were seated he asked them when they had eaten last, and Shapian told him,

"At trading post. Me, I have not that fear; but my sister, now, have plenty. So sit down all time one place, eat nothing. Me, I take care my sis-ter. That's never leave him alone, my sister. So nobody eat, only little bit Chilawee his bannock." And the policeman said,

"Ye're a brave lad. The O'Reillys, now—" But we are doomed never to hear just what the O'Reillys would have done about the matter, for at this moment the waiter came in with their order, and the children's eyes grew round as doorknobs, and very nearly as big, when they saw the tray piled high with cheerfully steaming eatables. These looked so tantalizing, and smelled so delicious, that when the dishes were set before them the chil-dren were quite overpowered. Sajo even felt a little faint, so excited was she, and soon they were too well occupied to talk, look, or listen, or to do anything else but eat, and eat; and there was some wonderfully fast work done around that table in the next few minutes. And while they were enjoying themselves, Sajo remembered that poor Chilawee must be hungry too, and she put tidbits from her plate into the basket, of bread and butter, and doughnuts, and pie and I don't know what all, and soon he was as busy as the rest of them, making up for a whole lot of lost time.

They were in one of those small private dining rooms that most restaurants have, and they were all by themselves, and now that the feast was pretty well over and nobody, not even Chilawee, could possibly have eaten one more mouthful, everybody sat back and began to feel exceedingly comfortable. Mr. O'Reilly lit a cigar, and being, if possible, in even better humour than before, beamed around on his guests in a state of the highest satisfaction. His helmet was off, and Shapian, being no longer busy, now had time to see that he was not quite so bald as he had claimed to be—bald as an egg, he had said—for a wide ring of hair started just above one of his ears and worked back, and around, till it came to the other ear; quite a respectable amount of hair, considering, far more than you will find on even the very best of eggs!

Sajo, like the good little housekeeper she was, piled all the dishes neatly away to one side, finding it great fun to handle these rich-looking things, although they were really nothing more than ordinary china tableware; but she, poor child, had never *seen* such dishes, as she told Shapian that night.

It was warm in the small room, and Sajo put back her bright head-shawl, showing her long, shining black braids and her soft, dark eyes, all alight with happiness just now, and the officer, who now saw her face properly for the first time, said she was the prettiest little girl he had ever seen since he'd "left Ireland, where they have the finest-lookin' gurrls in the wurrld!" And Shapian told her what he had said, and she blushed and hung her head, and pulled the head-shawl up again. But no one could be shy very long with this good-natured man, and she soon got over it and looked up at him, so that her shawl slipped back again, and this time she left it there, and she laughed at all the things he was saying although she couldn't understand a word of it. Shapian, glad to see his sister so light-hearted, laughed nearly as much as she. And Officer O'Reilly, mighty pleased at the success of his little party, laughed so heartily that he was obliged to open his coat, and mop his bald spot with a large red handkerchief that he pulled out of his sleeve; and taking it all around, they were all in uncommonly high spirits. Even Chilawee was heard from, and he and Sajo had a little private conversation of their own, while Mr. O'Reilly tried his hand at learning to talk Indian from Shapian. I'm afraid he didn't make very much progress; but there is one word that Indians use very often, "kaeget," which means "certainly," or "sure," or "indeed," and if you are *very* sure, you say "kae-*get.*" Now this was easy to say, and Pat caught on to it very soon, and when Shapian told him what it meant, he practised it until he had it right. From then on it was kae-*get* this, and kae-*get* that, and he was very proud indeed of his new word. And so he explained the plans he had made for the next day, talking, as nearly as he could, in Shapian's broken English:

"That park," he said, following Shapian's own style, "That park, closed." Here he closed the door of the room, very firmly. "Tomorrow, open park, give money, beaver come!" And opening wide the door, threw out his arm like a "go-ahead" traffic signal and stood aside, as though he expected a whole troop of beavers to come marching in through the opening. Then he brought out the letter, and tapping it said,

"Me, come this place. Tomorrow. You wait." And, with another flourish of the signal, "Kay-*get.*"

Shapian, whose English was not quite as bad as all that, found it hard to keep from smiling, understood very well, and said so, and the good Mr. O'Reilly was very pleased with his first lesson in Indian, and really felt that he began to understand something of the language.

He saw his "family" safely to their address, and turned them and the letter over to the manager of the place, making sure they understood that he would be back for them in the morning, telling them on no account to move until he came. The manager seemed to be expecting them; in fact, he had already received a telegram about them, and as soon as he had put them safely away for the night, he sent away a telegram himself. And at the same time, in his own modest home, Pat the policeman was holding a long conversation over the telephone about them; also, up at the distant fur post at Rabbit Portage, there was a considerable stir taking place on their account. And altogether, there was quite a fuss going on over these three little wanderers—a fuss about which they knew nothing whatever.

Upstairs, the two children talked excitedly, but in whispers, for some-how this grand, white-walled chamber gave them a feeling of being very small and out of place, like two mice that had stolen into somebody's pantry, or into a church.

But it was a place where no accidents could ever happen, that was cer-tain, so in the safety of this room, Shapian took out their little wad of money from a deerskin pouch that hung from a string about his neck. He spread it out and smoothed each bill very carefully on the table, while Sajo looked on, and nodded her shiny black head as if to say, "There you are, that's what my dream did!" They tried to make out just how much there was, Sajo standing by with her finger on her lips and her head on one side, looking very wise, while Shapian frowned and wondered, and looked closely at each bill; but the figures didn't mean a thing to them, and they had to give it up. But anyway, there was plenty, they agreed, more money than they had ever seen before; and Shapian folded it all up again and put it back into its little bag, under his shirt.

For this was the price of Chikanee's freedom and must never, for one single moment, be out of reach.

Meanwhile Chilawee, on the floor, was having the time of his life in the wash dish. He was having, at the same time, another feast, from a loaf of bread which the manager had kindly supplied, and what part of it he had not been able to eat, was slowly being transformed into a mushy, gooey, sticky mess, and you can take my word for it that the rug on which all this was taking place, was in no way improved by the performance.

Not one of them could sleep. The little beaver because there were far too many interesting things to be found under the bed, and in the clothes closet, and in corners, and the children because tomorrow was to be that great, that wonderful day of days, for which they had worked so hard and gone through so many dangers, and for which they had waited so long.

Tomorrow they would actually have Chikanee!

And neither one of them ever stopped to think that the park people might refuse, that they might never let the little beaver go, now that they had him. For, whatever misgivings Shapian may perhaps have had, Sajo, sure that her dream was coming true, never once doubted, and only said:

"Tomorrow we have Chikanee. I *know*."

Unto the Least of These

EARLY THE FOLLOWING DAY, PATRICK O'REILLY CALLED FOR his charges, as he had promised. But they did not go right away to the animal park as they had expected, but to a large building in the city, where the park owners had an office.

Afraid that at the last moment, some accident might happen to the money, Shapian felt often at the lump under his shirt, where the little bag was; they were going to need it very soon now, and he was getting nervous. In the other hand he carried Chilawee in his basket and beside him, never more than three feet away, Sajo walked with short, little-girl steps, her shawl wrapped about her head and shoulders.

There was a swift ride in an elevator, which they far from enjoyed, and then they found themselves, with the Irishman beside them, standing before a desk behind which sat a man.

And this was the man in whose hands was the fate of their little lost friend.

Sajo, who up till now had had such faith in her dream, became suddenly fearful and anxious, and trembled like a leaf. She had no idea what they were going to do if their offer was refused; and now that the moment had arrived she wanted to scream and run away. But she stood her ground bravely, determined to see it through, no matter what happened.

The man behind the desk was a youngish man with a pale narrow face and a weak-looking chin. He had a cigarette in the corner of his mouth, burnt almost down to his lips, and one of his eyes was screwed up unpleasantly, to keep the smoke out of it, while he looked around with the other, so that at times he appeared cross-eyed. He spoke without removing the cigarette, squinting sharply at them with the eye that was in working order; and a very colourless, unfriendly-looking eye it was.

"Well, what do you want?" he asked shortly.

There was a moment's silence, a very heavy, thick kind of a silence. I think that Sajo and Shapian had even stopped breathing. Then:

"Sorr," commenced Pat the policeman, "I telephoned Mr. H—— last night concerning me young friends there, and we were all to meet him here, to talk over a shmall matter of business, belike——"

"You can do your business with me," broke in the young man, in no very civil tone. "Mr. H—— is busy at present." And he glanced towards a door that led into another room, and which stood slightly open.

"You see, 'tis this way," began Pat once more, when the young man looked at his wrist watch and interrupted again.

"Make it snappy, constable; I'm busy this morning."

Pat got a little red in the face and again started his speech, this time successfully. It was a speech that he had carefully rehearsed the night before, the story that, as he had said at the railroad station, was going to "bring tears to the eyes of a heart of stone." Evidently the young man did not have a heart of stone, however, for there were no tears; in fact, while Pat was talking, this impatient personage looked several times at his wrist watch, and lit a fresh cigarette from the stump in his mouth. Far from having a heart of stone, it began to look very much as though he had no heart at all. And the honest policeman became a little discouraged towards the last, and finished his tale rather lamely:

". . . so the young people wants to buy the little baste back from ye: and I'll be so bold as to say that I think ye'll be doin' the Lord's own wurrk if ye let them have it." And having done his best he stood there, nervously wiping his face with the big red handkerchief. The man straightened some papers on the desk and leaned back in his chair.

"Are you quite done?" he inquired coldly.

"Yes," answered Pat, none too happily, for he began to fear, and with good reason, that he had lost the battle already.

"Oh," said the clerk, "thank you. Well, let me tell you"—his words fell like chips of ice on a plate of glass—"that beaver was bought in a fair and perfectly businesslike way, and not from these ragamuffins at all, but from a reputable trader. We paid fifty dollars for him, which was a great deal more than the little brute was worth, and we have no intention of selling him back—unless we can get a good profit on the deal, and"—here he looked at the two little Indians—"I don't think by their looks your red-skinned *friends*, as you call them, are very well off anyway."

Pat turned redder than ever, but shrewdly suspecting that money alone could talk to this hard-headed fellow, he pushed Shapian forward.

"Money," he whispered hoarsely. "That money. Money, give it now!" And Shapian, sick with fear, for he had understood nearly everything, stepped forward, fumbled for a moment in the pouch, and dropped his little wad of money on the desk.

The clerk took it, counted it. He sniffed.

"There's only fourteen dollars here." He handed it back. "Nothing doing!" he said, and to make sure that everybody understood, he added, for good measure, "All washed up; no sale; no good; no! Get me?"

They got him; every one of them.

Nobody spoke, nobody moved; but to Shapian it was the end of the world—but no—was this true? And then the silence seemed suddenly to be choking him; the white face of the man behind the desk was getting bigger and bigger, was rushing towards him—the floor seemed to be going from under his feet—was he going to fall like a woman, faint like a girl! He closed his eyes to shut out the sight of that pale, weak face with its one eye that leered at him so mockingly; he gritted his teeth, clenched his fists, and stiffened his young body upright in his old, proud way; and the dizzy feeling passed, leaving him cold and trembling. Meanwhile the policeman stood helplessly by in his dismay, mopping his bald head and mumbling huskily, "Oh, the shame it is! The pity of it! And it's me that's betrayed them that trusted in me; 'twill bring sorrow to the ould heart of me for many's the day!"

And Sajo? She had been watching every move with painful eagerness, her eyes flitting from face to face like two frightened birds in a cage; and she had seen. No one needed to tell her.

They had failed. In just two minutes they had failed.

She came softly over beside Shapian. "I know, my brother," she said very quietly, in such a strange little voice that Shapian looked at her quickly, and put his arm about her, while she stood close, looking up at him, "I know now. He is not going to give us Chikanee. I was wrong—about my dream. We have come to the city not to get Chikanee, after all. I think—perhaps—it was—to bring Chilawee to him. That must be what my mother meant; so they could be together—so they won't be lonesome any more. That must be it. So——"

And her childish voice fell to a whisper, and the little dark head drooped. "Tell this man—I—give him—Chilawee—too."

And she set Chilawee's basket upon the desk and stepped back, her face like a sheet of paper, her lips pale, and her eyes wide and dry, staring at the basket.

O'Reilly, cutting short his lament, stood aghast; *now* what was going on?

"What's this," exclaimed the clerk, becoming angry. And Shapian told him: "'Nother beaver, Chilawee. His brother, that Chikanee, very lonesome. You keep him Chilawee too; not be lonesome then. Those are words of my sister. Me—" his voice stuck in his throat, and he couldn't say any more.

"Well, now," said the clerk, smiling for the first time, though the smile improved his face very little. "That's a horse of a different colour! We'll fix that up very quickly," and he reached for his pen—

"NO!!" suddenly shouted the policeman in a terrific voice, bringing his fist down on the desk with a crash, so that everybody jumped, and the ink bottles and paperweights and the pens and the pencils all jumped. And even the pale young man jumped and turned a shade paler, and his cigarette jumped from his lips to the floor.

"No, you don't," bellowed Pat in a tremendous voice. "No son of an O'Reilly will stand by and see a couple of helpless kids bullyragged and put upon by ye, nor the likes o' ye. Ye're a black-hearted scoundrel!" he roared, "an I'm an officer of the law, an' I'll arrest ye for conspiracy, an' fraud, an' misdemeanour, an' highway robbery, an' assault, an'—" Here he ran out of the more attractive-sounding crimes, and growling fiercely started round the desk towards the badly scared young man, who was backing away as hastily as possible in the direction of the other room, while Sajo and Shapian stood by with eyes as big as saucers. Just what this rather violent son of the O'Reillys intended to do, never became known, for at that moment the other door opened, and the fleeing young man found his line of retreat cut off, as he stumbled backwards into yet another guest to the party, and a voice, a very quiet, low voice said: "Pardon me," as there appeared just inside the room a slim, grey-haired old gentleman, who stood peering over his spectacles at this astonishing scene.

He gave a slight cough, and said again: "Pardon me, if I appear to intrude," and then invited, very politely, "Won't you sit down?"

Pat still snorted angrily and glared at his intended prisoner, who was not at all sure if he *hadn't* committed some crime or another, so that his hands trembled a little as he fumbled with a new cigarette.

"Pray sit down, gentlemen," again invited the grey-haired man.

They sat down; somehow you felt that you must do as this mild-mannered old gentleman asked you. And he it was that owned the park; it was Mr. H—— himself.

"Now, let us talk matters over," he suggested, looking from the policeman to the clerk, then to the children, and back to the policeman again. "Now, constable, on the telephone last night I promised to hear these children's story, and to consider what should be done. I have heard everything—from the other room, far better than if I had been here; for then certain things *did* happen, that would not otherwise have done so. I had already learned from you how far they have come, and what hardships and dangers they have been through to try and regain their pet. But I had to be careful; I had to know that it was not a fraud, and as I cannot understand their language, I wanted to see what they would do, before I could even consider the matter. Now I know the *whole* story, and I see that matters are going to be very difficult—for me."

At this, the clerk looked around with a pleased expression, as if to say, "There now, didn't I tell you?" Mr. H—— looked around too, tapping his spectacles on his knee:

"Every one is listening, I hope?" he continued. "Yes?" It was plain to be seen that he was very well used to having people listen to him; and he held his glasses, which were of the pince-nez variety, across the thin bridge of his nose with his thumb and forefinger, and peered through them at each in turn, and the children found his gaze to be rather piercing, quite different from his voice.

"Ah," he said, finding that everybody was waiting to hear more (although Sajo did not understand a word he said, she was fascinated by his queer mannerisms and the smooth, even flowing of his speech). "Very good. Now, I heard these Indian children offer to give up their other pet, so the two little animals could be together, which proves to me their truthfulness. But, there is my side to be thought of. As George, here, says, it was a perfectly proper piece of business, and it cost me quite a sum of money. I cannot decide all at once. Moreover, it is not good for people, especially young people, for them to have everything they ask for, not, that is, unless they have worked for it." And he looked at them a trifle severely through his glasses, which he had put on again.

"And what are ye figurin' to do, Sorr?" asked O'Reilly anxiously, wishing that he would stop fidgeting with his spectacles and get down to business. But Mr. H—— turned to his clerk: "You are a good business man, George, almost too good, I sometimes think."

"I was only doing my duty, Sir," answered George, with some truth.

"Ah, our duty; yes," mused the thoughtful Mr. H——. "Well, no matter."

"But what are ye goin' to do about it, Sorr?" again asked Pat, nearly exploding with impatience.

"Do?" queried this exasperating old man. "Do? Oh, yes; I think I have decided what to do—just this!" and taking Chilawee's basket he beckoned the children over. "There," he said gently. "There is your small friend. Now," and becoming all at once very brisk and businesslike, he wrote something on a card and handed it to Pat. "And now, go down to the park with Mr. O'Reilly, *and get the other one. He is yours; you most certainly have earned him.*"

Shapian stared, his mouth open—did he hear aright? Or was this another one of Sajo's dreams in which he had become entangled? Or perhaps it was one of his own! But Sajo was very much awake, and she grabbed Chilawee's basket from him.

"Tell me, *tell* me," she clamoured excitedly, "what *is* it, what is it?" And seeing that they did not quite understand, Mr. H—— was about to speak again, when Pat burst out (he so wanted to be the first with the good news!).

"Pardon me, Sorr, I speak their langwidge," and he turned to Shapian: "Him," he said, giving Mr. H—— several good hearty slaps on the back, so that gentleman, caught unawares, almost went forward on his face, and his glasses went flying (much to every one's relief), "that's good feller. Him"—here he gave the astonished Mr. H—— a sound thump on the chest that nearly bowled him over backwards—"him, that's big chief, good. Me—'tis a difficult tongue, Sorr—you, catchem two beavers, chop, chop. Savvy?" And finishing in his very best Indian "Kaeget! Kae*get*!" he turned triumphantly to Mr. H—— "Langwidges was always a gift with the O'Reillys, Sorr."

"Quite," said Mr. H——. "Most decidedly—ah—yes!" And he smiled as he let the happy party out through the door, and closed it behind them, still smiling gently to himself. What an extremely pleasant little game it had been, he thought, even if he was, after all, the loser! And he rubbed his hands together very cheerfully, quite as though he had made rather a profitable bargain.

I greatly doubt if either Sajo or Shapian remembered very much about that trip to the amusement park, up to the time that Pat pointed out the entrance that could now be seen not far ahead of them. Then Sajo started to run. She was not pale now, and her eyes, that had been so dry and staring, were all aglow. Her shawl fell back unheeded, and her braids flew out and bobbed up and down on her shoulders, as her little moccasined feet pattered on the pavement. Behind her came Shapian, unable to keep up with her on account of carrying the basket, inside which Chilawee, tired of being cooped up for so long, was making a great uproar. Next came the stalwart Mr. O'Reilly, very red in the face, his helmet off, dabbing with his large red handkerchief at the head that had been "bald as an egg for twenty years," puffing and blowing like a tugboat that had a light touch of asthma.

Once he bellowed "Hey! What is this, a race?" But the youngsters kept right on going, and it is very doubtful if they ever heard him; so he fell to grumbling: "The little haythens, they'll be the death of me yet, so they will." But he kept valiantly on.

Several passers-by stopped to look at the young Indians in their forest clothes, racing along the street with the policeman apparently chasing them. They heard, too, the shrill cries and wails coming out of the basket, as Chilawee objected loudly to the shaking up he was getting in all this hurry; so a few of them turned and joined this strange parade, and followed this small, running, black-haired girl.

And behind them all, far, far behind, there came another person, a tall, brown-skinned man who strode along so softly, yet so swiftly through the city streets. And he looked so dark and stern that people were glad to step aside and let him pass, and stared after him and said to one another: "Who is that? What kind of a man is that?" But he never so much as glanced at any one of them.

There was some delay at the entrance, as the park was not yet open for the day, but O'Reilly soon caught up, and showed his card, and they were let in. Quite a respectable crowd had gathered, and pushed in with them as soon as the gates were opened. The attendant, who was none other than our friend Alec the keeper, already knew what to do, as Mr. H—— had decided, at the last moment, to come too and had given his orders and now stood in the crowd. At a nod from Mr. H—— the keeper led Sajo quickly over towards the beaver pen. And all at once she was pale as a ghost again. She seemed to be running in a great empty space at the end of which, miles away, was a dark, ugly looking row of iron bars, and now, now—she could see through them, and there—yes, there was a brown, furry little animal sitting up in the center of them, and was it?—could it be?—yes, it was—Chikanee!!

And Sajo, no longer shy, forgot the watching people, forgot the noisy city, forgot everything but the small furry body that was now so close, and rushing to the iron fence she threw herself on her knees in the gravel, thrust her two arms through the bars, and screamed: "Chikanee! CHIKANEE!! CHIKANEE!!!"

The little beaver, not believing, sat without a move, looking.

"It's me, Sajo; O! Chikanee!" The cry was almost a wail: Oh, had he forgotten?

For a moment longer the little creature stood there, stock still, his chubby brown head cocked to one side, listening, as Sajo cried out again:

"Chik-a-*nee-e-e-e!!!*"—and then he knew. And with a funny little noise in his throat, he scrambled as fast as his short legs would carry him, to the bars.

At that a little cheer broke out amongst the crowd, and there was a small commotion. Alec the keeper now came forward and opened a small iron gate, and said: "This way Miss—a—Mam'selle—a—Señorita—" for he didn't quite know how he should address her, and was rather excited himself. And she rushed in, and kneeling down gathered the so-long-lost Chikanee up on her lap and bent over him; and they both were very still. And the gay head-shawl hid everything; and neither you, nor I, nor any one else will ever know just what passed between those two on that fateful, that glorious, that never-to-be-forgotten morning.

And the grey-haired Mr. H—— took his handkerchief from his pocket and blew his nose rather loudly, and Alec the keeper had suddenly become troubled with a cough; "Humph," he said. "Hurrumph."

"You bet!" exclaimed Pat the policeman in a hearty voice, although the keeper hadn't really said anything at all.

And now was to come the biggest thrill of all. Chilawee and Chikanee were to have *their* party now. They were only ten feet apart, and didn't know it! What a thrill was there!

So it was with wildly beating heart that Sajo and Shapian carried the basket in; one of them alone could never have handled this affair; it took the two of them to pull off the lid, they were in such a state. And they lifted Chilawee out, and set him down facing Chikanee, a short distance away. Then they stood and watched, breathlessly. For a second or two neither of the kittens moved, just stared at each other. Then, the truth slowly dawning in the little twilight minds, they crept towards one another, eyes almost starting out of their heads, ears wide open, listening, sniffing, creeping slowly forward until the creep became a walk, and the walk became a little shuffling trot, and now, sure at last that they had found each other, the trot broke suddenly into a gallop and with a rush they met, head-on. And so violent was the collision, in a mild way of speaking, that, not being able to go any farther ahead, they went straight up on end, and with loud shrill cries they grasped each other tightly and there, in front of all those people, began to wrestle!

The ceaseless, hopeless searching, the daily disappointments, all the misery and longing, the dreary, empty nights of lonesomeness were over.

Big Small and Little Small were together again.

Before long they were disporting themselves all over the enclosure, and what had been a grim and ugly prison, had now become a playground, the best use that it had ever yet been put to, I'll guarantee! And the children clapped their hands, and shouted, and laughed and hallooed at them excitedly, while the wrestlers, or dancers, or whatever you have a mind to call them, stepped around in high feather, enjoying to the utmost what must have been to them the greatest moment in all their lives, up to that time and perhaps for ever after. Never before had they given quite such a brilliant performance; and the people cheered them on, and laughed, and the grey-haired Mr. H—— waved his handkerchief quite furiously in the air, and I am not at all sure that he didn't shout a little himself.

Mr. O'Reilly, just about dying to take a part in this happy occasion which he had helped so much to bring about, and very proud to think that he was the only one present who knew the whole story, appointed himself Master of Ceremonies, and while he performed his duties as a policeman and kept back the crowd, he also played the part of a modern radio announcer, and explained to them what it was all about, and cracked jokes, and beamed around on everybody in the most amiable fashion, and otherwise enjoyed himself immensely. And I think we will all agree that he was entitled to any credit he got, even if he did pretend to know a little more about it than he really did. And when the two Smalls commenced to do their queer-looking dance, he was not to be outdone, and was heard to say that it was the very first time in all his days that he had ever seen anything but an Irishman able to dance a good Irish jig; and he ended up by declaring for all to hear:

"Well, I'm seein' it, but, be japers, I'll never believe it."

For which he could have been very easily excused as, to any one who had never seen such a thing before, it must have been a most extraordinary sight.

ᘯᘯᘯ

AND THEN, HAVING BEEN THERE, WATCHING, FOR QUITE some time, for he had not wished to interrupt this little celebration, there now came out from behind the people another figure—a tall, dark man in moccasins. He was the same man who, a short time before, had been seen striding so swiftly through the city streets in this direction. A quietness fell upon the wondering crowd as he stepped forward. Sajo and Shapian, busy with their playfellows, never noticed him until a voice, *the* voice, the one they knew so very well, said softly there behind them, in the quiet, musical language of the Ojibways:

"O-way, the clouds have indeed gone from off the face of the sun. Now my sorrow has gone too, melted away like the mists of early morning. These people have done much, very much for us, my children. Let us thank them.

"My son, my daughter, take up your Nitchie-keewense,[*] your Little Brothers. O-pee-pee-soway is waiting."

Big Feather had come to take them, all four of them, back to The Place of Talking Waters, to the Land of the North West Wind.

And Sajo's dream had, after all, come true.

---

[*] Pronounced *Nit*-chie-*kee*-wense.

CHAPTER SIXTEEN

Mino-ta-kiyah!

SO THEY BID FAREWELL TO THE CITY, WITH ITS NOISE AND ITS bustle and its people who, after all, thought Sajo, seemed to be just about the same as any other folks—more good ones than bad ones. In fact, nearly all good ones, she decided, and made up her mind to tell the Indians just what they really *were* like.

And they said good-bye to Alec the keeper, who had been so kind to poor, lonely Chikanee, and who felt very relieved to see his little prisoner free once more; and to the whimsical, quietly smiling Mr. H——, who was happy for a long time after, in the knowledge that he had brought gladness to some very sorrowful hearts. Although Gitchie Meegwon had tried to pay him for Chikanee, he would not even hear of it, and said that it was worth the pleasure it had given him.

Patrick the policeman, stalwart son of the O'Reillys, brought them to the railroad station and saw them off; as he told his comrades afterwards, "Wid me own two hands I saw thim safely on their way. And whin their fayther heard me sp'akin' his langwidge to the youngsters, he smiled all over his face, so he did!" Which it is quite likely that he did. And as the train pulled out from the platform, the two children waved and waved to this friend who had been so good, and loyal, and true to them, and he stood there holding his helmet high in the air like a signal, his bald pate shining in the distance, leaving Shapian still firmly convinced that there was a whole nation of people living on a green island in a great salt lake, who called themselves Beavers.

When they arrived at Rabbit Portage, the first person they saw was Yellow Hair, who jumped aboard the boat before it was well landed, to welcome them. Right away, Shapian gave him the money that was left, and Yellow Hair told the Big Knives, who were all there to meet them, and offered it back to them. But one of them stepped out and made a little speech, and said that they were all very glad that things had turned out so well, and that the missionary was to keep the money and give it to some one amongst the Indians who might be poor, and needed it. And Gitchie Meegwon thanked them all for their kindness to his children, and said he hoped that some day it would come *his* turn to help some one, as your turn always came around some time, to do a good deed.

Yellow Hair told them that he was to accompany them back to the village, where he was going to work among the people. And at this the trader, who up till now had kept rather in the background, came forward and shook hands with all three of them and said that he was coming too, so that he could become better acquainted with his Indian customers, as all good traders should; though he never mentioned, never *would* mention, never *did* mention, that he too had helped. And it never would have been known if Yellow Hair had not seen him that time in the schoolhouse, and told Big Feather about it privately. Meanwhile, the two Smalls came in for a great deal of petting and attention, and they even consented to stage a wrestling bout for the assembled Gitchie Mokoman, though I doubt very much if they cared whether anybody saw them or not; and I think they were rather relieved when the party set out and they were left in their basket to themselves.

Big Feather paddled in his own canoe, which still showed the effects of the fire, and Shapian took the bow. Sajo, on this trip, did no work but was a passenger, along with Chilawee and Chikanee who never worked anyway, and she sat with her face stuck into the beaver box most of the time. Yellow Hair and the trader went with some more Indians in another and much larger canoe, one of those great birch-bark canoes called Rabishaws, with a high, proudly curving bow and stern, which gave it rather the appearance of some gallant charger, or a Spanish galleon.

At the first portage they found the old Chief, Stands First, encamped, awaiting them. He asked for an account of all that had happened, and listened very attentively as they told him, and at all the important points and especially interesting places, he said "Hoh!" and "Hah!" and "Hum!" in a deep, throaty voice, and there was a very knowing twinkle in his eye as he listened. After considering the matter for a while, he told Sajo and Shapian that they were an honour to their people, and that there would be a song made about them, and about their adventures with the Little Talking Brothers, as he called the Smalls, and that it would become a part of the history of the tribe. And he looked in on Chilawee and Chikanee and said that they too now belonged to the tribe, and would become a great tradition in the nation. And as he spoke there was a smile on his wise old wrinkled face, the first that had been there for many a long day; for he was rather a grim-looking old man, to tell the truth. And then, pulling his blanket about his waist he stood there very straight, with his long white hair about his shoulders, and made a sign with his hand towards the sun and said,

"Hah! Mino-ta-kiyah; kae*get* kee mino-ta-kiyah!—it is well, indeed, it is very well!"

And all the watching group of Indians, and Gitchie Meegwon, and Yellow Hair, repeated together like a chorus, "Mino-ta-kiyah!" and everybody seemed to be very solemn and impressed.

And as they journeyed on their way, on to O-pee-pee-soway, the trees beside the river seemed to wave to one another and to nod, and in the rustling of their branches and their leaves, they seemed to sigh "Kaeget mino-ta-kiyah, it is well"; the ravens in the air croaked "Mino-ta-kiyah!"[*] and the wind whispered through the grasses, "Se-e-e-e-ey mino-ta-kiyah"; and the racing water in the rapids, that once had seemed to be so fierce and wild, sang it over and over in that strange way that running water has; and the little swirling eddies that slipped from off the paddles, murmured it at every stroke, "Mino-ta-kiyah."

Never had the forest seemed more beautiful, never had the sky been quite so blue; and the sun had never shone so brightly, nor the squirrels frisked as gaily nor the birds sung half so sweetly, as they did for Sajo, on that journey back to O-pee-pee-soway. And never had she or Shapian, in all their lives, been quite so happy.

[*] Pronounced Mee-*no*-tak-*kiy*-ah.

When they arrived, Big Feather called all the people together, and at his cabin that night they held a dance of celebration. Everybody from the village came, including two or three half-breeds who were passing through (and who had *not* bothered anybody's hunting ground after all) and who, as usual, had their fiddles with them. And there were swift, clever step-dances while the fiddlers played old-time jigs and reels, the players putting into the tunes all kinds of queer twists and turns, after the fashion of the half-breeds; and there were Indian quadrilles with as many as twenty people on the floor at once. And the fun was fast and furious.

All the boys of the village wanted to dance with Sajo, so that she was kept pretty busy, and I can tell you, by the way, that she was quite a little dancer, for I myself was there and saw her, and saw Shapian, too, who was as proud as Punch to see his sister so much in demand. You may be sure that he had no trouble in finding dancing partners among the village maidens, and there were some very fine-looking young women to choose from, as could be plainly seen, because there was no ducking and hiding behind head-shawls, for none but the oldest ladies would ever think of wearing one to an affair of this kind.

Outside, a huge fire was kept burning, where tea was constantly being made, and before which had gathered a little group of old men who sat and smoked, and talked of olden days, whilst a crowd of youngsters played tag, and hide and seek among the flickering shadows. And Gitchie Meegwon passed among his guests, and talked with them, and his face, that was sometimes stern and often sad, was now very pleasant to took at as he smiled upon them all and bid them welcome. Every once in a while he went around with a large pail of tea, while Sajo and Shapian carried cups and served the people, and danced in between times.

Once during the evening the dancers cleared the floor, and sat back in a big circle against the wall as though expecting something to take place, and a hush fell on them. Soon two drummers took their place inside the circle with tom-toms, and commenced to beat. And then, through the door, came old Ne-Ganik-Abo, Stands First, the Chief, with a great bonnet of eagle feathers on his head and strange, wild-looking designs of paint upon his face, and danced to the sound of the drums. Below each of his knees there hung a circlet of hollow deer hoofs, that clinked and clanked at every step, and in his hand he held a rattle made of a whole turtle shell, painted red and black, and having the head and neck of the turtle for a handle. And as he danced, the hollow deer-hoofs fairly rang, like little copper bells, keeping time with the swift movements of his feet, and the fringes of his buckskins quivered and shook, and the great bonnet nodded, and opened wide across his shoulders, and closed and spread again, all in perfect time with the drums, which never stopped beating, and he shook his rattle very fiercely as he danced. And while he danced, he sang a low, weird chant, in which he told the adventures of Sajo and Shapian, and of Chilawee and Chikanee, as in the old days when the warriors had sung the story of a battle. And after each verse there was a chorus, given by a group of singers; and the song had a queer haunting melody that was somehow very exciting.

This was the song he had promised, and it would now be one of the legends of the tribe; for it was by means of such songs about various happenings, and by crudely painted pictures of events, that the old-time Indians kept a record of the history of their people. But the trader, who had never seen such goings on before and thought it was a war-dance, became the least bit alarmed, until Gitchie Meegwon explained to him that it was not a war-dance at all, but a Wabeno,[*] used only by the Medicine Men, or for the reciting of great events. Then with one loud, long yell the Wabeno came to an end.

And now the fiddles struck up a lively tune, and the floor filled up and the fun commenced where it had left off, and away went the quadrilles and the jigs again. Yellow Hair danced on nimble feet, and laughed the whole night through, and picked the homeliest old woman he could find for a partner; and when things slackened down for any length of time, he got them going again in very short order. And the trader, surrounded by all the merry throng, quite forgot his dignity, and let it be plainly seen that he could be just as jolly as the next man, and made no bones about it either, but footed it as merrily as the best of them. He even made friends with the Smalls, but still could never remember their names, though Shapian, who didn't hate him any more, did his best to tell him. But he kept on calling them Chilakee, and Cherokee, and Chikaroo and

[*] Pronounced *waw*-beno.

any number of other names that sounded something the same, but were always wrong, and of which he seemed to have an unlimited supply.

Chilawee and Chikanee themselves were by no means left out of things. They never would be left out of anything so long as they had two voices to shout with, and four legs apiece to run around on, and excited as they were by the music and the noise and all the fun, they tore about the floor, and scrambled between the dancers, and went around begging wherever they could find any one sitting down. Once Chilawee took the center of the room and stood there upright, fair and square in the people's way, and the dance had to be stopped in that particular set, because nobody wanted to trample on the little fellow, or fall over him. For a minute or two he had it all to himself, and held the floor, so to speak, and stood looking around as if to say, like Long John Silver: "Here I am, and here I stay, and you may lay to *that*." So Sajo finally had to carry the young ruffian bodily off the floor, kicking and squealing. Meanwhile Chikanee (the saint!), who had lived in the city and knew a thing or two, had found out where there was a case of apples that some one had brought up from the trading post, and discovering that one apple was about all he could cram into himself, he started carrying them away one by one and hiding them, and when he was found and arrested there was a real circus and another squealing match. Hoping to quiet them down, Sajo began giving them chunks of bannock to go to bed with. But they would not stay there and came bobbing out for more, so they were continually running back and forth with these bribes; and it is very certain that even if they had stuffed themselves all night, they could not possibly have eaten the half of it.

At last, tired out with the long journey, and the excitement, and this and that, and one thing and another, they finally retired to their own private chamber for good; and with their noses tight together, their little hands clutched in each other's fur, and entirely surrounded by bannock, they drifted off to sleep, all their troubles, all the long, weary days of lonesomeness, gone forever and forgotten.

From then on, all day and every day, the play-house and the lake shore rang with shouting and with laughter, as they had done before Chikanee had ever gone away. It began to seem as if such a thing had never really happened, but had been nothing but an ugly dream. The cabin, that for so many days had stood empty and forlorn, was once more filled with joy. And the soft ground at the landing bore again the print of little feet whose owners, those with two feet as well as those with four, had come so near to leaving no more footprints, ever, anywhere.

Chilawee, the scapegrace, became once again the bold, bad pirate, and was as wilful as he had ever been, or a little worse, if you ask me. He disappeared as regularly as ever, and could be depended on to be found just as regularly, and always up to some mischief or another, and when caught at it would do his absurd, wigglesome dance and fall on his back with a great outcry, either from delight at his prank, or just out of sheer naughtiness. Although they were both beginning to be quite a size by now, Chikanee had given up the race to see who could grow the fastest, and he had allowed Chilawee to get a little ahead of him. And there he stayed, so that Chikanee was still the Littlest Small and was as soft and gentle in his ways as he had ever been. Not that he was good *all* the time; that would have been too much to expect. But many and many was the time when he lay in Sajo's arms, as in the old days, with his nose pushed tight as could be against her throat in just one certain spot that he knew of. And there he would snuggle up, and close his eyes, and puff and blow a little, and make small whimpers of happiness, just as he had done so often in his dreams on his lonely little pallet in the keeper's kitchen. And now he was never to be lonely any more—and he would open one eye and take a look, to make quite sure that he was still there and that it was not just another of those dreams!

And now everything was the same as ever, and the days were very full, and busy, and exciting, with all the swimming and the burrowing, the puddling in the mud and the combing and scrubbing of coats, and the games of hide and seek under the canoe, and the wrestling and the amateur building operations on the tiny, crazy beaver house that just never *could* keep out the rain. And then, after all the work and the play was over for the day, the short, weary legs plodded up the water trail to the cabin; and there were the little dishes (the same little dishes!) full of boiled rice, or milk, or, on special occasions, even a little dash of preserves, and then a good stout chunk of bannock apiece to go to bed with, and the long sleep on a soft, warm bed——

And so the happy Summer passed.

Came the Autumn, and with it the Days of Falling Leaves, the Silent Days. The time had come to take Chilawee and Chikanee back to their old home. For they must now be allowed to take up again the life that was rightly theirs, and follow the way of all the Beaver People. In the Winter it would be impossible to supply them with enough water for their needs, nor could they be moved from place to place, as in the Summer. And Gitchie Meegwon called his children to him one day, and explained it all to them very carefully, and told them how the beavers, who would soon begin to grow up, could not much longer remain happily living in such an unnatural way, and that very soon they must be returned to their own folk, to live as the Great Spirit of the Wilderness had intended they should.

The children had known for some time that this must be so, though they had never mentioned it to one another. As the day for the parting drew near, Sajo became very quiet and thoughtful, and spent long hours with her small play-fellows, who would soon be hers no longer; while they, merry as a pair of sand-boys, played with her in the same old frolicsome way, with never a thought for the days to come, even though they should be happy ones.

And she loved them so much that she would not think of how lonesome *she* might be after they were gone, but of how glad *they* would be to see their father and their mother once again. So how can I be sad? she asked herself, and then said aloud, in rather a quavery little voice,

"I'm very happy. I *am*. I *know* I am!" So there!

Yes, Sajo, you were happy; happy as must be, always, those who give.

∾∾∾

AND SO, ONE MORNING IN OCTOBER, IN THE MONTH OF Falling Leaves, when the hills were all crimson, and brown, and golden in their Autumn colours, Chikanee and Chilawee, Little Small and Big Small, took their leave of their little private room and the cabin where they had spent the happy, carefree days of kittenhood. And they left the shaky little beaver lodge, and the play-house, and the water trail and all their landing places, left them there behind them on the shore, and climbed into their old birch-bark basket that had served them so well and for so long, and embarked on the last and most important journey they had ever made.

And little did they guess, as they settled themselves down on their scented sweet-grass beds, how great an event was waiting for them at the other end of it.

CHAPTER SEVENTEEN

In the Moon of Falling Leaves

IT WAS TO BE A BIG AFFAIR.

Sajo was gay in many-coloured tartan plaid, her newest, brightest head-shawl and her beautifully beaded moccasins. Shapian and Gitchie Meegwon had on their very best deerskin clothes, worn only on very special occasions, and newly smoked to a rich, velvety brown. On the famous basket Sajo had painted leaves and many-coloured flowers, and birds and little animals, to be company for Chilawee and Chikanee on this the last of all the journeys they would ever take in it; and with a big white feather hanging from the handle, and all the painted pictures, it looked no longer old, but like a new one. In it, with loving care, she had arranged a bed of sweet-scented grasses, and had tied to it, in a little leather bag all decorated with porcupine quills, the two small, but very precious dishes.

The canoe, that had carried them so staunchly and so well, and had shared so many of their adventures, had by no means been overlooked. No signs of the fire were left upon it. Its sides had been dyed a bright yellow, as before, and it had newly painted gunwales and a new eye, not so fierce as the one it had lost—rather a jolly-looking eye, come to look at it, and also a fine new tail. And a very proud appearance it made, as though it knew very well that this was to be no ordinary voyage; and out in the wind it wagged its new tail in a very frisky way indeed, and the eye, as the reeds and rushes blinked and nodded past it, seemed to be winking to itself as though its owner was very pleased about something or another.

And so they headed for the River of Yellow Birches, that lay far away in the blue distance among the Hills of the Whispering Leaves, where Chikanee and Chilawee had been born.

For six days they journeyed on. And ever, as they went, the air grew more still, the waters calmer. Every night long strings and lines of wild-geese flew overhead towards the South, the beat of their wings sounding very plainly in the darkness. Each morning the sun seemed a little larger and redder, the leaves more brilliant in their colouring. For the forest, in the days of Indian Summer, in the Moon of Falling Leaves, is very beautiful.

Sajo was really, truly happy; not at all as she had expected to feel. To keep herself that way, she kept remembering that her small, so-well-beloved friends, her Little Brothers, were going to be better off than they ever had been, and would soon be getting better care than she could ever give them—that they were going home, home amongst their own folks. Their play-days were almost over, she knew; they were becoming more sober-minded. Soon they would be going to work, as all the forest animals and nearly every kind of people must do sooner or later; that, she agreed (did you ever notice how easy it is to agree with yourself?), was what they were made for, not just to be pets, but to work; which was quite true. It was the only way that they could ever be really contented.

Yet there would come, once in a while, a little ache in her heart, and her eyes would get a little blurred and misty; but she would brush her hand across them quickly, and say to herself, "I'm just sorry for *me*. That's only being selfish. We must do what is best for *them*. That's how much I love them." And she would look bravely around at the trees and the lake, and peep into the basket, and tickle the funny, pursey ears, and think how lovely it would be if only she could just see what went on, and hear what they said to one another when they got inside the lodge.

If only their father and mother and the other little ones would come to meet them, so she could see them all together! And she hoped, oh! how she hoped, that no hunter would ever find them.

On the last night of the journey, they camped amongst the pine trees in that pleasant spot where we first saw Gitchie Meegwon making his noon meal, so long ago, beside the little stream that came down from the beaver pond. And on this memorable night, after supper had been eaten and everything put away, and it was dark and the campfire was blazing away cheerfully, Big Feather said that he had something of importance to tell them, something that he had been keeping for the very last.

And everything settled down to be very quiet, as the children sat and listened there beside the glowing fire. And Chilawee, as he sat beside his basket, not moving at all, his head cocked to one side, beaver fashion, seemed to be listening; and Chikanee, lying with his head on Sajo's knee, quiet as a mouse, must have been listening too. The broad, deep river that flowed so silently and swiftly by, must certainly have heard it all, and no doubt repeated it over and over to the very first rapids that it came to. Even the great, dark trees that stood so solemnly and still around the camp, the shadows from the firelight flickering in and out between them, seemed to stand and listen as he spoke.

"Sajo, Shapian," said Gitchie Meegwon, "this is the last night we will spend with Chikanee and Chilawee. Tomorrow they will be back with their own people, to live in their own way. Very pleasant have been the days they spent with us. They have brought much joy to our house, and the bright days of Summer have been brighter because they came to us.

"I found them at this place, sick and helpless—dying. Now they are back here again, well and strong, ready to carry on. Their adventures are over, and they will be happy as never before.

"One thing I can promise; they will never be killed."

Here Sajo made a little sound, a very little sound, but she put her finger to her lips to push it back. Gitchie Meegwon went on:

"You saw our Chief dance the She-she-gwun, the Dance of Rattles; it was a Wabeno, for a special sign, and he has commanded that no Indian shall hunt beaver in or near this place. And here no white man ever comes. This is my hunting ground, but I myself will never harm them, or their family; it would be like killing small, friendly people. For they have made my children happy; could they understand me, I would thank them. Come what may, they will be forever safe.

"Tomorrow, when you let them go, I will give the call of a beaver, the sound with which they call to one another. The young ones in the lodge will not listen, but perhaps the old ones may come and greet them. I cannot be sure, but I will try."

Sajo put her hand tightly across her mouth, so there was no sound *this* time.* Just then a low moaning cry came floating out from somewhere in the hills, became louder for a while, and faded again to silence; a wild, deep-toned, yet lonesome wail—the cry of a wolf. Gitchie Meegwon paused until the last echo had died away, while every one listened; for Indians do not fear the wolves as some do, but look on them as fellow hunters, calling them The Lonely Ones. Then he continued:

"Big Small and Little Small," he smiled at the names, "will never be quite lost to you. Beavers are different from other animals; they are very like persons, and do not quickly change. Once they know you and have become your friends, they do not forget. They will be yours, always.

"And now the best thing of all" (no sound from anybody; not even the wolf). "Once every year, in the Moon of Falling Leaves, when the leaves of the forest are falling all about us like brightly painted red and yellow snowflakes, and the wild geese fly in clouds across the sky, then you shall come here, to their home, and stay a little time and watch beside their home-pond in the evenings, and see them swimming, working, playing. It is very likely that they may come to you, so you may speak to them, perhaps may even touch them. They may not be able to remember every-thing, and many of the things they saw with you may pass from their minds, but *you* they will *never* forget. The old men, who are very wise, have told me. In my young days I, too, have seen it.

"My children, those are my words."

And they were words that took out from little Sajo's heart the last traces of sadness—not *quite* perhaps, for after all she was only a little girl, and she was giving up everything she had to give—these two tiny crea-tures that she loved as no one but a little girl *can* love. But they were not forgetful little people, her father had said, and, she thought, I will hang the basket on a tree, near the ground, and leave the little dishes too, where they can come and see them, so they *won't* forget. And that night, as she lay on her bed of balsam boughs, with Big Small and Little Small sleep-ing cuddled in her arms for the very last time, she thought over

---

* Indians exercise great care to avoid interrupting when any one is speaking. On an occasion such as this, for a young person to speak, unless directly addressed, would be counted as a serious misdemeanour.

everything that had ever happened, since they had come to her on that never-to-be-forgotten birthday, and of all the good times they had had together, and how happily everything had turned out at the last, and she thought of everything that her father had said—he was going to call them, and maybe the old ones would come out, and everything—and it seemed a shame to sleep away this very last night of all. So she lay awake as long as she possibly could, listening to the quiet breathing of Chilawee and Chikanee, and at last she laid her little head, that was so full of thoughts, down beside the two small damp noses that puffed, and blew, and sometimes were inclined to snore, and soon she passed with them into the Land of Forgetfulness.

෴ ෴ ෴

THE NEXT AFTERNOON, JUST AS THE SUN WAS SETTING, AT the time when wild beavers awake from sleep, they were all beside the home-pond of the Beaver People. It was from here that Chikanee and Chilawee, two tiny, lost mites, had started out on their Great Adventure.

In most ways the place was much as it had been when we first saw it in May, the Month of Flowers. The dam was full and running over, and in the best of shape, and the earthen house still reared itself like a huge, dark mound, high above the fen-land. But the pond no longer looked to be deserted. Fresh work showed everywhere, making it appear more than ever as though a gang of men had been busy with axe and shovel. Yet all this was the work of two beavers, for the little ones do not count for much during their first Summer. The sides of the lodge had been all heavily plastered to keep out the cold, and floating out in front of it was an immense raft of logs, and sticks, and branches, which had been col-lected for the beavers' Winter food supply. From different places along the shore smooth, well-kept, narrow roads wound their way up into the woods, and alongside them a number of freshly cut stumps were visi-ble, the very teeth marks plainly to be seen upon them. Most of the trees that had belonged to the stumps had disappeared, and were now hidden away under the raft, and a few others lay near the water partly cut into lengths, showing where the Beaver People were still at work, gathering in their harvest against the coming of Winter, which was soon to be upon them.

It was very quiet and peaceful there, and the ring of silent trees was reflected very clearly on the calm surface of the water, but their tops were no longer green, as they had been when we last saw them, but were red, and yellow, and brown, where the frost had painted them. And all around through the silent forest, the falling leaves came drifting, spinning, rustling slowly down.

Gitchie Meegwon drew away a short distance, while Sajo and Shapian carried the basket down to the water's edge between them. And there, beneath a tall, silvery poplar tree they opened it.

Shapian reached in and stroked the plump, silky little bodies, and said, "Farewell, Nitchie-kee-wense, good-bye, Little Brothers"; but not very loud, because his voice was a little shaky, and a man had to be careful about such things before the womenfolk. And then he took his sister's two hands in his own, and said to her:

"Do not sorrow, my sister. Every year when the leaves are falling, I will bring you here to see them. Many things have we four seen and done together; we will always remember, and *they* will not forget. Our father has said it. Now they will be happy, all their lives. It is well with them."

"Yes," Sajo answered in a whisper, "I know; they will be happy. So I must be happy, too." And she smiled up at him, "Thank you, my brother."

Then Shapian went over and stood with his father, and left Sajo there alone. She held the little beavers close, just for a moment, and whispered into the small black ears:

"Good-bye, Chilawee; good-bye, Chikanee, my Little Brothers. Don't let's forget—*ever.*"

And then she let them go.

She followed them to the very edge of the water, where she stood watching them as they floated off. On they swam, on across their own home pond, their two round, chubby heads side by side, as they had always been; sturdy Chilawee, jovial, wayward and full of whims; gentle Chikanee, wistful, winsome and affectionate. A few more minutes and they would be gone. And no matter how big they might grow to be, in one tender loving little heart they would still remain two tiny, helpless baby beavers.

To Sajo they would forever be the Smalls.

As they drew near to that great earthen stronghold across the way, Big Feather gave a long, clear call, the call of a beaver looking for his companions. Again the sound, like a note of music, stole out into the stillness; and again. And then, quite suddenly, a black head appeared on the surface of the water near the house, then another; great dark heads, with big furry brown bodies that floated high behind them.

Sajo scarcely breathed; it was just what she had hoped for, but had not dared to believe—the beaver father and mother were really coming, at Gitchie Meegwon's call, to meet them! Everything was coming true, *everything*—Oh!——

Every one stood as still as the trees themselves, while the old beavers came slowly towards Chikanee and Chilawee, passed around them once or twice, looking, sniffing at them, making some low, thrilling sounds, and then swam on beside them—big heads and little heads, all together now! Swimming steadily and swiftly on (oh, all too swiftly), they held on to their course, the water streaming out wide behind them in long, rippling V's; and once or twice there could be heard the faint, distant sound of childlike voices. The dark heads, the big ones still close beside the little ones, became smaller and smaller, farther and farther away, until, right before the entrance to the lodge, one by one, without a sound, they sank beneath the surface, out of sight.

Big Small and Little Small were home.

And Sajo stood there very still, like a many-coloured little statue, in her gay tartan dress and pretty moccasins, her head-shawl fallen back and her glossy black braids shining in the glow of the setting sun. And so she remained, looking out over the little pond, with her red lips parted and her dark eyes bright and starry, watching until the last brown head was gone, and the very last ripple on the water had disappeared.

And just then, from among the golden, whispering leaves above her head, there came the rippling notes of a small, white-throated singing-bird. As the tiny feathered songster trilled his melody so joyously, his voice seemed to fill the quiet valley, and, to the ears of Sajo, he sang a message, of hope, of happiness, and love:

"Mino-ta-kiyah, it is well," he seemed to sing. "*Me*-me-me-e—*no*-no-no-o-o—*no*-ta-kiy—*no*-ta-kiy—*no*-ta-kiy—ah!"[*]

And Sajo, standing there so quietly among the falling leaves, her eyes still fixed eagerly on the dark mound that was the last home of her Beaver People, repeated softly to herself, "Mee-no-ta-kiy-ah."

And the little basket, with its two wee dishes, its bed of scented grasses, and its gaily-painted animals and leaves and flowers, she hung upon a low branch near the ground, and left it there beside the clear, still water.

Then turning, with outstretched hands, and bravely smiling, she ran to meet her father and her brother.

∾ ∾ ∾

AND NOW THE FIGURES DISAPPEAR AND ALL ARE GONE. OUR journey is over; the tale is done.

While you have been listening to my story, the flickering fire in the center of the wigwam has burnt low, and only the gleaming coals remain. Behind us on the walls of skin our shadows fall big and dark.

We must go.

Yet sometimes, as you sit alone in the twilight of a Summer evening, and have nothing better to do, perhaps you may think of these two Indian children, who were real people, and had their fears and hopes, their troubles and their joys, very much the same as you yourself have; and think of Chilawee and Chikanee, two little beavers that loved them, and who really lived, and loved each other, and could be lonesome, and knew how to be happy too.

And so you may journey once more, in memory, to the Hills of the

[*] The song of the white-throat or song sparrow, or Canada, resembles in both rhythm and sound the effect I have attempted to reproduce above. The white woodsmen translate his song "o-o-o—Can-a-da—Can-a-da—Can-a-da-ah," while the Indians claim he sings, "*Me*-me-me—*no*-ta-kiy—*no*-ta-kiy *no*-ta-kiy-*ah*." His plaintive, unfinished melody is to be heard everywhere in the North Woods during the summer months, and to many of us he stands, with the beaver and the pine tree, as symbolic of the wilderness. And because his song, to the Indian ear, echoes the reassuring phrase "It is well," to have one of these birds sing in a tree under which a person may be standing, is considered to be an omen of future happiness.

Whispering Leaves, and see again the tall dark pines that seem to nod and beckon as you pass them; and you may make another voyage in the yellow bark canoe, with its peering eye and its bravely flying tail.

And perhaps, too, you may hear, as you sit so quietly and still, the rustle of falling leaves, hear the magic call of Talking Waters, and the soft low sound of voices, the voices of the Forest People, both large and small, who dwell in that great, lone land that is so far away, that is so wild, and yet so beautiful, the Land of the North West Wind.

Glossary of Ojibway Indian Words

Comprises common objects, etc., mentioned in the narrative. Spelled phonetically, with meanings.

A-*coon*-amee—A dam.

Ag-wah-*nee*-win—Shawl (bead shawl especially).

A-*jid*-a-mo—Squirrel ("head-downwards." Refers to a common attitude of squirrel when clinging to a tree-trunk).

Am-*mik*—Beaver.

Am-*mik*-onse—Kitten beaver.

A-*nish*-an-*ab*-ay—An Indian.

*Ap*ta—A half.

Ap*to*-zaan—Noon (half of the day).

Ap*to*-zee—Half-breed.

Bash-ka-*jig*an—Gun, rifle.

Baw-*wat*-ik—Rapids; Falls—Gitchie Baw-*wat*-ik (generally 'Chie Baw-*wat*-ik).

Bish*u*—Lynx.

Buck-*kway*-jigan—Bread (bannock).

Bu-da-way—To make fire.

Bush-*quay*-gan—Buckskin. Any kind of hide that has been tanned.

Dow-E-*nin*-ee—Store-man (Trader).

E-*nin*-ee—Man.

553

E-*quay*—Woman.

E-*quay*-sance—Girl.

E-*Quee*-way-sance—Boy.

Git-chie—Big, great.

Git-chie *Mo*-ko-maan—Americans (Big Knives).

Gwee-*gwee*-shee—Whisky-jack (Whistler). A camp-bird.

Jee-maun—Canoe.

Jing-*go*-bee—Any kind of evergreen boughs, or brush.

Jing-*watik*—Pine tree.

Mae-*hing*-gen—Wolf.

Mah-*tig*-'*kiz*-zin—*Boot* (wooden moccasin).

Mee-gwon—Feather.

Mo-ko-maan—Knife.

Moose—Moose.

Muk-*kiz*-zin—Moccasin.

Ne-*gan*-ik-*ab*-o—Man That Stands Ahead (Stands First).

Nee-*bah*—To sleep.

Nee-*bah*-gun—Tent.

Nee-*bay*-win—Bed.

Nee-beesh—Leaves.

Nee-beesh-*ab*-o—Tea (liquid leaves).

Nee-beesh-*abo*-gay—To make tea.

Nee-*gik* (hard G.)—Otter.

Nee-min—To dance.

No-po-ming—The forest, wild lands.

O-*ho*-mis-see—Laughing owl. (Cree language.) Also *Wap*-a-ho.

O-*jeshk*—Musk rat.

O-*nah*-gan—Dishes.

O-*nig*-gum—Portage.

O-pee-*pee*-soway—Place of Bubbling Water (Local dialect "Place of Talking Water").

Rab-a-shaw—Large Bark Canoe (generally twenty-two feet long. For freighting).

Sai-dee—Poplar tree.

Sak-a-*hig*-gan—Lake.

Schkoo-day—Fire.

Schkoo-day-*jee*maun—Steamboat (Fire canoe).

Schkoo-day-o-*da*bah—Railroad train (Fire-sleigh).

Shag-a-nash—White person (particularly English-speaking).

Shee-sheeb—Duck.

Shong-*gwis*-see—Mink.

Sho-nia—Money.

Sug-*gus*-wah—To smoke.

Tig-a-wash—Box.

Ub-wee—Paddle.

*Wab*igon-*oj*eense—Mouse (Little-runner-in-the-clay).

Waw-bigon—Flower.

Wawb-*wey*-an—Blanket.

Waw-*gok*-wet—Axe.

Waw-poose—Rabbit.

Waw-wash-*kay*-see—Deer.

Wig-wam—House, or *Tee*-pee. (Derived from Wigwas, meaning birch
    bark, as the Ojibway tee-pees are often made of sheets of birch bark.)

Wig-was—Birch bark.

Wig-was *Jee*-maun—Birch bark canoe.

Zak-a-tosh—Reeds and rushes (particularly bulrushes).

Zak-a-*tosh*-kah—Place of reeds and rushes.